CLYMER®

HONDA

XL/XR250 • 1978-2000, XL/XR350R • 1983-1985
XR200R • 1984-1985, XR250L • 1991-1996

CLYMER®

P.O. Box 12901, Overland Park, Kansas 66282-2901

Copyright ©2002 Penton Media, Inc.

FIRST EDITION
First Printing June, 1989
Second Printing January, 1990

SECOND EDITION
First Printing June, 1990
Second Printing November, 1991
Third Printing October, 1992
Fourth Printing November, 1993
Fifth Printing February, 1994
Sixth Printing March, 1995

THIRD EDITION
First Printing August, 1996
Second Printing September, 1997
Third Printing June, 1998
Fourth Printing October, 1999
Fifth Printing January, 2001

FOURTH EDITION
First Printing June, 2002
Second Printing October, 2003
Third Printing February, 2005
Fourth Printing April, 2007

Printed in U.S.A.

CLYMER and colophon are registered trademarks of Penton Media, Inc.

ISBN-10: 0-89287-821-5

ISBN-13: 978-0-89287-821-5

Library of Congress: 2002106232

AUTHOR: Ed Scott.

EDITOR: Alan Ahlstrand.

TOOLS AND EQUIPMENT: K & L Supply Co. at www.klsupply.com.

COVER: Mark Clifford Photography, Los Angeles, California. Honda XR250R courtesy of Rice Honda of La Puente, La Puente, California.

CLYMER ®

Publisher Shawn Etheridge

EDITORIAL

Managing Editor
James Grooms

Associate Editors
Rick Arens
Steven Thomas

Authors
Jay Bogart
Michael Morlan
George Parise
Mark Rolling
Ed Scott
Ron Wright

Technical Illustrators
Steve Amos
Errol McCarthy
Mitzi McCarthy
Bob Meyer

Group Production Manager
Dylan Goodwin

Production Manager
Greg Araujo

Senior Production Editor
Darin Watson

Production Editors
Justin Marciniak
Holly Messinger
Adraine Roberts

Production Designer
Jason Hale

MARKETING/SALES AND ADMINISTRATION

Marketing and Sales Representative
Erin Gribbin

Sales Managers
Justin Henton
Matt Tusken

Director, Operations–Books
Ron Rogers

Customer Service Manager
Terri Cannon

Customer Service Account Specialist
Courtney Hollars

Customer Service Representatives
Dinah Bunnell
April LeBlond

Warehouse & Inventory Manager
Leah Hicks

CLYMER ®

P.O. Box 12901, Overland Park, KS 66282-2901 • 800-262-1954 • 913-967-1719

More information available at *clymer.com*

CONTENTS

QUICK REFERENCE DATA

ENGINE OIL CAPACITY

Engine size	Oil drain		Rebuild	
	U.S. qt.	Liter	U.S. qt.	Liter
XR200R				
1984	1.2	1.1	1.3	1.2
1985	1.5	1.4	1.7	1.6
XL250S, XR250	1.6	1.5	2.1	2.0
XL250R				
1982-1983	1.6	1.5	2.1	2.0
1984-on	1.4	1.3	1.6	1.5
XR250L	1.4	1.3	1.6	1.5
XR250R				
1981-1982	1.8	1.7	2.1	2.0
1984	1.2	1.1	1.3	1.2
1985-on	1.5	1.4	1.7	1.6
XL350R	1.7	1.6	2.0	1.9
XR350R				
1983-1984	1.9	1.8	2.1	2.0
1985	1.6	1.5	2.1	2.0

MAINTENANCE AND TUNE-UP TORQUE SPECIFICATIONS

Item	N•m	ft.-lb.
Oil drain plug		
Wet-sump models	20-30	14-22
Dry-sump models		
Frame down tube	35-45	25-33
Crankcase	30-40	22-29
Front fork cap bolt		
XR350R	15-20	11-14
XR250R 1990-1995	25-35	18-25
XR250L	23	17
All other models	15-30	11-22
Rear axle nut (dual-shock models)		
XL250S	55-70	40-51
All other models	70-110	51-80
Rear axle nut (Pro-Link models)		
1981 models	70-110	51-80
1982-on	80-110	58-80
Balancer chain holder flange bolt		
XL250S, 1982-1983, XL250R	22-30	16-22
Fuel strainer cup (models so equipped)	3-5	2-4
Wheel rim locks	9-15	7-11
Valve adjuster locknut		
1984 XR200R, 1984-1989 XR250R	17-23	12-17
1990-1995 XR250R	21-25	16-18
XR250L	17-23	12-17
All other models	15-18	11-13

FRONT FORK OIL CAPACITY *

Model	Standard capacity		Standard distance from top of fork	
	cc	fl. oz.	mm	in.
XR200R	651	22.0		
Maximum	–	–	146	5.75
Minimum	–	–	186	7.32
XL250S	190	6.4	–	–
XL250R				
1982-1983	300	10.14	173	6.81
1984-on	293	9.91	195	7.68
XR250	202	6.8	–	–
XR250L	550	18.6	139	5.5
XR250R				
1981	368	12.4	152	6
1982	395	13.4	156	6.125
1984-1989	651	22.0		
Maximum	–	–	150	5.91
Minimum	–	–	190	7.48
1990-1995	492	16.6	128	5.0
XL350R	411	14.0	184	7.2
XR350R				
1983	553	18.7	132	5.2
1984-1985	563	19.0		
Maximum	–	–	152	5.98
Minimum	—	–	112	4.41

* Capacity for each fork leg.

FRONT FORK AIR PRESSURE

Model	psi	kg/cm2
XL250R	0-2.8	0-0.2
All other models	0	0

DRIVE CHAIN FREE PLAY

Model	mm	in.
Dual shock models		
XL series	15-20	0.6-0.8
XR series	20	0.8
Pro-Link models		
XL series	30-40	1 1/4-1 5/8
XR250L	20-30	3/4-1 1/4
All other XR series	35-45	1 3/8-1 3/4

DRIVE CHAIN REPLACEMENT NUMBERS

Model	Standard
XR200R	520VC-3-108FJ or 520MO-108FJ XL250S-102L
XL250R	
1982-1983	520VC-102L
1984-on	520MO-102LE or 520VC-102LE
XR250L	
1991-on	Diado 520VC6-104LE.
1991-1992	RK Excel RK520MO9-104LE.
1993-on	RK Excel RK520M29-104LE.
XR250	DIADO-102L
XR250R	
1981-1982	520DS-106RJ
1984-1989	20VC-3-108FJ or 520MO-108FJ
1990-1995	Diado 520VC.3-108FJ, Takasago 520MO-108FJ.
XL350R	520VC-102LE or 520SO-102LE
XR350R	
1983	520MS-104FJ
1984-1985	520MO-104FJ or 520VC-3-104FJ

DRIVE CHAIN SERVICE LENGTH SPECIFICATIONS

Model	Number of pins	Dimension	
		mm	in.
XR200R	107	1,716	67.55
XL250S	41	648	25.4
XL250R	NA		
XR250L	NA		
XR250	102	1,635	64.4
XR250R			
1981-1982	107	1,700	66.94
1984-on	107	1,716	67.55
XR350R	105	1,700	66.94

NA. Honda does not provide service information for all models.

TUNE-UP SPECIFICATIONS

Valve clearance
  1978-1989
    Intake
      All models   0.05 mm (0.002 in.)
    Exhaust
      200-350 cc   0.08 mm (0.003 in.)
  1990-on
    Intake   0.03-0.07 mm (0.001-0.003 in.)
    Exhaust   0.06-0.010 mm (0.002-0.004 in.)
Compression pressure
  XR200, 1981-1982 XR250R,   199 psi (14.0 kg/cm2)
    XL350R
  XR250L   156-185 psi (11.0-13.0 kg/cm2).
  XR250   192 psi (13.5 kg/cm2)
  XR250R
    1984-1989   192 psi (13.5 kg/cm2)
    1990-1991   184.9-213.3 psi (13.0-15.0 kg/cm2).
    1992-1995   170.7-184.9 psi (12.0-13.0 kg/cm2).
  All other models   175 psi (12.5 kg/cm2)

(continued)

TUNE-UP SPECIFICATIONS (continued)

Spark plug type
  Standard heat range
    1978-1981   ND X24ES-U or NGK D8EA
    1982   ND X24ESR-U or NGK DR8ES-L
    1983   ND X24EPR-U9 or NGK DPR8EA-9
    1984-on XR200R, XR250R   ND X27EPR-U or NGK DPR9EA-9
    1990-on
  Standard heat range
    XR250R   ND X27GRP-U or NGK DPR9Z
    XR250L   ND X24GRP-U or NGK DPR8Z
      For cold climate
        XR250R   ND X24GRP-U or NGK DPR8Z
        XR250L   ND X22GRP-U or NGK DPR7Z
      For extended high speed riding*
        XR250L   ND X27GRP-U or NGK DPR9Z
      All other models   ND X24EPR-U or NGK DPR8EA-9
Spark plug gap
  1978-1989   0.8-0.9 mm (0.032-0.036 in.)
  1990-on   0.6-0.7 mm (0.024-0.028 in.)
Ignition timing at "F" mark
  Engine rpm (200-350 cc)   1,300 $\pm$ 100 rpm
Idle speed
  1978-1989   1,200 $\pm$ 100 rpm
  1990-on   1,300 $\pm$ 100 rpm

MOTORCYCLE INFORMATION

MODEL:_____YEAR:_____

VIN NUMBER:_____

ENGINE SERIAL NUMBER:_____

CARBURETOR SERIAL NUMBER OR I.D. MARK:_____

NOTE: If you own a 1990 or later model, first check the Supplement at the back of the book for any new service information.

CHAPTER ONE

GENERAL INFORMATION

This detailed, comprehensive manual covers the Honda XL and XR 200-350 series singles from 1978-on. The XL series is street-legal but is also suited for the dirt. It has a quiet exhaust system, small carburetor(s) (some models have an accelerator pump) and conservative ignition timing. It has a heavier alternator flywheel than the XR models, which allows it to idle smoothly. The XL models have a battery and all the necessary lighting equipment for use on the street.

The XR series is strictly for off-road use. Being a competition-oriented machine, it has a noisier, less restrictive muffler, larger carburetor(s), tighter gearing and hotter ignition timing than the XL models. For better throttle response it has a lighter alternator flywheel.

The expert text gives complete information on maintenance, tune-up, repair and overhaul. Hundreds of photos and drawings guide you through every step. The book includes all you will need to know to keep your Honda running right. Throughout this book where differences occur among the models, they are clearly identified.

A shop manual is a reference. You want to be able to find information fast. As in all Clymer books, this one is designed with you in mind. All chapters are thumb tabbed. Important items are extensively indexed at the

rear of the book. All procedures, tables, photos, etc., in this manual are for the reader who may be working on the bike for the first time or using this manual for the first time. All the most frequently used specifications and capacities are summarized in the *Quick Reference Data* pages at the front of the book.

Keep the book handy in your tool box. It will help you better understand how your bike runs, lower repair costs and generally improve your satisfaction with the bike.

Tables 1-3 are at the end of this chapter.

MANUAL ORGANIZATION

All dimensions and capacities are expressed in English units familiar to U.S. mechanics as well as in metric units.

This chapter provides general information and discusses equipment and tools useful both for preventive maintenance and troubleshooting. **Table 1**, at the end of this chapter, contains model designation information.

Chapter Two provides methods and suggestions for quick and accurate diagnosis and repair of problems. Troubleshooting procedures discuss typical symptoms and logical methods to pinpoint the trouble.

Chapter Three explains all periodic lubrication and routine maintenance necessary to keep the Honda running well. Chapter Three also includes recommended tune-up procedures, eliminating the need to constantly consult chapters on the various assemblies.

Subsequent chapters describe specific systems such as the engine, clutch, transmission, fuel system, exhaust system, suspension and brakes. Each chapter provides disassembly, repair and assembly procedures in simple step-by-step form.

If a repair is impractical for a home mechanic, it is so indicated. It is usually faster and less expensive to take such repairs to a dealer or competent repair shop. Specifications concerning a particular system are included at the end of the appropriate chapter.

Some of the procedures in this manual specify special tools. In most cases, the tool is illustrated either in actual use or alone. Well equipped mechanics may find they can substitute similar tools already on hand or can fabricate their own.

NOTES, CAUTIONS AND WARNINGS

The terms NOTE, CAUTION and WARNING have specific meanings in this manual. A NOTE provides additional information to make a step or procedure easier or clearer. Disregarding a NOTE could cause inconvenience, but would not cause equipment damage or personal injury.

A CAUTION emphasizes areas where equipment damage could occur. Disregarding a CAUTION could cause permanent mechanical damage; however, personal injury is unlikely.

A WARNING emphasizes areas where personal injury or even death could result from negligence. Mechanical damage may also occur. WARNINGS *are to be taken seriously.* In some cases, serious injury or death has resulted from disregarding similar warnings.

Throughout this manual keep in mind 2 conventions. "Front" refers to the front of the bike. The front of any component, such as the engine, is the end which faces toward the front of the bike. The "left-" and "right-hand" sides refer to the position of the parts as viewed by a rider sitting on the seat facing forward. For example, the throttle control is on the right-hand side and the clutch lever is on the left-hand side. These rules are simple, but even experienced mechanics occasionally become disoriented.

SERVICE HINTS

Most of the service procedures covered are straightforward and can be performed by anyone reasonably handy with tools. It is suggested, however, that you consider your own capabilities carefully before attempting any operation involving major disassembly of the engine.

Some operations, for example, require the use of a press. It would be wiser to have these performed by a shop equipped for such work, rather than trying to do the job yourself with makeshift equipment. Other procedures require precise measurements. Unless you have the skills and equipment required, it would be better to have a qualified repair shop make the measurements for you.

There are many items available that can be used on your hands before and after working on your bike. A little preparation prior to getting "all greased up" will help when cleaning up later.

Before starting out, work Vaseline, soap or a product such as Invisible Glove (**Figure 1**) onto your forearms, into your hands and under your fingernails and cuticles. This will make cleanup a lot easier.

For cleanup, use a waterless hand soap such as Sta-Lube and then finish up with powdered Boraxo and a fingernail brush.

Repairs go much faster and easier if the bike is clean before you begin work. There are special cleaners, such as Gunk or Bel-Ray Degreaser (**Figure 2**) for washing the engine and related parts. Just spray or brush on the cleaning solution, let it stand, then rinse it away with a garden hose. Clean all oily or greasy parts with cleaning solvent as you remove them.

> *WARNING*
> ***Never*** *use gasoline as a cleaning agent. It presents an extreme fire hazard. Be sure to work in a well-ventilated area*

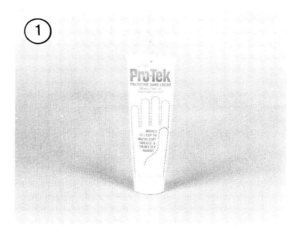

when using cleaning solvent. Keep a fire extinguisher, rated for gasoline fires, handy in any case.

Special tools are required for some repair procedures. These may be purchased from a dealer or motorcycle shop, rented from a tool rental dealer or fabricated by a mechanic or machinist (often at a considerable savings).

Much of the labor charged for repairs by mechanics is to for remove and disassemble other parts to reach the defective unit. It is usually possible to perform the preliminary operations yourself and then take the defective unit in to the dealer for repair.

Once you have decided to tackle the job yourself, read the entire section in this manual which pertains to it, making sure you have identified the proper one. Study the illustrations and text until you have a good idea of what is involved in completing the job satisfactorily. If special tools or replacement parts are required, make arrangements to get them before you start. It is frustrating and time-consuming to get partly into a job and then be unable to complete it.

Simple wiring checks can be easily made at home, but knowledge of electronics is almost a necessity for performing tests with complicated electronic testing gear.

During disassembly of parts keep a few general cautions in mind. Force is rarely needed to get things apart. If parts are a tight fit, such as a bearing in a case, there is usually a tool designed to separate them. Never use a screwdriver to pry parts with machined surfaces such as crankcase halves. You will mar the surfaces and end up with leaks.

Make diagrams (or take a Polaroid picture) wherever similar-appearing parts are found. For instance, crankcase bolts are often not the same

length. You may think you can remember where everything came from, but mistakes are costly. There is also the possibility you may be sidetracked and not return to work for days or even weeks, in which interval carefully laid out parts may have become disturbed.

Tag all similar internal parts for location and mark all mating parts for position. Record number and thickness of any shims as they are removed. Small parts such as bolts can be identified by placing them in plastic sandwich bags. Seal and label them with masking tape.

Wiring should be tagged with masking tape and marked as each wire is removed. Again, do not rely on memory alone.

Protect finished surfaces from physical damage or corrosion. Keep gasoline and hydraulic brake fluid off plastic parts or painted and plated surfaces.

Frozen or very tight bolts and screws can often be loosened by soaking with penetrating oil, such as WD-40 or Liquid Wrench, then sharply striking the bolt head a few times with a hammer and punch (or screwdriver for screws). Avoid heat unless absolutely necessary, since it may melt, warp or remove the temper from many parts.

No parts, except those assembled with a press fit, require unusual force during assembly. If a part is hard to remove or install, find out why before proceeding.

Cover all openings after removing parts to keep dirt, small tools, etc. from falling in.

When assembling 2 parts, start all fasteners, then tighten evenly.

Wiring connections and brake components should be kept clean and free of grease and oil.

When assembling parts, be sure all shims and washers are installed exactly as they came out.

Whenever a rotating part butts against a stationary part, look for a shim or washer. Use new gaskets if there is any doubt about the condition of the old ones. A thin coat of oil on gaskets may help them seal effectively.

Heavy grease can be used to hold small parts in place if they tend to fall out during assembly. However, keep grease and oil away from electrical and brake components.

High spots may be sanded off a piston with sandpaper, but fine emery cloth and oil will do a much more professional job.

Carbon can be removed from the head, the piston crown and the exhaust port with a dull screwdriver. Do *not* scratch machined surfaces. Wipe off the surface with a clean cloth when finished.

The carburetor is best cleaned by disassembling and soaking the parts in a commercial carburetor cleaner. Never soak gaskets and rubber parts in these cleaners. Never use wire to clean out jets and air passages; they are easily damaged. Use compressed air to blow out the carburetor *after* the float has been removed.

A baby bottle makes a good measuring device for adding oil to the front forks. Get one that is graduated in fluid ounces and cubic centimeters. After it has been used for this purpose, do *not* let a small child drink out of it as there will always be an oil residue in it.

Take your time and do the job right. Do not forget that a newly rebuilt engine must be broken in the same as a new one. Keep the rpm within the limits given in your owner's manual when you get back on the road.

TORQUE SPECIFICATIONS

Torque specifications throughout this manual are given in Newton meters (N•m) and foot-pounds (ft.-lb.). Newton meters have been adopted in place of meter kilograms (mkg) in accordance with the International Modernized Metric System. Tool manufacturers offer torque wrenches calibrated in Newton meters and Sears has a Craftsman line calibrated in both values.

Existing torque wrenches calibrated in meter kilograms can be used by performing a simple conversion. All you have to do is move the decimal point one place to the right; for example, 4.7 mkg = 47 N•m. This conversion is accurate enough for mechanical work even though the exact mathematical conversion is 3.5 mkg = 34.3 N•m.

Refer to **Table 2** for standard torque specifications for various size screws, bolts and nuts that may not be covered in the various chapters.

SAFETY FIRST

Professional mechanics can work for years and never sustain a serious injury. If you observe a few rules of common sense and safety, you can enjoy many hours servicing your own machine. If you ignore these rules you can hurt yourself or damage the bike.

1. *Never* use gasoline as a cleaning solvent.
2. Never smoke or use a torch in the vicinity of flammable liquids such as cleaning solvent in open containers.
3. If welding or brazing is required on the machine, remove the fuel tank to a safe distance, at least 50 feet away.

4. Use the proper size wrenches to avoid damage to nuts and injury to yourself.
5. When loosening a tight or stuck nut, think about what would happen if the wrench should slip. Be careful; protect yourself accordingly.
6. Keep your work area clean and uncluttered.
7. Wear safety goggles during all operations involving drilling, grinding or the use of a cold chisel.
8. Never use worn tools.
9. Keep a fire extinguisher handy and be sure it is rated for gasoline and electrical fires.

SPECIAL TIPS

Because of the extreme demands placed on a bike several points should be kept in mind when performing service and repair. The following items are general suggestions that may improve the overall life of the machine and help avoid costly failures.

1. Use a locking compound such as Loctite Lock N' Seal No. 242 (blue Loctite) on all bolts and nuts, even if they are secured with lockwashers.

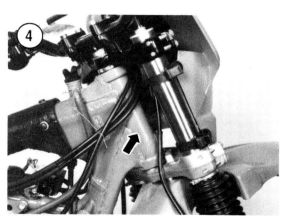

This type of Loctite does not harden completely and allows easy removal of the bolt or nut. A screw or bolt lost from an engine cover or bearing retainer could easily cause serious and expensive damage before its loss is noticed.

When applying Loctite, use a small amount. If too much is used, it can work its way down the threads and stick parts together not meant to be stuck.

Keep a tube of Loctite in your toolbox; when used properly it is cheap insurance.

2. Use a hammer-driven impact tool to remove tight fasteners, particularly engine cover screws. These tools help prevent damage to bolt heads and screw slots.

3. When replacing missing or broken fasteners (bolts, nuts and screws), especially on the engine or frame components, always use Honda replacement parts. They are specially hardened for each application. The wrong fastener could easily cause serious and expensive damage, not to mention rider injury.

4. When installing gaskets in the engine, always use Honda replacement gaskets *without* sealer,

unless designated. These gaskets are designed to swell when they come in contact with oil. Gasket sealer will prevent the gaskets from swelling as intended, which can result in oil leaks. These Honda gaskets are cut from material of the precise thickness needed. Installation of a too-thick or too-thin gasket in a critical area could cause engine damage.

EXPENDABLE SUPPLIES

Certain expendable supplies are required during maintenance and repair work. These include grease, oil, gasket cement, wiping rags and cleaning solvent. Ask your dealer for the special locking compounds, silicone lubricants and other products (**Figure 3**) which make vehicle maintenance simpler and easier. Cleaning solvent or kerosene is available at some service stations or hardware stores.

PARTS REPLACEMENT

Honda makes frequent changes during a model year—some minor, some relatively major. When you order parts from the dealer or other parts distributor, always order by engine and frame number. Write the numbers down and carry them with you. Compare new parts to old before purchasing them. If they are not alike, have the parts manager explain the difference to you.

SERIAL NUMBERS

You must know the model serial number and VIN number for registration purposes and when ordering replacement parts.

The frame serial number is stamped on the right-hand side of the steering head (**Figure 4**). The vehicle identification number (VIN) is on the left-hand side of the steering head (**Figure 5**). The engine serial number is located on the lower left-hand side of the crankcase adjacent to the shift lever (**Figure 6**) or on the top surface of the crankcase (**Figure 7**). The carburetor identification number is located on the carburetor body above the float bowl (**Figure 8**). On models so equipped, the color label is attached to the frame next to the air filter air box (**Figure 9**). When ordering color-coded parts always specify the color indicated on this label.

BASIC HAND TOOLS

A number of tools are required to maintain a bike in top riding condition. You may already have some of these tools for home or car repairs. There are also tools made especially for bike repairs these you will have to purchase. In any case, a wide variety of quality tools will make bike repair easier and more effective.

Top quality tools are essential; they are also more economical in the long run. If you are now starting to build your tool collection, stay away from the "advertised specials" featured at some parts houses, discount stores and chain drug stores. These are usually a poor grade tool that can be sold cheaply and that is exactly what they are – cheap. They are usually made of inferior material and are thick, heavy and clumsy. Their rough finish makes them difficult to clean and they usually don't last very long. Quality tools are made of alloy steel and are heat treated for greater strength. They are lighter and better balanced than cheap ones. Their surface is smooth, making them a pleasure to work with and easy to clean. The initial cost of good quality tools may be more but it is cheaper in the long run. Don't try to buy everything in all sizes in the beginning; do it a little at a time until you have the necessary tools.

Keep your tools clean and in a tool box. Keep them organized with the sockets and related drives together and the open end and box wrenches together, etc. After using a tool, wipe off dirt and grease with a clean cloth and place the tool in its correct place. Doing this will save a lot of time you would have spent trying to find a socket buried in a bunch of clutch parts. Also be careful when lending tools to "friends" – make sure they return them promptly; if not, your collection will soon disappear.

The following tools are required to perform virtually any repair job on a bike. Each tool is described and the recommended size given for starting a tool collection. Additional tools and some duplicates may be added as you become more familiar with the bike. Almost all motorcycles and bikes (with the exception of the U.S. built Harley and some English bikes) use metric size bolts and nuts.

If you are starting your collection now, buy metric sizes. Consider purchaising a set of basic tools (**Figure 10**) from a tool supplier. These offer a cost savings over individually purchased tools.

Screwdrivers

The screwdriver is a very basic tool, but if used improperly it will do more damage than good. The

slot on a screw has a definite dimension and shape. A screwdriver must be selected to conform with that shape. Use a small screwdriver for small screws and a large one for large screws or the screw head will be damaged.

Two basic types of screwdriver are required to repair the bike—a common (flat blade) screwdriver and the Phillips screwdriver.

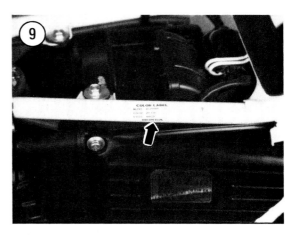

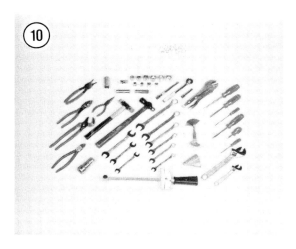

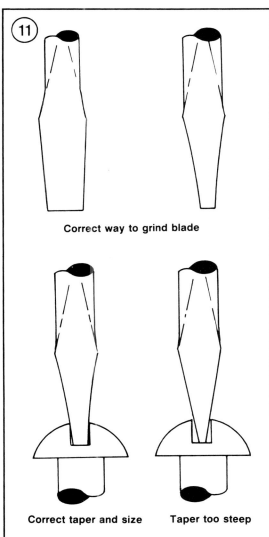

Correct way to grind blade

Correct taper and size   Taper too steep

Screwdrivers are available in sets which often include an assortment of common and Phillips blades. If you buy them individually, buy at least the following:

    a. Common screwdriver—5/16×6 in. blade.

    b. Common screwdriver—3/8×12 in. blade.

    c. Phillips screwdriver—size 2 tip, 6 in. blade.

Use screwdrivers only for driving screws. Never use a screwdriver for prying or chiseling. Do not try to remove a Phillips or Allen head screw with a common screwdriver; you can damage the head so that the proper tool will be unable to remove it.

Keep screwdrivers in the proper condition and they will last longer and perform better. Always keep the tip of a common screwdriver in good condition. **Figure 11** shows how to grind the tip to the proper shape if it becomes damaged. Note the symmetrical sides of the tip.

Pliers

Pliers come in a wide range of types and sizes. Pliers are useful for cutting, bending and crimping. They should never be used to cut hardened objects or to turn bolts or nuts. **Figure 12** shows several pliers useful in bike repairs.

Each type of pliers has a specialized function. Gas pliers are general purpose pliers and are used mainly for holding things and for bending. Vise Grips are used as pliers or to hold objects very tightly like a vise. Needlenose pliers are used to hold or bend small objects. Channel lock pliers can be adjusted to hold various sizes of objects; the jaws remain parallel to grip around objects such as pipe or tubing. There are many more types of pliers. The ones described here are most suitable for bike repairs.

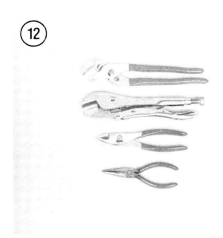

Box and Open-end Wrenches

Box and open-end wrenches are available in sets or separately in a variety of sizes. The size number stamped near the end refers to the distance between 2 parallel flats on the hex head bolt or nut.

Box wrenches are usually superior to open-end wrenches. Open-end wrenches grip the nut on only 2 flats. Unless it fits well, it may slip and round off the points on the nut. The box wrench grips all 6 flats. Both 6-point and 12-point openings on box wrenches are available. The 6-point gives superior holding power; the 12-point allows a shorter swing.

Combination wrenches (**Figure 13**) which are open on one side and boxed on the other are also available. Both ends are the same size.

Adjustable (Crescent) Wrenches

An adjustable wrench (also called crescent wrench) can be adjusted to fit nearly any nut or bolt head. See **Figure 14**. However, it can loosen and slip, causing damage to the nut and injury to your knuckles. Use an adjustable wrench only when other wrenches are not available.

Adjustable wrenches come in sizes ranging from 4-18 in. overall. A 6 or 8 in. wrench is recommended as an all-purpose wrench.

Socket Wrenches

This type is undoubtedly the fastest, safest and most convenient to use. See **Figure 15**. Sockets which attach to a ratchet handle are available with 6-point or 12-point openings and 1/4, 1/2, 3/8 and 3/4 in. drives. The drive size indicates the size of the square hole which mates with the ratchet handle.

Torque Wrench

A torque wrench is used with a socket to measure how tightly a nut or bolt is installed. They come in a wide price range and with either 3/8 or 1/2 in. square drive. The drive size indicates the size of the square drive which mates with the socket. Purchase one that measures 0-140 N•m (0-100 ft.-lb.).

Impact Driver

This tool might have been designed with the bike in mind. See **Figure 16**. It makes removal of engine and clutch parts easy and eliminates damage to bolts and screw slots. This tool is available at most large hardware, motorcycle or auto parts stores.

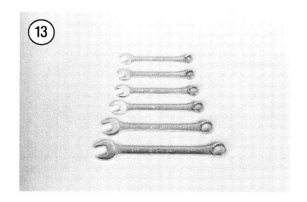

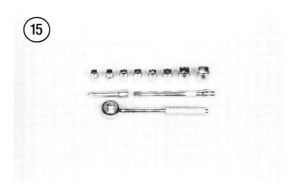

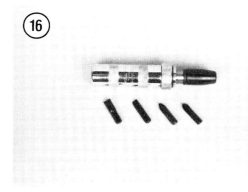

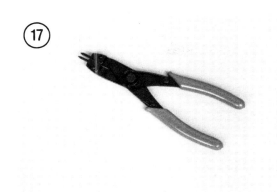

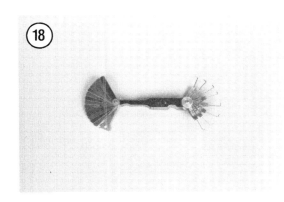

Circlip Pliers

Circlip pliers (sometimes referred to as snap-ring pliers) are necessary to remove the circlips used on the transmission shaft assemblies. See **Figure 17**.

Hammers

The correct hammer is necessary for bike repairs. Use only a hammer with a face (or head) of rubber or plastic or the soft-faced type that is filled with buckshot. These are sometimes necessary in engine teardowns. *Never* use a metal-faced hammer on the bike as severe damage will result in most cases. You can always produce the same amount of force with a soft-faced hammer.

Ignition Gauge

This tool (**Figure 18**) has both flat and wire measuring gauges and is used to measure spark plug gap. This device is available at most auto or motorcycle supply stores.

SPECIAL TOOLS

Special tools may be required for major service. These are described in the appropriate chapters and are available from Honda dealers or other sources as indicated.

TUNE-UP AND TROUBLESHOOTING TOOLS

Multimeter or Volt-ohm Meter

This instrument (**Figure 19**) is invaluable for electrical system troubleshooting and service. A few of its functions may be duplicated by homemade test equipment, but for the serious mechanic it is a must. Its uses are described in the applicable sections of the book.

Strobe Timing Light

This instrument is necessary for tuning. By flashing a light at the precise instant the spark plug fires, the position of the timing mark can be seen. Marks on the alternator flywheel line up with the stationary mark on the crankcase while the engine is running.

Suitable lights range from inexpensive neon bulb types to powerful xenon strobe lights (**Figure 20**). Neon timing lights are difficult to see and must be used in dimly lit areas. Xenon strobe timing lights can be used outside in bright sunlight. Both types work on the bike; use according to the manufacturer's instructions.

Portable Tachometer

A portable tachometer is necessary for tuning (**Figure 21**). Ignition timing and carburetor adjustments must be performed at the specified engine speed. The best instrument for this purpose is one with a low range of 0-1,000 or 0-2,000 rpm and a high range of 0-4,000 rpm. Extended range (0-6,000 or 0-8,000 rpm) instruments lack accuracy at lower speeds. The instrument should be capable of detecting changes of 25 rpm on the low range.

Compression Gauge

A compression gauge (**Figure 22**) measures the engine compression. The results, when properly interpreted, can indicate general ring and valve condition. They are available from motorcycle or auto supply stores and mail order outlets.

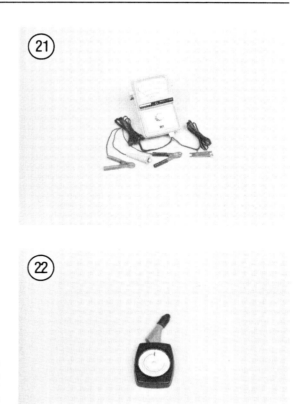

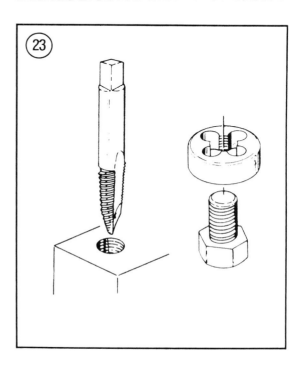

MECHANIC'S TIPS

Removing Frozen Nuts and Screws

When a fastener rusts and cannot be removed, several methods may be used to loosen it. First, apply penetrating oil such as Liquid Wrench or WD-40 (available at any hardware or auto supply store).

Apply it liberally and let it penetrate for 10-15 minutes. Rap the fastener several times with a small hammer; do not hit it hard enough to cause damage. Reapply the penetrating oil if necessary.

For frozen screws, apply penetrating oil as described, then insert a screwdriver in the slot and rap the top of the screwdriver with a hammer. This loosens the rust so the screw can be removed in the normal way. If the screw head is too chewed up to use a screwdriver, grip the head with Vise Grip pliers and twist the screw out.

Remedying Stripped Threads

Occasionally, threads are stripped though carelessness or impact damage. Often the threads can be cleaned up with a tap (for internal threads on nuts) or die (for external threads on bolts). See **Figure 23**.

Removing Broken Screws or Bolts

When the head breaks off a screw or bolt, several methods are available for removing the remaining portion.

If a large portion of the remainder projects out, try gripping it with Vise Grips. If the projecting portion is too small, file it to fit a wrench or cut a slot in it to fit a screwdriver. See **Figure 24**.

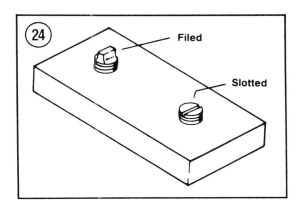

If the head breaks off flush, use a screw extractor. To do this, centerpunch the remaining portion of the screw or bolt. Drill a small hole in the screw and tap the extractor into the hole. Back the screw out with a wrench on the extractor. See **Figure 25**.

"OFF THE ROAD" RULES

Areas set aside by the federal government, state or local agencies for off-road riding are continuing to disappear. The loss of many of these areas is usually due to the few who really don't care and therefore ruin the sport of off-road fun for those who do. Many areas are closed off to protect

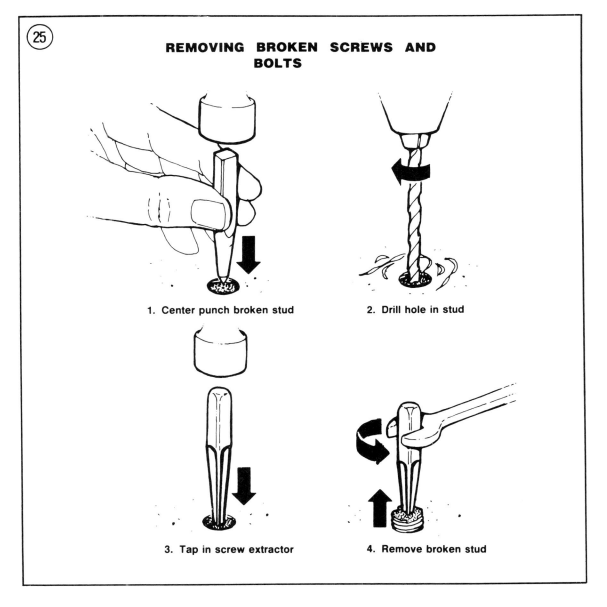

REMOVING BROKEN SCREWS AND BOLTS

1. Center punch broken stud

2. Drill hole in stud

3. Tap in screw extractor

4. Remove broken stud

wildlife habitat, vegetation and geological structures. Do not enter into these areas as it can result in an expensive citation and adds to the anti-off-road vehicle sentiment that can result in further land closures. By following these basic rules you and others will always have an area open for this type of recreation.

1. When riding, always observe the basic practice of good sportsmanship and recognize that other people will judge all off-road vehicle owners by your actions.

2. Don't litter the trails or camping areas. Leave the area cleaner than it was before you came.

3. Don't pollute lakes, streams or the ocean.

4. Be careful not to damage living trees, shrubs or other natural terrain.

5. Respect other people's rights and property.

6. Help anyone in distress.

7. Make yourself and your bike available for assistance in any search and rescue parties.

8. Don't harass other people using the same area as you are. Respect the rights of others enjoying the recreation area.

9. Be sure to obey all federal, state, provincial and other local rules regulating the operation of the bike.

10. Inform public officials when using public lands.

11. Don't harass wildlife and stay out of areas posted for the protection and feeding of wildlife.

12. Keep your exhaust noise to a minimum.

SAFETY

General Tips

1. Read your owner's manual and know your machine.

2. Check the throttle and brake controls before starting the engine.

3. Know how to make an emergency stop.

4. Know all state, federal and local laws concerning off-road riding. Respect private property.

5. Never add fuel while anyone is smoking in the area or when the engine is running.

6. Never wear loose scarves, belts or boot laces that could catch on moving parts or tree limbs.

7. Always wear protective clothing to protect your *entire* body. **Figure 26** shows a well-equipped off-road rider who is ready for almost any riding condition. Today's riding apparel is very stylish and you will be ready for action as well as being protected.

8. Riding in the winter months requires a good set of clothes to keep your body dry and warm, otherwise your entire trip may be miserable. If you dress properly, moisture will evaporate from your body. If you become too hot and if your clothes trap the moisture, you will become cold. **Figure 27** shows some recommended inner and outer layers of cold weather clothing. Even mild temperatures can be very uncomfortable and dangerous when combined with a strong wind or travel at high speed. Always dress according to what the wind chill factor is, not the ambient temperature.

9. Never allow anyone to operate the bike without proper instruction. This is for their bodily protection and to keep your machine from damage or destruction.

10. Use the "buddy system" for long trips, just in case you have a problem or run out of gas.

11. Never attempt to repair your machine with the engine running except when necessary for certain tune-up procedures.

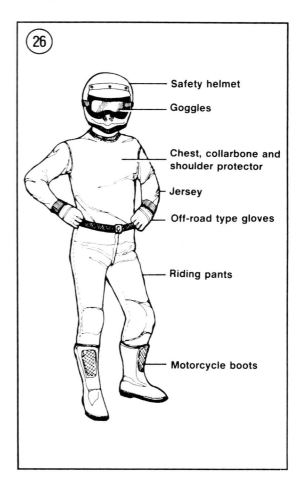

(26)

Safety helmet
Goggles
Chest, collarbone and shoulder protector
Jersey
Off-road type gloves
Riding pants
Motorcycle boots

(27)

Outer layers

Safety helmet

Goggles

Inner layers

Face mask

Insulated
suit

Wool shirt

Glove liners

Leather
gloves

Thermal
underwear

Heavy pants

Motorcycle or
snowmobile boots

Wool socks

WINTER PROTECTIVE CLOTHING

12. Check all of the machine components and hardware frequently, especially the wheels and the steering.

13. Push the bike onto a truck or trailer bed—never ride it on. Secure it firmly to the truck or trailer and if towing a trailer be sure that the trailer lights operate properly.

Operating Tips

1. Never operate the bike in crowded areas or steer toward persons.

2. Avoid dangerous terrain.

3. Cross highways (where permitted) at a 90 degree angle after looking in both directions. Post traffic guards if crossing in groups.

4. Do not ride the vehicle on or near railroad tracks. The bike engine and exhaust noise can drown out the sound of an approaching train.

5. Keep the headlight (if so equipped) free of dirt and never ride at night without the headlight on.

6. Always steer with both hands.

7. Be aware of the terrain and avoid operating the bike at excessive speed.

8. Do not panic if the throttle sticks. Turn the engine stop switch to the OFF position.

9. Do not speed through wooded areas. Hidden obstructions, hanging tree limbs, unseen ditches and even wild animals and hikers can cause injury and damage to the bike.

10. Do not tailgate. Rear end collisions can cause injury and machine damage.

11. Do not mix alcoholic beverages or drugs with riding—ride straight.

12. Check your fuel supply regularly. Do not travel farther than your fuel supply will permit you to return.

Tables are on the following pages.

Table 1 MODEL, YEAR AND FRAME NUMBER

Model	Year	Engine beginning Serial number	Frame beginning Serial number
XR200R	1984	ME05E-5000001-5006638	ME050-EK000001-EK005349
	1985*	ME05E-5100003-5105538	ME050-FK000001-FK105715
XL250S	1978	L250SE-5000094-on	L250S-500071-on
	1979	L250SE-5100007-on	L250S-510007-on
	1980	MD01E-5200001-on	MD01-5200001-on
	1981	MD01E-5300001-on	MD010-BM300001-on
XL250R	1982	MD03E-5000005-on	MD030-CM000002-on
	1983	MD03E-5100001-on	MD030-DM100001-on
CAL	1984	MD11E-5000044-5003180	MD111-EK000005-EK000758
49 STATE	1984	MD11E-5000039-5002895	MD110-EK000009-EK002307
CAL	1985	MD11E-5100022-5102020	MD111-FK100001-FK100500
49 STATE	1985	MD11E-5100016-5103798	MD110-FK100009-FK104428
CAL	1986	MD11E-5200001-5205254	MD111-GK100001-on GK201086
49 STATE	1986	MD11E-5200001-on 520554	MD110-GK100001-on GK204453
CAL	1987	MD11E-5300002-on	MD111-HK300002-on
49 STATE	1987	MD11E-5300002-on	MD110-HK300001-on
XR250	1979	ME01E-5000040-on	MD01-5000032-on
	1980	ME01E-5100001-on	MD01-5100001-on
XR250R	1981	ME01E-5200010-on	MD010-BM200010-on
	1982	ME01E-5300001-on	MD010-CM300001-on
	1983***		
	1984	ME06E-5000001-5007013	ME060-EK000001-EK006272
	1985	ME06E-5100003-5103830	ME060-FK100003-FK104453
	1986	ME06E-5200018-5206482	ME060-GK200014-GK206454
	1987	ME06E-5300002 5305129	ME060-HK300002 304481
	1988	ME06E-5400001-on	ME060-JK00001-on
	1989	ME06E-550001-on	
XL350R CAL	1984	ND03E-5000015-5006581	ND031-EM000001-EM001310
49 STATE	1984	ND03E-5000005-5005590	ND030-EM000001-EM004164
CAL	1985**	ND03E-5100075-on	ND031-FK100001-on
49 STATE	1985**	ND03E-5100001-on	ND030-FK100001-on

(continued)

Table 1 MODEL, YEAR AND FRAME NUMBER (continuee)

Model	Year	Engine beginning Serial number	Frame beginning Serial number
XR350R	1983	NE01E-5000033-5007074	NE010-DM000023-DM005646
	1984	NE01E-5100014-5105447	NE010-EM100006-EM105444
	1985**	NE01E-5000001-5005622	NE010-FK000015-FK205671

*Last year covered in this book.
**Last year of production for this model.
***No model produced this year.

Table 2 STANDARD TORQUE SPECIFICATIONS

Item	N•m	ft.-lb.
5 mm bolt and nut	4.5-6	3-4
6 mm bolt and nut	8-12	6-9
8 mm bolt and nut	18-25	13-18
10 mm bolt and nut	30-40	22-29
12 mm bolt and nut	50-60	36-43
5 mm screw	3.5-5	2-4
6 mm screw and 6 mm bolt with 8 mm head	7-11	5-8
6 mm flange bolt and nut	41-14	7-10
8 mm flange bolt and nut	24-30	17-22
10 mm flange bolt and nut	35-45	25-33

Table 3 CONVERSION FORMULAS

Multiply:	By:	To get the equivalent of:
Length		
Inches	25.4	Millimeter
Inches	2.54	Centimeter
Miles	1.609	Kilometer
Feet	0.3048	Meter
Millimeter	0.03937	Inches
Centimeter	0.3937	Inches
Kilometer	0.6214	Mile
Meter	3.281	Feet
Fluid volume		
U.S. quarts	0.9463	Liters
U.S. gallons	3.785	Liters
U.S. ounces	29.573529	Milliliters
Imperial gallons	4.54609	Liters
Imperial quarts	1.1365	Liters
Liters	0.2641721	U.S. gallons
Liters	1.0566882	U.S. quarts
Liters	33.814023	U.S. ounces
Liters	0.22	Imperial gallons
Liters	0.8799	Imperial quarts
Milliliters	0.033814	U.S. ounces
Milliliters	1.0	Cubic centimeters
Milliliters	0.001	Liters

(continued)

Table 3 CONVERSION FORMULAS (continued)

Multiply:	By:	To get the equivalent of:
Torque		
Foot-pounds	1.3558	Newton-meters
Foot-pounds	0.138255	Meters-kilograms
Inch-pounds	0.11299	Newton-meters
Newton-meters	0.7375622	Foot-pounds
Newton-meters	8.8507	Inch-pounds
Meters-kilograms	7.2330139	Foot-pounds
Volume		
Cubic inches	16.387064	Cubic centimeters
Cubic centimeters	0.0610237	Cubic inches
Temperature		
Fahrenheit	$(F - 32°) \times 0.556$	Centigrade
Centigrade	$(C \times 1.8) + 32$	Fahrenheit
Weight		
Ounces	28.3495	Grams
Pounds	0.4535924	Kilograms
Grams	0.035274	Ounces
Kilograms	2.2046224	Pounds
Pressure		
Pounds per square inch	0.070307	Kilograms per square centimeter
Kilograms per square centimeter	14.223343	Pounds per square inch
Kilopascals	0.1450	Pounds per square inch
Pounds per square inch	6.895	Kilopascals
Speed		
Miles per hour	1.609344	Kilometers per hour
Kilometers per hour	0.6213712	Miles per hour

CHAPTER TWO

TROUBLESHOOTING

Diagnosing mechanical problems is relatively simple if you use orderly procedures and keep a few basic principles in mind.

The troubleshooting procedures in this chapter analyze typical symptoms and show logical methods of isolating causes. These are not the only methods. There may be several ways to solve a problem, but only a systematic, methodical approach can guarantee success.

Never assume anything. Do not overlook the obvious. If you are riding along and the engine suddenly quits, check the easiest, most accessible problems first. Is there gasoline in the tank? Is the fuel valve in the ON position? Has a spark plug wire fallen off?

If nothing obvious turns up in a quick check, look a little further. Learning to recognize and describe symptoms will make repairs easier for you or a mechanic at the shop. Describe problems accurately and fully. Saying that "it won't run" isn't the same as saying "it quit at high speed and won't start" or that "it sat in my garage for 3 months and then wouldn't start."

Gather as many symptoms together as possible to aid in diagnosis. Note whether the engine lost power gradually or all at once. Remember that the more complicated a machine is, the easier it is to troubleshoot because symptoms point to specific problems.

After the symptoms are defined, areas which could cause the problems are tested and analyzed. Guessing at the cause of a problem may provide the solution, but it can easily lead to frustration, wasted time and a series of expensive, unnecessary parts replacements.

You do not need fancy equipment or complicated test gear to determine whether repairs can be attempted at home. A few simple checks could save a large repair bill and time lost while the bike sits in a dealer's service department. On the other hand, be realistic and don't attempt repairs beyond your abilities. Service departments tend to charge a lot for putting together a disassembled engine that may have been abused. Some dealers won't even take on such a job—so use common sense and don't get in over your head.

OPERATING REQUIREMENTS

An engine needs 3 basics to run properly: correct fuel-air mixture, compression and a spark at the correct time. If one or more are missing, the engine just won't run. The electrical system is the weakest link of the 3 basics. More problems result from electrical breakdowns than from any other source. Keep that in mind before you begin tampering with carburetor adjustments and the like.

If the bike has been sitting for any length of time and refuses to start, check and clean the spark plugs and then look to the gasoline delivery system. This includes the fuel tank, fuel shutoff valve and the fuel line to the carburetor. Gasoline deposits may have formed and gummed up the carburetor's jets and air passages. Gasoline tends to lose its potency after standing for long periods. Condensation may contaminate the fuel with water. Drain the old fuel and try starting with a fresh tankful.

EMERGENCY TROUBLESHOOTING

When the bike is difficult to start or won't start at all, it does not help to wear out your leg on the kickstarter. Check for obvious problems even before getting out your tools. Go down the following list step by step. Do each one; you may be embarrassed to find your kill switch is stuck in the OFF position. If it still will not start, refer to the appropriate troubleshooting procedure which follows in this chapter.

1. Is there fuel in the tank? Open the filler cap (**Figure 1**) and rock the bike. Listen for fuel sloshing around.

> *WARNING*
> *Do not use an open flame to check in*
> *the tank. A serious explosion is certain*
> *to result.*

2. Is the fuel shutoff valve (**Figure 2**) in the ON position?
3. Make sure the kill switch (**Figure 3**) is not stuck in the OFF position.
4. Is the spark plug wire (**Figure 4**) on tight? Push it on and slightly rotate it to clean the electrical connection between the plug and the connector.
5. Is the choke in the correct position:
   a. XR350R models: the choke lever should be in the *raised* position for a cold engine.

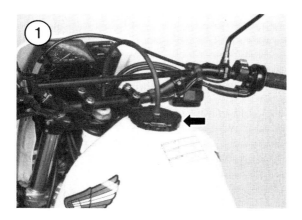

b. On XL350R and 1984-on XL250R models: the lever should be pulled *toward* the hand grip for a cold engine and pushed *away* for a warm engine (**Figure 5**).

c. On all other models: the knob should be pulled *up* (**Figure 6**) for a cold engine and pushed *down* for a warm engine.

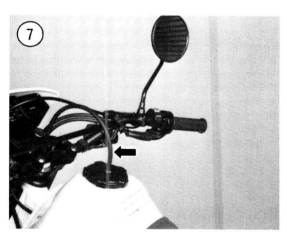

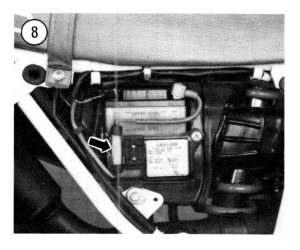

6. Is the vent tube (**Figure 7**) from the fuel filler cap blocked? Clean it out if necessary.

7. On models so equipped, has the main fuse blown (**Figure 8**)? Replace with a good one.

ENGINE STARTING

An engine that refuses to start or is difficult to start is very frustrating. More often than not, the problem is very minor and can be found with a simple and logical troubleshooting approach.

The following items show a beginning point from which to isolate engine starting problems.

Engine Fails to Start

Perform the following spark test to determine if the ignition system is operating properly.

1. Remove one of the spark plugs from the cylinder.

2. Connect the spark plug wire and connector to the spark plug and touch the spark plug's base to a good ground such as the engine cylinder head (**Figure 9**). Position the spark plug so you can see the electrodes.

> *WARNING*
> *If it is necessary to hold the high voltage lead during the next step, do so with an insulated pair of pliers. The high voltage generated by the ignition pulse generator and CDI unit could produce serious or fatal shocks.*

3. Crank the engine over with the kickstarter. A fat blue spark should be evident across the plug's electrodes.

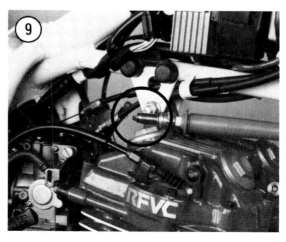

4. If the spark is good, check for one or more of the following possible malfunctions:
    a. Obstructed fuel line.
    b. Low compression.
    c. Leaking head gasket.
    d. Choke not operating properly.
    e. Throttle not operating properly.

5. If spark is not good, check for one or more of the following:
    a. Weak ignition coil.
    b. Weak CDI pulse generator.
    c. Broken or shorted high tension lead to the spark plug.
    d. Loose electrical connections.
    e. Loose or broken ignition coil ground wire.

Engine Is Difficult to Start

Check for one or more of the following possible malfunctions:
    a. Fouled spark plug.
    b. Improperly adjusted choke.
    c. Contaminated fuel system.
    d. Improperly adjusted carburetor.
    e. Weak ignition coil.
    f. Weak CDI pulse generator.
    g. Incorrect type ignition coil.
    h. Poor compression.

Engine Will Not Crank

Check for one or more of the following possible malfunctions:
    a. Discharged battery (models so equipped).
    b. Defective or broken kickstarter mechanism.
    c. Seized piston.
    d. Seized crankshaft bearings.
    e. Broken connecting rod.
    f. Locked-up transmission or clutch assembly.

ENGINE PERFORMANCE

In the following checklist, it is assumed that the engine runs, but is not operating at peak performance. This will serve as a starting point from which to isolate a performance malfunction.

The possible causes for each malfunction are listed in a logical sequence and in order of probability.

Engine Will Not Start Or Is Hard to Start

    a. Fuel tank empty.
    b. Obstructed fuel line or fuel shutoff valve.
    c. Sticking float valve in carburetor(s).
    d. Carburetor incorrectly adjusted.

    e. Improper choke operation.
    f. Fouled or improperly gapped spark plug.
    g. Weak CDI pulse generator.
    h. Ignition timing incorrect (faulty component in system).
    i. Broken or shorted ignition coil.
    j. Weak or faulty spark unit or pulse generator.
    k. Improper valve timing.
    l. Clogged air filter element.
    m. Contaminated fuel.

Engine Will Not Idle or Idles Erratically

    a. Carburetor(s) incorrectly adjusted.
    b. Fouled or improperly gapped spark plug.
    c. Leaking head gasket or vacuum leak.
    d. Weak CDI pulse generator.
    e. Ignition timing incorrect (faulty component in system).
    f. Improper valve timing.
    g. Obstructed fuel line or fuel shutoff valve.

Engine Misses at High Speed

    a. Fouled or improperly gapped spark plug.
    b. Improper ignition timing (faulty component in system).
    c. Improper carburetor main jet selection.
    d. Clogged jets in the carburetor(s).
    e. Weak ignition coil.
    f. Weak CDI pulse generator.
    g. Improper valve timing.
    h. Obstructed fuel line or fuel shutoff valve.

Engine Continues to Run with Ignition Off

    a. Excessive carbon build-up in engine.
    b. Vacuum leak in intake system.
    c. Contaminated or incorrect fuel octane rating.

Engine Overheating

    a. Obstructed cooling fins on the cylinder and cylinder head.
    b. Improper ignition timing (faulty component in system).
    c. Improper spark plug heat range.

Engine Misses at Idle

    a. Fouled or improperly gapped spark plug.
    b. Spark plug cap faulty.

c. Ignition cable insulation deteriorated (shorting out).
d. Dirty or clogged air filter element.
e. Carburetor(s) incorrectly adjusted (too lean or too rich).
f. Choke valve stuck.
g. Clogged jet(s) in the carburetor.
h. Carburetor float height incorrect.

Engine Backfires— Explosions in Mufflers

a. Fouled or improperly gapped spark plug.
b. Spark plug cap faulty.
c. Ignition cable insulation deteriorated (shorting out).
d. Ignition timing incorrect.
e. Improper valve timing.
f. Contaminated fuel.
g. Burned or damaged intake and/or exhaust valves.
h. Weak or broken intake and/or exhaust valve springs.

Pre-ignition (Fuel Mixture Ignites Before Spark Plug Fires)

a. Hot spot in combustion chamber (piece of carbon).
b. Valve(s) stuck in guide.
c. Overheating engine.

Smoky Exhaust and Engine Runs Roughly

a. Carburetor mixture too rich.
b. Choke not operating correctly.
c. Water or other contaminants in fuel.
d. Clogged fuel line.
e. Clogged air filter element.

Engine Loses Power at Normal Riding Speed

a. Carburetor incorrectly adjusted.
b. Engine overheating.
c. Improper ignition timing (faulty component in system).
d. Weak CDI pulse generator.
e. Incorrectly gapped spark plug.
f. Weak ignition coil.

g. Weak CDI pulse generator.
h. Obstructed mufflers.
i. Dragging brake(s).

Engine Lacks Acceleration

a. Carburetor mixture too lean.
b. Clogged fuel line.
c. Improper ignition timing (faulty component in system).
d. Improper valve clearance.
e. Dragging brake(s).

ENGINE NOISES

1. *Knocking or pinging during acceleration*— Caused by using a lower octane fuel than recommended. May also be caused by poor fuel. Pinging can also be caused by spark plugs of the wrong heat range. Refer to *Spark Plug Selection* in Chapter Three.
2. *Slapping or rattling noises at low speed or during acceleration*—May be caused by piston slap (excessive piston to cylinder wall clearance).
3. *Knocking or rapping while decelerating*— Usually caused by excessive rod bearing clearance.
4. *Persistent knocking and vibration*—Usually caused by excessive main bearing clearance.
5. *Rapid on-off squeal*—Compression leak around cylinder head gasket or spark plug.

EXCESSIVE VIBRATION

This can be difficult to find without disassembling the engine. Usually this is caused by loose engine mounting hardware.

FRONT SUSPENSION AND STEERING

Poor handling may be caused by improper tire pressure, a damaged or bent frame or front steering components, a worn front fork assembly, worn wheel bearings or dragging brakes.

BRAKE PROBLEMS

Sticking disc brakes may be caused by a stuck piston in a caliper assembly or warped pad shim.

A sticking drum brake may be caused by worn or weak return springs, dry pivot and cam bushings or improper adjustment. Grabbing brakes may be caused by greasy linings which must be replaced. Brake grab may also be due to an out-of-round drum. Glazed linings will cause loss of stopping power.

2

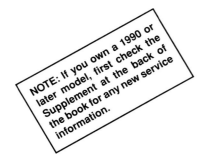

NOTE: If you own a 1990 or later model, first check the Supplement at the back of the book for any new service information.

CHAPTER THREE

LUBRICATION, MAINTENANCE AND TUNE-UP

A motorcycle, even in normal use, is subjected to tremendous heat, stress and vibration. When neglected, any bike becomes unreliable and actually dangerous to ride.

To gain the utmost in safety, performance and useful life from the Honda it is necessary to make periodic inspections and adjustments. Minor problems are often found during these inspections that are simple and inexpensive to correct at the time. If they are not found and corrected at this time they could lead to major and more expensive problems later on.

Start out by doing simple tune-up, lubrication and maintenance. Tackle more involved jobs as you become more acquainted with the bike.

Tables 1-12 are located at the end of this chapter.

ROUTINE CHECKS

The following simple checks should be performed at each stop at a service station for gas.

Engine Oil Level

Refer to *Engine Oil Level Check* under *Periodic Lubrication* in this chapter.

General Inspection

1. Quickly inspect the engine for signs of oil or fuel leakage.
2. Check the tires for embedded stones. Pry them out with your ignition key.
3. Make sure all lights work.

> *NOTE*
> *At least check the brake light. It can burn out at any time. Motorists cannot stop as quickly as you and need all the warning you can give.*

Tire Pressure

Tire pressure must be checked with the tires cold. Correct tire pressure varies with the load you are carrying. See **Table 1**.

Battery (XL Series)

On XL series models, remove the right-hand side cover and check the battery electrolyte level. The level must be between the upper and lower level marks on the case (**Figure 1**). For complete details see *Battery Removal, Installation and Electrolyte Level Check* in this chapter.

Check the level more frequently in hot weather; electrolyte will evaporate rapidly as heat increases.

Crankcase Breather Hose

Inspect the hoses for cracks and deterioration and make sure that all hose clamps are tight (**Figure 2**).

Evaporative Emission Control System (California XL Series)

Inspect the hoses (**Figure 3**) to make sure they are not kinked or bent and that they are securely connected to their respective parts.

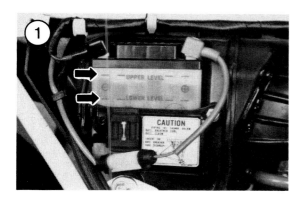

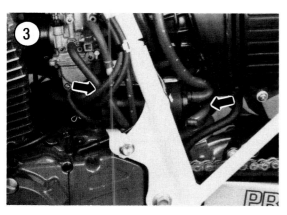

Lights and Horn

With the engine running, check the following.

NOTE
XR series bikes are equipped with only a headlight and taillight. The headlight is controlled by a dimmer switch.

3

1. Pull the front brake lever on and check that the brake light comes on.
2. Push the rear brake pedal down and check that the brake light comes on soon after you have begun depressing the pedal.
3A. On XL series, perform the following:
   a. Turn the headlight switch to the ON position. Check that both the headlight and taillight are on.
   b. Press the headlight dimmer switch to both the HI and LO positions and check to see that both headlight elements are working.
3B. On XR series, press the headlight dimmer switch to both the HI and LO positions and check to see that both headlight elements are working.
4. Turn the turn signal switch to the left and right positions and check that all 4 turn signals are working.
5. Push the horn button and make sure that the horn blows loudly.
6. If during the test, the rear brake pedal traveled too far before the brake light came on, adjust the rear brake light switch as described in Chapter Eight.
7. If the horn or any of the lights failed to operate properly, refer to Chapter Eight.

PRE-RIDE CHECKS

The following checks should be performed prior to the first ride of the day.
1. Inspect all fuel lines and fittings for wetness.
2. Make sure the fuel tank is full of fresh gasoline.
3. Make sure the engine oil level is correct.
4. Check the operation of the front brake. On disc brake models, add hydraulic fluid to the brake master cylinder if necessary.
5. Check the throttle and the rear brake pedal. Make sure they operate properly with no binding.
6. Inspect the front and rear suspension; make sure it has a good solid feel with no looseness.
7. Check tire pressure. Refer to **Table 1**.
8. Check the exhaust system for damage.
9. Check the tightness of all fasteners, especially engine mounting hardware.

SERVICE INTERVALS

The services and intervals shown in **Table 2** are recommended by the factory. Strict adherence to these recommendations will ensure long service from the Honda. If the bike is run in an area of high humidity, the lubrication services must be done more frequently to prevent possible rust damage.

Service intervals differ between the XL and XR series because the XR will be most likely be ridden harder and in dirtier areas. If your bike is an XL but is used off-road frequently you should follow the service recommended for the XR.

If you are riding your bike in competition events, refer to **Table 3** for suggested pre-race inspection areas and items.

For convenience when maintaining your motorcycle, most of the services shown in the table are described in this chapter. However, some procedures which require more than minor disassembly or adjustment are covered elsewhere in the appropriate chapter.

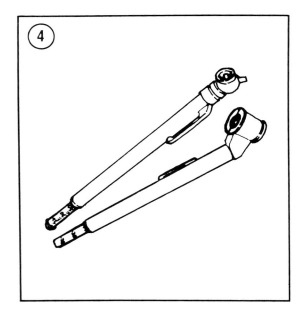

TIRES AND WHEELS

Tire Pressure

Tire pressure should be checked and adjusted to maintain the smoothness of the tire, good traction and handling and to get the maximum life out of the tire. A simple, accurate gauge (**Figure 4**) can be purchased for a few dollars and should be carried in your motorcycle tool kit. The appropriate tire pressures are shown in **Table 1**.

Tire Inspection

The tires take a lot of punishment so inspect them periodically for excessive wear, cuts, abrasions, etc. If you find a nail or other object in the tire, mark its location with a light crayon prior to removing it. This will help locate the hole for repair. Refer to Chapter Nine for tire changing and repair information.

Check local traffic regulations concerning minimum tread depth. Measure the tread depth at the center of the tire tread using a tread depth gauge (**Figure 5**) or small ruler. Honda recommends that original equipment tires be replaced when the depth is 8 mm (0.30 in.) or less.

Rim Inspection

Frequently inspect the wheel rims. If a rim has been damaged it might have been knocked out of

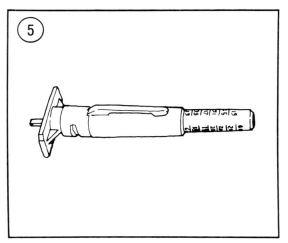

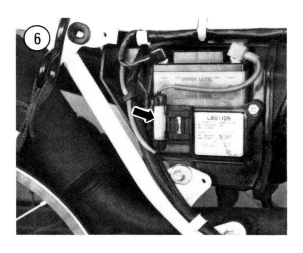

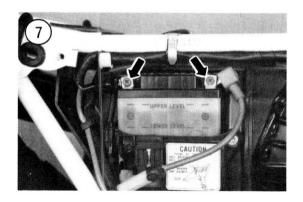

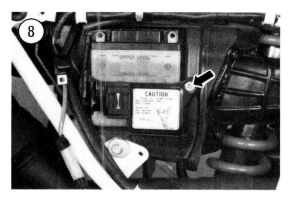

alignment. Improper wheel alignment can cause severe vibration and result in an unsafe riding condition.

3

Wheel Spoke Tension

1. Tap each spoke with a wrench. The higher the pitch of sound it makes, the tighter the spoke. The lower the sound frequency, the looser the spoke. A "ping" is good; a "clunk" says the spoke is too loose.
2. If one or more of the spokes are loose, tighten them as described under *Wheels* in Chapter Nine.

BATTERY
(XL SERIES)

Removal, Installation and
Electrolyte Level Check

The battery is the heart of the electrical system. Check and service the battery at the interval indicated in **Table 2**. Most electrical system troubles can be attributed to neglect of this vital component.

The electrolyte level may be checked with the battery in the frame. However, it is necessary to remove the right-hand side panel and the battery bracket. The electrolyte level should be maintained between the 2 marks on the battery case (**Figure 1**). If the electrolyte level is low, it's a good idea to remove the battery from the frame so it can be thoroughly serviced and checked.

> *NOTE*
> *Battery removal and installation vary slightly among the different models. This procedure shows a typical removal and installation procedure.*

1. Remove the right-hand side cover.
2. Pull the main fuse holder (**Figure 6**) out of the battery bracket.
3. First disconnect the battery negative lead and then the positive lead from the terminals (**Figure 7**).
4. Remove the bolt (**Figure 8**) securing the bracket and hinge it out of the way.
5. Pull the battery part way out of the compartment (**Figure 9**).
6. Disconnect the breather tube (**Figure 10**).

7. Slide the battery out the rest of the way and remove from the bike's frame.

WARNING
Protect your eyes, skin and clothing. If electrolyte gets into your eyes, flush your eyes thoroughly with clean water and get prompt medical attention.

CAUTION
Be careful not to spill battery electrolyte on plastic, painted or plated surfaces. The liquid is highly corrosive and will damage the finish. If it is spilled, wash it off immediately with soapy water and thoroughly rinse with clean water.

8. Remove the cap from the battery cells and add distilled water to correct the level. Never add electrolyte (acid) to correct the level.

NOTE
If distilled water has been added, reinstall the battery caps and gently shake the battery for several minutes to mix the existing electrolyte with the new water.

9. After the fluid level has been corrected and the battery allowed to stand for a few minutes, remove the battery caps and check the specific gravity of the electrolyte with a hydrometer (**Figure 11**). See *Battery Testing* in this chapter.
10. After the battery has been refilled, recharged or replaced, install it by reversing these removal steps.

CAUTION
If you removed the breather tube from the frame, be sure to route it so that residue will not drain onto any part of the bike's frame. The tube must be free of bends or twists as any restrictions may pressurize the battery and damage it.

Testing

Hydrometer testing is the best way to check battery condition. Use a hydrometer with numbered graduations from 1.100 to 1.300 rather than one with just color-coded bands. To use the hydrometer, squeeze the rubber ball, insert the tip into the cell and release the pressure on the ball. Draw enough electrolyte to float the weighted float inside the hydrometer. Note the number in line with the surface of the electrolyte; this is the specific gravity for this cell. Squeeze the rubber ball again and return the electrolyte to the cell from which it came.

The specific gravity of the electrolyte in each battery cell is an excellent indication of that cell's condition. A fully charged cell will read from 1.260-1.280, while a cell in good condition reads from 1.230-1.250 and anything below 1.140 is discharged.

If the cells test in the poor range, the battery requires recharging. The hydrometer is useful for checking the progress of the charging operation. **Table 4** shows approximate state of charge.

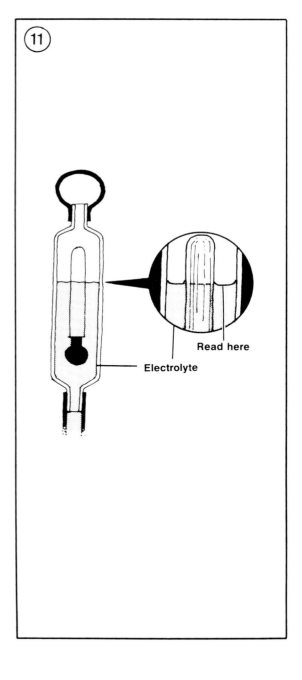

Read here

Electrolyte

Charging

WARNING
During the charging process, highly explosive hydrogen gas is released from the battery. The battery should be charged only in a well-ventilated area away from any open flames (including pilot lights on home gas appliances). Do not allow any smoking in the area. Never check the charge by arcing (connecting pliers or other metal objects) across the terminals; the resulting spark can ignite the hydrogen gas.

CAUTION
Always remove the battery from the bike's frame before connecting the battery charger. Never recharge a battery in the bike's frame; the corrosive mist that is emitted during the charging process will corrode all surrounding surfaces.

1. Connect the positive (+) charger lead to the positive (+) battery terminal and the negative (-) charger lead to the negative (-) battery terminal.

NOTE
Some models have a 6-volt battery (3 battery vent caps) and electrical system while models have a 12-volt battery (6 battery vent caps) and electrical system.

2. Remove all vent caps from the battery, set the charger to either 6 or 12 volts (depending on the bike's electrical system) and switch the charger. If the output of the charger is variable, it is best to select a low setting—1 1/2 to 2 amps.

CAUTION
The electrolyte level must be maintained at the upper level during the charging cycle; check and refill as necessary.

3. After the battery has been charged for about 8 hours, turn the charger, disconnect the leads and check the specific gravity of each cell. It should be within the limits specified in **Table 4**. If it is, and remains stable for 1 hour, the battery is considered charged.

4. Clean the battery terminals, electrical cable connectors and surrounding case and reinstall the battery in the frame, reversing the removal steps. Coat the battery terminals with Vaseline or silicone spray to retard corrosion and decomposition of the terminals.

CAUTION
Route the breather tube so that is does not drain onto any part of the frame. The tube must be free of bends or twists as any restriction may pressurize the battery and damage it.

New Battery Installation

When replacing the old battery with a new one, be sure to charge it completely (specific gravity 1.265-1.280) before installing it in the bike. Failure to do so or using the battery with a low electrolyte level will permanently damage the new battery.

PERIODIC LUBRICATION

Oil

Oil is graded according to its viscosity, which is an indication of how thick it is. The Society of Automotive Engineers (SAE) system distinguishes oil viscosity by numbers. Thick oils have higher viscosity numbers than thin oils. For example, an SAE 5 oil is a thin oil while an SAE 90 oil is relatively thick.

Grease

A good quality grease (preferably waterproof) should be used. Water does not wash grease off parts as easily as it washes oil off. In addition, grease maintains its lubricating qualities better than oil on long and strenuous rides. In a pinch, though, the wrong lubricant is better than none at all. Correct the situation as soon as possible.

Engine Oil Level Check
(Wet-sump Models)

Engine oil level is checked with the dipstick/oil filler cap, located at the front of the crankcase on the right-hand side (**Figure 12**).
1. Place the bike on level ground.
2. Start the engine and let it idle for 2-3 minutes.
3. Shut off the engine and let the oil settle.

4. Unscrew the dipstick and wipe it clean. Reinsert the dipstick onto the threads in the hole; do not screw it in.

5. Remove the dipstick and check the oil level. The level should be between the 2 lines and not above the upper one (**Figure 13**). If the level is below the lower line, add the recommended type engine oil (**Figure 14**) to correct the level.

Engine Oil Level Check (Dry-sump Models)

On dry-sump type engines, the major portion of the engine oil is stored in a closed-off section of the bike's frame while some of the oil is carried in the crankcase.

Engine oil level is checked in 2 places – the dipstick on the frame and the oil level check bolt on the crankcase.

1. Place wood block(s) under the skid plate to support the bike securely in a vertical position.

2. Start the engine and let it idle for 5 minutes. Let the engine warm up an additional 5 minutes if the air temperature is below 10° C (50° F)

3. Shut off the engine and let the oil settle.

4. Unscrew the dipstick (**Figure 15**).

5. Wipe the dipstick clean and reinsert the dipstick onto the threads in the hole; do *not* screw it in.

6. Remove the dipstick and check the oil level. The level should be between the 2 lines and not above the upper one. If the level is below the lower line, add the recommended type engine oil to correct the level.

7. Install the dipstick and tighten securely.

8. Restart the engine and allow it to run for a couple of minutes.

9. Shut off the engine and allow the oil to settle.

10. Unscrew the crankcase oil level check bolt (**Figure 16**).

11. The crankcase oil level is correct if the oil is up to the bottom surface of the threads in the hole.

12. If the oil level is correct on the dipstick but the crankcase oil level is incorrect, some part of the oil system is not operating properly. Do not operate the bike until you have found and fixed the problem. Perform the following:

    a. Recheck the oil level on the dipstick.

    b. Inspect the oil lines and fittings from the engine to the bike's frame.

    c. Inspect the oil pump as described in Chapter Five.

13. Reinstall the oil level check bolt and tighten securely.

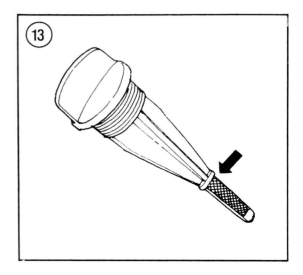

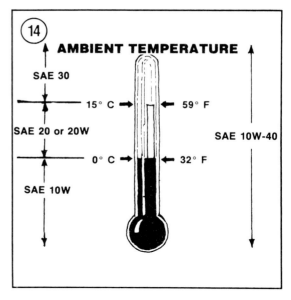

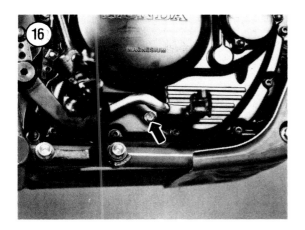

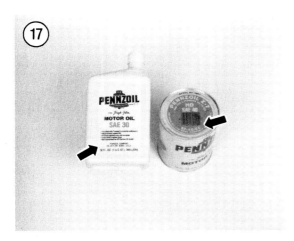

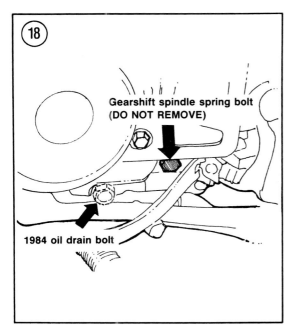

Engine Oil Change

Change the engine oil at the recommended oil change interval indicated in **Table 2**. This assumes that the motorcycle is operated in moderate climates. In extreme climates, oil should be changed every 30 days. The time interval is more important than the mileage interval because acids formed by combustion blowby will contaminate the oil even if the motorcycle is not run for several months. If the motorcycle is operated under dusty conditions, the oil will get dirty more quickly and should be changed more frequently than recommended.

Use only a high-quality detergent motor oil with an API classification of SE or SF. The classification is stamped on top of the can or printed on the label on the plastic bottle (**Figure 17**). Try to use the same brand of oil at each change. Use of oil additives is not recommended as it may cause clutch slippage. Refer to **Figure 14** for correct oil viscosity to use under anticipated ambient temperatures (not engine oil temperature).

> *CAUTION*
> *Do not add any friction-reducing additives to the oil as they will cause clutch slippage. Also do not use an engine oil with graphite added.*

> *CAUTION*
> *On 1985-on 250 cc engines, do **not** make the mistake of removing the gearshift spindle spring bolt (**Figure 18**). If this bolt is removed the gearshift spindle spring will move out of position, rendering the gearshift linkage useless. If this happens, the engine must be removed from the frame and the crankcase must be disassembled to reposition the spring onto the bolt.*

> *NOTE*
> *Never dispose of motor oil in the trash, on the ground, or down a storm drain. Many service stations accept used motor oil and waste haulers provide curbside used motor oil collection. Do not combine other fluids with motor oil to be recycled. To locate a recycler, contact the American Petroleum Institute (API) at **www.recycleoil.org**.*

To change the engine oil and filter you will need the following:

   a. Drain pan.
   b. Funnel.
   c. Can opener or pour spout (oil in cans).
   d. 17 mm wrench (drain plug).
   e. Oil (refer to **Table 5** for quantity).

There are a number of ways to discard the old oil safely. Some service stations and oil retailers will accept your used oil for recycling; some may even give you money for it. Never drain the oil onto the ground.

1. Start the engine and let it reach operating temperature; 15-20 minutes of stop-and-go riding is usually sufficient.

2. Turn the engine off and place the bike on level ground.

3A. On 1978-1984 models, place a drain pan under the crankcase and remove the drain plug (**Figure 19**). Remove the dipstick/oil filler cap; this will speed up the flow of oil.

3B. On 1985-on models, place a drain pan under the crankcase and remove the drain plug (**Figure 20**). Remove the dipstick/oil filler cap; this will speed up the flow of oil.

> *CAUTION*
> *Make sure the ignition switch is off. Do not let the engine start and run without oil in the crankcase.*

4. Let the oil drain for at least 15-20 minutes. During this time, kick the kickstarter a couple of times to help drain any remaining oil.

5. Inspect the sealing washer on the crankcase drain plug. Replace if its condition is in doubt.

6. Install the drain plug and washer and tighten to the torque specification listed in **Table 6**.

7. On dry-sump models, perform the following:

   a. Move the drain pan under the frame down tube and remove the drain plug (**Figure 21**) from the frame.
   b. Let the oil drain for at least 15-20 minutes.
   c. Inspect the sealing washer on the drain plug; replace if necessary.
   d. Install the drain plug and tighten to the torque specification listed in **Table 6**.

8. If the oil filter screen is to be cleaned, perform *Oil Filter Screen Cleaning* as described in this chapter.

9. On 1983-on 350 cc models, if the oil filter is going to be replaced, perform *Oil Filter Replacement (1983-on 350 cc Models)* as described in this chapter.

10. Insert a funnel into the oil fill hole and fill the engine with the correct viscosity and quantity of oil. Refer to **Table 5**.

11. Install the dipstick/oil filler cap.

12. Start the engine, let it run at idle speed and check for leaks.

13. Turn the engine off and check for correct oil level; adjust as necessary.

Oil Filter Screen Cleaning

The oil filter screen should be cleaned at the interval indicated in **Table 2**.

1. Drain the engine oil as described in this chapter.

2. Remove the bolts (**Figure 22**) securing the skid plate and remove the skid plate.

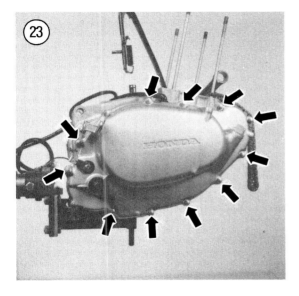

3. Remove the clamping bolt and remove the kickstarter arm.

4. Disconnect the clutch and decompression release cables from the right-hand crankcase cover.

5. Remove the bolts securing the right-hand footpeg and remove the footpeg assembly.

6. Remove the rear brake pedal.

7. Remove the bolts (**Figure 23**) securing the right-hand crankcase cover and remove the cover and gasket.

8. Remove the oil filter screen (**Figure 24**).

9. Clean the screen in solvent with a medium soft toothbrush and carefully dry with compressed air.

10. Inspect the screen; replace it if there are any breaks or holes in the screen.

11. Position the screen with the thick end facing toward the outside and install the screen into the crankcase.

NOTE
On models with a chain-driven balancer system, it is a good idea to adjust the balancer chain while the crankcase cover is removed. Refer to **Balancer Chain Adjustment** *in this chapter.*

12. Install by reversing these removal steps, noting the following.

13. Hold the compression release follower lever in the raised position, then install the crankcase cover and a new gasket.

14. Fill the crankcase with the recommended type and quantity of engine oil as described in this chapter.

15. Adjust the clutch, compression release and rear brake as described in this chapter.

Oil Filter Replacement
(350 cc Models)

1. Drain the engine oil as described in this chapter.

2. Place a drain pan under the right-hand crankcase cover.

3. Remove the bolts (**Figure 25**) securing the oil filter cover and remove the cover.

4. Remove the oil filter and spring. Discard the filter.

5. Wipe out the oil filter cavity with a shop rag and cleaning solvent. Remove any sludge.

6. Install the spring (**Figure 26**) and the filter element (**Figure 27**).

7. Inspect the O-ring seal on the cover and replace if necessary.

8. Install the cover and tighten the bolts securely.

9. Fill the crankcase with the recommended type and quantity of engine oil as described in this chapter.

Front Fork Oil Change
(Without Air-assist)

There is no recommended oil change interval but it's a good practice to change it at the recommended interval indicated in **Table 2**, or when it becomes contaminated.

1. Remove the upper plastic protective cap.

2. Use the 17 mm male socket provided in the factory tool kit or insert a 17 mm bolt head held with Vise Grip pliers and remove the upper fork cap bolt (**Figure 28**).

3. Place a drain pan under the fork and remove the drain screw (**Figure 29**). Allow the oil to drain for at least 5 minutes. Never reuse the oil.

> *CAUTION*
> *Do not allow the fork oil to come in contact with any of the brake components.*

4. With the bike's wheels on the ground and the front brake applied, push down on the handlebar grips to work the forks up and down. Continue until all oil is expelled.

5. Install the drain screw.

6. Fill the fork tube with DEXRON automatic transmission fluid or 10W fork oil. Refer to **Table 7** for fork oil capacities.

> *NOTE*
> *To measure the correct amount of fluid, use a plastic baby bottle. These have measurements in fluid ounces (oz.) and cubic centimeters (cc) on the side.*

7. After filling the fork tube, slowly pump the forks several times to expel air from the upper and lower fork chambers.

8. Install the fork cap bolt while pushing down on the spring. Start the bolt slowly; don't cross thread it. Tighten to the torque specifications listed in **Table 6**.

9. Repeat Steps 1-8 for the other fork.

10. Road test the bike and check for leaks.

Front Fork Oil Change
(With Air-assist)

There is no recommended fork oil change interval. However, it is a good practice to periodically change it to remove contaminates.

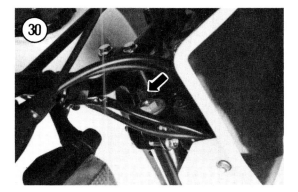

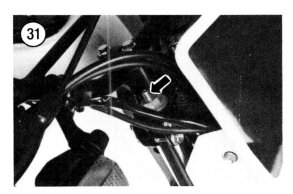

1. Place the bike on wood block(s) with the front wheel off the ground.

> *WARNING*
> *Release the air pressure gradually. If it is released too fast, oil will spurt out with the air. Protect your eyes and clothing accordingly.*

2. Unscrew the dust cap (**Figure 30**) and *bleed off all air pressure* by depressing the valve stem.
3. Slowly unscrew the fork cap bolt/air valve assembly (**Figure 31**); it is under pressure from the fork spring.
4. Place a drain pan under the fork and remove the drain screw (**Figure 32**). Allow the oil to drain for at least 5 minutes. *Never* reuse the oil.

> *CAUTION*
> *Do not allow the fork oil to come in contact with any of the brake components.*

5. Inspect the gasket on the drain screw; replace if necessary. Install the drain screw.
6. Place a shop cloth around the top of the fork tube to catch any residual fork oil on the fork spring. Withdraw the fork spring from the fork tube.
7. Fill the fork tube with DEXRON automatic transmission fluid or 10W fork oil. Refer to **Table 7** for fork oil capacities.

> *NOTE*
> *To measure the correct amount of fluid, use a plastic baby bottle. These have measurements in fluid ounces (oz.) and cubic centimeters (cc) on the side.*

8. Repeat Steps 1-7 for the other fork leg.
9. Remove the wood blocks(s) from under the engine.
10. After filling the fork tube, slowly pump the forks several times to expel air from the upper and lower fork chambers and to distribute the oil.
11. Apply the front brake and push down on the handlebar. Hold the handlebar in this position with the forks totally compressed. Have an assistant measure the distance from the top of the

fork tube to the top of the fork oil (**Figure 33**). Different fork damping characteristics will result from varying the amount of fork oil in the fork tube (using the standard air inflation pressure). Refer to **Table 7**.

12. Place the bike on wood block(s) with the front wheel off the ground.

13. Install the fork spring into each fork leg.

14. Inspect the O-ring seal on the fork cap bolt/air valve assembly; replace if necessary.

15. Install the fork cap bolt/air valve assembly while pushing down on the spring. Start the bolt slowly; don't cross thread it. Tighten to the torque specifications listed in **Table 6**.

> *WARNING*
> *Never use any type of compressed gas in Step 16 as an explosion may be lethal. Never heat the fork assembly with a torch or place it near an open flame or extreme heat as this will also result in an explosion. **Never** exceed the maximum air pressure of 14.0 psi (1.0 kg/cm²).*

16. Inflate the forks to the recommended air pressure listed in **Table 8**. Do not use compressed air; use only a small hand-operated air pump like the one shown in **Figure 34**.

17. Road test the bike and check for leaks.

Drive Chain Lubrication

Oil the drive chain at the interval indicated in **Table 2** or sooner if it becomes dry.

1. Place wood block(s) under the engine or frame to support the bike securely.

2. Oil the bottom run with a good grade of commercial chain lubricant. Concentrate on getting the oil down between the side plates of the chain links, into the pins, bushings and rollers.

3. Rotate the rear wheel to bring the non-oiled portion of the chain within reach. Continue until all the chain is lubricated.

Swing Arm Bearing Lubrication

Lubricate the swing arm bushings at the interval indicated in **Table 2**. Apply lubricant with a small hand-held grease gun. On dual-shock models, use a good grade multipurpose grease. On Pro-Link models, use molybdenum disulfide grease (NLGI No. 2).

1. Wipe the grease fittings clean of all road dirt and grease residue. Force the grease into the fitting until the grease runs out of both ends of the swing arm.

2. Clean off all excessive grease.

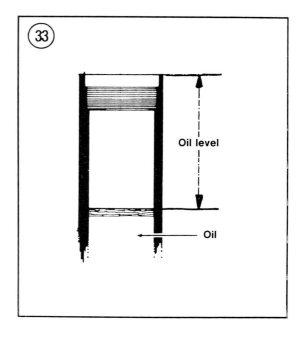

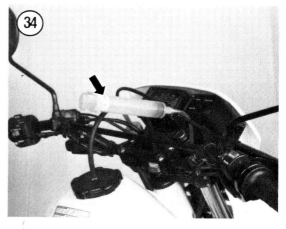

3. If the grease will not run out of the ends of the swing arm, unscrew the grease fitting from the swing arm. Clean it out with solvent; make sure the ball check valve is free. Reinstall the fitting or replace with a new one.

4. Apply the grease gun again. If the grease still does not run out of both ends of the swing arm, remove the swing arm as described in Chapter Ten. Disassemble the swing arm and thoroughly clean and re-grease.

Pro-Link Suspension Lubrication

Lubricate the Pro-Link suspension at the interval indicated in **Table 2**. Apply molybdenum disulfide grease (NLGI No. 2) with a small hand-held grease gun.

1. Wipe the grease fittings clean of all road dirt and grease residue. Force the grease into the fitting until the grease runs out past the dust seals on each of the links. There is one fitting where the shock arm is attached to the swing arm (**Figure 35**).

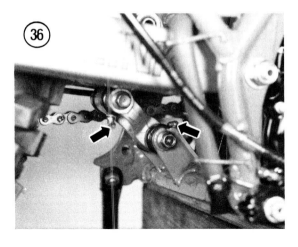

2. There is grease fitting where the shock arm attaches to the shock link and one where the shock link attaches to the frame. Refer to **Figure 36** or **Figure 37**.

3. Clean off all excessive grease.

4. If the grease will not run out of the ends of the joint, unscrew the grease fitting from the arm or link. Clean it out with solvent; make sure the ball check valve is free. Reinstall the fitting or replace with a new one.

5. Apply the grease gun again. If the grease still does not run out of both ends, remove the suspension components as described in Chapter Ten. Disassemble the arm and link and thoroughly clean and re-grease.

Control Cable Lubrication

The throttle, clutch and choke control cables (models so equipped) should be lubricated at the interval indicated in **Table 2**. They should also be inspected at this time for fraying and the cable sheath should be checked for chafing. The cables are relatively inexpensive and should be replaced when found to be faulty.

The control cables can be lubricated either with oil or with any of the popular cable lubricants and a cable lubricator. The first method requires more time and complete lubrication of the entire cable is less certain.

Examine the exposed end of the inner cable. If it is dirty or the cable feels gritty when moved up and down in its housing, first spray it with a lubricant/solvent such as LPS-25 or WD-40. Let this solvent drain out, then proceed with the following steps.

Oil method

1. Disconnect the cable from the lever.

> *NOTE*
> *On the throttle cable(s) it is necessary to remove the screws securing the right-hand switch assembly together to gain access to the throttle cable(s) ends.*

2. Make a cone of stiff paper and tape it to the end of the cable sheath (**Figure 38**).

3. Hold the cable upright and pour a small amount of thin oil (SAE 10W-30) into the cone. Work the cable in and out of the sheath for several minutes to help the oil work its way down to the end of the cable.

> *NOTE*
> *To avoid a mess, place a shop cloth at the end of the cable to catch the oil as it runs out.*

4. Remove the cone, reconnect the cable and adjust the cable(s) as described in this chapter.

NOTE
While the throttle cable(s) is removed and the switch assembly disassembled, apply a light coat of grease to the metal surfaces of the throttle grip assembly.

Lubricator method

1. Disconnect the cable from the lever.
2. Attach a lubricator following the manufacturer's instructions.
3. Insert the nozzle of the lubricant can in the lubricator, press the button on the can and hold it down until the lubricant begins to flow out of the other end of the cable.

NOTE
Place a shop cloth at the end of the cable(s) to catch all excess lubricant that will flow out.

4. Remove the lubricator, reconnect the cable(s) and adjust the cable as described in this chapter.

Miscellaneous Lubrication Points

Lubricate the clutch lever, front brake lever, rear brake pedal, side stand pivot points and footrest pivot points with SAE 10W/30 engine oil.

PERIODIC MAINTENANCE

Drive Chain Adjustment
(Dual-shock Models)

Check and adjust, if necessary, the drive chain at the recommended interval indicated in **Table 2**. The drive chain should be removed, cleaned and lubricated at the recommended interval listed in **Table 2**.
1. Place the transmission in NEUTRAL.
2. Remove the rear axle nut cotter pin. Discard the cotter pin.
3. Loosen the rear axle nut (A, **Figure 39**) and both axle adjusting locknuts (B, **Figure 39**).
4A. On XL250S models, perform the following:
   a. Place wood block(s) under the engine to support the bike with the rear wheel off the ground.

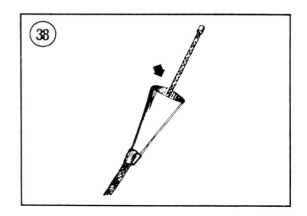

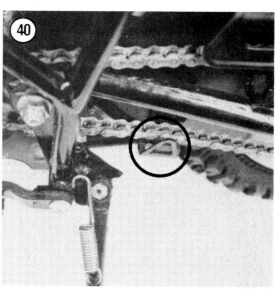

b. Screw the adjusters (C, **Figure 39**) in or out as required in equal amounts. Measure the free movement of the drive chain, pushed up mid-way on the lower run between both sprockets. Specifications for free play are listed in **Table 9**.

c. Rotate the rear wheel to move the chain to another position and recheck the adjustment; chains rarely wear or stretch evenly and as a result, the free play will not remain constant over the entire chain. If the chain cannot be adjusted within these limits, it is excessively worn and stretched and must be replaced as described in Chapter Ten.

d. If the drive chain cannot be adjusted within the limits in **Table 9**, it is excessively worn and stretched and should be replaced. Always replace both sprockets when replacing the drive chain; never install a new drive chain over worn sprocket. The replacement numbers are listed in **Table 10**.

WARNING
Excessive free play can result in chain breakage which could cause a serious accident.

e. After adjustment, tighten the axle adjuster locknuts securely.

4B. On XR250 models, perform the following:

a. Inspect the drive chain tensioner slider (**Figure 40**). If it is worn to the wear line, remove the screw and replace it before adjusting the drive chain.

b. Measure the distance between the bottom of the swing arm and top of the drive chain (**Figure 41**). Adjust if the distance is 20 mm (3/4 in.) or less.

c. Turn the adjuster bolt (C, **Figure 39**) until the distance shown in **Figure 41** is the same as listed in **Table 9**.

d. Rotate the rear wheel to move the chain to another position and recheck the adjustment; chains rarely wear or stretch evenly and as a result, the free play will not remain constant over the entire chain. If the chain cannot be adjusted within these limits, it is excessively worn and stretched and must be replaced as described in Chapter Ten. Always replace both sprockets when replacing the drive chain; never install a new drive chain over worn sprockets. The replacement numbers are listed in **Table 10**.

WARNING
Excessive free play can result in chain breakage which could cause a serious accident.

e. If the drive chain cannot be adjusted within the limits in **Table 9**, it is excessively worn and stretched and should be replaced.

f. After adjustment, tighten the axle adjuster locknuts securely.

5. On all models, make sure the index marks on the swing arm align with the same reference mark on both the right and left-hand sides (**Figure 42**).

6. When the adjustment is correct, sight along the chain from the rear sprocket to see that it is correctly aligned. It should leave the top of the rear sprocket in a straight line (A, **Figure 43**). If it cocked to one side or the other (B or C, **Figure 43**), the rear wheel is incorrectly aligned and must be corrected by turning the adjusters counter to one another until the chain and sprocket are correctly aligned.

7. Make sure the index mark aligns with the same graduation on the scale on both sides of the swing arm (**Figure 42**).

8. Tighten the rear axle nut to the torque specifications listed in **Table 6**.

9. Install a new cotter pin and bend the ends over completely.

10. Adjust the rear brake pedal free play as described in this chapter.

**Drive Chain Adjustment
(Pro-Link Models)**

Check and adjust, if necessary, the drive chain at the interval indicated in **Table 2**. The drive chain should be removed, cleaned and lubricated at the interval listed in **Table 2**.

1. Place wood block(s) under the engine to support the bike with the rear wheel off the ground.

2. Place the transmission in NEUTRAL.

3. Loosen the rear axle nut (A, **Figure 44**).

4. On 1985 XR350R models, loosen the holder nut (**Figure 45**) locking the snail adjuster in place.

5. Turn the snail adjusters (B, **Figure 44**) in equal amounts to either increase or decrease chain tension. After adjustment is complete, make sure that the same adjustment mark number on the snail adjuster aligns with the stopper pin on both sides of the swing arm (**Figure 46**).

6. Rotate the rear wheel to move the chain to another position and recheck the adjustment; chains rarely wear or stretch evenly and as a result, the free play will not remain constant over the entire chain. If the chain cannot be adjusted within these limits, it is excessively worn and stretched and must be replaced as described in Chapter Ten. Always replace both sprockets when replacing the drive chain; never install a new drive chain over worn sprocket. The replacement numbers are listed in **Table 10**.

> *WARNING*
> *Excessive free play can result in chain breakage which could cause a serious accident.*

7. When the adjustment is correct, sight along the chain from the rear sprocket to see that it is

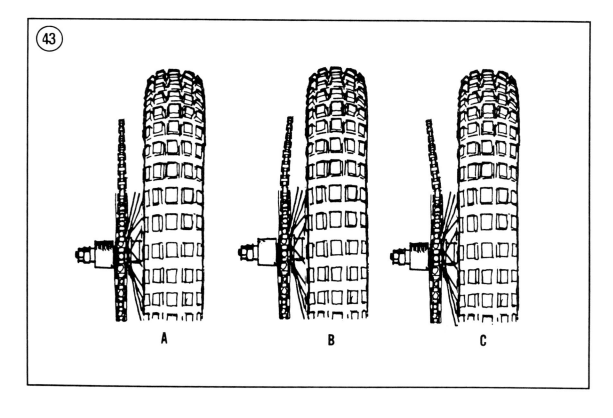

A   B   C

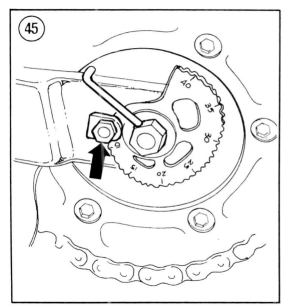

correctly aligned. It should leave the top of the rear sprocket in a straight line (A, **Figure 43**). If it cocked to one side or the other (B or C, **Figure 43**), the rear wheel is incorrectly aligned and must be corrected by turning the adjusters counter to one another until the chain and sprocket are correctly aligned.

8. When alignment is correct, readjust the free play as described in Step 3-7.

9. Tighten the self-locking rear axle nut to the torque specification listed in **Table 6**.

10. After the drive chain has been adjusted to the correct amount of free play, drill a small hole in the drive chain guard directly above the top of the chain. This can be used as a reference mark for further checking.

11. Adjust the rear brake pedal free play as described in this chapter.

Drive Chain Cleaning, Inspection and Lubrication

Clean and lubricate the drive chain at the interval indicated in **Table 2**.

1. Remove the drive chain as described under *Rear Wheel Removal/Installation* in Chapter Ten.

2. Immerse the drive chain in a pan of kerosene or non-flammable solvent and allow it to soak for about a half hour. Move it around and flex it during this period so that the dirt between the links, pins and rollers may work its way out.

3. Scrub the rollers and side plates with a stiff brush and rinse away loosened dirt. Rinse it a couple of times to make sure all dirt and grit is washed out. Dry the chain with a shop cloth and hang it up to thoroughly dry.

4. After cleaning the drive chain, examine it carefully for wear or damage. If any signs are visible, replace the drive chain.

5. Lay the drive chain against a ruler (**Figure 47**) and compress the links together. Then stretch them

apart. If more than 0.6 mm (1/4 in.) of movement is possible, the drive chain is worn and must be replaced.

6. One additional check is to lay the drive chain alongside a ruler with the links stretched apart completely. Measure the distance between the number of pins indicated in **Table 11**. Replace the drive chain if it has stretched to the service limit listed in **Table 11**.

> *NOTE*
> *Always inspect both sprockets (**Figure 48**) every time the chain is removed. If any wear is visible on the teeth, replace the sprocket(s). Never install a new chain over worn sprockets or a worn chain over new sprocket(s).*

7. Check the inner faces of the inner plates (**Figure 49**). They should be highly polished on both sides. If they show considerable wear on both sides, the sprockets are not aligned. Adjust alignment as described under *Drive Chain Adjustment* in this chapter.

8. Lubricate the drive chain with a good grade of chain lubricant, carefully following the manufacturer's instructions.

9. Reinstall the drive chain as described under *Rear Wheel Removal/Installation* in Chapter Ten.

10. Adjust drive chain free play as described in this chapter.

Drive Chain Sliders
(1986-on XR250R)

The drive chain is equipped with 3 different sliders. Two of the sliders are located at the pivot point of the swing arm and the other is located toward the rear of the swing arm.

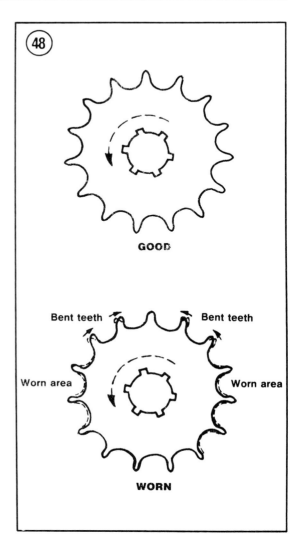

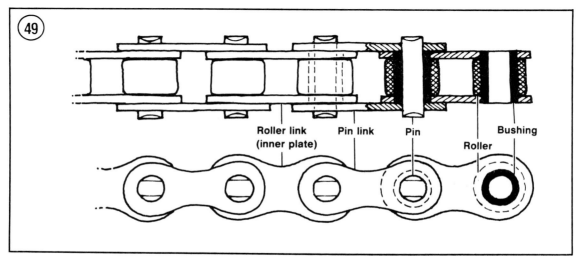

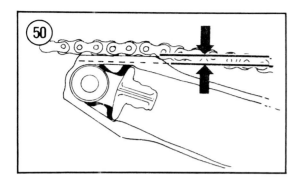

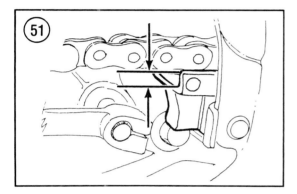

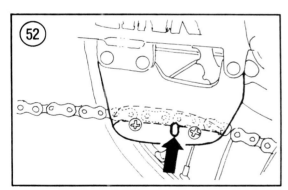

1. Inspect the slider attached to the front of the swing arm. If the wear groove is worn more than halfway through the material (**Figure 50**), replace the slider as follows:

    a. Remove the screws and washers securing the slider to the swing arm.

    b. Remove the slider and install a new slider.

    c. Tighten the screws securely.

2. Inspect the slider attached to the frame below the pivot point of the swing arm. If a groove is worn into the material by 15 mm (0.6 in.) (**Figure 51**), replace the slider as follows:

    a. Remove the bolt securing the slider to the mounting bracket.

    b. Remove the slider and the collar.

    c. Install the collar into the new slider and install the slider.

    d. Tighten the bolt securely.

3. Inspect the slider attached to the rear of the swing arm. If a slider is worn so the drive chain is visible through the wear limit opening on the mounting bracket (**Figure 52**), replace the slider as follows:

    a. Remove the bolts securing the slider to the mounting bracket.

    b. Remove the slider and install the new slider into the mounting bracket.

    c. Tighten the bolts securely.

Drive Chain Tensioners (Pro-Link Models)

On Pro-Link models there are either rollers or a slider on the chain tensioner arm. There is also a drive chain guide (A, **Figure 53**) and a flat slider (B, **Figure 53**) attached to left-hand side of the swing arm near the pivot point.

There are no factory-specified wear limit dimensions for the rollers. If they are worn unevenly or worn close to the attachment bolt, they should be replaced. Remove the bolt and nut securing the roller and replace with a new roller.

Inspect the slider attached to the swing arm. If the wear groove is worn more than halfway through the material, replace the slider as follows:

    a. Remove the screws and washers securing the slider to the swing arm.

    b. Remove the slider and install a new slider.

    c. Tighten the screws securely.

Brake Linings

Check the front and rear brake linings for wear. If the arrow on the brake arm aligns with the raised index mark on the brake backing plate (**Figure 54**) when the brake is applied, the brake linings require replacement.

If replacement is necessary, refer to Chapter Eleven.

Disc Brake Fluid Level

The fluid level in the front brake reservoir should be up to the upper mark within the reservoir. This upper level mark is visible only when the master cylinder top cover is removed. If the brake fluid level reaches the lower level mark, visible through the viewing port on the side of the master cylinder reservoir, the fluid level must be corrected by adding fresh brake fluid.
1. Place the bike on level ground and position the handlebars so the master cylinder reservoir is level.
2. Clean any dirt from the area around the top cover prior to removing the cover.
3. Remove the screws securing the top cover (**Figure 55**). Remove the top cover and the diaphragm. Add brake fluid until the level is to the upper level line within the master cylinder body. Use fresh brake fluid from a sealed brake fluid container.

> *WARNING*
> *Use brake fluid from a sealed container and clearly marked DOT 3 or DOT 4 only (specified for disc brakes). Others may vaporize and cause brake failure. Do not intermix different brands or types of brake fluid as they may not be compatible. Do not intermix a silicone based (DOT 5) brake fluid as it can cause brake component damage leading to brake system failure.*

> *CAUTION*
> *Be careful when handling brake fluid. Do not spill it on painted or plated surfaces or plastic parts as it will destroy the surface. Wash the area immediately with soapy water and thoroughly rinse it off.*

4. Reinstall the diaphragm and the top cover. Tighten the screws securely.

Disc Brake Lines

Check brake lines between the master cylinder and the brake caliper. If there is any leakage, tighten the connections and bleed the brakes as described in Chapter Eleven. If this does not stop the leak or if a brake line is obviously damaged, cracked or chafed, replace the brake line and bleed the system.

Disc Brake Pad Wear

Inspect the brake pads for excessive or uneven wear, scoring and oil or grease on the friction surface. Look up at the bottom of the caliper assembly and check the wear lines on the brake pads. Replace both pads if the wear line on the pads reaches the brake disc.

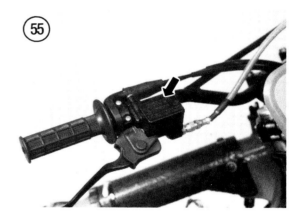

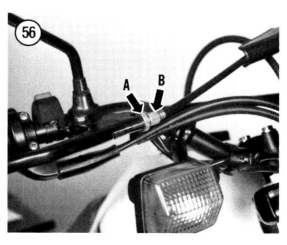

If any of these conditions exist, replace the pads as described in Chapter Eleven.

Disc Brake Fluid Change

Every time the reservoir cap is removed, a small amount of dirt and moisture enters the brake fluid. The same thing happens if a leak occurs or any part of the hydraulic system is loosened or disconnected. Dirt can clog the system and cause unnecessary wear. Water in the brake fluid vaporizes at high temperature, impairing the hydraulic action and reducing the brake's stopping ability.

To maintain peak performance, change the brake fluid as indicated in **Table 2**. To change brake fluid, follow the *Bleeding the Brake System* procedure in Chapter Eleven. Continue adding new fluid to the master cylinder and bleeding out at the caliper until the fluid leaving the caliper is clean and free of contaminants.

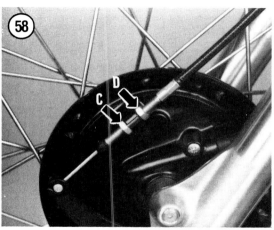

WARNING
Use brake fluid from a sealed container and clearly marked DOT 3 or DOT 4 only (specified for disc brakes). Others may vaporize and cause brake failure. Do not intermix different brands or types of brake fluid as they may not be compatible. Do not intermix a silicone based (DOT 5) brake fluid as it can cause brake component damage leading to brake system failure.

Front Brake Lever Adjustment
(Drum Brake Models)

The front brake cable should be adjusted so there will be 25-30 mm (1-1 1/4 in.) of brake lever movement required to actuate the brake, but it must not be so closely adjusted that the brake shoes contact the brake drum with the lever in the released position.

Minor adjustments should be made at the hand lever, but major adjustments should be made at the brake lever on the brake mechanism.

1. Loosen the locknut (A, **Figure 56**) and turn the adjusting barrel (B, **Figure 56**) in order to obtain the correct amount of free play. Tighten the locknut (A).
2. Because of normal brake wear, this adjustment will eventually be "used up." It is then necessary to loosen the locknut (A) and screw the adjusting barrel (B) all the way in toward the hand grip. Tighten the locknut (A).
3. At the lower adjustment on the front fork, loosen the locknut (C) and turn the adjuster nut (D), until the brake lever can once again be used for fine adjustment. Refer to **Figure 57** or **Figure 58**. Tighten the locknut (C).
4. When the 2 arrows on the brake arm and brake panel align (**Figure 54**) the brake shoes must be replaced as described in Chapter Eleven.

Front Brake Lever Free Play
(1985 XR350R Disc Brake Models)

A free play adjustment has been added to the brake lever. To increase or decrease brake lever free play, loosen the locknut and turn the adjuster in the desired direction (**Figure 59**). Tighten the locknut.

There is no factory recommended free play specification. Adjust to rider preference.

Front Brake Lever Free Play
(Disc Brake Models—Except 1985 XR350R)

The front disc brake lever has 2 free play positions.

1. Slide back the rubber protective boot from the brake lever pivot point area.

2. To increase free play, use a flat-bladed screwdriver and rotate the eccentric screw (**Figure 60**) until the single dot on the screw aligns with the index mark on the brake lever.

3. To decrease free play, use a flat-bladed screwdriver and rotate the eccentric screw (**Figure 60**) until the double dot on the screw aligns with the index mark on the brake lever.

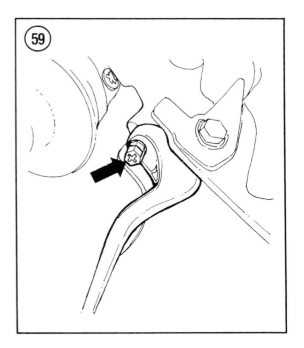

> *CAUTION*
> *Do not leave the eccentric screw between the 2 positions. It must always be aligned with one of the marks or the brake lever will not operate properly.*

Rear Brake Pedal
Height Adjustment

The rear brake pedal height should be adjusted at the interval listed in **Table 2**.

1. Make sure the brake pedal is in the at-rest position.

2A. Cable-operated brake: To change height position, loosen the locknut (A, **Figure 61**) and turn the adjuster bolt (B, **Figure 61**). Tighten the locknut (A).

2B. Rod-operated brake: To change height position, loosen the locknut (A, **Figure 62**) and turn the adjuster bolt (B, **Figure 62**). Tighten the locknut (A).

3. Adjust the pedal free play as described in this chapter.

Rear Brake Pedal Free Play Adjustment

Free play is the distance the rear brake pedal travels from the at-rest position to the applied position when the pedal is depressed by hand.

1. Adjust the rear brake to the correct height as described in this chapter.

2. Turn the adjust nut on the end of the brake rod until the pedal has 10-15 mm (3/8-5/8 in.) free play. Refer to **Figure 63** or **Figure 64**.

3. Rotate the rear wheel and check for brake drag.

4. Operate the brake pedal several times to make sure the pedal returns to the at-rest position immediately after release.

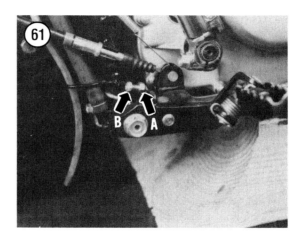

5. On XL series models, adjust the rear brake light switch as described in Chapter Eight.

Clutch Adjustment

Adjust the clutch at the interval indicated in **Table 2**. For the clutch to fully engage and disengage, there must be the following amount of free play:

    a. 1985 XR200R, 1985-on XR250R, XR350R: 10-20 mm (3/8-3/4 in.).

    b. All other models: 15-25 mm (5/8-1 in.).

1. Minor adjustments can be made at the upper adjuster at the hand lever as follows:

    a. Pull back the rubber protective boot.

    b. Loosen the locknut (A, **Figure 65**) and turn the adjuster (B, **Figure 65**) in or out to obtain the correct amount of free play. Tighten the locknut.

NOTE
If the proper amount of free play cannot be achieved at the hand lever, additional adjustment can be made at the clutch actuating lever on the engine or in-line adjuster on the clutch cable.

2. At the clutch lever, loosen the locknut (A, **Figure 65**) and turn the adjuster (B, **Figure 65**) in all the way toward the hand grip. Tighten the locknut (A).

3A. On 1983-1984 XR350R models, perform the following:

    a. On the left-hand crankcase cover, loosen the locknut (A, **Figure 66**) and turn the adjuster (B, **Figure 66**) until the correct amount of free play can be achieved.

    b. Tighten the locknut (A).

3B. On 1985 XR200R, 1985 XR250R and 1984-on XL250R models, perform the following:
  a. On the left-hand side of the frame down-tube below the fuel tank, loosen the locknut and turn the adjuster (**Figure 67**) until the correct amount of free play can be achieved.
  b. Tighten the locknut.

3C. On 1985 XR350R models, perform the following:
  a. On the cable between the clutch lever and the Enduro meter on the handlebar, loosen the locknut and turn the adjuster until the correct amount of free play can be achieved.
  b. Tighten the locknut.

3D. On 1986-on XR250R models, perform the following:
  a. On the right-hand side of the frame down-tube next to the right-hand crankcase cover, loosen the locknut and turn the adjuster until the correct amount of free play can be achieved.
  b. Tighten the locknut.

3E. On all other models, perform the following:
  a. Near the right-hand crankcase cover, loosen the locknut (A, **Figure 68**) and turn the adjuster (B, **Figure 68**) until the correct amount of free play can be achieved.
  b. Tighten the locknut (A).

4. If necessary, do some final adjusting at the clutch lever as described in Step 1.

5. After adjustment is complete, check that the locknuts are tight both at the hand lever and at the clutch actuating lever on the crankcase or at the cable in-line adjuster.

6. Road test the bike to make sure the clutch fully disengages when the lever is pulled in; if it does not, the bike will creep in gear when stopped. Also make sure the clutch fully engages; if it does not, the clutch will slip, particularly when accelerating in high gear.

7. If the proper amount of adjustment cannot be achieved using this procedure, the cable has stretched to the point where it needs replacing. Refer to Chapter Six for complete procedure.

Throttle Adjustment and Operation

The throttle grip should have 2-6 mm (1/8-1/4 in.) rotational free play (**Figure 69**). If adjustment is necessary, make minor adjustments at the throttle grip and major adjustments at the top of the carburetor.

NOTE
There are 2 throttle cables, but only the "pull" cable is adjustable.

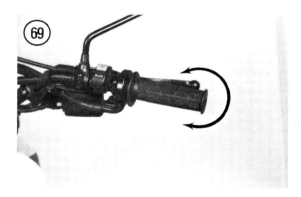

1A. On 1978-1982 models, perform the following:
  a. Loosen the locknut (A, **Figure 70**) and turn the adjuster (B, **Figure 70**) on the rear throttle cable at the throttle grip in or out to achieve proper free play rotation. Tighten the locknut.
  b. If additional adjustment is necessary, remove the fuel tank as described in Chapter Seven.

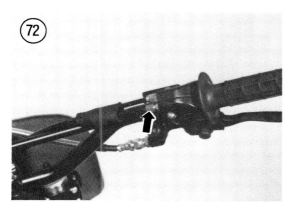

  c. Loosen the locknut and turn the adjuster (**Figure 71**) on the upper throttle cable at the carburetor assembly in or out to achieve proper free play rotation. Tighten the locknut and install the fuel tank.
1B. On 1982-on models, perform the following:
  a. Slide back the rubber protective boot.
  b. Loosen the locknut and turn the adjuster (**Figure 72**) on the lower throttle cable at the throttle grip in or out to achieve proper free play rotation. Tighten the locknut.
  c. If additional adjustment is necessary, remove the fuel tank as described in Chapter Seven.
  d. Loosen the locknut and turn the adjuster (**Figure 73**) on the lower throttle cable at the carburetor assembly in or out to achieve proper free play rotation. Tighten the locknut and install the fuel tank.
2. Check the throttle cables from the grip to the carburetor. Make sure they are not kinked or chafed. Replace as necessary.
3. Make sure the throttle grip rotates freely from a fully closed to fully open position. Check with the handlebar at center, at full right and at full left. If necessary, remove the throttle grip and apply a lithium base grease to it.

> *WARNING*
> *With the engine idling, move the handlebar from side to side. If idle speed increases during this movement, the throttle cable(s) may need adjusting or may be incorrectly routed through the frame. Correct this problem immediately. Do **not** ride the bike in this unsafe condition.*

Chain Tensioner Adjustment (XL250S, XL250 Models)

In time the camshaft chain and guide will wear and develop slack. This will cause engine noise and if neglected too long will cause engine damage. Adjust the camshaft chain tensioner as the interval indicated in **Table 2**.
1. Start the engine and let it reach normal operating temperature.

> *CAUTION*
> *Do **not** loosen the upper tensioner bolt or lower locknut more than 2 turns or the tensioner assembly within the engine may work loose and cause severe engine damage.*

2. Let the engine idle. Loosen the tensioner upper bolt (A, **Figure 74**) and the lower locknut (B, **Figure 74**) 1 1/2-2 turns.

3. When the tensioner bolt and locknut are loosened as described in Step 2, the tensioner will automatically adjust to the correct tension.

4. Tighten the tensioner bolt and locknut securely.

Cam Chain Tensioner Adjustment (All Except XL250S, XL250)

There is no provision for cam chain tensioner adjustment on these models. Chain tension is maintained automatically.

Starter Decompressor Adjustment (Single-cable Models)

> *NOTE*
> *Valve clearance must be correctly adjusted prior to adjusting the decompressor. Refer to **Valve Clearance Adjustment** in this chapter.*

1. Remove the 2 inspection covers on the left-hand crankcase cover (**Figure 75**).

2. Remove the spark plug. This will make it easier to rotate the engine by hand.

3. Rotate the crankshaft with the nut on the alternator rotor. Turn it *counterclockwise* until the piston is at top dead center (TDC) on the compression stroke.

> *NOTE*
> *A cylinder at TDC will have both its rocker arms loose, indicating that the exhaust and intake valves are closed. Remove the valve adjusting covers and make this test.*

4. Make sure the "T" timing mark on the alternator rotor aligns with the fixed notch in the case (**Figure 76**).

5. Measure the free play at the top of the decompressor valve lifter (A, **Figure 77**). The correct amount of free play is as follows:
   a. 250 cc models: 1-3 mm (0.04-0.12 in.).
   b. 500 cc models: 1-2 mm (0.04-0.08 in.).

6. To adjust the free play, loosen the locknut (B, **Figure 77**) and turn the adjuster (C, **Figure 77**) until the correct amount of free play is achieved.

> *CAUTION*
> *Excessive free play will result in hard starting. Insufficient free play will cause erratic engine idle and a burned exhaust valve.*

7. Tighten the locknut (B), install the valve adjusting covers, the spark plug and the 2 inspection covers.

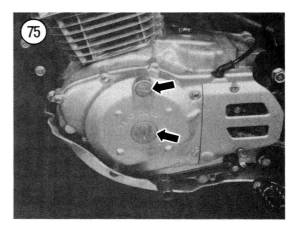

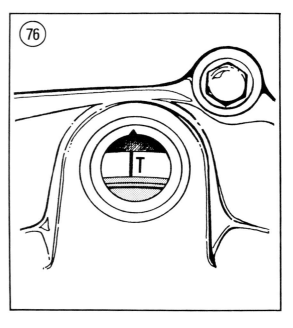

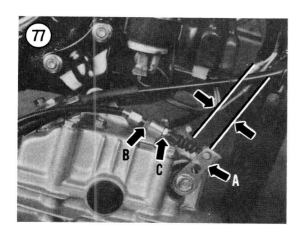

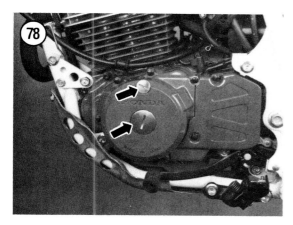

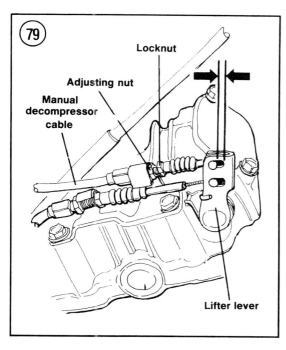

Locknut

Adjusting nut

Manual
decompressor
cable

Lifter lever

Starter Decompressor Adjustment
(Dual-cable Models)

NOTE
*Valve clearance must be correctly adjusted prior to adjusting the decompressor. Refer to **Valve Clearance Adjustment** in this chapter.*

The dual-cable models have a manual starter decompressor located on the left-hand handlebar and a decompressor that works directly with the kickstarter lever. Both the manual and kickstarter decompressor cables must be adjusted correctly or neither will work.

1. Place the bike on the sidestand.
2. Remove the fuel tank as described in Chapter Seven.
3. Remove the 2 inspection covers on the left-hand crankcase cover (**Figure 78**).
4. Remove the spark plug. This will make it easier to rotate the engine by hand.
5. Rotate the crankshaft with the nut on the alternator rotor. Turn it *counterclockwise* until the piston is at top dead center (TDC) on the compression stroke.

NOTE
A cylinder at TDC on its compression stroke will have both its rocker arms loose, indicating that the exhaust and intake valves are closed. Remove the valve adjusting covers and make this test. If the rocker arms are not loose, the piston is on the exhaust stroke. Rotate the crankshaft one full turn.

6. Make sure the "T" timing mark on the alternator rotor aligns with the fixed notch in the case (**Figure 76**).
7A. On 1984-on XL250R and XR350R models, the correct amount of free play is as follows:
    a. At the tip of the kickstarter decompressor lever: 1-2 mm (1/32-1/16 in.) as shown in **Figure 79**.
    b. At the tip of the manual decompressor lever: 5-8 mm (3/16-5/16 in.).
If adjustment is necessary, perform the following:
    a. Loosen the locknut and adjust nut and disconnect the manual decompressor cable from the actuating lever.
    b. If adjustment is necessary at the kickstarter, loosen the locknut and turn the adjust nut until the correct amount of free play is achieved.

c. Tighten the locknut and operate the kickstarter several times; recheck free play. Readjust if necessary.

d. Again rotate the crankshaft with the nut on the alternator rotor. Turn the nut *counterclockwise* until the piston is at top dead center (TDC) on the compression stroke with the "T" timing mark on the alternator rotor aligned with the fixed notch on the case (**Figure 76**).

e. Connect the manual starter decompressor cable to the lever.

f. If adjustment is necessary at the manual lever, loosen the locknut and turn the adjusting nut until the correct amount of free play is achieved. Tighten the locknut.

CAUTION
Excessive free play will result in hard starting. Insufficient free play will cause erratic engine idle and a burned exhaust valve.

7B. On all other models, the correct amount of free play is as follows:

a. At the tip of the kickstarter decompressor lever: 1-2 mm (1/32-1/16 in.).

b. At the tip of the manual decompressor lever: 5-8 mm (3/16-5/16 in.).

If adjustment is necessary, perform the following:

a. Loosen the manual cable locknut and adjust nut to gain slack in the cable.

b. Disconnect the manual cable from the decompressor starter valve lifter lever on the cylinder head cover.

c. Loosen the locknut on the kickstarter cable and turn the adjust nut until the correct amount of free play is achieved.

d. Tighten the locknut and operate the kickstarter several times and check the operation of the decompressor mechanism.

e. Reconnect the manual cable to the lever.

f. Loosen the locknut on the manual cable and turn the adjusting nut until the correct amount of free play is achieved. Tighten the locknut.

CAUTION
Excessive free play will result in hard starting. Insufficient free play will cause erratic engine idle and a burned exhaust valve.

8. Install the valve adjusting covers, the spark plug and the 2 inspection covers.

Balancer Chain Adjustment (XL250S, 1982-1983 XL250R)

The balancer chain should be adjusted at the interval listed in **Table 2**.

NOTE
All other models have a gear-driven balancer system that does not require routine adjustment.

1. Drain the engine oil as described in this chapter.
2. Remove the bolts securing the skid plate and remove the skid plate.
3. Remove the kickstarter arm.
4. Disconnect the clutch and starter decompressor lever cables from the right-hand crankcase cover.
5. Remove the bolts securing the right-hand footpeg assembly and remove the assembly.
6. Remove the brake pedal.
7. Remove the bolts securing the right-hand crankcase cover and remove it and the gasket.

8. Loosen the bolt (A, **Figure 80**) securing the balancer holder flange.

9. When the bolt is loosened, the spring (B, **Figure 80**) will pull the holder flange counterclockwise.

NOTE
If the holder flange bottoms out on the bolt, it will have to be repositioned. Refer to Steps 12-18.

10. Move the holder flange *clockwise* one graduation from where it stops (C, **Figure 80**).

NOTE
Align the graduations on the holder flange with the arrow on the crankcase.

11. Tighten the bolt to the torque specification listed in **Table 6**.

12. To reposition the holder flange, remove the small circlip (D, **Figure 80**) and slide off the balancer weight and thrust washer (E, **Figure 80**).

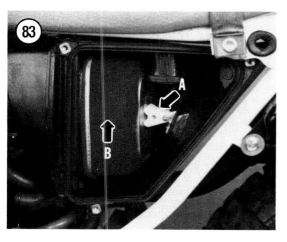

13. Remove the spring (A, **Figure 81**) and bolt (B, **Figure 81**).

14. Remove the large 38 mm circlip (C, **Figure 81**).

15. Note the original position of the holder flange on the shaft. Slide the holder flange off the shaft splines and reposition it one graduation to the left of the original position.

16. Install the large 38 mm circlip.

17. Install the thrust washer, balancer weight and circlip. Make sure the circlip is properly seated in the shaft groove.

CAUTION
The index mark on the balancer weight must align with the punch mark on the end of the shaft (E, Figure 80).

18. Install the spring (B, **Figure 80**) and bolt—do not tighten the bolt at this time.

19. Repeat Step 10 and Step 11.

20. Complete by reversing Steps 1-7. Tighten the holder bolt to the torque specification listed in **Table 6**.

21. Fill the crankcase with the recommended type and quantity of engine oil as described in this chapter.

**Air Filter Element
Removal/Installation
(1984-on XL250R)**

The air filter element should be removed and cleaned at the interval listed in **Table 2**.

The air filter removes dust and abrasive particles from the air before the air enters the carburetor and engine. Without the air filter, very fine particles could enter into the engine and cause rapid wear of the piston rings, cylinder and bearings and might clog small passages in the carburetor(s). Never run the bike without the air filter element installed.

Proper air filter servicing can do more to ensure long service from your engine than almost any other single item.

1. Place the bike on the sidestand.

2. Remove the left-hand side cover.

3. Remove the screws securing the air filter cover and remove the cover (**Figure 82**).

4. Push the element holder lever (A, **Figure 83**) up and withdraw the element assembly (B, **Figure 83**) from the air box.

5. Separate the air filter element (A, **Figure 84**) from the holder (B, **Figure 84**).

6. Wipe out the interior of the air box (**Figure 85**) with a shop rag dampened with cleaning solvent. Remove any foreign matter that may have passed through a broken element.

7. Clean and re-oil the element as described in this chapter.

8. Install by reversing these removal steps, noting the following.

9. Position the element holder with the "UP" mark facing up (**Figure 86**).

10. Make sure the element is correctly seated into the air box so there is no air leak.

Air Filter Element Removal/Installation (1985 XR200R, 1985-on XR250R, All 350 cc)

The air filter element should be removed and cleaned at the interval listed in **Table 2**.

The air filter removes dust and abrasive particles from the air before the air enters the carburetor and engine. Without the air filter, very fine particles could enter into the engine and cause rapid wear of the piston rings, cylinder and bearings and might clog small passages in the carburetor(s). Never run the bike without the air filter element installed.

Proper air filter servicing can do more to ensure long service from your engine than almost any other single item.

1. Place the bike on the sidestand.

2. Remove the left-hand side cover.

3. Unhook the element retaining strap (**Figure 87**).

4. Withdraw the element assembly from the air box.

5. Separate the air filter element from the holder (**Figure 88**).

6. Wipe out the interior of the air box with a shop rag dampened with cleaning solvent. Remove any foreign matter that may have passed through a broken element.

7. Clean and re-oil the element as described in this chapter.

8. Install by reversing these removal steps, noting the following.

9. Make sure the element is correctly seated into the air box so there is no air leak.

Air Filter Element Removal/Installation (All Other Models)

The air filter element should be removed and cleaned at the interval listed in **Table 2**.

The air filter removes dust and abrasive particles from the air before the air enters the carburetor and engine. Without the air filter, very fine particles could enter into the engine and cause rapid wear of the piston rings, cylinder and bearings and might clog small passages in the carburetor(s). Never run the bike without the air filter element installed.

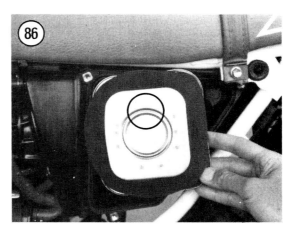

Proper air filter servicing can do more to ensure long service from your engine than almost any other single item.

1. Place the bike on the sidestand.
2. Remove the left-hand side cover.
3. Pull back the retainer and withdraw the element assembly from the air box.

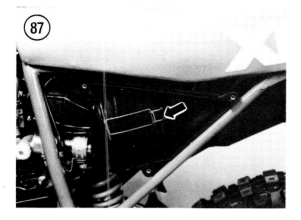

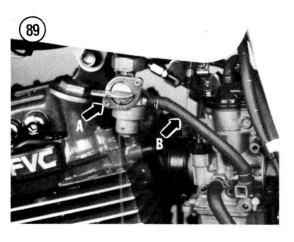

4. Separate the air filter element from the holder.
5. Wipe out the interior of the air box with a shop rag dampened with cleaning solvent. Remove any foreign matter that may have passed through a broken element.
6. Clean and re-oil the element as described in this chapter.
7. Install by reversing these removal steps, noting the following.
8. Make sure the element is correctly seated into the air box so there is no air leak.
9. Inspect the raised sealing ridge that fits into the perimeter gasket of the air box. If the ridge is cracked or broken, the side cover must be replaced.

Air Filter Element Cleaning and Re-oiling (All Models)

1. Clean the element gently in a non-flammable or high flash point cleaning solvent until all dirt is removed. Thoroughly dry in a clean shop cloth until all residue is removed. Let dry for about one hour.

> *CAUTION*
> *Inspect the element; if it is torn or broken in any area it should be replaced. Do not run with a damaged element as it may allow dirt to enter the engine.*

2. Pour a small amount of SAE 80W-90 gear oil or foam air filter oil onto the element and work it into the porous foam material. Do not oversaturate as too much oil will restrict air flow. The element should be discolored by the oil and should have an even color indicating that the oil is distributed evenly.
3. If foam air filter oil was used, let the element dry for another hour prior to installation. If installed too soon, the chemical carrier in the foam air filter oil will be drawn into the engine and may cause damage.

Fuel Shutoff Filter and Valve Removal/Installation

The fuel filter is built into the shutoff valve and removes particles which might otherwise enter into the carburetor and cause the float needle to stick open.

1. Turn the shutoff valve to the OFF position (A, **Figure 89**) and remove the fuel line (B, **Figure 89**) to the carburetor.

2. Place the loose end in a clean, sealable metal container. This fuel can be reused if it is kept clean.

3. Open the valve to the RESERVE position and remove the fuel filler cap. This will allow air to enter the fuel tank and speed up the flow of fuel. Drain the fuel tank completely.

4A. On metal fuel tanks, unscrew the locknut (A, **Figure 90**) securing the fuel shutoff valve to the fuel tank. Remove the valve.

4B. On plastic fuel tanks, remove the screw securing the fuel shutoff valve to the fuel tank. Remove the metal collars that surround the screws and remove the valve.

5. After removing the valve from the fuel tank, insert a corner of a shop cloth into the opening in the tank to stop the dribbling of fuel onto the engine and frame.

6. Remove the fuel filter (B, **Figure 90**) from the shutoff valve. Clean the filter with a medium soft toothbrush and blow out with compressed air. Replace the filter if it is broken in any area.

7. Install by reversing these removal steps, noting the following.

8A. On metal fuel tanks, be sure to install a gasket (C, **Figure 90**) between the shutoff valve and the fuel tank. Tighten the locknut securely.

8B. On plastic fuel tanks, be sure to install the O-ring seal onto the valve. Do not forget to install the collars that surround the screws. Tighten the screws securely.

9. Turn the fuel shutoff valve to the ON position (**Figure 91**) and check for leaks.

Fuel Strainer Cleaning
(1984-on XL Series Models)

The fuel strainer is built into the shutoff valve and removes particles which might otherwise enter into the carburetor and may cause the float needle to remain in the open position.

Refer to **Figure 92** for this procedure.

1. Turn the shutoff valve to the OFF position (A, **Figure 93**).

2. Unscrew the fuel cup (B, **Figure 93**), O-ring and screen from the shutoff valve. Dispose of fuel remaining in the fuel cup properly.

3. Clean the screen with a medium-soft toothbrush and blow out with compressed air. Replace the screen if it is broken in any area.

4. Align the index marks on the screen and shutoff valve body.

5. Install the O-ring seal and screw on the fuel cup.

6. Hand-tighten the fuel cup to the torque specification listed in **Table 6**. Do *not* overtighten the fuel cup as it may be damaged.

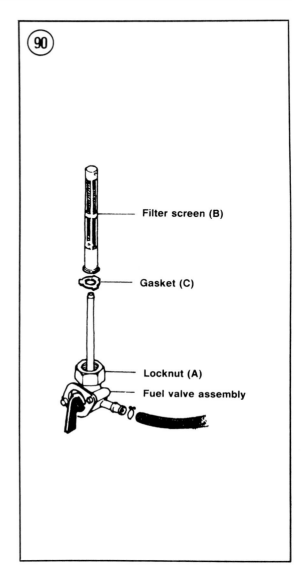

Filter screen (B)

Gasket (C)

Locknut (A)
Fuel valve assembly

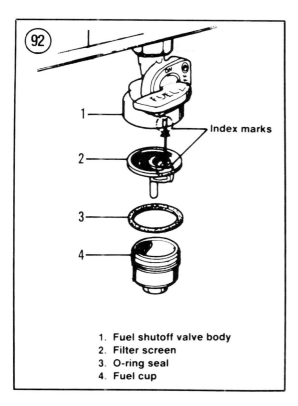

1. Fuel shutoff valve body
2. Filter screen
3. O-ring seal
4. Fuel cup

Index marks

7. Turn the fuel shutoff valve to the ON position (**Figure 93**) and check for leaks.

Fuel Line Inspection

Inspect the fuel line (B, **Figure 89**) from the fuel shutoff valve to the carburetor. If it is cracked or starting to deteriorate it must be replaced. Make sure the hose clamps are in place and holding securely.

> *WARNING*
> *A damaged or deteriorated fuel line presents a very dangerous fire hazard to both the rider and the vehicle if fuel should spill onto a hot engine or exhaust pipe.*

Crankcase Breather
(U.S. Only)

At the interval listed in **Table 2**, or sooner if a considerable amount of riding is done at full throttle or in the rain, remove the drain plug (**Figure 94**) and drain out all residue. Install the cap.

Refer to Chapter Seven for detailed information on the breather system.

Evaporative Emission Control System
(1984-on California XL Series Only)

Fuel vapor from the fuel tank is routed into a charcoal canister when the engine is stopped. When the engine is started these vapors are drawn into the air filter, through the carburetor and into the engine to be burned. Make sure all vacuum hoses are correctly routed and attached. Inspect the hoses (**Figure 95**) and replace any if necessary. The charcoal canister must be inspected at the interval indicated in **Table 2**.

Refer to Chapter Seven for detailed information on the evaporative emission control system and for vacuum hose routing.

**Spark Arrester Cleaning
(U.S. Only)**

The spark arrester should be cleaned at the interval listed in **Table 2**.

> *WARNING*
> *To avoid burning your hands do not perform this cleaning operation with the exhaust system hot. Work in a well-ventilated area (outside your garage) that is free from fire hazards. Be sure to protect your eyes with safety goggles or glasses.*

XR250, XL250S, 1982-1983 XL250R

On these models a special tool is required to remove the spark arrester from the muffler as shown in **Figure 96**. Use an auto body slide hammer fitted with a special hook adapter. Use Honda part No. 07936-428000 or equivalent. This tool may be available from mail order parts houses or a motorcycle dealer.

1. Remove the arrester with the special tools.
2. Start the engine and rev it up about 20-25 times to blow out carbon deposits. Continue to rev up the engine until carbon stops coming out.

3. Paint the spark arrester with a heat-resistant paint prior to installation. Tap the arrester into place with a hammer and piece of wood.

*All except XR250, XL250S,
1982-1983 XL250R*

1. Remove the bolts securing the muffler rear port cover (**Figure 97**). Remove the cover and the gasket.

> *WARNING*
> *Wear heavy gloves to protect your hands in the next step.*

2. Wad up a couple of heavy shop cloths or rags and plug the end of the muffler to create back pressure. This will force the exhaust and carbon deposits out of the rear port.
3. Start the engine and rev it up a couple of times.
4. Continue revving the engine until carbon stops coming out.
5. Install a new gasket onto the port cover and install the port cover. Tighten the bolts securely.

Wheel Bearings

There is no factory-recommended mileage interval for cleaning and repacking the wheel bearings. They should be inspected and serviced if necessary every time the wheel is removed or

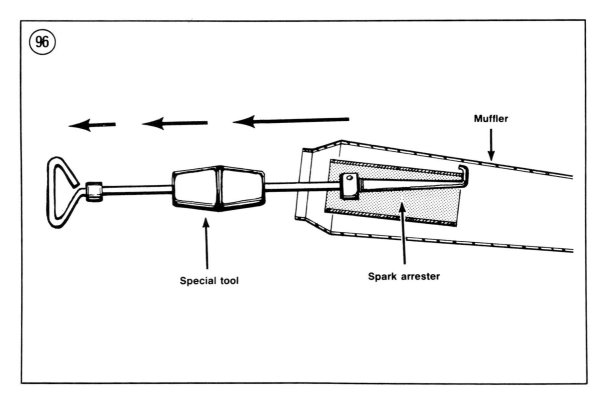

Muffler

Special tool

Spark arrester

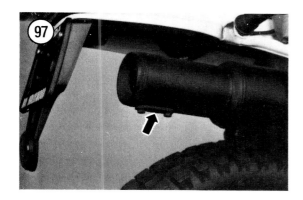

whenever there is a likelihood of water contamination. The correct service procedures are covered in Chapter Nine and Chapter Ten.

Wheel Hubs, Rims and Spokes

Check the wheel hubs and rims for bends and other signs of damage. Check both wheels for broken or bent spokes. Replace damaged or broken spokes as described in Chapter Nine. Plunk each spoke with your finger like a guitar string or tap each one lightly with a small metal tool. All spokes should emit the same sound. A spoke that is too tight will have a higher pitch than others; one that is too loose will have a lower pitch. If only one or two spokes are slightly out of adjustment, adjust with a spoke wrench made for this purpose. If more are affected, the wheel should be removed and trued as described in Chapter Nine.

On models so equipped, make sure the rim locks are tight. If necessary, tighten to the torque specification listed in **Table 6**.

Front Suspension Check

1. Apply the front brake and pump the forks up and down as vigorously as possible. Check for smooth operation and check for any oil leaks.
2. Make sure the upper and lower fork bridge bolts are tight (**Figure 98**).
3. Make sure the bolts securing the handlebar holders (**Figure 99**) are tight and that the handlebar is secure.
4. Make sure the front axle, or axle nut is tight and on models so equipped, make sure the cotter pin is in place.
5. On model so equipped, make sure axle pinch bolt and the nuts securing the axle holder nuts are tight.

> *CAUTION*
> *If any of the previously mentioned bolts and nuts are loose, refer to Chapter Nine for correct procedures and torque specifications.*

Rear Suspension Check

1. Place a wood block(s) under the engine to support it securely with the rear wheel off the ground.
2. Push hard on the rear wheel (sideways) to check for side play in the rear swing arm bearings. Remove the wood block(s).
3A. On dual-shock models, check the tightness of the upper and lower mounting nuts on each shock absorber (**Figure 100**).

3B. On Pro-Link models, check the tightness of the upper (**Figure 101**) and lower mounting bolts and nuts (**Figure 102**) nuts on the shock absorber.
4. Make sure the swing arm pivot bolt and nut (**Figure 103**) are tight.
5. On Pro-Link models, check the tightness of the suspension pivot arm assembly bolts and nuts (**Figure 104**).
6. Make sure the rear axle nut (**Figure 105**) is tight and that the cotter pin is in place.
7. On models so equipped, check the tightness of the rear brake torque arm bolt. Make sure the cotter pin is in place.

> *CAUTION*
> *If any of the previously mentioned bolts and nuts are loose, refer to Chapter Ten for correct procedures and torque specifications.*

Nuts, Bolts and Other Fasteners

Constant vibration can loosen many of the fasteners on the motorcycle. Check the tightness of all fasteners, especially those on:
   a. Engine mounting hardware.
   b. Engine crankcase covers.
   c. Handlebar and front forks.
   d. Gearshift lever.
   e. Brake pedal and lever.
   f. Exhaust system.
   g. Lighting equipment (XL series only).

Sidestand Rubber (XL Series Only)

The rubber pad on the sidestand kicks the sidestand up if you should forget. If it wears down to the molded line, replace the rubber as it will no longer be effective and must be replaced.

Steering Head Adjustment Check

Check the steering head ball bearings for looseness at the interval listed in **Table 2**.
Place a wood block(s) under the engine to support it securely with the front wheel off the ground.
Hold onto the front fork tube and gently rock the fork assembly back and forth. If you feel looseness, refer to *Steering Head Adjustment* in Chapter Nine.

TUNE-UP

Perform a complete tune-up at the interval listed in **Table 2** for bikes used in normal riding. More frequent tune-ups may be required if the bike is ridden in stop-and-go traffic. If the bike is used for racing, it should be tuned up prior to each race.

The purpose of the tune-up is to restore the performance lost due to normal wear and deterioration of parts.

The spark plugs should be routinely replaced at every other tune-up or if the electrodes show signs of erosion. In addition, this is a good time to clean the air filter element. Have the new parts on hand before you begin.

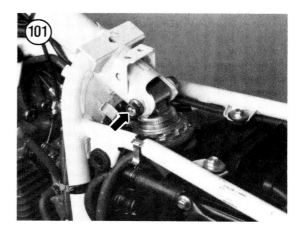

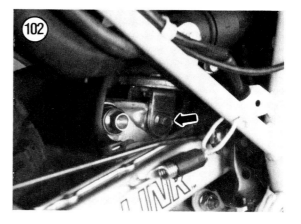

Because the different systems in an engine interact, the procedures should be done in the following order:

    a. Tighten the cylinder head nuts and bolts (except Radial Four Valve Combustion engines).

    b. Adjust valve clearances.

    c. Run a compression test.

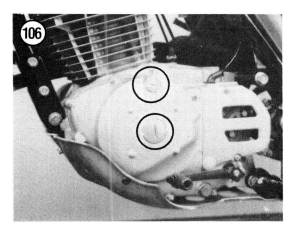

    d. Check and adjust the ignition components and timing.

    e. Set the idle speed.

Table 12 summarizes tune-up specifications.

To perform a tune-up on your Honda, you will need the following tools and equipment:

    a. 18 mm (5/8 in.) spark plug wrench.

    b. Socket wrench and assorted sockets.

    c. Flat feeler gauge.

    d. Compression gauge.

    e. Spark plug wire feeler gauge and gapper tool.

    f. Ignition timing light.

Cylinder Head Nuts
(Except Radial Four Valve Combustion Engines)

The cylinder head (not the cylinder head cover) is held in place with 4 acorn nuts. The 2 on the left-hand side are exposed but the 2 on the right-hand side are within the cylinder head cavity.

The nuts should be tightened only on the first tune-up after purchase of a new bike or after the cylinder head has been removed for service. If you wish to tighten the 4 nuts, remove the cylinder head cover and tighten the nuts as described in Chapter Four.

Valve Clearance Adjustment

Valve clearance measurement and adjustment must be performed with the engine cool, at room temperature (below 35° C/95° F). The correct valve clearance for all models is listed in **Table 12**. The exhaust valves are located at the front of the engine and the intake valves are located at the rear of the engine.

> *NOTE*
> *Make sure there is free play in the starter decompressor lever. If not, it will hold down the exhaust valves and make the exhaust valve clearance incorrect. If necessary, adjust the starter decompressor as described in this chapter to allow sufficient slack. Readjust the starter decompressor clearance after the valve clearance is correctly adjusted.*

1. Place the bike on the side stand.
2. Remove the seat.
3. Remove the fuel tank as described in Chapter Seven.
4. Remove the 2 inspection covers (**Figure 106**) on the left-hand crankcase cover.
5A. On XR350R models, unscrew each valve adjustment cover.

5B. On all other models, remove the bolts (**Figure 107**) securing the front and rear valve adjustment covers and remove the covers and gaskets.

6. Remove the spark plug. This will make it easier to rotate the engine.

7. Rotate the engine with the bolt or nut on the alternator rotor. Rotate the engine *counterclockwise* until the engine is at top dead center (TDC) on the compression stroke.

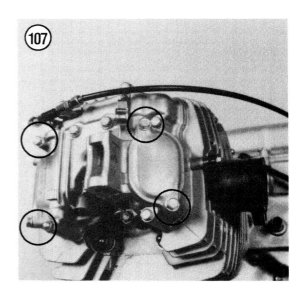

> *NOTE*
> *A cylinder at TDC on its compression stroke will have free play in all of its rocker arms, indicating that all intake and exhaust valves are closed. If the rocker arms do not have free play the piston is on its exhaust stroke. Rotate the crankshaft one full turn.*

8. Make sure the ignition timing mark "T" aligns with the index mark on the crankcase (**Figure 108**).

9. With the engine timing mark on the "T," if the all rocker arms are not loose, rotate the engine *counterclockwise* an additional 180° until all rocker arms have free play.

10. Again make sure the ignition timing mark "T" aligns with the index mark on the crankcase (**Figure 108**).

11. Check the clearance of both intake and exhaust valves by inserting a flat feeler gauge between the adjusting screw and the valve stem (**Figure 109**). When the clearance is correct, there will be a slight drag on the feeler gauge when it is inserted and withdrawn.

12. To correct the clearance, perform the following:

   a. Loosen the adjuster locknut.

   b. Screw the adjuster in or out so there is a slight resistance felt on the feeler gauge (**Figure 110**).

   c. Hold the adjuster to prevent it from turning further and tighten the locknut (**Figure 111**) to the torque specification listed in **Table 6**.

   d. Recheck the clearance to make sure the adjuster did not turn after the correct clearance was achieved. Readjust if necessary.

   e. Repeat for all 4 valves.

13. Inspect the rubber gaskets on all valve adjusting covers. Replace any that are starting to deteriorate or harden; replace as a set even if only one is bad. Install all covers.

14. Install all items removed.

15. Adjust the starter decompressor as described in this chapter.

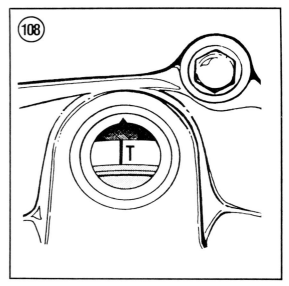

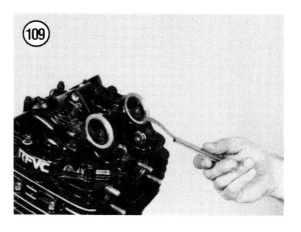

Compression Test

Check the cylinder compression at the interval indicated in **Table 2**. Record the results and compare them to the results at the next interval. A running record will show trends in deterioration so that corrective action can be taken before complete failure.

The results, when properly interpreted, can indicate general cylinder, piston ring and valve condition.

1. Warm the engine to normal operating temperature, then shut it off. Make sure the choke valve and throttle valve are completely open.

2. Remove the spark plug.

3. Connect the compression tester to one cylinder following the manufacturer's instructions.

4. Have an assistant crank the engine over until there is no further rise in pressure.

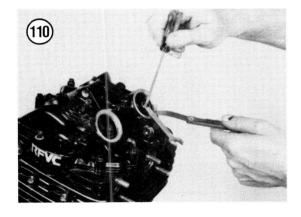

5. Remove the tester and record the reading. When interpreting the results, actual readings are not as important as the difference between the readings. The recommended cylinder compression is listed in **Table 12**. Greater differences than that listed in **Table 12** indicate broken rings, leaky or sticking valves, a blown head gasket or a combination of all.

If the compression readings do not differ between the cylinders by more than 10 psi, the rings and valves are in good condition.

A low reading (10% or more) indicates valve or ring trouble. To determine which, pour about a teaspoon of engine oil through the spark plug hole onto the top of the piston. Turn the engine over once to clear the oil, then take another compression test and record the reading. If the compression returns to normal, the valves are good but the rings are defective. If the compression does not increase, the valves require servicing. A valve(s) could be hanging open or burned or a piece of carbon could be on a valve seat.

Spark Plug Selection

Spark plugs are available in various heat ranges, hotter or colder than plugs originally installed at the factory.

Select plugs of a heat range designed for the loads and temperature conditions under which the bike will be run. The use of incorrect heat ranges can cause seized pistons, scored cylinder walls or damaged piston crowns.

In general, use a hot plug for low speeds, low engine loads and low temperatures. Use a cold plug for high speeds, high engine loads and high temperatures. The plug should operate hot enough to burn off unwanted deposits, but not so hot that it is damaged or causes preignition. A spark plug of the correct heat range will show a light tan color on the portion of the insulator within the cylinder after the plug has been in service.

In areas where seasonal temperature variations are great, the factory recommends a "2-plug system"—cold plugs for hard summer riding and hot plugs for slower winter operation.

The reach (length) of a plug is also important (**Figure 112**). A longer than normal plug could interfere with the valves and pistons, causing permanent and severe damage. The recommended standard spark plugs are listed in **Table 12**.

Spark Plug Removal/Cleaning

1. Grasp the spark plug lead (**Figure 113**) as near to the plug as possible and pull it off the plug. If the boot is stuck to the plug, twist it slightly to break it loose.

2. Blow away any dirt that has accumulated in the spark plug well.

> *CAUTION*
> *The dirt could fall into the cylinder when the plug is removed, causing serious engine damage.*

3. Remove spark plug with an 18 mm spark plug wrench.

> *NOTE*
> *If plugs are difficult to remove, apply penetrating oil around base of plugs and let it soak in about 10-20 minutes.*

4. Inspect the spark plug carefully. Look for a plug with broken center porcelain, excessively eroded electrodes and excessive carbon or oil fouling. Replace such a plug. If deposits are light, the plug may be cleaned in solvent with a wire brush or in a special spark plug sandblast cleaner. Regap the plug as explained in this chapter.

Spark Plug Gaping and Installation

A new plug should be carefully gapped to ensure a reliable, consistent spark. You must use a special spark plug gapping tool with a wire feeler gauge.

1. Remove the new plug from the box.

2. Insert a wire feeler gauge between the center and the side electrode of each plug (**Figure 114**). The correct gap is listed in **Table 12**. If the gap is correct, you will feel a slight drag as you pull the wire through. If there is no drag or the gauge won't pass through, bend the side electrode *with the gapping tool* (**Figure 115**) to set the proper gap.

3. Put a *small* amount of anti-seize compound on the threads of the spark plug.

4. Screw each spark plug in by hand until it seats. Very little effort is required. If force is necessary, you have the plug cross-threaded; unscrew it and try again.

5. Tighten the spark plugs an additional 1/2 turn after the gasket has made contact with the head. If you are reinstalling old, regapped plugs and are reusing the old gasket, tighten only an additional 1/4 turn.

> *CAUTION*
> *Do not overtighten. This will only squash the gasket and destroy its sealing ability.*

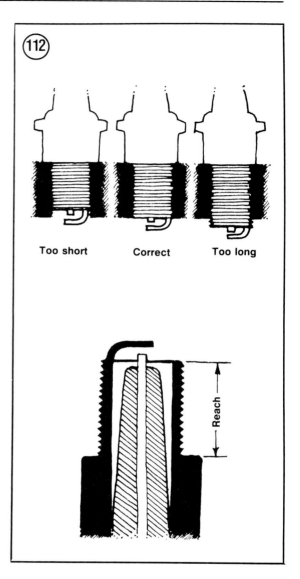

Too short   Correct   Too long

Reach

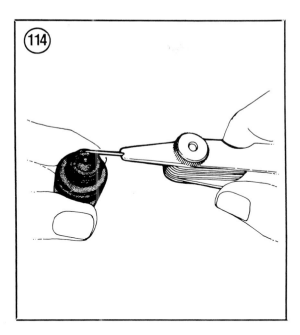

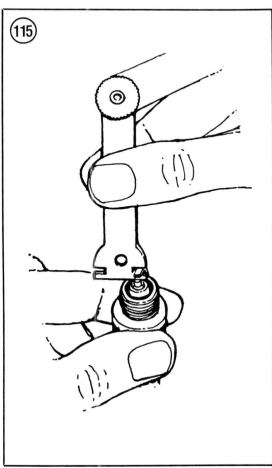

6. Install the spark plug lead; make sure the lead is on tight.

Reading Spark Plugs

Much information about engine and spark plug performance can be determined by careful examination of the spark plugs. This information is more valid after performing the following steps.

1. Ride the bike a short distance at full throttle in any gear.

2. Turn the engine kill switch (**Figure 116**) to the OFF position before closing the throttle and simultaneously pull in the clutch or shift to NEUTRAL; coast and brake to a stop.

3. Remove the spark plug and examine it. Compare it to **Figure 117**. If the insulator is white or burned, the plug is too hot and should be replaced with a colder one.

A too-cold plug will have sooty or oily deposits ranging in color from dark brown to black. Replace with a hotter plug and check for too-rich carburetion or evidence of oil blowby at the piston rings.

If the plug has a light tan or gray colored deposit and no abnormal gap wear or electrode erosion is evident, the plug and the engine are running properly.

If the plug exhibits a black insulator tip, a damp and oily film over the firing end and a carbon layer over the entire nose, it is oil fouled. An oil fouled plug can be cleaned, but it is better to replace it.

CDI Ignition Timing

All models are equipped with a capacitor discharge ignition (CDI) system. This system uses no breaker points and is non-adjustable. The ignition timing should be checked to make sure all ignition components are operating correctly.

Incorrect ignition timing can cause a drastic loss of engine performance and efficiency. It may also cause overheating.

⑴⑴⑺ **SPARK PLUG CONDITION**

NORMAL
- Identified by light tan or gray deposits on the firing tip.
- Can be cleaned.

GAP BRIDGED
- Identified by deposit buildup closing gap between electrodes.
- Caused by oil or carbon fouling. If deposits are not excessive, the plug can be cleaned.

OIL FOULED
- Identified by wet black deposits on the insulator shell bore and electrodes.
- Caused by excessive oil entering combustion chamber through worn rings and pistons, excessive clearance between valve guides and stems, or worn or loose bearings. Can be cleaned. If engine is not repaired, use a hotter plug.

CARBON FOULED
- Identified by black, dry fluffy carbon deposits on insulator tips, exposed shell surfaces and electrodes.
- Caused by too cold a plug, weak ignition, dirty air cleaner, too rich a fuel mixture, or excessive idling. Can be cleaned.

LEAD FOULED
- Identified by dark gray, black, yellow, or tan deposits or a fused glazed coating on the insulator tip.
- Caused by highly leaded gasoline. Can be cleaned.

WORN
- Identified by severely eroded or worn electrodes.
- Caused by normal wear. Should be replaced.

FUSED SPOT DEPOSIT
- Identified by melted or spotty deposits resembling bubbles or blisters.
- Caused by sudden acceleration. Can be cleaned.

OVERHEATING
- Identified by a white or light gray insulator with small black or gray brown spots and with bluish-burnt appearance of electrodes.
- Caused by engine overheating, wrong type of fuel, loose spark plugs, too hot a plug, or incorrect ignition timing. Replace the plug.

PREIGNITION
- Identified by melted electrodes and possibly blistered insulator. Metallic deposits on insulator indicate engine damage.
- Caused by wrong type of fuel, incorrect ignition timing or advance, too hot a plug, burned valves, or engine overheating. Replace the plug.

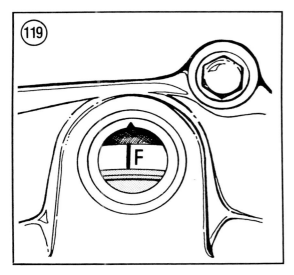

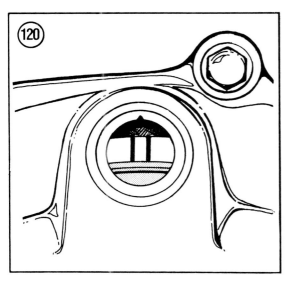

Before starting on this procedure, check all electrical connections related to the ignition system. Make sure all connections are tight and free of corrosion and that all ground connections are tight.

1. Start the engine and let it reach normal operating temperature. Shut the engine off.
2. Place the bike on the side stand or centerstand.
3. Remove the ignition timing cap (**Figure 118**).
4. Connect a portable tachometer following the manufacturer's instructions.
5. Connect a timing light following the manufacturer's instructions.
6. Fill in the timing marks on the pulse generator rotor or alternator rotor with white grease pencil or typewriter white correction fluid. This will make the marks more visible.
7. Start the engine and let it idle at the idle speed listed in **Table 12**. If necessary, readjust the idle speed as described in this chapter.
8. Aim the timing light at the timing hole and pull the trigger. If the timing mark "F" aligns with the fixed pointer on the crankcase cover (**Figure 119**), the timing is correct.
9. Increase engine speed to slightly above 3,500 rpm.
10. Aim the timing light at the timing hole and pull the trigger. If the fixed pointer aligns between the full advance timing marks (**Figure 120**) the timing is correct.
11. If timing at either idle or full advance is not correct, refer to Chapter Eight and check the pulse generator and CDI unit.
12. There is no method for adjusting ignition timing.
13. Shut off the engine and disconnect the timing light and portable tachometer.
14. Make sure the O-ring seal is in place and install the ignition timing cap.

Carburetor Idle Speed Adjustment

Before making this adjustment, the air filter element must be clean and the engine must have adequate compression. See *Compression Test* in this chapter. Otherwise this procedure cannot be done properly.

1. Start the engine and let it reach normal operating temperature. Make sure the choke knob or lever is in the open position.
2. Connect a portable tachometer following the manufacturer's instructions.

3A. On RFVC engines, turn the idle adjust screw (**Figure 121**) in or out to adjust idle speed. Idle speed is listed in **Table 12**.

3B. On all other models, turn the idle adjust knob (**Figure 122**) in or out to adjust idle speed.

4. The correct idle speed is listed in **Table 12**.

5. Open and close the throttle a couple of times; check for variations in idle speed. Readjust if necessary.

> *WARNING*
> *With the engine running at idle speed, move the handlebar from side to side. If the idle speed increases during this movement, the throttle cable may need adjusting or it may be incorrectly routed through the frame. Correct this problem immediately. Do **not** ride the bike in this unsafe condition.*

Carburetor Idle Mixture

The idle mixture (pilot screw) is preset at the factory and *is not to be reset.* Do not adjust the pilot screw unless the carburetor has been overhauled. If so, refer to Chapter Seven for service procedures.

Table 1 TIRE INFLATION PRESSURE*

Tire Size	Air Pressure	
	psi	kg/cm²
Front tire		
3.00-21 6PR	14	1.0
3.00-21 4PR	21	1.5
3.00-23 6PR	15	1.03
3.00-23 4PR	21	1.5
90/80-21 6PR	15	1.03
90/90-21 6PR	14	1.0
Rear tire		
4.60-17 4PR	21	1.5
5.10-17 6PR		
1985 XR350R	11	0.8
All other models	15	1.03
5.10-17 4PR	21	1.5
4.60-18 4PR	21	1.5
4.60-18 6PR	17	1.2
110/90-17 6PR	14	1.0
130/80-17 6PR	14	1.0

* Tire inflation pressure for factory equipped tires. Aftermarket tire inflation pressure may vary according to manufacturer's instructions.

Table 2 MAINTENANCE SCHEDULE

XL SERIES MODELS

Every 300 miles (500 km) or when dry

- Lubricate and adjust the drive chain

Every 500 miles (800 km) or 6 months

- Clean air filter element
- Check engine oil level
- Lubricate all control cables
- Lubricate rear brake pedal and shift lever
- Lubricate side stand pivot point
- Inspect front steering for looseness
- Check wheel bearings for smooth operation
- Check battery electrolyte level and condition
- Check ignition timing
- Check and adjust idle speed
- Check clutch lever free play
- Check fuel shutoff valve and filter
- Check wheel spoke condition
- Check wheel runout
- Clean and lubricate drive chain

Every 1,000 miles (1,600 km)

- Lubricate swing arm bushings

Every 1,800 miles (3,000 km)

- Change engine oil

Every 4,000 miles (6,400 km)

- Clean air filter element
- Replace engine oil filter
- Inspect spark plug, regap if necessary
- Check and adjust valve clearance
- Adjust cam chain tension (models so equipped)
- Adjust balancer chain tension (models so equipped)
- Inspect decompressor free play, adjust if necessary
- Inspect fuel lines for chafed, cracked or swollen ends
- Inspect and repack wheel bearings
- Inspect crankcase ventilation hoses for cracks or loose hose clamps- drain out all residue
- Check engine mounting bolts for tightness
- Check steering for free play
- Check all suspension components
- Adjust front and rear brake levers (including free-play)

(continued)

Table 2 MAINTENANCE SCHEDULE (cont.)

XL SERIES MODELS
Every 6,000 miles (10,000 km)
• Complete engine tune-up • Check and adjust valve clearance • Adjust the cam chain tension (models so equipped) • Check and adjust ignition timing • Check and adjust the carburetor(s) • Replace spark plug • Perform a compression test • Dismantle and clean carburetor(s) • Change front fork oil • Inspect and repack swing arm bushings • Replace air filter element • Lubricate speedometer cable • Inspect brake shoes (or pads) for wear • Check engine mounting bolts for tightness • Check all suspension components • Inspect all drive chain roller tensioners and sliders • Lubricate control cables • Inspect and repack steering head bearings • Check and adjust rear brake pedal height
Every 8,000 miles (12,800 km)
• Remove and clean engine oil filter screen • Replace the spark plug • Inspect the evaporative emission control system hoses and canister for damage (California models only) • Change brake fluid
XR SERIES MODELS
Every 300 miles (500 km) or when dry
• Lubricate and adjust the drive chain
Every 500 miles (800 km) or 6 months
• Clean air filter element • Check engine oil level • Lubricate all control cables • Lubricate rear brake pedal and shift lever • Lubricate side stand pivot point • Check steering head bearings for looseness • Check wheel bearings for smooth operation • Check ignition timing • Check and adjust idle speed • Check clutch lever free play • Check fuel shutoff valve and filter • Check wheel spoke condition • Check wheel runout • Clean and lubricate drive chain

(continued)

Table 2 MAINTENANCE SCHEDULE (cont.)

XR SERIES MODELS

Every 1,000 miles (1,600 km)	• Change engine oil • Lubricate swing arm bushings • Clean engine oil filter screen • Replace engine oil filter (models so equipped) • Inspect spark plug, regap if necessary • Check and adjust valve clearance • Adjust cam chain tension (models so equipped) • Adjust balancer chain tension (models so equipped) • Inspect decompressor free play, adjust if necessary • Inspect fuel lines for chafed, cracked or swollen ends • Inspect and repack wheel bearings • Inspect crankcase ventilation hoses for cracks or loose hose clamps- drain out all residue • Check engine mounting bolts for tightness • Check steering for free play • Check all suspension components • Adjust front and rear brake levers (including freeplay)
Every 4,000 miles (6,400 km)	• Complete engine tune-up • Check and adjust valve clearance • Adjust the cam chain tension (models so equipped) • Check and adjust ignition timing • Check and adjust the carburetor(s) • Replace spark plug • Dismantle and clean carburetor(s) • Change front fork oil • Inspect and repack swing arm bushings • Replace air filter element • Lubricate speedometer cable • Change brake fluid • Check and adjust rear brake pedal height • Perform a compression test • Inspect brake shoes (or pads) for wear • Check engine mounting bolts for tightness • Check all suspension components • Inspect all drive chain roller tensioners and sliders • Lubricate control cables • Inspect and repack steering head bearings

*This Honda factory maintenance schedule should be considered as a guide to general maintenance and lubrication intervals. Harder than normal use and exposure to mud, water, sand, high humidity, etc. will naturally dictate more frequent attention to most maintenance items.

Table 3 COMPETITION PRE-RACE INSPECTION

Item	Inspection
Engine oil	Check for contamination, change if dirty
Fuel line	Check for leakage and deterioration, replace
Air cleaner	Check for tears and contamination, replace or clean
Valve clearance	Adjust if necessary to correct clearance
Cam chain tension	Check for abnormal noise, adjust if necessary
Carburetor idle speed	Check and adjust if necessary
Balancer chain tension	Adjust if necessary (check while inspecting the clutch disc)
Starter decompressor	Check for correct free play, adjust if necessary
Clutch disc wear	Check for abnormal wear and/or discoloration
Spark plug	Check for proper heat range, gap tightness and plug tightness
Steering head	Check for free rotation of handlebar, check tightness of steering stem nut, adjust and/or tighten if necessary
Front suspension	Check for oil leaks, tight boot clamps and smooth action of forks
Rear suspension	Check for oil leaks and smooth operation
Swing arm bushings	Check for abnormal side play, replace if necessary
Brake shoes	Check wear indicators for wear beyond limits, replace brake shoes
Drive chain	Inspect for damage and chain stretch replace if necessary
Sprockets (both)	Inspect for wear and tightness of installation
Seat	Check for tightness of mounting hardware
Control cables	Check for smooth operation and frayed outer sheath, lubricate or replace
Engine mounting bolts	Check for tightness and fractures on mounting hardware
Headlight	Proper headlight adjustment
Instrument lights	Check for proper operation
Tires	Check for proper inflation and inspect for cuts and deep abrasions, replace if necessary
Exterior engine	Clean the entire engine and frame prior to a race

Table 4 BATTERY STATE OF CHARGE

Specific Gravity	State of Charge
1.110-1.130	Discharged
1.140-1.160	Almost discharged
1.170-1.190	One-quarter charged
1.200-1.220	One-half charged
1.230-1.250	Three-quarters charged
1.260-1.280	Fully charged

Table 5 ENGINE OIL CAPACITY

Engine size	Oil drain		Rebuilt	
	U.S. qt.	Liter	U.S. qt.	Liter
XR200R				
1984	1.2	1.1	1.3	1.2
1985	1.5	1.4	1.7	1.6
XL250S, XR250	1.6	1.5	2.1	2.0
XL250R				
1982-1983	1.6	1.5	2.1	2.0
1984-1987	1.4	1.3	1.6	1.5
XR250R				
1981-1982	1.8	1.7	2.1	2.0
1984	1.2	1.1	1.3	1.2
1985-on	1.5	1.4	1.7	1.6
XL350R	1.7	1.6	2.0	1.9
XR350R				
1983-1984	1.9	1.8	2.1	2.0
1985	1.6	1.5	2.1	2.0

3

Table 6 MAINTENANCE AND TUNE-UP TORQUE SPECIFICATIONS

Item	N•m	ft.-lb.
Oil drain plug		
Wet-sump models	20-30	14-22
Dry-sump models		
Frame down tube	35-45	25-33
Crankcase	30-40	22-29
Front fork cap bolt		
XR350R	15-20	11-14
All other models	15-30	11-22
Rear axle nut (dual-shock models)		
XL250S	55-70	40-51
All other models	70-110	51-80
Rear axle nut (Pro-Link models)		
1981 models	70-110	51-80
1982-1983 models	80-110	58-80
Balancer chain holder flange bolt		
XL250S, 1982-1983	22-30	16-22
XL250R		
Fuel strainer cup	3-5	2-4
(models so equipped)		
Wheel rim locks	9-15	7-11
Valve adjuster locknut		
1984 XR200R, 1984-on XR250R	17-23	12-17
All other models	15-18	11-13

Table 7 FRONT FORK OIL CAPACITY *

Model	Standard Capacity		Standard distance from top of fork	
	cc	fl. oz.	mm	in.
XR200R	651	22.0		
Maximum	-	-	146	5.75
Minimum	-	-	186	7.32
XL250S	190	6.4	-	-
XL250R				
1982-1983	300	10.14	173	6.81
1984-on	293	9.91	195	7.68
XR250	202	6.8	-	-
XR250R				
1981	368	12.4	152	6
1982	395	13.4	156	6.125
1984-on	651	22.0		
Maximum	-	-	150	5.91
Minimum	-	-	190	7.48
XL350R	411	14.0	184	7.2
XR350R				
1983	553	18.7	132	5.2
1984-1985	563	19.0		
Maximum	-	-	152	5.98
Minimum	-	-	112	4.41

* Capacity for each fork leg.

Table 8 FRONT FORK AIR PRESSURE

Model	psi	kg/cm²
XL250R	0-2.8	0-0.2
All other models	0	0

Table 9 DRIVE CHAIN FREE PLAY

Model	mm	in.
Dual shock models		
XL series	15-20	0.6-0.8
XR series	20	0.8
Pro-Link models		
XL series	30-40	1 1/4-1 5/8
XR series	35-45	1 3/8-1 3/4

Table 10 DRIVE CHAIN REPLACEMENT NUMBERS

Model	Standard
XR200R	520VC-3-108FJ or 520MO-108FJ
XL250S	-102L
XL250R	
1982-1983	520VC-102L
1984-on	520MO-102LE or 520VC-102LE
XR250	-102L
XR250R	
1981-1982	520DS-106RJ
1984-on	520VC-3-108FJ or 520MO-108FJ
XL350R	520VC-102LE or 520SO-102LE
XR350R	
1983	520MS-104FJ
1984-1985	520MO-104FJ or 520VC-3-104FJ

Table 11 DRIVE CHAIN SERVICE LENGTH SPECIFICATIONS

Model	Number of pins	Dimension mm	in.
XR200R	107	1,716	67.55
XL250S	41	648	25.4
XL250R	NA		
XR250	102	1,635	64.4
XR250R			
1981-1982	107	1,700	66.94
1984-on	107	1,716	67.55
XL350R	NA	NA	NA
XR350R	105	1,700	66.94

NA. Honda does not provide service information for all models.

Table 12 TUNE-UP SPECIFICATIONS

Valve clearance	
Intake	
All models	0.05 mm (0.002 in.)
Exhaust	
200-350 cc	0.08 mm (0.003 in.)
Compression pressure	
XR200, 1981-1982 XR250R,	199 psi (14.0 kg/cm²)
XL350R	
XR250, 1984-on XR250R	192 psi (13.5 kg/cm²)
All other models	175 psi (12.5 kg/cm²)
Spark plug type	
Standard heat range	
1978-1981	ND X24ES-U or NGK D8EA
1982	ND X24ESR-U or NGK DR8ES-L
1983	ND X24EPR-U9 NGK DPR8EA-9
1984-on XR200R, XR250R	ND X27EPR-U or NGK DPR9EA-9
All other models	ND X24EPR-U or NGK DPR8EA-9
Spark plug gap	0.8-0.9 mm (0.032-0.036 in.)
Ignition timing @ "F" mark	
Engine rpm	
200-350 cc	1,300 ± 100 rpm
Idle speed	1,200 ± 100 rpm

4

1978-1983 250 CC ENGINE

All models covered in this chapter are equipped with an air-cooled, 4-stroke, single cylinder engine with a single overhead camshaft. The cylinder head incorporates a pair of dual valves with each set having its own rocker arm. Each valve has its own adjuster.

The crankshaft is supported by 2 large ball bearings and engine vibration is minimized by 2 counter-rotating balancers that are driven off the crankshaft by a chain or gears.

The engine has a decompressor to ease starting. As the kickstarter pedal is depressed, a cam on the pedal operates a lever that transmits movement via a cable to the decompressor valve lifter on the cylinder head. This lifter opens the exhaust valves momentarily and then allows them to close as the pedal continues its downward travel.

Engine lubrication is provided by the oil pump located on the right-hand side of the engine. The oil pump is driven by the kickstarter idle gear.

The camshaft is chain-driven from the sprocket on the right-hand side of the crankshaft.

This chapter contains removal, inspection, service and reassembly procedures for the engine. Although the clutch and transmission are located within the engine, they are covered in Chapter Six to simplify this material.

Table 1 provides complete specifications for the engine and **Table 2** lists all of the engine torque specifications. **Table 1** and **Table 2** are located at the end of this chapter.

Before beginning work, re-read Chapter One of this book. You will do a better job with this information fresh in your mind.

Throughout the text there is frequent mention of the right-hand and left-hand side of the engine. This refers to the engine as it sits in the bike's frame, *not* as it sits on your workbench. The right- and left-hand refers to a rider sitting on the seat facing forward.

ENGINE PRINCIPLES

Figure 1 explains how the engine works. This will be helpful when troubleshooting or repairing the engine.

ENGINE COOLING

Cooling is provided by air passing over the cooling fins on the engine cylinder head and cylinder. It is very important to keep these fins free from buildup of dirt, oil, grease and other foreign matter. Brush out the fins with a whisk broom or small stiff paint brush.

CAUTION
Remember, these fins are thin in order to dissipate heat and may be damaged if struck too hard.

① **4-STROKE OPERATING PRINCIPLES**

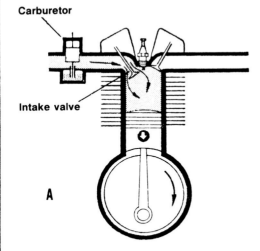

Carburetor

Intake valve

A

As the piston travels downward,
the exhaust valve is closed and the intake
valve opens, allowing the new fuel/air
mixture from the carburetor to be drawn
into the cylinder. When the piston reaches
the bottom of its travel (BDC), the intake
valve closes and remains closed for
the next revolution-and-a-half of the
crankshaft.

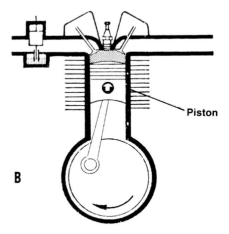

Piston

B

While the crankshaft continues to
rotate, the piston moves upward,
compressing the fuel/air mixture.

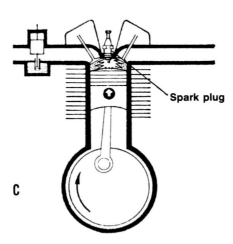

Spark plug

C

As the piston almost reaches the top
of its travel, the spark plug fires, igniting
the compressed fuel/air mixture. The
piston continues to top dead center
(TDC) and is pushed downward by the
expanding gases.

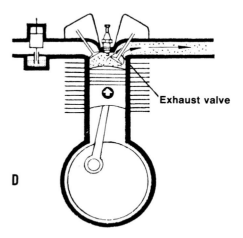

Exhaust valve

D

When the piston almost reaches BDC,
the exhaust valve opens and remains
open until the piston is near TDC. The
upward travel of the piston causes
the exhaust gases to be pushed out
of the cylinder. After the piston has
reached TDC, the exhaust valve closes
and the cycle starts all over again.

SERVICING ENGINE IN FRAME

The following components can be serviced while the engine is mounted in the frame (the bike's frame is a great holding fixture for breaking loose stubborn bolts and nuts):
   a. Camshaft.
   b. Cylinder head.
   c. Cylinder.
   d. Carburetor.
   e. Kickstarter.
   f. Alternator.
   g. Clutch assembly
   h. External shift mechanism.

4

ENGINE REMOVAL/INSTALLATION

1. Remove the right- and left-hand side covers and the seat.

NOTE
*On XL250S models, reinstall the seat strap bolts as they also hold the upper portion of the shock absorbers in place (**Figure 2**). Remove and install one bolt at a time.*

2. Drain the engine oil as described in Chapter Three.
3. Remove the fuel tank as described in Chapter Seven.
4. Remove the exhaust system as described in Chapter Seven.
5. Remove the carburetor as described in Chapter Seven.
6. Disconnect the spark plug lead and tie it up out of the way.
7. Remove the bolts (**Figure 3**) securing the skid plate and remove the skid plate.
8. On models so equipped, disconnect the battery negative lead or the main fuse (**Figure 4**).
9. Remove the kickstarter pedal.
10. Disconnect the rear brake light switch return spring and cable.
11. Remove the left-hand front footpeg and the gearshift lever.
12. Slacken the clutch cable at the hand lever. Disconnect the clutch cable at the crankcase cover.
13. Disconnect the alternator electrical connector.
14. Disconnect the ignition pulse generator wires at the electrical connector. Refer to **Figure 5** or **Figure 6**.

15. Remove the screws (**Figure 7**) securing the drive sprocket cover and remove the cover.

16. Remove the bolts and keeper (**Figure 8**) securing the drive sprocket and remove the sprocket and drive chain.

NOTE
If you are just removing the engine and are not planning to disassemble it, do not perform Step 17. The engine is small enough that external components can be left on during engine removal.

17. If the engine is going to be disassembled, remove the following parts:

   a. Remove the alternator as described in Chapter Eight.

   b. Remove the clutch assembly as described in Chapter Six.

   c. Remove the external shift mechanism as described in Chapter Six.

   d. Remove the cylinder head cover, camshaft, cylinder head, cylinder, piston and oil pump assembly as described in this chapter.

18. Disconnect the crankcase breather hose from the engine.

19. Take a final look all over the engine to make sure everything has been disconnected.

20. Place a suitable size jack, with a piece of wood to protect the crankcase, under the engine (A, **Figure 9**). Apply a small amount of jack pressure to the engine.

21. Remove the engine front hanger bolts (B, **Figure 9**) and nuts and remove the hanger.

22. Remove the upper rear mounting bolt and nut (**Figure 10**).

NOTE
*Don't lose the spacers (**Figure 10**) between the frame and the engine. Be sure to reinstall them.*

23. Remove the lower rear mounting bolt and nut (C, **Figure 9**).

24. Remove the upper bolts, nuts and plates (**Figure 11**).

> *CAUTION*
> *Continually adjust jack pressure during engine removal and installation to prevent damage to the mounting bolt threads and hardware.*

> *WARNING*
> *The following steps require the aid of a helper to safely remove the engine assembly from the frame.*

25. Lower the engine assembly to clear the frame mounting brackets and pull the engine out through the right-hand side of the frame. Take it to a workbench for further disassembly.
26. Install by reversing these removal steps, noting the following.
27. Tighten the mounting bolts to the torque specifications in **Table 2** and **Figure 12**.

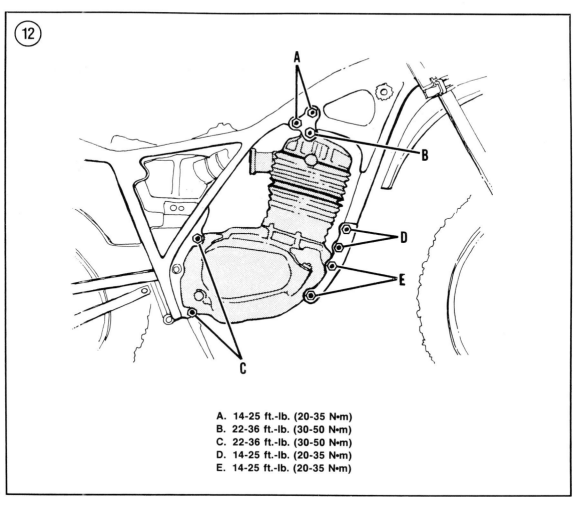

A. 14-25 ft.-lb. (20-35 N•m)
B. 22-36 ft.-lb. (30-50 N•m)
C. 22-36 ft.-lb. (30-50 N•m)
D. 14-25 ft.-lb. (20-35 N•m)
E. 14-25 ft.-lb. (20-35 N•m)

28. Fill the engine with the recommended type and quantity of oil; refer to Chapter Three.

29. Adjust the starter decompression lever free play, the clutch, drive chain and rear brake pedal as described in Chapter Three.

30. Start the engine and check for leaks.

CYLINDER HEAD COVER

Removal

> *CAUTION*
> *To prevent any warpage and damage, remove the cylinder head cover only when the engine is at room temperature.*

1. Remove the side covers and the seat.

2. Remove the fuel tank as described in Chapter Seven.

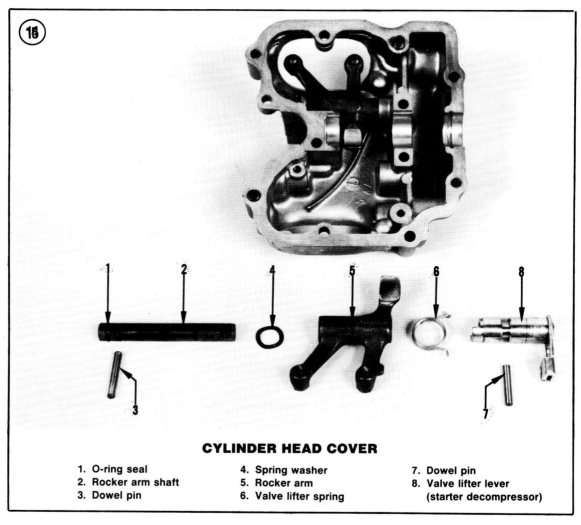

CYLINDER HEAD COVER

1. O-ring seal	4. Spring washer	7. Dowel pin
2. Rocker arm shaft	5. Rocker arm	8. Valve lifter lever
3. Dowel pin	6. Valve lifter spring	(starter decompressor)

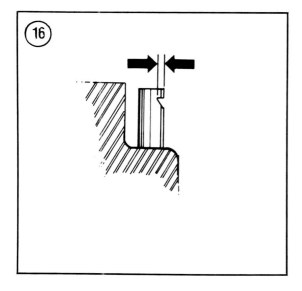

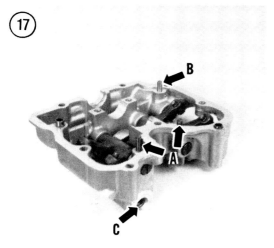

3. Disconnect the starter decompressor cable from the cylinder head cover.

4. Remove the upper bolts, nuts and mounting plates (**Figure 11**).

5. Remove the valve adjuster covers.

6. Remove the bolts (**Figure 13**) and one acorn nut (A, **Figure 13**) securing the cylinder head cover. Remove the cover and gasket. Don't lose the locating dowels.

Disassembly/Inspection/Assembly

Refer to **Figure 14** for this procedure.

1A. On XR250R models, to remove the dowel pins (**Figure 15**) securing the rocker arm shaft perform the following:

   a. Cut a 2 mm notch (**Figure 16**) in each dowel pin with a small rotary grinder.

> *CAUTION*
> *In the following step, do **not** overtighten the vise holding the cylinder head cover. Use the vise only as a holding fixture.*

   b. Very carefully place the cylinder head cover in a vise with soft jaws.

   c. Insert a drift or chisel in through the valve adjustment cover opening in the cylinder head cover and tap out the dowel pins. Remove the dowel pins and discard them.

> *CAUTION*
> *Be careful not to damage the cylinder head cover or rocker arms during the removal procedure.*

> *NOTE*
> *If these pins are difficult to remove, apply Liquid Wrench to the base of the pins and let sit for 10-15 minutes. This may help to loosen them.*

1B. On all other models, remove the dowel pins securing the rocker arm shafts (A, **Figure 17**).

2. Remove the dowel pin securing the valve lifter lever (B, **Figure 17**).

3. Hold the cover upside down in your hand and tap on the engine mounting boss (C, **Figure 17**) with a plastic mallet several times. Tap on the side where the rocker shaft ends are exposed. This tapping will cause the rocker arm shafts to work their way out enough to get hold of with your fingers. Do not use pliers as there is an O-ring seal on each shaft end.

> *CAUTION*
> *Do not use a metal hammer as the cover will be damaged.*

NOTE
In Step 4, mark the shafts with an "I"
(intake) or "E" (exhaust) as they must
be reinstalled into their original
*position. The rocker arms are **not***
identical and must be identified.

4. Pull the rocker arm shaft out and remove the rocker arm and spring washer. Repeat for the other shaft.

5. Pull the valve lifter lever out with the spring.

6. Wash all parts in solvent and dry thoroughly with compressed air.

7. Inspect the rocker arm pad where it rides on the cam lobe (A, **Figure 18**) and where the adjuster rides on the valve stem (B, **Figure 18**). If the pad is scratched or unevenly worn, inspect the cam lobe for scoring, chipping or flat spots. Replace the rocker arm if defective.

8. Measure the inside diameter of the rocker arm bore (A, **Figure 19**) with an inside micrometer and check against the dimensions in **Table 1**. Replace if worn to the service limit or larger.

9. Inspect the rocker arm shaft for signs of wear or scoring. Measure the outside diameter (B, **Figure 19**) with a micrometer and check against the dimensions in **Table 1**. Replace if worn to the service limit or smaller.

10. Inspect the camshaft bearing surfaces (**Figure 20**) for excessive wear.

11. Check the spring washers for breakage or distortion; replace if necessary.

12. Inspect the O-ring seals on the rocker arm shafts and valve lifter lever shaft. Replace if they have lost their resiliency.

13. Inspect the valve lifter lever shaft and the bearing surface in which it rides in the cover. Replace the valve lifter shaft if necessary.

14. Coat the rocker arm shaft, rocker arm bore and the shaft receptacles in the cover with assembly oil or clean engine oil.

15. Make sure the O-ring seal is in place on each rocker arm shaft.

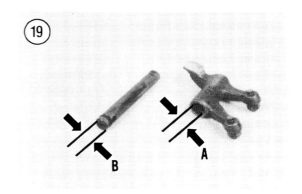

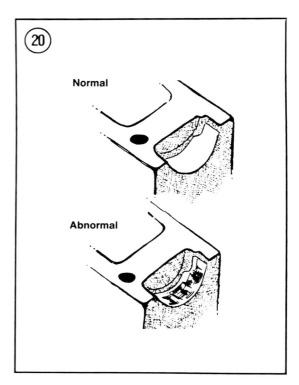

Normal

Abnormal

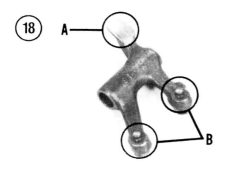

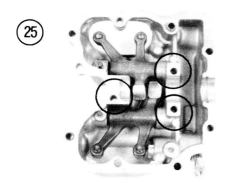

16. Refer to marks made in Step 3, *Removal*, and be sure to install the rocker arm shafts into their original location.

17. Install the rocker arm shaft with the O-ring end facing out. Partially insert the rocker arm shaft into the cylinder head.

18. Install the spring washer (**Figure 21**) on the left-hand side of the rocker arm. Push the rocker arm shaft through the spring washer and the rocker arm.

19. After the shaft is installed, rotate it to align the locating notch with the bolt hole (**Figure 22**) in the cover. Rotate the shaft using the slot (**Figure 23**) in the exposed end of the shaft.

20A. On XR250R models, install new dowel pins (**Figure 15**). Tap them into place with a hammer. *Never* reuse a dowel pin that has a removal notch ground into it.

20B. On all other models, install the dowel pins to secure the shafts in place.

21. Repeat Steps 15-19 for the other rocker arm assembly.

22. Coat the decompression valve lifter shaft with assembly oil and install the lever and spring as shown in **Figure 24**. Install the locating dowel (B, **Figure 17**) securing it in place.

Installation

1. Make sure all sealant residue is removed from the sealing surfaces of the cylinder head and cylinder head cover. Spray both sealing surfaces with contact cleaner and wipe dry with a clean cloth.

> *CAUTION*
> *Do not apply sealant to the areas surrounding the camshaft bearing surfaces (**Figure 25**).*

2. Apply a thin, even coat of Three Bond 1104 or equivalent to the cylinder head sealing surface.

3. If removed, install the camshaft plug (**Figure 26**).

4. Add fresh engine oil into the camshaft pocket in the cylinder head. The camshaft lobes must be submerged in oil or they will be damaged when the engine is first started up. Also lubricate the camshaft bearing journals and bearing surfaces in the cylinder head cover.

5. Make sure the locating dowels are in place.

6. Install the cylinder head cover and press it into position.

7. Install the cylinder head cover bolts and acorn nut.

8. Tighten the cylinder head bolts and nut in 2-3 stages in the torque pattern indicated in **Figure 27**. Tighten to the torque specification listed in **Table 2**.

9. Install the engine upper mounting plates, bolts and nuts. Tighten the bolts and nuts to the torque specification listed in **Table 2**.

10. Attach the starter decompressor cable to the lever on the cylinder head cover.

11. Install the fuel tank, valve adjuster covers, seat and side covers.

CYLINDER HEAD

NOTE
Cylinder head removal and inspection are the same for all engines. Installation differs because of a different camshaft chain tensioner design. Be sure to use the correct installation procedure for your particular bike.

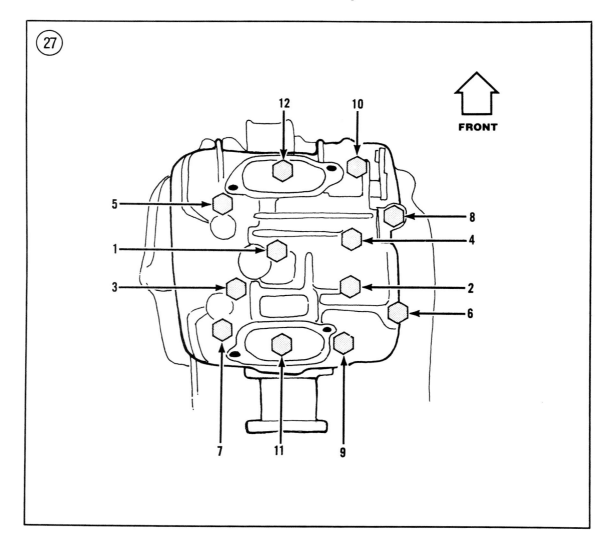

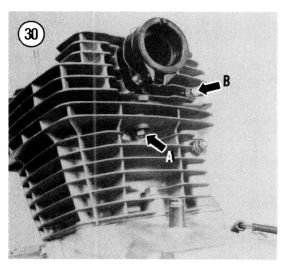

Removal (All Models)

> *CAUTION*
> *To prevent any warpage and damage, remove the cylinder head only when the engine is at room temperature.*

> *NOTE*
> *The cylinder head can be removed with the engine in the frame. The engine is shown removed in this procedure for clarity.*

1. Remove the cylinder head cover as described in this chapter.
2. Remove the carburetor as described in Chapter Seven.
3. Remove the exhaust system as described in Chapter Seven.
4. If still installed, remove the camshaft plug (A, **Figure 28**).
5. Remove both timing hole caps (**Figure 29**).
6. Rotate the engine with the bolt on the alternator rotor (bottom timing hole) until one of the camshaft sprocket bolts is exposed. Remove that bolt (B, **Figure 28**).

> *NOTE*
> *During Step 7, don't drop the bolts in the camshaft cavity as they will fall into the crankcase.*

7. Again rotate the engine until the other camshaft sprocket bolts is exposed. Remove that bolt.
8. Leave the sprocket in this position with one of the bolt holes at the 12 o'clock position. Gently pry the camshaft sprocket to the right, off the boss on the camshaft.
9. Attach a piece of wire to the camshaft chain and tie it to the exterior of the engine. This will prevent the chain from falling into the crankcase.
10. Disengage the chain from the sprocket and place the chain to the left, behind the sprocket. Remove the sprocket.
11. Remove the camshaft.

> *CAUTION*
> *If the crankshaft must be rotated when the camshaft is removed, pull up on the camshaft chain and keep it taut while rotating the crankshaft. Make certain that the drive chain is positioned correctly on the crankshaft timing sprocket. If this is not done, the drive chain may become kinked and may damage both the chain and the timing sprocket on the crankshaft.*

12. Remove the lower nuts and washers (A, **Figure 30**), one at the front and one at the rear.

13. Remove the camshaft chain tensioner upper lockbolt and washer (B, **Figure 30**). On XL250S and XL250 models, don't lose the O-ring seal.

14. Loosen the cylinder head bolts in a crisscross pattern in 2-3 stages. Remove the bolts.

15. Loosen the cylinder head by tapping around the perimeter with a rubber or soft-faced mallet. If necessary, *gently* pry the head loose with a broad-tipped screwdriver.

CAUTION
Remember the cooling fins are fragile and may be damaged if tapped or pried on too hard. Never use a metal hammer.

16. Lift the cylinder head straight up and off the cylinder. Guide the camshaft chain through the opening in the cylinder head and retie the wire to the exterior of the engine. This will prevent the drive chain from falling down into the crankcase.

17. Remove the cylinder head gasket and discard it. Don't lose the locating dowels.

18. Place a clean shop cloth into the camshaft chain opening in the cylinder to prevent the entry of foreign matter.

Inspection (All Models)

Because the cylinder head and cylinder head cover are machined as a set during manufacture, they must be replaced as a set if either is damaged or defective.

1. Remove all traces of gasket material from the cylinder head mating surfaces.

2. *Without removing the valves,* remove all carbon deposits from the combustion chamber and valve ports with a wire brush. A blunt screwdriver or chisel may be used if care is taken not to damage the head, valves and spark plug threads.

3. After the carbon is removed from the combustion chamber and the valve intake and exhaust ports, clean the entire head in cleaning solvent. Blow dry with compressed air.

4. Clean away all carbon from the piston crown. Do not remove the carbon ridge at the top of the cylinder bore.

5. Check for cracks in the combustion chamber and exhaust ports. A cracked head must be replaced.

6. After the head has been thoroughly cleaned, place a straightedge across the cylinder head/cylinder gasket surface at several points (**Figure 31**). Measure the warp by inserting a flat feeler gauge between the straightedge and the cylinder head at each location. There should be no warpage; if a small amount is present, it can be

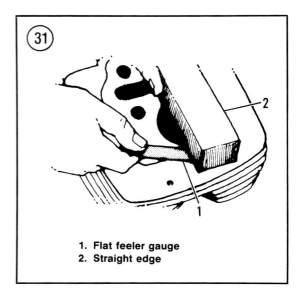

1. **Flat feeler gauge**
2. **Straight edge**

resurfaced by a dealer or qualified machine shop. Replace the cylinder head and cylinder head cover as a set if the gasket surface is warped to or beyond the limit listed in **Table 1**.

7. Check the cylinder head cover mating surface using the procedure in Step 6. There should be no warpage.

8. Check the valves and valve guides as described in this chapter.

9. Check the end seal plug (A, **Figure 28**). Make sure it fits tightly; if not, replace it.

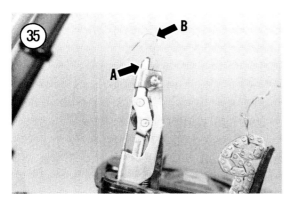

10. Inspect the camshaft bearing surfaces in the cylinder head and cylinder head cover for wear or scoring. Replace the cylinder head and cylinder head cover as a set if the bearing surfaces are worn or scored.

11. Inspect the oil groove (**Figure 32**) in each camshaft bearing surface. Make sure they are clean.

Installation (XL250R, XR250R)

1. Install the dowel pins (**Figure 33**). Install the O-ring seal on the dowel pin adjacent to the camshaft chain tensioner.

2. Install a new cylinder head gasket. Make sure the holes align exactly.

3. Push down on the camshaft chain tensioner wedge "B" (**Figure 34**) and pull up on wedge "A." Pull wedge "A" (A, **Figure 35**) up enough to expose the 2 mm hole in the wedge.

4. Insert a piece of wire (approximately 2 mm in diameter) into the hole to hold wedge "A" in the up position. Refer to B, **Figure 35**. A straightened No. 2 paper clip will work.

> *NOTE*
> *Be careful that the piece of wire holding the camshaft tensioner wedge does not work loose while installing the cylinder head. If the wire jumps out of place it will fall down into the crankcase.*

5. Untie the wire securing the camshaft drive chain from exterior of the engine and remove the shop rag from the opening in the cylinder.

6. Carefully slide the cylinder head onto the cylinder. Feed the camshaft chain through the chain cavity in the cylinder head and secure the other end of the wire again.

7. Apply oil to the threads of the cylinder head bolts.

8. Install the cylinder head bolts and washers and tighten in a crisscross pattern, in 2-3 stages. Tighten to the torque specification listed in **Table 2**.

9. Install the lower washers and nuts (A, **Figure 30**) and tighten securely.

10. Install the camshaft chain tensioner set bolt and sealing washer (**Figure 36**).

11. Lubricate all camshaft lobes and bearing journals with assembly oil. Also coat the camshaft bearing surfaces in the cylinder head and cylinder head cover.

> *CAUTION*
> *When rotating the crankshaft, keep the camshaft chain taut and engaged with the timing sprocket on the crankshaft.*

12. The engine must be at top dead center (TDC) for the following steps for correct valve timing. Hold the camshaft chain out and taut while rotating the crankshaft to avoid damage to the chain and/or the crankcase.

13. Pull up on the chain, making sure it is properly engaged on the crankshaft sprocket. Rotate the engine until the "T" timing mark on the alternator rotor aligns with the fixed notch on the crankcase cover (**Figure 37**).

14. Position the camshaft sprocket so the 2 timing marks face toward the center of the engine and with the elongated notch up toward the top (**Figure 38**).

15. Hold the camshaft sprocket and chain in this position and feed the camshaft through both parts. Rest the camshaft on the bearing surfaces in the cylinder head.

16. Rotate the camshaft sprocket until the 2 timing marks on the backside align with the top surface of the cylinder head (**Figure 39**).

17. Rotate the camshaft until the bolt mounting holes align with the camshaft sprocket—do not place the sprocket up on the camshaft boss at this time.

NOTE
*The camshaft can be installed with the lobes up or down as long as the bolt holes align with the camshaft sprocket and the timing marks on the sprocket align with the cylinder head (**Figure 39**). It is easier if the lobes are facing down as this will place less of a load on the rocker arms during cylinder head cover installation.*

NOTE
If the engine is relatively new or a new camshaft chain has been installed, Step 18 may be difficult. Carefully insert a long, broad-tipped screwdriver down into the camshaft chain cavity and depress the tensioner from the inside. This will give you additional chain slack, enabling the camshaft sprocket and chain to slide up onto the camshaft boss. Be careful not to damage anything in the camshaft cavity with the screwdriver.

18. Install the chain onto the sprocket without rotating the sprocket. Slide the sprocket and chain up and onto the camshaft boss. Recheck the following:

a. Refer to Step 13 and make sure the "T" mark is still properly aligned (**Figure 37**). Readjust if necessary.

b. Make sure the index marks on the camshaft sprocket are perfectly aligned with the top surface of the cylinder head (**Figure 39**).

19. If alignment is incorrect, reposition the camshaft chain on the sprocket and recheck the alignment. Refer to **Figure 37** and **Figure 39**.

CAUTION
Very expensive damage could result from improper camshaft and camshaft chain alignment. Recheck your work several times to be sure alignment is correct.

20. When alignment is correct, perform the following:

a. Install the bolt into the exposed bolt hole. Tighten only finger-tight at this time.

b. Rotate the engine to expose the other bolt hole and install the other bolt.

c. Make sure the camshaft sprocket is correctly seated on the camshaft boss.

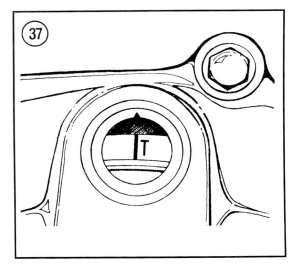

d. Tighten both bolts to the torque specification listed in **Table 2**.

CAUTION
If there is any binding while rotating the crankshaft, ***stop***. *Determine the cause before proceeding.*

21. After installation is complete, rotate the crankshaft several times using the bolt on the alternator rotor.

22. Make one final check to make sure alignment is correct. The "T" timing mark must be aligned with the crankcase cover notch and the timing marks on the camshaft sprocket must be perfectly aligned with the top surface of the cylinder head.

23. Remove the piece of 2 mm wire from the hole in wedge "A." Make sure the camshaft chain tensioner wedge "A" slides down into the released position (**Figure 40**).

24. Fill the oil pocket in the cylinder head with new engine oil so the cam lobes are submerged in the oil.

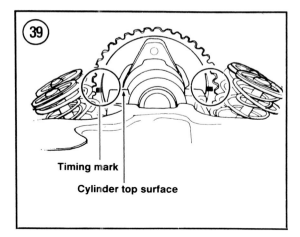

Timing mark

Cylinder top surface

25. Install the cylinder head cover as described in this chapter.

26. Install the carburetor and exhaust system as described in Chapter Seven.

27. Adjust the valves and camshaft chain tension as described in Chapter Three.

Installation (All Other Models)

1. Install the camshaft chain tensioner locknut; pull the tensioner assembly all the way up and tighten the locknut.

2. Install the dowel pins. Install the O-ring seal on the rear right-hand side.

3. Install a new cylinder head gasket. Make sure the holes align exactly.

4. Remove the shop rag from the opening in the cylinder.

5. Carefully slide the cylinder head onto the cylinder. Feed the camshaft chain through the chain cavity in the cylinder head and secure the other end of the wire again.

6. Apply oil to the threads of the cylinder head bolts.

7. Install the cylinder bolts and washers and tighten in a crisscross pattern, in 2-3 stages. Tighten to the torque specification listed in **Table 2**.

8. Install the lower washers and nuts (A, **Figure 30**) and tighten securely.

NOTE
Make sure the O-ring seal is installed on the lockbolt.

9. Install the camshaft chain tensioner lockbolt and washer (B, **Figure 30**).

10. Lubricate all camshaft lobes and bearing journals with assembly oil. Also coat the camshaft bearing surfaces in the cylinder head and cylinder head cover.

CAUTION
When rotating the crankshaft, keep the camshaft chain taut and engaged with the timing sprocket on the crankshaft.

11. The engine must be at top dead center (TDC) for the following steps for correct valve timing. Hold the camshaft chain out and taut while rotating the crankshaft to avoid damage to the chain and/or the crankcase.

12. Pull up on the chain, making sure it is properly engaged on the crankshaft sprocket. Rotate the engine until the "T" timing mark on the alternator rotor aligns with the fixed notch on the crankcase cover (**Figure 37**).

13. Position the camshaft sprocket so the 2 timing marks face toward the center of the engine.

14. Hold the camshaft sprocket and chain in this position and feed the camshaft through both parts. Rest the camshaft on the bearing surfaces in the cylinder head.

15. Rotate the camshaft sprocket until the 2 timing marks on the backside align with the top surface of the cylinder head (**Figure 39**).

16. Rotate the camshaft until the bolt mounting holes align with the camshaft sprocket—do not place the sprocket up on the camshaft boss at this time.

NOTE
*The camshaft can be installed with the lobes up or down as long as the bolt holes align with the camshaft sprocket and the timing marks on the sprocket align with the cylinder head (**Figure 39**). It is easier if the lobes are facing down as this will place less of a load on the rocker arms during cylinder head cover installation.*

NOTE
If the engine is relatively new or a new camshaft chain has been installed, Step 17 may be difficult. Carefully insert a long, broad-tipped screwdriver down into the camshaft chain cavity and depress the tensioner from the inside. This will give you additional chain slack, enabling the camshaft sprocket and chain to slide up onto the camshaft boss. Be careful not to damage anything in the camshaft cavity with the screwdriver.

17. Install the chain onto the sprocket without rotating the sprocket. Slide the sprocket and chain up and onto the camshaft boss. Recheck the following:
   a. Refer to Step 13 and make sure the "T" mark is still properly aligned (**Figure 37**). Readjust if necessary.
   b. Make sure the index marks on the camshaft sprocket are perfectly aligned with the top surface of the cylinder head (**Figure 39**).

18. If alignment is incorrect, reposition the camshaft chain on the sprocket and recheck the alignment. Refer to **Figure 37** and **Figure 39**.

CAUTION
Very expensive damage could result from improper camshaft and camshaft chain alignment. Recheck your work several times to be sure alignment is correct.

19. When alignment is correct, perform the following:
   a. Install the bolt into the exposed bolt hole. Tighten only finger-tight at this time.
   b. Rotate the engine to expose the other bolt hole and install the other bolt.
   c. Make sure the camshaft sprocket is correctly seated on the camshaft boss.
   d. Tighten both bolts to the torque specification listed in **Table 2**.

CAUTION
*If there is any binding while rotating the crankshaft, **stop**. Determine the cause before proceeding.*

20. After installation is complete, rotate the crankshaft several times using the bolt on the alternator rotor.

21. Make one final check to make sure alignment is correct. The "T" timing mark must be aligned

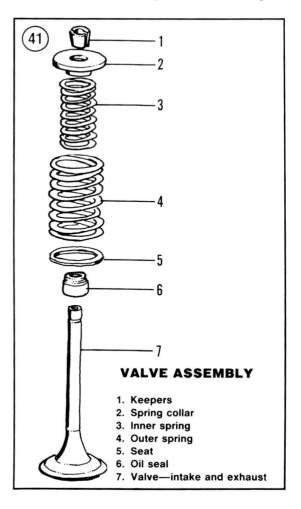

VALVE ASSEMBLY

1. Keepers
2. Spring collar
3. Inner spring
4. Outer spring
5. Seat
6. Oil seal
7. Valve—intake and exhaust

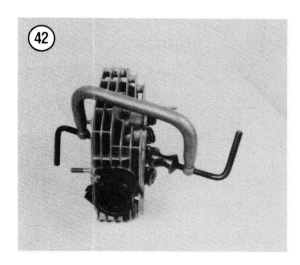

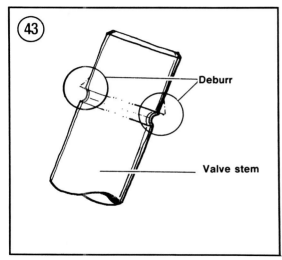

Deburr

Valve stem

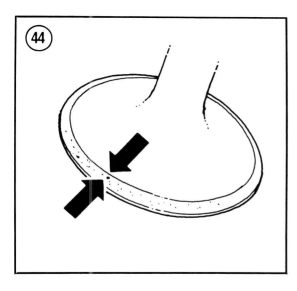

with the mark and the timing marks on the camshaft sprocket must be perfectly aligned with the top surface of the cylinder head.

22. Fill the oil pocket in the cylinder head with new engine oil so the cam lobes are submerged in the oil.

23. Install the cylinder head cover as described in this chapter.

24. Install the carburetor and exhaust system as described in Chapter Seven.

25. Adjust the valves and camshaft chain tension as described in Chapter Three.

> *NOTE*
> *A general practice among those who do their own service is to remove the cylinder head and take it to a machine shop or dealer for inspection and service. Since the cost is low relative to the required effort and equipment, this is the best approach, even for experienced mechanics. The following procedures are included in case you choose to perform these tasks yourself.*

VALVES AND VALVE COMPONENTS

Removal

Refer to **Figure 41** for this procedure.

1. Remove the cylinder head as described in this chapter.

> *CAUTION*
> *To avoid loss of spring tension, do not compress the springs any more than necessary to remove the keepers.*

2. Compress the valve springs with a valve compressor tool (**Figure 42**). Remove the valve keepers and release the compression. Remove the valve compressor tool.

3. Remove the valve spring collar and valve springs.

4. Prior to removing the valve, remove any burrs from the valve stem (**Figure 43**). Otherwise the valve guide will be damaged.

5. Remove the valve.

6. Mark all parts as they are disassembled so that they will be installed in their original locations.

Inspection

1. Clean the valves with a wire brush and solvent.

2. Inspect the contact surface of each valve for burning or pitting (**Figure 44**). Unevenness of the contact surface is an indication that the valve is not serviceable. The valve contact surface can *not* be ground and must be replaced if defective.

3. Inspect the valve stem for wear and roughness and measure the vertical runout of the valve stem as shown in **Figure 45**. The runout should not exceed the service limit listed in **Table 1.**

4. Measure the valve stem for wear (**Figure 46**). If worn to the wear limit listed in **Table 1** or less, the valve must be replaced.

5. Remove all carbon and varnish from the valve guide with a stiff spiral wire brush.

6. Insert each valve in its guide. Hold the valve with the head just slightly off the valve seat and rock it sideways. If it rocks more than slightly, the guide is probably worn and should be replaced. As a final check, take the cylinder to a dealer and have the valve guides measured.

7. Measure each valve spring free length with a vernier caliper (**Figure 47**). All should be within the length specified in **Table 1** with no signs of bending or distortion. Replace defective springs in pairs (inner and outer).

8. Check the valve spring retainer and valve keepers. If they are in good condition they may be reused; replace as necessary.

9. Inspect the valve seats. If worn or burned, they must be reconditioned. This should be performed by a dealer or qualified machine shop.

Installation

1. Coat the valve stems with molybdenum disulfide grease. To avoid damage to the valve stem seal, turn the valve slowly while inserting the valve into the cylinder head.

2. Install the bottom spring retainers and new seals.

3. Install the valve springs with their closer wound coils facing the cylinder head and install the valve spring retainer.

> *CAUTION*
> *To avoid loss of spring tension, do not compress the springs any more than necessary to install the keepers.*

4. Compress the valve springs with a compressor tool (**Figure 42**) and install the valve keepers. Remove the compression tool.

5. After all springs have been installed, gently tap the end of the valve stem with a soft aluminum or brass drift and hammer. This will ensure that the keepers are properly seated.

6. Install the cylinder head as described in this chapter.

Valve Guide Replacement

When valve guides are worn so that there is excessive stem-to-guide clearance or valve tipping,

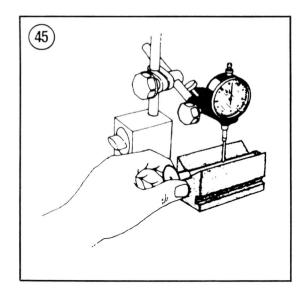

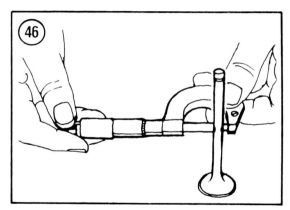

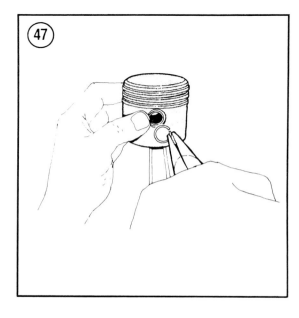

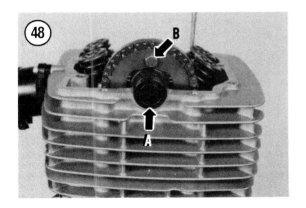

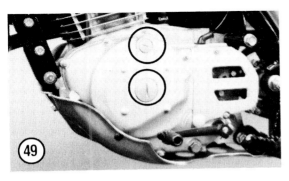

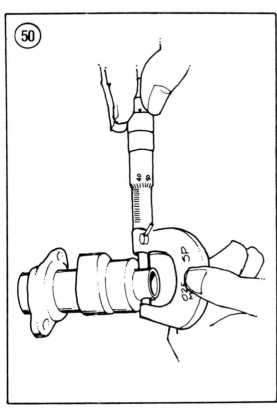

the guides must be replaced. Replace all, even if only one is worn. This job should be done only by a dealer or machine shop as special tools are required. If the valve guides are replaced; replace the valves also.

Valve Seat Reconditioning

This job is best left to a dealer or qualified machine shop. They have special equipment and knowledge for this exacting job. You can still save considerable money by removing the cylinder head and taking the head to the shop for repairs.

CAMSHAFT

Removal/Installation

1. Remove the cylinder head cover as described in this chapter.
2. Remove the carburetor as described in Chapter Seven.
3. Remove the exhaust system as described in Chapter Seven.
4. If still installed, remove the camshaft plug (A, **Figure 48**).
5. Remove both timing hole caps (**Figure 49**).
6. Rotate the engine with the bolt on the alternator rotor (bottom timing hole) until one of the camshaft sprocket bolts is exposed. Remove that bolt (B, **Figure 48**).

NOTE
In Step 7, don't drop the bolts in the camshaft cavity as they will fall into the crankcase.

7. Again rotate the engine until the other camshaft sprocket bolt is exposed. Remove that bolt.
8. Leave the sprocket in this position with one of the bolt holes at the 12 o'clock position. Gently pry the camshaft sprocket to the right, off the boss on the camshaft.
9. Attach a piece of wire to the camshaft chain and tie it to the exterior of the engine. This will prevent the chain from falling into the crankcase.
10. Disengage the chain from the sprocket and place the chain to the left, behind the sprocket. Remove the sprocket.
11. Remove the camshaft.

Inspection

1. Measure both the right- and left-hand camshaft bearing journals (**Figure 50**) for wear and scoring. Compare to the dimensions given in **Table 1**. If worn to the service limit or less, the camshaft must be replaced.

NOTE
*Don't mistake the sprocket boss area (A, **Figure 51**) for the right-hand bearing journal (B, **Figure 51**).*

2. Check the camshaft lobes for wear. The lobes should show no signs of scoring and the edges should be square. Slight damage may be removed with a silicone carbide oilstone. Use No. 100-120 grit stone initially, then polish with a No. 280-320 grit stone.

NOTE
The cam is dark in color due to the manufacturing heat treating process. It is not due to lack of oil pressure or excessive engine heat.

3. Even though the camshaft lobe surface appears to be satisfactory, with no visible signs of wear, the camshaft lobes must be measured with a micrometer (**Figure 52**). Compare to the dimensions given in **Table 1**.

4. Inspect the camshaft bearing surfaces in the cylinder head and cylinder head cover. They should not be scored or excessively worn (**Figure 53**). Replace the cylinder head and cylinder head cover as a set if the bearing surfaces are worn or scored.

5. Remove the camshaft plug from the cylinder head. Install the cylinder head cover and tighten the bolts in the torque sequence shown in **Figure 54**. Tighten to the torque specification listed in **Table 2**.

6. Measure the inside diameter of the bearing surfaces, both the right- and left-hand side. Compare to dimensions listed in **Table 1**. If either dimension exceeds the wear limit in **Table 1**, the cylinder head and cylinder head cover must be replaced as a set. Remove the cylinder head cover.

7. Inspect the camshaft sprocket for wear; replace if necessary.

Installation

1. Lubricate all camshaft lobes and bearing journals with assembly oil. Also coat the camshaft bearing surfaces in the cylinder head and cylinder head cover.

CAUTION
When rotating the crankshaft, keep the camshaft chain taut and engaged with the timing sprocket on the crankshaft.

2. The engine must be at top dead center (TDC) for the following steps for correct valve timing. Hold the camshaft chain out and taut while rotating the crankshaft to avoid damage to the chain and/or the crankcase.

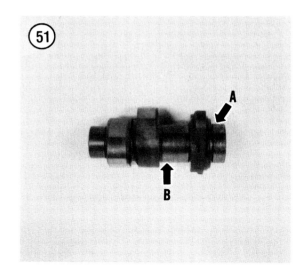

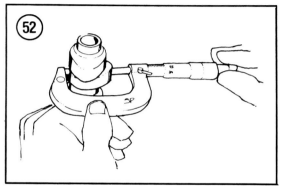

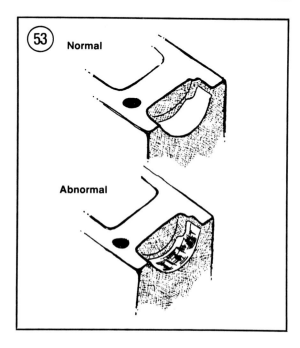

Normal

Abnormal

3. Pull up on the chain, making sure it is properly engaged on the crankshaft sprocket. Rotate the engine until the "T" timing mark on the alternator rotor aligns with the fixed notch on the crankcase cover (**Figure 37**).

4. Position the camshaft sprocket so the 2 timing marks face toward the center of the engine.

5. Hold the camshaft sprocket and chain in this position and feed the camshaft through both parts. Rest the camshaft on the bearing surfaces in the cylinder head.

6. Rotate the camshaft sprocket until the 2 timing marks on the backside align with the top surface of the cylinder head (**Figure 39**).

7. Rotate the camshaft until the bolt mounting holes align with the camshaft sprocket—do not place the sprocket up on the camshaft boss at this time.

NOTE
*The camshaft can be installed with the lobes up or down as long as the bolt holes align with the camshaft sprocket and the timing marks on the sprocket align with the cylinder head (**Figure 39**).*

It is easier if the lobes are facing down as this will place less of a load on the rocker arms during cylinder head cover installation.

NOTE
If the engine is relatively new or a new camshaft chain has been installed, Step 8 may be difficult. Carefully insert a long, broad-tipped screwdriver down into the camshaft chain cavity and depress the tensioner from the inside. This will give you additional chain slack, enabling the camshaft sprocket and chain to slide up onto the camshaft boss. Be careful not to damage anything in the camshaft cavity with the screwdriver.

8. Install the chain onto the sprocket without rotating the sprocket. Slide the sprocket and chain up and onto the camshaft boss. Recheck the following:

a. Refer to Step 13 and make sure the "T" mark is still properly aligned (**Figure 37**). Readjust if necessary.

b. Make sure the index marks on the camshaft sprocket are perfectly aligned with the top surface of the cylinder head (**Figure 39**).

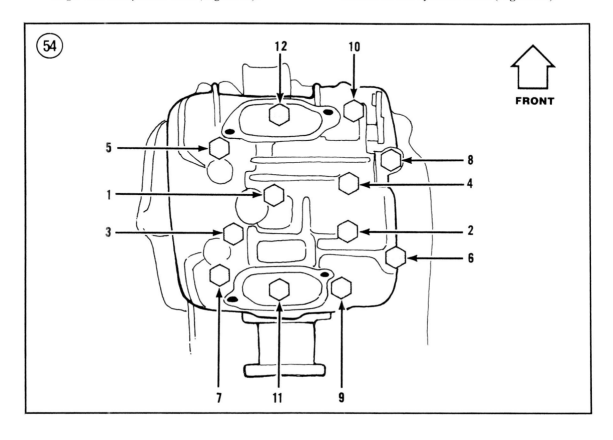

9. If alignment is incorrect, reposition the camshaft chain on the sprocket and recheck the alignment. Refer to **Figure 37** and **Figure 39**.

> *CAUTION*
> *Very expensive damage could result from improper camshaft and camshaft chain alignment. Recheck your work several times to be sure alignment is correct.*

10. When alignment is correct, perform the following:
    a. Install the bolt into the exposed bolt hole. Tighten only finger-tight at this time.
    b. Rotate the engine to expose the other bolt hole and install the other bolt.
    c. Make sure the camshaft sprocket is correctly seated on the camshaft boss.
    d. Tighten both bolts to the torque specification listed in **Table 2**.

> *CAUTION*
> *If there is any binding while rotating the crankshaft, **stop**. Determine the cause before proceeding.*

11. After installation is complete, rotate the crankshaft several times using the bolt on the alternator rotor.

12. Make one final check to make sure alignment is correct. The "T" timing mark must be aligned with the mark and the timing marks on the camshaft sprocket must be perfectly aligned with the top surface of the cylinder head.

13. Fill the oil pocket in the cylinder head with new engine oil so the cam lobes are submerged in the oil.

14. Install the cylinder head cover as described in this chapter.

CAMSHAFT CHAIN AND DAMPERS

Removal/Installation

1. Remove the cylinder head cover, cylinder head and cylinder as described in this chapter.

2. Remove the clutch assembly as described in Chapter Six.

3. Remove the ignition advance assembly as described in this chapter.

4. Remove the bolt (A, **Figure 55**) securing the cam chain tensioner and remove it.

> *NOTE*
> *The cam chain guide was removed in the cylinder removal sequence.*

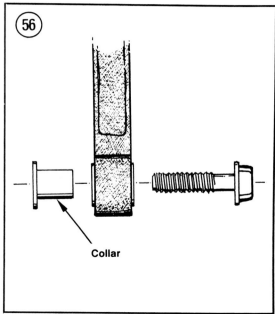

Collar

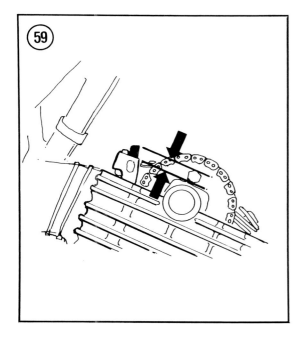

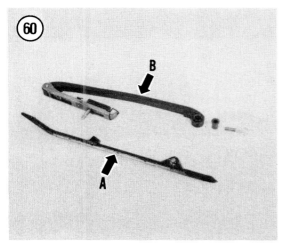

6. Disengage the cam chain from the crankshaft sprocket and remove it (B, **Figure 55**).

7. Install by reversing these removal steps. Tighten the cam chain tensioner bolt to the torque specifications listed in **Table 2**.

> *CAUTION*
> *Make sure the collar (**Figure 56**) is in place in the tensioner assembly prior to installation.*

Inspection (XR250R)

The upper end of the cam chain tensioner assembly is a set of sliding wedges that work together to maintain the correct tension on the cam chain, eliminating the need for periodic adjustment.

1. Inspect the mating surfaces of both wedges (**Figure 57**) for uneven wear or damage. If either is damaged to the extent that they do not slide smoothly against each other, the tensioner must be replaced.

2. Check the small spring (**Figure 58**) that holds the upper wedge up. If it is weak or broken, the tensioner must be replaced.

The camshaft chain is a Hy-vo type and rarely wears out, but will stretch with prolonged use. To check for chain wear, remove the cylinder head cover as described in this chapter. Measure the distance that the upper wedge (wedge "B") protrudes above the upper surface of the tensioner assembly bracket (**Figure 59**). The chain must be replaced if the dimension is 9.0 mm (0.35 in.) or more.

If the chain is worn, check the drive and driven sprockets for wear also; they may also require replacement.

Inspection (All Except XR250R)

Check the top surface of the guide (A, **Figure 60**) and the tensioner assembly (B, **Figure 60**). If either is worn or damaged it must be replaced. This may indicate a worn chain or improper chain adjustment.

Check all of the components of the tensioner assembly (B, **Figure 60**); if any part is defective, replace the assembly.

The camshaft chain is a Hy-vo type and rarely wears out, but will stretch with prolonged use. Check it thoroughly and if damaged, replace it. If it needs replacing, also check the drive sprocket on the crankshaft and the cam sprocket. They also may be defective.

CYLINDER

Removal

1. Remove the cylinder head cover and cylinder head as described in this chapter.

2. Remove the cylinder head gasket, locating dowels and O-ring seal.

3A. On XL250R and XR250R models, perform the following:

    a. Remove the camshaft chain guide (**Figure 61**).

    b. Remove the camshaft chain tensioner set bolt and copper washer (**Figure 62**) and push the tensioner assembly forward.

    c. Remove the bolts (**Figure 63**) securing the cylinder on the right-hand side.

3B. On all other models, perform the following:

    a. Remove the camshaft chain tensioner locknut and sealing washer. Remove the O-ring seal from the threaded stud on the tensioner assembly.

    b. Push the tensioner assembly forward to move the threaded stud out of the hole in the cylinder.

    c. Remove the bolts securing the cylinder on the right-hand side.

4. Loosen the cylinder by tapping around the perimeter with a rubber or plastic mallet. If necessary, *gently* pry the cylinder loose with a broad-tipped screwdriver.

> *CAUTION*
> *Remember, the cooling fins are fragile and may be damaged if tapped or pried on too hard. Never use a metal hammer.*

5. Pull the cylinder straight out and off of the piston. Work the camshaft chain wire through the opening in the cylinder. Reattach the wire to the exterior of the crankcase.

6. Remove the cylinder base gasket and discard it. Remove the dowel pins from the crankcase receptacles.

7. Install a piston holding fixture under the piston to protect the piston skirt from damage. This fixture may be purchased or may be a homemade unit of wood. See **Figure 64** for dimensions.

Inspection

The following procedure requires the use of highly specialized and expensive measuring instruments. If such equipment is not readily available, have the measurements performed by a dealer or qualified machine shop.

1. Soak with solvent any old cylinder head gasket material on the cylinder. Use a broad-tipped *dull* chisel and gently scrape off all gasket residue. Do not gouge the sealing surface as oil and air leaks will result.

2. Measure the cylinder bore with a cylinder gauge (**Figure 65**) or inside micrometer at the points shown in **Figure 66**. Measure in 2 axes—in line with the piston pin and at 90° to the pin. If the taper or out-of-round is 0.05 mm (0.002 in.) or greater, the cylinder must be rebored to the next oversize and a new piston installed.

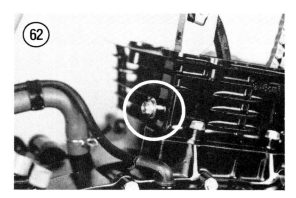

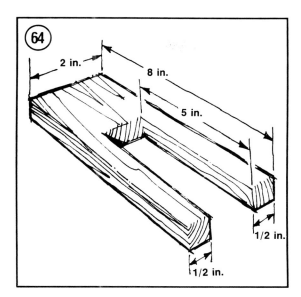

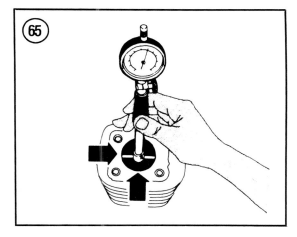

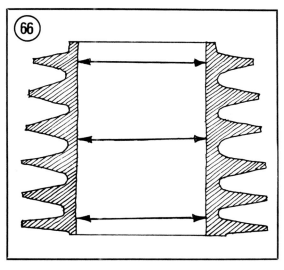

NOTE
The new piston should be obtained before the cylinder is rebored so that the piston can be measured; slight manufacturing tolerances must be taken into account to determine the actual size and working clearance.

3. Check the cylinder wall for scratches; if evident, the cylinder should be rebored.

NOTE
*The maximum wear limit on the cylinder is listed in **Table 1**. If the cylinder is worn to this limit, it must be replaced. Never rebore a cylinder if the finished rebore diameter will be this dimension or greater.*

NOTE
After having the cylinder rebored, wash it thoroughly in hot soapy water. This is the best way to clean the cylinder of all fine grit material left from the bore job. After washing the cylinder, run a clean white cloth through it. The cloth should show no traces of dirt or other debris. If the rag is dirty, the cylinder is not clean enough and must be rewashed. After the cylinder is thoroughly clean, dry and lubricate the cylinder wall with clean engine oil to protect the cylinder liner from rust.

Installation

1. Check that the top surface of the crankcase and the bottom surface of the cylinder are clean prior to installing a new base gasket.
2. Install a new cylinder base gasket and dowel pins.
3. Make sure the oil control orifice (**Figure 67**) is clean (not clogged) and is in place in the receptacle in the crankcase.

4. Install a piston holding fixture under the piston.

5. Make sure the end gaps of the piston rings are *not* lined up with each other—they must be staggered. Lightly oil the piston rings and the inside of the cylinder bore with assembly oil.

6. Carefully feed the camshaft chain and wire up through the opening in the cylinder and tie it to the engine.

7. Start the cylinder down over the piston. Compress each piston ring with your fingers as it enters the cylinder.

8. Slide the cylinder down until it bottoms on the piston holding fixture.

9. Remove the piston holding fixture and slide the cylinder down into place on the crankcase.

10. Install the bolts securing the cylinder to the crankcase on the right-hand side and tighten to the torque specification listed in **Table 2**.

11A. On XL250R and XR250R models, pull the camshaft chain tensioner to the rear and up. Then install the tensioner set bolt and copper washer (**Figure 62**).

11B. On all other models, perform the following:
  a. Pull the camshaft chain tensioner to the rear until the threaded stud comes through the hole in the cylinder.
  b. Install the O-ring seal, sealing washer and locknut onto the threaded stud.

12. Install the camshaft chain guide. Make sure the lower end of the guide is properly indexed into the receptacle in the crankcase. If improperly installed, it will interfere with and bind with the camshaft chain.

13. Install the cylinder head and cylinder head cover as described in this chapter.

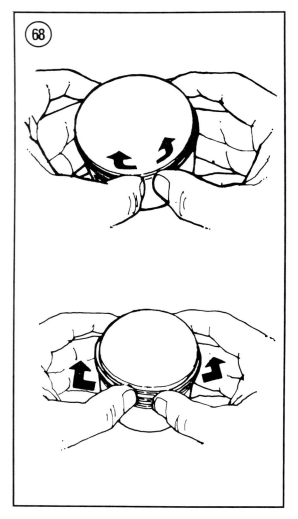

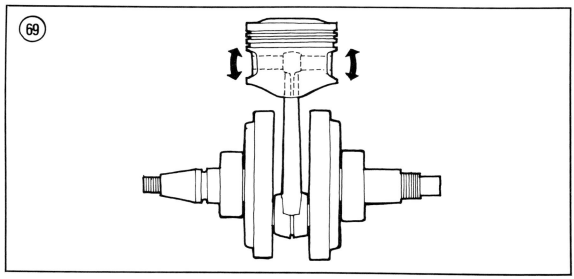

14. Adjust the valves and the camshaft chain tensioner as described in Chapter Three.

15. Follow the *Break-in Procedure* in this chapter if the cylinder was rebored or honed or a new piston or piston rings were installed.

PISTON, PISTON PIN AND PISTON RINGS

The piston is made of an aluminum alloy. The piston pin is made of steel and is a precision fit. The piston pin is held in place by a clip at each end.

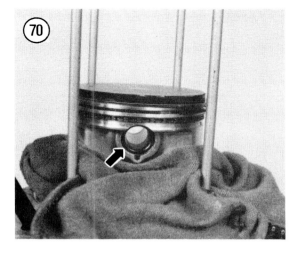

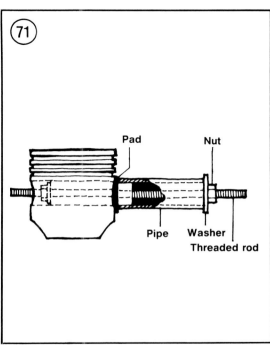

Pad   Nut

Pipe   Washer
Threaded rod

Piston Removal

1. Remove the cylinder head cover, cylinder head and cylinder as described in this chapter.

> *WARNING*
> *The edges of all piston rings are very sharp. Be careful when handling them to avoid cutting fingers.*

2. Remove the top ring with a ring expander tool or by spreading the ends with your thumbs just enough to slide the ring up over the piston (**Figure 68**). Repeat for the remaining rings.

3. Before removing the piston, hold the rod tightly and rock the piston as shown in **Figure 69**. Any rocking motion (do not confuse with the normal sliding motion) indicates wear on the piston pin, piston pin bore or connecting rod small-end bore (more likely a combination of these).

> *NOTE*
> *Wrap a clean shop cloth under the piston so that the piston pin clip will not fall into the crankcase.*

4. Remove the clips from each side of the piston pin bore (**Figure 70**) with a small screwdriver or scribe. Hold your thumb over one edge of the clip when removing it to prevent the clip from springing out.

5. Use a proper size wooden dowel or socket extension and push out the piston pin.

> *CAUTION*
> *Be careful when removing the pin to avoid damaging the connecting rod. If it is necessary to gently tap the pin to remove it, be sure that the piston is properly supported so that lateral shock is not transmitted to the lower connecting rod bearing.*

6. If the piston pin is difficult to remove, heat the piston and pin with a hair dryer. The pin will probably push right out. Heat the piston to only about 140° F (60° C), i.e., until it is too warm to touch, but not excessively hot. If the pin is still difficult to push out, use a homemade tool as shown in **Figure 71**.

7. Lift the piston off the connecting rod.

8. If the piston is going to be left off for some time, place a piece of foam insulation tube over the end of the rod to protect it.

Inspection

1. Carefully clean the carbon from the piston crown with a chemical remover or with a soft scraper (**Figure 72**). Do not remove or damage the carbon ridge around the circumference of the piston above the top ring. If the piston, rings and cylinder are found to be dimensionally correct and can be reused, removal of the carbon ring from the top of the piston or the carbon ridge from the top of the cylinder will promote excessive oil consumption.

> *CAUTION*
> *Do not wire brush the piston skirts.*

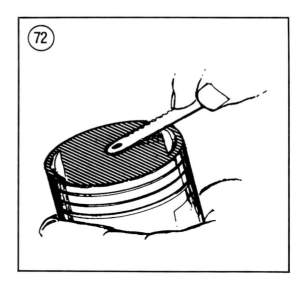

2. Examine each ring groove for burrs, dented edges and wide wear. Pay particular attention to the top compression ring groove as it usually wears more than the others.
3. If damage or wear indicates piston replacement, select a new piston as described under *Piston Clearance* in this chapter.
4. Oil the piston pin and install it in the connecting rod. Slowly rotate the piston pin and check for play (**Figure 73**). If any play exists, the piston pin should be replaced, providing the rod bore is in good condition.
5. Measure the inside diameter of the piston pin bore with a snap gauge (**Figure 74**) and measure the outside diameter of the piston pin with a micrometer (**Figure 75**). Compare with dimensions given in **Table 1**. Replace the piston and piston pin as a set if either or both are worn.
6. Check the piston skirt for galling and abrasion which may have been caused by piston seizure. If light galling is present, smooth the affected area with No. 400 emery paper and oil or a fine oilstone. However, if galling is severe or if the piston is deeply scored, replace it.

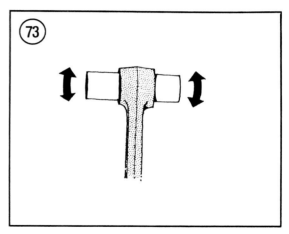

Piston Clearance

1. Make sure the piston and cylinder walls are clean and dry.
2. Measure the inside diameter of the cylinder bore at a point 13 mm (1/2 in.) from the upper edge with a bore gauge.
3. Measure the outside diameter of the piston across the skirt (**Figure 76**) at right angles to the piston pin. Measure at a distance 18 mm (0.70 in.) up from the bottom of the piston skirt.
4. Piston clearance is the difference between the maximum piston diameter and the minimum cylinder diameter. Subtract the dimension of the piston from the cylinder dimension and compare

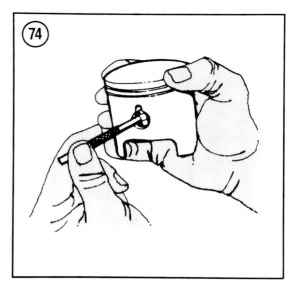

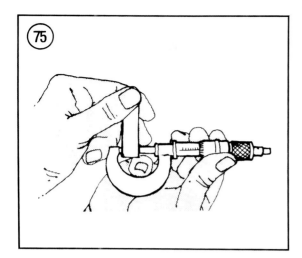

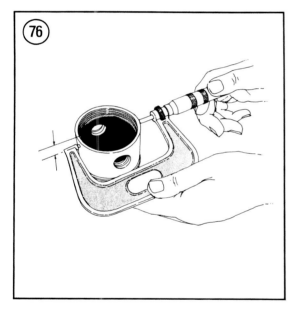

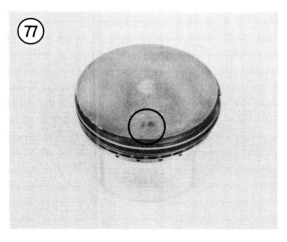

to the dimension listed in **Table 1**. If the clearance exceeds that specified, the cylinder should be rebored to the next oversize and a new piston installed.

5. To establish a final overbore dimension with a new piston, add the piston skirt measurement to the specified clearance. This will determine the dimension for the cylinder overbore size. Remember, do not exceed the cylinder maximum service limit inside diameter indicated in **Table 1**.

Piston Installation

1. Apply molybdenum disulfide grease to the inside surface of the connecting rod.
2. Oil the piston pin with assembly oil and install it in the piston until its end extends slightly beyond the inside of the boss.
3. Place the piston over the connecting rod with the "IN" mark (**Figure 77**) on the piston crown directed toward the rear of the engine.
4. Line up the piston pin with the hole in the connecting rod. Push the piston pin through the connecting rod and into the other side of the piston until it is even with the piston pin clip grooves.

> *CAUTION*
> *If it is necessary to tap the piston pin into the connecting rod, do so gently with a block of wood or a soft-faced hammer. Make sure you support the piston to prevent the lateral shock from being transmitted to the connecting rod bearing.*

> *NOTE*
> *In the next step, install the clips with the gap away from the cutout in the piston.*

5. Install new piston pin clips in both ends of the pin boss. Make sure they are seated in the grooves in the piston.
6. Check the installation by rocking the piston back and forth around the pin axis and from side to side along the axis. It should rotate freely back and forth but not from side to side.
7. Install the piston rings as described in this chapter.
8. Install the cylinder, cylinder head and cylinder head cover as described in this chapter.

Piston Ring
Removal/Inspection/Installation

> *WARNING*
> *The edges of all piston rings are very sharp. Be careful when handling them to avoid cutting fingers.*

1. Remove the top ring by spreading the ends with your thumbs just enough to slide the ring up over the piston (**Figure 68**). Repeat for the remaining rings.

2. Carefully remove all carbon buildup from the ring grooves with a broken piston ring (**Figure 78**). Inspect the grooves carefully for burrs, nicks or broken and cracked lands. Recondition or replace the piston if necessary.

3. Roll each ring around its piston groove as shown in **Figure 79** to check for binding. Minor binding may be cleaned up with a fine-cut file.

4. Measure the side clearance of each ring in its groove with a flat feeler gauge (**Figure 80**) and compare to dimensions given in **Table 1**. If the clearance is greater than specified, the rings must be replaced. If the clearance is still excessive with the new rings, the piston must also be replaced.

5. Measure each ring for wear. Place each ring, one at a time, into the cylinder and push it in about 20 mm (3/4 in.) with the crown of the piston to ensure that the ring is square in the cylinder bore. Measure the gap with a flat feeler gauge (**Figure 81**) and compare to dimensions in **Table 1**. If the gap is greater than specified, the rings should be replaced. When installing new rings, measure their end gap in the same manner as for old ones. If the gap is less than specified, carefully file the ends (**Figure 82**) with a fine-cut file until the gap is correct.

6. Install the piston rings in the order shown in **Figure 83**.

7. Install the oil ring spacer first, then the side rails. New oil ring side rails do not have top and bottom designations. If reassembling used parts, install the side rails as they were removed.

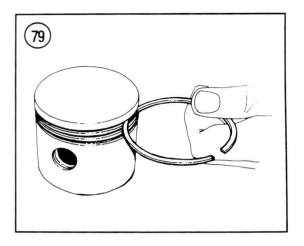

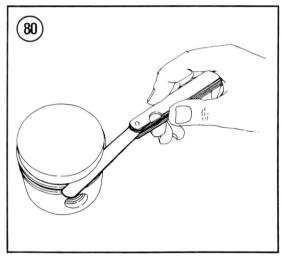

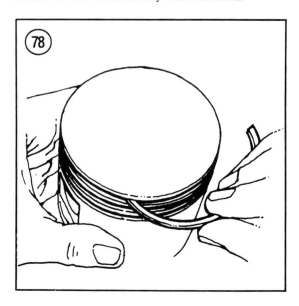

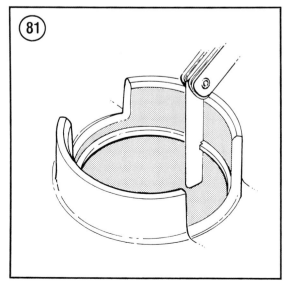

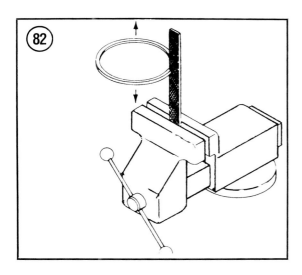

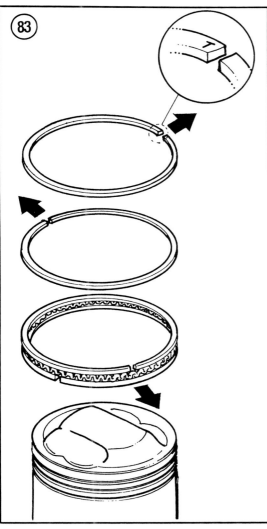

8. Install second compression ring, then the top compression ring, by carefully spreading the ends of the ring with your thumbs and slipping the ring over the top of the piston. Remember that the marks on the piston rings are toward the top of the piston.

9. Make sure the rings are seated completely in their grooves all the way around the piston and that the ends are distributed around the piston. The important thing is that the ring gaps are not aligned with each other when installed.

10. If new rings were installed, measure the side clearance of each ring in its groove with a flat feeler gauge (**Figure 80**) and compare to dimensions given in **Table 1**.

11. Follow the *Break-in Procedure* in this chapter if a new piston or piston rings have been installed or the cylinder was rebored or honed.

IGNITION ADVANCE MECHANISM

Removal

1. Remove both side covers and the seat.

> *NOTE*
> *On XL250S models, reinstall the seat strap bolts as they also hold the upper portion of the shock absorber to the frame (**Figure 84**). Remove and reinstall one bolt at a time.*

2. Remove the bolts securing the skid plate and remove the skid plate.

3. Drain the engine oil as described in Chapter Three.

4. Place wood block(s) under the frame to support the bike securely.

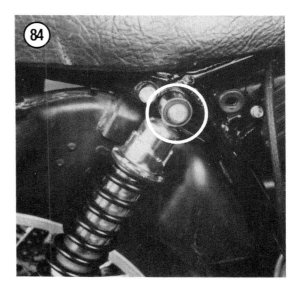

5. On XL models, disconnect the battery negative lead or disconnect the main fuse (**Figure 85**).

6. Remove the fuel tank as described in Chapter Seven.

7. Remove the kickstarter pedal (A, **Figure 86**).

8. Disconnect the rear brake light switch return spring and cable (B, **Figure 86**), the right-hand foot peg (C, **Figure 86**) and the rear brake pedal (D, **Figure 86**).

9. Slacken the clutch cable at the hand lever and disconnect the clutch cable at the crankcase cover (E, **Figure 86**).

10. Disconnect the starter decompressor cable at the crankcase cover (F, **Figure 86**).

11. Disconnect the ignition pulse generator electrical connector. Refer to **Figure 87** for XL series models or **Figure 88** for XR series models.

12. Remove the bolts securing the right-hand crankcase cover and remove the cover and gasket. Don't lose the locating dowels.

13. Place a copper washer (or penny) between the primary drive gear and the clutch outer housing gear. This will prevent the primary drive gear from turning while removing the locknut in Step 14.

14A. On 1982-1983 XL250R models (**Figure 89**), perform the following:

    a. Remove the 14 mm locknut and washer.

    b. Remove the stopper pin securing the oil pressure pad.

    c. Remove the oil pressure pad and spring.

    d. Slide the pulse generator rotor off of the crankshaft.

14B. On all other models, perform the following:

    a. Remove the 14 mm locknut (**Figure 90**).

    b. Remove the stopper pin securing the oil pressure pad (**Figure 91**).

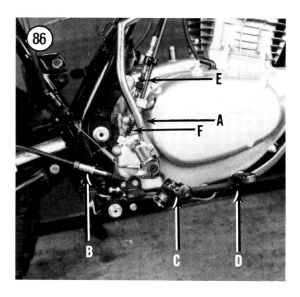

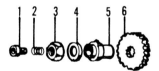

PULSE GENERATOR ROTOR

1. Oil pressure pad
2. Spring
3. Locknut
4. Lockwasher
5. Pulse generator rotor
6. Primary drive gear

c. Remove the oil pressure pad and spring (A, **Figure 92**) and washer (B, **Figure 92**).

d. Slide the pulse generator rotor off of the crankshaft.

15. Remove the copper washer (or penny) from the gears.

16. Inspect all components as described in Chapter Eight.

Installation

NOTE
*If either the advance rotor or pulse generator have been replaced with new units, they must have the same identification mark (**Figure 93**). Failure to do so will result in poor engine performance.*

4

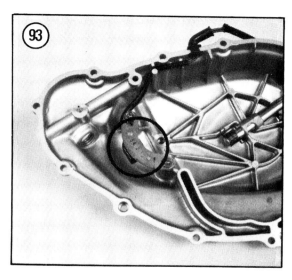

1A. On 1982-1983 XL250R models, align the cutout notch on the rotor with the dowel pin (**Figure 94**) on the crankshaft and slide on the rotor. Install the stopper pin (**Figure 95**).

1B. On all other models, align the cutout notch on the rotor with the dowel pin on the crankshaft and slide on the rotor.

2. Install the washer and the locknut. Tighten the locknut to the torque specification listed in **Table 2**.

3. Make sure the locating dowels are in place and install a new gasket.

4. Hold the starter decompressor lever in the raised position and install the right-hand crankcase cover. Tighten the screws securely.

> *CAUTION*
> *After the crankcase cover is installed, check the operation of the clutch and the starter decompressor levers. They should operate without binding; if they do bind, remove the cover and correct the problem.*

5. Connect the ignition pulse generator electrical connector. Make sure it is pushed together tightly.

6. On XL series models, connect the battery negative lead or reconnect the main fuse.

7. Connect the clutch and starter decompressor cables.

8. Install the rear brake pedal, right-hand foot peg and kickstarter arm.

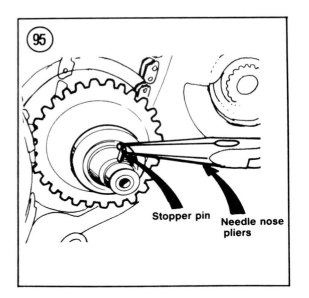

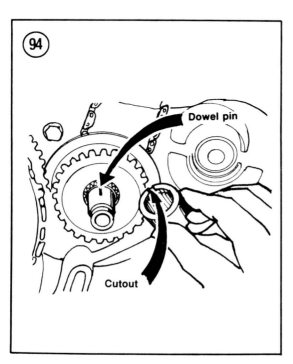

9. Connect the rear brake switch return spring and cable.

10. Install the skid plate, seat and side covers.

11. Install the fuel tank as described in Chapter Seven.

12. Fill the crankcase with the recommended type and quantity of engine oil as described in Chapter Three.

13. Adjust the clutch cable, starter decompressor and rear brake as described in Chapter Three.

OIL PUMP AND OIL FILTER SCREEN

The oil pump is located on the right-hand side of the engine. The oil pump can be removed with the engine in the frame. This procedure is shown with the engine removed for clarity.

Removal/Installation

1. Remove the clutch assembly as described in Chapter Six.

2. Remove the bolts (**Figure 96**) securing the set plate and remove it.

3. Remove the kickstarter idle gear (A, **Figure 97**) from the shift fork shaft (B, **Figure 97**).

4. Slide the oil pump assembly off the shaft and remove the O-ring seals (A, **Figure 98**).

5. Slide out the oil filter screen (B, **Figure 98**) and clean it with a medium soft toothbrush. Dry it carefully with compressed air. Inspect the screen; replace it if there are any breaks or holes in it.

6. Thoroughly clean out the oil filter screen cavity (**Figure 99**) in the crankcase. Wipe it clean with a cloth saturated in solvent and dry with compressed air.

7. Install the oil filter screen with the thick side facing out (**Figure 100**).

8. Install the O-ring seals (A, **Figure 98**) and make sure the locating dowel (**Figure 101**) is in place in the oil pump assembly.

9. Install the oil pump assembly and kickstarter idle gear.

10. Rotate the shift fork shaft (B, **Figure 97**) so that it aligns with the oil pump set plate. Install the set plate and bolts (**Figure 102**). Tighten the bolts securely.

> *CAUTION*
> *The set plate must align with the shift fork shaft as shown in **Figure 102**. Set it flush against the shaft so there is no clearance. If the shift fork shaft rotates, the lubrication passages within it will be blocked causing oil starvation to the transmission, resulting in transmission damage.*

11. Install the clutch assembly as described in Chapter Six.

Disassembly/Inspection/Assembly

Refer to **Figure 103** for XR250R models or **Figure 104** for all other models.

1. Inspect the outer housing and cover for cracks.
2. Remove the locating dowel (A, **Figure 105**) and screw (B, **Figure 105**) securing the cover to the body and separate the two parts.
3. Remove the inner and outer rotors. Inspect both parts for scratches and abrasions. Replace both parts if these are found.
4. Clean all parts in solvent and thoroughly dry. Coat all parts with fresh engine oil prior to assembly.
5. Install the outer rotor into the pump body and measure the clearance between the outer rotor and the oil pump body with a flat feeler gauge (**Figure 106**). If worn to the wear limit listed in **Table 1** or greater, replace the worn part.

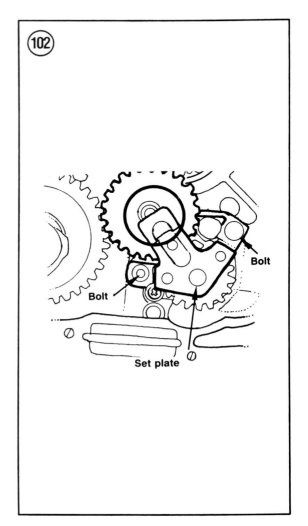

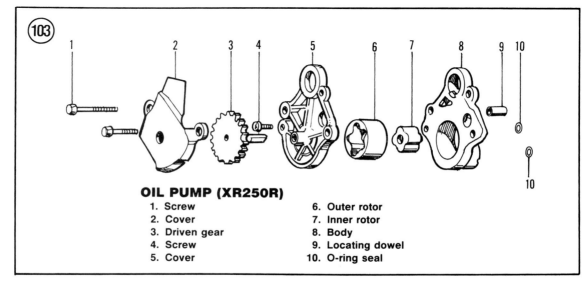

OIL PUMP (XR250R)

1. Screw
2. Cover
3. Driven gear
4. Screw
5. Cover
6. Outer rotor
7. Inner rotor
8. Body
9. Locating dowel
10. O-ring seal

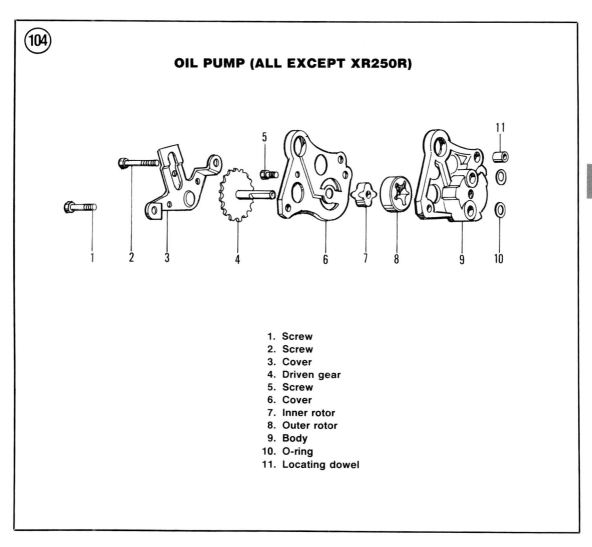

OIL PUMP (ALL EXCEPT XR250R)

1. Screw
2. Screw
3. Cover
4. Driven gear
5. Screw
6. Cover
7. Inner rotor
8. Outer rotor
9. Body
10. O-ring
11. Locating dowel

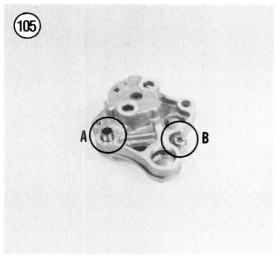

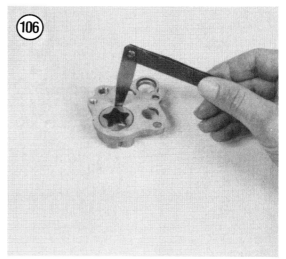

6. Install the inner rotor and measure the clearance between the inner rotor tip and the outer rotor with a flat feeler gauge (**Figure 107**). If worn to the wear limit listed in **Table 1** or greater, replace the worn part.

7. Measure the clearance between the rotor end and the pump body with a straight edge and a flat feeler gauge (**Figure 108**). If worn to the wear limit listed in **Table 1** or greater, replace either the rotors or the oil pump assembly.

8. Remove the inner and outer rotor from the pump body.

9. Install pump drive gear and shaft into the pump cover (**Figure 109**).

NOTE
Align the flat side on the pump shaft
with the flat within the inner rotor.

10. Install the pump housing, locating dowel (A, **Figure 105**) and screw. Tighten the screw securely.

11. Measure the inside diameter of the kickstarter idle gear. Replace if worn to the wear limit in **Table 1**, or larger. Inspect the gear for excessive wear, burrs, pitting or chipped teeth. Replace if necessary.

12. Inspect the O-ring seals (A, **Figure 98**). Replace as a set if either has lost its resiliency or is deteriorated.

KICKSTARTER

Removal

Refer to **Figure 110** for this procedure.
1. Remove the engine from the frame as described in this chapter.
2. Remove the thrust washer, kickstarter cam, spring and spring seat (**Figure 111**).
3. Split the crankcase as described in this chapter.
4. From within the crankcase, disconnect the kickstarter return spring from the spring hook pin.
5. Remove the kickstarter assembly from the crankcase.

Disassembly/Inspection/Assembly

Refer to **Figure 110** for this procedure.
1. Remove the kickstarter return spring.
2. Remove the 16 mm circlip, thrust washer and collar from the shaft.
3A. On XR250R models, slide off the thrust washer, return spring and kickstarter ratchet from the shaft (**Figure 112**).
3B. On all other models, slide off the return spring, thrust washer and kickstarter ratchet from the shaft.
4. Remove the 22 mm circlip, thrust washer, kickstarter gear, thrust washer and 24 mm circlip.

5. Measure the inside diameter of the kickstarter gear. If worn to the wear limit listed in **Table 1**, or larger, replace the gear.

6. Measure the outside diameter of the kickstarter shaft where the gear rides. If worn to the wear limit listed in **Table 1**, or smaller, replace the shaft.

7. Check for chipped or missing teeth on all gears.

8. Inspect the internal splines on all gears.

9. Check all parts for uneven wear; replace as necessary.

10. Inspect the splines on the kickstarter shaft.

11. Check the ratchet surfaces on both the kickstarter ratchet and the kickstarter gear for wear; replace if necessary.

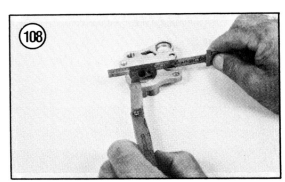

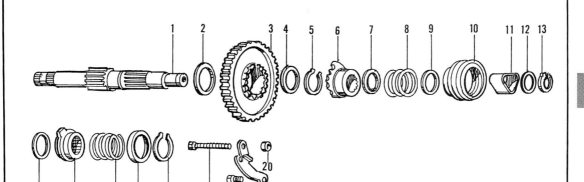

KICKSTARTER

1. Kickstarter spindle
2. Thrust washer
3. Kickstarter gear
4. Thrust washer
5. Circlip
6. Kickstarter ratchet
7. Thrust washer
   (all models except XR250R)
8. Spring
9. Thrust washer
   (XR250R models only)
10. Return spring
11. Collar
12. Thrust washer
13. Circlip
14. Kickstarter cam
15. Spring
16. Spring seat
17. Bolt
18. Screw
19. Stopper plate
20. Nut

12. Apply clean engine oil to all sliding surfaces of all parts prior to assembly and installation.

13. Install the 24 mm circlip on the right-hand side where the kickstarter gear rides. Slide on the thrust washer.

14. Position the kickstarter gear with the ratchet side going on last and slide on the gear.

15. Slide on the thrust washer and the 22 mm circlip.

16. Align the punch mark on the ratchet and shaft and slide on the kickstarter ratchet (**Figure 113**).

17A. On XR250R models, perform the following:
  a. Install the ratchet spring and thrust washer (**Figure 111**).
  b. Slide on the collar.

17B. On all other models, perform the following:
  a. Install the thrust washer and ratchet spring.
  b. Slide on the collar.

> *NOTE*
> *Prior to installing the shaft assembly into the crankcase, check with **Figure 114** for correct placement of all components.*

Installation

1. Install the assembled shaft into the crankcase with the oil and spring holes facing up.

2. Pour a small amount of clean engine oil into the oil hole (**Figure 115**).

3. Install the return spring (**Figure 116**) and hook the end into the hole in the shaft.

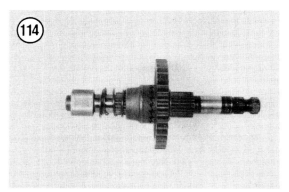

> *NOTE*
> *Install the circlip with the chamfered edge toward the end of the shaft. Make sure the circlip is completely seated in the groove in the shaft.*

4. Install the thrust washer and 16 mm circlip.

5. Pull the spring into position using a motorcycle muffler spring hook (**Figure 117**) or use Vise Grip pliers.

6. Install the spring seat and spring.

7. Align the punch mark on the shaft with the mark on the kickstarter cam (**Figure 118**), then slide the cam down onto the shaft splines.

8. Install the thrust washer (**Figure 119**).

9. Assemble the crankcase and install the engine in the frame as described in this chapter.

CRANKCASE
(XL250S AND XR250)

Crankcase disassembly (splitting the cases) requires that the engine be removed from the frame.

13. Pull the front balancer sprocket and chain forward and align the punch mark on the crankshaft sprocket with the 9th pin's link plate on the chain (**Figure 130**). Let the front balancer sprocket and chain hang from the crankshaft sprocket.

14. Thoroughly clean the sealing surfaces of both crankcase halves with contact cleaner and wipe dry with a lint-free cloth.

15. Apply a light coat of Three Bond 1104, or equivalent, to the sealing surfaces of the upper crankcase half. Coat only flat surfaces, not the

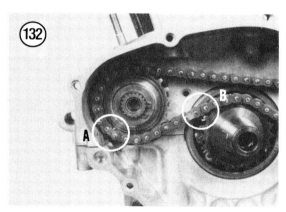

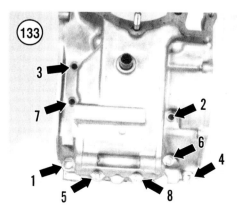

curved bearing surfaces. Cover the surfaces completely, but apply the coating as thin as possible, or the case can shift and hammer out the bearings. Use only a non-hardening sealant.

16. Make sure all alignments made in Steps 11-13 are still correct. If not, repeat Steps 11-13 until all are correct. Position the upper crankcase onto the rear of the lower crankcase.

17. Align the punch mark on the front balancer shaft with the punch mark on the sprocket and install the front balancer sprocket onto the balancer unit (A, **Figure 131**).

18. Install the circlip securing the sprocket to the balancer unit. Make sure the circlip is properly seated in the groove.

19. Completely join the 2 crankcase halves together. Again check the alignment of the punch marks and chain pins on the front balancer (A, **Figure 132**) and crankshaft (B, **Figure 132**). If alignment is incorrect, correct it before proceeding.

20. Make sure that the transmission bearing races are engaged into the dowel pins and set rings. If not seated correctly, this will keep the crankcase from seating completely.

CAUTION
*Do **not** install any crankcase bolts until the sealing surface around the entire crankcase perimeter has seated completely.*

21. Lightly tap the case halves together with a plastic or rubber mallet until they seat.

CAUTION
Crankcase halves should fit together without force. If the crankcase halves do not fit together completely, do not attempt to pull them together with the crankcase bolts. Separate the crankcase halves and investigate the cause of the interference. If the transmission shafts were disassembled, recheck to make sure that a gear is not installed backwards. Do not risk damage by trying to force the cases together.

22. Prior to installing the bolts, slowly spin the transmission shafts and shift through all gears. Also spin the crankshaft to make sure there is no binding.

23. Apply oil to all crankcase bolt threads.

24. Install the upper crankcase bolts and tighten only finger-tight.

25. Tighten the upper crankcase bolts in 2-3 stages in the sequence shown in **Figure 133**. Tighten the bolts to the torque specification listed in **Table 2**.

There are 2 different size bolts, 6mm and 8mm. Be sure to tighten them to their correct torque specifications.

26. Turn the engine over and install the lower crankcase bolts and tighten only finger-tight.

27. Tighten the lower crankcase bolts in 2-3 stages in the sequence shown in **Figure 134**. Tighten the bolts to the torque specification listed in **Table 2**.

28. After the crankcase halves are completely assembled, and the bolts tightened, again rotate the crankshaft and transmission shafts to make sure there is no binding. If any is present, disassemble the crankcase and correct the problem.

29. Install the balancer chain guide (B, **Figure 131**).

30. Install the camshaft drive chain, front balancer holder lockbolt and spring (**Figure 122**). Tighten the bolt to the torque specification listed in **Table 2**.

31. Be sure to install the small oil pipe (C, **Figure 120**) prior to installing the right-hand crankcase cover.

32. Install all exterior engine assemblies as described in this chapter and other related chapters:
   a. Cylinder head cover and cylinder head.
   b. Cylinder and piston.
   c. Clutch assembly.
   d. Alternator.
   e. External shift mechanism.
   f. Oil pump.
   g. External portion of the kickstarter mechanism.

33. Install the engine as described in this chapter.

34. Refill the crankcase with the recommended type and quantity of engine oil as described in Chapter Three.

CRANKCASE
(1982-1983 XL250R AND 1981-1982 XR250R)

Crankcase disassembly (splitting the cases) requires that the engine be removed from the frame.

The crankcase is made in 2 halves of precision diecast aluminum alloy and is of the "thin-walled" type. To avoid damage, do not hammer or pry on any of the interior or exterior projected walls. These areas are easily damaged. The cases are split horizontally down the centerline of the crankshaft. The cases are assembled *without* a gasket between the 2 halves. Dowel pins align the halves when they are bolted together.

The procedure which follows is presented as a complete, step-by-step, major lower end rebuild that should be followed if an engine is to be completely reconditioned. However, if you're replacing a part that you know is defective, the disassembly should be carried out only until the failed part is accessible; there is no need to disassemble the engine beyond that point so long as you know the remaining components are in good condition and that they were not affected by the failed part.

Crankcase Disassembly

1. Remove all exterior engine assemblies as described in this chapter and other related chapters:
   a. Cylinder head cover and cylinder head.
   b. Cylinder and piston.
   c. Clutch assembly.
   d. Alternator.
   e. External shift mechanism.
   f. Oil pump.
   g. External portion of the kickstarter assembly.

2. Remove the engine as described in this chapter.

3. Remove the bolt securing the camshaft chain tensioner and remove the camshaft chain tensioner assembly.

4. Remove the camshaft drive chain and the balancer holder lockbolt.

5. Turn the engine upside down on the work bench on blocks of wood to protect the connecting rod.

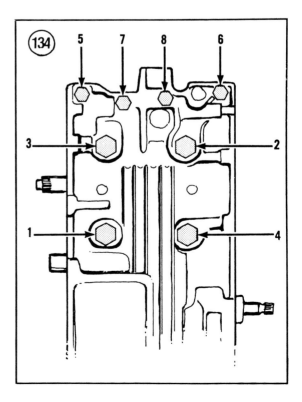

6. Loosen the lower crankcase bolts in 2-3 stages in a crisscross pattern to avoid warpage. Remove all bolts.

7. Turn the engine right side up and set it on wooden blocks.

8. Loosen the upper crankcase bolts in 2-3 stages in a crisscross pattern to avoid warpage. Remove all bolts.

9. Tap around the perimeter of the crankcase halves with a plastic or soft-faced mallet—do not use a metal hammer as it will cause damage.

CAUTION
Honda's thin-walled crankcase castings are just that—thin. To avoid damage to the cases do not hammer on the projected walls that surround the clutch and alternator. These areas are easily damaged if stressed.

CAUTION
If it is necessary to pry the crankcase halves apart, do it very carefully so that you do not mar the gasket sealing surfaces. If you do, they will leak and the crankcase halves must be replaced.

10. Lift up on the upper crankcase half and remove it from the lower one.

11. Remove the crankshaft assembly and both transmission shaft assemblies from the lower crankcase half.

12. Remove the balancer assembly from the upper crankcase half as described in this chapter.

13. Remove the shift drum and shift forks as described in Chapter Six.

14. Remove the internal portion of the kickstarter assembly as described in this chapter.

15. Remove the bolts securing the crankcase breather separator baffle plate and remove the plate.

16. Don't lose the locating dowels if they came out of the case. They do not have to be removed from the case if they are secure.

17. Inspect the crankcase halves and crankshaft as described in this chapter.

Crankcase Assembly

1. Before installing parts, coat all surfaces with assembly oil or clean engine oil. Do not get any oil on the sealing surfaces of the case halves.

2. Install the crankcase breather separator baffle plate and tighten the screws securely.

3. Apply assembly oil to the crankshaft bearings.

4. Install the inner portion of the kickstarter assembly and crankshaft assembly into the lower crankcase half.

5. Install the transmission assemblies as described in Chapter Six.

6. Install the balancer assembly as described in this chapter.

7. If removed, install the locating dowels in the lower crankcase half. Make sure the transmission bearing set rings are also in position.

NOTE
Make sure the mating surfaces are clean and free of all old sealant material. Make sure you get a leak-free seal.

8. Thoroughly clean the sealing surfaces of both crankcase halves with contact cleaner and wipe dry with a lint-free cloth.

9. Apply a light coat of Three Bond 1104, or equivalent, to the sealing surfaces of the upper crankcase half. Coat only flat surfaces, not the curved bearing surfaces. Cover the surfaces completely, but make the coating as thin as possible, or the case can shift and hammer out the bearings. Use only a non-hardening sealant.

10. The crankshaft counterbalancer weights will locate the crankshaft at approximately bottom dead center (BDC). This will locate the punch mark on the balancer drive gear (attached to the crankshaft) at about the 10 o'clock position.

11. Position the upper crankcase half onto the lower half while aligning the punch mark (1981 models) or index line (1982-1983 models) on the balancer driven gear with the punch mark on the drive gear (**Figure 135**).

NOTE
***Figure 135** shows a 1982 balancer gear. The 1981 model is slightly different but the alignment procedure is the same.*

12. Install the upper crankcase onto the lower case half. Make sure that the transmission bearing races are engaged into the dowel pins and set rings. If not seated correctly this will keep the crankcase from seating completely.

CAUTION
*Do **not** install any crankcase bolts until the sealing surface around the entire crankcase perimeter has seated completely.*

13. Lightly tap the case halves together with a plastic or rubber mallet until they seat.

CAUTION
Crankcase halves should fit together without force. If the crankcase halves do not fit together completely, do not attempt to pull them together with the crankcase bolts. Separate the crankcase halves and investigate the cause of the interference. If the transmission shafts were disassembled, recheck to make sure that a gear is not installed backwards. Do not risk damage by trying to force the cases together.

14. Prior to installing the bolts, slowly spin the transmission shafts and shift through all gears. Also spin the crankshaft to make sure there is no binding.
15. Apply oil to all crankcase bolt threads.
16. Install the upper crankcase bolts and tighten only finger-tight.
17. Tighten the upper crankcase bolts in 2-3 stages in the sequence shown in **Figure 136**. Tighten the bolts to the torque specification listed in **Table 2**.
18. Turn the engine over and install the lower crankcase bolts and tighten only finger-tight.
19. Tighten the lower crankcase bolts in 2-3 stages in the sequence shown in **Figure 137**. Tighten the bolts to the torque specification listed in **Table 2**.
20. After the crankcase halves are completely assembled, and the bolts tightened, again rotate the crankshaft and transmission shafts to make sure there is no binding. If any is present, disassemble the crankcase and correct the problem.
21. Make sure the collar is in place in the tensioner assembly prior to installation (**Figure 138**). Install the camshaft chain tensioner assembly and tighten the bolt to the torque specification listed in **Table 2**.
22. Install the balancer holder lockbolt (**Figure 139**), but do not tighten at this time.
23. Adjust the balancer backlash as described in this chapter.
24. Install the camshaft drive chain and if removed, the oil pipe.

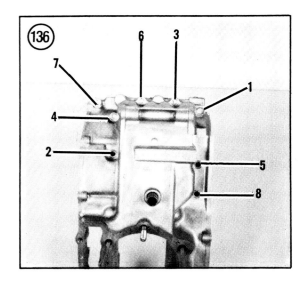

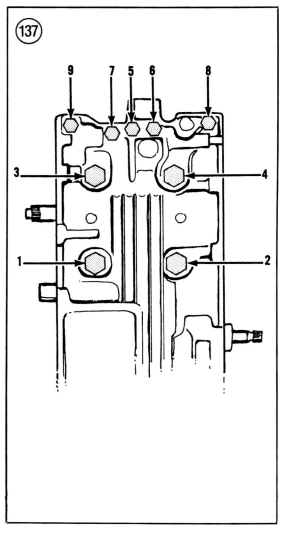

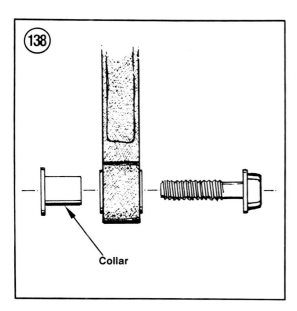

Collar

25. Install all exterior engine assemblies as described in this chapter and other related chapters:
   a. Cylinder head cover and cylinder head.
   b. Cylinder and piston.
   c. Clutch assembly.
   d. Alternator.
   e. External shift mechanism.
   f. Oil pump.
   g. External portion of the kickstarter mechanism.
26. Install the engine as described in this chapter.
27. Refill the crankcase with the recommended type and quantity of engine oil as described in Chapter Three.

Crankcase Inspection

1. Clean both crankcase halves inside and out with cleaning solvent. Thoroughly dry with compressed air and wipe off with a clean shop cloth. Be sure to remove all traces of old gasket material from all mating surfaces.
2. Make sure all oil passages are clean; be sure to blow them out with compressed air.
3. Carefully inspect the cases for cracks and fractures, especially in the lower areas; they are vulnerable to rock damage. Inspect the mating surfaces of both halves. They must be free of gouges, burrs or any damage that could cause an oil leak.
4. If damage is found, have the cases repaired by a shop specializing in the repair of precision aluminum castings or replace them.
5. Inspect the balancer system as described in this chapter.

CRANKSHAFT AND CONNECTING ROD

The crankshaft assembly is made up of 2 full-circle flywheels pressed together on a hollow crankpin. The connecting rod big end bearing on the crankpin is a needle bearing assembly. The crankshaft assembly is supported in 2 ball bearings in the crankcase. Service to the crankshaft assembly is limited to removal and replacement.

Removal/Installation

1. Disassemble the crankcase as described in this chapter.
2. Remove the crankshaft assembly from the lower crankcase half.
3. Prior to installing the crankshaft, lubricate the large ball bearings and connecting rod large end bearing with assembly oil.
4. Make sure the crankshaft bearing set ring (**Figure 140**) is in place in the lower crankcase half.

5. Install the crankshaft assembly into the lower crankcase half. Make sure the set ring is properly seated into the bearing outer race.

6. Assemble the crankcase as described in this chapter.

Crankshaft Inspection

1. Measure the inside diameter of the connecting rod small end with a snap gauge and an inside micrometer (**Figure 141**). Compare to dimensions given in **Table 1**. If worn to the service limit or greater the crankshaft assembly must be replaced.

2. Check the connecting rod-to-crankshaft side clearance with a flat feeler gauge (**Figure 142**). Compare to dimensions given in **Table 1**. If the clearance is greater than specified, the crankshaft assembly must be replaced.

3. Check the crankshaft main bearings (**Figure 143**) for roughness, pitting, galling and play by rotating them slowly by hand. If any roughness or play can be felt in the bearing, it must be replaced. This must be entrusted to a dealer as special tools are required.

4. Check the connecting rod big end bearing by grasping the rod in one hand and lifting up on it. With the heel of your other hand, rap sharply on the top of the rod. A sharp metallic sound, such as a click, is an indication that the bearing or crankpin or both are worn and the crankshaft assembly should be replaced.

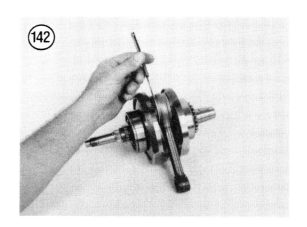

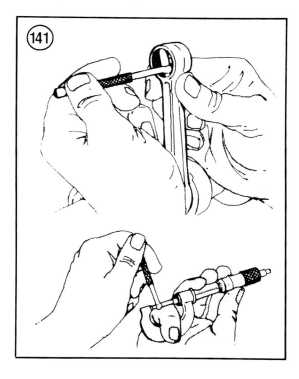

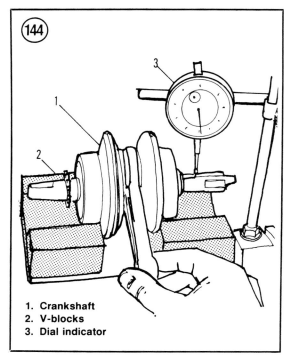

1. Crankshaft
2. V-blocks
3. Dial indicator

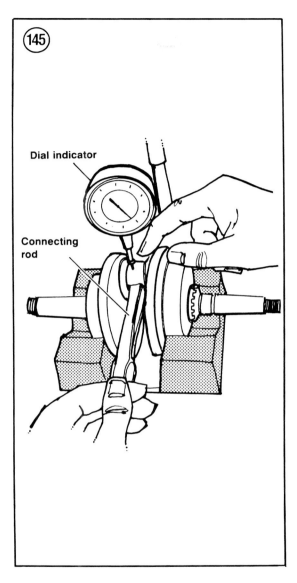

Dial indicator

Connecting rod

5. Mount the crankshaft assembly in a pair of V-blocks and use a dial indicator as shown in **Figure 144**. Rotate the crankshaft slowly several complete revolutions. Measure the runout, using the dial indicator, at each end. Replace the crankshaft assembly if the runout exceeds 0.1 mm (0.0004 in.) at either end.

6. Mount the crankshaft assembly as in Step 5 and measure the clearance between the connecting rod and crankpin (**Figure 145**). Replace the crankshaft assembly if the clearance exceeds the wear limit dimension listed in **Table 1**.

7. Inspect the balancer drive sprocket or gear (**Figure 146**) for wear or missing teeth. If the sprocket or gear is damaged, it must be replaced. This must be entrusted to a dealer as special tools are required.

8. Inspect the camshaft drive sprocket for wear or missing teeth. If the sprocket is damaged, it must be replaced. This must be entrusted to a dealer as special tools are required.

BALANCER SYSTEM

The balancer system eliminates the vibration normally associated with a large displacement single cylinder engine. The engine and motorcycle frame are designed for use with this balancer system. If the balancers are disconnected or eliminated, excessive engine vibration will occur. This vibration will result in major fatigue to engine and frame components. Do *not* eliminate this feature by disconnecting it.

CAUTION
Any applicable manufacturer's warranty will be voided if the balancer system is modified, disconnected or removed.

Front Balancer
(XL250S, XR250 and 1981 XR250R)

Removal/installation

1. Remove the engine and disassemble the crankcase as described in this chapter.

NOTE
The right- and left-hand side refers to the engine as it sits in the bike's frame—not as it sits on your workbench.

2. Remove the 20 mm circlip from the balancer shaft on the left-hand side of the engine.

3A. On XL250S and XR250 models, remove the chain sprocket and the thrust washer.

3B. On 1981 XR250R models, remove the drive gear and the thrust washer.

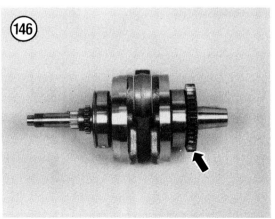

4. Slide the balancer shaft (**Figure 147**) out the right-hand side.

5. Slide the balancer shaft holder (**Figure 148**) out the right-hand side.

6. Install by reversing these removal steps, noting the following.

7. Apply assembly oil to all needle bearings and rotating surfaces prior to installation.

8. On 1981 XR250R models, perform the following:

   a. Align the punch marks on the balancer shaft and balancer driven gear, then slide the balancer driven gear onto the shaft.

   b. Make sure these 2 marks (**Figure 149**) align.

   c. Install the circlip with the sharp side facing toward the outside.

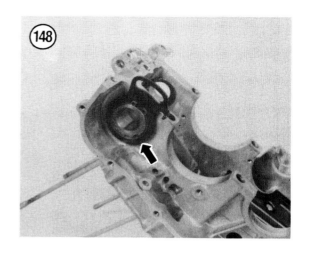

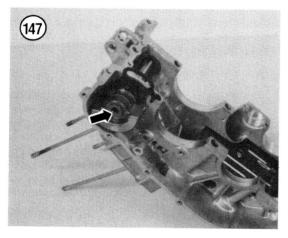

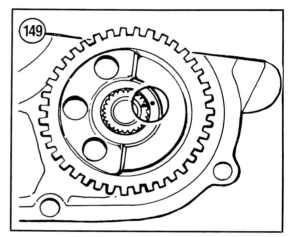

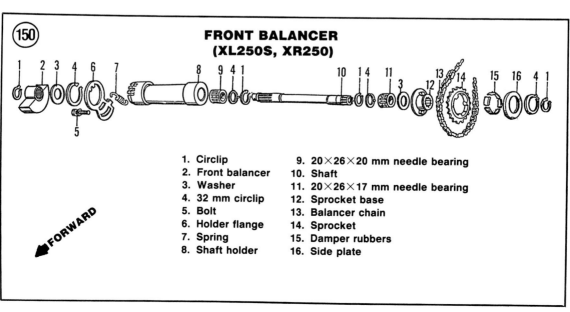

**FRONT BALANCER
(XL250S, XR250)**

FORWARD

1. Circlip
2. Front balancer
3. Washer
4. 32 mm circlip
5. Bolt
6. Holder flange
7. Spring
8. Shaft holder
9. 20×26×20 mm needle bearing
10. Shaft
11. 20×26×17 mm needle bearing
12. Sprocket base
13. Balancer chain
14. Sprocket
15. Damper rubbers
16. Side plate

Disassembly/assembly

Refer to **Figure 150** (XL250S and XR250 models) or **Figure 151** (1981 XR250R models) for this procedure.

1. If necessary, remove the circlip (**Figure 152**) securing the balancer holder flange to the shaft and remove the flange.

> *NOTE*
> *The needle bearings on the shaft have different widths. They must be reinstalled on the correct side of the shaft.*

> *NOTE*
> *Once all of the components have been removed from the balancer shaft it is difficult to know one end of the shaft from the other. Next to the inner circlip grooves, mark the shaft with an "R" (right-hand side) and "L" (left-hand side) to avoid confusion during assembly.*

2. Perform the following on the right-hand side of the shaft:
   a. Remove the circlip (**Figure 153**) securing the balancer weight to the shaft.
   b. Remove the balancer weight and the thrust washer.
   c. Slide off the wide needle bearing and special washer.
3. Slide off the narrow needle bearing and special washer from the left-hand side of the shaft.
4. If necessary, remove the inner circlips from the shaft.

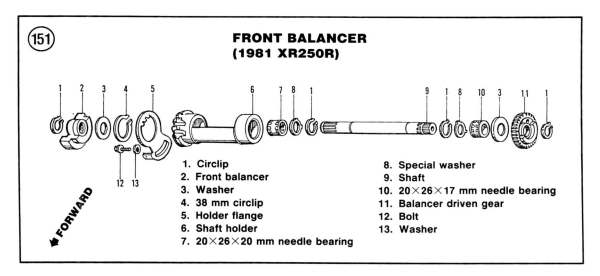

**FRONT BALANCER
(1981 XR250R)**

FORWARD

1. Circlip
2. Front balancer
3. Washer
4. 38 mm circlip
5. Holder flange
6. Shaft holder
7. 20×26×20 mm needle bearing
8. Special washer
9. Shaft
10. 20×26×17 mm needle bearing
11. Balancer driven gear
12. Bolt
13. Washer

5. On XL250S and XR250 models, refer to **Figure 154** and disassemble and assemble the sprocket/balancer weight assembly as follows:

   a. Remove the circlip and side plate.

   b. Note the location of the rubber dampers in relationship to the sprocket and sprocket base. The rubber dampers must be reinstalled in the same locations. Remove the 6 rubber dampers from the sprocket base.

   c. Remove the sprocket from the sprocket base.

   d. Inspect the rubber dampers. If any are worn or starting to deteriorate, replace all 6 as a set.

   e. To reassemble, align the punch mark (**Figure 155**) of the sprocket and the sprocket base. Then install the sprocket onto the sprocket base.

   f. Install the rubber dampers, the side plate, then the circlip. Make sure the circlip is properly seated in the groove.

6. If removed, install the inner circlips into the inner grooves in the shaft.

> *NOTE*
> *In the following step, there are 2 different width needle bearings. The narrow bearing (marked 20 X 26 X 17) is to be installed on the left-hand side (next to the driven sprocket or gear). Refer to **Figure 156**. If the wrong bearing is installed it will be impossible to install the circlip as the circlip groove will not be exposed.*

7. Slide the special washer and the narrow needle bearing onto the left-hand side of the shaft. Align the special washer tabs with the circlip so they are locked in place and will not spin.

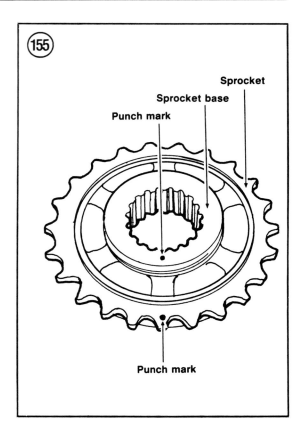

(155)

Sprocket

Sprocket base

Punch mark

Punch mark

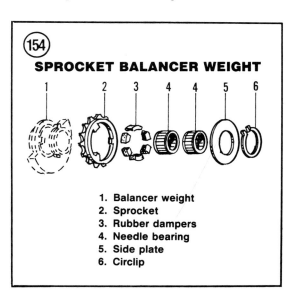

(154)

SPROCKET BALANCER WEIGHT

1   2   3   4 4   5   6

1. Balancer weight
2. Sprocket
3. Rubber dampers
4. Needle bearing
5. Side plate
6. Circlip

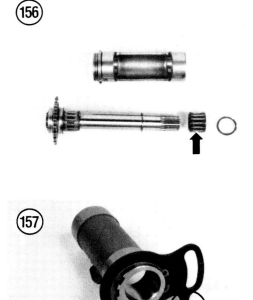

(156)

(157)

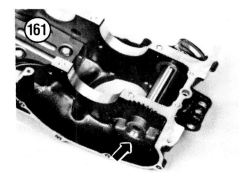

8. Perform the following on the right-hand side of the shaft:

    a. Slide on special washer and the wide needle bearing. Align the special washer tabs with the circlip so they are locked in place and will not spin.

    b. Align the punch mark on the balancer weight with the punch mark on the shaft. Slide on the thrust washer and balancer weight.

    c. Install the circlip.

9. If removed, install the balancer holder flange with the bent-over ear (**Figure 157**) facing outward away from the shaft. Install the circlip with the sharp edge facing toward the outside.

Front Balancer
(1982-1983 XL250R and 1982 XR250R)

Removal/installation

1. Remove the engine and disassemble the crankcase as described in this chapter.

> *NOTE*
>
> *The right- and left-hand side refers to the engine as it sits in the bike's frame—not as it sits on your workbench.*

2. On the right-hand side of the engine, perform the following:

    a. Remove the circlip (**Figure 158**) securing the right-hand balancer weight to the balancer shaft/weight unit.

    b. Slide off the right-hand balancer weight and thrust washer (**Figure 159**).

    c. Slide off the needle bearing and washer (**Figure 160**) located on the balancer shaft behind the thrust washer.

3. On the left-hand side, withdraw the balancer shaft/gear unit (**Figure 161**).

4. On the right-hand side, remove the balancer shaft holder assembly (**Figure 162**).

5. Install by reversing these removal steps, noting the following.

6. Apply assembly oil to needle bearings and all rotating surfaces prior to installation.

7. Align the punch marks (**Figure 163**) on the balancer shaft/gear unit with the right-hand balancer and install the right-hand balancer onto the balancer shaft/gear unit. Make sure these 2 punch marks align and install the circlip with the sharp side facing toward the outside.

Disassembly/assembly

Refer to **Figure 164** for this procedure.

1. If necessary, remove the circlip (**Figure 152**) securing the balancer holder flange to the shaft and remove the flange.

2. Remove both circlips (A, **Figure 165**).

3. Slide off the washer.

4. Remove the needle bearing (B, **Figure 165**) and thrust washer next to the left-hand balancer weight/driven gear.

5. Slide on the thrust washer.

NOTE
In the following step, there are 2 different width needle bearings. The narrow bearing (marked 20 X 26 X 17) is to be installed on the left-hand side (next to the gear-driven balancer). Refer to Figure 166.

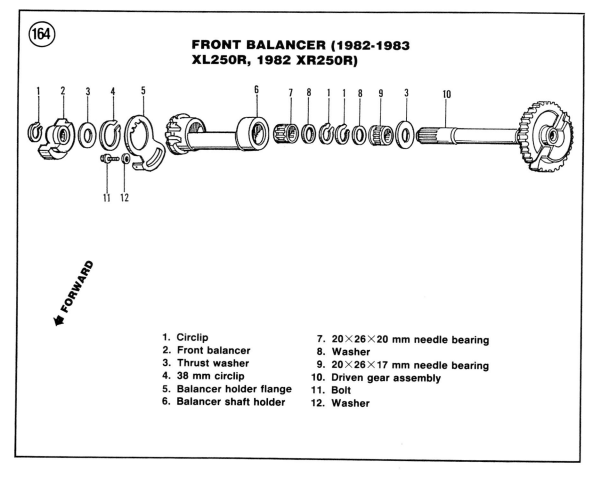

FRONT BALANCER (1982-1983 XL250R, 1982 XR250R)

1. Circlip
2. Front balancer
3. Thrust washer
4. 38 mm circlip
5. Balancer holder flange
6. Balancer shaft holder
7. 20×26×20 mm needle bearing
8. Washer
9. 20×26×17 mm needle bearing
10. Driven gear assembly
11. Bolt
12. Washer

FORWARD

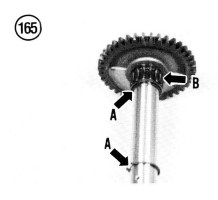

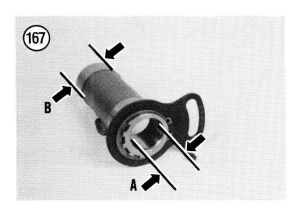

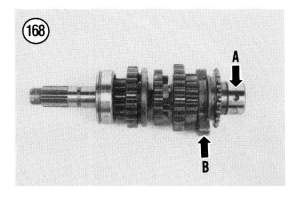

6. Slide the narrow needle bearing and washer onto the shaft.

7. Install the circlips.

8. Slide on the washer and the wide needle bearing.

9. If removed, install the balancer holder flange with the bent-over ear (**Figure 157**) facing outward away from the shaft. Install the circlip with the sharp edge facing toward the outside.

Front Balancer Inspection (All Models)

1. Inspect the needle bearings. Make sure they rotate smoothly with no signs of wear or damage. Replace as necessary.

2. Measure the inside diameter (A, **Figure 167**) of the balancer shaft holder. Replace if the diameter is worn to the wear limit in **Table 1**, or greater.

3. Measure the outside diameter (B, **Figure 167**) of the bearing surfaces at each end of the balancer shaft holder. Replace if the diameter is worn to the wear limit in **Table 1** or smaller.

4. Inspect the sprocket teeth for wear or damage. Replace if necessary.

5. Inspect the teeth of the driven gear (models so equipped). Check for excessive wear, burrs pitting or chipped or missing teeth. Replace if necessary.

NOTE
On some models, the gear is part of the shaft and cannot be removed. If damaged the entire unit must be replaced.

Rear Balancer (XL250S and XR250)

Removal/installation

1. Remove the engine from the frame and disassemble the crankcase as described in this chapter.

2. Remove the transmission main shaft as described in Chapter Six.

3. Slide off the outer race and needle bearing (A, **Figure 168**) and thrust washer.

4. Slide off the rear balancer assembly (B, **Figure 168**).

5. Slide off the 2 needle bearings and thrust washer from the shaft. The 2 needle bearings may have come off with the rear balancer in Step 4.

6. Install by reversing these removal steps, noting the following.

7. Install the parts in this exact order; thrust washer, needle bearing, needle bearing, rear balancer, thrust washer, needle bearing and outer race.

Assembly/inspection/assembly

1. To disassemble the rear balancer, remove the circlip, side plate, sprocket and 6 rubber dampers.
2. Inspect the rubber dampers. If they are worn or starting to deteriorate, replace all 6 as a set.
3. Measure the inside diameter of the rear balancer. Replace if worn to the wear limit dimension listed in **Table 1** or larger.
4. Inspect the teeth on the sprocket for wear or damage. Replace if necessary.
5A. On XL250S models, assemble as follows:
  a. Place the sprocket into the rear balancer. Position it so the tabs on the sprocket are centered between the tabs on the rear balancer. When positioned correctly there will be 6 places for the rubber dampers.

> *CAUTION*
> *Do **not** position the sprocket into the balancer so that the metal tabs are touching each other. They must be separated with a rubber damper in between each one.*

  b. Insert a rubber damper into each space between one of the tabs on the sprocket and one of the tabs on the balancer. Install all 6 rubber dampers.
  c. Install the side plate and circlip. Make sure the circlip is correctly seated in the groove.
5B. On XR250 models, assemble as follows:
  a. Align the punch mark on the sprocket with one of the tabs on the balancer weight (**Figure 169**) and place the sprocket into the rear balancer.
  b. Insert all 6 rubber dampers. Make sure they are not pinched after installation.
  c. Install the side plate and circlip. Make sure the circlip is correctly seated in the groove.

Balancer Backlash Adjustment (1982-1983 XL250R and 1981-1982 XR250R)

Whenever the balancer assembly has been removed (or if the balancer lockbolt is loosened or removed) the backlash must be adjusted. The most accurate way to measure is with a dial indicator; however, if you do not have an indicator, a modified flat feeler gauge can be used as described in this section.

> *NOTE*
> *This adjustment is required only on gear-driven models.*

> *NOTE*
> *The engine must be at room temperature for this procedure to be accurate (below 35° C/95° F).*

With dial indicator

To measure the backlash with a dial indicator perform the following:
1. Set the pointer of the dial indicator on a gear tooth of the balancer driven gear (A, **Figure 170**).
2. Align the zero (B, **Figure 170**) on the dial indicator face exactly with the gauge needle. By hand, rotate the drive gear back and forth to make sure the gauge is centered on zero. Readjust the gauge face if necessary.
3. By hand, rotate the driven gear (C, **Figure 170**) back and forth slightly and check the amount of backlash between the driven gear and the drive gear. The specified backlash is 0.05-0.13 mm (0.0002-0.005 in.).
4. If the backlash is not within tolerance, adjust as described in this chapter.

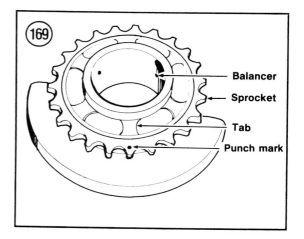

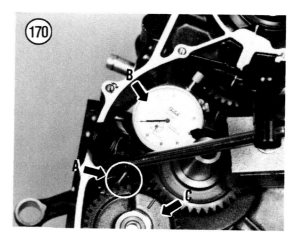

With flat feeler gauge

If you are unable to obtain a dial indicator, a modified flat feeler gauge will work. This method is not as accurate but it is better than guessing at the tolerance and being wrong. Perform the following:
1. The flat feeler gauge must be cut so it is narrow enough to fit in between the meshed gear teeth.
2. Insert the flat feeler gauge between the mating surfaces of the gear teeth (**Figure 171**).
3. Nothing thicker than a 0.13 mm (0.005 in.) gauge should fit.
4. If the backlash is not within tolerance, adjust as described in this chapter.

Balancer Backlash Adjustment
(1982-1983 XL250R and 1981-1982 XR250R)

CAUTION
The most important thing is that there is some amount of backlash. If there is no backlash and the gears are tight against each other, gear wear will be rapid and excessive. If the backlash is greater than specified, the gears will be noisy.

If the backlash is not within tolerance, perform the following.
1. Loosen the balancer holder lockbolt (**Figure 172**).
2. Rotate the balancer holder in either direction to achieve the correct amount of gear backlash.
3. Tighten the balancer holder lockbolt to the torque specification listed in **Table 2**.

BREAK-IN PROCEDURE

If the rings were replaced, a new piston installed, the cylinder rebored or honed or major lower end work performed, the engine should be broken in just as though it were new. The performance and service life of the engine depends greatly on a careful and sensible break-in.

For the first 5-10 hours of operation, no more than one-third throttle should be used and speed should be varied as much as possible within the one-third throttle limit. Prolonged steady running at one speed, no matter how moderate, is to be avoided as well as hard acceleration.

Following the first 5-10 hours of operation more throttle should not be used until the bike has run for 100 hours and then it should be limited to short bursts of speed until 150 hours have been logged.

During this period, oil consumption will be higher than normal. It is therefore important to frequently check and correct oil level. At no time, during the break-in or later, should the oil level be allowed to drop below the bottom line on the dipstick; if the oil level is low, the oil will become overheated resulting in insufficient lubrication and increased wear.

Service After 10 Hours Of Operation

It is essential that the oil be changed and the oil filter rotor and filter screen be cleaned after the first 10 hours of operation. In addition, it is a good idea to change the oil and clean the oil filter rotor and filter screen at the completion of 100 hours of operation to ensure that all of the particles produced during break-in are removed from the lubrication system. The small added expense may be considered a smart investment that will pay off in increased engine life.

Table 1 250 CC ENGINE SPECIFICATIONS

Item	Specifications	Wear limit
General		
Type	4-stroke, air-cooled, SOHC	
Number of cylinders	1	
Bore and stroke	74.0 $\times$ 57.8 mm (2.91 $\times$ 2.27 in.)	
Displacement	249 cc (15.1 cu. in.)	
Compression ratio		
XL series	9.1 to 1	
XR series	9.6 to 1	
Compression pressure		
XR250	192 ± 21 psi (13.5 ± 1.5 kg/cm^2)	
Alll other models	175 psi (12.5 kg/cm^2)	
Cylinder head warpage	–	0.1 mm (0.004 in.)
Cylinder		
Bore	74.00-74.01 mm (2.913-2.914 in.)	74.11 mm (2.918 in.)
Out of round	–	0.05 mm (0.002 in.)
Piston/cylinder clearance	0.01-0.04 mm (0.0004-0.0016 in.)	0.1 mm (0.004 in.)
Warpage across top	–	0.1 mm (0.004 in.)
Piston		
Diameter	73.97-73.99 mm (2.912-2.913 in.)	73.89 mm (2.909 in.)
Clearance in bore	0.01-0.04 mm (0.0004-0.0016 in.)	0.10 mm (0.004 in.)
Piston pin bore	19.002-19.008 mm (0.7481-0.7483 in.)	19.08 mm (0.751 in.)
Piston pin outer diameter	18.994-19.000 mm (0.7478-0.7480 in.)	18.96 mm (0.747 in.)
Piston rings		
Number of rings		
Compression	2	
Oil control	1	
Ring end gap		
Top and second	0.15-0.35 mm (0.0006-0.014 in.)	0.5 mm (0.02 in.)
Oil (side rail)	0.2-0.9 mm (0.007-0.035 in.)	NA
Ring side clearance		
Top and second ring	0.015-0.045 mm (0.0006-0.0018 in.)	0.12 mm (0.006 in.)
Oil control	0.017 mm (0.0007 in.)	NA
Crankshaft/connecting rod		
Small end inner diameter	19.020-19.041 mm (0.7488-0.7496 in.)	19.07 mm (0.751 in.)
Connecting rod big end side clearance	0.05-0.45 mm (0.002-0.017 in.)	0.60 mm (0.024 in.)
Connecting rod big end radial clearance	0.006-0.018 mm (0.0002-0.0007 in.)	0.05 mm (0.002 in.)

(continued)

Table 1 250 CC ENGINE SPECIFICATIONS (cont.)

Item	Specifications	Wear limit
Camshaft		
Cam lobe height		
Intake	36.362 mm (1.4316 in.)	36.30 mm (1.429 in.)
Exhaust	36.256 mm (1.4274 in.)	36.20 mm (1.425 in.)
Cam journal O.D.		
Left-hand end	19.954-19.975 mm (0.7856-0.7864 in.)	19.9 mm (0.78 in.)
Right-hand end	23.954-23.975 mm (0.9431-0.9439 in.)	23.9 mm (0.94 in.)
Cam bearing surface in cylinder head and cylinder head cover		
Left-hand side	20.000-20.021 mm (0.7874-0.7882 in.)	20.05 mm (0.789 in.)
Right-hand side	24.000-24.021 mm (0.9449-0.9457 in.)	24.05 mm (0.947 in.)
Valves		
Valves stem outer diameter		
Intake	5.475-5.490 mm (0.2156-0.2161 in.)	5.465 mm (0.2152 in.)
Exhaust	5.455-5.470 mm (0.2148-0.2154 in.)	5.445 mm (0.2144 in.)
Valve stem runout	–	0.05 mm (0.002 in.)
Valve guide inner diameter		
Intake and exhaust	5.500-5.512 mm (0.2166-0.2170 in.)	5.53 mm (0.218 in.)
Stem to guide clearance	0.010-0.047 mm (0.0004-0.0019 in.)	0.06 mm (0.0024 in.)
Valve face width		
Intake and exhaust	1.2-1.4 mm (0.048-0.055 in.)	2.0 mm (0.08 in.)
Valve springs free length		
Intake and exhaust		
Inner	43.6 mm (1.72 in.)	42.5 mm (1.67 in.)
Outer	35.58 mm (1.40 in.)	34.5 mm (1.36 in.)
Rocker arm assembly		
Rocker arm bore ID	12.000-12.018 mm (0.4724-0.4731 in.)	12.05 mm (0.474 in.)
Rocker arm shaft OD	11.966-11.984 mm (0.4711-0.4718 in.)	11.91 mm (0.469 in.)
Oil pump		
Inner to outer rotor tip clearance	0.15 mm (0.006 in.)	0.20 mm (0.008 in.)
Outer rotor to body clearance	0.15-0.18 mm (0.006-0.007 in.)	0.25 m (0.010 in.)
Rotor to body clearance	0.01-0.07 mm (0.0004-0.0028 in.)	0.12 mm (0.0047 in.)
Counter balancer system		
Front		
Shaft holder ID	26.007-26.020 mm (1.0239-1.0244 in.)	26.05 mm (1.026 in.)
Shaft holder OD	39.964-39.980 mm (1.5734-1.5740 in.)	39.91 mm (1.571 in.)

(continued)

Table 1 250 CC ENGINE SPECIFICATIONS (cont.)

Item	Specifications	Wear limit
Rear		
Balancer ID	26.007-26.020 mm	26.05 mm (1.026 in.)
	(1.0239-1.0244 in.)	
Kickstarter		
Gear ID	22.000-22.021 mm	22.10 mm (0.870 in.)
	(0.8661-0.8670 in.)	
Shaft OD	21.959-21.980 mm	21.91 mm (0.863 in.)
(where gear rides)	(0.8645-0.8654 in.)	

NA: Honda does not provide service information for all items or all models. All available information is included in this table.

Table 2 ENGINE TORQUE SPECIFICATIONS

Item	N•m	ft.-lb.
Engine mounting bolts (upper 3)		
8 mm bolts–all models	20-35	14-25
10 mm bolts		
XL series	30-50	22-36
XR series	45-60	33-44
Engine hanger bolts (front 4)		
Upper 8 mm bolts–all models	30-50	22-36
Lower 10 mm bolts		
XL series	30-50	22-36
XR series	45-60	33-43
Engine mounting bolts		
10 mm–XL series	30-50	22-36
12 mm–XR series	70-100	51-72
Valve adjuster cover bolts	10-14	7-10
Cylinder head studs	35-40	25-29
Cyinder head bolts and nuts		
All other models	35-40	25-29
Cylinder head cover bolts and nuts	10-14	7-10
Cylinder side bolts	10-14	7-10
Cylinder front, rear and		
side bolts	22-28	16-20
Cam sprocket bolts	17-23	12-17
Cam chain tensioner bolt	22-28	16-20
Balancer shaft locknut	18-25	13-18
Ignition advance mechanism nut	45-60	33-43
Right- and left-hand crankcase		
cover bolts	8-12	6-9
Alternator rotor bolt		
XL250S	85-105	61-76
XR250, XR250R	95-105	69-76
Upper crankcase bolts		
6 mm bolts	10-14	7-10
8 mm bolts	22-28	16-20
Lower crankcase bolts		
6 mm bolts	10-14	7-10
8 mm bolts	22-28	16-20
9 mm bolts	27-32	20-23
10 mm bolts	33-37	24-27

CHAPTER FIVE

NOTE: If you own a 1990 or later model, first check the Supplement at the back of the book for any new service information.

200 THRU 350 CC RFVC ENGINES

All models covered in this chapter are equipped with an unusual 4-valve, air-cooled, 4-stroke, single cylinder engine with a single overhead camshaft. The engine is called the Radial Four Valve Combustion (RFVC) engine. The cylinder head incorporates 2 intake and 2 exhaust valves arranged radially. This design allows the largest possible valves to maximize the intake and exhaust efficiency. Each pair of dual valves has its own set of rocker arms and each valve has its own adjuster.

The crankshaft is supported by 2 large ball bearings and engine vibration is minimized by a counter-rotating balancer that is driven off the crankshaft.

To ease starting, the engine has a starter decompressor. As the kickstarter pedal is depressed, a cam on the pedal operates a lever that transmits movement via a cable to the decompressor valve lifter on the cylinder head. This lifter opens the exhaust valves momentarily and then allows them to close as the pedal continues its downward travel.

Engine lubrication is provided by the oil pump, located on the right-hand side of the engine and gear driven by the crankshaft.

This chapter contains information for removal, inspection, service and installation of the engine. Although the clutch and transmission are located within the engine, they are covered in Chapter Six to simplify this material.

Table 1 provides complete specifications for the engine and **Table 2** lists all of the engine torque specifications. **Table 1** and **Table 2** are located at the end of this chapter.

Before beginning work, re-read Chapter One of this book. You will do a better job with this information fresh in your mind.

Throughout the text there is frequent mention of the right-hand and left-hand sides of the engine. This refers to the engine as it sits in the bike's frame, *not* as it sits on your workbench. "Right-" and "left-hand" refers to a rider sitting on the seat facing forward.

ENGINE PRINCIPLES

Figure 1 explains how the engine works. This will be helpful when troubleshooting or repairing the engine.

4-STROKE PRINCIPLES

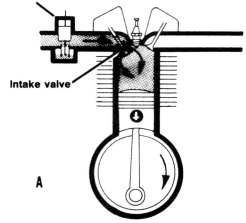

A

As the piston travels downward, the exhaust valve is closed and the intake valve opens, allowing the new air-fuel mixture from the carburetor to be drawn into the cylinder. When the piston reaches the bottom of its travel (BDC), the intake valve closes and remains closed for the next 1 1/2 revolutions of the crankshaft.

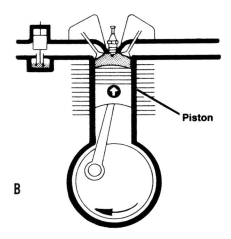

B

While the crankshaft continues to rotate, the piston moves upward, compressing the air-fuel mixture.

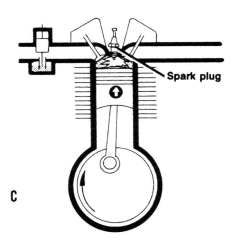

C

As the piston almost reaches the top of its travel, the spark plug fires, igniting the compressed air-fuel mixture. The piston continues to top dead center (TDC) and is pushed downward by the expanding gases.

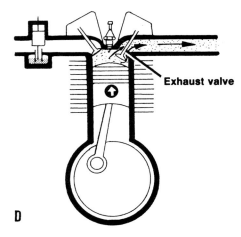

D

When the piston almost reaches BDC, the exhaust valve opens and remains open until the piston is near TDC. The upward travel of the piston forces the exhaust gases out of the cylinder. After the piston has reached TDC, the exhaust valve closes and the cycle starts all over again.

ENGINE COOLING

Cooling is provided by air passing over the cooling fins on the engine cylinder head and cylinder. It is very important to keep these fins free from buildup of dirt, oil, grease and other foreign matter. Brush out the fins with a whisk broom or small stiff paint brush.

CAUTION
Remember, these fins are thin in order to dissipate heat and may be damaged if struck too hard.

SERVICING ENGINE IN FRAME

The following components can be serviced while the engine is mounted in the frame (the bike's frame is a great holding fixture for breaking loose stubborn bolts and nuts):
   a. Cylinder head cover and camshaft (except XL350R and 1983-1984 XR350R).
   b. Cylinder head (except XL350R and 1983-1984 XR350R).
   c. Cylinder and piston (except XL350R and 1983-1984 XR350R).
   d. Carburetor.
   e. Kickstarter.
   f. Alternator.
   g. Clutch assembly.
   h. External shift mechanism.

ENGINE REMOVAL/INSTALLATION

1. Drain the engine oil as described in Chapter Three.
2A. On 1985 XR350R models, remove the bolts (**Figure 2**) securing the engine protector and remove the protector.
2B. On all other models, remove the bolts securing the skid plate and remove the skid plate.
3. Remove both side covers and the seat.
4. Remove the bolts securing the right-hand foot peg and remove the foot peg.
5. Remove the pivot bolt on the rear brake pedal. Move the brake pedal assembly to the rear. It is not necessary to completely remove the assembly.
6. Place wood block(s) under the frame to support the bike securely.
7. Remove the fuel tank as described in Chapter Seven.
8. Remove the exhaust system as described in Chapter Seven.
9. Remove the carburetor as described in Chapter Seven.
10. Disconnect the spark plug lead and tie it up out of the way.
11. Remove the bolts (**Figure 3**) securing the external oil pipe and remove the oil pipe from the engine. Don't lose the sealing washers on each side of the fittings on the oil pipe.

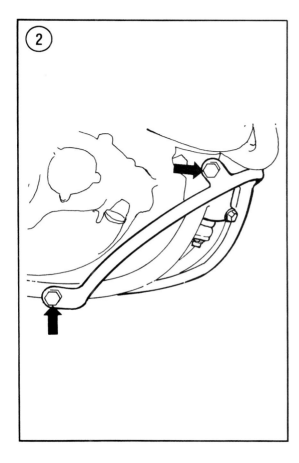

12. Disconnect the starter decompressor cables (A, **Figure 4**) from the cylinder head cover.

13. On dry-sump models, disconnect the oil tank breather tube (B, **Figure 4**) from the cylinder head cover.

14. Remove the bolt securing the gear shift lever and remove the gear shift lever.

15. Slacken the clutch cable at the hand lever. Disconnect the clutch cable at the crankcase cover.

16. Disconnect the alternator electrical connector.

17. Disconnect the ignition pulse generator wires at the electrical connector.

18. Remove the bolts securing the drive sprocket cover and remove the cover.

19. Remove the bolts (A, **Figure 5**) securing the drive sprocket.

20. Rotate the drive sprocket holder (B, **Figure 5**) in either direction and slide it off the shaft.

21. Loosen the rear axle nut and move the snail adjusters to loosen the drive chain.

22. Push the rear wheel forward and remove the drive sprocket and drive chain from the shaft.

23. Disconnect the crankcase breather tube from the crankcase.

24. On dry-sump models, perform the following:
   a. Hold onto the fittings either on the metal oil line or the frame and unscrew the flexible oil lines from the frame (**Figure 6**).
   b. Remove the bolts securing the oil line assemblies to the engine (**Figure 7**) and remove the oil lines. Don't lose the O-ring seals on the oil lines.

NOTE
If you are just removing the engine and are not planning to disassemble it, do not perform Step 25. The engine is small enough that external components can be left on during engine removal.

25. If the engine is going to be disassembled, remove the following parts:
   a. Remove the alternator as described in Chapter Eight.
   b. Remove the clutch assembly as described in Chapter Six.
   c. Remove the external shift mechanism as described in Chapter Six.
   d. On 1984-1985 XR200R, XR250R, XL250R and 1985 XR350R models, remove the cylinder head cover, camshaft, cylinder head, cylinder and piston as described in this chapter.
   e. Remove the oil pump assembly as described in this chapter.

26. Take a final look all over the engine to make sure everything has been disconnected.

27. Place a suitable size jack, with a piece of wood to protect the crankcase, under the engine. Apply a small amount of jack pressure up on the engine.

28. Remove the engine upper hanger bolts (**Figure 8**) and nuts and remove the hanger plates.

29. Remove the bolts (A, **Figure 9**) securing the front hanger plates to the frame on each side.

30. Remove the front through-bolt and nut (B, **Figure 9**). Remove the hanger plates.

31. Remove the bolts (**Figure 10**) securing the upper rear hanger plates on the right-hand side.

32. Remove the upper rear through-bolt and nut (**Figure 11**) from the left-hand side. Remove the hanger plate on the right-hand side.

33. Remove the lower front through-bolt (A, **Figure 12**) from the right-hand side. Don't lose the spacer (B, **Figure 12**) on the right-hand side.

CAUTION
Continually adjust jack pressure during engine removal and installation to prevent damage to the mounting bolt threads and hardware.

WARNING
The following steps require the aid of a helper to safely remove the engine assembly from the frame.

34. Pull the engine assembly up and slightly forward. Remove the engine from the right-hand side. Take it to a workbench for further disassembly.

35. Install by reversing these removal steps, noting the following.

36. Be sure to install the spacer (B, **Figure 12**) on the right-hand side of the lower front through-bolt.

37. Tighten the mounting bolts and nuts to the torque specifications in **Table 2**.

38. Be sure to install a sealing washer on each side of the fittings on the external oil pipe. Tighten the union bolt securely.

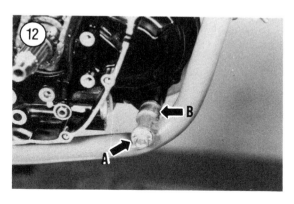

39. Fill the engine with the recommended type and quantity of oil; refer to Chapter Three.

40. Refer to Chapter Three and adjust the following:

    a. Clutch.

    b. Starter decompressor.

    c. Throttle grip free play.

    d. Drive chain slack.

    e. Rear brake pedal free play.

41. Start the engine and check for leaks.

CYLINDER HEAD COVER AND CAMSHAFT

The cylinder head cover carries the rocker arm assemblies and the starter decompressor lever.

The camshaft is held in place between the cylinder head cover and the cylinder head. The camshaft is chain-driven by a sprocket on the crankshaft.

Removal

> *NOTE*
> *On 1984-1985 XR200R, XR250R, XL250R and 1985 XR350R models, the cylinder head cover and camshaft can be removed with the engine in the frame. On all other models the engine must be removed from the frame for upper end service.*

> *CAUTION*
> *To prevent any warpage and damage, remove the cylinder head cover only when the engine is at room temperature.*

1. On XL350R and 1983-1984 XR350R models, remove the engine from the frame as described in this chapter.

2. Remove the side covers and the seat.

3. Remove the fuel tank as described in Chapter Seven.

> *NOTE*
> *Step 4 applies only to models where upper end service can be performed with the engine in the frame.*

4. On 1984-1985 XR200R, XR250R, XL250R and 1985 XR350R models, perform the following:

    a. Disconnect the starter decompressor cable(s) from the cylinder head cover.

    b. Remove the engine upper hanger bolts and nuts (**Figure 8**). Remove the upper hanger plates.

    c. Disconnect the spark plug wire and tie it up out of the way.

5. Remove the valve adjuster covers.

6. If removed, reinstall the alternator rotor and the left-hand crankcase cover. Remove the inspection covers (**Figure 13**) on the left-hand crankcase cover.

7. Using the bolt on the alternator rotor, rotate the crankshaft *counterclockwise* until the piston is at

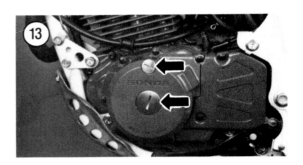

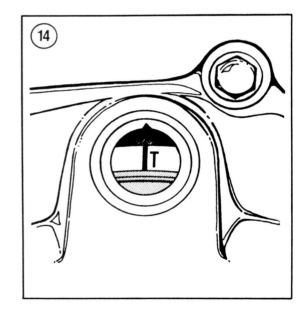

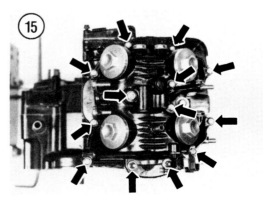

top dead center (TDC) on the compression stroke. Check that the "T" mark on the alternator rotor aligns with the stationary pointer on the crankcase cover (**Figure 14**).

> *NOTE*
> *A cylinder at TDC on its compression stroke will have free play in all of its rocker arms, indicating that both the intake and exhaust valves are closed.*

8. Using a crisscross pattern, loosen the bolts (**Figure 15**) securing the cylinder head cover. Remove the bolts.
9. Remove the cylinder head cover and gasket. Don't lose the locating dowel.
10A. On 1983 200-250 cc and all 350 cc models, remove the camshaft chain tensioner as described in this chapter.
10B. On 1984-on 200-250 cc models, relieve the tensioner tension and remove the upper plate of the camshaft chain tensioner as described in this chapter.
11. Using the alternator rotor, rotate the engine until one of the camshaft sprocket bolts is visible. Remove that bolt.
12. Again rotate the engine until the other camshaft sprocket bolt is visible. Remove that bolt.

13. Pull the camshaft chain sprocket and camshaft chain toward the center of the engine and off of the shoulder on the camshaft.
14. Tie a piece of wire to the camshaft chain and secure the loose end to the exterior of the engine. This will prevent the camshaft chain from falling into the crankcase.
15. Remove the camshaft and sprocket from the cylinder head.

> *CAUTION*
> *If the crankshaft must be rotated when the camshaft is removed, pull up on the camshaft chain and keep it taut while rotating the crankshaft. Make certain that the chain is positioned correctly on the crankshaft sprocket. If this is not done, the chain may become kinked and may damage both the chain and the sprocket on the crankshaft.*

Camshaft Inspection

1. Check the camshaft bearings (A, **Figure 16**) for roughness, pitting, galling and play by rotating them by hand. If any roughness or play can be felt in the bearing(s) it must be replaced.
2. Check the camshaft lobes for wear. The lobes should show no signs of scoring and the edges should be square. Slight damage may be removed with a silicon carbide oilstone. Use a No. 100-120 grit stone initially, then polish with a No. 280-320 grit stone.

> *NOTE*
> *The cam is dark in color due to the manufacturing heat treating process. It is not due to lack of oil pressure or excessive engine heat.*

3. Even though the camshaft lobe surface appears to be satisfactory, with no visible signs of wear, the camshaft lobes must be measured with a micrometer or vernier caliper as shown in **Figure 17**.

> *NOTE*
> *Position the camshaft with the camshaft sprocket boss on the right-hand side. The camshaft lobe locations from left to right are as follows: exhaust, intake, exhaust, intake.*

4. Measure both the intake (B, **Figure 16**) and exhaust (C, **Figure 16**) lobes of the camshaft. Compare to the dimensions given in **Table 1**. If any lobes are worn to the wear limit or less the camshaft must be replaced.

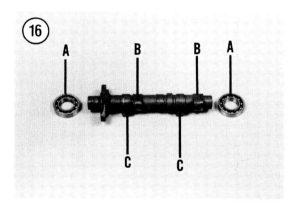

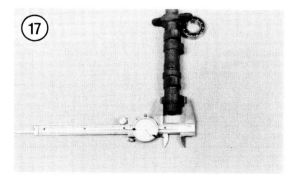

5. Inspect the camshaft sprocket for wear; replace if necessary.

Cylinder Head Cover
Disassembly/Inspection/Assembly

It is recommended that one rocker arm assembly be disassembled, inspected and then assembled to avoid the intermixing of parts. This is especially true of a well run-in engine as different sets of parts have taken a set and wear pattern.

1. To remove the starter decompressor valve lifter lever, perform the following:
    a. Remove the dowel pin (**Figure 18**) securing the lever.
    b. Remove the lifter lever and return spring from the cylinder head cover.

2. Unscrew the valve adjuster covers.

3. To remove the sub-rocker arm assembly, perform the following:
    a. Unscrew the exhaust valve sub-rocker arm shaft (**Figure 19**).
    b. Remove the rocker arm shaft, copper sealing washer and wave washer.
    c. Remove the sub-rocker arm (A, **Figure 20**).
    d. Repeat Steps a-c for the intake valve sub-rocker arm shaft and sub-rocker arm.

4. To remove the main rocker arm assemblies, perform the following:
    a. Unscrew the main rocker arm shaft (**Figure 21**).

> *NOTE*
> *On 1986-on XR250R models, the wave washers have been eliminated on the main rocker arm shafts.*

    b. Remove the main rocker arm shaft, copper sealing washer and wave washers.
    c. Remove the main rocker arms.

5. Wash all parts in cleaning solvent and thoroughly dry.

6. Inspect the sub-rocker arm components as follows:
    a. Inspect the sub-rocker arm pad where it rides on the main rocker arm adjuster. If the pad is scratched or unevenly worn, inspect the main rocker arm where the sub-rocker arm rides for scoring, chipping or flat spots. Replace the rocker arm if defective.
    b. Measure the inside diameter of the sub-rocker arm bore with a snap gauge and check against the dimensions in **Table 1**. Replace if worn to the service limit or larger.
    c. Inspect the rocker arm shaft for signs of wear or scoring. Measure the outside diameter with

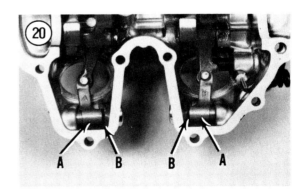

a micrometer and check against the dimensions in **Table 1**. Replace if worn to the service limit or smaller.

7. Inspect the main rocker arm components as follows:

   a. Inspect the main rocker arm pad where it rides on the cam lobe and where the adjuster rides on the sub-rocker arm. If the pad is

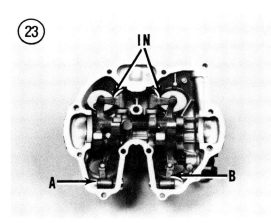

scratched or unevenly worn, inspect the cam lobe for scoring, chipping or flat spots. Replace the rocker arm if defective.

   b. Measure the inside diameter of the main rocker arm bore with a snap gauge and check against the dimensions in **Table 1**. Replace if worn to the service limit or larger.

   c. Inspect the rocker arm shaft for signs of wear or scoring. Measure the outside diameter with a micrometer and check against the dimensions in **Table 1**. Replace if worn to the service limit or smaller.

8. Coat the rocker arm shaft and rocker arm bores with assembly oil.

9. To install the main rocker arm assemblies, perform the following:

   a. Position the main rocker arms as shown in **Figure 22**. Each main rocker arm has its own identifying mark. The exhaust valves are marked "A" (A, **Figure 22**) and the intake valves are marked "B" (B, **Figure 22**).

NOTE
On 1986-on XR250R models, the wave washers have been eliminated on the main rocker arm shafts.

   b. Place a wave washer on the inboard side of each rocker arm (C, **Figure 22**).

   c. Place a copper sealing washer on each rocker arm shaft.

   d. Push the main rocker arm shaft through the cylinder head cover, rocker arm, wave washer (models so equipped), cover boss, wave washer and rocker arm.

   e. Screw in the main rocker arm shaft and tighten to the torque specification listed in **Table 2**.

10. To install the sub-rocker arm assemblies, perform the following:

   a. Position the main rocker arms as shown in **Figure 23**. Each sub-rocker arm has its own identifying mark. The exhaust valves are marked "A" (A, **Figure 23**) (left-hand side) or "B" (B, **Figure 23**) (right-hand side). The intake valves are marked with an "IN".

   b. Place a wave washer on the intake valve sub-rocker arm as shown in **Figure 24** and on the exhaust valve sub-rocker arm as shown in B, **Figure 20**.

   c. Place a copper sealing washer on each rocker arm shaft.

   d. On the intake valve sub-rocker arm, push the sub-rocker arm shafts through the cylinder head cover, rocker arm, wave washer and cover boss.

e. On the exhaust valve sub-rocker arm, push the sub-rocker arm shafts through the cylinder head cover, wave washer, rocker arm and cover boss.

f. Screw in each sub-rocker arm shaft and tighten to the torque specification listed in **Table 2**.

11. Perform Steps 3-10 for each rocker arm or sub-rocker arm assembly.

12. Inspect the cam chain tensioner lifter assembly (A, **Figure 25**) for wear or damage. Replace the O-ring seal (B, **Figure 25**) if it is starting to harden or deteriorate.

13. To install the starter decompressor lever, perform the following:

a. Install the spring into the lifter lever.

b. Install the lifter lever into the cylinder head cover and position the spring onto the boss.

c. Align the cutout in the lifter lever shaft with the dowel pin hole in the cylinder head cover.

d. Apply a light coat of grease to the dowel pin. This will hold the dowel in place when the cylinder head cover is turned upside down during installation.

e. Install the dowel pin (**Figure 18**) into the cylinder head cover and past the lifter lever shaft.

Installation

1. Lubricate all camshaft lobes with molybdenum disulfide grease. Apply assembly oil or clean engine oil to the camshaft bearings.

2. If removed, install the bearings onto the camshaft. The sealed bearing goes onto the sprocket boss end of the cam with the sealed side facing out.

CAUTION
When rotating the crankshaft, keep the camshaft chain taut and engaged with the timing sprocket on the crankshaft.

3. If removed, temporarily install the alternator cover and remove the timing mark hole cap.

4. The engine must be at top dead center (TDC) during the following steps for correct valve timing. Hold the camshaft chain out and taut while rotating the crankshaft to avoid damage to the chain and/or the crankcase.

5. Pull up on the chain, making sure it is properly engaged on the crankshaft sprocket. Rotate the engine until the "T" timing mark on the alternator rotor aligns with the fixed notch on the crankcase cover (**Figure 14**).

6. If removed, install the camshaft bearing stopper pins (**Figure 26**) into the cylinder head. They *must* be installed as they control camshaft bearing end-float.

7. Position the camshaft with the sprocket boss toward the left-hand side. Install the camshaft through the camshaft chain and into position in the cylinder head.

8. Position the camshaft sprocket with the flush side toward the left-hand side and install the camshaft sprocket onto the camshaft.

9. Position the camshaft sprocket so the alignment marks are aligned with the top surface of the cylinder head.

10. Make sure the camshaft chain is meshed properly with the drive sprocket on the crankshaft.

11. Hold the camshaft sprocket in this position and install the chain onto the camshaft sprocket.

NOTE
The camshaft can be positioned with the lobes up or down as long as the bolt holes align with the camshaft sprocket

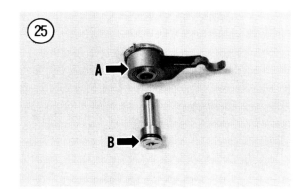

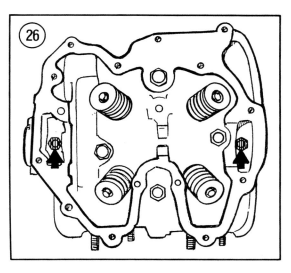

*and the timing marks on the sprocket
align with the cylinder head (**Figure 27**).
It is easier if the lobes are facing down
as this will place less of a load on the
rocker arms during cylinder head cover
installation.*

12. Pull the camshaft chain and sprocket assembly
up onto the shoulder on the camshaft. Check that
the alignment marks are still aligned with the top
surface of the cylinder head (**Figure 27**) and that
the alternator rotor "T" mark is still aligned
(**Figure 14**).

13. If alignment is incorrect, reposition the
camshaft chain on the sprocket and recheck the
alignment.

> *CAUTION*
> *Very expensive damage could result
> from improper camshaft and camshaft
> chain alignment. Recheck your work
> several times to be sure alignment is
> correct.*

14. Rotate the camshaft until the sprocket boss
bolt hole aligns with the exposed bolt in the
camshaft sprocket.

15. When alignment is correct, perform the
following:
   a. Install the bolt into the exposed bolt hole.
   Tighten only finger-tight at this time.
   b. Rotate the engine to expose the other bolt
   hole and install the other bolt.
   c. Make sure the camshaft sprocket is correctly
   seated on the camshaft boss.
   d. Tighten both bolts to the torque specification
   listed in **Table 2**.

> *CAUTION*
> *If there is any binding while rotating
> the crankshaft, **stop**. Determine the
> cause before proceeding.*

16. After installation is complete, rotate the
crankshaft several times using the bolt on the
alternator rotor.

17. Make one final check to make sure alignment
is correct. The "T" timing mark must be aligned
with the fixed timing mark and the timing marks
on the camshaft sprocket must be perfectly aligned
with the top surface of the cylinder head.

18A. On 1983 200-250 cc and all 350 cc models,
install the camshaft chain tensioner as described in
this chapter.

18B. On 1984-on 200-250 cc models, install the
upper plate and remove the wire from the
tensioner as described in this chapter. This will
allow the tensioner to apply the correct amount of
force on the camshaft chain.

19. Fill the oil pocket in the cylinder head with
new engine oil so the cam lobes are submerged in
the oil for the initial startup.

20. Make sure all locating dowels are in place in
the cylinder head.

21. Loosen the valve adjusters fully. This to
relieve strain on the rocker arms and cylinder head
cover during installation.

22. Wrap a small rubber band (**Figure 28**) around
each sub-rocker arm and then attach it to the
exterior of the cylinder head cover. This is to
hold the main and sub-rocker arms up during
cylinder head cover installation.

23. Make sure all sealing surfaces of the cylinder
head and the cylinder head cover are completely
clean. Spray both sealing surfaces with contact
cleaner and wipe dry with a clean lint-free cloth.

> *CAUTION*
> *Do not destroy the silicone surface on
> the cylinder head cover gasket as it will
> destroy its sealing ability.*

24. Install a new cylinder head cover gasket.

25. Preload the starter decompressor lever and install the cylinder head cover.

26. Remove the rubber bands.

27. Install the 6 mm and 8 mm bolts and tighten in a crisscross pattern in 2-3 steps to the torque specification listed in **Table 2**.

28. Adjust the valves and starter decompressor as described in Chapter Three.

CAMSHAFT CHAIN TENSIONER

Removal
(1983 200-250 cc and All 350 cc Engines)

1. Remove the dowel pin (**Figure 29**) securing the camshaft chain tensioner.

2. Screw a 6 mm bolt into the threaded hole (**Figure 30**) in the camshaft chain tensioner.

3. Withdraw the camshaft chain tensioner shaft.

> *WARNING*
> *In the next step, the camshaft chain tensioner is under spring tension. As the tensioner is removed from the cylinder head the spring will snap but will **not** fly out. It is captured in the tensioner. Do **not** put your fingers down into the cylinder cavity during this procedure as they may get cut by the spring.*

4. Carefully withdraw the camshaft chain tensioner from the cylinder head.

> *NOTE*
> *Do not drop the camshaft sprocket bolts as they may become lodged in the camshaft tensioner slippers. If this happens, further engine disassembly will be necessary to retrieve them.*

Installation
(1983 200-250 cc and All 350 cc Engines)

The camshaft chain tensioner can be installed with or without special tools. Both ways are included in this procedure.

If removed, install the camshaft chain tensioner spring onto the tensioner as shown in **Figure 31**.

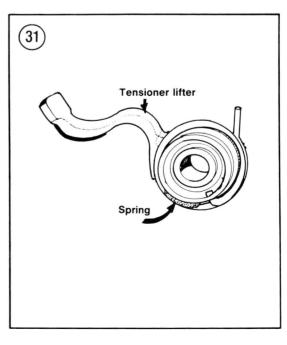

Tensioner lifter

Spring

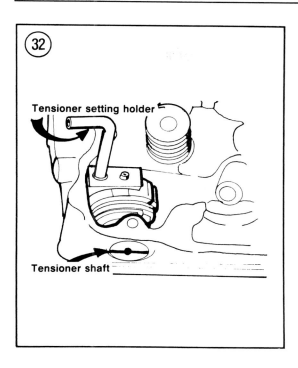

Tensioner setting holder

Tensioner shaft

With special tool

1. Partially install the tensioner lifter assembly into the cylinder head with the curved surface on the arm facing toward the camshaft chain.

2. Insert Honda special tool (tensioner setting holder, part No. 07973-MG3000) onto the tensioner as shown in **Figure 32**.

3. Push the tensioner lifter assembly down until the hole aligns with the hole in the cylinder head.

4. Apply clean engine oil to the O-ring seal on the tensioner shaft and install the tensioner shaft. Use a wide-bladed screwdriver and rotate the shaft until the shaft hole aligns with the hole in the cylinder head cover. Install the dowel pin (**Figure 33**) securing the tensioner shaft; push it down all the way.

5. Remove the special tool.

Without special tool

1. Wrap a piece of wire around the tensioner lifter and the spring and compress the spring (**Figure 34**).

2. Partially install the tensioner lifter assembly into the cylinder head with the curved surface on the arm facing toward the camshaft chain.

3. Push the tensioner lifter assembly down until the hole aligns with the hole in the cylinder head. You may have to use a long narrow-bladed screwdriver to help push the spring down into position onto the flat surface within the cylinder head.

4. Apply clean engine oil to the O-ring seal on the tensioner shaft and install the tensioner shaft. Use a wide-bladed screwdriver and rotate the shaft until the shaft hole aligns with the hole in the cylinder head cover. Install the dowel pin (**Figure 33**) securing the tensioner shaft; push it down all the way.

5. Cut the wire and pull it out. Make sure that all pieces of wire are removed from the engine.

Removal
(1984-on 200-250 cc Engines)

1. Cut a piece of wire approximately 2 mm (0.08 in.) in diameter and about 38 mm (1 1/2 in.) long. A straightened No. 2 paper clip will work.

2. Pull up on the tip of the tensioner with a pair of pliers until the hole in the tip is exposed.

3. Hold the tip up and insert the piece of cut wire into the hole in the tip (**Figure 35**).

4. Bend each end of the wire over a little so it will not accidentally fall out during this procedure.

5. Remove the bolts (**Figure 36**) securing the holder plate on the camshaft chain tensioner and remove the plate.

6. Remove the cylinder head and cylinder as described in this chapter.

7. Remove the clutch as described in Chapter Six.

8. Remove the bolt securing the tensioner assembly to the crankcase and remove the tensioner assembly.

Installation
(1984-on 200-250 cc Engines)

1. Install the tensioner assembly into the crankcase.

2. Install the bolt securing the tensioner assembly to the crankcase. Tighten to the torque specification listed in **Table 2**.

3. Install the clutch as described in Chapter Six.

4. Install the cylinder and cylinder head as described in this chapter.

5. Install the holder plate and bolts (**Figure 36**) securing the camshaft chain tensioner to the cylinder head.

6. Straighten the ends of the wire in the tensioner tip.

7. Using a pair of pliers, pull up on the tip of the camshaft chain tensioner and remove the wire from the tip.

8. Make sure the tip slides down after the wire is removed. If necessary, gently tap on the tip with a plastic or soft faced mallet. The tip must move down to apply the proper tension on the camshaft chain. If the tip will not move down correctly, replace the tensioner assembly.

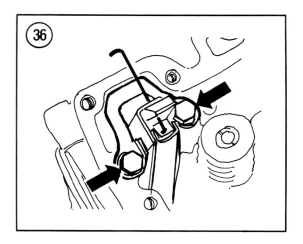

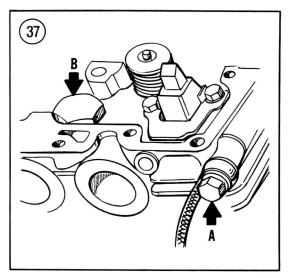

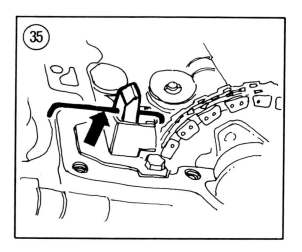

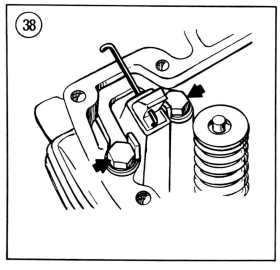

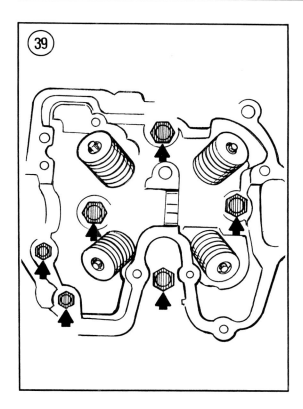

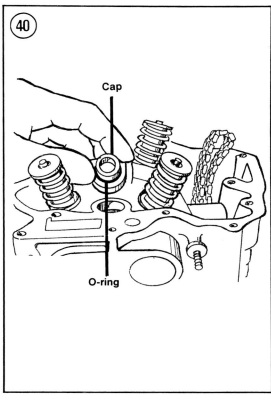

CYLINDER HEAD

Removal/Installation

CAUTION
To prevent any warpage and damage, remove the cylinder head only when the engine is at room temperature.

NOTE
On 1984-1985 XR200R, XR250R, XL250R and 1985 XR350R models, the cylinder head can be removed with the engine in the frame. It is shown removed in this procedure for clarity.

1. Remove the cylinder head cover and camshaft as described in this chapter.
2. On 1984-1985 XR200R, XR250R, XL250R and 1985 XR350R models, perform the following:
   a. Remove the carburetor as described in Chapter Seven.
   b. Remove the exhaust system as described in Chapter Seven.
3A. On 200-250 cc models, perform the following:
   a. Remove the union bolt and sealing washers (A, **Figure 37**) securing the external oil line to the rear right-hand side of the cylinder head. Gently pull the oil line away from the cylinder head.
   b. Remove the cylinder head bolt hole plug and O-ring (B, **Figure 37**).
   c. Remove the bolts (**Figure 38**) securing the holder plate on the camshaft chain tensioner. Remove the holder plate only—the tensioner assembly will not come out.
   d. Loosen the cylinder head bolts (**Figure 39**) in a crisscross pattern in 2-3 stages. Remove the bolts.
3B. On XL350R and 1983-1984 XR350R models, perform the following:
   a. Remove the cylinder head bolt hole plug and O-ring (**Figure 40**).
   b. Loosen the cylinder head bolts (A, **Figure 41**) in a crisscross pattern in 2-3 stages. Remove the bolts and washers. The washers may stay in the bolt receptacles in the cylinder head. After the cylinder head is removed, turn the cylinder head upside down and remove the washers.

NOTE
In the next step, your bike may have all nuts or a combination of bolts and nuts. Honda made a running change during the 1985 model year.

3C. On 1985 XR350R models, loosen the cylinder head bolts and/or nuts (A, **Figure 41**) in a crisscross pattern in 2-3 stages. Remove the bolts and/or nuts.

4. On all models, if the camshaft bearing stopper pins (B, **Figure 41**) are loose, remove them. If they are secure in the cylinder head, do not remove them.

5. Loosen the cylinder head by tapping around the perimeter with a rubber or soft-faced mallet. If necessary, *gently* pry the head loose with a broad-tipped screwdriver.

> *CAUTION*
> *Remember, the cooling fins are fragile and may be damaged if tapped or pried on too hard. Never use a metal hammer.*

6. Untie the wire securing the camshaft chain and retie it to the cylinder head.

7. Lift the cylinder head straight up and off the cylinder. Guide the camshaft chain through the opening in the cylinder head and retie the wire to the exterior of the engine. This will prevent the drive chain from falling down into the crankcase.

8. Remove the cylinder head gasket and discard it. Don't lose the locating dowels.

9. Place a clean shop cloth into the camshaft chain opening in the cylinder to prevent the entry of foreign matter.

10. Install by reversing these removal steps, noting the following.

11. Clean the mating surface of the cylinder and cylinder head of any old gasket material.

12. If removed, install the locating dowels in the cylinder.

13. Install a new cylinder head gasket. Make sure the holes align exactly.

14. Apply oil to the threads of the cylinder head bolts and/or nuts.

15. Install the cylinder head bolts and washers and/or nuts and tighten in a crisscross pattern, in 2-3 stages. Tighten to the torque specification listed in **Table 2**.

16. On models so equipped, make sure the O-ring seal is in good condition and install the cylinder head plug and O-ring seal (B, **Figure 37**).

17. If removed, install the camshaft bearing stopper pins (B, **Figure 41**). They *must* be installed as they control the end float of both camshaft bearings.

18. Install the cylinder head cover as described in this chapter.

Inspection

1. Remove all traces of gasket material from the cylinder head mating surfaces.

2. *Without removing the valves,* remove all carbon deposits from the combustion chamber and valve ports with a wire brush. A blunt screwdriver or chisel may be used if care is taken not to damage the head, valves and spark plug threads.

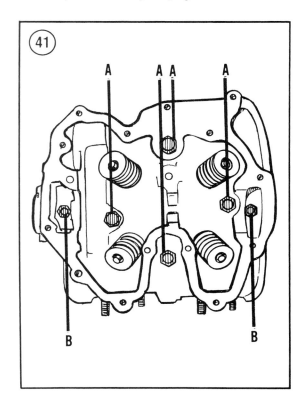

(41)

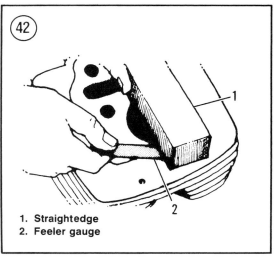

(42)

1. **Straightedge**
2. **Feeler gauge**

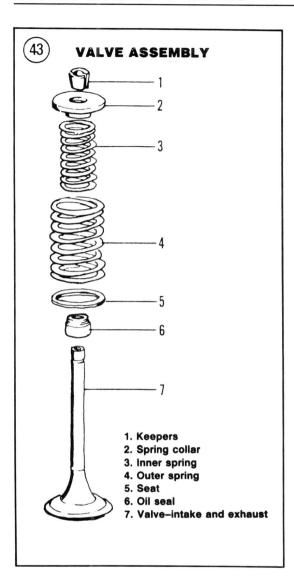

VALVE ASSEMBLY

1. Keepers
2. Spring collar
3. Inner spring
4. Outer spring
5. Seat
6. Oil seal
7. Valve–intake and exhaust

3. After the carbon is removed from the combustion chamber and the valve intake and exhaust ports, clean the entire head in cleaning solvent. Blow dry with compressed air.

4. Clean away all carbon from the piston crown. Do not remove the carbon ridge at the top of the cylinder bore.

5. Check for cracks in the combustion chamber and exhaust ports. A cracked head must be replaced.

6. After the head has been thoroughly cleaned, place a straightedge across the cylinder head/cylinder gasket surface at several points (**Figure 42**). Measure the warpage by inserting a flat feeler gauge between the straightedge and the cylinder head at each location. There should be no warpage; if a small amount is present, it can be resurfaced by a dealer or qualified machine shop. Replace the cylinder head and cylinder head cover as a set if the gasket surface is warped to or beyond the limit listed in **Table 1**.

7. Check the cylinder head cover mating surface using the procedure in Step 6. There should be no warpage.

8. Check the valves and valve guides as described in this chapter.

VALVES AND VALVE COMPONENTS

NOTE
General practice among those who do their own service is to remove the cylinder head and take it to a machine shop or dealer for inspection and service. Since the cost is low relative to the required effort and equipment, this is the best approach, even for experienced mechanics. The following procedures are included if you choose to perform these tasks yourself.

Removal

Refer to **Figure 43** for this procedure.

1. Remove the cylinder head as described in this chapter.

CAUTION
To avoid loss of spring tension, do not compress the springs any more than necessary to remove the keepers.

2. Compress the valve springs with a valve spring compressor tool (**Figure 44**). Remove the valve keepers and release the compression. Remove the valve spring compressor tool.

3. Remove the valve spring collar and valve springs (**Figure 45**).

4. The spring seat (**Figure 46**) and the valve stem seal (**Figure 47**) may stay in the cylinder head. Remove them if they do.

5. Prior to removing the valve, remove any burrs from the valve stem (**Figure 48**). Otherwise the valve guide will be damaged.

6. Remove the valve.

7. Mark all parts as they are disassembled so that they will be installed in their original locations.

Inspection

1. Clean the valves with a wire brush and solvent.

2. Inspect the contact surface of each valve for burning or pitting (**Figure 49**). Unevenness of the contact surface is an indication that the valve is not serviceable. The valve contact surface can *not* be ground and must be replaced if defective.

3. Inspect the valve stem for wear and roughness and measure the vertical runout of the valve stem as shown in **Figure 50**. The runout should not exceed the service limit listed in **Table 1**.

4. Measure the valve stem for wear (**Figure 51**). If worn to the wear limit listed in **Table 1** or smaller, the valve must be replaced.

5. Remove all carbon and varnish from the valve guide with a stiff spiral wire brush.

6. Insert each valve in its guide. Hold the valve with the head just slightly off the valve seat and rock it sideways. If it rocks more than slightly, the guide is probably worn and should be replaced. As a final check, take the cylinder to a dealer and have the valve guides measured.

7. Measure each valve spring free length with a vernier caliper (**Figure 52**). All should be within the length specified in **Table 1** with no signs of bending or distortion. Replace defective springs in pairs (inner and outer).

8. Check the valve spring retainer and valve keepers. If they are in good condition they may be reused; replace as necessary.

9. Inspect the valve seats. If worn or burned, they must be reconditioned. This should be performed by a dealer or qualified machine shop.

Installation

1. Coat the valve stems with molybdenum disulfide grease. To avoid damage to the valve stem seal, turn the valve slowly while inserting the valve into the cylinder head.

2. Install the bottom spring retainers and new seals.

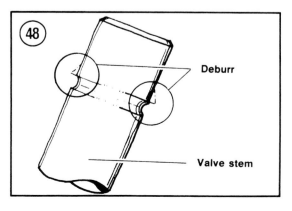
Deburr

Valve stem

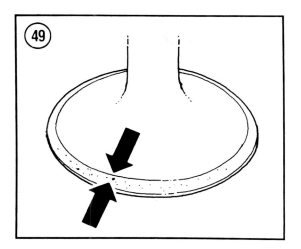

3. Install the valve springs with their closer wound coils facing the cylinder head and install the valve spring retainer.

CAUTION
To avoid loss of spring tension, do not compress the springs any more than necessary to install the keepers.

4. Compress the valve springs with a compressor tool (**Figure 44**) and install the valve keepers. Remove the compressor tool.

5. After all springs have been installed, gently tap the end of the valve stem with a soft aluminum or brass drift and hammer. This will ensure that the keepers are properly seated.

6. Install the cylinder head as described in this chapter.

Valve Guide Replacement

When valve guides are worn so that there is excessive stem-to-guide clearance or valve tipping, the guides must be replaced. Replace all, even if only one is worn. This job should be done only by a dealer as special tools are required. If the valve guides are replaced, replace the valves also.

Valve Seat Reconditioning

This job is best left to a dealer or qualified machine shop. They have special equipment and knowledge for this exacting job. You can still save considerable money by removing the cylinder head and taking the head to the shop for repairs.

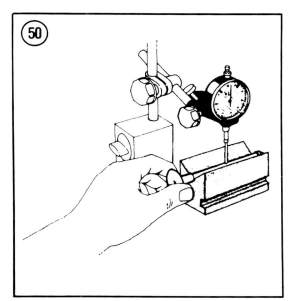

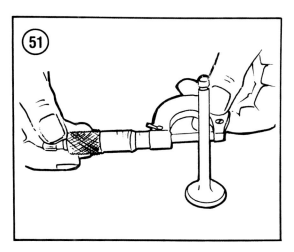

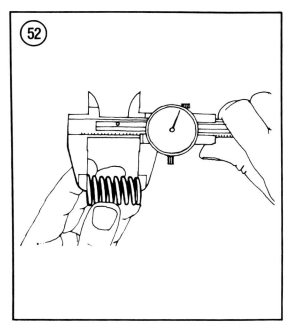

CYLINDER

Removal

1. Remove the cylinder head cover and cylinder head as described in this chapter.
2. On 200-250 cc models, remove the bolts securing the cylinder base to the crankcase on the right-hand side.
3. Loosen the cylinder bolts (**Figure 53**) in a crisscross pattern in 2-3 stages.
4. Remove the cylinder bolts and washers.
5. Loosen the cylinder by tapping around the perimeter with a rubber or plastic mallet. If necessary, *gently* pry the cylinder loose with a broad-tipped screwdriver.

> *CAUTION*
> *Remember, the cooling fins are fragile and may be damaged if tapped or pried on too hard. Never use a metal hammer.*

6. Pull the cylinder straight out and off of the piston. Work the camshaft chain wire through the opening in the cylinder. Reattach the wire to the exterior of the crankcase.
7. Remove the cylinder base gasket and discard it. Remove the dowel pins from the crankcase receptacles.
8. Install a piston holding fixture under the piston to protect the piston skirt from damage. This fixture may be purchased or may be a homemade unit of wood. See **Figure 54** for dimensions.

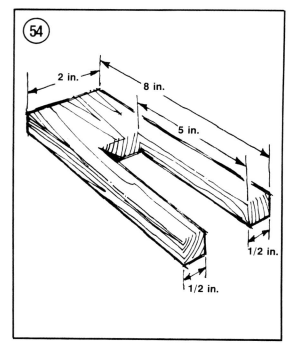

> *NOTE*
> *If the following items are to be removed, remove the clutch as described in Chapter Six and the oil pump as described in this chapter.*

9. Remove the camshaft chain guide (**Figure 55**).
10. Remove the bolt (**Figure 56**) securing the cam chain tensioner assembly. Remove the tensioner assembly, bushing and washer.

Inspection

The following procedure requires the use of highly specialized and expensive measuring instruments. If such equipment is not readily available, have the measurements performed by a dealer or qualified machine shop.

1. Soak with solvent any old cylinder head gasket material on the cylinder. Use a broad-tipped *dull* chisel and gently scrape off all gasket residue. Do not gouge the sealing surface as oil and air leaks will result.

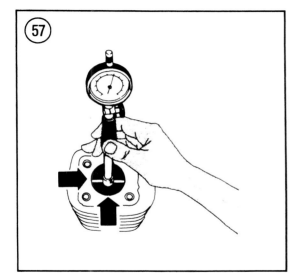

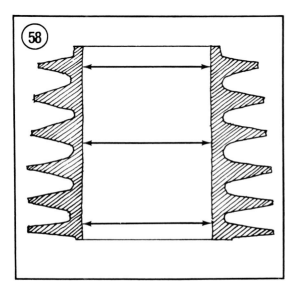

2. Measure the cylinder bore with a cylinder gauge (**Figure 57**) or inside micrometer at the points shown in **Figure 58**. Measure in 2 axes—in line with the piston pin and at 90° to the pin. If the taper or out-of-round is 0.10 mm (0.004 in.) or greater, the cylinder must be rebored to the next oversize and a new piston installed.

NOTE
The new piston should be obtained before the cylinder is rebored so that the piston can be measured; slight manufacturing tolerances must be taken into account to determine the actual size and working clearance.

3. Check the cylinder wall for scratches; if evident, the cylinder should be rebored.

NOTE
*The maximum wear limit on the cylinder is listed in **Table 1**. If the cylinder is worn to this limit, it must be replaced. Never rebore a cylinder if the finished rebore diameter will be this dimension or greater.*

NOTE
After having the cylinder rebored, wash it thoroughly in hot soapy water. This is the best way to clean the cylinder of all fine grit material left from the bore job. After washing the cylinder, run a clean white cloth through it. The cloth should show no traces of dirt or other debris. If the rag is dirty, the cylinder is not clean enough and must be rewashed. After the cylinder is thoroughly clean, dry and lubricate the cylinder wall with clean engine oil to protect the cylinder liner from rust.

Installation

1. Check that the top surface of the crankcase and the bottom surface of the cylinder are clean prior to installing a new base gasket.
2. If removed, install the following:
   a. Install the washer, bushing and the camshaft chain tensioner assembly. Install the bolt (**Figure 56**) and tighten to the torque specification listed in **Table 2**.

b. Install the camshaft chain guide (**Figure 55**). Make sure it seats correctly in the notch in the right-hand crankcase (**Figure 59**).

c. Install the oil pump as described in this chapter.

d. Install the clutch as described in Chapter Six.

3. On 200-250 cc models, apply a small amount of liquid sealant to the mating surfaces of the crankcase halves in the area where the cylinder base gasket fits. This will help prevent an oil leak.

4. Install a new cylinder base gasket. Make sure all holes align.

5. Install the dowel pins into the receptacles in the crankcase.

6. Install a piston holding fixture under the piston.

7. Make sure the end gaps of the piston rings are *not* lined up with each other—they must be staggered. Lightly oil the piston rings and the inside of the cylinder bore with assembly oil.

8. Carefully feed the camshaft chain and wire up through the opening in the cylinder and tie it to the engine.

9. Start the cylinder down over the piston. Compress each piston ring with your fingers as it enters the cylinder.

10. Slide the cylinder down until it bottoms on the piston holding fixture.

11. Remove the piston holding fixture and slide the cylinder down into place on the crankcase.

12. Install the cylinder bolts and washers. Tighten in a crisscross pattern in 2-3 steps to the torque specification listed in **Table 2**.

13. Install the bolts securing the cylinder to the crankcase on the right-hand side and tighten to the torque specification listed in **Table 2**.

14. Install the cylinder head, camshaft and cylinder head cover as described in this chapter.

15. Adjust the valves and the camshaft chain tensioner as described in Chapter Three.

16. Follow the *Break-in Procedure* in this chapter if the cylinder was rebored or honed or a new piston or piston rings were installed.

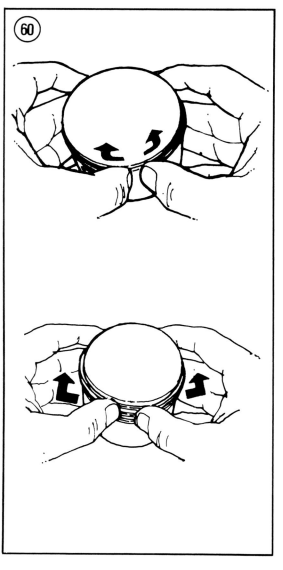

PISTON, PISTON PIN AND PISTON RINGS

The piston is made of an aluminum alloy. The piston pin is made of steel and is a precision fit. The piston pin is held in place by a clip at each end.

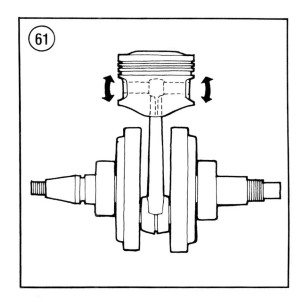

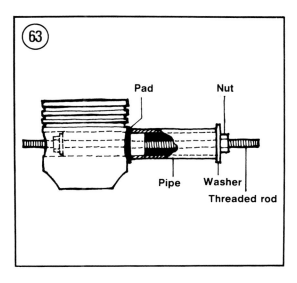

Piston Removal

1. Remove the cylinder head cover, cylinder head and cylinder as described in this chapter.

WARNING
The edges of all piston rings are very sharp. Be careful when handling them to avoid cutting fingers.

2. Remove the top ring with a ring expander tool or by spreading the ends with your thumbs just enough to slide the ring up over the piston (**Figure 60**). Repeat for the remaining rings.

3. Before removing the piston, hold the rod tightly and rock the piston as shown in **Figure 61**. Any rocking motion (do not confuse with the normal sliding motion) indicates wear on the piston pin, piston pin bore or connecting rod small-end bore (more likely a combination of these).

NOTE
Wrap a clean shop cloth under the piston so that the piston pin clip will not fall into the crankcase.

4. Remove the clips from each side of the piston pin bore (**Figure 62**) with a small screwdriver or scribe. Hold your thumb over one edge of the clip when removing it to prevent the clip from springing out.

5. Use a proper size wooden dowel or socket extension and push out the piston pin.

CAUTION
Be careful when removing the pin to avoid damaging the connecting rod. If it is necessary to gently tap the pin to remove it, be sure that the piston is properly supported so that lateral shock is not transmitted to the lower connecting rod bearing.

6. If the piston pin is difficult to remove, heat the piston and pin with a hair dryer. The pin will probably push right out. Heat the piston to only about 140° F (60° C), i.e., until it is too warm to touch, but not excessively hot. If the pin is still difficult to push out, use a homemade tool as shown in **Figure 63**.

7. Lift the piston off the connecting rod.

8. If the piston is going to be left off for some time, place a piece of foam insulation tube over the end of the rod to protect it.

Inspection

1. Carefully clean the carbon from the piston crown with a chemical remover or with a soft scraper (**Figure 64**). Do not remove or damage the carbon ridge around the circumference of the piston above the top ring. If the piston, rings and cylinder are found to be dimensionally correct and can be reused, removal of the carbon ring from the top of the piston or the carbon ridge from the top of the cylinder will promote excessive oil consumption.

CAUTION
Do not wire brush the piston skirts.

2. Examine each ring groove for burrs, dented edges and wide wear. Pay particular attention to the top compression ring groove as it usually wears more than the others.

3. If damage or wear indicates piston replacement, select a new piston as described under *Piston Clearance* in this chapter.

4. Oil the piston pin and install it in the connecting rod. Slowly rotate the piston pin and check for play (**Figure 65**). If any play exists, the piston pin should be replaced, providing the rod bore is in good condition.

5. Measure the inside diameter of the piston pin bore with a snap gauge (**Figure 66**) and measure the outside diameter of the piston pin with a micrometer (**Figure 67**). Compare with dimensions given in **Table 1**. Replace the piston and piston pin as a set if either or both are worn.

6. Check the piston skirt for galling and abrasion which may have been caused by piston seizure. If light galling is present, smooth the affected area with No. 400 emery paper and oil or a fine oilstone. However, if galling is severe or if the piston is deeply scored, replace it.

Piston Clearance

1. Make sure the piston and cylinder walls are clean and dry.

2. Measure the inside diameter of the cylinder bore at a point 13 mm (1/2 in.) from the upper edge with a bore gauge (**Figure 57**).

3. Measure the outside diameter of the piston across the skirt (**Figure 68**) at right angles to the piston pin. Measure at a distance 10 mm (0.40 in.) up from the bottom of the piston skirt.

4. Piston clearance is the difference between the maximum piston diameter and the minimum cylinder diameter. Subtract the dimension of the piston from the cylinder dimension and compare

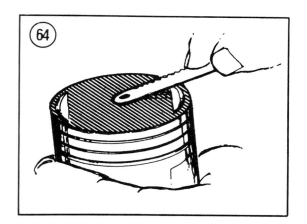

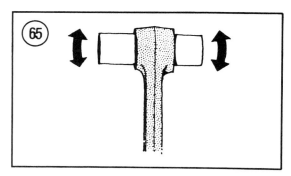

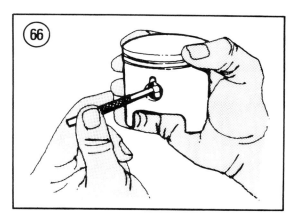

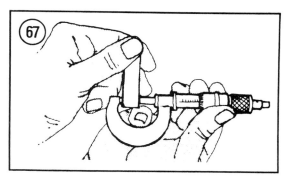

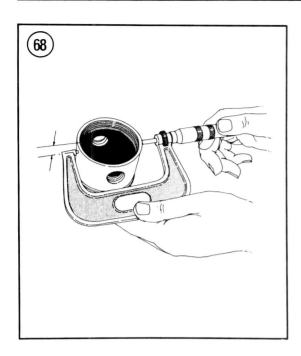

to the dimension listed in **Table 1**. If the clearance exceeds that specified, the cylinder should be rebored to the next oversize and a new piston installed.

5. To establish a final overbore dimension with a new piston, add the piston skirt measurement to the specified clearance. This will determine the dimension for the cylinder overbore size. Remember, do not exceed the cylinder maximum service limit inside diameter indicated in **Table 1**.

Piston Installation

1. Apply molybdenum disulfide grease to the inside surface of the connecting rod.
2. Oil the piston pin with assembly oil and install it in the piston until its end extends slightly beyond the inside of the boss (**Figure 69**).
3. Place the piston over the connecting rod with the "IN" mark (**Figure 70**) on the piston crown directed toward the rear of the engine.
4. Line up the piston pin with the hole in the connecting rod. Push the piston pin through the connecting rod and into the other side of the piston until it is even with the piston pin clip grooves.

> *CAUTION*
> *If it is necessary to tap the piston pin into the connecting rod, do so gently with a block of wood or a soft-faced hammer. Make sure you support the piston to prevent the lateral shock from being transmitted to the connecting rod bearing.*

> *NOTE*
> *In the next step, install the clips with the gap away from the cutout in the piston (**Figure 71**).*

5. Install new piston pin clips in both ends of the pin boss. Make sure they are seated in the grooves in the piston.

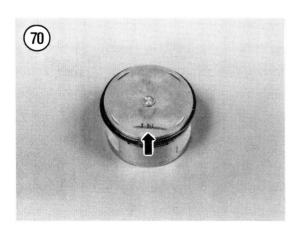

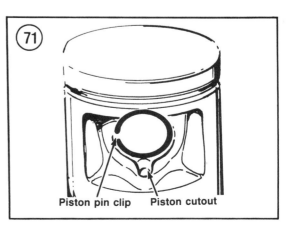

Piston pin clip   **Piston cutout**

6. Check the installation by rocking the piston back and forth around the pin axis and from side to side along the axis. It should rotate freely back and forth but not from side to side.

7. Install the piston rings as described in this chapter.

8. Install the cylinder, cylinder head and cylinder head cover as described in this chapter.

Piston Ring
Removal/Inspection/Installation

> *WARNING*
> *The edges of all piston rings are very sharp. Be careful when handling them to avoid cutting fingers.*

1. Remove the top ring by spreading the ends with your thumbs just enough to slide the ring up over the piston (**Figure 72**). Repeat for the remaining rings.

2. Carefully remove all carbon buildup from the ring grooves with a broken piston ring (**Figure 73**). Inspect the grooves carefully for burrs, nicks or broken and cracked lands. Recondition or replace the piston if necessary.

3. Roll each ring around its piston groove as shown in **Figure 74** to check for binding. Minor binding may be cleaned up with a fine-cut file.

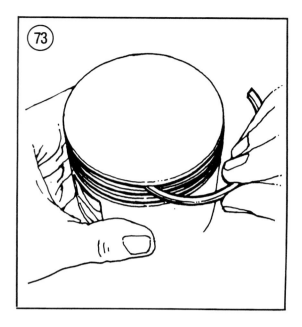

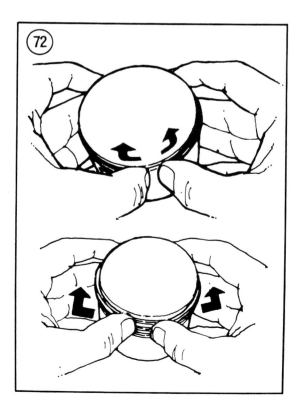

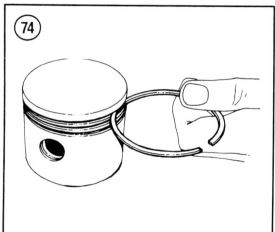

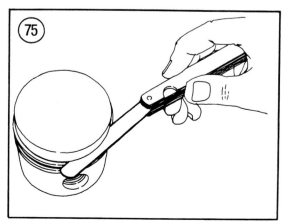

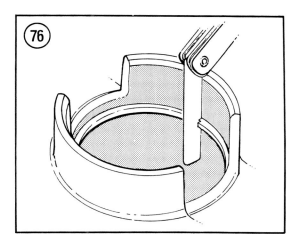

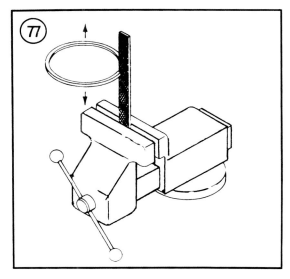

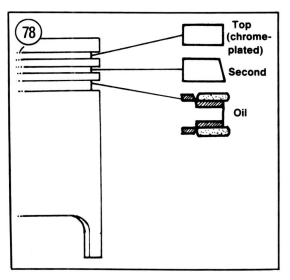

4. Measure the side clearance of each ring in its groove with a flat feeler gauge (**Figure 75**) and compare to dimensions given in **Table 1**. If the clearance is greater than specified, the rings must be replaced. If the clearance is still excessive with the new rings, the piston must also be replaced.

5. Measure each ring for wear. Place each ring, one at a time, into the cylinder and push it in about 20 mm (3/4 in.) with the crown of the piston to ensure that the ring is square in the cylinder bore. Measure the gap with a flat feeler gauge (**Figure 76**) and compare to dimensions in **Table 1**. If the gap is greater than specified, the rings should be replaced. When installing new rings, measure their end gap in the same manner as for old ones. If the gap is less than specified, carefully file the ends (**Figure 77**) with a fine-cut file until the gap is correct.

6. Install the piston rings in the order shown in **Figure 78**.

7. Install the oil ring spacer first, then the side rails. New oil ring side rails do not have top and bottom designations. If reassembling used parts, install the side rails as they were removed.

8. Install second compression ring, then the top compression ring, by carefully spreading the ends of the ring with your thumbs and slipping the ring over the top of the piston. Remember that the marks on the piston rings are toward the top of the piston.

9. Make sure the rings are seated completely in their grooves all the way around the piston and that the ends are distributed around the piston as shown in **Figure 79**. The important thing is that the ring gaps are not aligned with each other when installed.

10. If new rings were installed, measure the side clearance of each ring in its groove with a flat feeler gauge (**Figure 75**) and compare to dimensions given in **Table 1**.

11. Follow the *Break-in Procedure* in this chapter if a new piston or piston rings have been installed or the cylinder was rebored or honed.

PRIMARY DRIVE GEAR
(200-250 CC)

Removal/Installation

1. Remove the clutch assembly as described in Chapter Six.

2A. On 1986-on XR250R models, remove the oil pump as described in this chapter.

NOTE
In Step 2B on XL250R models, do not allow the oil pump drive shaft to come out of the oil pump assembly. If the shaft does come out, the oil pump will have to be disassembled to correctly reposition the drive shaft.

2B. On all models except 1986-on XR250R, remove the oil pump cover and the oil pump driven gear.

3. Temporarily install the clutch outer housing. Place a copper washer (or penny) between the clutch outer housing gear and the primary drive gear.

4. Loosen the primary drive gear locknut.

5. Remove the copper washer (or penny) and the clutch outer housing.

6. Remove the primary drive gear locknut (**Figure 80**).

7. Remove the lockwasher (A, **Figure 81**), the pulse generator rotor (B, **Figure 81**) and the primary drive gear (C, **Figure 81**).

NOTE
The primary drive gear and pulse generator rotor can be installed onto the crankshaft in only one position. During installation match up the wide spline groove on the gear and rotor with the 2 matching splines on the crankshaft.

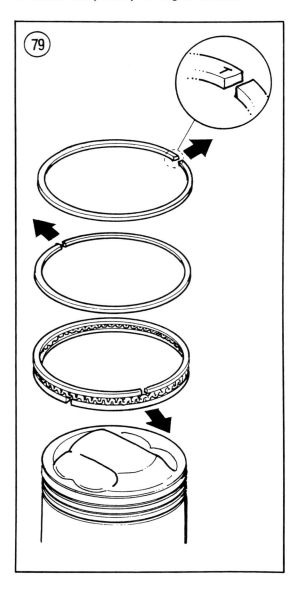

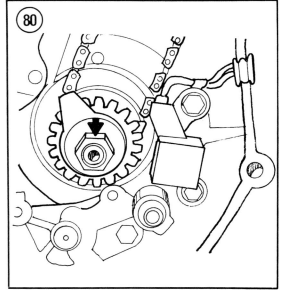

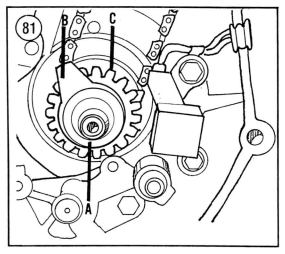

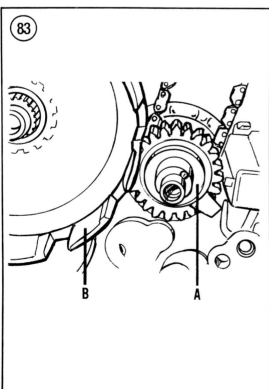

8. Inspect the primary drive gear and ignition pulse generator rotor for wear or damage. Replace any worn or damaged part.

9. Align the splines of the primary drive gear and slide it onto the crankshaft.

10. Position the pulse generator with the "OUTSIDE" mark facing toward the outside.

11. Align the splines of the pulse generator rotor and slide it onto the crankshaft.

12. Install the lockwasher with the "OUTSIDE" mark facing toward the outside.

13. Install the locknut and tighten only finger-tight at this time.

14. Temporarily install the clutch outer housing. Place a copper washer (or penny) between the clutch outer housing gear and the primary drive gear.

15. Tighten the primary drive gear locknut to the torque specification listed in **Table 2**. Remove the copper washer (or penny).

16A. On 1986-on XR250R models, install the oil pump as described in this chapter.

NOTE
In Step 16B on XL250R models, make sure the oil pump drive shaft is still properly installed in the oil pump assembly. If the shaft does come out, the oil pump will have to be disassembled to correctly reposition the drive shaft.

16B. On all models except 1986-on XR250R, install the oil pump driven gear and the oil pump cover.

17. Install the clutch assembly as described in Chapter Six.

PRIMARY DRIVE GEAR (1985 XR350R)

Removal/Installation

1. Remove the clutch assembly as described in Chapter Six.

2. Remove the oil pump as described in this chapter.

3. Remove the circlip (A, **Figure 82**) securing the oil pump drive gear and remove the drive gear (B, **Figure 82**).

4. Temporarily install the clutch outer housing. Place a copper washer (or penny) between the clutch outer housing gear and the primary drive gear.

5. Loosen the primary drive gear locknut.

6. Remove the locknut and lockwasher (A, **Figure 83**).

7. Remove the copper washer (or penny) and the clutch outer housing (B, **Figure 83**).

8. Remove pulse generator rotor (A, **Figure 84**) and the primary drive gear (B, **Figure 84**).

9. Install the primary drive gear.

10. Align the cutout in the pulse generator rotor with the dowel pin on the crankshaft and install the pulse generator rotor.

11. Install the lockwasher with the "OUTSIDE" mark facing toward the outside.

12. Install the locknut and tighten only finger-tight at this time.

13. Temporarily install the clutch outer housing. Place a copper washer (or penny) between the clutch outer housing gear and the primary drive gear.

14. Tighten the primary drive gear locknut to the torque specification listed in **Table 2**. Remove the copper washer.

15. Align the cutout in the oil pump drive gear with the dowel pin on the crankshaft and install the oil pump drive gear.

16. Install the circlip. Make sure the circlip is properly seated in the groove in the crankshaft.

17. Install the oil pump as described in this chapter.

18. Install the clutch assembly as described in Chapter Six in the main body of this book.

PRIMARY DRIVE GEAR (XL350R AND 1983-1984 XR350R)

Removal/Installation

1. Place a copper washer (or penny) between the clutch outer housing gear and the primary drive gear.

2. Loosen the primary drive gear locknut and remove the copper washer (or penny).

3. Remove the clutch assembly as described in Chapter Six.

4. Remove the oil pump drive gear (**Figure 85**).

5. Remove the primary drive gear locknut (**Figure 86**) and lockwasher.

6. Remove the oil pump drive gear and pulse generator rotor.

7. Install the primary drive gear.

8. Inspect the primary drive gear, pulse generator rotor and oil pump drive gear for wear or damage. Replace any worn part.

NOTE
The primary drive gear, pulse generator rotor and oil pump drive gear can be installed onto the crankshaft in only one position. During installation match

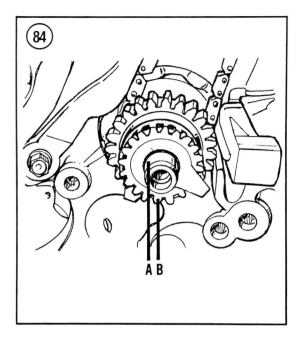

up the wide spline groove on the gear and rotor with the 2 matching splines on the crankshaft.

9. Align the splines of the primary drive gear and slide it onto the crankshaft (**Figure 87**).
10. Position the pulse generator with the "OUTSIDE" mark facing toward the outside.
11. Align the splines of the pulse generator rotor and slide it onto the crankshaft.
12. Install the lockwasher with the "OUTSIDE" mark facing toward the outside (**Figure 88**).
13. Install the locknut (**Figure 86**) and tighten only finger-tight at this time.
14. Install the clutch as described in Chapter Six. Place a copper washer (or penny) between the clutch outer housing gear and the primary drive gear.
15. Tighten the primary drive gear locknut to the torque specification listed in **Table 2**. Remove the copper washer (or penny).

OIL PUMP
(1984-1985 XR200R AND 1984-ON XR250R)

The oil pump is located on the right-hand side of the engine. The oil pump can be removed with the engine in the frame.

Removal/Installation

1. Remove the clutch assembly as described in Chapter Six.
2. Remove the bolts securing the oil pump cover and remove the cover.
3. Remove the oil pump driven gear from the oil pump assembly.
4. Remove the dowel pin and O-ring.
5. Remove the bolts securing the oil pump to the crankcase and remove the oil pump assembly from the crankcase.
6. Remove the dowel pins and the oil pump seat.
7. Install by reversing these removal steps, noting the following.
8. Inspect the O-ring seals; replace any that have started to harden or deteriorate.

Disassembly/Inspection/Assembly (1984)

Refer to **Figure 89** for this procedure.
1. On the backside of the oil pump assembly, remove the Phillips head screws securing the pump body to the pump cover.
2. Separate the assembly and remove the drive shaft and the inner and outer rotors.
3. Inspect the oil pump components as described under *Inspection (Single Cavity Oil Pumps)* in this chapter.
4. Make sure the dowel pin is installed in the oil pump body.
5. Install the drive shaft into front of the cover.
6. Align the flat on the pump shaft with the flat on the inner rotor and install the cover and shaft onto the body.
7. Hold onto the shaft and turn the assembly over.
8. Install the Phillips head screws and tighten securely.
9. Rotate the pump and make sure there is no binding.
10. Install the driven gear and rotate the pump to make sure there is no binding.

Disassembly/Inspection/Assembly (1985-on)

This oil pump has dual cavities with main and sub-rotor assemblies. In the inspection steps, the clearance measurements are the same for both the main and sub-rotor assemblies. The main set of rotors is the thicker of the two and is assembled into the main oil pump body.

Refer to **Figure 90** for this procedure.

1. On the backside of the oil pump assembly, remove the Phillips head screws securing the main- and sub-oil pump bodies together.

2. Separate the assembly and remove the drive shaft, the pair of inner and outer rotors and the pump plate.

3. Inspect the oil pump components as described under *Inspection (Single Cavity Oil Pumps)* in this chapter.

4. Make sure the dowel pin is installed in the sub-oil pump body.

5. Install the drive shaft into front of the main oil pump body and align the flat on the pump shaft with the flat on the inner rotor. Push the pump shaft through the inner rotor.

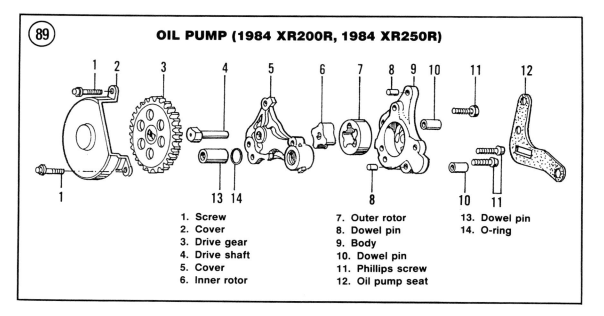

OIL PUMP (1984 XR200R, 1984 XR250R)

1. Screw	7. Outer rotor
2. Cover	8. Dowel pin
3. Drive gear	9. Body
4. Drive shaft	10. Dowel pin
5. Cover	11. Phillips screw
6. Inner rotor	12. Oil pump seat

13. Dowel pin
14. O-ring

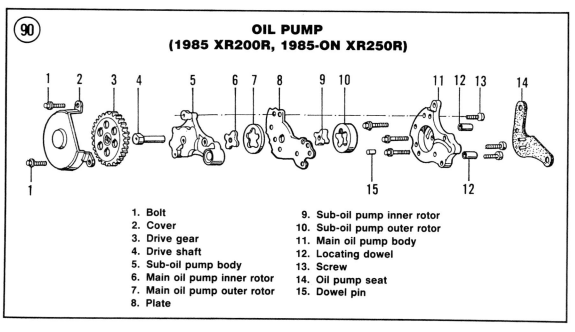

OIL PUMP (1985 XR200R, 1985-ON XR250R)

1. Bolt	9. Sub-oil pump inner rotor
2. Cover	10. Sub-oil pump outer rotor
3. Drive gear	11. Main oil pump body
4. Drive shaft	12. Locating dowel
5. Sub-oil pump body	13. Screw
6. Main oil pump inner rotor	14. Oil pump seat
7. Main oil pump outer rotor	15. Dowel pin
8. Plate	

6. Install the oil pump plate onto the main oil pump body.

7. Remove the inner and outer rotors from the sub-oil pump body.

8. Align the flat on the inner rotor with the flat on the shaft and install the inner rotor on the pump drive shaft.

9. Install the outer rotor onto the inner rotor and the pump shaft.

10. Install the sub-oil pump body onto the outer rotor assembly and install the Phillips head screws. Tighten the screws securely.

11. Rotate the pump and make sure there is no binding.

OIL PUMP
(1983 XR350R)

The oil pump is located on the right-hand side of the engine next to the clutch. The oil pump can be removed with the engine in the frame.

Removal/Installation

1. Remove the clutch as described in Chapter Six.

2. Remove the oil pump driven gear/shaft.

3. Remove the bolt securing the oil line to the crankcase.

4. Remove the oil line (including the large dowel and O-rings) from the crankcase.

5. Remove the bolts securing the oil pump to the crankcase and remove the oil pump assembly from the crankcase.

6. Install by reversing these removal steps, noting the following.

7. Make sure the large O-ring seal is installed in the inlet on the crankcase and that the locating dowels are in place on the crankcase.

8. Make sure the O-ring is in place on the end of the oil pickup pipe.

9. Install the driven gear/shaft, aligning the flat on the shaft with the flat on the inner rotor.

Disassembly/Inspection/Assembly

Refer to **Figure 91** for this procedure.

1. On the backside of the oil pump assembly, remove the Phillips head screws securing the pump body to the pump cover.

2. Separate the assembly and remove the inner and outer rotors.

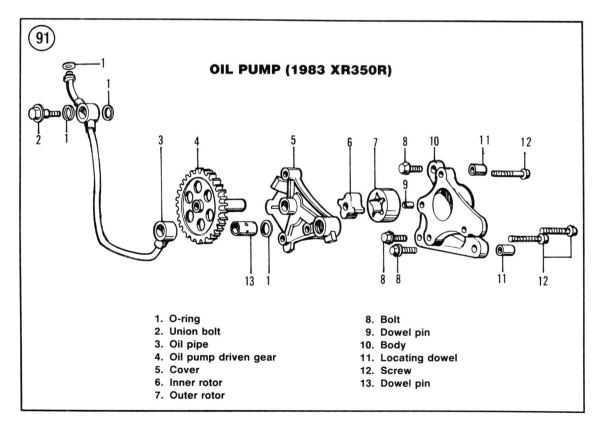

OIL PUMP (1983 XR350R)

1. O-ring	8. Bolt
2. Union bolt	9. Dowel pin
3. Oil pipe	10. Body
4. Oil pump driven gear	11. Locating dowel
5. Cover	12. Screw
6. Inner rotor	13. Dowel pin
7. Outer rotor	

3. Inspect the oil pump components as described under *Inspection (Single Cavity Oil Pumps)* in this chapter.

4. Make sure the dowel pin is installed in the oil pump body.

5. Install the inner and outer rotor in the oil pump body.

6. Align the flat on the pump shaft with the flat on the inner rotor and install the cover and driven gear/shaft onto the body.

7. Hold onto the driven gear and turn the assembly over.

8. Install the Phillips head screws and tighten securely.

9. Rotate the pump and make sure there is no binding.

10. Remove the driven gear/shaft from the assembly.

OIL PUMP (ALL OTHER MODELS)

The oil pump is located on the right-hand side of the engine next to the clutch. The oil pump can be removed with the engine in the frame.

Removal/Installation

1. Remove the clutch as described in Chapter Six.

2A. On XL250R models, perform the following:
    a. Remove the bolt securing the oil pump cover and remove the cover.
    b. Remove the oil pump driven gear from the oil pump assembly.

2B. On XL350R and 1984-1985 XR350R models, perform the following:
    a. Remove the bolt(s) securing the oil line to the crankcase.
    b. Remove the oil line (including the large dowel and O-rings) from the crankcase.
    c. On 1985 XR350R models, don't lose the O-ring and locating dowel on the outside surface of the oil pump next to the drive gear.

3. Remove the bolts securing the oil pump to the crankcase and remove the oil pump assembly from the crankcase.

4. Remove the locating dowels and on XL250R models, the oil pump seat.

5. Install by reversing these removal steps, noting the following.

6A. On XL350R and 1984 XR350R models, make sure the large O-ring seal is installed in the inlet on the crankcase and the O-ring is in place on the oil pickup pipe on the crankcase.

6B. On 1985 XR350R models, make sure the large O-ring seal is installed in the inlet on the crankcase

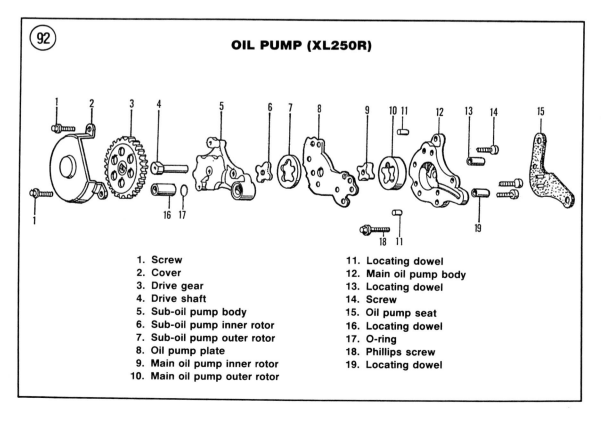

(92)

OIL PUMP (XL250R)

1. Screw
2. Cover
3. Drive gear
4. Drive shaft
5. Sub-oil pump body
6. Sub-oil pump inner rotor
7. Sub-oil pump outer rotor
8. Oil pump plate
9. Main oil pump inner rotor
10. Main oil pump outer rotor
11. Locating dowel
12. Main oil pump body
13. Locating dowel
14. Screw
15. Oil pump seat
16. Locating dowel
17. O-ring
18. Phillips screw
19. Locating dowel

and the oil control orifice and O-ring are in place on the crankcase. Also make sure the O-ring is in place on the oil pickup pipe.

Disassembly/Assembly
(XL250R, XL350R and 1984 XR350R)

Refer to **Figure 92** (XL250R) or **Figure 93** (XL350R and 1984 XR350R) for this procedure. These oil pumps have dual cavities with main and sub-rotor assemblies. In the inspection steps, the clearance measurements are the same for both the main and sub-rotor assemblies. The main set of rotors is the thicker of the two and is assembled into the main oil pump body.

1. On the backside of the oil pump assembly, remove the Phillips head screws securing the main and sub-oil pump bodies together.

2. Separate the assembly and remove the drive gear/shaft, the pair of inner and outer rotors and the check valve housing.

3. Inspect the oil pump components as described under *Inspection (Dual Cavity Oil Pumps)* in the chapter.

4. Make sure the dowel pin is installed in the sub-oil pump body.

5A. On XL250R models, install the pump drive shaft through the front of the sub-oil pump body and align the flat on the pump shaft with the flat on the inner rotor. Push the pump shaft through the inner rotor.

5B. On XL350R and 1984 XR350R models, install the pump drive shaft and driven gear through the front of the sub-oil pump body and align the flat on the pump shaft with the flat on the inner rotor. Push the pump shaft through the inner rotor.

6. Install the pump plate onto the sub-oil pump body.

7. Remove the inner and outer rotors from the main oil pump body.

8. Align the flat on the inner rotor with the flat on the shaft and install the inner rotor on the pump drive shaft.

9. Install the outer rotor onto the inner rotor and the pump drive shaft.

10. Install the main oil pump outer rotor onto the pump shaft.

11. Install the main oil pump body and install the Phillips head screws. Tighten the screws securely.

12. On XL250R models, install the driven gear on the drive shaft.

13. Rotate the pump and make sure there is no binding.

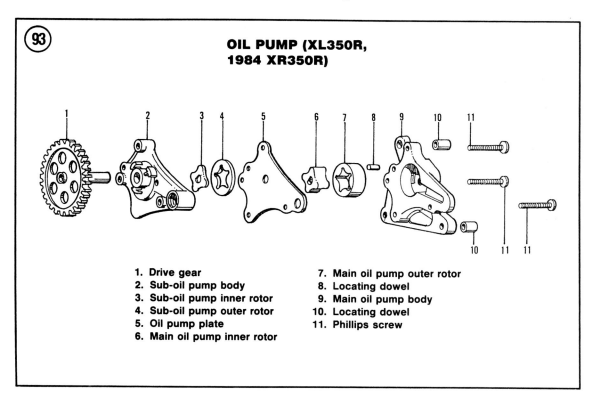

93

OIL PUMP (XL350R, 1984 XR350R)

1. Drive gear
2. Sub-oil pump body
3. Sub-oil pump inner rotor
4. Sub-oil pump outer rotor
5. Oil pump plate
6. Main oil pump inner rotor
7. Main oil pump outer rotor
8. Locating dowel
9. Main oil pump body
10. Locating dowel
11. Phillips screw

5

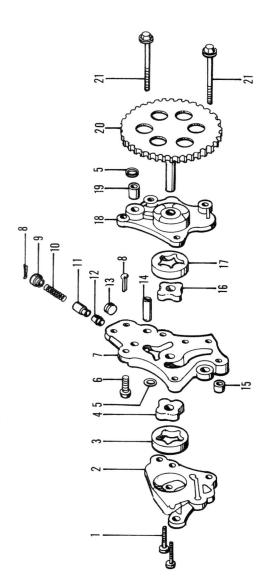

OIL PUMP (1985 XR350R)

1. Screw
2. Main oil pump body
3. Main oil pump outer rotor
4. Main oil pump inner rotor
5. O-ring
6. Bolt
7. Check valve housing
8. Cotter pin
9. Spring seat
10. Spring
11. Check valve
12. Oil seal
13. Plug
14. Locating dowel
15. Dowel pin
16. Sub-oil pump inner rotor
17. Sub-oil pump outer rotor
18. Sub-oil pump body
19. Dowel pin
20. Drive gear/drive shaft
21. Bolt

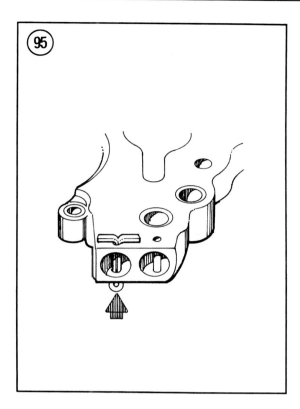

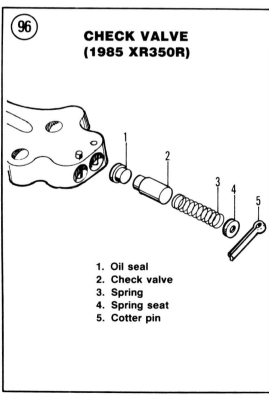

**CHECK VALVE
(1985 XR350R)**

1. Oil seal
2. Check valve
3. Spring
4. Spring seat
5. Cotter pin

**Disassembly/Assembly
(1985 XR350R)**

This oil pump has two cavities with main and sub-rotor assemblies. In the inspection steps, the clearance measurements are the same for both the main and sub-rotor assemblies. The main set of rotors is the thicker of the two and is assembled into the main oil pump body.

Refer to **Figure 94** for this procedure.

1. On the backside of the oil pump assembly, remove the Phillips head screws securing the main and sub-oil pump bodies together.

2. Separate the assembly and remove the drive gear/shaft, the pair of inner and outer rotors and the check valve housing.

3. Inspect the oil pump components as described under *Inspection (Dual Cavity Oil Pumps)* in this chapter.

4. To disassemble the check valve, perform the following:

   a. Remove the cotter pin at the end of the check valve housing (**Figure 95**). Discard the cotter pin.

   b. Remove the spring seat, spring, check valve and oil seal (**Figure 96**).

5. Clean all parts in solvent and thoroughly dry. Coat all parts with fresh engine oil prior to installation.

6. To assemble the check valve, perform the following:

   a. Install the oil seal (large end in first), check valve (small end in first), spring and spring seat.

   b. Install a new cotter pin and bend the ends over completely.

7. Make sure the dowel pin is installed in the sub-oil pump body.

8. Install the drive gear/shaft into front of the sub-oil pump body and align the flat on the pump shaft with the flat on the inner rotor. Push the pump shaft through the inner rotor.

9. Install the check valve housing onto the sub-oil pump body. Install the one Phillips head screw that secures the check valve housing to the sub-oil pump body. Tighten only finger-tight at this time.

10. Remove the inner and outer rotors from the main oil pump body.

11. Align the flat on the inner rotor with the flat on the shaft and install the inner rotor on the pump drive shaft.

5

12. Install the outer rotor onto the inner rotor and the pump shaft.

13. Install the main-oil pump body onto the outer rotor assembly and install the 2 remaining Phillips head screws. Securely tighten these screws and the one installed in Step 9.

14. Rotate the pump and make sure there is no binding.

Inspection
(Single Cavity Oil Pumps)

1. Inspect the inner and outer rotors for scratches and abrasions. Replace both parts if these are found.

2. Clean all parts in solvent and thoroughly dry. Coat all parts with fresh engine oil prior to installation.

3. Inspect the teeth on the driven gear. Replace the driven gear if the teeth are damaged or any are missing.

4. Install the outer rotor into the oil pump body.

5. Measure the clearance between the outer rotor and the oil pump body with a flat feeler gauge (**Figure 97**). If the clearance is 0.25 mm (0.010 in.) or greater, replace the worn part.

6. Install the inner rotor into the outer rotor.

7. Measure the clearance between the tip of the inner rotor and the outer rotor with a flat feeler gauge (**Figure 98**). If the clearance is 0.20 mm (0.008 in.) or greater, replace the worn part.

8. Measure the end clearance between both rotors and the oil pump body with a straightedge and a flat feeler gauge (**Figure 99**). If the clearance is 0.12 mm (0.005 in.) or greater, replace the worn part.

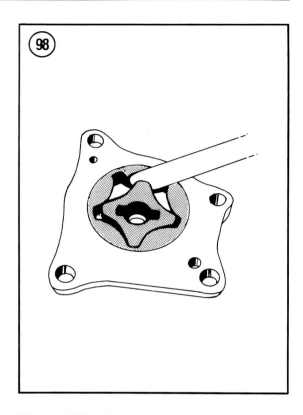

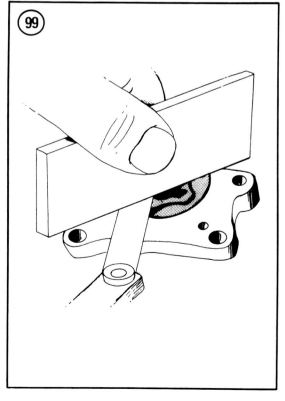

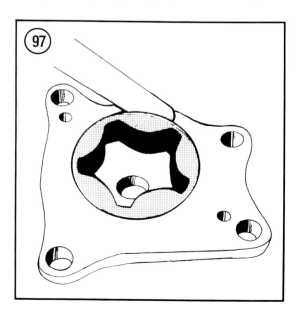

Inspection
(Dual Cavity Oil Pumps)

1. Inspect both sets of inner and outer rotors for scratches and abrasions. Replace parts of each set if evidence of these are found.
2. Clean all parts in solvent and thoroughly dry. Coat all parts with fresh engine oil prior to installation.

3. Inspect the teeth on the driven gear. Replace the driven gear if the teeth are damaged or if any are missing.
4. Install the correct outer rotor into each oil pump body.
5. Measure the clearance between the outer rotor and the oil pump body with a flat feeler gauge (**Figure 97**). If the clearance is 0.010 in. (0.25 mm) or greater, replace the worn part.
6. Install the correct inner rotor into each oil pump body and outer rotor.
7. Measure the clearance between the tip of the inner rotor and the outer rotor with a flat feeler gauge (**Figure 98**). If the clearance is 0.008 in. (0.20 mm) or greater, replace the worn part.
8. Measure the end clearance between both rotors and the oil pump body with a straightedge and a flat feeler gauge (**Figure 99**). If the clearance is 0.005 in. (0.12 mm) or greater, replace the worn part.

OIL LINES
(DRY-SUMP MODELS)

With a dry sump engine, the engine oil is stored in the bike's frame. Engine oil is transferred from the bike's frame to the engine via flexible and metal oil lines.

Removal/Inspection/Installation

1. Drain the engine oil as described in Chapter Three.
2. Hold onto the fitting, either on the frame or on the metal oil line, with a wrench and unscrew the flexible oil lines from these fittings (**Figure 100**).
3. Remove the bolts (**Figure 101**) securing the plate that secures the oil lines to the crankcase.
4. Remove the plate and the oil lines.
5. Inspect the oil lines for damage or leakage. If damaged, replace both lines.
6. Inspect the O-ring seals (**Figure 102**) on the engine end of the oil lines. If damaged or starting to deteriorate, replace the O-ring on each oil line.
7. To remove the metal oil line, perform the following:
   a. Remove the clamping band on the frame.
   b. Disconnect the fitting on the metal oil line from the bike's frame.
8. Install by reversing these removal steps, noting the following.
9. When installing the flexible oil lines, hold onto the fitting, either on the frame or the metal oil line with a wrench and screw the flexible oil lines onto these fittings. Let the flexible oil lines flow in a natural curve; make sure they are not kinked. Tighten the fittings securely.

5

OIL COOLER SYSTEM
(1986-ON XR250R)

An oil cooler system is built in on 1986-on XR250R models. A small oil cooler is located at the base of the steering head assembly and is attached to the frame.

Oil pipes carry the hot engine oil from the engine up through the oil cooler, then bring it back to the engine.

System Inspection

1. Inspect the cooling fins on the oil cooler (A, **Figure 103**) for oil leaks, damage or caked-on mud or dirt.
2. Carefully remove any dirt from the cooling fins, then blow them out with compressed air.
3. Make sure the union bolts (B, **Figure 103**) are tight. Refer to **Table 2** for torque specifications. Tighten if necessary.
4. Check the oil pipes for damage or leaks. Tighten all fittings and replace the oil pipe(s) if necessary.

Removal/Installation

Refer to **Figure 104** for this procedure.
1. Remove the fuel tank as described in Chapter Seven.
2. Remove the headlight as described in Chapter Eight.

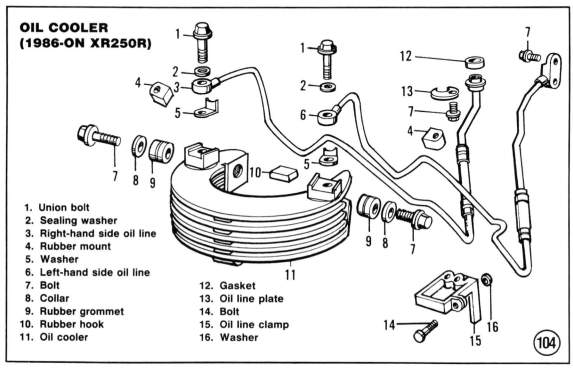

**OIL COOLER
(1986-ON XR250R)**

1. Union bolt
2. Sealing washer
3. Right-hand side oil line
4. Rubber mount
5. Washer
6. Left-hand side oil line
7. Bolt
8. Collar
9. Rubber grommet
10. Rubber hook
11. Oil cooler
12. Gasket
13. Oil line plate
14. Bolt
15. Oil line clamp
16. Washer

3. Remove the union bolts and sealing washers (B, **Figure 103**) securing the oil pipes to the oil cooler. Note that the sealing washer on top of the fitting is round and the sealing washer on the bottom of the fitting is D-shaped. They must be reinstalled in the correct locations.

4. Remove the bolts and washers securing the oil cooler to the frame and remove the oil cooler. Don't lose the rubber grommets that fit between the oil cooler and the bolt mounting bosses on the frame.

5. Remove the screw on the clamp securing both oil pipes to the frame front down tube. Open the clamp.

6. Remove the screw securing each set plate that holds each oil pipe to the crankcase cover (clutch cover).

7. Withdraw the oil pipes from the crankcase cover. Remove the O-rings at the end of each oil pipe where they attach to the crankcase cover. Discard the O-rings.

8. Remove the oil pipes from the frame.

9. Install by reversing these removal steps, noting the following.

10. Tighten the union bolts securing the oil pipes to the oil cooler to the torque specification listed in **Table 2**.

11. Install new O-ring seals where the oil pipes attach to the crankcase cover (clutch cover).

12. Tighten each oil pipe set plate screw securely.

13. Be sure to position the pulse generator electrical wire and the oil pipes into the clamp on the frame down tube. Tighten the clamp screw securely.

14. Start the engine and check for oil leaks.

CAMSHAFT CHAIN

Removal/Installation

1. Remove the cylinder head cover and camshaft as described in this chapter.

2. Remove the clutch assembly as described in Chapter Six.

3. Remove the primary drive gear as described in this chapter.

4. Let the camshaft chain drop down through the passageway in the cylinder head and cylinder and into the outer portion of the right-hand crankcase.

5. Remove the camshaft chain from the camshaft chain sprocket on the crankshaft.

6. Remove the camshaft chain sprocket from the crankshaft.

7. Inspect the camshaft chain for wear and damage. If the chain needs replacing, also check the drive sprocket and the camshaft sprocket. They may require replacement also.

8. Install by reversing these removal steps.

9. The camshaft chain drive gear can be installed onto the crankshaft in only one position. Align the wide spline groove on the camshaft drive gear (A, **Figure 105**) with the 2 matching splines on the crankshaft (B, **Figure 105**) and slide it onto the crankshaft.

10. Attach a piece of wire to the camshaft chain and pull the chain up through the passageway in the cylinder and cylinder head.

CRANKCASE AND CRANKSHAFT

Crankcase disassembly (splitting the cases) and crankshaft removal require that the engine be removed from the frame.

The crankcase is made in 2 halves of precision diecast aluminum alloy and is of the "thin-walled" type. To avoid damage, do not hammer or pry on any of the interior or exterior projected walls. These areas are easily damaged. The cases are split vertically down the centerline of the connecting rod. The cases are assembled with a gasket between the 2 halves. Dowel pins align the halves when they are bolted together.

The crankshaft assembly is made up of 2 full-circle flywheels pressed together on a hollow crankpin. The connecting rod big end bearing on the crankpin is a needle bearing assembly. The crankshaft assembly is supported in 2 ball bearings in the crankcase. Service to the crankshaft assembly is limited to removal and replacement.

The procedure which follows is presented as a complete, step-by-step, major lower end rebuild that should be followed if an engine is to be completely reconditioned. However, if you're replacing a part that you know is defective, the disassembly should be carried out only until the failed part is accessible; there is no need to disassemble the engine beyond that point so long as you know the remaining components are in good condition and that they were not affected by the failed part.

Crankcase Disassembly

1. Remove all exterior engine assemblies as described in this chapter and other related chapters:
   a. Cylinder head cover, camshaft and cylinder head.
   b. Cylinder and piston.
   c. Camshaft chain and tensioner.
   d. Clutch assembly.
   e. Kickstarter.
   f. Alternator.
   g. External shift mechanism.
   h. Oil pump.
2. Remove the engine as described in this chapter.
3. On 1984-on 200-250 cc engines, if not already removed, remove the union bolt securing the external oil line to the top of the crankcase. Don't lose the sealing washer on each side of the fitting.
4. Before removing the crankcase screws, cut a cardboard template approximately the size of the crankcase and punch holes in the template for each screw location. Place each screw in the template hole as it is removed. This will speed up assembly by eliminating the search for the correct length screw.
5A. On 200-250 cc models, remove the bolts from the left-hand crankcase side that secure the crankcase halves together (**Figure 106**). To prevent warpage, loosen them in a crisscross pattern.
5B. On 350 cc models, remove the bolts from the left-hand crankcase side that secure the crankcase halves together (**Figure 107**). To prevent warpage, loosen them in a crisscross pattern.

NOTE
*Set the engine on wooden blocks or fabricate a holding fixture of 2×4 inch wood as shown in **Figure 108**.*

6A. On 200-250 cc models, remove the single bolt from the right-hand crankcase side (**Figure 109**).
6B. On 350 cc models, remove the bolts from the right-hand crankcase side (**Figure 110**).

CAUTION
*Perform the next step directly over and close to the workbench as the crankcase halves may separate easily. **Do not** hammer on the crankcase halves or they will be damaged.*

7. Set the crankcase down on the left-hand side. Hold onto the right-hand crankcase and tap on the right-hand end of the crankshaft and transmission shafts with a plastic or soft-faced mallet until the crankshaft and crankcase separate.
8. If the crankcase and crankshaft will not separate using this method, check to make sure that all screws are removed. If you still have a problem, it may be necessary to use a puller to remove the right-hand crankcase half. If the proper tools are not available, take the crankcase assembly to a dealer and have it separated. Do not risk expensive crankcase damage with improper tools or techniques.

NOTE
Never pry between case halves. Doing so may result in oil leaks, requiring replacement of the case halves.

9. Remove the crankcase gasket. Don't lose the locating dowels if they came out of the case. They do not have to be removed from the case if they are secure.

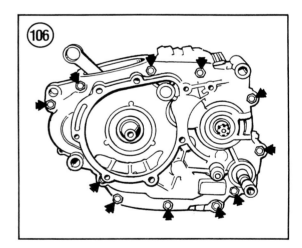

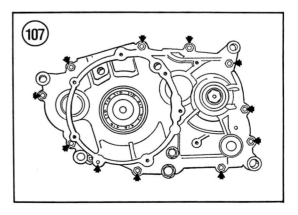

10. Lift up and carefully remove the transmission, shift drum and shift fork shaft assemblies.

CAUTION
The crankshaft is pressed into the left-hand crankcase half. Do not try to remove it or the crankcase will be damaged. If removal is necessary, take the crankcase and crankshaft to a dealer and have them press it out. The balancer will come out at the same time.

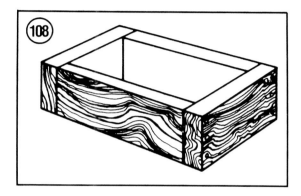

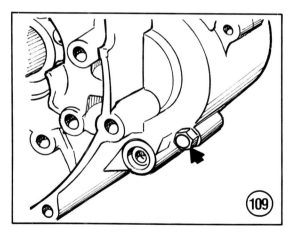

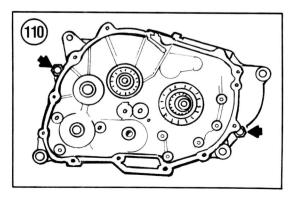

CAUTION
Do not try to drive the crankshaft out of the main bearing with a hammer or crankshaft alignment may be disturbed.

11. If the crankshaft left-hand ball bearing comes out of the crankcase with the crankshaft, it must be replaced. Have it removed and a new one installed by a dealer.
12. Inspect the crankcase halves and crankshaft as described in this chapter.

Crankcase Assembly

1. Apply assembly oil to the inner race of all bearings in both crankcase halves and to the crankshaft ball bearings.
2. If the crankshaft and balancer were removed, have them installed by a Honda dealer as special tools are required to pull the crankshaft and balancer into the left-hand crankcase half. Also the balancer and crankshaft must be properly aligned to each other for correct balance.

CAUTION
Do not attempt to drive the crankshaft into the left-hand main bearing with a hammer or mallet or the crankshaft alignment will be disturbed.

NOTE
Set the crankcase half assembly on wood blocks or the wood holding fixture shown in the disassembly procedure.

3. Install the transmission assemblies, shift shafts and shift drum in the left-hand crankcase half and lightly oil all shaft ends. Refer to Chapter Six for the correct procedure.

NOTE
Make sure the mating surfaces are clean and free of all old sealant material. Make sure you get a leak-free seal.

4. Install the locating dowels if they were removed and install a new crankcase gasket.
5. Set the right-hand crankcase half over the left-hand crankcase half on the blocks. Push it down squarely into place until it reaches the crankshaft bearing. There is usually about 1/2 inch left to go.

6. Lightly tap the case halves together with a plastic or rubber mallet until they seat.

CAUTION
Crankcase halves should fit together without force. If the crankcase halves do not fit together completely, do not attempt to pull them together with the crankcase screws. Separate the crankcase halves and investigate the cause of the interference. If the transmission shafts were disassembled, recheck to make sure that a gear is not installed backwards. Do not risk damage by trying to force the cases together.

7. After the crankcase halves are completely assembled, rotate the crankshaft and transmission shafts to make sure there is no binding. If any is present, disassemble the crankcase and correct the problem.

NOTE
*Set the engine on wooden blocks or fabricate a holding fixture of 2×4 inch wood as shown in **Figure 108**.*

8A. On 200-250 cc models, install the bolts on the left-hand crankcase side that secure the crankcase halves together (**Figure 106**). Tighten only finger-tight.
8B. On 350 cc models, install the bolts on the left-hand crankcase side that secure the crankcase halves together (**Figure 107**). Tighten only finger-tight.
9. Securely tighten the bolts in 2 stages in a crisscross pattern to the torque specification listed in **Table 2**.
10A. On 200-250 cc models, install the single bolt on the right-hand crankcase side (**Figure 109**) and tighten to the torque specification listed in **Table 2**.
10B. On 350 cc models, install the bolts on the right-hand crankcase side (**Figure 110**) and tighten to the torque specification listed in **Table 2**.
11. After the crankcase halves are completely assembled, again rotate the crankshaft and transmission shafts to make sure there is no binding. If any is present, disassemble the crankcase and correct the problem.

12. After a new crankcase gasket has been installed it must be trimmed. Carefully trim off all excess gasket material where the cylinder base gasket comes in contact with the crankcase. If it is not trimmed, the cylinder base gasket will not seal properly.
13. Feed the camshaft chain down through the top of the chain opening in the crankcase and install the chain onto the crankshaft sprocket (**Figure 111**). Make sure it is correctly engaged with the sprocket.
14. On 1984-on 200-250 cc engines, perform the following:

  a. Install the external oil line onto the top of crankcase.

  b. Be sure to install a sealing washer on each side of the fitting prior to installing the union bolt.

  c. Tighten the union bolt securely.

15. Install all exterior engine assemblies as described in this chapter and other related chapters:
   a. Cylinder head, camshaft and cylinder head cover.
   b. Cylinder and piston.
   c. Camshaft chain and tensioner assembly.
   d. Clutch assembly.
   e. Kickstarter
   f. Alternator.
   g. External shift mechanism.
   h. Oil pump.

Crankcase and Crankshaft Inspection

1. Clean both crankcase halves inside and out with cleaning solvent. Thoroughly dry with compressed air and wipe off with a clean shop cloth. Be sure to remove all traces of old gasket material from all mating surfaces.
2. Check the transmission bearings (A, **Figure 112**) for roughness, pitting, galling and play by rotating them slowly by hand. If any roughness or play can be felt in the bearing it must be replaced.
3. Carefully inspect the cases for cracks and fractures, especially in the lower areas; they are vulnerable to rock damage. Also check the areas around the stiffening ribs, around bearing bosses and threaded holes. If damage is found, have them repaired by a shop specializing in the repair of precision aluminum castings or replace them.
4. Check the crankshaft main bearings (B, **Figure 112**) for roughness, pitting, galling and play by rotating them slowly by hand. If any roughness or play can be felt in the bearing, it must be replaced. This must be entrusted to a dealer as special tools are required. The cam chain sprocket and oil pump drive gear must also be removed and realigned properly upon installation.

5. Check the balancer bearing (C, **Figure 112**) for roughness, pitting, galling and play by rotating it slowly by hand. If any roughness or play can be felt in the bearing it must be replaced.
6. Inspect the cam chain sprocket for wear or missing teeth. If the sprocket is damaged, the left-hand portion of the crankshaft or the entire crankshaft must be replaced.
7. Measure the inside diameter of the connecting rod small end with a snap gauge and an inside micrometer (**Figure 113**). Compare to dimensions given in **Table 1**. If worn to the service limit, the crankshaft assembly must be replaced.
8. Check the connecting rod big end bearing by grasping the rod in one hand and lifting up on it. With the heel of your other hand, rap sharply on the top of the rod. A sharp metallic sound, such as a click, is an indication that the bearing or crankpin or both are worn and the crankshaft assembly should be replaced.
9. Check the connecting rod-to-crankshaft side clearance with a flat feeler gauge (**Figure 114**). Compare to dimensions given in **Table 1**. If the clearance is greater than specified, the crankshaft assembly must be replaced.
10. Other inspections of the crankshaft assembly involve accurate measuring equipment and should be entrusted to a dealer or competent machine shop. The crankshaft assembly operates under severe stress and dimensional tolerances are critical. These dimensions are given in **Table 1**. If any are off by the slightest amount, severe damage or destruction of the engine may occur. The crankshaft assembly must be replaced as a unit as it cannot be serviced without the aid of a 10-12 ton (9,000-11,000 kilogram) capacity press, holding fixtures and crankshaft jig.
11. Inspect the oil seals. They should be replaced every time the crankcase is disassembled. Refer to *Bearing and Oil Seal Replacement* in this chapter.

5

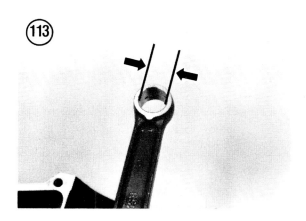

(113)

(114)

Bearing and Oil Seal Replacement

1. Pry out the oil seals with a small screwdriver, taking care not to damage the crankcase bore. If the seals are old and difficult to remove, heat the cases as described in Step 2 and use an awl to punch a small hole in the steel backing of the seal. Install a small sheet metal screw partway into the seal and pull the seal out with a pair of pliers.

> *CAUTION*
> *Do not install the screw too deep or it may contact and damage the bearing behind it.*

2. On bearings so equipped, remove the screws securing the bearing retainer plate (**Figure 115**) and remove the retainer plate.

3. The bearings are installed with a slight interference fit. The crankcase must be heated in an oven to a temperature of about 212° F (100° C). An easy way to check the proper temperature is to drop tiny drops of water on the case; if they sizzle and evaporate immediately, the temperature is correct. Heat only one case at a time.

> *CAUTION*
> *Do **not** heat the cases with a torch (propane or acetylene); never bring a flame into contact with the bearing or case. The direct heat will destroy the case hardening of the bearing and will likely cause warpage of the case.*

4. Remove the case from the oven and hold onto the 2 crankcase studs with a kitchen pot holder, heavy gloves or heavy shop cloths—*it is hot.*

5. Remove the oil seals if not already removed (see Step 1).

6. Hold the crankcase with the bearing side down and tap it squarely on a piece of soft wood. Continue to tap until the bearing(s) fall out. Repeat for the other half.

> *CAUTION*
> *Be sure to tap the crankcase squarely on the piece of wood. Avoid damaging the sealing surface of the crankcase.*

7. If the bearings are difficult to remove, they can be gently tapped out with a socket or piece of pipe the same size as the bearing outer race.

> *CAUTION*
> *If the bearings or seals are difficult to remove or install, do not take a chance on expensive damage. Have the work performed by a dealer or competent machine shop.*

8. While heating up the crankcase halves, place the new bearings in a freezer if possible. Chilling them will slightly reduce their overall diameter while the hot crankcase is slightly larger due to heat expansion. This will make bearing installation much easier.

9. While the crankcase is still hot, press each new bearing(s) into place in the crankcase by hand until it seats completely. Do not hammer it in. If the bearing will not seat, remove it and cool it again. Reheat the crankcase and install the bearing again.

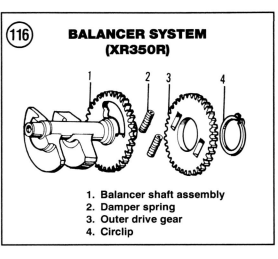

BALANCER SYSTEM (XR350R)

1. Balancer shaft assembly
2. Damper spring
3. Outer drive gear
4. Circlip

10. Oil seals are best installed with a special tool available at a dealer or motorcycle supply store. However, a proper size socket or piece of pipe can be substituted. Make sure that the bearings and seals are not cocked in the crankcase hole and that they are seated properly.

BALANCER SYSTEM

The balancer system eliminates the vibration normally associated with a large displacement single cylinder engine. The engine and the frame are designed to be compatible with the balancer system. If the balancer is eliminated it will result in an excessive amount of vibration. This vibration will result in major fatigue to engine and frame components. Do *not* eliminate this feature.

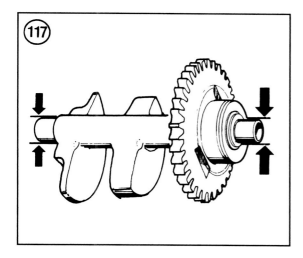

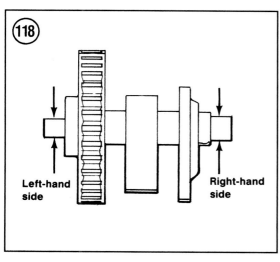

CAUTION
Any applicable manufacturer's warranty will be voided if the balancer system is modified, disconnect or removed.

The balancer system consists of a balancer weight that is gear-driven by the crankshaft assembly. The balancer construction varies with the different models.

Removal/Installation

The balancer must be removed along with the crankshaft. This procedure must be entrusted to a Honda dealer as special tools are required for removal and installation.

The balancer and crankshaft must be properly aligned to each other during installation for correct balance.

Disassembly/Inspection/Assembly
(XL250R, XL350R and 1983-1984 XR350R)

Refer to **Figure 116** for this procedure.

1. Remove the circlip and remove the outer driven gear and damper springs from the balancer shaft assembly.

2. Check for broken, chipped or missing teeth on the outer driven gear and the gear on the balancer shaft.

3. Check the damper springs. Make sure they are not broken or sagging. Replace as a set even if only one requires replacement.

4. On 350cc models, measure the outside diameter of the balancer shaft at each end (**Figure 117**) with a micrometer. Replace if worn to the service limit dimension listed in **Table 1** or less.

5. Install the damper springs into the balancer shaft assembly.

6A. On XL250R models, align the hole of both gears and install the outer drive gear.

6B. On all other models, align the index marks of \ both gears and install the outer drive gear.

7. Install the circlip with the sharp side facing out. Make sure it is completely seated in the groove in the shaft assembly.

Inspection
(1985 XR350R)

The balancer on this model cannot be disassembled as on previous models.

Measure the outside diameter of the balancer shaft at each end (**Figure 118**) with a micrometer. Replace

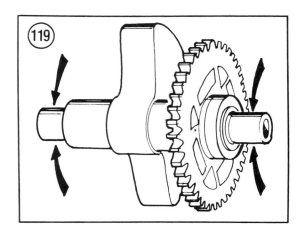

KICKSTARTER

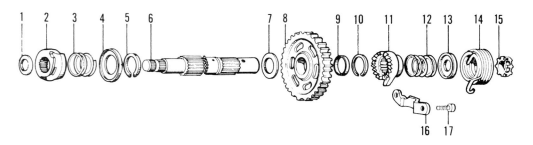

1. Thrust washer
2. Kickstarter cam
3. Spring
4. Spring seat
5. Circlip
6. Kickstarter shaft
7. Thrust washer
8. Kickstarter gear
9. Thrust washer

10. Circlip
11. Ratchet
12. Ratchet spring
13. Spring seat
14. Return spring
15. Spring collar
16. Stopper plate
17. Bolt

Inspection
(All Other Models)

The balancer on these models cannot be disassembled.

Inspect the balancer shaft at each end (**Figure 119**) for wear or damage. Honda does not provide service limit information for these models. Replace if worn or damaged in any way.

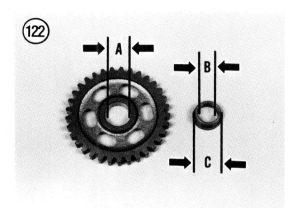

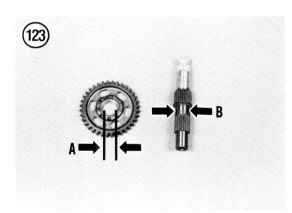

KICKSTARTER

Removal

1. Remove the clutch as described in Chapter Six.
2. Remove the kickstarter idle gear and bushing (**Figure 120**).
3. Using Vise Grip pliers, carefully unhook the return spring from the boss on the crankcase.
4. Withdraw the kickstarter assembly from the crankcase.

Disassembly/Inspection

Refer to **Figure 121** for this procedure.
1. Clean the assembled shaft in solvent and thoroughly dry with compressed air.
2. Slide off the thrust washer, kickstarter cam, spring and spring seat.
3. Remove the circlip.
4. From the other end of the shaft, remove the spring collar, return spring and spring seat.
5. Remove the kickstarter ratchet.
6. Remove the circlip and slide off the thrust washer, the kickstarter gear and the other thrust washer.
7. Measure the inside diameter of the kickstarter idle gear (A, **Figure 122**). Replace if worn to the service limit demension listed in **Table 1** or greater.
8. Measure the inside diameter (B, **Figure 122**) and outside diameter (C, **Figure 122**) of the kickstarter idle gear bushing. Replace if worn to the service limit dimension listed in **Table 1** or less or greater.
9. Measure the inside diameter of the kickstarter gear (A, **Figure 123**). Replace if worn to the service limit dimension listed in **Table 1** or greater.
10. Measure the outside diameter of the kickstarter shaft where the kickstarter gear rides (B, **Figure 123**). Replace if worn to the service limit dimension listed in **Table 1** or less.
11. Inspect the gears for chipped or missing teeth. Replace any gears as necessary.
12. Inspect the splines on the kickstarter shaft for wear or damage. Replace as necessary.
13. Make sure the ratchet gear operates properly and smoothly on its shaft.
14. Check all parts for uneven wear; replace any that are questionable.

Assembly

1. Apply assembly oil or fresh engine oil to all sliding surfaces of all parts.
2. Install the thrust washer and kickstarter gear onto the shaft (**Figure 124**).

5

3. Install the thrust washer and circlip (**Figure 125**). Make sure the circlip is correctly seated in the groove in the shaft.

4. Align the punch marks on the kickstarter shaft and the drive ratchet (**Figure 126**). Slide on the ratchet.

5. Install the ratchet spring and spring seat (**Figure 127**).

6. Install the return spring. Place the hook into the hole in the shaft (**Figure 128**).

7. Slide on the collar and push the collar into place within the return spring (**Figure 129**).

8. Onto the other end of the shaft, install the spring seat and spring (**Figure 130**).

9. Align the punch mark on the kickstarter cam and the punch mark on the shaft (**Figure 131**) and slide on the cam.

10. Install the thrust washer (**Figure 132**).

11. Prior to installing the assembled shaft into the crankcase, check **Figure 133** for correct placement of all components.

Installation

1. Install the assembled shaft into the crankcase.

2. Insert the drive ratchet pawl against the rachet guide plate on the crankcase.

3. Temporarily install the kickstarter pedal onto the shaft.

4. Hook the return spring onto the crankcase.

5. Rotate the assembly *counterclockwise* until the ratchet pawl clears the stopper plate. Then push the kickstarter shaft all the way in.

6. Remove the kickstarter pedal.

7. Install the kickstarter idle gear bushing with the shoulder side on first (**Figure 134**).

8. Install the kickstarter idle gear onto the bushing (**Figure 120**).

9. Install the clutch assembly as described in Chapter Six.

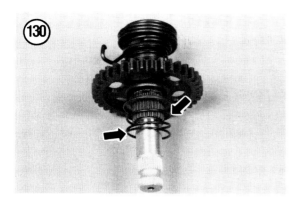

BREAK-IN PROCEDURE

If the rings were replaced, a new piston installed, the cylinder rebored or honed or major lower end work performed, the engine should be broken in just as though it were new. The performance and service life of the engine depends greatly on a careful and sensible break-in.

For the first 5-10 hours of operation, no more than one-third throttle should be used and speed should be varied as much as possible within the one-third throttle limit. Prolonged steady running at one speed, no matter how moderate, is to be avoided as well as hard acceleration.

The mono-grade oils recommended for break-in and normal use provide a better bedding pattern for rings and cylinder than do multi-grade oils. As a result, piston ring and cylinder bore life are greatly increased. During this period, oil consumption will be higher than normal. It is therefore important to frequently check and correct oil level. At no time, during the break-in or later, should the oil level be allowed to drop below the bottom line on the dipstick; if the oil level is low, the oil will become overheated resulting in insufficient lubrication and increased wear.

Service After 10 Hours Of Operation

It is essential that the oil be changed and the oil filter rotor and filter screen be cleaned after the first 10 hours of operation. In addition, it is a good idea to change the oil and clean the oil filter rotor and filter screen at the completion of 100 hours of operation to ensure that all of the particles produced during break-in are removed from the lubrication system. The small added expense may be considered a smart investment that will pay off in increased engine life.

Table 1 RFVC ENGINE SPECIFICATIONS

200-250 CC		
Item	**Specifications**	**Wear limit**
General		
Type	4-Stroke, air-cooled SOHC	
Number of cylinders	1	
Bore and stroke		
200 cc	67.0 × 56.6 mm (2.6 × 2.2 in.)	
250 cc		
1984-on XL250R,		
1984-1985 XR250R	75.0 × 56.5 mm (2.9 × 2.2 in.)	
1986-on XR250R	73.0 × 59.5 mm (2.87 × 2.34 in.)	
Displacement		
200 cc	199 cc (12.1 cu. in.)	
250 cc	249 cc (15.2 cu. in.)	
Compression ratio		
200 cc	11.0 to 1	
250 cc	10.2 to 1	
Compression pressure	199 psi (14 kg/cm^2)	
Cylinder head warpage	–	0.1 mm (0.004 in.)
Cylinder		
Bore		
200 cc	67.00-67.01 mm	67.11 mm (2.642 in.)
	(2.6381-2.6939 in.)	
250 cc		
1984-on XL250R,		
1984-1985 XR250R	75.00-75.01 mm	75.11 mm (2.957 in.)
	(2.953-2.954 in.)	
1986-on XR250R	73.00-73.01 mm	73.11 mm (2.878 in.)
	(2.8740-2.8744 in.)	
Out of round	–	0.05 mm (0.002 in.)
Piston/cylinder clearance	0.01-0.04 mm	0.1 mm (0.004 in.)
	(0.0004-0.0016 in.)	
Warpage across top	–	0.1 mm (0.004 in.)
Piston		
Diameter		
200 cc	66.960-66.985 mm	66.89 mm (2.632 in.)
	(2.6362-2.6372 in.)	
250 cc		
1984-on XL250R,		
1984-1985 XR250R	74.960-74.985 mm	74.88 mm (2.948 in.)
	(2.9512-2.9522 in.)	
1986-on XR250R	72.960-73.985 mm	72.88 mm (2.869 in.)
	(2.87424-2.8734 in.)	
Clearance in bore	0.01-0.04 mm	0.10 mm (0.004 in.)
	(0.0004-0.0016 in.)	
Piston pin bore	17.002-17.008 mm	17.07 mm (0.672 in.)
	(0.6694-0.6696 in.)	
Piston pin outer diameter	17.000-17.006 mm	16.97 mm (0.668 in.)
	(0.6693-0.6695 in.)	
Piston rings		
Number of rings		
Compression	2	
Oil control	1	

(continued)

Table 1 RFVC ENGINE SPECIFICATIONS (cont.)

200-250 CC		
Item	**Specifications**	**Wear limit**
Ring end gap		
Top and second		
1986-on XR250R	0.25-0.45 mm (0.010-0.018 in.)	0.56 mm (0.022 in.)
All other models	0.10-0.30 mm (0.004-0.012 in.)	0.41 mm (0.016 in.)
Oil (side rail)	0.2-0.7 mm (0.008-0.028 in.)	0.86 mm (0.034 in.)
Ring side clearance		
Top ring	0.015-0.045 mm (0.0006-0.0018 in.)	0.12 mm (0.006 in.)
Second ring	0.015-0.045 mm (0.0006-0.0018 in.)	0.12 mm (0.006 in.)
Crankshaft/connecting rod		
Small end inner diameter	17.016-17.034 mm (0.6699-0.6706 in.)	17.06 mm (0.672 in.)
Connecting rod big end side clearance	0.05-0.65 mm (0.002-0.0256 in.)	0.80 mm (0.031 in.)
Connecting rod big end radial clearance	0.006-0.018 mm (0.002-0.0007 in.)	0.05 mm (0.002 in.)
Camshaft		
Cam lobe height		
Intake		
200 cc	29.252 mm (1.152 in.)	29.06 mm (1.144 in.)
250 cc	29.529 mm (1.163 in.)	29.34 mm (1.155 in.)
Exhaust		
200 cc	29.196 mm (1.149 in.)	29.01 mm (1.142 in.)
250 cc	29.330 mm (1.155 in.)	29.14 mm (1.147 in.)
Runout	–	0.04 mm (0.002 in.)
Valves		
Valve stem outer diameter		
Intake	5.475-5.490 mm (0.2155-0.2161 in.)	5.46 mm (0.215 in.)
Exhaust	5.467-5.477 mm (0.2152-0.2156 in.)	5.45 mm (0.214 in.)
Valve stem runout	–	0.05 mm (0.002 in.)
Valve guide inner diameter		
Intake and exhaust	5.500-5.512 mm (0.2166-0.2170 in.)	5.53 mm (0.218 in.)
Stem to guide clearance	0.010-0.037 mm 0.0004-0.0015 in.)	0.07 mm (0.0027 in.)
Valve face width		
Intake and exhaust	1.2-1.4 mm (0.05-0.06 in.)	2.0 mm (0.08 in.)
Valves spring free length intake and exhaust		
Inner	38.83 mm (1.529 in.)	37.9 mm (1.49 in.)
Outer	38.30 mm (1.508 in.)	37.1 mm (1.46 in.
Main rocker arm assembly		
Rocker arm bore ID	11.500-11.518 mm (0.4528-0.4535 in.)	11.53 mm (0.454 in.)
Rocker arm shaft OD	11.46-11.484 mm (0.4514-0.4521 in.)	11.41 mm (0.449 in.)
Rocker arem to shaft clearance	0.016-0.052 mm (0.0006-0.0020 in.)	0.10 mm (0.004 in.)

(continued)

5

Table 1 RFVC ENGINE SPECIFICATIONS (cont.)

200-250 CC		
Item	**Specifications**	**Wear limit**
Sub-rocker arm assembly		
Rocker arm bore ID		
Intake and exhaust	7.00-7.015 mm	7.05 mm (0.278 in.)
	(0.2756-0.2762 in.)	
Rocker arm shaft OD		
Intake and exhaust	6.972-6.987 mm	6.92 mm (0.272 in.)
	(0.2745-0.2751 in.)	
Rocker arm to shaft clearance	0.013-0.043 mm	0.10 mm (0.004 in.)
	(0.0005-0.0017 in.)	
Oil pump		
Inner to outer		
rotor tip clearance	0.15 mm (0.006 in.)	0.20 mm (0.008 in.)
Outer rotor to body clearance	0.10-0.21 mm	0.25 mm (0.010 in.)
	(0.004-0.008 in.)	
Rotor to body clearance	0.02-0.09 mm	0.12 mm (0.005 in.)
	(0.0008-0.003 in.)	
Kickstarter		
Starter gear ID	22.020-22.041 mm	22.12 mm (0.871 in.)
	(0.8669-0.8679 in.)	
Starter gear shaft OD		
(where gear rides)	21.959-21.980 mm	21.91 mm (0.863 in.)
	(0.8645-0.8654 in.)	
Idle gear ID	19.010-19.034 mm	19.13 mm (0.753 in.)
	(07484-0.7494 in.)	
Idle gear bushing		
ID	15.000-15.018 mm	14.97 mm (0.589 in.)
	(0.5906-0.5913 in.)	
OD	18.959-18.980 mm	18.92 mm (0.745 in.)
	(0.7464-0.7472 in.)	

350 CC		
Item	**Specifications**	**Wear limit**
General		
Type	4-Stroke, air-cooled, SOHC	
Number of cylinders	1	
Bore and stroke	84.0 × 61.3 mm (3.31 × 2.41 in.)	
Displacement	339 cc (20.7 cu. in.)	
Compression ratio	9.5 to 1	
Compression pressure	175 psi (12.5 kg/cm^2)	
Cylinder head warpage	–	0.1 mm (0.004 in.)
Cylinder		
Bore	84.00-84.01 mm	84.11 mm (3.311 in.)
	(3.3071-3.3074 in.)	
Out of round	–	0.05 mm (0.002 in.)
Piston/cylinder clearance	0.01-0.04 mm	0.1 mm (0.004 in.)
	(0.0004-0.0016 in.)	
Warpage across top	–	0.1 mm (0.004 in.)
Piston		
Diameter	83.96-83.98 mm	83.87 mm (3.302 in.)
	(3.3055-3.3063 in.)	
Clearance in bore	0.01-0.04 mm	0.10 mm (0.004 in.)
	(0.0004-0.0016 in.)	

(continued)

Table 1 RFVC ENGINE SPECIFICATIONS (cont.)

350 CC		
Item	**Specifications**	**Wear Limit**
Piston pin bore		
1983-1984 XR350R	19.002-19.008 mm (0.7481-0.7483 in.)	19.08 mm (0.751 in.)
All other models	21.002-21.008 mm (0.8268-0.8271 in.)	21.08 mm (0.830 in.)
Piston pin outer diameter		
1983-1984 XR350R	20.994-21.000 mm (0.8265-0.8268 in.)	20.96 mm (0.825 in.)
All other models	18.994-19.000 mm (0.7478-0.7480 in.)	18.96 mm (0.746 in.)
Piston rings		
Number of rings		
Compression	2	
Oil control	1	
Ring end gap		
Top and second	0.20-0.40 mm (0.0079-0.0157 in.)	0.55 mm (0.0216 in.)
Oil (side rail)	0.2-0.9 mm (0.007-0.035 in.)	NA
Ring side clearance		
Top ring	0.030-0.065 mm (0.0012-0.0026 in.)	0.12 mm (0.006 in.)
Second ring	0.015-0.045 mm (0.0006-0.0018 in.)	0.12 mm (0.006 in.)
Oil control	NA	
Crankshaft/connecting rod		
Small end inner diameter	19.020-19.041 mm 0.7488-0.7496 in.)	19.07 mm (0.751 in).
Connecting rod big end side clearance	0.05-0.65 mm (0.002-0.0256 in.)	0.80 mm (0.031 in.)
Connecting rod big radial clearance	0.006-0.018 mm (0.0002-0.0007 in.)	0.05 mm (0.002 in.)
Camshaft		
Cam lobe height		
Intake	30.569 mm (1.2035 in.)	30.37 mm (1.195 in.)
Exhaust	30.575 mm (1.2037 in.)	30.38 mm (1.196 in.)
Cam journal OD both ends	19.972-19.993 mm (0.7863-0.7871 in.)	19.92 mm (0.784 in.)
Camshaft bearing ID	19.99-20.00 mm 0.7870-0.7874 in.)	20.049 mm (.0789 in.)
Valves		
Valve stem outer diameter		
Intake	5.475-5.490 mm (0.2155-0.2161 in.)	5.46 mm (0.215 in.)
Exhaust	5.467-5.477 mm (0.2152-0.2156 in.)	5.45 mm (0.214 in.)
Valve stem runout	-	0.05 mm (0.002 in.)
Valve guide inner diameter		
Intake and exhaust	5.500-5.512 mm (0.2166-0.2170 in.)	5.53 mm (0.218 in.)
Stem to guide clearance	0.010-0.047 mm (0.0004-0.0019 in.)	0.06 mm (0.0024 in.)

(continued)

Table 1 RFVC ENGINE SPECIFICATIONS (cont.)

350 CC		
Item	Specifications	Wear limit
Valve face width		
Intake and exhaust	1.2-1.4 mm (0.048-0.055 in.)	2.0 mm (0.08 in.)
Valve springs free length		
intake and exhaust		
1985 XR350R		
Inner	37.2 mm (1.46 in.)	36.3 mm (1.43 in.)
Outer	42.9 mm(1.69 in.)	42.0 mm (1.65 in.)
All other models		
Inner	35.7 mm (1.4055 in.)	34.6 mm (1.362 in.)
Outer	41.1 mm (1.6181 in.)	40.16 mm (1.581 in.)
Main rocker arm assembly		
Rocker arm bore ID	11.482-11.500 mm (0.4520-0.4527 in.)	10.53 mm (0.415 in.)
Rocker arm shaft OD	11.466-11.484 mm (0.4514-0.4521 in.)	11.41 mm (0.449 in.)
Sub-rocker arm assembly		
Rocker arm bore ID		
Intake	8.00-8.015 mm (0.3150-0.3155 in.)	8.05 mm (0.317 in.)
Exhaust	7.00-7.015 mm (0.2756-0.2761 in.)	7.05 mm (0.277 in.)
Rocker arm shaft OD		
Intake	7.969-7.972 mm (0.3137-0.3139 in.)	7.916 mm (0.312 in.)
Exhaust	6.969-6.972 mm (0.2744-0.2745 in.)	6.916 mm (0.272 in.)
Rocker arm to shaft clearance		
both assemblies	0.016-0.052 mm (0.0006-0.0020 in.)	0.14 mm (0.006 in.)
Oil pump		
Inner to outer rotor tip clearance	0.15 mm (0.006 in.)	0.20 mm (0.008 in.)
Outer rotor to body clearance	0.15-0.21 mm (0.006-0.008 in.)	0.25 mm (0.010 in.)
Rotor to body clearance	0.02-0.08 mm (0.0008-0.003 in.)	0.12 mm (0.005 in.)
Counter balancer system		
Shaft OD each end		
1983-1984 XR350R	11.972-11.99 mm (0.4713-0.4720 in.)	11.95 mm (0.471 in.)
System shaft OD (all other models)		
Right-hand end	14.972-14.990 mm (0.5894-0.5902 in.)	14.95 (0.589 in.)
Left-hand end	11.983-11.994 mm (0.4718-0.4722 in.)	11.95 mm (0.471 in.)
Kickstarter		
Gear ID	22.020-22.041 mm (0.8669-0.8679 in.)	22.12 mm (0.871 in.)
Shaft OD (where gear rides)	21.959-21.980 mm (0.8645-0.8653 in.)	21.91 mm (0.863 in.)

*NA: Honda does not provide service for all items or all models. All available information is included in this table. NA = not available.

Table 2 200-350 CC RFVC ENGINE TORQUE SPECIFICATIONS

Item	N•m	ft.-lb.
Engine mounting bolts and nuts		
8 mm bolts and nuts	30-37	22-27
8 mm bolt (1986-on CR250R)	24-30	17-22
10 mm bolt (1986-on XR250R)	35-45	25-33
Engine mounting bolts 10 mm		
Upper rear through bolt,		
lower front through bolt	55-65	40-48
Valve adjuster locknuts		
200-250 cc	17-23	12-17
350 cc	15-18	11-13
Cylinder head cover bolts		
200-250 cc		
6 mm	8-12	6-9
8 mm	26-30	19-22
350 cc		
6 mm		
Normal sized head	10-14	7-10
Small size head	8-12	6-9
8 mm	24-30	17-22
Cylinder head bolts	47-53	34-38
Cylinder head nuts	37-43	27-31
Cylinder bolts		
250 cc		
6 mm	10-14	7-10
10 mm	37-43	27-31
350 cc		
6 mm	10-14	7-10
10 mm	47-53	34-38
Cam sprocket bolts	17-23	12-17
Camshaft chain tensioner bolt		
(1984-on 200-350 cc)	10-14	7-10
Main rocker arm shafts	25-30	18-22
Oil pipe union bolts	10-14	7-10
Sub-rocker arm shafts		
Intake	25-30	18-22
Exhaust	20-25	15-18
Primary drive gear locknut		
200-250 cc	50-60	36-43
350 cc	50-60	36-43
Crankcase bolts	8-12	6-9
Right- and left-hand crankcase		
cover bolts	8-12	6-9
Alternator cover bolts	8-12	6-9
Alternator rotor bolt	100-200	78-87
Drive sprocket bolts	8-12	6-9

5

CHAPTER SIX

CLUTCH AND TRANSMISSION

The clutch is a wet multi-plate type which operates immersed in the engine oil. It is mounted on the right-hand end of the transmission main shaft. The inner clutch hub is splined to the main shaft and the outer housing can rotate freely on the main shaft. The outer housing is geared to the crankshaft.

The clutch release mechanism is mounted within the right-hand crankcase cover and is operated by the clutch cable and hand lever mounted on the handlebar.

Clutch specifications are listed in **Table 1** at the end of this chapter. **Tables 1-7** are located at the end of this chapter.

CLUTCH

The clutch assembly used on these models is basically the same but minor differences exist among the various models. Where differences occur they are identified.

Refer to the following illustrations for this procedure:

   a. **Figure 1**: 1978-1980 XL250S and XR250.
   b. **Figure 2**: 1981 XL250S, XL250R and 1981-1982 XR250R.

Removal/Disassembly

The clutch can be removed with the engine in the frame.

1. Remove the seat and side covers.

> *NOTE*
> *On XL250S models, reinstall the seat strap bolts as they also hold the upper portion of the shock absorbers to the frame (**Figure 3**). Remove and install one bolt at a time.*

2. Remove the bolts securing the skid plate and remove the skid plate.
3. Drain the engine oil as described in Chapter Three.
4. Place wooden block(s) under the engine to support it freely.
5. On XL series models, disconnect the batter negative lead or disconnect the main fuse (**Figure 4**).
6. Remove the fuel tank as described in Chapter Seven.
7. Remove the bolt securing the kickstarter pedal and remove the kickstarter pedal.
8. Disconnect the rear brake switch return spring and cable, the front right-hand foot peg and the rear brake pedal.

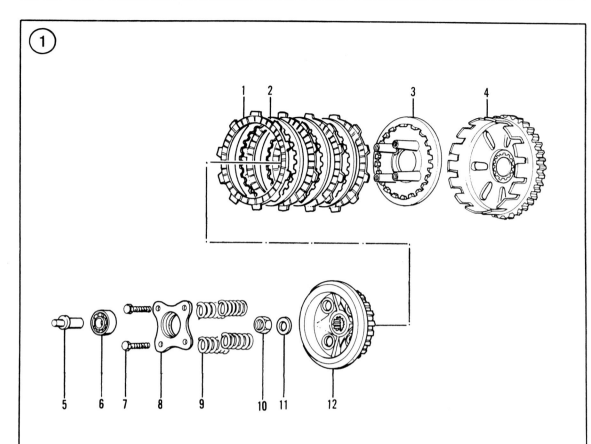

**CLUTCH ASSEMBLY
(1978-1980 XL250S, XR250)**

1. Friction disc (4)
2. Clutch plate (3)
3. Pressure plate
4. Clutch outer housing
5. Lifter rod
6. Bearing
7. Bolts
8. Lifter plate
9. Clutch springs
10. Clutch nut
11. Lockwasher
12. Clutch center

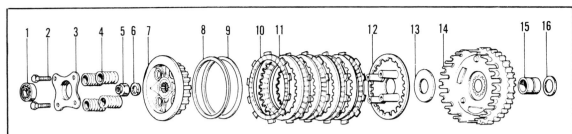

CLUTCH ASSEMBLY (1981 XL250S, XL250R, 1981-1982 XR250R)

1. Bearing
2. Clutch bolts
3. Lifter plate
4. Clutch springs
5. Clutch nut
6. Locknut
7. Clutch center
8. Damper seat
9. Damper spring
10. Clutch friction disc
11. Clutch plate
12. Pressure plate
13. Thrust washer
14. Clutch outer housing
15. Clutch outer housing guide
16. Thrust collar

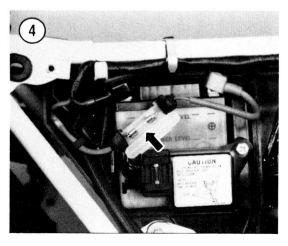

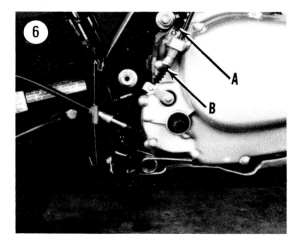

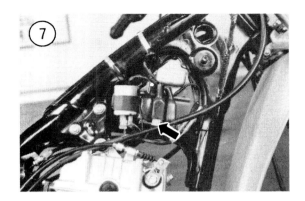

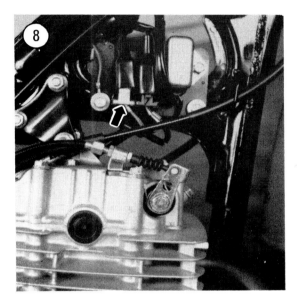

9. Slacken the clutch cable at the hand lever (**Figure 5**).

10. Disconnect the clutch cable from the clutch release arm (A, **Figure 6**).

11. Disconnect the starter decompressor cable at the crankcase cover (B, **Figure 6**).

12. Disconnect the pulse generator 2-pin electrical connector. Refer to **Figure 7** or **Figure 8**.

13. Remove the bolts (**Figure 9**) securing the clutch cover and remove the clutch cover and gasket. Don't lose the locating dowels.

14. Remove the lifter rod and bearing (**Figure 10**).

15. Using a crisscross pattern, remove the clutch bolts (**Figure 11**) securing the clutch lifter plate and remove the lifter plate.

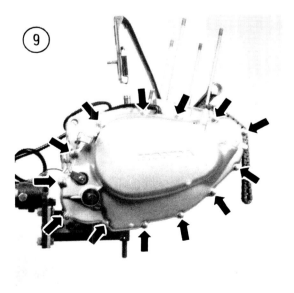

16. Remove the clutch springs (**Figure 12**).

17A. To loosen the clutch nut with a special tool, perform the following:

    a. Hold onto the clutch center to prevent it from turning. Use Honda special tool (Clutch Center Holder—part No. 07923-4280000) or equivalent (**Figure 13**).

    b. Loosen the clutch nut. Remove the nut and lockwasher.

17B. To remove the clutch nut without special tool, perform the following:

    a. Hold onto the clutch center to prevent it from turning.

    b. Use an impact driver and loosen the clutch nut. Remove the nut and lockwasher.

18. Slide the entire clutch assembly (clutch center, clutch plates, friction discs, pressure plate and clutch outer housing) off of the transmission main shaft.

19. On models so equipped, remove the clutch outer housing guide and thrust washer.

20. Separate the components removed in Step 18.

21. Inspect all components as described in this chapter.

Assembly/Installation

> *NOTE*
> *If new friction discs and clutch plates are being installed, apply new engine oil to all surfaces to avoid having the clutch lock up when used for the first time.*

> *NOTE*
> *The number of friction plates and clutch discs varies among the different models.*

1A. On models equipped with a judder spring, perform the following:

    a. Place the clutch center on your workbench with the splines facing up and perform the following:

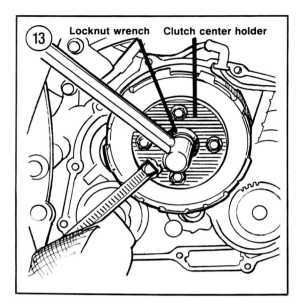

13   Locknut wrench   Clutch center holder

14

12

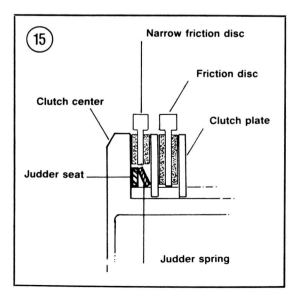

15   Narrow friction disc

Friction disc

Clutch center

Clutch plate

Judder seat

Judder spring

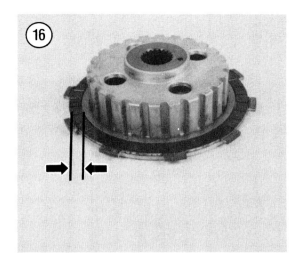

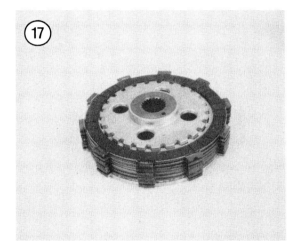

b. Install the flat judder seat (**Figure 14**) onto the clutch center.

c. Install the judder spring on the clutch center with the dished side facing up as shown in **Figure 15**.

d. Install the only *narrow* friction disc (**Figure 16**) onto the clutch center with the judder seat and spring inboard of it. Refer to **Figure 15**.

e. Onto the narrow friction disc, install a clutch plate and then a friction disc.

f. Continue to install a clutch plate and then a friction disc, alternating them until all are installed. The last item installed is a friction disc (**Figure 17**).

1B. On all other models, perform the following:

a. Place the clutch center on your workbench with the splines facing up and perform the following:

b. Onto the clutch center, install first a friction disc then a clutch plate.

c. Continue to install the friction discs and clutch plates, alternating them until all are installed. The last item installed is a friction disc (**Figure 17**).

2. Onto this assembly, install the pressure plate.

3. On models so equipped, install the thrust washer and clutch outer housing guide (**Figure 18**) onto the transmission main shaft.

4. Install the clutch outer housing onto the transmission shaft (**Figure 19**). Make sure the gears mesh properly with the drive gear on the crankshaft.

NOTE
In the following step, do not tighten the bolts too tight as some play is needed for final alignment when the friction plate tabs slide into the clutch outer housing.

5. Install a couple of clutch springs, washers and bolts (A, **Figure 20**) to hold the assembly made up in Step 1 and Step 2 together. This will aid in installation of these parts. Slide this assembly (B, **Figure 20**) into the clutch outer housing.

6. Remove the bolts, washers and springs.

7. Install the lockwasher with the "OUTSIDE" mark facing toward the outside (**Figure 21**).

8. Use the same tool set-up used in *Removal/Disassembly*, Step 17. Install the clutch nut and tighten to the torque specification listed in **Table 2**.

9. Install the clutch springs and the lifter plate.

10. Install the clutch bolts. Tighten the bolts securely in a crisscross pattern in 2-3 stages.

11. Install the ball bearing and lifter rod (A, **Figure 22**).

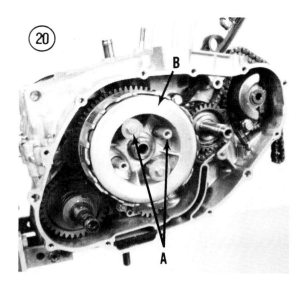

> *NOTE*
> *Make sure the oil screen (B, **Figure 22**) is still in place. This is a good time to remove and clean the screen as described in Chapter Three.*

12. Install a new clutch cover gasket and locating dowels onto the crankcase.

13. Hold the decompressor cam follower in the down position and install the clutch cover. Tighten the bolts to the torque specification listed in **Table 2**.

> *CAUTION*
> *After the clutch cover is installed, check the operation of the clutch and starter decompressor levers. They should operate without binding; if they bind, remove the cover and correct the problem.*

14. Connect the clutch and starter decompressor cables (**Figure 6**).

15. Install the rear brake lever, front foot pegs and kickstarter lever.

> *NOTE*
> *On XR250 models, make sure all rubber spacers (**Figure 23**) are installed onto the skid plate prior to installation.*

16. Install the skid plate and tighten the bolt securely.

17. Install the side covers and the seat.

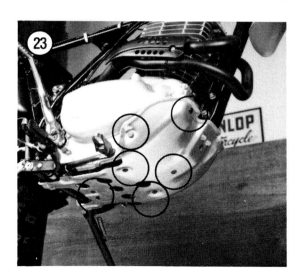

18. Refill the engine with the recommended type and quantity of engine oil as described in Chapter Three.

19. Adjust the clutch, starter decompressor and rear brake as described in Chapter Three.

CLUTCH
(XR200R, 1984-ON XR250R, XL350R, XR350R)

Removal/Disassembly

Refer to **Figure 24** for 200 and 250 cc models or **Figure 25** for 350 cc models for this procedure.

The clutch assembly can be removed with the engine in the frame.

1. Remove the seat and side covers.

2. Remove the exhaust pipe as described in Chapter Seven.

6

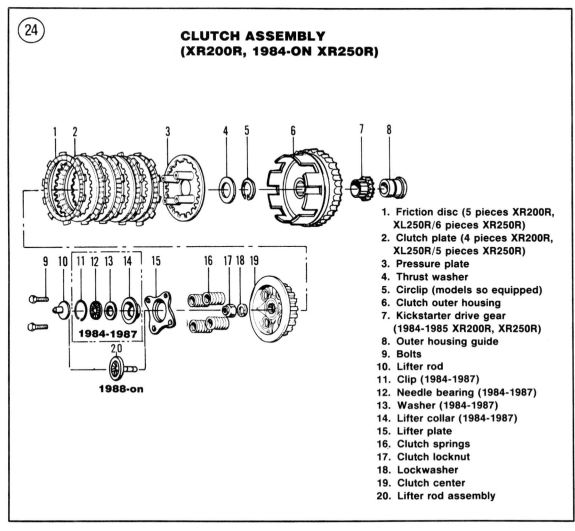

CLUTCH ASSEMBLY
(XR200R, 1984-ON XR250R)

1. Friction disc (5 pieces XR200R, XL250R/6 pieces XR250R)
2. Clutch plate (4 pieces XR200R, XL250R/5 pieces XR250R)
3. Pressure plate
4. Thrust washer
5. Circlip (models so equipped)
6. Clutch outer housing
7. Kickstarter drive gear (1984-1985 XR200R, XR250R)
8. Outer housing guide
9. Bolts
10. Lifter rod
11. Clip (1984-1987)
12. Needle bearing (1984-1987)
13. Washer (1984-1987)
14. Lifter collar (1984-1987)
15. Lifter plate
16. Clutch springs
17. Clutch locknut
18. Lockwasher
19. Clutch center
20. Lifter rod assembly

1984-1987

1988-on

CLUTCH ASSEMBLY
(350 CC MODELS)

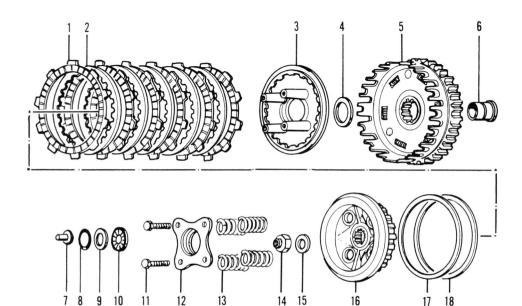

1. Friction disc
2. Clutch plate
3. Pressure plate
4. Thrust washer
5. Clutch outer housing
6. Outer housing guide
7. Lifter rod
8. Clip
9. Washer

10. Needle bearing
11. Bolts
12. Lifter collar
13. Clutch springs
14. Clutch locknut
15. Lockwasher
16. Clutch center
17. Judder seat—Models XL350R only
18. Judder spring—Models XL350R only

3. Drain the engine oil as described in Chapter Three.

4. Remove the bolt securing the kickstarter pedal and remove the kickstarter pedal.

5. Disconnect the clutch cable from the clutch release arm (**Figure 26**).

6. Remove the bolts securing the right-hand foot peg assembly and remove the assembly.

7. Loosen the brake adjust nut on the end of the brake rod (**Figure 27**).

8. Disconnect the brake pedal return spring from the brake pedal.

9. Disconnect the brake light switch spring from the brake pedal.

10. Remove the rear brake pedal pinch bolt on the pivot shaft.

11. Remove the brake pedal pivot shaft. Move the brake pedal assembly back and out of the way. It is not necessary to remove the assembly from the frame.

12. On 1986-on XR250R models, perform the following:

    a. Remove the oil pipe union bolt from the top of the clutch cover. Don't lose the sealing washers on each side of the oil pipe fitting.

    b. Disconnect the oil cooler lines from the clutch cover as described under *Oil Cooler System (1986-on XR250R)* in Chapter Five.

13. Disconnect the starter decompressor cable (A, **Figure 28**) from the lever on the crankcase cover.

14. Remove the bolts and nuts securing the clutch cover (B, **Figure 28**) and remove the clutch cover and gasket. Don't lose the locating dowels.

15. Remove the bolts (A, **Figure 29**) securing the clutch pressure plate in a crisscross pattern and remove the pressure plate (B, **Figure 29**) along with the thrust bearing (C, **Figure 29**).

16. Remove the clutch springs.

17A. To loosen the clutch nut with a special tool, perform the following:

    a. Hold onto the clutch center to prevent it from turning. Use Honda special tool (Clutch Center Holder—part No. 07923-KE10001) or equivalent (**Figure 13**).

6

b. Loosen the clutch nut. Remove the nut and lockwasher.

c. Use an impact driver to loosen the clutch nut. Remove the nut and lockwasher.

18. Slide the entire clutch assembly (clutch center, clutch plates, friction discs, pressure plate and clutch outer housing) off of the transmission main shaft.

19. On models so equipped, remove the circlip securing the clutch outer housing to the transmission shaft.

20A. On 250 cc models, withdraw the clutch outer housing, kickstarter driven gear and guide as an assembly.

20B. On 350 cc models, withdraw the clutch outer housing and guide as an assembly.

21. Separate the components removed in Step 18.

22. Inspect all components as described in this chapter.

Assembly/Installation

Refer to **Figure 24** for 200 and 250 cc models or **Figure 25** for 350 cc models for this procedure.

> *NOTE*
> *If new friction discs and clutch plates are being installed, apply new engine oil to all surfaces to avoid having the clutch lock up when used for the first time.*

1. Position the clutch outer housing guide with the flange side on first and slide it onto the transmission shaft (**Figure 30**).

2. If removed, install the kickstarter driven gear into the backside of the clutch outer housing.

3A. On 250 cc models, install the clutch outer housing and kickstarter driven gear assembly onto the clutch outer housing guide. Slightly rotate the kickstarter idle gear to align the gear teeth of both kickstarter gears.

3B. On 350 cc models, install the clutch outer housing onto the clutch outer housing guide.

4. On models so equipped, install the circlip onto the transmission shaft. Make sure the circlip is correctly seated in the groove in the transmission shaft.

5. Slide on the thrust washer.

6. Place the clutch center on your workbench with the splines facing up and perform the following:

a. Onto the clutch center, install first a friction disc then a clutch plate.

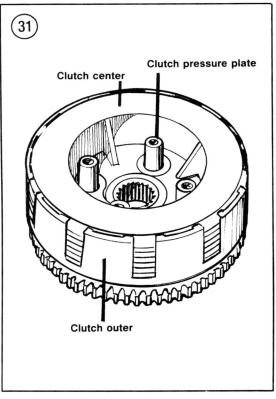

Clutch center
Clutch pressure plate
Clutch outer

b. Continue to install the friction discs and clutch plates, alternating them until all are installed. The last item installed is a friction disc (**Figure 17**).

c. Onto this assembly, install the pressure plate.

7. Install the parts assembled in Step 6 into the clutch outer housing (**Figure 31**).

8. Install the lockwasher with the "OUTSIDE" mark facing toward the outside (**Figure 21**).

9. Use the same tool set-up used in *Removal* Step 17A or Step 17B. Install the clutch nut (**Figure 32**) and tighten to the torque specification listed in **Table 2**.

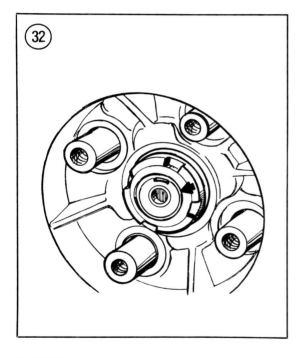

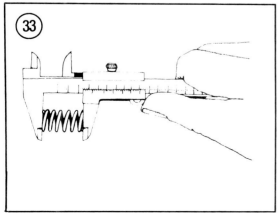

10. Install the clutch springs and the lifter plate and thrust bearing.

11. Install the clutch bolts. Tighten the bolts securely in a crisscross pattern in 2-3 stages.

12. Install a new clutch cover gasket and locating dowels onto the crankcase. Make sure the O-ring seal is in place on the oil pump.

13. Hold the starter decompressor cam follower in the down position and install the clutch cover. Tighten all bolts and nuts to the torque specification listed in **Table 2**.

14. Install the kickstarter lever and bolt. Tighten the bolt to the torque specifications listed in **Table 2**.

15. Connect the starter decompressor cable onto the lever on the crankcase cover.

16. On 1986-on XR250R models, perform the following:

a. Install a new sealing washer on each side of the oil pipe fitting and install the union bolt to the top of the clutch cover. Tighten the union bolt securely.

b. Connect the oil cooler lines onto the clutch cover as described under *Oil Cooler System (1986-on XR250R)* in Chapter Five.

17. Move the brake pedal assembly back into position and install the brake pedal pivot shaft.

18. Install the rear brake pedal pinch bolt onto the pivot shaft and tighten securely.

19. Connect the brake light switch spring and the brake pedal return spring onto the brake pedal.

20. Install the right-hand foot peg assembly and tighten the bolts to the torque specification listed in **Table 2**.

21. Connect the clutch cable onto the clutch release arm.

22. Refill the engine with the recommended type and quantity of engine oil as described in Chapter Three.

23. Install the exhaust pipe as described in Chapter Seven.

24. Install the seat and side covers.

25. Adjust the clutch and rear brake as described in Chapter Three.

Inspection (All Models)

Refer to **Table 1** for clutch specifications.

1. Clean all clutch parts in petroleum-based solvent such as kerosene and thoroughly dry with compressed air.

2. Measure the free length of each clutch spring as shown in **Figure 33**. Compare to the specifications listed in **Table 1**. Replace any springs that have sagged to the service limit or less.

3. Measure the thickness of each friction disc at several places around the disc as shown in **Figure 34**. Compare to the specifications listed in **Table 1**. Replace any disc that is worn to the service limit or less.

4. Check the clutch plates for warpage on a surface plate such as a piece of plate glass (**Figure 35**). Compare to the specifications listed in **Table 1**. Replace any plate that is warped to the service limit or more.

> *NOTE*
> *If any of the friction discs, clutch plates or clutch springs require replacement, you should consider replacing all of them as a set to retain maximum clutch performance.*

5. Inspect the slots in the clutch outer housing (**Figure 36**) for cracks, nicks or galling where they come in contact with the friction disc tabs. If any severe damage is evident, the housing must be replaced.

6. Inspect the gear teeth (**Figure 37**) on the outer housing for damage. Remove any small nicks with an oilstone. If damage is severe, the housing must be replaced. Also check the teeth on the driven gear of the crankshaft; if damaged, the driven gear may also need replacing.

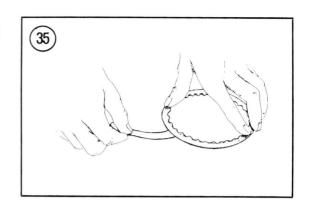

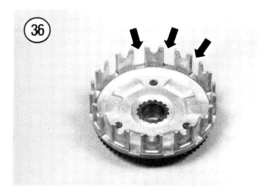

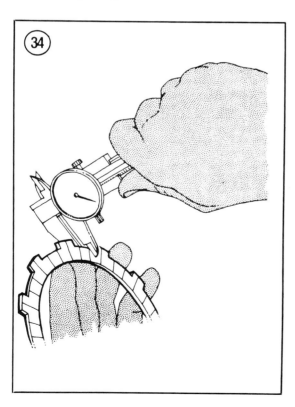

7. On 350 cc models, perform the following:

 a. Inspect the damper springs (**Figure 38**). If they are sagged or broken the housing must be replaced.

 b. Inspect the inner splines (A, **Figure 39**) of the clutch outer housing and the outer splines of the kickstarter driven gear (B, **Figure 39**). Replace any damaged parts.

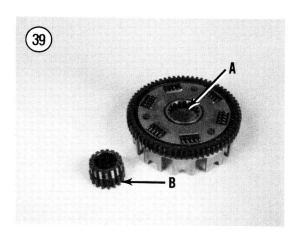

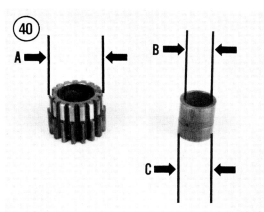

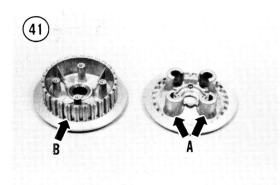

8A. On 1984-1985 XR200R and XR250R models, measure the outside diameter of the kickstarter for drive gear (A, **Figure 40**). Compare to dimensions listed in **Table 1**.

8B. On all other models, measure the inside diameter (B, **Figure 40**) and the outside diameter (C, **Figure 40**) of the outer guide. Compare to the service limit dimensions listed in **Table 1**. Replace any worn part.

9. Inspect the grooves and studs in the pressure plate (A, **Figure 41**). If either shows signs of wear or galling, the pressure plate should be replaced.

10. Inspect the inner splines and outer grooves in the clutch center (B, **Figure 41**). If damaged the clutch center should be replaced.

11. Inspect the clutch lifter rod for bending. Roll it on a surface plate or piece of plate glass. Honda does not provide service information for this component, but if the rod is bent or deformed in any way it must be replaced. Otherwise it may hang up in the channel within the transmission shaft, causing erratic clutch operation.

12A. On 1988-on XR250R models, inspect the bearing in the lifter rod assembly. Make sure the bearing rotates smoothly with no signs of wear or damage. If the bearing is faulty, replace the lifter rod assembly.

12B. On all other models, check the bearing in the lifter guide (**Figure 42**). Make sure the bearing rotates smoothly with no signs of wear or damage. If necessary, remove the circlip and replace the bearing.

6

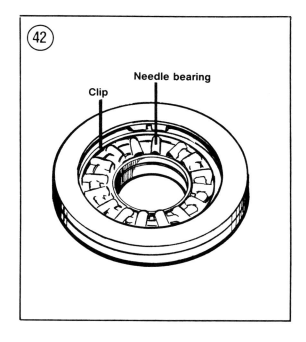

13. Check the movement of the clutch lifter arm assembly in the crankcase cover. If the arm binds or the return spring is weak or broken, it must be replaced. To remove the mechanism perform the following:

  a. Remove the clutch lifter from the lifter arm.
  b. Remove the spring (A, **Figure 43**) and withdraw the lifter arm (B, **Figure 43**) from the cover.
  c. Remove the spring.
  d. Inspect the O-ring seal on the clutch lifter mechanism. Replace if necessary.
  e. Check that the return spring is not bent or broken. Replace if necessary.
  f. Apply multipurpose grease to the clutch lifter mechanism and install it into the crankcase cover. Secure the mechanism with the spring pin.

CLUTCH CABLE REPLACEMENT

In time the clutch cable will stretch to the point where it is no longer useful and will have to be replaced.

1. Remove the right- and left-hand side covers and seat.

> *NOTE*
> *On XL250S models, reinstall the seat strap bolts as they also hold the upper portion of the shock to the frame. Remove and reinstall one bolt at a time.*

2. Remove the fuel tank as described in Chapter Six.
3. On XL series models, disconnect the battery negative lead or disconnect the main fuse (**Figure 4**).
4. Remove the fuel tank as described in Chapter Seven.
5. Loosen the locknut (A, **Figure 44**) and adjusting barrel (B, **Figure 44**) at the clutch hand lever and remove the cable from the lever.
6A. On RFVC engine models, perform the following:

  a. Remove the clutch cable from the retainer on top of the crankcase.
  b. Slip the cable end out of the release arm (**Figure 26**).
  c. Pull the clutch cable from the retaining clip (A, **Figure 45**) on the cylinder head cover.
  d. Pull the cable out from behind the headlight/steering head area (B, **Figure 45**).

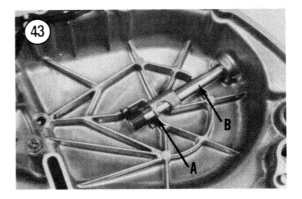

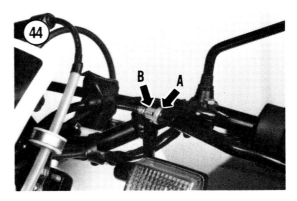

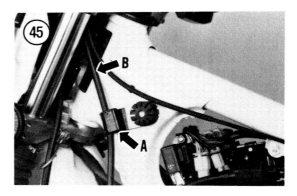

6B. On all other models, perform the following:
   a. Loosen the locknut and adjusting nut (A, **Figure 46**) at the frame lower bracket.
   b. Slip the cable end out of the clutch activating arm (B, **Figure 46**).
   c. Pull the clutch cable from the retaining clip (A, **Figure 47**) on the cylinder head cover.
   d. Pull the cable out from behind the headlight/steering head area and out of the retaining loop on the frame (B, **Figure 47**).

NOTE
Prior to removing the cable, make a drawing of the cable routing through the frame. It is very easy to forget how it was, once it has been removed. Replace the cable exactly as it was, avoiding any sharp turns.

7. Remove the cable and replace it with a new cable.
8. Install by reversing these removal steps, noting the following.
9. Adjust the clutch as described in Chapter Three.

EXTERNAL SHIFT MECHANISM (ALL RFVC ENGINE MODELS)

The shifting mechanism is located on the same side of the crankcase as the clutch assembly. To remove the internal shift mechanism (shift levers, shift drum and shift forks), it is necessary to remove the engine and split the crankcase. This procedure is covered in this chapter.

Removal

1. Remove the clutch assembly as described in this chapter.
2. Remove the kickstarter assembly as described in Chapter Five.
3. Remove the bolts securing the oil line to the oil pump and the crankcase.
4. Remove the bolt (**Figure 48**) securing the shift drum stopper plate and remove the stopper plate.
5. Remove the bolt (**Figure 49**) securing the neutral stopper arm and remove the arm.

Inspection

1. Inspect the ramps of the shift drum stopper plate (A, **Figure 50**). They must be smooth and free from burrs or wear. Replace as necessary.
2. Inspect the roller on the neutral stopper arm (B, **Figure 50**). It must rotate smoothly with no signs of wear or binding. Replace as necessary.

Installation

1. Install the neutral stopper arm, spring and bolt (**Figure 48**) onto the crankcase. Tighten the bolt securely.

2. Hold the neutral stopper arm back and out of the way with a screwdriver (A, **Figure 51**).

3. Align the bolt hole in the backside of the shift drum stopper plate with the dowel pin on the shift drum (**Figure 52**). Install the shift drum stopper plate and bolt (B, **Figure 51**). Tighten the bolt securely.

4. Remove the screwdriver and index the stopper arm onto the shift drum stopper plate.

5. Install the oil line from the oil pump to the crankcase. Install and tighten the bolts securely.

6. Install the kickstarter as described in Chapter Five.

7. Install the clutch assembly as described in this chapter.

8. Refill the engine with the recommended type and quantity of engine oil as described in Chapter Three.

9. Adjust the clutch as described in Chapter Three.

EXTERNAL SHIFT MECHANISM (ALL EXCEPT RFVC ENGINE MODELS)

The shifting mechanism is located under the left-hand crankcase cover. Removal and installation can be accomplished with the engine in the frame. This procedure is shown with the engine removed for clarity.

To remove the internal shift mechanism (shift levers, shift drum and shift forks), it is necessary to remove the engine and split the crankcase. This procedure is covered in this chapter.

Removal/Installation

1. Remove the alternator as described in this chapter.

> *CAUTION*
> *On XL models, shift the transmission into **1st gear**. This will align the neutral indicator rotor with the open area of the shift plate. Do **not** damage this rotor during removal and installation as it will have to be replaced.*

2. Remove the thrust washer (A, **Figure 53**) and carefully remove the gearshift spindle assembly (B, **Figure 53**) and inner thrust washer.

3. Unhook the shift pawl spring (A, **Figure 54**) and remove the bolt (B, **Figure 54**) securing the shift pawl. Remove the shift pawl.

4. If necessary, remove the stopper plate bolt (C, **Figure 54**) and remove the neutral indicator rotor.

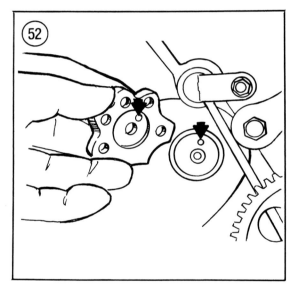

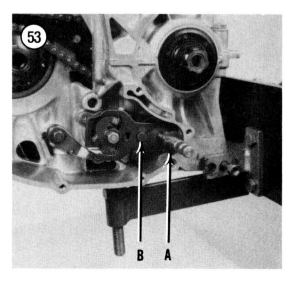

5. Remove the bolt (**Figure 48**) securing the neutral stopper arm and remove the arm.

6. If spindle disassembly is necessary, remove the circlips (**Figure 55**) at each end and remove all components. Assemble in the order shown in **Figure 55**.

7. Install by reversing these removal steps, noting the following.

8. Make sure the transmission is in 1st gear when installing the gearshift spindle.

9. Make sure the inner thrust washer is installed on the spindle assembly prior to installation.

TRANSMISSIONS

Many different transmissions are used among the various models. Some have only small variations and all variations are noted in each procedure. Be sure to use the correct procedure for your specific bike—including model year.

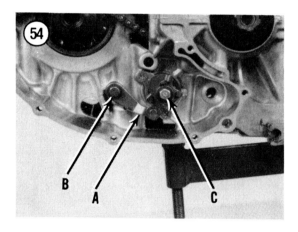

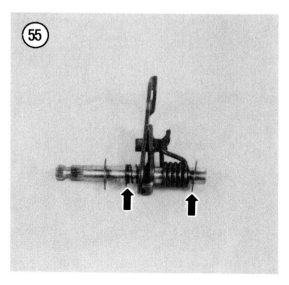

Refer to the **Tables 3-7** at the end of the chapter for transmission and internal shift mechanism specifications.

To gain access to the transmission and internal shift mechanism it is necessary to remove the engine and split the crankcase as described either in Chapter Four or Chapter Five.

The transmissions used with the RFVC (Radial Four Valve Combustion) engines are removed and installed together with their internal shift mechanisms.

The transmissions used on all other models can be removed and installed without having to remove the internal shift mechanism since the crankcase is split horizontally. Once the crankcase is split, removal and installation of the transmission assemblies is a simple task of pulling the assemblies up and out of the lower crankcase.

Preliminary Inspection (All Models)

After the transmission shaft assemblies have been removed from the crankcase, clean and inspect the assemblies prior to disassembling them. Place the assembled shaft into a large can or plastic bucket and thoroughly clean with a petroleum-based solvent such as kerosene and a stiff brush. Dry with compressed air or let it sit on rags to drip dry. Repeat for the other shaft assembly.

1. After they have been cleaned, visually inspect the components of the assemblies for excessive wear. Any burrs, pitting or roughness on the teeth of a gear will cause wear on the mating gear. Minor roughness can be cleaned up with an oilstone but there's little point in attempting to remove deep scars.

NOTE
Defective gears should be replaced. It's a good idea to replace the mating gear on the other shaft even though it may not show as much wear or damage.

2. Carefully check the engagement dogs. If any are chipped, worn, rounded or missing, the affected gear must be replaced.

3A. On RFVC engines, rotate the transmission bearings in both crankcase halves by hand. Check for roughness, noise and radial play. Any bearing that is suspect should be replaced as described in Chapter Four.

3B. On all other engines, rotate the transmission bearings on the transmission shafts by hand. Check for roughness, noise and radial play. Any bearing that is suspect should be replaced as described in this chapter.

4. If the transmission shafts are satisfactory and are not going to be disassembled, apply assembly oil or engine oil to all components and reinstall them in the crankcase as described in this chapter.

NOTE
If disassembling a used, well run-in (high mileage) transmission for the first time, pay particular attention to any additional shims that may have been added by a previous owner. These may have been added to take up the tolerance of worn components and must be reinstalled in the same position since the shims have developed a wear pattern. If new parts are going to be installed these shims may be eliminated. This is something you will have to determine upon reassembly.

5-SPEED TRANSMISSION
(XL250S, 1979-1980 XR250)

Removal/Installation

1. Remove the engine and split the crankcase as described in Chapter Four.
2. Remove the main shaft assembly (A, **Figure 56**) and countershaft assembly (B, **Figure 56**).
3. Install by reversing these removal steps, noting the following.

NOTE
Prior to installation, coat all friction surfaces with assembly oil.

4. Position the shift forks as shown in A, **Figure 57**.
5. Install the 2 bearing set rings (B, **Figure 57**) and bearing locating dowel (C, **Figure 57**).
6. Engage the balance chain onto the sprocket on the left-hand end of the main shaft assembly and install it (**Figure 58**).

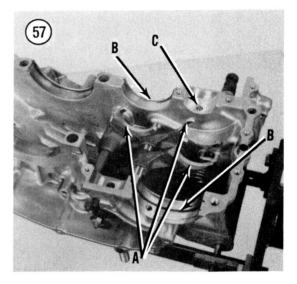

NOTE
*During the next step, make sure the shift fork engages properly. Also make sure the bearings are properly indexed into the set ring and locating dowel. The sealing ring on the oil seal must be correctly seated into the groove (A, **Figure 59**) or the crankcase halves will not join properly.*

NOTE
When a new oil seal is installed, apply a light coat of multipurpose grease to the lips prior to installation.

7. Install the countershaft assembly (**Figure 59**).

8. After both transmission assemblies are installed, rotate them by hand. Make sure there is no binding. Also shift through all 5 gears using the shift drum. Make sure the shift forks are operating properly and that you can shift through all gears. This is the time to find that something may be installed incorrectly—not after the crankcase is completely assembled.

9. Reassemble the crankcase and install the engine as described in Chapter Four.

Main Shaft
Disassembly/Inspection/Assembly

Refer to **Figure 60** for this procedure.

6

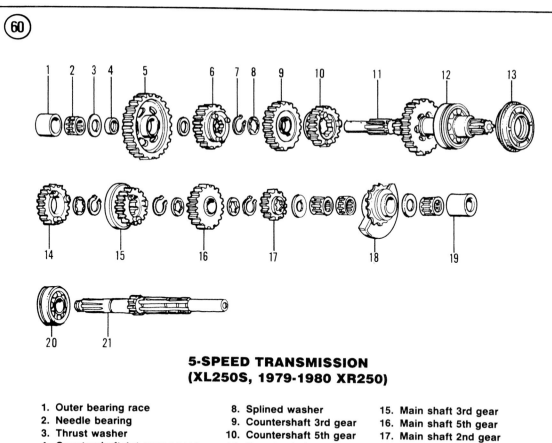

5-SPEED TRANSMISSION
(XL250S, 1979-1980 XR250)

1. Outer bearing race	8. Splined washer	15. Main shaft 3rd gear
2. Needle bearing	9. Countershaft 3rd gear	16. Main shaft 5th gear
3. Thrust washer	10. Countershaft 5th gear	17. Main shaft 2nd gear
4. Countershaft 1st gear spacer	11. Countershaft	18. Rear balancer
5. Countershaft 1st gear	12. Ball bearing	19. Outer bearing race
6. Countershaft 4th gear	13. Oil seal	20. Ball bearing
7. Circlip	14. Main shaft 4th gear	21. Main shaft

NOTE
A helpful "tool" that should be used for transmission disassembly is a large egg flat (the type that restaurants get their eggs in). As you remove a part from the shaft set it in one of the depressions in the same position from which it was removed. This is an easy way to remember the correct relationship of all parts.

1. If not cleaned in the *Preliminary Inspection* sequence, place the assembled shaft into a large can or plastic bucket and thoroughly clean with solvent and a stiff brush. Dry with compressed air or let it sit on rags to dry.
2. Remove the outer bearing race, needle bearing(s) and thrust washer (1, **Figure 61**).
3. Remove the rear balancer weight (2).
4. Remove the needle bearings (3).
5. Slide off the thrust washer (3).
6. Slide off the 2nd gear (4).
7. Remove the circlip and splined washer, then slide off the 5th gear (5).

8. Slide off the splined washer and remove the circlip, then slide off the 3rd gear (6).
9. Remove the circlip and splined washer, then slide off the 4th gear (7).
10. If necessary, remove the ball bearing from the shaft (**Figure 62**).
11. Check each gear for excessive wear, burrs, pitting, or chipped or missing teeth. Make sure the lugs on the gears are in good condition.

NOTE
Defective gears should be replaced. It is a good idea to replace the mating gear on the countershaft even though it may not show as much wear or damage.

12. Make sure that all gears slide smoothly on the main shaft splines.

NOTE
All circlips should be replaced every time the transmission is disassembled to ensure proper gear alignment. Do not expand a circlip more than necessary to slide it over the shaft.

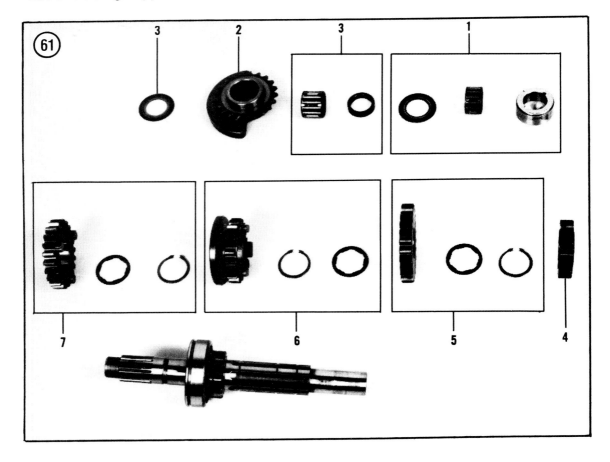

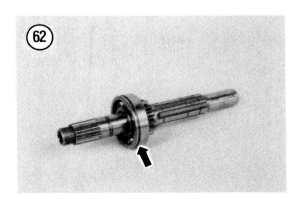

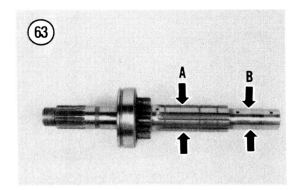

13. Measure the outside diameter of the main shaft at points "A" and "B". Refer to **Figure 63**. If the shaft is worn to the service limit listed in **Table 3** or smaller at either location, the shaft must be replaced. The clearance between any gear and shaft is 0.15 mm (0.006 in.).

14. Check the bearings. Make sure they rotate smoothly with no signs of wear or damage. Replace as necessary.

15. Assemble by reversing the disassembly steps, noting the following.

16. Refer to **Figure 64** for correct placement of all gears. Make sure all circlips are seated correctly in the main shaft grooves.

17. Make sure each gear engages properly to the adjoining gear where applicable.

18. Be sure to install the 2nd gear with the recess (**Figure 65**) facing in toward the 5th gear. This recess is necessary to clear the splined washer and circlip securing the 5th gear.

Countershaft
Disassembly/Inspection/Assembly

Refer to **Figure 60** for this procedure.

NOTE
Use the same large egg flat (used on the main shaft disassembly) during the countershaft disassembly. This is an easy way to remember the correct relationship of all parts.

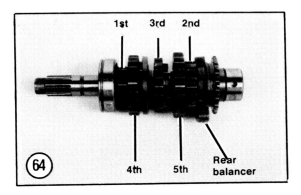

1. If not cleaned in the *Preliminary Inspection* sequence, place the assembled shaft into a large can or plastic bucket and thoroughly clean with solvent and a stiff brush. Dry with compressed air or let it sit on rags to dry.

2. Remove the outer bearing race, needle bearing and thrust washer (1, **Figure 66**).

3. Slide off the 1st gear, 1st gear spacer and the thrust washer (2).

4. Slide off the 4th gear (3).

5. Remove the circlip and splined washer. Then slide off the 3rd gear (4).

6. Slide off the 5th gear (5).

7. Remove the 2nd gear and/or the ball bearing if necessary (**Figure 67**). These 2 components are pressed into place on the countershaft and removal should be entrusted to a Honda dealer or machine shop.

8. Carefully slide off the oil seal (6).

9. Check each gear for excessive wear, burrs, pitting, or chipped or missing teeth. Make sure the lugs on the gears are in good condition.

> *NOTE*
> *Defective gears should be replaced. It is a good idea to replace the mating gear on the main shaft even though it may not show as much wear or damage.*

10. Make sure that all gears slide smoothly on the main shaft splines.

> *NOTE*
> *All circlips should be replaced every time the transmission is disassembled to ensure proper gear alignment. Do not expand a circlip more than necessary to slide it over the shaft.*

11. Measure the outside diameter of the countershaft at points "A," "B" and "C". Refer to **Figure 68**. If the shaft is worn to the service limit

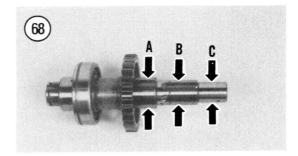

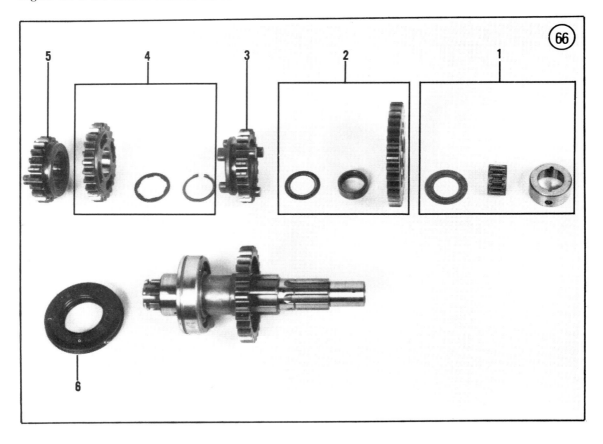

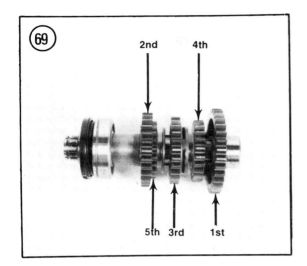

Figure 69

listed in **Table 3** or smaller at any location, the shaft must be replaced. The clearance between any gear and shaft is 0.15 mm (0.006 in.).

12. Measure the inside diameter (ID) and outside (OD) of the 1st gear spacer. If either dimension is to the service limit listed in **Table 3** the spacer must be replaced.

13. Check the bearings. Make sure they rotate smoothly with no signs of wear or damage. Replace as necessary.

14. Assemble by reversing these removal steps, noting the following.

15. Refer to **Figure 69** for correct placement of all gears. Make sure all circlips are seated correctly in the countershaft grooves.

16. Make sure each gear engages properly to the adjoining gear where applicable.

6-SPEED TRANSMISSION (1982-1983 XL250R, XR250R)

Removal/Installation

1. Remove the engine and split the crankcase as described in Chapter Four.

2. Remove the countershaft assembly (A, **Figure 70**).

3. Remove the main shaft assembly (B, **Figure 70**).

4. Install by reversing these removal steps, noting the following.

NOTE
Prior to installation, coat all bearing surfaces with assembly oil.

5. Turn the shift drum to the neutral position (**Figure 71**). This will correctly position the shift forks (**Figure 72**) to allow easy installation of the transmission shaft assemblies.

6. Install the 2 bearing set rings (A, **Figure 73**) and roller bearing locating dowels (B, **Figure 73**) in the lower crankcase half.

NOTE
The locating dowel on the left-hand side is also an oil control orifice (Figure 74).

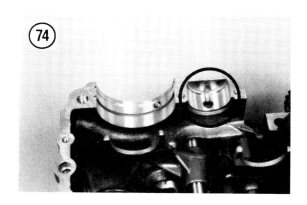

7. Install the main shaft assembly (**Figure 75**). Make sure the shift fork engages properly with the groove in the gear and that the bearings are properly indexed into the set ring and oil control orifice on the left-hand side.

8. Install the countershaft assembly (**Figure 76**). Make sure the shift forks engage properly with the groove in the gears and that the bearings are properly indexed into the set ring and oil control orifice on the left-hand side.

NOTE
Make sure the shift fork engages properly. Also make sure the bearings are properly indexed into the set ring and locating dowel. The sealing ring on the oil seal must be correctly seated into the groove (Figure 77) or the crankcase halves will not join properly.

NOTE
When a new oil seal is installed, apply a light coat of multipurpose grease to the lips prior to installation.

9. After both transmission assemblies are installed, rotate them by hand. Make sure there is no binding. Also shift through all 6 gears using the shift drum. Make sure the shift forks are operating properly and that you can shift through all gears. This is the time to find that something may be installed incorrectly—not after the crankcase is completely assembled.

10. Reassemble the crankcase and install the engine as described in Chapter Four.

Main Shaft
Disassembly/Inspection/Assembly

Refer to **Figure 78** for 1982-1983 XL250R or **Figure 79** for 1981-1982 XR250R models for this procedure.

NOTE
A helpful "tool" that should be used for transmission disassembly is a large egg flat (the type that restaurants get their eggs in). As you remove a part from the shaft set it in one of the depressions in the same position from which it was removed (Figure 80). This is an easy way to remember the correct relationship of all parts.

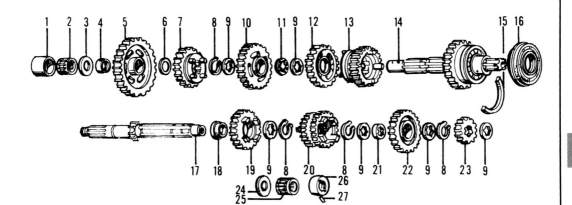

6-SPEED TRANSMISSION
(1982-1983 XL250R)

1. Needle bearing outer race
2. Needle bearing
3. Washer
4. Countershaft 1st gear bushing
5. Countershaft 1st gear
6. Washer
7. Countershaft 5th gear
8. Circlip
9. Splined washer
10. Countershaft 3rd gear
11. Splined lockwasher
12. Countershaft 4th gear
13. Countershaft 6th gear
14. Countershaft/2nd gear

15. 1/2 clip
16. Oil seal
17. Main shaft
18. Main shaft 5th gear bushing
19. Main shaft 5th gear
20. Main shaft 3rd/4th combination gear
21. Main shaft 6th gear bushing
22. Main shaft 6th gear
23. Main shaft 2nd gear
24. Thrust washer
25. Needle bearing
26. Needle bearing outer race
27. Pin

6

1. If not cleaned in the *Preliminary Inspection* sequence, place the assembled shaft into a large can or plastic bucket and thoroughly clean with solvent and a stiff brush. Dry with compressed air or let it sit on rags to dry.

2. Slide off the needle bearing outer race and the needle bearing.

3. Slide off the thrust washer, the splined washer and the 2nd gear.

4. Remove the circlip.

5A. On XL250R models, slide off the splined washer, the 6th gear and the 6th gear bushing.

5B. On XR250R models, slide off the splined washer and the 6th gear.

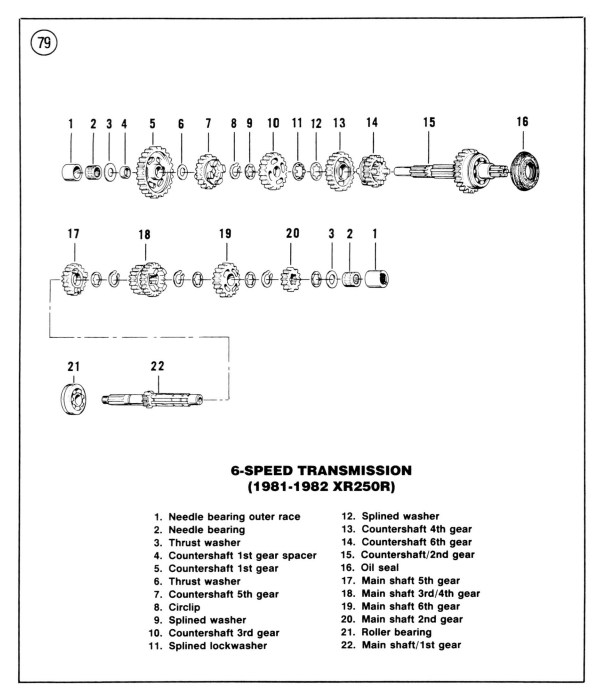

**6-SPEED TRANSMISSION
(1981-1982 XR250R)**

1. Needle bearing outer race
2. Needle bearing
3. Thrust washer
4. Countershaft 1st gear spacer
5. Countershaft 1st gear
6. Thrust washer
7. Countershaft 5th gear
8. Circlip
9. Splined washer
10. Countershaft 3rd gear
11. Splined lockwasher
12. Splined washer
13. Countershaft 4th gear
14. Countershaft 6th gear
15. Countershaft/2nd gear
16. Oil seal
17. Main shaft 5th gear
18. Main shaft 3rd/4th gear
19. Main shaft 6th gear
20. Main shaft 2nd gear
21. Roller bearing
22. Main shaft/1st gear

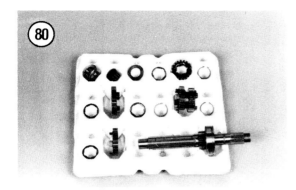

6. Slide off the splined washer and remove the circlip.

7. Slide off the 3rd/4th combination gear.

8. Remove the circlip and splined washer.

9A. On XL250R models, slide off the 5th gear and 5th gear bushing.

9B. On XR250R models, slide off the 5th gear.

10. If necessary, remove the ball bearing from the shaft (A, **Figure 81**).

11. Check each gear for excessive wear, burrs, pitting, or chipped or missing teeth. Make sure the lugs on the gears are in good condition.

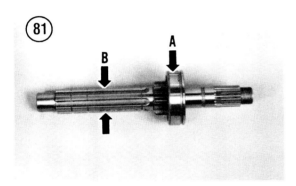

NOTE
Defective gears should be replaced. It is a good idea to replace the mating gear on the countershaft even though it may not show as much wear or damage.

NOTE
The 1st gear is part of the main shaft. If the gear is defective the shaft must be replaced.

12. Make sure that all gears slide smoothly on the main shaft splines.

NOTE
All circlips should be replaced every time the transmission is disassembled to ensure proper gear alignment. Do not expand a circlip more than necessary to slide it over the shaft.

13. Measure the outside diameter of the main shaft (B, **Figure 81**). If the shaft is worn to the service limit listed in **Table 4** or smaller at either location, the shaft must be replaced.

14. Check the bearing (A, **Figure 81**). Make sure it rotates smoothly with no signs of wear or damage. Replace as necessary.

15A. On XL250R models, slide on the 5th gear bushing and the 5th gear. Install the splined washer and circlip.

15B. On XR250R models, slide on the 5th gear and install the splined washer and circlip (**Figure 82**).

16. Position the 3rd/4th combination gear with the smaller 3rd gear going on first. Slide on the 3rd/4th combination gear (**Figure 83**).

17. Install the circlip and the splined washer (**Figure 84**).

18. Slide on the 6th gear, the splined washer and circlip (**Figure 85**).

19. Slide on the 2nd gear and the splined washer (**Figure 86**).

20. Slide on the thrust washer, needle bearing and needle bearing outer race (**Figure 87**).

21. After the assembly is complete, refer to **Figure 88** for correct placement of all gears. Make sure all circlips are seated correctly in the main shaft grooves.

22. Make sure each gear engages properly to the adjoining gear where applicable.

Countershaft
Disassembly/Inspection/Assembly

Refer to **Figure 78** for 1982-1983 XL250R or **Figure 79** for XR250R models for this procedure.

> *NOTE*
> *Use the same large egg flat (used on the main shaft disassembly) during the countershaft disassembly. This is an easy way to remember the correct relationship of all parts.*

1. If not cleaned in the *Preliminary Inspection* sequence, place the assembled shaft into a large can or plastic bucket and thoroughly clean with solvent and a stiff brush. Dry with compressed air or let it sit on rags to dry.

2. Slide off the needle bearing outer race and the needle bearing.

3. Slide off the thrust washer, 1st gear, 1st gear bushing and the thrust washer.

4. Slide off the 5th gear.

5. Remove the circlip, splined washer and slide off the 3rd gear.

6. Slide off the splined lockwasher. Rotate the splined washer in either direction to disengage the tangs from the raised splines on the transmission shaft. Slide off the splined washer.

7. Slide off the 4th gear.

8. Slide off the 6th gear.

9. Check each gear for excessive wear, burrs, pitting, or chipped or missing teeth. Make sure the lugs on the gears are in good condition.

> *NOTE*
> *Defective gears should be replaced. It is a good idea to replace the mating gear on the main shaft even though it may not show as much wear or damage.*

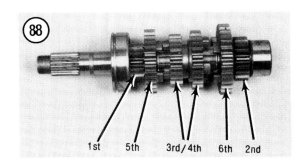

1st   5th   3rd/4th   6th   2nd

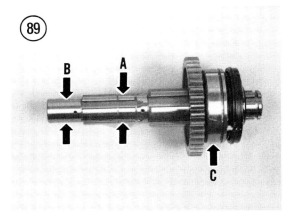

NOTE
The 2nd gear is part of the shaft. If the gear is defective the shaft must be replaced.

10. Make sure that all gears slide smoothly on the main shaft splines.

NOTE
It is recommended that all circlips be replaced every time the transmission is disassembled to ensure proper gear alignment. Do not expand a circlip more than necessary to slide it over the shaft.

11. Measure the outside diameter of the countershaft at points "A" and "B". Refer to **Figure 89**. If the shaft is worn to the service limit listed in **Table 4** or smaller at either location, the shaft must be replaced. The clearance between any gear and shaft is 0.15 mm (0.006 in.).

12. Measure the inside diameter (ID) and outside (OD) of the 1st gear bushing. Replace if worn to or beyond the service limit dimensions listed in **Table 4**.

13. Check the bearing (C, **Figure 89**). Make sure it rotates smoothly with no signs of wear or damage. Replace as necessary.

14. Slide on the 6th gear (**Figure 90**).

15. Slide on the 5th gear (flush side on last) and the splined washer (**Figure 91**). Rotate the splined washer in either direction so its tangs are engaged into the groove in the raised splines of the transmission shaft.

16. Slide on the splined lockwasher (**Figure 92**) so that the tangs go into the open areas of the splined washer and lock the washer in place (**Figure 93**).

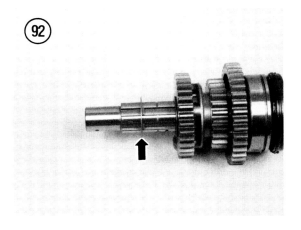

17. Slide on the 3rd gear (with the shoulder side on first) (**Figure 94**).

18. Install the splined washer and circlip (**Figure 95**).

19. Slide on the 5th gear, the thrust washer and the 1st gear bushing (**Figure 96**).

20. Slide on the 1st gear (flush side on last), thrust washer, needle bearing and needle bearing outer race (**Figure 97**).

21. After the assembly is complete, refer to **Figure 98** for correct placement of all gears. Make sure all circlips are seated correctly in the main shaft grooves.

22. Make sure each gear engages properly to the adjoining gear where applicable.

6-SPEED TRANSMISSION AND INTERNAL SHIFT MECHANISM (1984-1985 XR200R, 1984-ON XL250R, 1984-ON XR250R)

Removal/Installation

1. Remove the engine and split the crankcase as described in Chapter Five.

2. Pull the shift fork shaft out of the crankcase.

3. Pivot the shift forks away from the shift drum to allow for shift drum removal.

4. Remove the shift drum and the shift forks.

5. Remove the gearshift assembly.

6. Remove both transmission assemblies.

7. Inspect the shift fork assembly as described in this chapter.

8. Install the transmission assemblies as follows:

  a. Mesh both transmission assemblies together in their proper relationship to each other.

  b. Hold the thrust washer in place with your fingers on the countershaft assembly.

  c. Install the assembled shafts into the left-hand crankcase.

  d. Make sure the countershaft thrust washer is still positioned correctly after the assemblies are completely installed.

  e. After both assemblies are installed, tap on the end of both shafts with a plastic or soft-faced mallet to make sure they are completely seated.

NOTE
If the thrust washer on the end of the countershaft is not seated correctly it will hold the transmission shaft up a little and prevent the crankcase halves from seating completely.

1st 5th 3rd 4th 6th 2nd

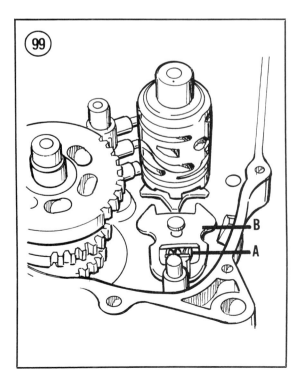

9. Each shift fork is marked with an "R" (right-hand side), "C" (center) or "L" (left-hand side). Install the shift forks with these marks facing *down* toward the left-hand crankcase.

10. Install the shift forks in this sequence—"L," "C" and then "R." Engage each shift fork into the groove in each gear but do not insert the shift fork shaft at this time.

11. Prior to installation, coat all sliding surfaces of the shift drum with assembly oil, then install the shift drum. Make sure it engages properly with the gearshift assembly.

12. Pivot each shift fork into mesh with the shift drum.

13. Install the shift fork shaft.

14. Make sure all 3 cam pin followers are in mesh with the shift drum grooves.

15. Spin both transmission shafts. Make sure there is no binding.

16. Tilt the left-hand crankcase half and transmission assemblies up to about a 45° angle from horizontal. This is to relieve some of the weight of the gears onto each other. If the next step is done with the left-hand crankcase half horizontal you may not be able to shift the transmission through the gears, even though all parts have been installed correctly.

NOTE
The following step is best done with the aid of a helper as the assemblies are loose and won't spin very easily. Have the helper spin the transmission shafts while you turn the shift drum through all the gears.

17. Spin the transmission shafts and shift through all 6 gears using the shift drum. Make sure the shift forks are operating properly and that you can shift through all gears. This is the time to find that something may be installed incorrectly—not after the crankcase is completely assembled.

18. Install the gearshift assembly as follows:
  a. Position the assembly with the splined end (for the gearshift pedal) going into the left-hand crankcase half and partially install the assembly.
  b. Align the return spring (A, **Figure 99**) with the pin bolt in the crankcase.
  c. Pull back on the shift plate (B, **Figure 99**) and push the gearshift assembly all the way in. Release the shift plate.

19. Make sure the thrust washer is installed on the end of the countershaft.

20. Reassemble the crankcase and install the engine as described in Chapter Five.

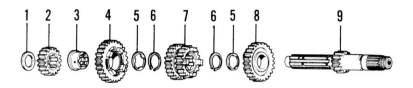

**6-SPEED TRANSMISSION
(1984-1985 XR200R, 1984-ON
XL250R, 1984-ON XR250R)**

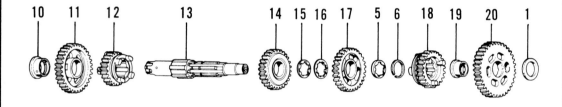

1. Thrust washer
2. Main shaft 2nd gear
3. Main shaft 6th gear bushing
4. Main shaft 6th gear
5. Splined washer
6. Circlip
7. Main shaft 3rd/4th gear

8. Main shaft 5th gear
9. Main shaft/1st gear
10. Countershaft 2nd gear bushing
11. Countershaft 2nd gear
12. Countershaft 6th gear
13. Countershaft
14. Countershaft 4th gear

15. Splined lockwasher
16. Splined washer
17. Countershaft 3rd gear
18. Countershaft 5th gear
19. Countershaft 1st gear bushing
20. Countershaft 1st gear

Main Shaft
Disassembly/Inspection/Assembly

Refer to **Figure 100** for this procedure.

NOTE
A helpful "tool" that should be used for transmission disassembly is a large egg flat (the type that restaurants get their eggs in). As you remove a part from the shaft, set it in one of the depressions in the same position from which it was removed. This is an easy way to remember the correct relationship of all parts.

1. If not cleaned in the *Preliminary Inspection* sequence, place the assembled shaft into a large can or plastic bucket and thoroughly clean with solvent and a stiff brush. Dry with compressed air or let it sit on rags to dry.
2. Slide off the thrust washer and the 2nd gear.
3. Slide off the 6th gear, the 6th gear bushing and the splined washer.
4. Remove the circlip.
5. Slide off the 3rd/4th combination gear.
6. Remove the circlip and splined washer.
7. Slide off the 5th gear.
8. Check each gear for excessive wear, burrs, pitting, or chipped or missing teeth. Make sure the lugs on the gears are in good condition.

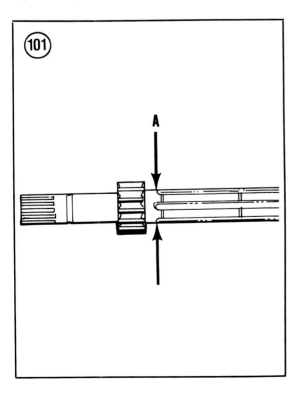

NOTE
Defective gears should be replaced. It is a good idea to replace the mating gear on the countershaft even though it may not show as much wear or damage.

NOTE
The 1st gear is part of the main shaft. If the gear is defective the shaft must be replaced.

9. Make sure that all gears slide smoothly on the main shaft splines.

NOTE
It is recommended that all circlips be replaced every time the transmission is disassembled to ensure proper gear alignment. Do not expand a circlip more than necessary to slide it over the shaft.

10. Measure the outside diameter of the main shaft (A, **Figure 101**). If the shaft is worn to the service limit listed in **Table 5** or smaller at either location, the shaft must be replaced.
11. Measure the inside diameter of the main shaft 5th and 6th gears. If the gear(s) is worn to the service limit listed in **Table 5** or larger, the gear(s) must be replaced.
12. Measure the outside diameter of the main shaft 6th gear bushing. If the bushing is worn to the service limit listed in **Table 5** or larger, the bushing must be replaced.
13. Slide on the 5th gear (flush side on first). Install the splined washer and circlip.
14. Position the 3rd/4th combination gear with the smaller diameter 3rd gear going on first. Slide on the 3rd/4th combination gear.
15. Install the circlip and the splined washer.
16. Align the oil hole in the 6th gear bushing with the oil hole in the main shaft and slide the bushing onto the shaft. This alignment is necessary for proper oil flow.
17. Slide on the 6th gear, the 2nd gear and the thrust washer.
18. Before installation, double-check the placement of all gears. Make sure all circlips are seated correctly in the main shaft grooves.
19. Make sure each gear engages properly to the adjoining gear where applicable.

Countershaft
Disassembly/Inspection/Assembly

Refer to **Figure 100** for this procedure.

NOTE
Use the same large egg flat (used on the main shaft disassembly) during the countershaft disassembly. This is an easy way to remember the correct relationship of all parts.

1. If not cleaned in the *Preliminary Inspection* sequence, place the assembled shaft into a large can or plastic bucket and thoroughly clean with solvent and a stiff brush. Dry with compressed air or let it sit on rags to dry.
2. Slide off the 2nd gear and the 2nd gear bushing.
3. Slide off the 6th gear.
4. From the other end of the shaft, slide off the thrust washer, the 1st gear and the 1st gear bushing.
5. Slide off the 5th gear.
6. Remove the circlip and slide off the splined washer.
7. Slide off the 3rd gear.
8. Slide off the splined lockwasher. Rotate the splined washer in either direction to disengage the tangs from the raised splines on the transmission shaft. Slide off the splined washer.
9. Slide off the 4th gear.
10. Check each gear for excessive wear, burrs, pitting, or chipped or missing teeth. Make sure the lugs on the gears are in good condition.

NOTE
Defective gears should be replaced. It is a good idea to replace the mating gear on the main shaft even though it may not show as much wear or damage.

11. Make sure that all gears slide smoothly on the counter shaft splines.

NOTE
All circlips should be replaced every time the transmission is disassembled to ensure proper gear alignment. Do not expand a circlip more than necessary to slide it over the shaft.

12. Measure the inside diameter of the 1st, 2nd, 3rd and 4th gears. Replace if worn to or beyond the service limit dimensions listed in **Table 5**.
13. Measure the inside diameter and outside diameter of the 1st and 2nd gear bushings. Replace if worn to or beyond the service limit dimensions listed in **Table 5**.
14A. On XR200R and XR250R models, measure the outside diameter of the countershaft at points "B" and "C". Refer to **Figure 102**. If the shaft is worn to the service limit listed in **Table 5** or less at either location, the shaft must be replaced.

14B. On XL250R models, measure the outside diameter of the countershaft at points "B," "C" and "D". Refer to **Figure 103**. If the shaft is worn to the service limit listed in **Table 5** or less at either location, the shaft must be replaced.
15. Slide on the 6th gear.
16. Install the 2nd gear bushing into the flush side of the 2nd gear.
17. Slide the 2nd gear (flush side on last) and 2nd gear bushing onto the shaft.
18. Onto the other end of the shaft, slide on the 4th gear (flush side on last).
19. Slide on the splined washer. Rotate the splined washer in either direction so its tangs are engaged into the groove in the raised splines of the transmission shaft.
20. Slide on the splined lockwasher so that the tangs go into the open areas of the splined washer and lock the washer in place.
21. Slide on the 3rd gear and splined washer.
22. Install the circlip.
23. Slide on the 5th gear.
24. Slide on the 1st gear bushing with the flange side on first.
25. Slide on the 1st gear (flush side on last) and thrust washer.
26. Before installation, double-check the placement of all gears. Make sure all circlips are seated correctly in the main shaft grooves.
27. Make sure each gear engages properly to the adjoining gear where applicable.
28. After both transmission assemblies have been assembled, mesh the 2 assemblies together in the correct position. Check that all gears meet correctly. This is your last check prior to installing the assemblies in the crankcase; make sure they are correctly assembled.

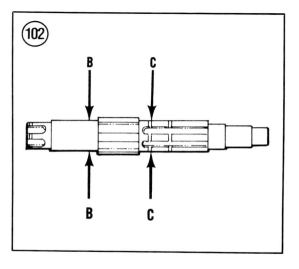

6-SPEED TRANSMISSION
AND INTERNAL SHIFT MECHANISM
(XL350R AND XR350R)

Removal/Installation

1. Remove the engine and split the crankcase as described in Chapter Five.
2. Pull the shift fork shaft out of the crankcase.
3. Pivot the shift forks away from the shift drum to allow for shift drum removal.
4. Remove the shift drum and the shift forks.
5. Remove the gearshift assembly.
6. Remove both transmission assemblies.
7. Inspect the shift fork assembly as described in this chapter.
8. Install the transmission assemblies as follows:
   a. Mesh both transmission assemblies together in their proper relationship to each other.
   b. Hold the thrust washer in place with your fingers on the countershaft assembly.
   c. Install the assembled shafts into the left-hand crankcase.
   d. Make sure the countershaft thrust washer is still positioned correctly after the assemblies are completely installed.
   e. After both assemblies are installed, tap on the end of both shafts with a plastic or soft-faced mallet to make sure they are completely seated.

NOTE
If the thrust washer on the end of the countershaft is not seated correctly it will hold the transmission shaft up a little and prevent the crankcase halves from seating completely.

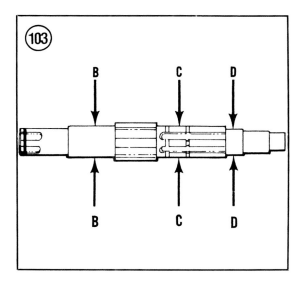

9. Each shift fork is marked with an "R" (right-hand side), "C" (center) or "L" (left-hand side). Install the shift forks with these marks facing *down* toward the left-hand crankcase.
10. Install the shift forks in this sequence—"L," "C" and then "R." Engage each shift fork into the groove in each gear but do not insert the shift fork shaft at this time.
11. Prior to installation, coat all sliding surfaces of the shift drum with assembly oil, then install the shift drum. Make sure it engages properly with the gearshift assembly.
12. Pivot each shift fork into mesh with the shift drum.
13. Install the shift fork shaft.
14. Make sure all 3 cam pin followers are in mesh with the shift drum grooves.
15. Spin both transmission shafts. Make sure there is no binding.
16. Tilt the left-hand crankcase half and transmission assemblies up to about a 45° angle from horizontal. This is to relieve some of the weight of the gears onto each other. If the next step is done with the left-hand crankcase half horizontal you may not be able to shift the transmission through the gears, even though all parts have been installed correctly.

NOTE
The following step is best done with the aid of a helper as the assemblies are loose and won't spin very easily. Have the helper spin the transmission shaft while you turn the shift drum through all the gears.

17. Spin the transmission shafts and shift through all 6 gears using the shift drum. Make sure the shift forks are operating properly and that you can shift through all gears. This is the time to find that something may be installed incorrectly—not after the crankcase is completely assembled.
18. Install the gearshift assembly as follows:
   a. Position the assembly with the splined end (for the gearshift pedal) going into the left-hand crankcase half and partially install the assembly.
   b. Align the return spring (A, **Figure 99**) with the pin bolt in the crankcase.
   c. Pull back on the shift plate (B, **Figure 99**) and push the gearshift assembly all the way in. Release the shift plate.
19. Make sure the thrust washer is installed on the end of the countershaft.
20. Reassemble the crankcase and install the engine as described in Chapter Five.

Main Shaft
Disassembly/Inspection/Assembly

Refer to **Figure 104** for this procedure.

NOTE
A helpful "tool" that should be used for transmission disassembly is a large egg flat (the type that restaurants get their eggs in). As you remove a part from the shaft, set it in one of the depressions in the same position from which it was removed. This is an easy way to remember the correct relationship of all parts.

1. If not cleaned in the *Preliminary Inspection* sequence, place the assembled shaft into a large can or plastic bucket and thoroughly clean with solvent and a stiff brush. Dry with compressed air or let it sit on rags to dry.
2. Slide off the 2nd gear, the 5th gear and 5th gear bushing.
3. Slide off the splined washer and remove the circlip.
4. Slide off the 3rd/4th combination gear.
5. Remove the circlip and splined washer.
6. Slide off the 6th gear.
7. Check each gear for excessive wear, burrs, pitting, or chipped or missing teeth. Make sure the lugs on the gears are in good condition.

6-SPEED TRANSMISSION
(XL350R, XR350R)

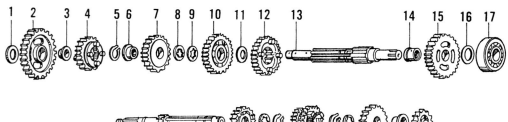

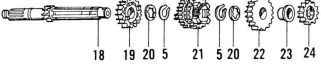

1. Washer
2. Countershaft 1st gear
3. Countershaft 1st gear bushing
4. Countershaft 6th gear
5. Circlip
6. Countershaft 3rd gear bushing
7. Countershaft 3rd gear
8. Splined lockwasher
9. Lockwasher
10. Countershaft 4th gear
11. Thrust washer
12. Countershaft 5th gear
13. Countershaft
14. Countershaft 2nd gear bushing (1985 XR350R only)
15. Countershaft 2nd gear
16. Thrust washer
17. Ball bearing
18. Main shaft/1st gear
19. Main shaft 6th gear
20. Splined washer
21. Main shaft 3rd/4th combination gear
22. Main shaft 5th gear
23. Main shaft 5th gear bushing
24. Main shaft 2nd gear

NOTE

Defective gears should be replaced. It is a good idea to replace the mating gear on the countershaft even though it may not show as much wear or damage.

NOTE

The 1st gear is part of the main shaft. If the gear is defective the shaft must be replaced.

8. Make sure that all gears slide smoothly on the main shaft splines.

NOTE

All circlips should be replaced every time the transmission is disassembled to ensure proper gear alignment. Do not expand a circlip more than necessary to slide it over the shaft.

9A. On 1983-1984 XR350R models, measure the outside diameter of the main shaft at locations "A" and "B" (**Figure 105**). If the shaft is worn to the service limit listed in **Table 6** or smaller at either location, the shaft must be replaced.

9B. On 1985 XR350R and 1984-1985 XL350R models, measure the outside diameter of the main shaft at location "A" (**Figure 101**). If the shaft is worn to the service limit listed in **Table 6** or smaller, the shaft must be replaced.

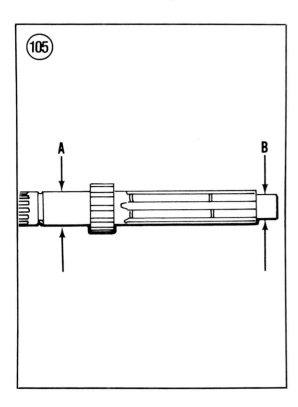

10. Measure the inside diameter of the main shaft 5th gear. If the gear(s) is worn to the service limit listed in **Table 6** or larger, the gear must be replaced.

11. Slide on the 6th gear.

12. Install the splined washer and circlip.

13. Position the 3rd/4th combination gear with the smaller diameter 3rd gear going on first. Slide on the 3rd/4th combination gear.

14. Install the circlip and the splined washer.

15. Slide on the 5th gear and 5th gear bushing.

16. Slide on the 2nd gear.

17. Before installation, double-check the placement of all gears. Make sure all circlips are seated correctly in the main shaft grooves.

18. Make sure each gear engages properly to the adjoining gear where applicable.

Countershaft
Disassembly/Inspection/Assembly

Refer to **Figure 104** for this procedure.

NOTE

Use the same large egg flat (used on the main shaft disassembly) during the countershaft disassembly. This is an easy way to remember the correct relationship of all parts.

1. If not cleaned in the *Preliminary Inspection* sequence, place the assembled shaft into a large can or plastic bucket and thoroughly clean with solvent and a stiff brush. Dry with compressed air or let it sit on rags to dry.

2. Slide off the thrust washer.

3A. On 1985 XR350R models, slide off the 2nd gear and the 2nd gear bushing.

3B. On all other models, slide off the 2nd gear.

4. From the other end of the shaft, slide off the thrust washer, the 1st gear and the 1st gear bushing.

5. Slide off the 6th gear.

6. Remove the circlip.

7. Slide off the 3rd gear and the 3rd gear bushing.

8. Slide off the splined lockwasher. Rotate the splined washer in either direction to disengage the tangs from the raised splines on the transmission shaft. Slide off the splined washer.

9. Slide off the 4th gear.

10A. On 1985 XR350R models, slide off the thrust washer and the 5th gear.

10B. On all other models, slide off the 5th gear.

11. Check each gear for excessive wear, burrs, pitting, or chipped or missing teeth. Make sure the lugs on the gears are in good condition.

NOTE
Defective gears should be replaced. It is a good idea to replace the mating gear on the main shaft even though it may not show as much wear or damage.

12. Make sure that all gears slide smoothly on the countershaft splines.

NOTE
All circlips should be replaced every time the transmission is disassembled to ensure proper gear alignment. Do not expand a circlip more than necessary to slide it over the shaft.

13A. On 1983-1984 XR350R models, measure the outside diameter of the countershaft at locations "C" and "D" (**Figure 106**). If the shaft is worn to the service limit listed in **Table 6** or smaller at either location, the shaft must be replaced.

13B. On 1985 XR350R and 1984-1985 XL350R models, measure the outside diameter of the countershaft at locations "B," "C" and "D" (**Figure 103**). If the shaft is worn to the service limit listed in **Table 6** or smaller, at any of the locations the shaft must be replaced.

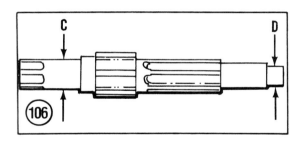

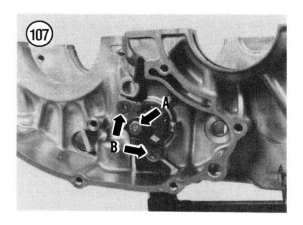

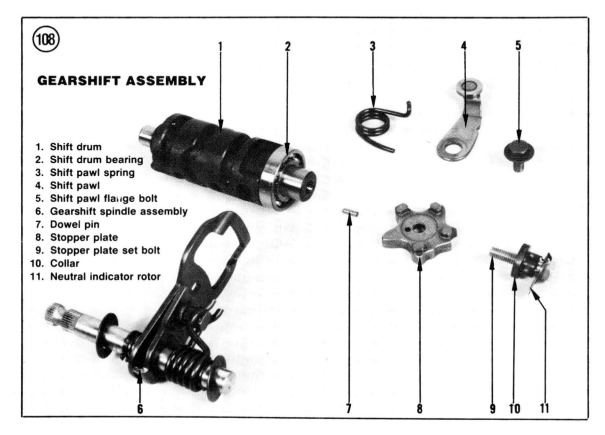

GEARSHIFT ASSEMBLY

1. Shift drum
2. Shift drum bearing
3. Shift pawl spring
4. Shift pawl
5. Shift pawl flange bolt
6. Gearshift spindle assembly
7. Dowel pin
8. Stopper plate
9. Stopper plate set bolt
10. Collar
11. Neutral indicator rotor

14. Measure the inside diameter of the 1st, 2nd, 3rd and 4th gears. Replace if worn to or beyond the service limit dimensions listed in **Table 6**.

15A. On 1985 XR350R models, slide on the 5th gear and the thrust washer.

15B. On all other models, slide on the 5th gear.

16. Slide on the 4th gear.

17. Slide on the splined washer. Rotate the splined washer in either direction so its tangs are engaged into the groove in the raised splines of the transmission shaft.

18. Slide on the splined lockwasher so that the tangs go into the open areas of the splined washer and lock the washer in place.

19. Slide on the 3rd gear (flush side on first) and the 3rd gear bushing.

20. Install the circlip.

21. Slide on the 6th gear.

22. Slide on the 1st gear bushing.

23. Slide on the 1st gear (flush side on last) and thrust washer.

24A. On 1985 XR350R models, onto the other end of the shaft, slide on the 2nd gear bushing and 2nd gear (flush side on last).

24B. On all other models, slide on the 2nd gear.

25. Slide on the thrust washer.

26. Before installation, double-check the placement of all gears. Make sure all circlips are seated correctly in the main shaft grooves.

27. Make sure each gear engages properly to the adjoining gear where applicable.

28. After both transmission assemblies have been assembled, mesh the 2 assemblies together in the correct position. Check that all gears meet correctly. This is your last check prior to installing the assemblies in the crankcase; make sure they are correctly assembled.

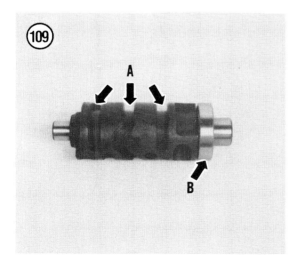

INTERNAL SHIFT MECHANISM (XL250S, XR250, 1982-1983 XL250R, 1981-1982 XR250R)

Removal/Disassembly

1. Remove the transmission assemblies as described in this chapter.

2. Hold onto the shift fork(s) and withdraw one shift fork at a time. Remove both shift fork shafts and the shift fork(s).

3. Remove the bolt (A, **Figure 107**) securing the neutral indicator rotor, collar and stopper plate. Remove all parts.

4. Remove the screws (B, **Figure 107**) securing the bearing set plate and remove the plate.

5. Carefully withdraw the shift drum from the left-hand side.

6. Thoroughly clean all parts in solvent and dry with compressed air.

Inspection

Refer to **Figure 108** for this procedure.

1. Inspect each shift fork for signs of wear or cracking. Check for bending and make sure each fork slides smoothly on the shaft. Replace any worn or damaged forks.

2. Check for any arc-shaped wear or burned marks on the shift forks. This indicates that the shift fork has come in contact with the gear. The fork fingers have become excessively worn and the fork must be replaced.

3. Check the grooves in the shift drum (A, **Figure 109**) for wear or roughness. If any of the groove profiles have excessive wear or damage, replace the shift drum.

4. Check the shift drum bearing (B, **Figure 109**). Make sure it operates smoothly with no signs of wear or damage.

5. Check the cam pin followers on each shift fork. It should fit snugly but not too tightly. Check the end that rides in the shift drum for wear or damage. Replace as necessary.

6. Measure the outside diameter of the gearshift fork shafts with a micrometer. Replace the ones worn to the service limit listed in **Table 7** or less.

7. Roll each shift fork shaft on a flat surface such as a piece of plate glass and check for any bends. If the shaft is bent, it must be replaced.

6

8. Measure the width of the gearshift fork fingers with a micrometer (**Figure 110**). Replace the ones worn to the service limit listed in **Table 7** or less.

> *CAUTION*
> *It is recommended that marginal shift forks be replaced. Worn forks can cause the transmission to slip out of gear, leading to more serious and expensive damage.*

9. Measure the inside diameter of the gearshift forks with a micrometer (**Figure 111**). Replace the ones worn to the service limit listed in **Table 7** or greater.
10. Check the stopper plate for wear; replace as necessary.

Assembly/Installation

1. Apply a light coat of oil to the shift fork shafts and the inside bores of the shift forks prior to installation.
2. Install the shift drum from the left-hand side.
3. Install the bearing set plate and screws (B, **Figure 107**). Tighten the screws to 9-13 N•m (7-9 ft.-lb.).

> *NOTE*
> *After installing the shift drum, make sure it rotates smoothly with no binding.*

4. Align the dowel pin in the stopper plate with the notch on the end of the shift drum and install the stopper plate.
5. Install the collar, neutral indicator rotor and stopper plate set bolt (A, **Figure 107**). Tighten the bolt securely.

> *NOTE*
> *The shift forks have cast identification marks: "L" left-hand side, "C" center and "R" right-hand side. Refer to* ***Figure 112***.

6. Install the right- and left-hand shift forks and shaft (A, **Figure 113**).
7. Install the center shift fork and shaft (B, **Figure 113**).

> *NOTE*
> ***Figure 114*** *is shown with the shift forks and shafts removed for clarity.*

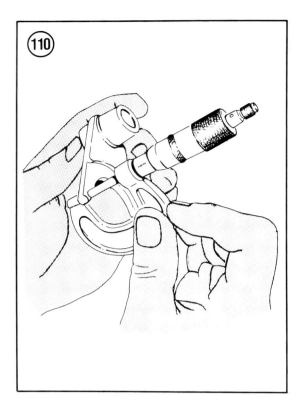

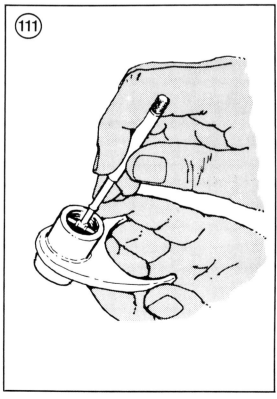

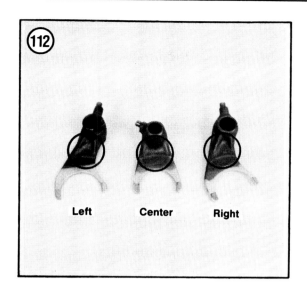

Left   Center   Right

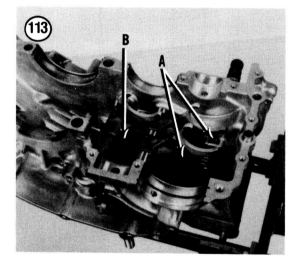

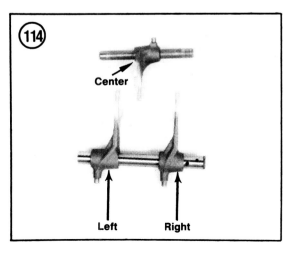

Center

Left   Right

8. Make sure the shift fork guide pins are properly meshed with the grooves in the shift drum and are correctly positioned on their respective shafts as shown in **Figure 114**.

9. Install the transmission assemblies as described in this chapter.

INTERNAL SHIFT MECHANISM (ALL OTHER MODELS)

The internal shift mechanism on these models is removed and installed during the transmission removal and installation procedures described in this chapter.

Inspection

1. Inspect each shift fork for signs of wear or cracking. Check for bending and make sure each fork slides smoothly on the shaft. Replace any worn or damaged forks.

2. Check for any arc-shaped wear or burned marks on the shift forks. This indicates that the shift fork has come in contact with the gear. The fork fingers have become excessively worn and the fork must be replaced.

3. Check the grooves in the shift drum (**Figure 115**) for wear or roughness. If any of the groove profiles have excessive wear or damage, replace the shift drum.

4. Check the cam pin followers on each shift fork. It should fit snugly but not too tightly. Check the end that rides in the shift drum for wear or damage. Replace as necessary.

5. Measure the outside diameter of the gearshift fork shafts with a micrometer. Replace the ones worn to the service limit listed in **Table 7** or smaller.

6. Roll each shift fork shaft on a flat surface such as a piece of plate glass and check for any bends. If the shaft is bent, it must be replaced.

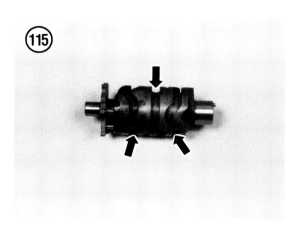

7. Measure the width of the gearshift fork fingers with a micrometer (**Figure 110**). Replace the ones worn to the service limit listed in **Table 7** or smaller.

> *CAUTION*
> *Marginal shift forks should be replaced. Worn forks can cause the transmission to slip out of gear, leading to more serious and expensive damage.*

8. Measure the inside diameter of the gearshift forks with a micrometer (**Figure 111**). Replace the ones worn to the service limit listed in **Table 7** or larger.

9. Apply a light coat of oil to the shift fork shafts and the inside bores of the shift forks prior to installation.

10. Inspect the shift mechanism for wear or damage. Make sure the return springs (**Figure 116**) have not sagged or broken. Replace as necessary.

11. Move the shift plate back and forth (**Figure 117**). It must move freely with no binding. Replace the shift mechanism if necessary.

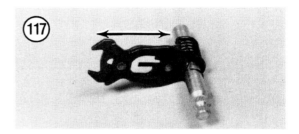

Table 1 CLUTCH SPECIFICATIONS

Item	Standard	Wear limit
Friction disc thickness		
200 cc	2.92-30.8 mm (0.115-0.121 in.)	2.6 mm (0.10 in.)
250 cc		
1978-1983	2.62-2.78 mm (0.102-1.09 in.)	2.3 mm (0.091 in.)
1984-on	2.92-3.08 mm (0.115-0.121 in.)	2.6 mm (0.10 in.)
350 cc	2.92-3.08 mm (0.115-0.121 in.)	2.6 mm (0.10 in.)
Clutch plate warpage	–	0.30 mm (0.01 in.)
Clutch springs free length		
200 cc	33.7 mm (1.32 in.)	32.2 mm (1.27 in.)
250 cc		
1978-1983	37.3 mm (1.46 in.)	35.8 mm (1.41 in.)
1984-on	33.7 mm (1.32 in.)	32.2 mm (1.27 in.)
350 cc		
XL350R	35.4 mm (1.39 in.)	33.7 mm (1.33 in.)
1983-1984 XR350R	35.9 mm (1.41 in.)	34.4 mm (1.35 in.)
1985 XR350R	36.0 mm (1.42 in.)	33.7 mm (1.33 in.)
Clutch outer guide		
Outer diameter		
200 cc	24.959-24.980 mm (0.9826-0.9835 in.)	24.17 mm (0.952 in.)
250 cc		
1978-1983	26.959-26.980 mm (1.0614-1.0622 in.)	26.91 mm (1.059 in.)
1984-on	24.959-24.980 mm (0.9826-0.9835 in.)	24.17 mm (0.952 in.)
XL350R	27.959-27.998 mm (1.1007-1.1023 in.)	27.05 mm (1.065 in.)
XR350R	27.098-27.959 mm (1.0668-1.1007 in.)	27.05 mm (1.065 in.)
Clutch outer guide		
Inner diameter		
200 cc	20.010-20.035 mm (0.7878-0.7888 in.)	20.05 mm (0.807 in.)
250 cc		
1978-1983	22.000-22.035 mm (0.8661-0.8675 in.)	22.05 mm (0.868 in.)
1984-on	20.010-20.035 mm (0.7878-0.7888 in.)	20.05 mm (0.807 in.)
350 cc	22.010-22.035 mm (0.8665-0.8675 in.)	22.05 mm (0.868 in.)
Clutch outer housing		
Inner diameter		
200 cc	25.000-25.021 mm (0.9843-0.9851 in.)	25.04 mm (0.986 in.)
250 cc		
1978-1983	27.000-27.021 mm (1.0630-1.0638 in.)	27.05 mm (1.065 in.)
1984-on	25.000-25.021 mm (0.9843-0.9851 in.)	25.04 mm (0.986 in.)
350 cc	28.000-28.021 mm (1.1024-1.1032 in.)	28.04 mm (1.104 in.)
Kickstarter gear outer diameter (1984-1985 XR200R, XR250R)	25.000-25.021 mm (0.9843-0.9851 in.)	25.04 mm (1.065 mm)

6

Table 2 CLUTCH TORQUE SPECIFICATIONS (cont.)

Item	N•m	ft.-lb.
Clutch nut		
XL250S, XR250, 1981-1982 XR250R	45-60	33-43
All other models (200-350 cc)	55-65	40-47
Clutch cover bolts and nuts	8-12	6-9
Kickstarter lever bolt	20-35	14-25
Footpeg bolts	35-45	25-33

Table 3 5-SPEED TRANSMISSION SPECIFICATIONS (XL250S, XR250)

Item	Standard	Service limit
Transmission gears ID		
Mainshaft		
4th, 5th gear	25.020-25.041 mm (0.9850-0.9859 in.)	25.10 mm (0.988 in.)
Countershaft		
1st, 3rd gear	25.020-25.041 mm (0.9850-0.9859 in.)	25.10 mm (0.988 in.)
Countershaft 1st gear bushing		
ID	20.020-20.041 mm (0.7881-0.7890 in.)	20.10 mm (0.791 in.)
OD	25.005-25.016 mm (0.9846-0.9849 in.)	24.96 mm (0.982 in.)
Shaft to bushing clearance	0.020-0.054 mm (0.0008-0.0021 in.)	0.15 mm (0.006 in.)
Mainshaft OD @ locations:		
A	24.959-24.980 mm (0.9826-0.9835 in.)	24.91 mm (0.981 in.)
B	19.987-20.000 mm (0.7869-0.7874 in.)	19.95 mm (0.785 in.)
Countershaft OD @ locations:		
A	26.959-26.980 mm (1.0614-1.0622 in.)	26.91 mm (1.059 in.)
B	24.959-24.980 mm (0.9826-0.9835 in.)	24.91 mm (0.981 in.)
C	19.987-20.000 mm (0.7869-0.7874 in.)	19.95 mm (0.785 in.)

Table 4 6-SPEED TRANSMISSION SPECIFICATIONS

Item	Standard	Service limit
1982-1983 XL250R		
Transmission gears ID		
Mainshaft		
5th gear	28.020-28.041 mm (1.1032-1.1040 in.)	28.10 mm (1.106 in.)
6th gear	28.020-28.053 mm (1.1032-1.1045 in.)	28.12 mm (1.107 in.)
Countershaft		
1st, 4th gear	25.020-25.041 mm (0.9850-0.9859 in.)	25.10 mm (0.988 in.)
2nd gear	27.020-27.053 mm (1.0638-1.0651 in.)	27.12 mm (1.068 in.)
3rd gear	28.020-28.053 mm (1.1032-1.1045 in.)	28.12 mm (1.107 in.)
Gear bushing OD		
Mainshaft 6th, Countershaft 3rd	27.969-27.980 mm (1.1011-1.1016 in.)	27.90 mm (1.098 in.)
1981-1982 XR250R		
Transmission gears ID		
Mainshaft		
5th, 6th gear	25.020-25.041 mm (0.9850-0.9859 in.)	25.10 mm (0.988 in.)
Countershaft		
1st, 2nd, 3rd gear	25.020-25.041 mm (0.9850-0.9859 in.)	25.10 mm (0.988 in.)
Gear bushing		
Counter shaft 1st gear		
ID	20.020-20.041 mm (0.7881-0.7890 in.)	20.10 mm (0.791 in.)
OD	25.005-25.016 mm (0.9846-0.9849 in.)	24.96 mm (0.982 in.)
Gear to bushing clearance	0.004-0.036 mm (0.0002-0.0014 in.)	0.15 mm (0.006 in.)
Mainshaft OD @ location B	24.959-24.980 mm (0.9826-0.9835 in.)	24.91 mm (0.981 in.)
Counter shaft OD @ locations:		
A	24.959-24.980 mm (0.9826-0.9835 in.)	24.91 mm (0.981 in.)
B	19.987-20.000 mm (0.7869-0.7874 in.)	19.95 mm (0.785 in.)

6

Table 5 6-SPEED TRANSMISSION SPECIFICATIONS

1984-1985 XR200R, 1984-ON XL250R, 1984-ON XR250R		
Item	**Standard**	**Service limit**
Transmission gears ID		
Main shaft		
5th gear	22.020-22.041 mm	22.08 mm (0.869 in.)
	(0.8669-0.8678 in.)	
6th gear	23.020-23.041 mm	23.09 mm (0.909 in.)
	(0.9063-09071 in.)	
Countershaft		
1st gear	23.000-23.021 mm	23.07 mm (0.908 in.)
	(0.9055-0.9063 in.)	
2nd gear	25.020-25.041 mm	25.09 mm (0.988 in.)
	(09850-0.9859 in.)	
3rd, 4th gear (200 cc)	22.020-22.041 mm	22.08 mm (0.869 in.)
	(0.8669-0.8678 in.)	
3rd gear (250 cc)	22.020-22.041 mm	22.08 mm (0.869 in.)
	(0.8669-0.8678 in.)	
4th gear (250 cc)	22.014-22.020 mm	22.08 mm (0.869 in.)
	(0.8667-0.8669 in.)	
Gear bushing OD		
Main shaft 6th	22.959-22.980 mm	22.92 mm (0.902 in.)
	(0.9039-0.9047 in.)	
Countershaft		
1st gear	22.951-22.980 mm	22.90 mm (0.901 in.)
	(0.9035-0.9047 in.)	
2nd gear	24.962-24.993 mm	24.90 mm (0.980 in.)
	(0.9828-0.9840 in.)	
Gear bushing ID		
Countershaft 1st gear	18.000-18.018 mm	18.08 mm (0.712)
	(0.7087-0.7094 in.)	
Countershaft 2nd gear	22.020-22.041 mm	21.98 mm (0.865 in.)
	(0.8669-0.8678 in.)	
Gear to bushing clearance		
Main shaft 6th gear	0.040-0.082 mm	0.10 mm (0.004 in.)
	(0.0016-0.0032 in.)	
Countershaft		
1st gear	0.020-0.070 mm	0.10 mm (0.004 in.)
	(0.0008-0.0028 in.)	
2nd gear	0.027-0.069 mm	0.10 mm (0.004 in.)
	(0.0011-0.0027 in.)	
Main shaft OD @ location A	21.959-21.980 mm	21.91 mm (0.863 in.)
	(0.8645-0.8654 in.)	
Countershaft OD @ locations		
B and C	21.959-21.980 mm	21.91 mm (0.863 in.)
	(0.8645-0.8654 in.)	
Shaft to gear clearance		
Main shaft 5th gear,		
countershaft 3rd, 4th gears	0.040-0.082 mm	0.15 mm (0.006 in.)
	(0.0016-0.0032 in.)	
Shaft to bushing clearance		
Countershaft 2nd gear	0. 061-0.082 mm	0.15 mm (0.006 in.)
	(0.0024-0.0032 in.)	

Table 6 5-SPEED TRANSMISSION SPECIFICATIONS

Item	Standard	Service limit
XL350R		
Transmission gears ID		
Main shaft		
6th gear	22.020-22.041 mm (0.8669-0.8678 in.)	22.10 mm (0.870 in.)
5th gear	24.020-24.041 mm (0.9457-0.9465 in.)	24.10 mm (0.949 in.)
Countershaft		
1st gear and 4th gears	22.020-22.041 mm (0.8669-0.8678 in.)	22.10 mm (0.870 in.)
2nd and 3rd gears	24.020-24.041 mm (0.9457-0.9465 in.)	24.10 mm (0.949 in.)
Gear bushing OD		
Main shaft 5th and 3rd gears	23.984-24.005 mm (0.9443-0.9451 in.)	23.93 mm (0.942 in.)
Countershaft 1st gear	21.984-22.005 mm (0.8655-0.8663 in.)	21.93 mm (0.863 in.)
Gear bushing ID		
Countershaft 1st gear	17.014-17.020 mm (0.6698-0.6701 in.)	17.08 mm (0.672 in.)
Gear to bushing clearance		
Main shaft 5th gear	0.015-0.057 mm (0.0006-0.0022 in.)	0.10 mm (0.004 in.)
Countershaft		
1st and 3rd gear	0.015-0.057 mm (0.0006-0.0022 in.)	0.10 mm (0.004 in.)
Main shaft OD @ location A	21.959-21.980 mm (0.8645-0.8654 in.)	21.91 mm (0.863 in.)
Countershaft OD @ locations:		
B	23.959-23.980 mm (0.9433-0.9441 in.)	23.91 mm (0.941 in.)
C	21.959-21.980 mm (0.8645-0.8654 in.)	21.91 mm (0.863 in.)
D	16.966-6.984 mm (0.6680-0.6687 in.)	16.93 mm (0.667 in.)
Shaft to gear clearance		
Main shaft 6th gear	0.040-0.082 mm (0.0016-0.0032 in.)	0.15 mm (0.006 in.)
Countershaft 2nd gear	0.040-0.082 mm (0.0016-0.0032 in.)	0.15 mm (0.006 in.)
Shaft to bushing clearance		
Countershaft 1st gear	0.020-0.054 mm (0.0008-0.0021 in.)	0.10 mm (0.004 in.)
1983-1984 XR350R		
Transmission gears ID		
Mainshaft		
5th gear	24.020-24.041 mm (0.9457-0.9465 in.)	24.10 mm (0.949 in.)
Countershaft		
1st, 4th gear	22.020-22.041 mm (0.8669-0.8678 in.)	22.10 mm (0.870 in.)
2nd, 3rd gear	24.020-24.041 mm (0.9457-0.9465 in.)	24.10 mm (0.949 in.)

(continued)

6

Table 6 5-SPEED TRANSMISSION SPECIFICATIONS (cont.)

	1983-1984 XR350R	
Item	**Standard**	**Service limit**
Gear bushing		
Countershaft		
1st gear ID	17.014-17.020 mm	17.08 mm (0.672 in.)
	(0.6698-0.670 in.)	
OD	21.984-22.000 mm	21.93 mm (0.863 in.)
	(0.8655-0.8663 in.)	
Shaft to clearance 1st		
gear bushing clearance	0.020-0.054 mm	0.10 mm (0.004 in.)
	(0.0008-0.0021 in.)	
Mainshaft OD @ locations:		
A	21.959-21.980 mm	21.91 mm (0.862 in.)
	(0.8645-0.8653 in.)	
B	16.966-16.984 mm	16.93 mm (0.667 in.)
	(0.6680-0.6687 in.)	
Countershaft OD @ locations:		
C	19.959-19.980 mm	19.92 mm (0.784 in.)
	(0.7858-0.7866 in.)	
D	16.966-16.984 mm	16.93 mm (0.667 in.)
	(0.6680-0.6687 in.)	
	1985 XR350R	
Transmission gears ID		
Main shaft		
6th gear	22.020-22.041 mm	22.10 mm (0.870 in.)
	(0.8669-0.8678 in.)	
5th gear	24.020-24.041 mm	24.10 mm (0.949 in.)
	(0.9457-0.9465 in.)	
Countershaft		
1st gear	23.020-23.041 mm	23.10 mm (0.909 in.)
	(0.9063-0.9071 in.)	
2nd gear	27.020-27.041 mm	27.10 mm (1.067 in.)
	(1.0638-1.0646 in.)	
3rd gear	28.020-28.041 mm	28.10 mm (1.106 in.)
	(1.1031-1.1040 in.)	
4th gear	25.020-25.041 mm	25.10 mm (0.988 in.)
	(0.9850-0.9859 in.)	
Gear bushing OD		
Main shaft 5th	23.984-24.005 mm	23.93 mm (0.942 in.)
	(0.9443-0.9451 in.)	
Countershaft		
1st gear	22.984-23.005 mm	22.93 mm (0.903 in.)
	(0.9049-0.9057 in.)	
2nd gear	26.959-26.980 mm	26.91 mm (1.059 in.)
	(1.0614-1.0622 in.)	
3rd gear	27.979-28.000 mm	27.93 mm (1.100 in.)
	(1.1015-1.1024 in.)	
Gear bushing ID		
Countershaft		
1st gear	20.000-20.021 mm	20.08 mm (0.791 in.)
	(0.7874-0.7882 in.)	
2nd gear	24.000-24.021 mm	24.08 mm (0.948 in.)
	(0.9449-0.9457 in.)	

(continued)

Table 6 5-SPEED TRANSMISSION SPECIFICATIONS (cont.)

	1985 XR350R	
Item	Standard	Service limit
Gear to bushing clearance		
Main shaft 5th gear	0.015-0.057 mm (0.0006-0.0022 in.)	0.10 mm (0.004 in.)
Countershaft		
1st, 2nd and 3rd gears	0.015-0.057 mm (0.0006-0.0022 in.)	0.10 mm (0.004 in.)
Mainshaft OD @ locations A	21.959-21.980 mm (0.8645-0.8654 in.)	21.91 mm (0.863 in.)
Countershaft OD @ locations:		
B	23.959-23.980 mm (0.9433-0.9441 in.)	23.91 mm (0.941 in.)
C	24.959-24.980 mm (0.9826-0.9835 in.)	24.91 mm (0.981 in.)
D	19.959-19.980 mm (0.7858-0.7866 in.)	19.91 mm (0.784 in.)
Shaft to gear clearance		
Main shaft 6th gear	0.040-0.082 mm (0.0016-0.0032 in.)	0.15 mm (0.006 in.)
Countershaft 2nd gear	0.040-0.082 mm (0.0016-0.0032 in.)	0.15 mm (0.006 in.)
Shaft to bushing clearance		
Countershaft 1st and 2nd gear	0.020-0.054 mm (0.0008-0.0021 in.)	0.10 mm (0.004 in.)

6

Table 7 SHIFT FORK AND SHAFT SPECIFICATIONS

Item	Specifications	Wear limit
	200-250 CC	
Shift fork I.D.		
Center fork	12.000-12.021 mm (0.4724-0.4733 in.)	12.05 mm (0.474 in.)
Right-hand, left-hand	15.000-15.021 mm (0.5906-0.5914 in.)	15.05 mm (0.592 in.)
Shift fork finger thickness	4.93-5.00 mm (0.194-0.197 in.)	4.50 mm (0.18 in.)
Shift fork shaft OD		
Center fork	11.966-11.984 mm (0.4711-0.4718 in.)	11.91 mm (0.469 in.)
Right-hand, left hand	14.966-14.984 mm (0.5892-0.5899 in.)	14.91 mm (0.587 in.)
Gear shift drum OD	11.966-11.984 mm (0.4711-0.4718 in.)	11.91 mm (0.469 in.)

(continued)

Table 7 SHIFT FORK AND SHAFT SPECIFICATIONS (cont.)

Item	Specifications	Wear limit
350 CC		
Shift fork I.D.		
All	13.000-13.021 mm	13.05 mm (0.514 in.)
	(0.5118-0.5126 in.)	
Shift fork finger thickness	4.93-5.00 mm	4.50 mm (0.18 in.)
	(0.194-0.197 in.)	
Shift fork shaft OD	12.966-12.984 mm	12.90 mm (0.508 in.)
	(0.5105-0.5111 in.)	
Gear shift drum OD	11.966-11.984 mm	11.91 mm (0.469 in.)
	(0.4711-0.4718 in.)	

CHAPTER SEVEN

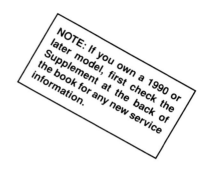

NOTE: If you own a 1990 or later model, first check the Supplement at the back of the book for any new service information.

FUEL AND EXHAUST SYSTEMS

7

The fuel system consists of the fuel tank, the shutoff valve, a single or dual carburetor and an air filter.

The exhaust system consists of a dual exhaust pipe and a muffler.

This chapter includes service procedures for all parts of the fuel and exhaust systems. Air filter service is covered in Chapter Three.

Carburetor specifications are covered in **Table 1** at the end of this chapter.

CARBURETOR OPERATION

For proper operation a gasoline engine must be supplied with fuel and air mixed in proper proportions by weight. A mixture in which there is excess fuel is said to be rich. A lean mixture is one which contains insufficient fuel. A properly adjusted carburetor supplies the proper mixture to the engine under all operating conditions.

The carburetor consists of several major systems. A float and float valve mechanism maintain a constant fuel level in the float bowl(s). The pilot system supplies fuel at low speeds. The main fuel system supplies fuel at medium and high speeds. A starter (choke) system supplies the very rich mixture needed to start a cold engine.

Some models are equipped with dual carburetors. The primary carburetor operates alone

at low- to mid-range for smooth, precise throttle control. The secondary carburetor opens (along with the primary carburetor) at high-range to provide a large volume of fuel-air mixture for maximum power.

The progressive linkage connecting the 2 carburetors is mechanical. Linkage adjustment is covered in this chapter.

CARBURETOR SERVICE

Major carburetor service (removal and cleaning) should be performed at the intervals indicated in **Table 2** in Chapter Three or when poor engine performance, hesitation and little or no response to mixture adjustment is observed. Alterations in jet size, throttle slide cutaway, and changes in jet needle position, etc., should be attempted only if you're experienced in this type of "tuning" work; a bad guess could result in costly engine damage or, at least, poor performance. If, after servicing the carburetor and making the adjustments described in this chapter, the bike does not perform correctly (and assuming that other factors affecting performance are correct, such as ignition timing and condition, etc.), the bike should be checked by a dealer or a qualified performance tuning specialist.

Dual Carburetor
Removal/Installation

1. Remove both side covers and the seat.
2. On XL series models, disconnect the battery negative lead or disconnect the main fuse (**Figure 1**).
3. Remove the fuel tank as described in this chapter.
4. Loosen the screw on the clamping band (A, **Figure 2**) on each end of both carburetors. Slide the clamping bands away from the carburetors.
5. Remove the bolts (B, **Figure 2**) securing the intake tube and insulator to the cylinder head. Remove the intake tube and insulator from the engine and carburetor assembly.

> *NOTE*
> *There is 1 bolt on the bottom in the center of the intake tubes. It is very difficult to remove.*

6. Pull the carburetor assembly forward and out of the air filter intake tube (**Figure 3**).
7. Loosen the throttle cable locknuts (**Figure 4**) at the carburetor assembly.
8. On 1984-on XL250R, 1984-on XR250R and XL350R models, perform the following:
   a. Loosen the screw (A, **Figure 5**) on the choke cable clamp.
   b. Disconnect the choke cable (B, **Figure 5**) from the carburetor.
9. Partially pull the carburetor assembly out through the left-hand side.
10. Disconnect the "pull" cable (A, **Figure 6**) and the "push" cable (B, **Figure 6**) from the throttle wheel.
11. Note the routing of the carburetor drain tube through the frame. Carefully pull the tube free from the frame and leave it attached to the carburetor.
12. Carefully remove the carburetor from the engine and frame and take it a workbench for disassembly and cleaning.
13. Install by reversing these removal steps, noting the following.
14. Inspect the O-ring seals in the intake tube (A, **Figure 7**) and the insulator (B, **Figure 7**). Replace if necessary.
15. When installing the throttle cables be sure to install the "pull" cable (A, **Figure 6**) to the bottom

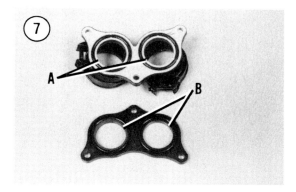

receptacle on the throttle wheel and the "push" cable (B, **Figure 6**) to the upper receptacle on the throttle wheel.

16. Make sure the screws on the clamping bands are tight to avoid a vacuum loss and possible valve damage.

17. Adjust the throttle cables and on models so equipped, the choke cable as described in Chapter Three.

Single Carburetor
Removal/Installation

1. Remove both side covers and the seat.

> *NOTE*
> *On XL250S models, reinstall the seat strap bolts as they also hold the upper portion of the shocks to the frame. Remove and install one bolt at a time.*

2. On XL series models, disconnect the battery negative lead or disconnect the main fuse (**Figure 1**).

3. Remove the fuel tank as described in this chapter.

4. It is recommended that the air filter air box be removed as it makes carburetor removal and installation much easier.

5. Disconnect the breather hose (A, **Figure 8**) from the air box.

6. Loosen the screw on the clamping bands on the rear rubber boot (**Figure 9**) and slide the clamping band away from the carburetor.

7

7. Remove the bolts securing the air box to the frame (B, **Figure 8** and **Figure 10**) and remove the air box.

8. Disconnect the "pull" cable and the "push" cable from the throttle wheel (**Figure 11**).

9. Loosen the screw (**Figure 12**) on the cable clamp and disconnect the choke cable end from the link plate on the carburetor (A, **Figure 13**).

10. Loosen the screw on the clamping band on the rubber intake tube (B, **Figure 13**) and slide the clamping band away from the carburetor.

11. Note the routing of the carburetor drain tube through the frame. Carefully pull the tube free from the frame and leave it attached to the carburetor.

12. Carefully pull the carburetor assembly to the rear and remove it from the engine and frame and take it a workbench for disassembly and cleaning.

13. Install by reversing these removal steps, noting the following.

14. Install the carburetor so that the boss on the carburetor aligns with the notch in the rubber intake tube.

15. When installing the throttle cables be sure to install the "pull" cable to the bottom receptacle on the throttle wheel and the "push" cable to the upper receptacle on the throttle wheel.

16. Make sure the screws on the clamping bands are tight to avoid a vacuum loss and possible valve damage.

17. Adjust the throttle and choke cables as described in Chapter Three.

Carburetor
Disassembly/Assembly

The carburetor on all models is basically the same unit. Slight variations exist on the dual-carburetor design. The XL models are equipped with an accelerator pump system.

On models with dual carburetors, only one carburetor should be disassembled at a time. This will prevent a mixup of parts. The primary carburetor is located on the left-hand side and the secondary carburetor is on the right-hand side.

Refer to **Figure 14** for dual-carburetor models or **Figure 15** for single-carburetor models.

1. On dual-carburetor models, separate the carburetors as described in this chapter.

NOTE
Carburetor separation is necessary to gain access to the air cutoff valve on the left-hand carburetor.

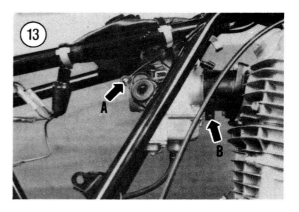

DUAL CARBURETORS

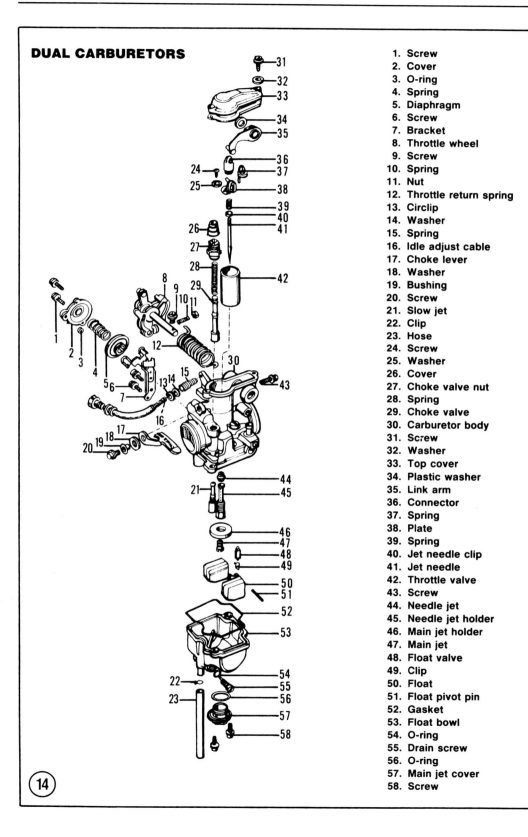

1. Screw
2. Cover
3. O-ring
4. Spring
5. Diaphragm
6. Screw
7. Bracket
8. Throttle wheel
9. Screw
10. Spring
11. Nut
12. Throttle return spring
13. Circlip
14. Washer
15. Spring
16. Idle adjust cable
17. Choke lever
18. Washer
19. Bushing
20. Screw
21. Slow jet
22. Clip
23. Hose
24. Screw
25. Washer
26. Cover
27. Choke valve nut
28. Spring
29. Choke valve
30. Carburetor body
31. Screw
32. Washer
33. Top cover
34. Plastic washer
35. Link arm
36. Connector
37. Spring
38. Plate
39. Spring
40. Jet needle clip
41. Jet needle
42. Throttle valve
43. Screw
44. Needle jet
45. Needle jet holder
46. Main jet holder
47. Main jet
48. Float valve
49. Clip
50. Float
51. Float pivot pin
52. Gasket
53. Float bowl
54. O-ring
55. Drain screw
56. O-ring
57. Main jet cover
58. Screw

7

14

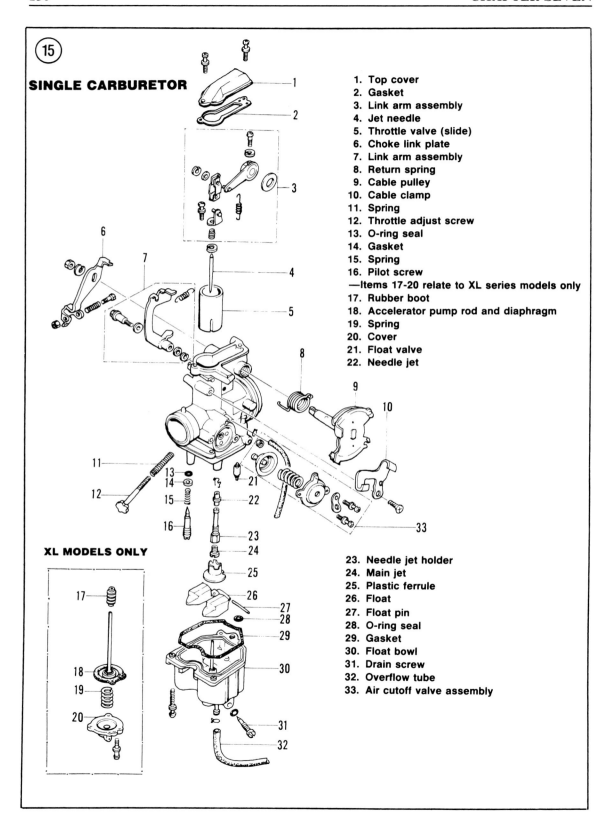

15

SINGLE CARBURETOR

XL MODELS ONLY

1. Top cover
2. Gasket
3. Link arm assembly
4. Jet needle
5. Throttle valve (slide)
6. Choke link plate
7. Link arm assembly
8. Return spring
9. Cable pulley
10. Cable clamp
11. Spring
12. Throttle adjust screw
13. O-ring seal
14. Gasket
15. Spring
16. Pilot screw
—Items 17-20 relate to XL series models only
17. Rubber boot
18. Accelerator pump rod and diaphragm
19. Spring
20. Cover
21. Float valve
22. Needle jet

23. Needle jet holder
24. Main jet
25. Plastic ferrule
26. Float
27. Float pin
28. O-ring seal
29. Gasket
30. Float bowl
31. Drain screw
32. Overflow tube
33. Air cutoff valve assembly

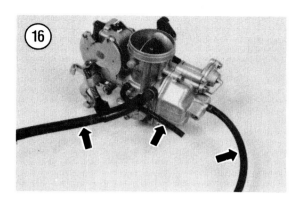

2. Remove the vent and overflow tubes (**Figure 16**).

3. Remove the screws (**Figure 17**) securing the top cover and remove cover and the gasket.

4. Remove the screws (**Figure 18**) securing the link arm assembly to the throttle valve and pivot the link arm assembly out of the way.

5. Remove the throttle valve and needle valve from the carburetor.

6. On models equipped with an air cutoff valve, perform the following:

   a. Remove the screws (**Figure 19**) securing the air cutoff valve cover and remove the cover.

   b. Remove the spring and diaphragm (**Figure 20**).

   c. Remove the small O-ring seal (**Figure 21**).

7

7. On models equipped with an accelerator pump, perform the following:

    a. Remove the screw (**Figure 22**) securing the accelerator pump cover and remove the cover.

    b. Remove the spring (**Figure 23**).

    c. Carefully withdraw the accelerator pump rod assembly (A, **Figure 24**) and remove the rubber boot (B, **Figure 24**).

8. Remove the screws securing the float bowl and remove the float bowl. Refer to **Figure 25** for models with an accelerator pump or A, **Figure 26** for all other models.

9. On models so equipped, unscrew the main jet cover (B, **Figure 26**) from the float bowl.

10. Remove the plastic ferrule (**Figure 27**) from the main jet stanchion.

NOTE

*Prior to removing the pilot screw, carefully screw it in until it **lightly** seats. Count and record the number of turns so it can be installed in the same position.*

11. Unscrew the pilot screw and spring (**Figure 28**).

12. Remove the small O-ring seal (**Figure 29**) located within the pilot screw receptacle.

13. Remove the float pivot pin (**Figure 30**).

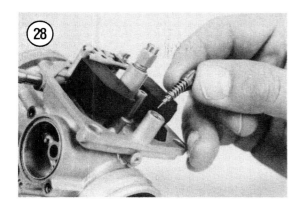

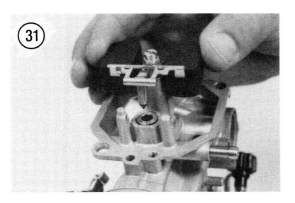

14. Remove the float and float valve needle (**Figure 31**).

> *NOTE*
> *Prior to removing the air screw, carefully screw it in until it **lightly** seats. Count and record the number of turns so it can be installed in the same position.*

15. Remove the air screw on dual-carburetor models; the secondary carburetor is not equipped with an air screw.

16. Remove the main jet (A, **Figure 32**), needle jet holder (**Figure 33**) and the needle jet.

17. Turn the carburetor over and gently tap the side of the body. Catch the needle jet as it falls out into your hand. If the needle jet does not fall out, use a plastic or fiber tool and gently push the needle jet out. Do not use any metal tools for this purpose.

18. On models equipped with a removable slow jet, remove the slow jet (B, **Figure 32**).

19A. On dual-carburetor models, on the primary carburetor only, remove the screw securing the starter choke and remove the choke assembly.

7

19B. On all other models, unhook the choke return spring and remove the plastic link arm (A, **Figure 34**).

20. Unscrew the throttle adjust screw (B, **Figure 34**) and remove the spring and the throttle adjust screw.

21. Remove the float bowl seal from the float bowl.

22. Remove the main jet cover and O-ring seal.

NOTE
Further disassembly is neither necessary nor recommended. If throttle or choke shafts or butterflies are damaged, take the carburetor body to a dealer for replacement.

23. Clean and inspect all parts as described in this chapter.

24. Assembly is the reverse of these disassembly steps, noting the following.

25. Install the needle jet (**Figure 35**) with the chamfered end facing *up* toward the needle jet holder.

26. If removed, install the needle jet clip in the correct groove; refer to **Table 1** at the end of this chapter.

27. Install the plastic ferrule (**Figure 27**) with the cutout notch facing toward the float pin. This notch is for the overflow tube in the float bowl.

28. Check the float height and adjust if necessary as described in this chapter.

29. On models equipped with an accelerator pump, perform the following:
   a. Make sure the tabs on the accelerator pump diaphragm are positioned correctly in the float bowl (**Figure 36**).
   b. Make sure that the rubber boot is completely seated in the carburetor body flange (**Figure 37**).

CAUTION
This boot must be correctly seated as it seals off the pump shaft to keep dirt out of the diaphragm area.

30. Make sure that any small O-ring seals removed are correctly installed and not forgotten.

31. On dual-carburetor models, repeat for the other carburetor.

32. After the carburetor(s) has been assembled, the pilot screw, air screw and the idle speed should be adjusted.

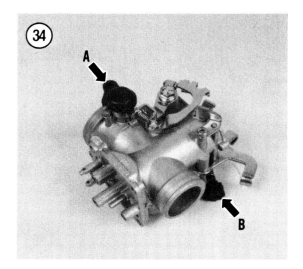

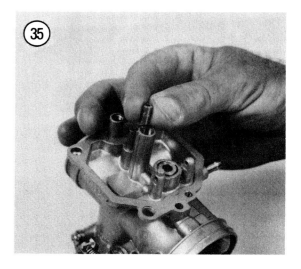

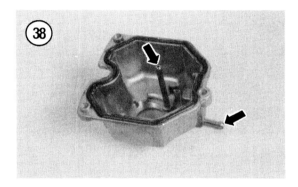

Cleaning/Inspection
(All Models)

1. Clean all parts, except rubber or plastic parts, in a good grade of carburetor cleaner. This solution is available at most automotive or motorcycle supply stores in a small, resealable tank with a dip basket for just a few dollars. If it is tightly sealed when not in use, the solution will last for several cleanings. Follow the manufacturer's instructions for correct soak time (usually about 1/2 hour).

2. Remove all parts from the cleaner and blow dry with compressed air. Blow out the jets and needle jet holder with compressed air.

> *CAUTION*
> *If compressed air is not available, allow the parts to air dry or use a clean lint-free cloth. Do **not** use a paper towel to dry carburetor parts, as small paper particles may plug openings in the carburetor body or jets.*

> *CAUTION*
> *Do **not** use a piece of wire to clean jets or passages as minor gouges can alter flow rate and upset the fuel/air mixture.*

3. Be sure to clean out the overflow tube in the float bowl from both ends (**Figure 38**).

4. Inspect the end of the float valve needle (**Figure 39**) for wear or damage. Also check the inside of the needle valve body. If either part is damaged, replace as a set. A damaged needle valve or a particle of dirt or grit in the needle valve assembly will cause the carburetor to flood and overflow fuel.

5. Inspect all O-ring seals. O-ring seals tend to become hardened after prolonged use and heat and therefore lose their ability to seal properly.

6. Examine the end of the pilot screw and the throttle adjust screw. If any grooves or roughness are present on either screw, replace it. A damaged end will prevent smooth low-speed engine operation.

Dual Carburetor Separation

1. Remove the carburetor assembly as described in this chapter.

2. Remove the screw (**Figure 40**) securing the throttle adjust screw bracket and remove the bracket assembly.

3. Remove the screws (A, **Figure 41**) securing the 2 carburetor bodies together.

4. Carefully separate the ball stud from the ball-joint (**Figure 42**) on the throttle drum of the secondary carburetor.

5. Carefully pull the 2 carburetor bodies apart. Do not damage the air joint (**Figure 43**) or the fuel joint (B, **Figure 41**) joining the 2 carburetors.

6. Install new O-ring seals on both the air and fuel joints.

7. Apply a light coat of multipurpose grease to the O-ring seals on the air and fuel joints.

8. Insert the air and fuel joints into their receptacles on the primary carburetor.

9. Place the secondary carburetor onto the primary carburetor, carefully aligning the air joint (**Figure 43**) and fuel joint (B, **Figure 41**). Make sure that the O-ring seals are in place on both joints.

10. Push the 2 carburetor bodies together until they are completely seated.

11. Push the ball stud onto the ball joint (**Figure 42**).

12. Install the screws (A, **Figure 41**) securing the 2 carburetor bodies together.

13. Align the groove in the throttle adjust screw bracket with the tab on the air vent tube. Install the screws and tighten securely.

14. Check the operation of the throttle as follows:
  a. Move the throttle plate and open and close the throttle a couple of times. It should move freely from open to closed with no binding.
  b. If movement is not free, make sure the ball stud is correctly seated on the throttle drum.
  c. Loosen the carburetor attachment screws a little and slightly move each carburetor body.
  d. Retighten the screws and recheck the movement.

Float Adjustment

The carburetor assembly has to be removed and partially disassembled for this adjustment.

1. Remove the carburetor assembly as described in this chapter.

2A. On dual-carburetor models, remove the screws securing both float bowls and remove the float bowls.

2B. On single-carburetor models, remove the screws securing the float bowl and remove the float bowl (**Figure 44**).

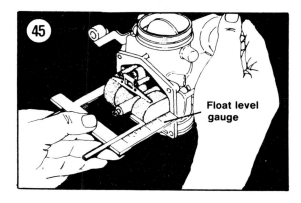

Float level gauge

3. Hold the carburetor assembly with the carburetor inclined 15-45° from vertical so that the float arm is just touching the float needle—not pushing it down. Use a float gauge (**Figure 45**), vernier caliper or small ruler and measure the distance from the carburetor body to the bottom surface of the float body (**Figure 46**). The correct height is listed in **Table 1**.

4. Adjust by carefully bending the tang on the float arm. If the float level is too high, the result will be a rich fuel/air mixture. If it is too low, the mixture will be too lean.

NOTE
On dual-carburetor models, the floats on both carburetors must be adjusted at the same height to maintain the same fuel/air mixture.

5. Reassemble and install the carburetors.

Needle Jet Adjustment (XR Models)

NOTE
On XL series models, the needle has only one groove for the clip so it is non-adjustable.

Needle position can be adjusted to affect the fuel-air mixture for medium throttle openings.

The carburetor assembly has to be removed and partially disassembled for this adjustment.

1. Remove the carburetor assembly as described in this chapter.

2. Remove the screws (**Figure 47**) securing the top cover and remove the cover and gasket.

3. Remove the screws (**Figure 48**) securing the link arm assembly to the throttle valve. Then pivot the link arm assembly back out of the way.

4. Remove the throttle valve and needle jet.

5. Remove the needle valve and note the original position of the needle clip. The standard setting is listed in **Table 1**.

6. Raising the needle (lowering the clip) will enrich the mixture during mid-throttle openings, while lowering the needle (raising the clip) will lean out the mixture.

7. Reassemble and install the carburetor by reversing these steps.

Pilot Screw Adjustment (1978-1979)

The air filter element must be cleaned before starting this procedure or the results will be inaccurate. Refer to Chapter Three.

NOTE
The pilot jet is pre-set at the factory and adjustment is not necessary unless the carburetor(s) has been overhauled or someone has misadjusted it.

1. For the preliminary adjustment, carefully turn the pilot screw (**Figure 49**) in until it seats *lightly* and then back it out the number of turns listed in **Table 2**.

CAUTION
The pilot screw seat can be damaged if the pilot screw is tightened too hard against the seat.

2. Start the engine and let it reach normal operating temperature. Approximately 5-10 minutes of stop and go riding is usually sufficient. Shut the engine off.
3. Connect a portable tachometer following the manufacturer's instructions.
4. Turn the idle adjust screw in or out to obtain the idle speed listed in **Table 1**.
5A. On XL series models, turn the pilot screw *clockwise* until the engine stops running. Back the pilot screw out 2 full turns. Restart the engine and proceed to Step 6.
5B. On XR series models, turn the pilot screw in either direction until the highest idle speed is obtained.
6. Reset the idle speed; refer to Step 4. Open and close the throttle a couple of times; check for variation in idle speed. Readjust if necessary.

WARNING
With the engine idling, move the handlebar from side to side. If idle speed increases during this movement, the throttle cable needs adjustment or it may be incorrectly routed through the frame. Correct this problem immediately. Do not ride the bike in this unsafe condition.

7. If necessary, repeat Step 5 and Step 6 until the engine runs smoothly at the correct idle speed.
8. Disconnect the portable tachometer.

**New Pilot Screw Adjustment and
New Limiter Cap Installation
(1980-1981 XL250S)**

In order to comply with U.S. and Canadian emission control standards, a limiter cap is attached to the end of the pilot screw. This is to prevent the owner from readjusting the pilot screw from the factory setting. The limiter cap will allow a maximum of 7/8 of a turn of the pilot screw *to a leaner mixture only*.

The pilot jet is pre-set at the factory and adjustment is not necessary unless the carburetor(s) has been overhauled or someone has misadjusted it.

The air filter element must be cleaned before starting this procedure or the results will be inaccurate. Refer to Chapter Three.

CAUTION
Do not try to remove the limiter cap from the old pilot screw, as it is bonded in place. It will break off and damage the pilot screw if removal is attempted.

1. For the preliminary adjustment, carefully turn the new pilot screw in until it seats *lightly* and then back it out the number of turns listed in **Table 2**.

CAUTION
The pilot screw seat can be damaged if the pilot screw is tightened too hard against the seat.

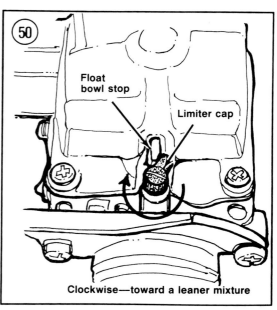

Float
bowl stop

Limiter cap

Clockwise—toward a leaner mixture

2. Start the engine and let it reach normal operating temperature. Approximately 5-10 minutes of stop and go riding is usually sufficient. Shut the engine off.

3. Connect a portable tachometer following the manufacturer's instructions.

4. Turn the idle adjust screw in or out to obtain the idle speed listed in **Table 1**.

5. Turn the pilot screw *in* slowly until the engine stops.

6. Turn the pilot screw *out* the number of turns listed in **Table 1**.

7. Start the engine and turn the idle adjust screw in or out to achieve the idle speed listed in **Table 1**.

WARNING
With the engine idling, move the handlebar from side to side. If idle speed increases during this movement, the throttle cable needs adjustment or it may be incorrectly routed through the frame. Correct this problem immediately. Do not ride the bike in this unsafe condition.

8. Disconnect the portable tachometer.

9. Perform this step only if a new limiter cap is to be installed. Install the limiter caps as follows:
   a. Apply Loctite No. 601, or equivalent, to the new limiter cap.
   b. Position the limiter cap against the stop on the float bowl (**Figure 50**) so that the pilot screw can only turn *clockwise*, not counterclockwise.
   c. Install the limiter cap on the pilot screw. Make sure the pilot screw does not move while installing the limiter cap.

10. After this adjustment is completed, test ride the bike. Throttle response from idle should be rapid and without any hesitation.

Air Screw Adjustment
(1984-1985 XR200R, 1984-on XR250R, XR350R)

The air filter element must be cleaned before starting this procedure or the results will be inaccurate. Refer to Chapter Three.

1. For the preliminary adjustment, carefully turn the air screw (**Figure 51**) in until it seats *lightly* and then back it out the number of turns listed in **Table 2**.

CAUTION
The air screw seat can be damaged if the air screw is tightened too hard against the seat.

2. Start the engine and let it reach normal operating temperature. Approximately 5-10 minutes of stop and go riding is usually sufficient. Shut the engine off.

3. Connect a portable tachometer following the manufacturer's instructions.

4. Turn the idle adjust screw (**Figure 52**) in or out to obtain the idle speed listed in **Table 1**.

5. Open and close the throttle a couple of times. Engine speed should increase smoothly with no hesitation.

6. Turn the air screw in or out to obtain the highest idle speed.

7. Turn the idle adjust screw (**Figure 52**) in or out to obtain the idle speed listed in **Table 1**.

WARNING
With the engine idling, move the handlebar from side to side. If idle speed increases during this movement, the throttle cable needs adjustment or it may be incorrectly routed through the frame. Correct this problem immediately. Do not ride the bike in this unsafe condition.

8. Turn the engine off and disconnect the portable tachometer.

9. After this adjustment is completed, test ride the bike. Throttle response from idle should be rapid and without any hesitation.

Secondary Carburetor Touch Lever Adjustment (XR350R)

Refer to **Figure 53** for this procedure.

1. Turn the throttle adjust screw (**Figure 52**) *counterclockwise* until it stops. Record the number of turns.

2. Turn the secondary touch lever adjust screw *out* until the stopper on the secondary touch lever lightly bottoms out on the lug on the throttle lever.

3. Turn the secondary touch lever adjust screw *in* until the clearance (dimension A) between the stopper and the lug is 4.5-5.0 mm (0.177-0.207 in.).

4. Turn the throttle adjust screw (**Figure 52**) *clockwise* to the position recorded in Step 1.

5. Adjust idle speed as described in this chapter.

Secondary Carburetor Touch Lever Adjustment (1984-1985 XR200R, 1984-1985 XR250R)

Refer to **Figure 54** for this procedure.

1. Turn the idle adjust screw (**Figure 55**) *counterclockwise* until it stops. Record the number of turns.

2. Loosen the locknut on the secondary touch lever adjust screw.

3. Turn the secondary touch lever adjust screw *out* until the stopper on the secondary touch lever lightly bottoms out on the lug on the throttle lever.

4. Turn the secondary touch lever adjust screw *in* until the clearance (dimension A) between the stopper and the lug is as follows:

    a. XR200R: 4.5-5.0 mm (0.177-0.207 in.).

    b. XR250R: 3.5-4.0 mm (0.137-0.157 in.).

5. Tighten the locknut.

6. Turn the idle adjust screw (**Figure 55**) *clockwise* to the position recorded in Step 1.

7. Adjust idle speed as described in this chapter.

Secondary Carburetor Touch Lever Adjustment (XL350R)

Refer to **Figure 54** for this procedure.

Positive closure adjustment

1. Turn the idle adjust screw (**Figure 55**) *counterclockwise* until it stops. Record the number of turns.

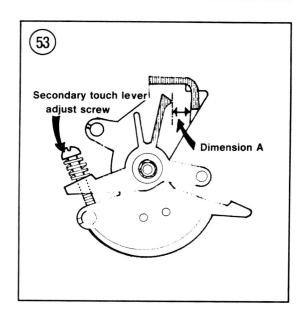

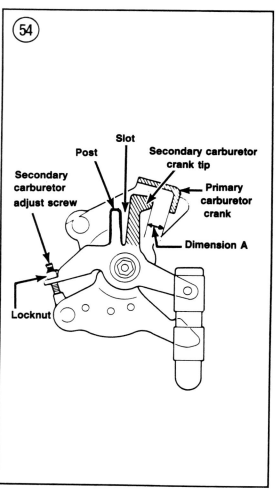

2. Loosen the locknut on the secondary touch lever adjust screw.

3. Turn the secondary touch lever adjust screw *in* until it just contacts the primary carburetor crank.

4. Tighten the locknut.

Opening clearance adjustment

1. Turn the idle adjust screw (**Figure 55**) *counterclockwise* until it no longer contacts the primary carburetor crank.

2. Completely close the throttle.

3. Measure the clearance (dimension A) between the primary carburetor crank and the secondary carburetor tip (**Figure 55**). The specified clearance is 4.5-5.0 mm (0.18-0.20 in.).

4. If the clearance is not within specification, carefully bend the secondary carburetor crank tip as follows:

    a. To reduce the clearance, insert a flat-bladed screwdriver blade in the slot behind the secondary carburetor crank tip. Gently twist the screwdriver against the post. This will open up the gap in the slot and move the crank tip closer to the primary carburetor crank.

    b. To reduce the clearance, use a pair of gas pliers and gently squeeze the secondary carburetor crank tip back against the post behind the crank tip. This will close the gap in the slot and move the crank tip away from the primary carburetor crank.

5. Adjust idle speed as described in this chapter.

Fast Idle Adjustment (XL250S)

1. Start the engine and let it reach normal operating temperature. Approximately 5-10 minutes of stop and go riding is usually sufficient. Shut the engine off.

2. Connect a portable tachometer following the manufacturer's instructions.

3. Start the engine and pull the choke knob out (**Figure 56**) to its detent position. The correct high speed idle is 2,000-2,500 rpm.

> *NOTE*
> *Figure 57 is shown with the fuel tank and side covers removed for clarity only; do not remove them for this adjustment.*

> *NOTE*
> *The locknut and adjusting screw are covered with locking paint at the factory so they will be difficult to adjust the first time.*

4. Adjust by loosening the locknut and turning the adjust screw (**Figure 57**) until the fast idle speed is correct.
5. Open and close the throttle a couple of times and check for variations. Readjust if necessary.
6. Turn the engine off and disconnect the portable tachometer.

Choke Adjustment
(1984-on XL Series)

First make sure the choke operates smoothly with no binding. If the cable binds, lubricate it as described under *Control Cables* in Chapter Three. If the cable still does not operate smoothly it must be replaced as described in this chapter.
1. Remove the seat and both side covers.
2. Remove the fuel tank as described in this chapter.
3. Operate the choke lever and check for smooth operation of the cable and choke mechanism.

> *NOTE*
> *The choke circuit is a "bystarter" system in which the choke lever opens a valve rather than closing a butterfly in the venturi area as on many carburetors. In the open position, the slow jet discharges a stream of fuel into the carburetor venturi to enrich the mixture when the engine is cold.*

4. Pull the choke lever (**Figure 58**) all the way back to the fully open position and then to the fully closed position.
5. Measure the choke valve stroke (**Figure 59**). The correct stroke is 5-7 mm (3/16-1/4 in.).
6. To adjust, loosen the cable clamping screw (A, **Figure 5**) and move the cable sheath either up or down to achieve the correct amount of stroke.
7. Repeat Steps 4 through 6 until the correct stroke can be achieved.
8. If proper adjustment cannot be achieved using this procedure the cable has stretched and must be replaced as described in this chapter.
9. Reinstall the fuel tank, seat and the side covers.

High Altitude Adjustment
(XR250)

Make sure the air screw is adjusted properly before performing this procedure.

If the bike is going to be ridden for any sustained period of time at high elevations (2,000 m/6,500 ft.) the carburetor must be readjusted to improve performance and decrease exhaust emissions.

> *CAUTION*
> *When the bike is returned to lower elevations (near sea level), the main jet must be changed back to the original size and the idle speed readjusted to idle speed listed in* ***Table 1****.*

1. Remove the carburetor assembly as described in this chapter.
2. Remove the screws securing the float bowl and remove the bowl.
3. Remove the standard main jet (**Figure 60**) and install the new smaller one. The sizes are listed in **Table 1**.
4. Reassemble and install the carburetor.
5. Adjust idle speed as described in Chapter Three. The idle speed is the same as with the standard main jet.
6. If the engine idle is rough or the engine misses or stalls, adjust the pilot screw as described in this chapter except for the following. The pilot screw must be backed out 1 3/4 turns (not 2 1/2 turns as with the standard main jet).

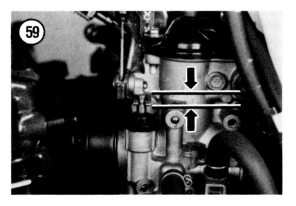

High Altitude Adjustment (XL250R, XL350R)

If the bike is going to be ridden for any sustained period of time at high elevations (2,000 m/6,500 ft.) the carburetor must be readjusted to improve performance and decrease exhaust emissions.

CAUTION
When the bike is returned to lower elevations (near sea level), the main jet must be changed back to the original size and the idle speed readjusted to idle speed listed in Table 1.

1. Remove the carburetor assembly as described in this chapter.
2. Remove the screws securing the float bowls and remove both bowls.
3. Remove the standard main jet (**Figure 61**) and install a new smaller jet in each carburetor. The sizes are listed in **Table 1.**
4. Turn the air screw *counterclockwise* as follows:
   a. XL250R:
   1984—2 full turns.
   1985—3/8 turn.
   1986-on—1 full turn.
   b. XL350R: 1/2 turn.
5. Reassemble and install the carburetor.

6. Adjust idle speed as described in Chapter Three. The idle speed is the same as with the standard main jet.

High-altitude and Temperature Adjustment (1984-on XR200R and 1981-on XR250R)

High-altitude and temperature adjustments consists of 3 different changes to the carburetor: main jet size change, a different location of the clip on the jet needle and a different pilot screw setting. Refer to **Figure 62**.

If the bike is going to be ridden for any sustained period of time at high elevations (above 2,000 m/6,500 ft.), the main jet should be changed to a 1-step smaller jet. Never change a jet by more than one size at a time without test riding the bike and running a spark plug test as described in Chapter Three.

CAUTION
If the carburetor has been adjusted for higher elevations, it must be changed back to the standard settings when the bike is returned to lower elevations (near sea level). Engine overheating and piston seizure will occur if the engine runs too lean.

Rejetting The Carburetors

Do not try to solve a poor running engine problem by rejetting the carburetors if all of the following conditions hold true:
   a. The engine has held a good tune in the past with the standard jetting.
   b. The engine has not been modified.
   c. The motorcycle is being operated in the same geographical region under the same general climatic conditions as in the past.
   d. The motorcycle was and is being ridden at average highway speeds.

If those conditions all hold true, the chances are that the problem is due to a malfunction in the carburetor or in another component that needs to be adjusted or repaired. Changing carburetor jet size probably won't solve the problem. Rejetting the carburetors may be necessary if any of the following conditions hold true:
   a. A non-standard type of air filter element is being used.
   b. A non-standard exhaust system is installed on the motorcycle.
   c. Any of the top end components in the engine (pistons, cams, valves, compression ratio, etc.) have been modified.

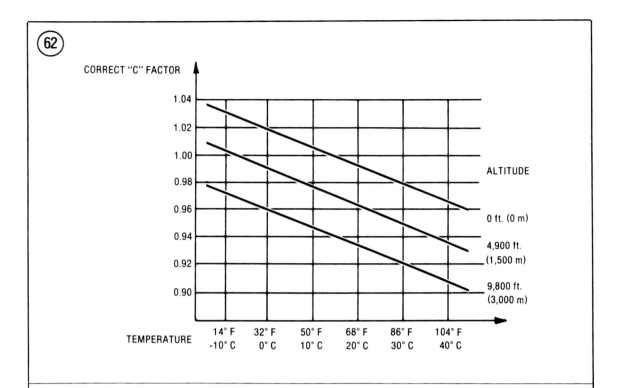

Use the information in this table to determine what carburetor adjustments are necessary for proper engine operation in various areas.

The cart in the table is divided in 2 directions:

    Horizontal—for various ambient temperatures
    Vertical (right-hand side)—various altitudes
    Vertical (left-hand side)—for the "C" factor

Determine the approximate altitude and surrounding air temperature of the area where you are going to ride. Locate these 2 factors on the cart. Where these 2 factors intersect (vertical and horizontal), closest to one of the angled lines, will establish the "C" factor. Use this established "C" factor for the following steps:

To Determine Main Jet Size
Multiply the standard main jet number (No. 138) by the "C" factor. Use the main jet number closest to the number in the answer.

EXAMPLE
Main jet number times the "C" factor—i.e.
(138 × 0.96 = 132.48)—use main jet number 132.

To Determine the Pilot Screw Setting and Jet Needle Clip Position
If the determined "C" factor is above 0.95 (left-hand side of the chart) no adjustment is necessary to the pilot screw or clip position change on the jet needle for proper engine operation.

If the determined "C" factor is 0.95 (left-hand side of the chart) or anywhere below, turn the pilot screw *out* by ½ turn and raise the clip on the jet needle by one groove.

EXAMPLE
Pilot screw opening (+) plus ½ turn—i.e.
(2½ + ½ turn = 3). Turn the pilot screw out 3 turns from the *lightly seated position.*

EXAMPLE
Jet needle clip standard position minus 1 position—i.e.
4 − 1 = 3). Move the jet needle clip to the No. 3 position on the jet needle.

d. The motorcycle is in use at considerably higher or lower altitudes or in a considerably hotter or colder climate than in the past.

e. The motorcycle is being operated at considerably higher speeds than before and changing to colder spark plugs does not solve the problem.

f. Someone has previously changed the carburetor jetting.

g. The motorcycle has never held a satisfactory engine tune.

If it is necessary to rejet the carburetors, check with a dealer or motorcycle performance tuner for recommendations as to the size of jets to install for your specific situation.

If you do change the jets, do so only one size at a time. After rejetting, test ride the bike and perform a spark plug test; refer to *Reading Spark Plugs* in Chapter Three.

THROTTLE CABLE REPLACEMENT

1. Remove both side covers and the seat.
2. Remove the fuel tank as described in this chapter.
3. Remove the screws securing the throttle housing together and disengage the throttle cables from the throttle grip.

4. In order to gain access to the throttle wheel on the carburetor, partially remove the carburetor assembly as described in this chapter.
5. Loosen both throttle cable locknuts (**Figure 63**) at the carburetor assembly.
6. Disconnect the "pull" cable (A, **Figure 64**) and the "push" cable (B, **Figure 64**) from the throttle wheel.

NOTE
The piece of string attached in the next step will be used to pull the new throttle cables back through the frame so they will be routed in exactly the same position as the old ones were.

7. Tie a piece of heavy string or cord (approximately 7 ft./2 m long) to the carburetor end of both throttle cables. Wrap this end with masking or duct tape. Do not use an excessive amount of tape as it must be pulled through the frame loop during removal. Tie the other end of the string to the frame or air box.
8. At the throttle grip end of the cables, carefully pull the cables (and attached string) out through the frame. Make sure the attached string follows the same path as the cables through the frame.
9. Remove the tape and untie the string from the old cables.
10. Lubricate the new cables as described in Chapter Three.
11. Tie the string to the new throttle cables and wrap it with tape.
12. Carefully pull the string back through the frame, routing the new cables through the same path as the old cables.
13. Remove the tape and untie the string from the cables and the frame.

CAUTION
*The throttle cables are the push/pull type and must be installed as described and shown in Step 14 and Step 15. Do **not** interchange the 2 cables.*

14. Attach the throttle "pull" cable to the bottom receptacle in the throttle wheel (A, **Figure 64**).
15. Attach the throttle "push" cable to the top receptacle in the throttle wheel (B, **Figure 64**).
16. Install the throttle/switch housing and tighten the screws securely.
17. Operate the throttle grip and make sure the carburetor throttle linkage is operating correctly, with no binding. If operation is incorrect or there is binding, carefully check that the cables are attached correctly and there are no tight bends in the cables.

18. Install the carburetor assembly, fuel tank and seat.

19. Adjust the throttle cables as described in Chapter Three.

20. Test ride the bike slowly at first and make sure the throttle is operating correctly.

CHOKE CABLE REPLACEMENT

1. Remove both side covers and the seat.

2. Remove the fuel tank as described in this chapter.

3A. On single-carburetor models, loosen the cable clamp screw (**Figure 65**) and disconnect the cable from the link plate on the carburetor.

3B. On dual-carburetor models, loosen the cable clamp screw (A, **Figure 66**) and disconnect the cable from the carburetor (B, **Figure 66**).

4A. On 1978-1983 models, loosen the locknut and remove the choke cable from the bracket on the upper fork bridge.

4B. On 1984-on models, remove the screw (**Figure 67**) securing the cable lever and cable to the housing and remove the cable end from the lever.

NOTE
The piece of string attached in the next step will be used to pull the new choke cable back through the frame so it will be routed in the same position as the old cable.

5. Tie a piece of heavy string or cord (approximately 7 ft./2 m long) to the carburetor end of the choke cable. Wrap this end with masking or duct tape. Do not use an excessive amount of tape as it must be pulled through the frame loop during removal. Tie the other end of the string to the frame or air box.

6. At the choke lever end of the cable, carefully pull the cable (and attached string) out through the frame. Make sure the attached string follows the same path that the cable does through the frame.

7. Remove the tape and untie the string from the old cable.

8. Lubricate the new cable as described in Chapter Three.

9. Tie the string to the new choke cable and wrap it with tape.

10. Carefully pull the string back through the frame, routing the new cable through the same path as the old cable.

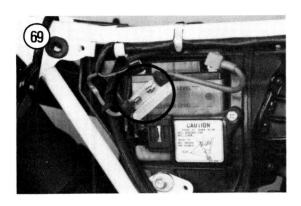

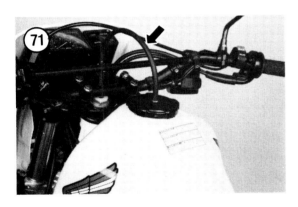

11. Remove the tape and untie the string from the cable and the frame.

12A. On 1978-1983 models, install the cable into the bracket on the upper fork bridge. Tighten the locknut.

12B. On 1984-on models, attach the cable to the lever and install the lever and screw onto the housing. Tighten the screw securely.

13A. On single-carburetor models, connect the cable onto the link plate on the carburetor. Tighten the cable clamp screw (**Figure 68**).

13B. On dual-carburetor models, connect the cable onto the carburetor. Tighten the cable clamp screw (A, **Figure 66**).

14. Operate the choke lever and make sure the carburetor choke linkage is operating correctly, with no binding. If operation is incorrect or there is binding, carefully check that the cable is attached correctly and there are no tight bends in the cable.

15. Adjust the choke cable as described in this chapter.

7

FUEL TANK (METAL)

Removal/Installation

1. Remove both side covers and the seat.

> *NOTE*
> *On XL250S models, reinstall the seat strap bolts as they also hold the upper portion of the shocks to the frame. Remove and install one bolt at a time.*

2. On XL series models, disconnect the battery negative lead or disconnect the main fuse (**Figure 69**).

3. Turn the fuel shutoff valve to the OFF position (A, **Figure 70**).

4. Remove the fuel line to the carburetor assembly (B, **Figure 70**).

5. Pull the fuel filler cap vent tube (**Figure 71**) from the steering head receptacle or filler cap.

6. Remove the bolt and washer (**Figure 72**) securing the rear of the fuel tank. Don't lose the metal spacer in the rubber cushion.

7. Lift up and pull the tank to the rear and remove the fuel tank.

8. Install by reversing these removal steps, noting the following.

9. Inspect the rubber cushions (**Figure 73**) where the front of the fuel tank attaches to the frame. Replace if they are damaged or starting to deteriorate.

10. Turn on the fuel shutoff valve (**Figure 74**) and check for fuel leaks.

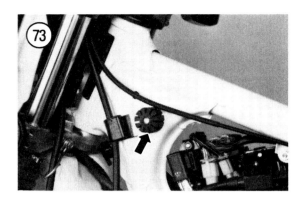

FUEL TANK (PLASTIC)

Removal/Installation

1. Remove both side covers and the seat.
2. Turn the fuel shutoff valve to the OFF position.
3. Remove the fuel line that runs to the carburetor assembly.
4. Unhook the rubber strap (A, **Figure 75**) securing the rear of the tank.
5. Remove the bolt and spacer on each side of the front of the fuel tank (B, **Figure 75**).
6. Pull the fuel filler cap vent tube (C, **Figure 75**) from the steering head receptacle.
7. Lift up and pull the tank to the rear and remove the fuel tank.
8. Inspect the rubber protective bands (**Figure 76**) or rubber covers (**Figure 77**) on the nuts of the engine upper hanger plate. Replace as a set if any are damaged or starting to deteriorate.

> *WARNING*
> *If the protective bands or rubber covers are worn through or not installed, the bolt heads or nuts may wear a hole through the fuel tank. This presents a real fire danger.*

9. Install by reversing these removal steps.

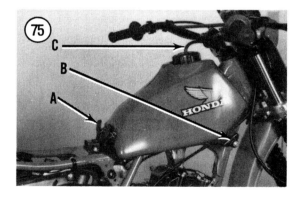

FUEL FILTER

The bike is equipped with a small fuel filter screen in the fuel shutoff valve. Considering the dirt and residue that is often found in today's gasoline, it is good idea to install an inline fuel filter to help keep the carburetor clean.

A good quality inline fuel filter (A.C. part No. GF453 or equivalent) is available at most auto and motorcycle supply stores. Just cut the fuel line from the fuel tank to the carburetor and install the filter. Cut out a section of the fuel line the length of the filter so the fuel line does not kink and restrict fuel flow. Insert the fuel filter and make sure the fuel line is secured to the filter at each end.

GASOLINE/ALCOHOL BLEND TEST

Gasoline blended with alcohol is available in many areas. Most states and most fuel suppliers require labeling of gasoline pumps that dispense gasoline containing a certain percentage of alcohol (methyl or wood). If in doubt, ask the service station operator if their fuel contains any alcohol. A gasoline/alcohol blend, even if it contains co-solvents and corrosion inhibitors for methanol, may be damaging to the fuel system. It may also cause poor performance, hot engine restart or hot-engine running problems.

If you are not sure if the fuel you purchased contains alcohol, run this simple and effective test.

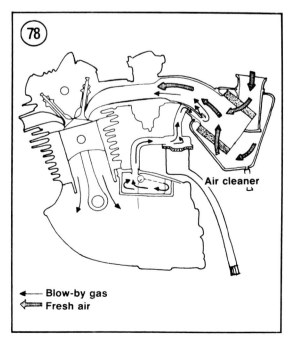

← **Blow-by gas**
← **Fresh air**

A blended fuel doesn't look any different from straight gasoline so it must be tested.

WARNING
Gasoline is very volatile and presents an extreme fire hazard. Be sure to work in a well-ventilated area away from any open flames (including pilot lights on household appliances). Do not allow anyone to smoke in the area and have a fire extinguisher rated for gasoline fires handy.

During this test keep the following facts in mind:
  a. Alcohol and gasoline mix together.
  b. Alcohol mixes *easier* with water.
  c. Gasoline and water do *not* mix.

NOTE
If cosolvents have been used in the gasoline, this test may not work with water. Repeat this test using automotive antifreeze instead of water.

Use an 8 oz. transparent baby bottle with a sealable cap.
1. Set the baby bottle on a level surface and add water up to the 1.5 oz mark. Mark this line on the bottle with a fine-line permanent marking pen. This will be the reference line used later in this test.
2. Add the suspect fuel into the baby bottle up to the 8 oz. mark.
3. Install the sealable cap and shake the bottle vigorously for about 10 seconds.
4. Set the baby bottle upright on the level surface used in Step 1 and wait for a few minutes for the mixture to settle down.
5. If there is *no* alcohol in the fuel the gasoline/water separation line will be exactly on the 1.5 oz reference line made in Step 1.
6. If there *is* alcohol in the fuel the gasoline/water separation line will be *above* the 1.5 oz. reference line made in Step 1. The alcohol has separated from the gasoline and mixed in with the water (remember it is easier for the alcohol to mix with water than gasoline).

WARNING
*After the test, discard the baby bottle or place it out of reach of small children. There will always be a gasoline and alcohol residue in it and should **not** be used to drink out of.*

CRANKCASE BREATHER SYSTEM (U.S. ONLY)

To comply with air pollution standards, the XL series models are equipped with a closed crankcase breather system. The system shown in **Figure 78** has a breather separator unit (A, **Figure 79**) and the blowby gases from crankcase are recirculated into the fuel/air mixture and thus into the engine to be burned. The system used on the XR series models differs in that the gases are not routed to the air filter air box nor are they burned in the engine. They are routed as shown in **Figure 80** and are vented to the atmosphere.

Inspection/Cleaning

Make sure all hose clamps (B, **Figure 79**) are tight. Check all hoses for deterioration and replace as necessary.

Remove the plug on the XL series (**Figure 81**) or XR series (**Figure 82**) from the drain hose and drain out all residue. This cleaning procedure should be done more frequently if a considerable amount of riding is done at full throttle or in the rain.

> *NOTE*
> *Be sure to install the drain plug and clamp.*

EVAPORATIVE EMISSION CONTROL SYSTEM (1984-ON CALIFORNIA XL SERIES MODELS ONLY)

Fuel vapor from the fuel tank is routed into a charcoal canister (**Figure 83**). This vapor is stored when the engine is not running. When the engine is running, these vapors are drawn through a purge control valve and into the carburetors.   Make sure all hose clamps are tight. Check all hoses for deterioration and replace as necessary (**Figure 84**).

Refer to **Figure 85** for correct hose routing to the PC valve. When removing the hoses from the PC valve, mark the hose and the fitting with a piece of masking tape and identify where the hose goes. There are so many vacuum hoses on these models that reconnection can be very confusing.

The charcoal canister and the PC valve are located just forward of the rear wheel.

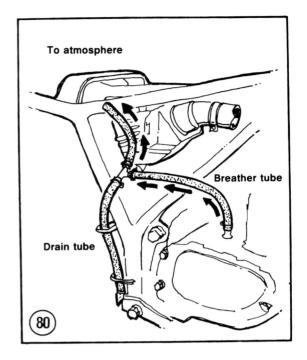

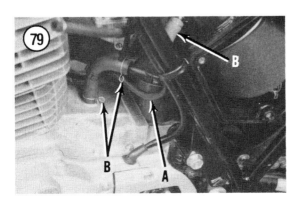

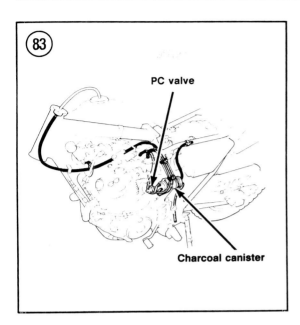

PC valve

Charcoal canister

Removal/Installation

1. Remove both side covers and the seat.
2. Remove the fuel tank as described in this chapter.
3. Remove the rear wheel as described in Chapter Nine.

> *NOTE*
> *Prior to removing the hoses from the PC valve, mark the hose and the fitting with a piece of masking tape and identify where the hose goes.*

4. Disconnect the hoses (**Figure 84**) going to the charcoal canister from the PC valve.
5. Remove the bolt(s) (**Figure 86**) securing the charcoal canister to the canister bracket on the frame and remove the canister assembly.
6. Install by reversing these removal steps.
7. Be sure to install the hoses to their correct fittings on the PC valve.
8. Make sure the hoses are not kinked, twisted or in contact with any sharp surfaces.

AIR FILTER CASE

Removal/Installation

> *NOTE*
> *On some models, the air filter case must be removed for rear shock absorber removal and installation. This procedure represents a typical air filter case removal and installation. Minor variations exist among the various models.*

1. Remove the seat and both side covers.
2. On California models, remove the charcoal canister and the PC valve as described in this chapter.
3. Remove the battery as described in Chapter Three.

7

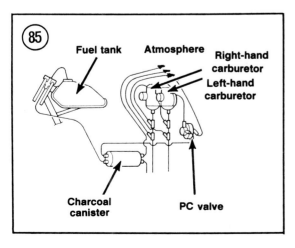

Fuel tank   Atmosphere   Right-hand carburetor
Left-hand carburetor

Charcoal canister   PC valve

4. Loosen the screws on the clamping bands on each carburetor at the back where they attach to the air box inlet tube (A, **Figure 87**).

5. Remove the bolt securing the air box (B, **Figure 87**) on the side.

6. Remove the bolts (A, **Figure 88**) securing the top of the air box to the frame.

7. On some models, remove the muffler as described in this chapter.

8. Unhook the metal band (B, **Figure 88**) securing the electrical harness to the air box. Move the wiring harness out of the way.

9. Disconnect the crankcase breather hose (C, **Figure 88**) from the air box.

10. Remove the air filter air box from the frame.

11. Install by reversing these removal steps.

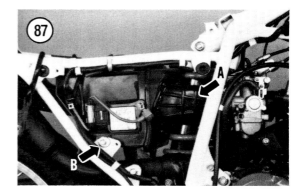

EXHAUST SYSTEM

The exhaust system is a vital performance component and frequently, because of its design, it is a vulnerable piece of equipment. Check the exhaust system for deep dents and fractures and repair or replace them immediately. Check the muffler frame mounting flanges for fractures and loose bolts. Check the cylinder head mounting flanges for tightness. A loose exhaust pipe connection can rob the engine of power.

The exhaust system consists of a dual exhaust pipe, single muffler and a spark arrestor.

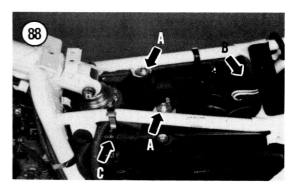

Removal/Installation

1. Remove the side covers and the seat.

2. Remove the fuel tank as described in this chapter.

3. Remove the nuts (**Figure 89**) securing the exhaust pipe flanges to the cylinder head.

4. Loosen the clamping bolts (**Figure 90**) securing the exhaust pipe to the muffler. Withdraw the exhaust pipe from the muffler and the cylinder head and remove it.

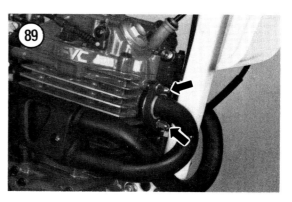

NOTE
Don't lose the 2 collars at each exhaust port when the exhaust pipe is removed from the cylinder head.

5. Remove the bolt(s) and washer(s) (**Figure 91**) securing the muffler to the frame. Withdraw the muffler out through the rear and remove it.

6. Inspect the gaskets at all joints; replace as necessary.

7. Be sure to install a new gasket in each exhaust port in the cylinder head.

8. Install the muffler onto the frame.

9. Install the exhaust pipe assembly into position and install one cylinder head nut (at each exhaust port) only finger-tight until the muffler bolts and washers are installed.

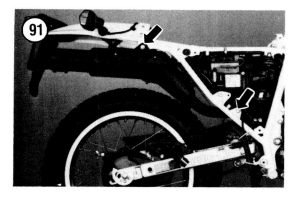

10. Install the muffler mounting bolt(s) and washer(s); do not tighten at this time. Make sure the head pipe inlet is correctly seated in the exhaust port.

11. Remove both cylinder head nuts. Install the 4 collars into place (2 collars per exhaust port) and slide the exhaust flange into position. Make sure the collars are correctly seated into the cylinder head exhaust port.

NOTE
Tightening the cylinder head nuts first will minimize exhaust leaks at the cylinder head.

12. Tighten the muffler bolts securely.

13. Install the fuel tank, seat and side covers.

14. After installation is complete, start the engine and make sure there are no exhaust leaks.

7

Table 1 CARBURETOR SPECIFICATIONS

Item	XR200R	
Model No.		
1984	PH31A	
1985-on	PH32A	
Main jet No.		
Primary carb	98	
Secondary		
1984	95	
1985	98	
High altitude main jet No.		
See High-altitude and Temperature Adjustment in text.		
Slow jet	42	
Initial pilot screw opening		
1984	1 3/8 turns	
1985	1 1/8 turns	
Needle jet clip position from top		
Primary carb	4th groove	
Secondary carb	3rd groove	
Float level	18 mm (0.71 in.)	
Idle speed	1,300 ± 100 rpm	

Item	1978-1979 XL250S	1980-1981 XL250S
Model No.	PD 03A	PD 10A
Main jet No.	120	115
Slow jet	40	38
Initial pilot screw opening	1 3/8 turns	1 3/4 turns
Needle jet clip position from top	fixed	fixed
Float level	14.5 mm (0.57 in.)	15.5 mm (0.57 in.)
Idle speed	1,200 ± 100 rpm	1,200 ± 100 rpm

(continued)

Table 1 CARBURETOR SPECIFICATIONS (cont.)

Item	1982-1983 XL250R	
Model No.	PD 74A	
Main jet No.	110	
High altitude jet	NA	
Slow jet	38	
Initial pilot	1 3/4 turns	
screw opening		
Needle jet clip clip	fixed	
position from top		
Float level	14.0 mm (0.55 in.)	
Idle speed	1,200 ± 100 rpm	

Item	1984-ON XL250R (49-STATE)	1984-ON XL250R (CALIF)
Model No.		
1984	PH28A	PH85A
1985-on	PH10A	PH10B
Main jet No.		
Primary carb		
1984	108	108
1985	102	102
1986	102	105
Secondary carb	122	122
High altitude main jet		
Primary carb	100	100
Secondary carb	115	115
Slow jet	42	42
Initial pilot	1 1/2 turns	1 1/2 turns
screw opening		
Needle jet clip position from top		
Primary carb	2nd groove	2nd groove
Secondary carb	2nd groove	2nd groove
Float level	18 mm (0.71 in.)	18 mm (0.71 in.)
Idle speed	1,300 ± 100 rpm	1,300 ± 100 rpm

Item	1979 XR250	
Model No.	PD 02A	
Main jet No.	122	
High altitude jet	118	
Slow jet	40	
Initial pilot	2 1/8 turns	
screw opening		
Needle jet clip clip	4th groove	
position from top		
Float level	14.5 mm (0.57 in.)	
Idle speed	1,200 ± 100 rpm	

Item	1980 XR250	1981-1982 XR250R
Model No.	PD 12A	PD 71A
Main jet No.	120	130
High altitude jet	115	115, 118, 120, 122,
	125, 128, 132, 135	
Slow jet	40	40

(continued)

Table 1 CARBURETOR SPECIFICATIONS (cont.)

Item	1980 XR250	1981-1982 XR250R
Initial pilot screw opening	1 1/4 turns	2 1/2 turns
Needle jet clip clip position from top	4th groove	3rd groove
Float level	14.5 mm (0.57 in.)	12.5 mm (0.49 in.)
Idle speed	1,300 ± 100 rpm	1,300 ± 100 rpm

Item	1984-1985 XR250R	1986-ON XR250R*
Model No.		
1984	PH42A	
1985	PH41A	
1986	—	PD05A
Main jet No.		
Primary carb	108	
Secondary		
1984	105	
1985	98	
Main jet	—	125
High altitude main jet No.		
See High-altitude and Temperature Adjustment in text.		
Slow jet	45	40
Initial pilot screw opening		
1984	1 1/4 turns	
1985	1 full turn	
1986	—	2 1/4 turns
Needle jet clip position from top		
Primary carb	2nd groove	
Secondary carb	2dd groove	
Needle jet clip position from top	3rd groove	
Float level	18 mm (0.71 in.)	12.5 mm (0.49 in.)
Idle speed	1,300 ± 100 rpm	1,300 ± 100 rpm

Item	XL350R (49-STATE)	XL350R (CALIF)
Model No.	PH80A	PH81A
Main jet No.		
Primary carb	112	112
Secondary carb	110	110
High altitude main jet		
Primary carb	105	105
Secondary carb	102	102
Slow jet	42	42
Initial pilot screw opening	2 1/8 turns	2 1/8 turns
Needle jet clip position from top		
Primary carb	NA	NA
Secondary carb	NA	NA
Float level	18 mm (0.71 in.)	18 mm (0.71 in.)
Idle speed	1,300 ± 100 rpm	1,300 ± 100 rpm

Item	1983 XR350R
Model No.	PD 01A
Main jet No.	
Primary carb.	112
Secondary carb.	105 (continued)

7

Table 1 CARBURETOR SPECIFICATIONS (cont.)

Item	1983 XR350R
High altitude jet	90, 98, 100, 102, 108, 110 115, 118, 120
Slow jet	45
Initial pilot screw opening	1 1/4 turns
Needle jet clip position from top	
Primary carb.	2nd groove
Secondary carb.	3rd groove
Float level	18.0 mm (0.71 in.)
Idle speed	1,300 ± 100 rpm

Item	1984-1985 XR350R*
Model No.	
1984	PH05A
1985	PD11D
Main jet No.	
Primary carb	112
Secondary carb	105
1985	150
High altitude main jet	
See High-altitude and Temperature Adjustment in test.	
Slow jet	
1984	42
1985	50
Initial pilot screw opening	
1984	1 3/4 turns
1985	1 1/2 turns
Needle jet clip position from top	
Primary carb	3rd groove
Secondary carb	1st groove
1985	3rd groove
Float level	
1984	18 mm (0.71 in.)
1985	12.5 mm (0.49 in.)
Idle speed	1,300 ± 100 rpm

NA: Honda does not provide service information for all items or all models.
*The 1986-on XR250R and 1985 XR350R are equipped with a single carburetor.

Table 2 CARBURETOR PILOT (OR AIR) SCREW INITIAL OPENING

Model	Turns out
XR200R	
1984	1 3/8
1985	1 1/8
XL250S	
1978-1979	1 3/8
1980-1981	1 3/4
XL250R	
1982-1983	1 3/4
1984-on	1 1/2
XR250	
1979	2 1/8
1980	1 1/4
XR250R	
1982-1983	2 1/2
1984	1 1/4
1985	1 full turn
1986-on	2 1/14
XL350R	2 1/8
XR350R	
1983	1 1/4
1984	1 3/4
1985	1 1/2

7

NOTE: If you own a 1990 or later model, first check the Supplement at the back of the book for any new service information.

CHAPTER EIGHT

ELECTRICAL SYSTEM

This chapter describes operating principles, service and test procedures for all electrical and ignition components, except the battery and spark plug. These are covered in Chapter Three.

The electrical systems vary between the XL and XR series models. The XL series is equipped with components approved for a street legal bike. The XR series is equipped only with a headlight and taillight (no battery) and is for off-road use only.

Where differences occur between the XL and XR series they are identified.

The electrical system includes the following systems:

    a. Charging system (XL series models).
    b. Ignition system.
    c. Lighting system.

Tables 1-7 are at the end of this chapter.

CHARGING SYSTEM (XL SERIES MODELS)

The charging system consists of the battery, alternator and a solid-state voltage regulator/rectifier. See **Figures 1-3**.

Alternating current generated by the alternator is rectified to direct current. The voltage regulator maintains the voltage to the electrical load (lights, ignition, etc.) within a specified range regardless of variations in engine speed and load.

Charging System Test

Whenever charging system trouble is suspected, make sure the battery is fully charged and in good condition before going any further. Clean and test the battery as described in Chapter Three. Make sure all electrical connectors are tight and free of corrosion.

1. Start the engine and let it reach normal operating temperature; shut off the engine.
2. Disconnect both battery wires leading to the voltage regulator/rectifier.
3. Connect a 0-15 DC voltmeter and 0-15 DC ammeter as shown in **Figure 4**.
4. Start the engine and let it idle.
5. Increase engine speed and check output at the engine speeds indicated in **Table 1**.
6. If the charging current is considerably lower than specified, check the alternator and/or the voltage regulator/rectifier.
7. If the charging current is too high, the voltage regulator/rectifier is probable at fault.
8. Test these components as described in this chapter. If found faulty they must be replaced as described in this chapter.
9. After the test is completed, disconnect the voltmeter and ammeter. Reconnect the voltage regulator/rectifier wires to the battery.

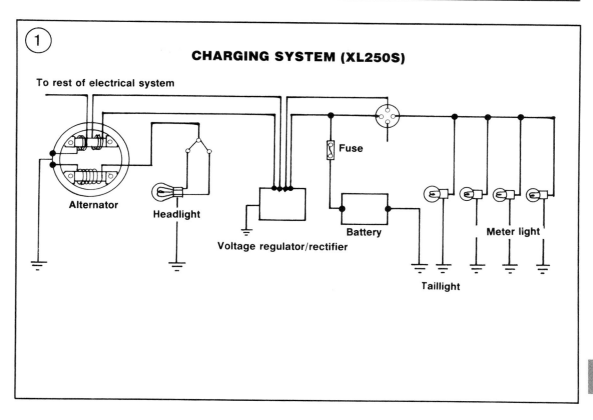

CHARGING SYSTEM (XL250S)

To rest of electrical system

Alternator

Headlight

Fuse

Voltage regulator/rectifier

Battery

Meter light

Taillight

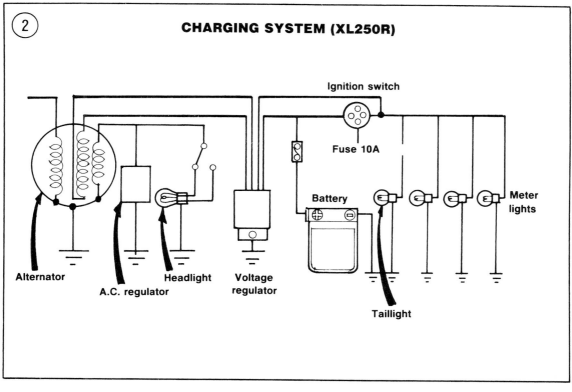

CHARGING SYSTEM (XL250R)

Ignition switch

Fuse 10A

Battery

Meter lights

Alternator

A.C. regulator

Headlight

Voltage regulator

Taillight

8

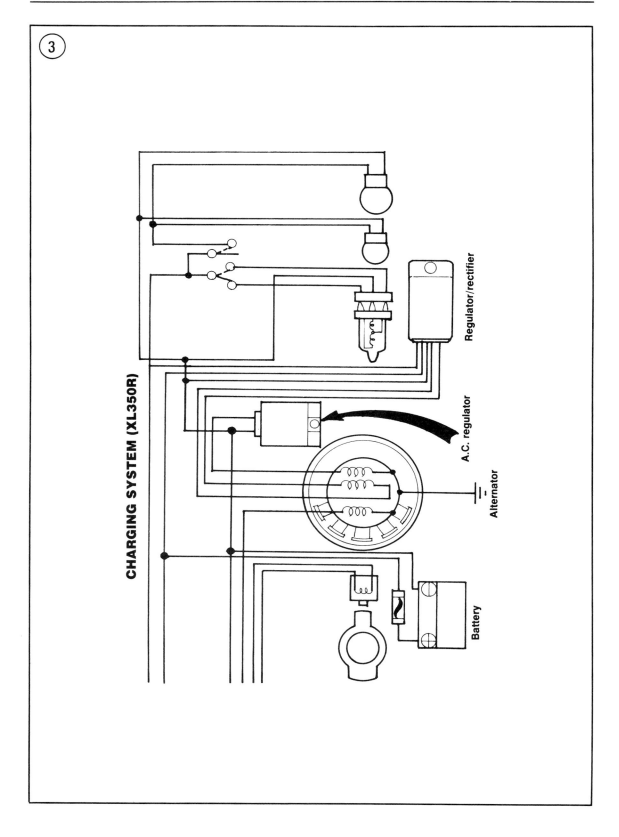

③

CHARGING SYSTEM (XL350R)

Regulator/rectifier

A.C. regulator

Alternator

Battery

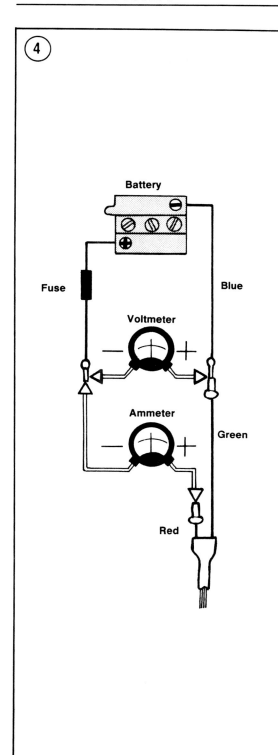

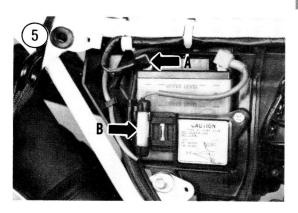

ALTERNATOR ROTOR

Removal/Installation

1. Remove the bolts securing the skid plate and remove the skid plate.
2. Remove the seat and both side covers.

> *NOTE*
> *On XL250S models, remove the seat strap bolts as they also hold the upper portion of the shock to the frame. Remove and reinstall one bolt at a time.*

3. Drain the engine oil as described in Chapter Three.
4. Remove the fuel tank as described in Chapter Seven.
5. On XL series models, disconnect the battery negative lead (A, **Figure 5**) or the main fuse (B, **Figure 5**).
6. Disconnect the alternator stator's 3-wire alternator electrical connector.
7. Shift the transmission into 5th gear.
8. Remove the clamping bolt on the gearshift lever (A, **Figure 6**) and remove the gearshift lever.
9. On 350 cc models, perform the following:

8

a. Loosen the locknut on the clutch cable at the hand lever. This will allow slack in the clutch cable.

b. Disconnect the clutch cable from the actuating arm (B, **Figure 6**) on the alternator cover.

10. Remove the bolts securing the drive sprocket cover (**Figure 7**) and remove the cover.

11. Remove the bolts securing the alternator cover and stator assembly (**Figure 8**) and remove the cover and gasket. Don't lose the locating dowels.

12. Have an assistant apply the rear brake. This will keep the rotor from rotating while removing the nut.

13. Remove the shoulder bolt (**Figure 9**) securing the alternator rotor.

14. Screw in a flywheel puller (**Figure 10**) until it stops. Use the Honda flywheel puller (part No. 07733-0020001), K & N (part No. 81-0170) or equivalent. Refer to **Figure 11** for 1983 models or **Figure 12** for all other models.

> *CAUTION*
> *Don't try to remove the rotor without a puller; any attempt to do so will ultimately lead to some form of damage to the engine and/or rotor. Many aftermarket pullers are available from motorcycle dealers or mail order houses. These pullers cost about $10 and they make an excellent addition to any mechanic's tool box. If you can't buy or borrow one, have a dealer remove the rotor.*

15. Hold the puller with a wrench and gradually tighten the center bolt until the rotor disengages from the crankshaft.

> *NOTE*
> *If the rotor is difficult to remove, strike the puller center bolt with a hammer a few times. This will usually break it loose.*

> *CAUTION*
> *Never strike the rotor with a hammer as this could demagnetize the rotor. If demagnetized, the rotor must be replaced.*

> *CAUTION*
> *If normal rotor removal attempts fail, do not force the puller as the threads may be stripped out of the rotor causing expensive damage. Take the vehicle to a dealer and have the rotor removed.*

16. Remove the rotor and the puller. Remove the puller from the rotor.

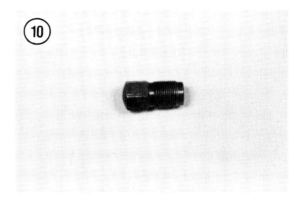

17. Make sure the Woodruff key is still in place in the slot in the crankshaft. Refer to **Figure 13** for RFVC engine models or **Figure 14** for all other models.

> *CAUTION*
> *Carefully inspect the inside of the rotor* ***(Figure 15)*** *for small bolts, washers or other metal "trash" that may have been picked up by the magnets. These small metal bits can cause severe damage to the alternator stator plate components.*

18. Install by reversing these removal steps, noting the following.
19. Make sure the Woodruff key is in place on the crankshaft and align the keyway in the rotor with the key when installing the rotor.
20. Have an assistant apply the rear brake. This will keep the rotor from rotating while tightening the bolt.
21. Install and tighten the rotor bolt to the torque specification listed in **Table 2**.
22. Install the locating dowels and a new gasket.
23. Adjust the clutch as described in Chapter Three.

8

ALTERNATOR STATOR

Removal/Installation

1. Perform Steps 1-11, *Alternator Rotor Removal/Installation* in this chapter.
2A. On 350 cc models, perform the following:
   a. Remove the bolts (A, **Figure 16**) securing the stator assembly to the alternator cover.
   b. Pull the electrical harness and rubber grommet (B, **Figure 16**) from the notch in the cover.
   c. Remove the stator assembly.

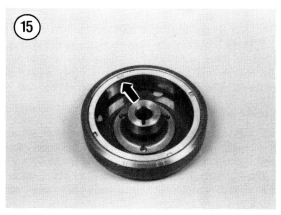

2B. On all other models, perform the following:
   a. Remove the bolts (A, **Figure 17**) securing the stator assembly and set plates to the alternator cover.
   b. Remove the bolt (B, **Figure 17**) securing the wire clamp and remove the wire clamp.
   c. Pull the electrical harness and both rubber grommets from the 2 notches in the cover.
   d. Remove the stator assembly.
3. Install by reversing these removal steps, noting the following.
4. On all models except the RFVC engine models, be sure to install the stator assembly with the "F" mark (C, **Figure 17**) toward the front of the alternator cover.
5. Make sure all electrical connectors are free of corrosion and are tight.

Stator Coil Testing

It is not necessary to remove the stator plate to perform the following tests. It is shown removed in the following procedure for clarity.

In order to get accurate resistance measurements, the stator assembly and coil must be approximately 20° C (68° F).
1. Remove the seat and side covers.
2. Remove the fuel tank as described in Chapter Seven.
3. On XL series models, disconnect the battery negative lead (A, **Figure 5**) or disconnect the main fuse (B, **Figure 5**).
4. Disconnect the alternator electrical connector coming from the alternator stator assembly and make the following tests:

Lighting coil

Use an ohmmeter set at R×1 and check for continuity between the following wires (A, **Figure 18**):
   a. XL series: White/yellow wire and ground.
   b. XR series: Blue wire and ground.
If there is continuity (low resistance) the coil is good. If there is no continuity (infinite resistance) the coil is bad and the stator assembly must be replaced. The individual coil cannot be replaced.

Exciter coil

On XL series models, use an ohmmeter set at R×1 and check for continuity between the pink/yellow wire and ground (B, **Figure 18**).

On XR series models, use an ohmmeter set at R×1 and check for continuity between the black/red wire and ground.

If there is continuity (low resistance) the coil is good. If there is no continuity (infinite resistance) the coil is bad and the stator assembly must be replaced. The individual coil cannot be replaced.
5. Connect the electrical connectors. Make sure all connectors are free of corrosion and are tight.
6. Install all items removed.

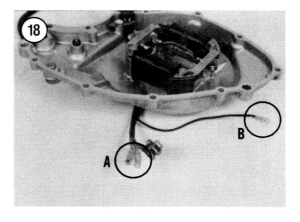

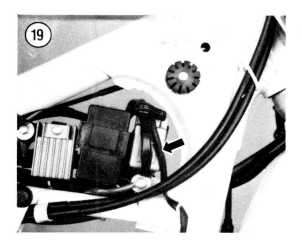

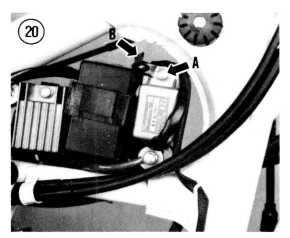

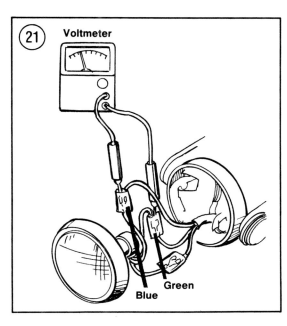

Voltmeter

Green
Blue

VOLTAGE REGULATOR/RECTIFIER (XL SERIES MODELS)

Removal/Installation

1. Remove the seat and both side covers.
2. Remove the fuel tank as described in Chapter Seven.
3. Disconnect the negative battery lead (A, **Figure 5**) or disconnect the main fuse (B, **Figure 5**).
4. Disconnect the electrical connector going to the voltage regulator (**Figure 19**) from the wiring harness.
5. Remove the bolt (A, **Figure 20**) securing the voltage regulator to the frame and remove the voltage regulator.
6. Install by reversing these removal steps, noting the following.
7. Make sure all electrical connectors are free of corrosion and are tight.
8. On models so equipped, don't forget to install the electrical wire harness (B, **Figure 20**) onto the bolt.

Performance Test (XL250S)

1. Remove the right-hand side cover.
2. Connect a voltmeter to the battery negative and positive terminals. Leave the battery cables attached.
3. Start the engine and let it idle; increase engine speed until the voltage going to the battery reaches 8.0-8.9 volts (usually at 5,000 rpm).
4. At this point the voltage regulator should prevent any further increase in voltage. If this does not happen and the voltage increases above the specified amount, the voltage regulator/rectifier is faulty and must be replaced.
5. Disconnect the voltmeter and shut off the engine.
6. Install the right-hand side cover.

Performance Test (XL250R, XL350R)

1. Remove the headlight lens assembly from the housing as described in Chapter Seven. Leave the electrical connector attached to the headlight bulb.
2. Turn the headlight dimmer switch to the HI position.
3. Connect a voltmeter to the headlight green and blue electrical wires. Refer to **Figure 21** for XL250R models or **Figure 22** for XL350R models.
4. Start the engine and let it idle; increase engine speed slowly until engine speed reaches 5,000 rpm.
5. The voltage should be 13.5-14.5 volts at this engine speed.

8

6. At this point the voltage regulator should prevent any further increase in voltage. If this does not happen and the voltage increases above the specified amount, the voltage regulator/rectifier is faulty and must be replaced.

7. Disconnect the voltmeter and shut off the engine.

8. Install the headlight lens assembly.

CAPACITOR DISCHARGE IGNITION

All models are equipped with a capacitor discharge ignition (CDI) system, a solid-state system that uses no breaker points. The ignition circuit is shown in the following illustrations:

a. **Figure 23**: XL250S.

b. **Figure 24**: XR250.

c. **Figure 25**: 1981-1982 XR250R, XR350R.

d. **Figure 26**: XL250R.

e. **Figure 27**: 1984-1985 XR200R, 1984-on XR250R.

f. **Figure 28**: XL350R.

As the rotor is turned by the crankshaft, the permanent magnets within the rotor cause an

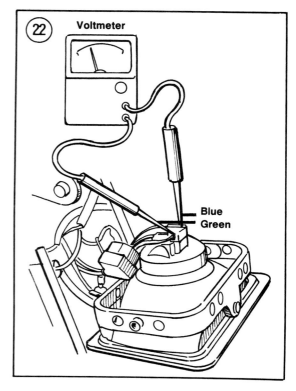

Voltmeter

Blue
Green

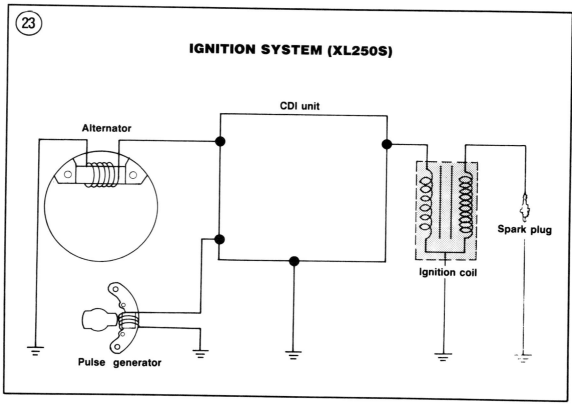

IGNITION SYSTEM (XL250S)

CDI unit

Alternator

Spark plug

Ignition coil

Pulse generator

**IGNITION SYSTEM
(XR250)**

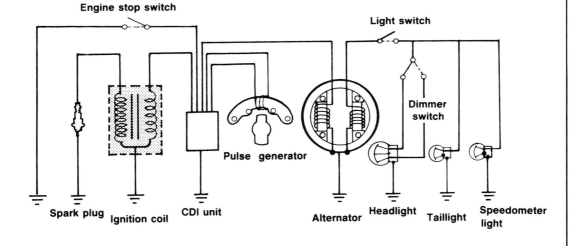

Engine stop switch

Light switch

Dimmer
switch

Pulse generator

Spark plug Ignition coil CDI unit Alternator Headlight Taillight Speedometer
light

8

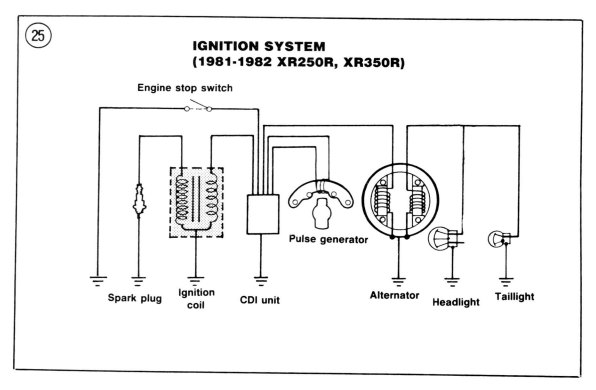

(25)

IGNITION SYSTEM
(1981-1982 XR250R, XR350R)

Engine stop switch

Pulse generator

Spark plug   Ignition coil   CDI unit   Alternator   Headlight   Taillight

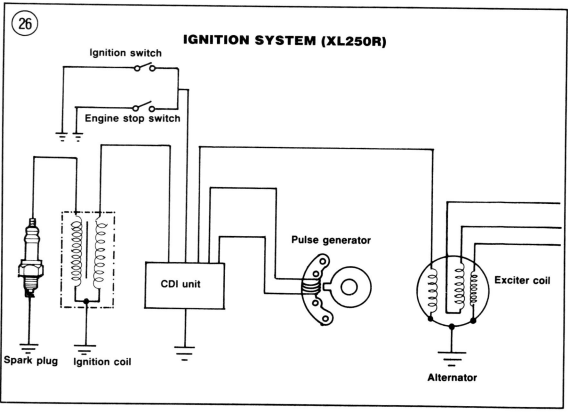

(26)

IGNITION SYSTEM (XL250R)

Ignition switch

Engine stop switch

Pulse generator

CDI unit

Exciter coil

Spark plug   Ignition coil

Alternator

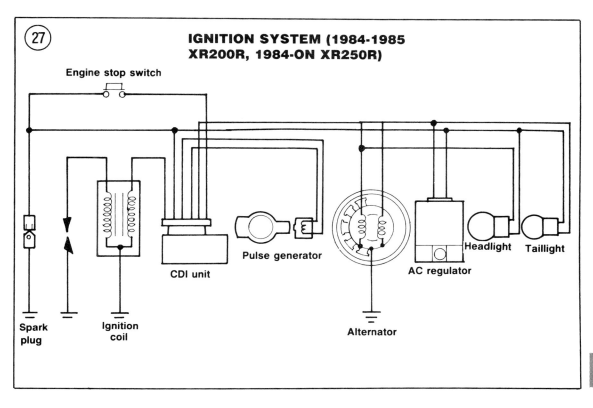

(27) **IGNITION SYSTEM (1984-1985 XR200R, 1984-ON XR250R)**

Engine stop switch

Spark plug

Ignition coil

CDI unit

Pulse generator

Alternator

AC regulator

Headlight

Taillight

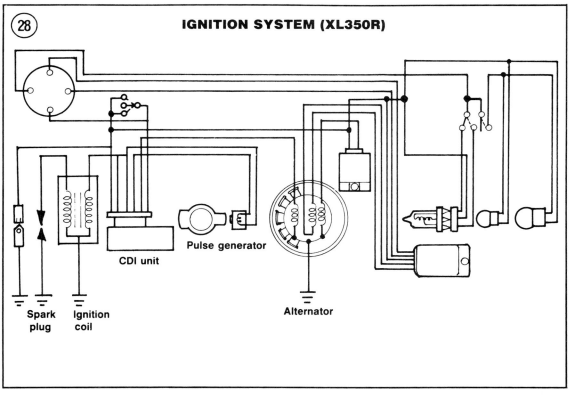

(28) **IGNITION SYSTEM (XL350R)**

Spark plug

Ignition coil

CDI unit

Pulse generator

Alternator

8

electronic pulse to develop in the primary coil of the stator assembly. This pulse is then routed to the CDI unit where it is amplified. A pulse from the pickup coil in the stator assembly is used to trigger the output of the CDI unit which in turn triggers the output of the ignition coil and fires the spark plug.

CDI Precautions

Certain measures must be taken to protect the capacitor discharge system.

1. Never disconnect any of the electrical connections while the engine is running.

2. Keep all connections between the various units clean and tight. Be sure that the wiring connectors are pushed together firmly to help keep out moisture.

3. Do not substitute another type of ignition coil.

4. The CDI unit is mounted to the frame in a rubber mount. Always be sure the CDI unit is mounted by this means as it is designed to help isolate vibrations.

CDI Troubleshooting

Problems with the capacitor discharge system fall into one of the following categories. See **Table 3**.
  a. Weak spark.
  b. No spark.

CDI Testing
(1984-on XL250R, 1986-on XR250R)

NOTE
This procedure covers only these specific models. On models not listed, if you suspect a faulty CDI unit, take your bike to a dealer and have it tested. Chances are they will perform a "remove and replace" test to see if the CDI unit is faulty. This type of test is expensive if performed by yourself. Remember if you purchase a new CDI unit and it does not solve your particular ignition system problem, you cannot return the CDI unit for refund. Most motorcycle dealers will not accept returns on any electrical component since they could be damaged internally even though they look okay externally.

Honda does not recommend the CDI test procedures previously used by the factory. This test procedure was to measure the resistance values between the various connector pins on the CDI unit. This inspection method has been determined to be unreliable because of the following:
  a. The wrong type of multimeter was used and would give incorrect resistance value readings.
  b. The multimeter's battery voltage was low and would result in an incorrect resistance value reading.
  c. Human error occurred in performing the test and/or reading the specifications in the resistance value table.
  d. Manufacturing tolerances varied among CDI units of the same type for the same model.

1. Test the CDI unit's ability to produce a spark. Perform the following:
  a. Disconnect the high voltage lead from the spark plug. Remove the spark plug from the cylinder head.

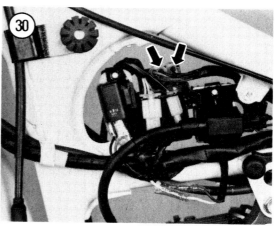

b. Connect a new or known good spark plug to the high voltage lead and place the spark plug base on a good ground like the engine cylinder head (**Figure 29**). Position the spark plug so you can see the electrodes.

WARNING
If it is necessary to hold the high voltage lead, do so with an insulated pair of pliers. The high voltage generated by the CDI could produce serious or fatal shocks.

NOTE
The engine must be kicked over rapidly since the ignition system does not produce a spark at a low rpm.

c. Kick the engine over rapidly with the kickstarter and check for a spark. If there is a fat blue spark, replace the spark plug.
d. If a weak spark or no spark is obtained continue with this procedure.
e. Reinstall the spark plug and connect the high voltage lead onto the spark plug.
2. Remove the seat and both side covers.
3. Remove the fuel tank as described in Chapter Seven.
4. Disconnect the electrical connector(s) (**Figure 30**) from the backside of the CDI unit.

NOTE
For best results, in the following step, use a quality digital multimeter (Honda part No. KS-AHM-32-003) or equivalent. Install a fresh battery in the multimeter prior to performing these tests.

5. Refer to **Table 4** and measure the resistance values between each of the electrical connector(s) terminals on the wire harness side of the electrical connector(s). Do not perform these tests on the terminals of the CDI unit.

6. If any of the tests results do not meet the specifications, then test and inspect the following ignition system components as described in this chapter.
   a. Ignition coil: primary and secondary resistance.
   b. Alternator exciter coil.
   c. Pulse generator.
   d. Engine stop switch.
7. If all of the ignition components are okay, then check the following:
   a. Check for an open or short in the wire harness between each component.
   b. Make sure all connections between the various components are clean and tight. Be sure that the wiring connectors are pushed together firmly to help keep out moisture.
8. If Steps 1-7 meet all specifications, then the CDI unit is faulty and must be replaced as described in this chapter.

CDI Replacement

1. Remove the seat and side covers.
2. Remove the fuel tank as described in Chapter Seven.
3. Disconnect the electrical connectors (**Figure 30**) from the backside of the CDI unit.
4. On models so equipped, remove the screws securing the CDI unit to the frame. On all other models, remove the CDI unit from the rubber isolator (**Figure 31**) on the frame.
5. Remove the CDI unit.
6. Install a new CDI unit onto the frame and attach the electrical wires to it. Make sure all electrical connectors are free of corrosion and are tight.
7. Install all parts removed.

MECHANICAL IGNITION ADVANCE MECHANISM (XL250S, XR250, 1981-1982 XR250R)

NOTE
All models not listed here have an ignition advance circuit built into the CDI unit. This circuit senses speed of the pulse generator rotor as it passes the pulse generator and changes ignition timing accordingly.

The mechanical ignition advance mechanism advances the ignition (fires the spark plug sooner) as engine speed increases. If it does not advance properly and smoothly, the ignition will be incorrect at high engine rpm. It must be inspected periodically to make certain it operates smoothly.

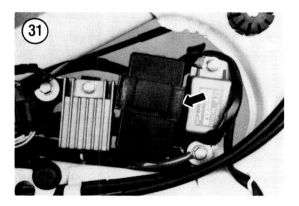

1. Remove the ignition advance mechanism as described in Chapter Four.

2. Inspect the rotor pivot points (A, **Figure 32**) of each weight. The rotor must pivot smoothly to maintain the proper ignition advance. Apply lightweight grease to the pivot pins.

3. Inspect the rotor return springs (B, **Figure 32**). Make sure they are taut and return the rotor to its fully seated position completely.

4. If the rotor is removed from the base, install it, aligning the punch mark (C, **Figure 32**) with the hole in the base.

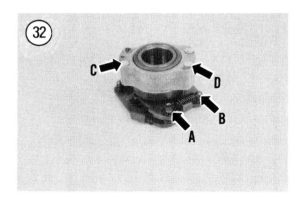

> *NOTE*
> *If the ignition advancer rotor is replaced, the new one must have the same letter designation. Refer to D, **Figure 32**. Failure to do so will result in poor engine performance.*

5. Install by reversing these removal steps.

STARTING DIFFICULTIES
(1984 XL250R)

If you have experienced starting difficulties and the kickstarter has "kicked back" there may be damage to the countershaft bearing in the right-hand crankcase. Refer to Chapter Five regarding this problem as it relates to the engine.

When riding in deep water or when washing down the bike, water may get into the area under the fuel tank where the CDI unit is located. The moisture may find its way into the electrical connector which will result in starting difficulties.

To keep moisture out of the electrical connector, perform the following.

1. Remove the fuel tank as described in Chapter Seven.

2. Disconnect the electrical connector from the backside of the CDI unit (**Figure 30**).

3. Thoroughly dry both the CDI unit and the electrical connector, first with electrical contact cleaner and then blow dry with compressed air.

4. Check for corrosion on the electrical terminals and clean if necessary. Reclean with contact cleaner.

> *CAUTION*
> *In the following step do not use silicone sealer; use silicone **grease**.*

5. Squeeze out about 2-3 mm (1/16-1/8 in.) of silicone grease from the tube. Apply the grease to the end of the electrical connector on the electrical harness.

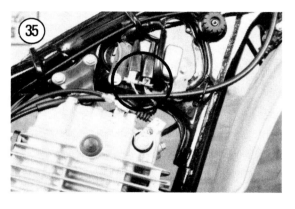

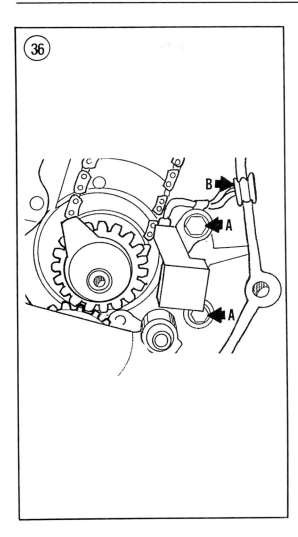

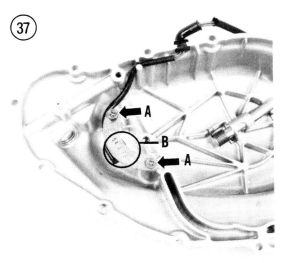

6. Make sure that the rubber seal on the end of the electrical harness is pressed into the connector about 1-2 mm (1/32-1/16 in.).

7. Install the electrical connector into the CDI unit and press it all the way in.

8. Install the fuel tank.

PULSE GENERATOR

Testing

1A. On RFVC engine models, disconnect the electrical connector going to the pulse generator (**Figure 33**).

1B. On all other models, disconnect the electrical connector going to the pulse generator. Refer to **Figure 34** for XL series models or **Figure 35** for XR series models.

2A. On XL250S and XR250 models, use an ohmmeter set at $R \times 10$ and check the resistance between both wires in the electrical connector. The specified resistance is listed in **Table 5**.

2B. On all other models, use an ohmmeter set at $R \times 100$ and check the resistance between both wires in the electrical connector. The specified resistance is listed in **Table 5**.

3. If the resistance shown is greater or there is no indicated resistance (infinity) between the 2 terminals, the pulse generator has an open or short and must be replaced as described in this chapter.

Removal/Installation
(RFVC Engine)

1. Remove the right-hand crankcase cover (clutch cover) as described under *Clutch Removal/ Disassembly* in Chapter Six.

2. Remove the bolts (A, **Figure 36**) securing the pulse generator to the crankcase.

3. Carefully remove the electrical harness and rubber grommet (B, **Figure 36**) from the crankcase.

4. Install by reversing these removal steps, noting the following.

5. Make sure all electrical connectors are free of corrosion and are tight.

Removal/Installation
(All Other Models)

1. Remove the right-hand crankcase cover (clutch cover) as described under *Clutch Removal/ Disassembly* in Chapter Six.

2. Remove the Phillips head screws (A, **Figure 37**) securing the pulse generator to the right-hand crankcase cover.

3. Carefully remove the electrical harness and rubber grommet from the right-hand crankcase cover.

4. Install by reversing these removal steps, noting the following.

> *NOTE*
> *If the pulse generator is replaced, the new one must have the same letter designation stamped on it (B, **Figure 37**). Failure to do so will result in poor engine performance.*

5. Route the electrical harness through the crankcase cover and out the rubber grommet as shown in **Figure 37**.
6. Make sure all electrical connectors are free of corrosion and are tight.

IGNITION COIL

Removal/Installation

1. Remove the seat and side covers.
2. Remove the fuel tank as described in Chapter Seven.
3. On XL series models, disconnect the battery negative lead (A, **Figure 5**) or disconnect the main fuse (B, **Figure 5**).
4. Disconnect the high voltage lead (**Figure 38**) from the spark plug.
5. Disconnect the electrical wires (**Figure 39**) from the ignition coil.
6A. On models so equipped, remove the bolts (**Figure 40**) or screw (**Figure 41**) securing the ignition coil to the frame and remove the coil.
6B. On all other models, withdraw the ignition coil and rubber isolator from the frame.
7. Install by reversing these removal steps, noting the following.
8. Make sure all electrical connections are free of corrosion and are tight.

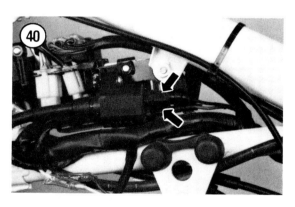

Testing (XL250S, 1982-1983 XL250R, XR250, 1981-1983 XR250R)

Refer to **Figure 42** for this procedure.

The ignition coil is a form of transformer which develops the high voltage required to jump the spark plug gap. The only maintenance required is that of keeping the electrical connections clean and tight and occasionally checking to see that the coil is mounted securely.

If the condition of the coil is doubtful, there are several checks which may be made.

First as a quick check of coil condition, disconnect the high voltage lead from the spark plug. Remove the spark plug from the cylinder head. Connect a new or known good spark plug to the high voltage lead and place the spark plug base on a good ground like the engine cylinder head (**Figure 29**). Position the spark plug so you can see the electrode.

> *WARNING*
> *If it is necessary to hold the high voltage lead, do so with an insulated pair of pliers. The high voltage generated by the CDI could produce serious or fatal shocks.*

Turn the engine over with the kickstarter. If a fat, blue spark occurs, the coil is in good condition; if not, proceed as follows. Make sure that you are using a known good spark plug for this test. If the spark plug used is defective the test results will be incorrect.

Reinstall the spark plug in the cylinder head.

Disconnect all ignition coil wires (including the spark plug lead from the spark plug) before testing.

> *NOTE*
> *In order to get accurate resistance measurements, the coil must be at 20° C (68° F).*

1. Use an ohmmeter set at R × 1 and measure the primary coil resistance between the primary terminal and the mounting flange. Refer to specified resistance values listed in **Table 6**.

2. Use an ohmmeter set at R × 1 and measure the secondary lead (spark plug lead with the spark plug cap attached) and the mounting flange. Refer to specified resistance values listed **Table 6**.

3. If the coil resistance does not meet either of these specifications, the coil must be replaced. If the coil exhibits visible damage, it should be replaced.

4. Reconnect all ignition coil wires to the ignition coil.

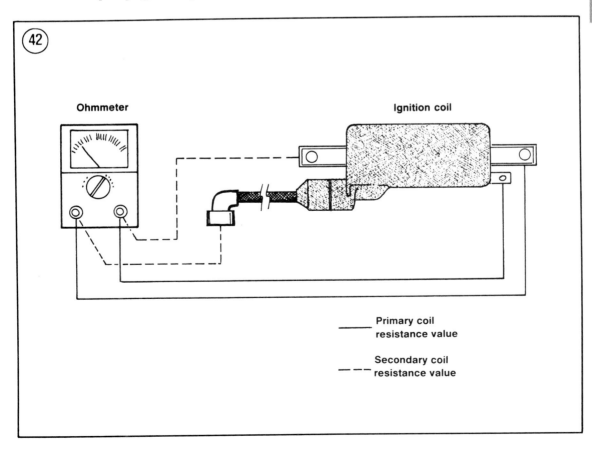

Testing (XR200, 1984-on XL250R, 1984-on XR250R, 1984-1985 XL350R, 1985 XR350R)

Refer to **Figure 43** for this procedure.

The ignition coil is a form of transformer which develops the high voltage required to jump the spark plug gap. The only maintenance required is that of keeping the electrical connections clean and tight and occasionally checking to see that the coil is mounted securely.

If the condition of the coil is doubtful, there are several checks which may be made.

First as a quick check of coil condition, disconnect the high voltage lead from the spark plug. Remove the spark plug from the cylinder head. Connect a new or known good spark plug to the high voltage lead and place the spark plug base on a good ground like the engine cylinder head (**Figure 29**). Position the spark plug so you can see the electrode.

> *WARNING*
> *If it is necessary to hold the high voltage lead, do so with an insulated pair of pliers. The high voltage generated by the CDI could produce serious or fatal shocks.*

Turn the engine over with the kickstarter. If a fat, blue spark occurs, the coil is in good condition; if not, proceed as follows. Make sure that you are using a known good spark plug for this test. If the spark plug used is defective the test results will be incorrect.

Reinstall the spark plug in the cylinder head.

Disconnect all ignition coil wires (including the spark plug lead from the spark plug) before testing.

> *NOTE*
> *In order to get accurate resistance measurements, the coil must be at 20° C (68° F).*

1. Use an ohmmeter set at R × 1 and measure the primary coil resistance between the positive (+) and the negative (−) terminals on the top of the ignition coil. Refer to specified resistance values listed in **Table 6**.

2. Use an ohmmeter set at $R \times 1,000$ to measure the secondary coil resistance between the positive (+) terminal on the top of the ignition coil and spark plug lead (with the spark plug cap attached). Refer to specified resistance values listed in **Table 6**.

3. On 1984-on XL250R and 1986-on XR250R models, use an ohmmeter set at $R \times 1,000$ to measure the secondary coil resistance between the positive (+) terminal on the top of the ignition coil and spark plug lead (with the spark plug cap removed). Refer to specified resistance values listed in **Table 6**. Reconnect the spark plug cap.

4. If the coil resistance does not meet any of these specifications, the coil must be replaced. If the coil exhibits visible damage, it should be replaced.

5. Reconnect all ignition coil wires to the ignition coil.

LIGHTING SYSTEM

The lighting system consists of a headlight and taillight.

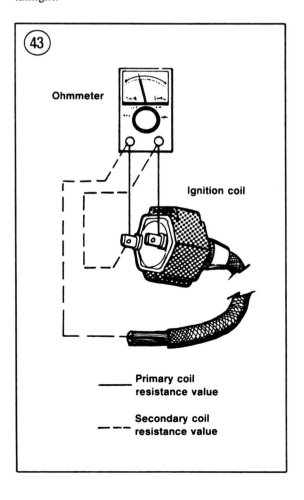

43

Ohmmeter

Ignition coil

——— Primary coil resistance value

- - - Secondary coil resistance value

XL series models are also equipped with directional lights, indicator lights and a speedometer illumination light. **Table 7** lists replacement bulbs for these components. Always use the correct wattage bulb as indicated in this section. The use of a larger wattage bulb will give a dim light and a smaller wattage bulb will burn out prematurely.

Headlight Replacement and Headlight Housing Removal/Installation (XL250S, 1982-1983 XL250R)

Refer to **Figure 44** for this procedure.
1. Remove the screw (**Figure 45**) on each side of the headlight housing.

8

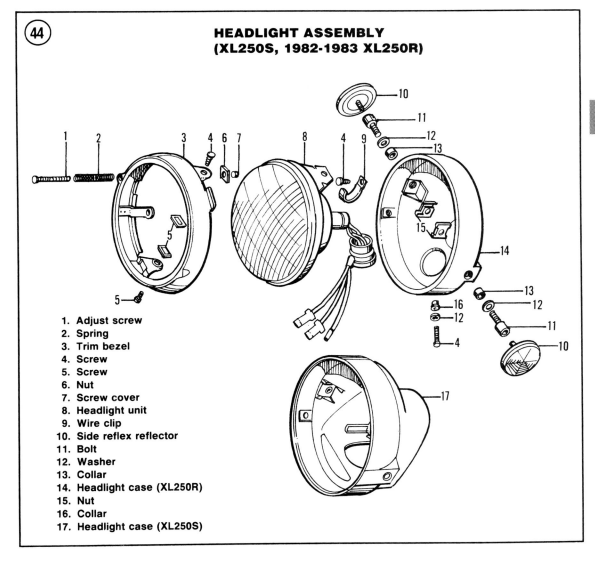

HEADLIGHT ASSEMBLY
(XL250S, 1982-1983 XL250R)

1. Adjust screw
2. Spring
3. Trim bezel
4. Screw
5. Screw
6. Nut
7. Screw cover
8. Headlight unit
9. Wire clip
10. Side reflex reflector
11. Bolt
12. Washer
13. Collar
14. Headlight case (XL250R)
15. Nut
16. Collar
17. Headlight case (XL250S)

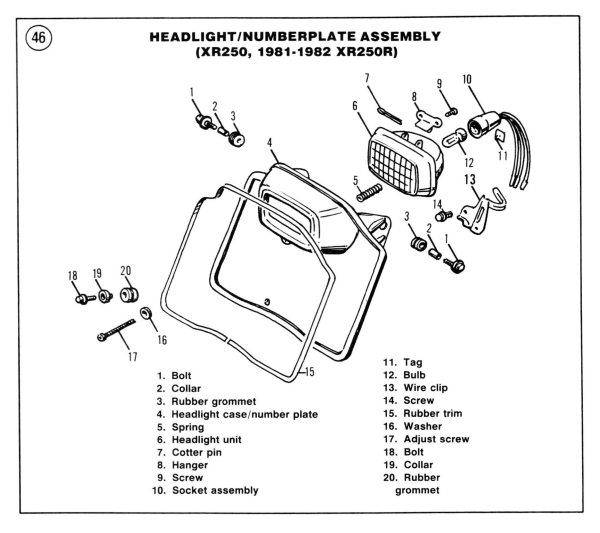

46 **HEADLIGHT/NUMBERPLATE ASSEMBLY**
(XR250, 1981-1982 XR250R)

1. Bolt
2. Collar
3. Rubber grommet
4. Headlight case/number plate
5. Spring
6. Headlight unit
7. Cotter pin
8. Hanger
9. Screw
10. Socket assembly
11. Tag
12. Bulb
13. Wire clip
14. Screw
15. Rubber trim
16. Washer
17. Adjust screw
18. Bolt
19. Collar
20. Rubber
    grommet

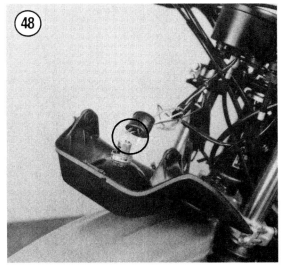

2. Pull the trim bezel and headlight unit up and out of the housing.

3. Disconnect the electrical connector from the backside of the headlight unit.

4. Remove the retainer securing the sealed beam unit and remove the unit.

5. To remove the headlight housing, perform the following:

   a. Mark all electrical connectors prior to disconnecting them. This will ensure correct reconnection of all wires.

   b. Disconnect all electrical connectors within the headlight housing.

   c. Unscrew the reflex reflector on each side.

   d. Unscrew the bolt, washer, collar and nut on each side securing the headlight housing to the front fork.

   e. Carefully withdraw the electrical wires out through the opening in the backside of the headlight housing.

   f. Remove the headlight housing.

6. Install by reversing these removal steps.

7. Adjust the headlight as described in this chapter.

Headlight Replacement and Headlight Holder Removal/Installation (XR250, 1981-1982 XR250R)

Refer to **Figure 46** for this procedure.

1. Remove the bolts and washers (**Figure 47**) securing the headlight holder.

2. Pivot the holder and headlight assembly down.

3. Rotate the electrical connector/socket (**Figure 48**) and remove it from the backside of the headlight lens unit.

4. Remove the headlight holder.

5. Remove the bulb from the electrical connector/socket and replace with a new bulb.

6. Install by reversing these removal steps.

7. Adjust the headlight as described in this chapter.

Headlight Replacement and Number Plate Removal/Installation (1984-1985 XR200R, 1984-on XR250R, XR350R)

Refer to **Figure 49** for this procedure.

8

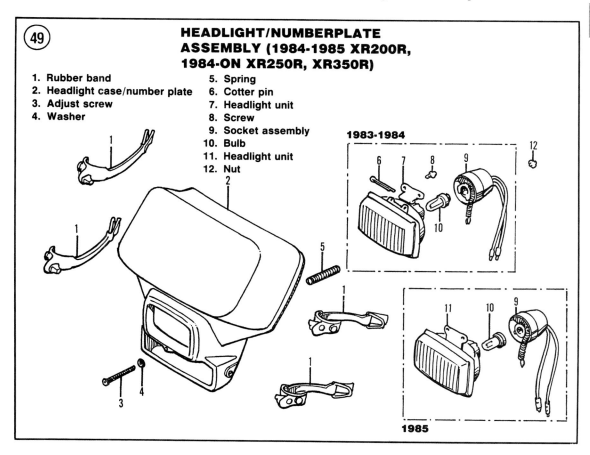

(49) **HEADLIGHT/NUMBERPLATE ASSEMBLY (1984-1985 XR200R, 1984-ON XR250R, XR350R)**

1. Rubber band
2. Headlight case/number plate
3. Adjust screw
4. Washer
5. Spring
6. Cotter pin
7. Headlight unit
8. Screw
9. Socket assembly
10. Bulb
11. Headlight unit
12. Nut

1983-1984

1985

1. Unhook the rubber mounting bands (**Figure 50**) securing the number plate/headlight assembly to the front forks.

2. Pivot the number plate/headlight assembly out away from the forks and disconnect the electrical connectors going to the bulb socket (**Figure 51**).

3. Remove the number plate.

4. Unhook the spring securing the electrical connector/socket to the backside of the headlight lens unit.

5. Remove the bulb from the electrical connector/socket and replace with a new bulb.

6. Install by reversing these removal steps.

7. Adjust the headlight as described in this chapter.

Headlight Replacement and
Number Plate Removal/Installation
(1984-on XL250R, XL350R)

Refer to **Figure 52** for this procedure.

1. Remove the mounting bolt (**Figure 53**) on each side securing the number plate/headlight assembly to the mounting brackets on the front forks.

2. Pivot the number plate/headlight assembly down and away from the forks.

3A. On 1984-on XL250R models, perform the following:

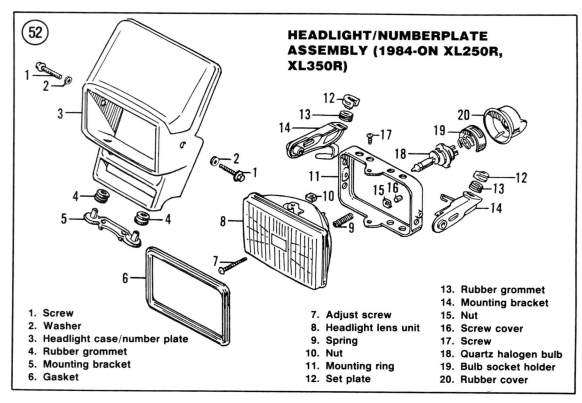

HEADLIGHT/NUMBERPLATE ASSEMBLY (1984-ON XL250R, XL350R)

1. Screw
2. Washer
3. Headlight case/number plate
4. Rubber grommet
5. Mounting bracket
6. Gasket
7. Adjust screw
8. Headlight lens unit
9. Spring
10. Nut
11. Mounting ring
12. Set plate
13. Rubber grommet
14. Mounting bracket
15. Nut
16. Screw cover
17. Screw
18. Quartz halogen bulb
19. Bulb socket holder
20. Rubber cover

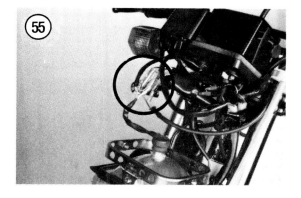

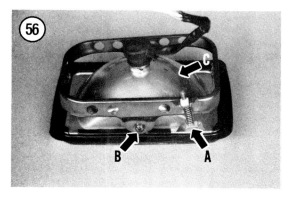

a. Remove the bolt (**Figure 54**) securing the headlight assembly to the mounting bracket on each side.

b. Disconnect the electrical connectors going to the sealed beam unit (**Figure 55**).

c. Completely unscrew the adjusting screw (A, **Figure 56**).

d. Remove the screws (B, **Figure 56**) securing the sealed beam unit to the mounting ring.

e. Remove the sealed beam unit (C, **Figure 56**).

f. If in good condition, remove the rubber gasket (**Figure 57**) from the perimeter of the sealed beam unit and reinstall on the new sealed beam unit. Install a new gasket if necessary.

3B. On XL350R models, perform the following:

a. Disconnect the electrical connector from the backside of the socket assembly.

b. Rotate the socket holder and remove the socket holder and bulb from the lens unit.

CAUTION
Carefully read all instructions shipped with the replacement quartz halogen bulb. Do not touch the new bulb glass with your fingers because of oil on your skin. Any traces of oil on the glass will drastically reduce the life of the bulb. Clean any traces of oil from the new bulb with a cloth moistened in alcohol or lacquer thinner.

c. Remove the bulb from the socket.

4. Install by reversing these removal steps.

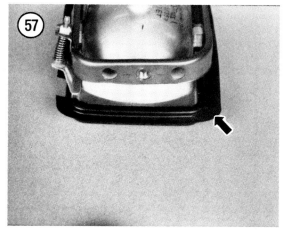

8

5. On 1984-on XL250R models, align the index marks (**Figure 58**) on the headlight assembly and the mounting bracket on each side. Tighten the bolts securely.

6. Adjust the headlight as described in this chapter.

Headlight Adjustment (XL250S, 1982-1983 XL250R)

Adjust the headlight horizontally and vertically according to Department of Motor Vehicles regulations in your area.

To adjust the headlight horizontally, turn the screw (A, **Figure 59**). Screwing it in turns the light to the right and loosening it will turn the light to the left.

For vertical adjustment, unscrew the front reflex reflectors, then loosen the mounting bolts on each side (B, **Figure 59**). Tilt the headlight housing and tighten the mounting bolts. Install the reflex reflectors.

Headlight Adjustment (XR250, 1981-1982 XR250R, 1984-1985 XR200R, 1984-on XR250R, XR350R)

The headlight on these models is limited to vertical adjustment only. Adjust to your own personal preference.

For vertical adjustment, turn the adjust screw at the base of the headlight lens.

Headlight Adjustment (1984-on XL250R, XL350R)

Adjust the headlight horizontally and vertically according to Department of Motor Vehicles regulations in your area.

To adjust the headlight horizontally, turn the screw (A, **Figure 60**). Screwing it in turns the light to the right and loosening it will turn the light to the left.

For vertical adjustments loosen the mounting bolts on each side (B, **Figure 60**). Tilt the headlight housing and tighten the mounting bolts.

Taillight/Brakelight Replacement (XL250S, XL250R, XL350R)

1A. On XL250S models, remove the screws (**Figure 61**) securing the lens and remove the lens and gasket.

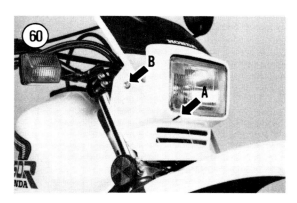

1B. On all other models, remove the screws (**Figure 62**) securing the lens and remove the lens and gasket.

2. Wash out the inside and outside of the lens with a mild detergent and wipe dry.

3. Inspect the lens gasket and replace it if damaged or deteriorated.

4. Replace the bulb (**Figure 63**) and install the lens; do not overtighten the screws as the lens may crack.

Taillight Replacement
(XR250)

1. Remove the screws (**Figure 64**) securing the lens and remove the lens and gasket.

2. Wash out the inside and outside of the lens with a mild detergent and wipe dry.

3. Inspect the lens gasket and replace it if damaged or deteriorated.

4. Replace the bulb and install the lens; do not overtighten the screws as the lens may crack.

Taillight Replacement
(All Other XR Series Models)

1. From underneath the rear fender, remove the screws, washers and metal collars securing the lens and remove the lens.

2. Wash out the inside and outside of the lens with a mild detergent and wipe dry.

3. Replace the bulb and install the lens; do not overtighten the screws as the lens may crack.

Directional Signal Light Replacement
(XL Series Models)

1. Remove the screws securing the lens and remove the lens. Refer to **Figure 65** for front lights and **Figure 66** for rear lights.

2. Wash out the inside and outside of the lens with a mild detergent and wipe dry.

3. Replace the bulb and install the lens; do not overtighten the screws as the lens may crack.

Speedometer Illumination Light Replacement (1978-1980 XL250S)

1. Remove the headlight housing (A, **Figure 67**) as described in this chapter.
2. Disconnect the speedometer drive cable (B, **Figure 67**).
3. Remove the acorn nuts and washers (C, **Figure 67**) and pull the instrument cluster forward and turn it upside down.
4. Pull the defective lamp holder/electrical wire assembly up and out of the housing.
5. Remove and replace the defective bulb.

> *NOTE*
> *If a new bulb will not work, check the wire connections for loose or broken wires. Also check the bulb socket for corrosion. Replace as necessary.*

6. Install by reversing these removal steps.

Speedometer Illumination Light Replacement (1981 XL250S, XL250R)

1. Remove the headlight/number plate assembly as described in this chapter.
2. Remove the nuts and collars (**Figure 68**) securing the speedometer housing to the mounting bracket.
3. Carefully pull the speedometer housing away from the mounting bracket.
4. Carefully pull the defective lamp holder/electrical wire assembly from the backside of the housing.
5. Remove and replace the defective bulb.

> *NOTE*
> *If a new bulb will not work, check the wire connections for loose or broken wires. Also check the bulb socket for corrosion. Replace as necessary.*

6. Push the lamp socket/electrical wire assembly back into the housing. Make sure it is completely seated to prevent the entry of water and moisture.
7. Install the speedometer housing onto the mounting bracket and install the collars and nuts. Tighten the nuts securely.
8. Install the headlight/number plate assembly as described in this chapter.

Speedometer Illumination Light Replacement (XR250)

1. Remove the headlight housing as described in this chapter.
2. Carefully pull the lamp holder/electrical wire assembly (**Figure 69**) down and out of the housing.

3. Remove and replace the defective bulb.

> *NOTE*
> *If a new bulb will not work, check the
> wire connections for loose or broken
> wires. Also check the bulb socket for
> corrosion. Replace as necessary.*

4. Install by reversing these removal steps.

Neutral, High Beam and Directional Signal Indicator Light Replacement (1978-1980 XL250S)

Follow the procedure for replacement of the speedometer illumination light as described in this chapter.

Neutral, High Beam and Turn Signal Indicator Light Replacement (1981-on XL Series Models)

1. Remove the headlight/number plate assembly as described in this chapter.
2. Carefully pull the lamp holder/electrical wire assembly (**Figure 70**) down and out of the backside of the instrument cluster.

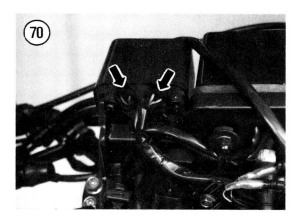

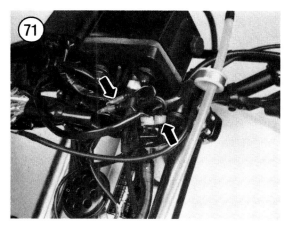

3. Remove and replace the defective bulb.

> *NOTE*
> *If a new bulb will not work, check the
> wire connections for loose or broken
> wires. Also check the bulb socket for
> corrosion. Replace as necessary.*

4. Push the lamp socket/electrical wire assembly back into the housing. Make sure it is completely seated to prevent the entry of water and moisture.
5. Install the headlight/number plate assembly as described in this chapter.

SWITCHES

Ignition Switch Continuity Test (XL Series Models)

1A. On 1982-1983 XL250R models, remove the coupler box cover at the base of the headlight.
1B. On all other models, perform the following:
   a. Remove the headlight/number plate assembly as described in this chapter.
   b. In the area in front of the steering stem, locate and disconnect the necessary electrical connectors.

> *NOTE*
> *Some models have a 4-pin electrical
> connector while others have a 3-pin
> electrical connector and one separate
> connector. On all models, there are 4
> wires to be tested.*

2. Locate the electrical connector(s) containing 3 or 4 wires (1 black, 1 red, 1 black/white, 1 green). Disconnect the electrical connector(s) (**Figure 71**).
3. Use an ohmmeter and check for continuity. Connect the test leads to the ignition switch side of the electrical connector as follows:
   a. Turn the ignition switch ON: there should be continuity (low resistance) between the black and red wires.
   b. Turn the ignition switch OFF: there should be continuity (low resistance) between the black/white and green wires.
   c. On 1982-1983 XL250R models, turn the ignition switch to LOCK: there should be continuity (low resistance) between the black/white and green wires.
4. If the ignition switch fails any one of these tests, the electrical contact portion of the switch must be replaced as described in this chapter.
5. Reconnect the 4-pin electrical connector and install all items removed.

Ignition Switch
Removal/Installation

1. Remove the headlight/number plate assembly as described in this chapter.
2. On XL250S and 1982-1983 XL250R models, remove the instrument cluster (XL250S) or speedometer assembly as described in this chapter.
3. Disconnect the electrical connector from the ignition switch (**Figure 68**).
4. Remove the mounting bolts (**Figure 72**) securing the ignition switch and remove the switch assembly from the upper fork bridge.
5. Install by reversing these removal steps.

Ignition Switch
Disassembly/Assembly

1. Remove the ignition switch as described in this chapter.
2. Insert the ignition key in the switch and turn the tumbler so it is part way between the ON and OFF positions.
3A. On XL250S and 1982-1983 XL250R models, push in on the lugs (**Figure 73**) of the electrical contact switch portion, depressing them enough to clear the slots in the mechanical portion of the switch assembly.
3B. On 1984-1986 XL250R and XL350R models, perform the following:
    a. Open the wire retainer (A, **Figure 74**) securing the electrical harness to the switch.
    b. Push in on the lugs (B, **Figure 74**) of the electrical contact switch portion, depressing them enough to clear the slots in the mechanical portion of the switch assembly.
3C. On 1987 XL250R models, perform the following:
    a. Open the wire retainer (A, **Figure 75**) securing the electrical harness to the switch.
    b. Remove the screws (B, **Figure 75**) securing the electrical contact portion.
    c. Push in on the lug of the electrical contact switch portion, depressing it enough to clear the slot in the mechanical portion of the switch assembly.
4. Withdraw the electrical portion of the switch from the mechanical portion of the ignition switch.
5. Replace the defective component.
6. Assemble by reversing these disassembly steps, noting the following.
7. Make sure the lugs are completely indexed into the slots in the mechanical portion of the switch.

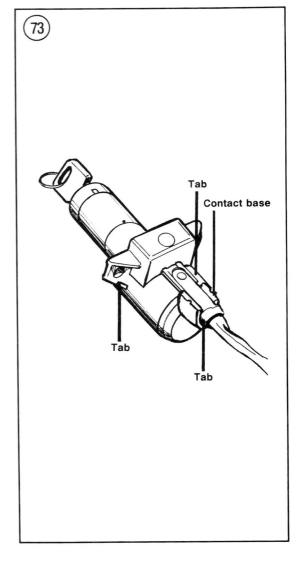

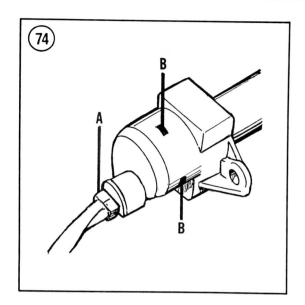

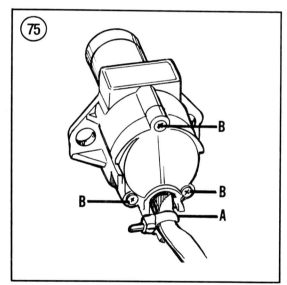

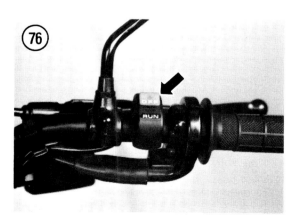

Engine Kill Switch Testing

1A. On 1984-on XL250R models, disconnect the electrical connector from the engine kill switch (**Figure 76**) on the handlebar.

1B. On XL250S models, remove the headlight assembly as described in this chapter.

2A. On XR series models, disconnect the green and the black/white electrical connectors going to the engine kill switch.

2B. On XL series other than 1984-on XL250R models, perform the following:

    a. In the area in front of the steering stem, locate and disconnect the 3-pin electrical connector that contains the green wire for the engine kill switch.

    b. Also disconnect the individual black/white wire from a connector.

3. Use an ohmmeter set at R×1 and connect the 2 leads of the ohmmeter to the black/white and green wires. Turn the kill switch button to one of the OFF positions and then to the other OFF position. If the switch is good there will be continuity (very low resistance) in both OFF positions.

4. Turn the kill switch button to the RUN position. If the switch is good there will be no continuity (infinite resistance).

5. If the switch fails to pass any of these tests, the switch is faulty and must be replaced.

6. Reconnect the electrical connectors.

7. Install all items removed.

Headlight Dimmer Switch Testing

XL250S

1. Remove the headlight as described in this chapter.

2. Within the headlight housing disconnect the black, black/white and white electrical connectors from the dimmer switch.

3. Turn the dimmer switch to the HI position. Use an ohmmeter set at R×1 and connect the 2 leads of the ohmmeter to the black and black/white wires. If the switch is good, there will be continuity (very low resistance).

4. Turn the dimmer switch to the N position. Use an ohmmeter set at R×1 and connect the 2 leads of the ohmmeter to the following colors:

    a. Black/white and white.

    b. Black and white.

    c. Black and black/white.

If the switch is good, there will be continuity (very low resistance) between each of these wires.

5. Turn the dimmer switch to the LO position. Use an ohmmeter set at R×1 and connect the 2 leads of the ohmmeter to the black/white and white wires. If the switch is good there will be continuity (very low resistance).

6. If the switch fails to pass any of these tests, the switch is faulty and must be replaced.

7. Reconnect the disconnected wires and install the headlight as described in this chapter.

1982-1983 XL250R

1. Remove the coupler box cover at the base of the headlight.

2. Within the coupler box, disconnect the blue, white/yellow and white electrical connectors from the dimmer switch.

3. Turn the dimmer switch to the HI position. Use an ohmmeter set at R×1 and connect the 2 leads of the ohmmeter to the blue and white/yellow wires. If the switch is good there will be continuity (very low resistance).

4. Turn the dimmer switch to the N position. Use an ohmmeter set at R×1 and connect the 2 leads of the ohmmeter to the following colors:
   a. Blue and white/yellow.
   b. Blue and white.
   c. White/yellow and white.
   If the switch is good there will be continuity (very low resistance) between each of these wires.

5. Turn the dimmer switch to the LO position. Use an ohmmeter set at R×1 and connect the 2 leads of the ohmmeter to the white/yellow and white wires. If the switch is good there will be continuity (very low resistance).

6. If the switch fails to pass any of these tests, the switch is faulty and must be replaced.

7. Reconnect the disconnected wires and install the couple box cover.

1984-on XL250R

Honda does not provide service information for these models.

XR250

1. Remove the headlight as described in this chapter.

2. Within the headlight housing disconnect the white/yellow, brown, blue and white electrical connectors from the dimmer switch.

3. Turn the dimmer switch to the HI position. Use an ohmmeter set at R×1 and connect the 2 leads of the ohmmeter to the following colors:
   a. White/yellow and brown.
   b. White/yellow and blue.
   c. Brown and blue wires.

If the switch is good, there will be continuity (very low resistance).

4. Turn the dimmer switch to the N position. Use an ohmmeter set at R×1 and connect the 2 leads of the ohmmeter to the following colors:
   a. White/yellow and brown.
   b. White/yellow and blue.
   c. White/yellow and white.
   Then to the following colors:
   a. Brown and blue.
   b. Brown and white.
   c. Blue and white.
   If the switch is good, there will be continuity (very low resistance) between each of these wires.

5. Turn the dimmer switch to the LO position. Use an ohmmeter set at R×1 and connect the 2 leads of the ohmmeter to the following colors:
   a. White/yellow and brown.
   b. White/yellow and white.
   c. Brown and white wires.
   If the switch is good, there will be continuity (very low resistance).

6. If the switch fails to pass any of these tests, the switch is faulty and must be replaced.

7. Reconnect the disconnected wires and install the headlight as described in this chapter.

XL350

1. Remove the headlight housing as described in this chapter.

2. In the area in front of the steering stem locate and disconnect the white/yellow, blue and white electrical connectors from the dimmer switch.

3. Turn the dimmer switch to the HI position. Use an ohmmeter set at R×1 and connect the 2 leads of the ohmmeter to the white/yellow and blue wires. If the switch is good there will be continuity (very low resistance).

4. Turn the dimmer switch to the N position. Use an ohmmeter set at R×1 and connect the 2 leads of the ohmmeter to the following colors:
   a. White/yellow and blue.
   b. White/yellow and white.
   c. Blue and white.
   If the switch is good, there will be continuity (very low resistance) between each of these wires.

5. Turn the dimmer switch to the LO position. Use an ohmmeter set at R×1 and connect the 2 leads of the ohmmeter to the white/yellow and white wires. If the switch is good, there will be continuity (very low resistance).

6. If the switch fails to pass any of these tests, the switch is faulty and must be replaced.

7. Reconnect the disconnected wires and install the headlight assembly as described in this chapter.

Turn Signal Switch Testing (XL Series Models)

1A. On XL250S models, perform the following:
   a. Remove the headlight as described in this chapter.
   b. Within the headlight housing disconnect the light blue, gray and orange electrical connectors from the turn signal switch.
1B. On all other models, perform the following:
   a. Remove the headlight housing as described in this chapter.
   b. In the area in front of the steering stem, locate and disconnect the light blue, gray and orange electrical connectors from the turn signal switch.

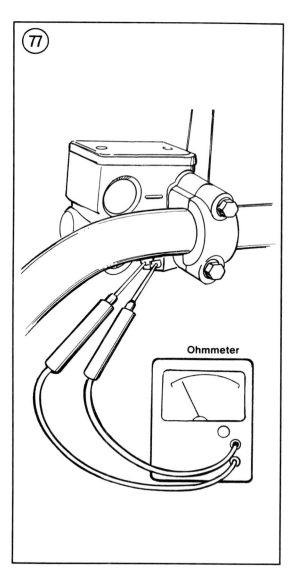

Ohmmeter

2. Turn the turn signal switch to the R position. Use an ohmmeter set at R×1 and connect the 2 leads of the ohmmeter to the light blue and gray wires. If the switch is good, there will be continuity (very low resistance).
3. Turn the turn signal switch to the L position. Use an ohmmeter set at R×1 and connect the 2 leads of the ohmmeter to the gray and orange wires. If the switch is good, there will be continuity (very low resistance) between each of these wires.
4. If the switch fails to pass any of these tests, the switch is faulty and must be replaced.
5. Reconnect the disconnected wires and install the headlight assembly as described in this chapter.

Front Brake Light Switch Testing

XL250S and 1982-1983 XL250R

1. Remove the headlight as described in this chapter.
2A. On XL250S models, perform the following:
   a. Within the headlight housing, disconnect the brown and green/yellow electrical connectors from the front brake light switch.
   b. Have an assistant apply the front brake. Use an ohmmeter set at R×1 and connect the 2 leads of the ohmmeter to the brown and green/yellow wires. If the switch is good, there will be continuity (very low resistance).
2B. On 1982-1983 XL250R models, perform the following:
   a. Within the headlight housing disconnect the black and green/yellow electrical connectors from the front brake light switch.
   b. Have an assistant apply the front brake. Use an ohmmeter set at R×1 and connect the 2 leads of the ohmmeter to the black and green/yellow wires. If the switch is good, there will be continuity (very low resistance).
3. If the switch fails to pass this test, the switch is faulty and must be replaced.
4. Reconnect the disconnected wires and install the headlight assembly as described in this chapter.

1984-on XL250R, XL350R

1. Disconnect the electrical wires from the front brake lever switch.
2. Have an assistant apply the front brake. Use an ohmmeter set at R×1 and connect the 2 leads of the ohmmeter to the terminals of the switch (**Figure 77**).
3. If the switch is good, there will be continuity (very low resistance).
4. If the switch fails to pass this test, the switch is faulty and must be replaced.

5. To remove the switch, remove the screw and the switch from the lever assembly. Install a new switch.

6. Connect the electrical wires to the front brake lever switch.

Rear Brake Light Switch Testing (All XL Series Models)

1. Disconnect the electrical connector wires going to the rear brake pedal switch.

2. Have an assistant apply the rear brake. Use an ohmmeter set at R×1 and connect the 2 leads of the ohmmeter to the electrical wires of the switch connector.

3. If the switch is good, there will be continuity (very low resistance).

4. If the switch fails to pass this test, the switch is faulty and must be replaced.

5. To remove the switch, completely unscrew the adjust nut and remove the switch body (**Figure 78**) from the chassis.

6. Install a new switch and adjust as described in this chapter.

7. Connect the electrical connector wires to the rear brake pedal switch.

ELECTRICAL COMPONENTS

Instrument Cluster Removal/Installation (XL250S)

1. Disconnect the battery negative lead or the main fuse.

2. Remove the headlight (A, **Figure 79**) as described in this chapter.

3. Disconnect the speedometer drive cable (B, **Figure 79**).

4. Remove the acorn nuts and washers (C, **Figure 79**), pull the instrument cluster forward and turn upside down.

5. Carefully pull the lamp holder/electrical wire assemblies.

6. Disconnect the ignition switch 4-pin electrical connector located within the headlight housing.

7. Pull the ignition switch (D, **Figure 79**) and electrical harness out from the cluster and remove the ignition switch from the cluster.

8. Remove the instrument cluster assembly.

9. Install by reversing these removal steps, noting the following.

10. Be sure the rubber isolators are in place on the mounting studs (C, **Figure 79**).

Speedometer Removal/Installation

1982-1983 XL250R, XR250, 1981-1982 XR250R

1. Disconnect the speedometer cable from the base of the speedometer.

2. Carefully pull the lamp holder/electrical wire assembly down and out of the backside of the speedometer housing.

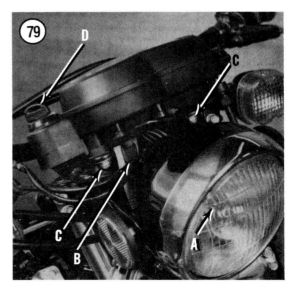

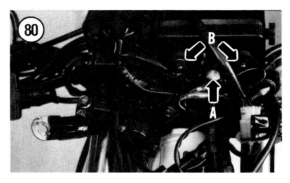

3. Remove the acorn nut and washer (models so equipped) securing the speedometer to the mounting bracket on the upper fork bridge.
4. Remove the speedometer housing assembly.
5. Install by reversing these removal steps.

1984-1985 XR200, 1984-1985 XR250R, XL350R, 1983-1984 XR350R

1. Remove the headlight housing as described in this chapter.
2. Disconnect the speedometer cable from the base of the speedometer.
3. Carefully pull the lamp holder/electrical wire assemblies down and out of the backside of the speedometer housing.
4. Remove the nuts and washers securing the speedometer to the mounting bracket on the upper fork bridge.
5. Remove the speedometer housing assembly.
6. Install by reversing these removal steps.

1984-on XL250R

1. Remove the headlight/number plate assembly as described in this chapter.

2. Disconnect the speedometer cable (A, **Figure 80**) from the base of the speedometer.
3. Carefully pull up and remove the electrical wire coupler cover (**Figure 81**).
4. Disconnect the electrical connector (**Figure 82**).
5. Remove the bolts (B, **Figure 80**) securing the speedometer to the mounting bracket on the upper fork bridge.
6. Remove the speedometer housing and electrical wire harness assembly.
7. To remove the speedometer housing from the mounting bracket, remove the nuts and collars securing the housing and remove the housing and the gasket.
8. Install by reversing these removal steps.

1986-on XR250R

1. Remove the headlight housing as described in this chapter.
2. Disconnect the speedometer cable from the base of the speedometer.
3. Remove the wiring harness from the clamp next to the speedometer mounting bracket.
4. Remove the bolts securing the speedometer to the mounting bracket on the upper fork bridge.
5. Remove the speedometer housing assembly.
6. Install by reversing these removal steps.

Digital Enduro Meter (XR350R)

Meter removal/installation and battery replacement

1. Remove the headlight housing as described in this chapter.
2. Disconnect the electrical wires going to the meter from the sensor on top of the speedometer drive bracket (attached to the upper fork bridge).
3. Remove the bolt on each side of the front hold-down bracket and remove the bracket.
4. Remove the meter assembly from the upper mounting bracket that is attached to the handlebar upper holders.

> *NOTE*
> *Disassembly of the meter is not recommended since replacement parts are not available. If the meter is faulty, the entire meter must be replaced.*

5. To replace the batteries, perform the following:
   a. Turn the lockscrew on the bottom of the meter assembly and open the access door.
   b. Replace the three AA batteries, close the door and turn the lock screw.
6. Install by reversing these removal steps.

8

Sensor removal/installation

1. Remove the meter assembly as described in this chapter.
2. Disconnect the speedometer cable from the sensor.
3. Remove the bolt securing the sensor and mounting bracket to the upper fork bridge. Remove the assembly.
4. Install by reversing these removal steps.

Sensor inspection

1. Remove the sensor as described in this chapter.
2. Using an ohmmeter, connect the test leads to the electrical wires on the sensor.
3. Have an assistant insert a narrow flat-bladed screwdriver into the base of the sensor (where the speedometer cable attaches).
4. Rotate the sensor with the screwdriver and observe the needle on the ohmmeter. The ohmmeter needle should swing back and forth twice for every single complete revolution of the screwdriver and sensor.
5. If the sensor fails this test, the sensor must be replaced.

Horn (XL Series Models)

Removal/Installation

1. Remove the headlight housing as described in this chapter.
2. Disconnect the electrical connectors (A, **Figure 83**) from the horn.
3. Remove the bolt (B, **Figure 83**) securing the horn to the bracket.
4. Install by reversing these removal steps.

Testing

1. Disconnect horn wires from harness.
2. Depending on model, connect a 6-volt or 12-volt battery to the horn.
3. If the horn is good it will sound. If not, replace it.

FUSE (XL SERIES MODELS)

NOTE
There is one 10-amp main fuse in the electrical system on XL series models. The fuse (A, Figure 84) is located next to the battery under the right-hand side cover.

The XR series models are not equipped with a fuse.

NOTE
Always carry a spare fuse. On some later models, there is a spare fuse (B, Figure 84) next to the main fuse.

Whenever the fuse blows, find out the reason for the failure before replacing the fuse. Usually, the trouble is a short circuit in the wiring. This may be caused by worn-through insulation or a disconnected wire shorted to ground.

CAUTION
Never substitute metal foil or wire for a fuse. Never use a higher amperage fuse than specified. An overload could result in a fire and complete loss of the bike.

WIRING DIAGRAMS

Wiring diagrams for all models are located at the end of this book.

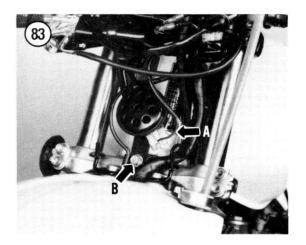

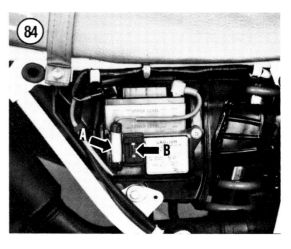

Table 1 CHARGING CURRENT

XL250S	
Disconnect black wire @ voltage regulator	
Light switch OFF	
5,000 rpm	4.0A/8.9V
8,000 rpm	5.5A/8.0V
Light switch ON (high beam)	
5,000 rpm	2.6A/7.5V
8,000 rpm	4.0A/8.0V
1982-1983 XL250R	
Disconnect black wire @ voltage regulator	
2,500 rpm	2.5A/16.8V
8,000 rpm	5.5A/18.4V
1984-on XL250R	
Information not available from Honda.	
XL350R	
Disconnect voltage regulator/rectifier connector. Disconnect black wire then reconnect connector.	
2,500 rpm	2.7A/16.8V
8,000 rpm	5.5A/18.4V

Table 2 ALTERNATOR ROTOR BOLT TORQUE SPECIFICATIONS

Model	N•m	ft.-lb.
XR200R	80-100	58-72
XL250S	85-105	61-76
XR250	95-105	69-76
XR250R		
1981-1982	95-105	69-76
1984-1985	80-100	59-73
1986-on	100-110	72-80
XL350R, XR350R	100-120	72-87

Table 3 CDI TROUBLESHOOTING

Symptoms	Probable Cause
Weak spark	Low battery
	Poor connections (clean and tighten)
	High voltage linkage (replace defective wire)
	Defective coil
No spark	Discharged battery
	Fuse burned out
	Wiring broken
	Defective coil
	Defective signal generating coil (replace)

8

Table 4 IGNITION SYSTEM TEST POINTS

1985-ON XL250R AND 1986-ON XR250R ONLY		
Item	**Terminal**	**Standard resistance values**
Ignition coil primary circuit	Green and black/yellow wires	0.1-0.3 ohms*
Ignition coil secondary circuit with spark plug cap installed	Green wire and spark plug cap	7.4-11 k ohms*
Ignition coil secondary circuit with spark plug cap removed	Green wire and spark plug lead	3.7-4.5 k ohms*
Alternator exciter coil	Black/red and green wires	50-250 ohms*
Pulse generator	Green/white and blue/yellow wires	460-580 ohms*
Engine stop switch (In RUN position)	Black/white and green wires	No continuity
Ignition switch (In ON position)	Black/white and green wires	No continuity
*For accurate readings, the components must be at 20° C (68° F).		

Table 5 PULSE GENERATOR SPECIFIED RESISTANCE

Model	Standard resistance values
XR200R	468-572
XL250S, XR250	20-60 ohms
XL250R	
1982-1983	510-570
1984-on	460-580
XR250R	
1981-1982	90-110
1984-1985	468-572
1986-on	460-580
XL350R, XR350R	460-580

Table 6 IGNITION COIL SPECIFIED RESISTANCE

Model	Primary	Secondary
XR200R	0.16-0.19 ohms	3.69-4.51 k ohms
XL250S, XR250	0.2-0.8 ohms	8-15 k ohms
XL250R		
1982-1983	0.2-0.8 ohms	8-15 k ohms
1984-on	0.1-0.3 ohms	–
With spark plug cap installed	–	7.4-11 k ohms
With spark plug cap removed	–	3.7-4.5 k ohms
XR250R		
1981-1982	0.2-0.8 ohms	8-15 k ohms
1984-1985	0.16-0.19 ohms	3.69-4.51 k ohms
1986-on	0.1-0.3 ohms	–
With spark plug cap installed	–	7.4-11 k ohms
With spark plug cap removed	–	3.7-4.5 k ohms
XL350R	0.1-0.3	3.5-4.7 k ohms
XR350R		
1983	0.2-0.3 ohms	3.2-4.2 k ohms
1984-1985	0.16-0.2 ohms	3.7-4.5 k ohms

Table 7 REPLACEMENT BULBS

Model	Headlight	Taillight-Brakelight	Turn Signal
XR200R			
1984-1985	6V 25/25W	6V/3W	.
Optional	12V/55W	12V/4W	.
XL250S	6V 35/36.5W	6V/32W	6V/18W
XL250R			
1982-1983	12V 35/36.5W	12V/32W	12V/23W
1984-on	12V 35/35W	12V/8/27W	12V/23W
XR250	6V 25/25W	6V/6/3	.
XR250R			
1981-on	6V 25/25W	6V/3W	.
1984-on optional	12V/55W	12V/4W	.
XL350	12/55/60W	12V 8/27W	12V/23W
XR350	6V/35W	6V/3W	.
Optional	12V/55W	12V/3.4W	.

All indicator and illumination bulbs 6V or 12V and 1.7W or 3.4W.

8

NOTE: If you own a 1990 or later model, first check the Supplement at the back of the book for any new service information.

CHAPTER NINE

FRONT SUSPENSION AND STEERING

This chapter describes repair and maintenance procedures for the front wheel, forks and steering components.

Front suspension torque specifications are covered in **Table 1**. **Tables 1-4** are at the end of this chapter.

FRONT WHEEL
(DRUM BRAKE)

Removal (XL250S, XR250R)

1. Place wood block(s) under the skid plate to support the bike securely with the front wheel off the ground.
2. Slacken the brake cable at the hand lever (**Figure 1**).
3. Remove the speedometer cable set screw (A, **Figure 2**).
4. Pull the speedometer cable (B, **Figure 2**) free from the speedometer gear box.
5. Loosen the locknut (A, **Figure 3**) at the fork leg bracket.
6. Remove the cable end from the brake arm (B, **Figure 3**).
7A. On XL250S models, perform the following:
  a. Remove the cotter pin, then the axle nut. Discard the cotter pin—never reuse a cotter pin as it may break and fall out.

  b. Loosen the axle pinch bolt (**Figure 4**).
7B. On XR250 models, perform the following:
  a. Remove the axle nut (**Figure 5**).
  b. Loosen the axle holder nuts (**Figure 6**) and loosen the axle holder. It is not necessary to remove the axle holder, just loosen it enough to clear the front axle.
8. Remove the front axle from the left-hand side.
9. Pull the wheel down and forward. This allows the brake panel to disengage from the boss on the left-hand fork slider.
10. Remove the front wheel.
11. Inspect the wheel as described in this chapter.

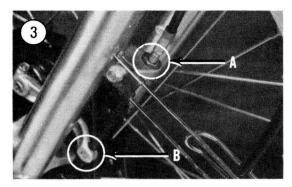

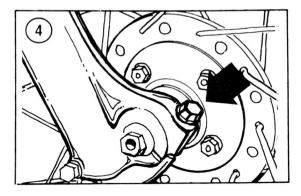

Installation (XL250S, XR250R)

1. Make sure the axle bearing surfaces of the fork slider and axle are free from burrs and nicks.

2. Clean the axle in solvent and thoroughly dry. Make sure all surfaces that the axle comes in contact with are clean and free from road dirt and old grease prior to installation.

3. Position the wheel into place, carefully inserting the groove in the brake panel into the groove in the left-hand fork slider. This is necessary for proper brake operation.

4. Insert the front axle from the right-hand side through the axle holder and the wheel hub and install the axle nut.

5A. On XL250S models, perform the following:
    a. Tighten the front axle nut to the torque specification listed in **Table 1**.
    b. Install a new cotter pin and bend the ends over completely.

5B. On XR250 models, perform the following:
    a. If removed, install the axle holder with the "UP" mark facing upward. Install the axle holder nuts and tighten finger-tight at this time.
    b. Tighten the front axle nut to the torque specification listed in **Table 1**.
    c. Tighten the front axle holder nuts a little tighter—but not to the final torque specification.

6. Install the front brake cable to the brake arm.

7. Slowly rotate the wheel and install the speedometer cable into the speedometer housing. Install the cable set screw.

8. Remove the wood block(s) from under the skid plate.

9. With the front brake applied, push down hard on the handlebars and pump the forks several times to seat the front axle.

9

10A. On XL250S models, tighten the front axle pinch bolt to the torque specification listed in **Table 1**.

> *WARNING*
> *During Step 10B, the axle holder nuts must be tightened in the specified manner and to the correct torque value. After installation is complete, there will be slight gap at the bottom, with no gap at the top. If done incorrectly, the studs in the fork slider may fail, resulting in loss of control of the bike when riding.*

10B. On XR250 models, tighten the axle holder upper nuts first and then the lower nuts to the torque specification listed in **Table 1**.

11. After the wheel is completely installed, rotate it several times and apply the brakes a couple of times to make sure that it rotates freely and that the brake is operating correctly.

12. Adjust the front brake as described in Chapter Three.

Removal (1981-1982 XR250R, 1983 XR350R)

1. Place wood block(s) under the skid plate to support the bike securely with the front wheel off the ground.

2. Slacken the brake cable at the hand lever.

3. Remove the speedometer cable set screw (A, **Figure 7**).

4. Pull the speedometer cable free from the speedometer gear box.

5. On 1983 XR350R models, loosen the screws on the brake cable clamp on the left-hand fork slider. This is to allow movement of the cable for the next step.

6. At the brake panel, perform the following:
   a. Loosen the locknut (A, **Figure 8**).
   b. Remove the cable end from the brake arm (B, **Figure 8**).
   c. Remove the brake cable from the bracket on the brake panel.

7. Loosen the axle holder nuts (B, **Figure 7**) and loosen the axle holder. It is not necessary to remove the axle holder, just loosen it enough to clear the front axle.

8. Unscrew the front axle (C, **Figure 7**) from the left-hand fork leg. Withdraw the front axle.

9. Pull the wheel down and forward. This allows the brake panel to disengage from the boss on the left-hand fork slider.

10. Remove the front wheel.

11. Inspect the wheel as described in this chapter.

Installation (1981-1982 XR250R, XR350R)

1. Make sure the axle bearing surfaces of the fork slider and axle are free from burrs and nicks.

2. Clean the axle in solvent and thoroughly dry. Make sure all surfaces that the axle comes in contact with are clean and free from road dirt and old grease prior to installation.

3. Position the wheel into place, carefully inserting the groove in the brake panel into the groove in the left-hand fork slider. This is necessary for proper brake operation.

4. Position the tang on the speedometer gear box under the lip on the fork slider.

5. Insert the front axle from the right-hand side through the axle holder, the speedometer gear box and the wheel hub. Screw the axle into the left-hand fork slider and temporarily tighten the axle.

6. If removed, install the axle holder with the "UP" mark facing upward. Install the axle holder nuts and tighten only finger-tight at this time.

7. Tighten the front axle to the torque specification listed in **Table 1**.

8. Tighten the front axle nuts a little tighter, but not to the final torque specification.

9. Install the front brake cable to the brake arm.

10. Tighten the screws on the brake cable clamp on the left-hand fork slider.

11. Slowly rotate the wheel and install the speedometer cable into the speedometer housing. Install the cable set screw.

12. Remove the wood block(s) from under the skid plate.

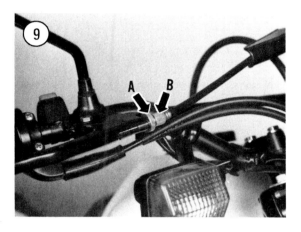

13. With the front brake applied, push down hard on the handlebars and pump the forks several times to seat the front axle.

WARNING
During Step 14, the axle holder nuts must be tightened in the specified manner and to the correct torque value. After installation is complete, there will be a slight gap at the bottom, with no gap at the top. If done incorrectly the studs in the fork slider may fail, resulting in the loss of control of the bike when riding.

14. Tighten the axle holder upper nuts first and then the lower nuts to the torque specification listed in **Table 1**.

15. After the wheel is completely installed, rotate it several times and apply the brakes a couple of times to make sure that it rotates freely and that the brake is operating correctly.

16. Adjust the front brake as described in Chapter Three.

Removal (XL250R, 1984-1985 XR200R, 1984-1985 XR250R)

1. Place wood block(s) under the skid plate to support the bike securely with the front wheel off the ground.

2. Loosen the locknut (A, **Figure 9**) and unscrew the adjuster (B, **Figure 9**) at the brake hand lever.

3. Remove the speedometer cable set screw (A, **Figure 10**).

4. Pull the speedometer cable free from the speedometer gear box.

5. Loosen the screws on the brake cable clamp (**Figure 11**) on the left-hand fork slider. This is to allow movement of the cable for the next step.

6. At the brake panel, perform the following:
   a. Loosen the locknut (B, **Figure 10**).
   b. Remove the cable end from the brake arm (C, **Figure 10**).
   c. Remove the brake cable from the bracket on the brake panel.
   d. On 1984-1985 XR200R and XR250R models, don't lose the coil spring at the end of the brake cable.

7. Loosen the axle holder nuts (A, **Figure 12**) and loosen the axle holder. It is not necessary to remove the axle holder, just loosen it enough to clear the front axle.

8. Unscrew the front axle (B, **Figure 12**) from the left-hand fork leg. Withdraw the front axle.

9. Pull the wheel down and forward. This allows the brake panel to disengage from the boss on the left-hand fork slider.

10. Remove the front wheel.

11. Inspect the wheel as described in this chapter.

Installation (XL250R, 1984-1985 XR200R, 1984-1988XR250R)

1. Make sure the axle bearing surfaces of the fork slider and axle are free from burrs and nicks.

2. Clean the axle in solvent and thoroughly dry. Make sure all surfaces that the axle comes in contact with are clean and free from road dirt and old grease prior to installation.

3. Position the wheel into place, carefully inserting the groove in the brake panel into the groove in the left-hand fork slider (**Figure 13**). This is necessary for proper brake operation.

4. Insert the front axle from the right-hand side through the axle holder and the wheel hub. Screw the axle into the left-hand fork slider and temporarily tighten the axle.

5. If removed, install the axle holder with the "UP" mark facing upward (C, **Figure 12**). Install the axle holder nuts and tighten only finger-tight at this time.

6. Tighten the front axle to the torque specification listed in **Table 1**.

7. Tighten the front axle holder nuts a little tighter—but not to the final torque specification.

8A. On 1984-1985 XR200R and XR250R models, be sure to install the coil spring on the end of the brake cable before inserting the front brake cable onto the brake arm.

8B. On 1984-on XL250R models, install the front brake cable to the brake arm.

9. Tighten the screws on the brake cable clamp on the left-hand fork slider.

10. Slowly rotate the wheel and install the speedometer cable into the speedometer housing. Install the cable set screw.

11. Remove the wood block(s) from under the skid plate.

12. With the front brake applied, push down hard on the handlebars and pump the forks several times to seat the front axle.

> *WARNING*
> *During Step 13, the axle holder nuts must be tightened in the specified manner and to the correct torque value. After installation is complete, there will be a slight gap at the bottom, with no gap at the top. If done incorrectly the studs in the fork slider may fail, resulting in loss of control of the bike when riding.*

13. Tighten the axle holder upper nuts first and then the lower nuts to the torque specification listed in **Table 1**.

14. After the wheel is completely installed, rotate it several times and apply the brakes a couple of times to make sure that it rotates freely and that the brake is operating correctly.

15. Adjust the front brake as described in Chapter Three.

FRONT WHEEL (DISC BRAKE)

Removal

1. Place wood block(s) under the skid plate to support it securely with the front wheel off the ground.
2. Remove the speedometer cable set screw (**Figure 14**). Pull the speedometer cable free from the speedometer gear box.
3. Loosen the axle holder nuts (A, **Figure 15**) and loosen the axle holder. It is not necessary to remove the axle holder, just loosen it enough to clear the front axle.
4. Unscrew the front axle (B, **Figure 15**) from the left-hand fork leg. Withdraw the front axle.
5. Pull the wheel down and forward and remove it. This allows the brake disc to slide out of the caliper assembly.
6. Remove the wheel.

CAUTION
Do not set the wheel down on the disc surface as it may get scratched or warped. Set the sidewalls on 2 wood blocks.

NOTE
Insert a piece of vinyl tubing or wood in the caliper in place of the brake disc. That way if the brake lever is inadvertently squeezed, the piston will not be forced out of the cylinder. If this does happen, the caliper may have to be disassembled to reseat the piston and the system will have to be bled. By using the wood, bleeding the brake is not necessary when installing the wheel.

Installation

1. Make sure the axle bearing surfaces of the fork slider and axle are free from burrs and nicks.
2. Remove the vinyl tubing or pieces of wood from the brake calipers.
3. Position the wheel into place and carefully insert the brake disc between the brake pads in the caliper assembly.
4. Align the speedometer housing with the tang on the right-hand fork slider.
5. Insert the front axle from the right-hand side through the speedometer gear box and the wheel hub. Screw it into the left-hand fork leg.
6. If removed, install the axle holder with the "UP" mark facing upward. Install the axle holder nuts and tighten only finger-tight at this time.
7. Tighten the front axle to the torque specification listed in **Table 1**.
8. Tighten the front axle holder nuts a little tighter—but not to the final torque specification.
9. Slowly rotate the wheel and install the speedometer cable into the speedometer housing. Install the cable set screw.
10. Remove the wood block(s) from under the skid plate.
11. With the front brake applied, push down hard on the handlebars and pump the forks several times to seat the front axle.

WARNING
During Step 12, the axle holder nuts must be tightened in the specified manner and to the correct torque value. After installation is complete, there will be a slight gap at the bottom, with no gap at the top. If done incorrectly the studs in the fork slider may fall, resulting in the loss of control of the bike when riding.

12. Tighten the axle holder upper nuts first and then the lower nuts to the torque specification listed in **Table 1**.

13. After the wheel is completely installed, rotate it several times and apply the brakes a couple of times to make sure that it rotates freely and that the brake pads are against the disc correctly.

WHEEL INSPECTION (ALL MODELS)

Measure the axial and radial runout of the wheel with a dial indicator as shown in **Figure 16**. The maximum axial and radial runout is 2.0 mm (0.08 in.). If the runout exceeds this dimension, check the wheel bearing condition.

If the wheel bearings are okay, tighten or replace bent or loose spokes as described in this chapter.

Check the front axle runout as described under *Front Hub* in this chapter.

FRONT HUB

Inspection

Inspect each wheel bearing prior to removing it from the wheel hub.

> *CAUTION*
> *Do not remove the wheel bearings for inspection purposes as they will be damaged during the removal process. Remove wheel bearings only if they are to be replaced.*

1. Perform Steps 1-7 of *Disassembly* in this chapter.
2. Turn each bearing by hand. Make sure bearings turn smoothly.
3. On non-sealed bearings, check the balls for evidence of wear, pitting or excessive heat (bluish tint). Replace the bearings if necessary; always replace as a complete set. When replacing the bearings, be sure to take your old bearings along to ensure a perfect matchup.

> *NOTE*
> *Fully sealed bearings are available from many bearing specialty shops. Fully sealed bearings provide better protection from dirt and moisture that may get into the hub.*

4. Check the axle for wear and straightness. Use V-blocks and a dial indicator as shown in **Figure 17**. If the runout is 0.2 mm (0.01 in.) or greater, the axle should be replaced.

Disassembly

Refer to **Figure 18** for drum brake models or **Figure 19** for disc brake models for this procedure.
1. Remove the front wheel as described in this chapter.
2. On drum brake models, pull the brake assembly straight up and out of the brake drum.
3. On models so equipped, remove the speedometer gear box.

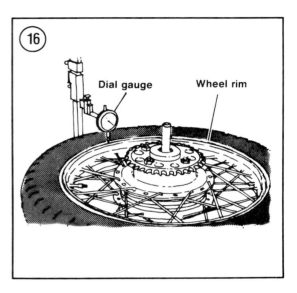
Dial gauge   Wheel rim

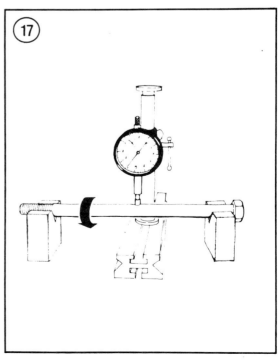

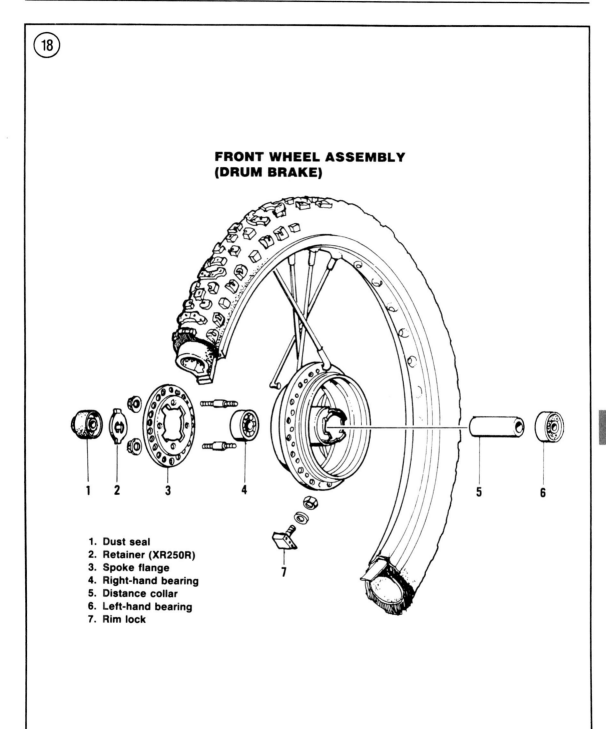

**FRONT WHEEL ASSEMBLY
(DRUM BRAKE)**

1. Dust seal
2. Retainer (XR250R)
3. Spoke flange
4. Right-hand bearing
5. Distance collar
6. Left-hand bearing
7. Rim lock

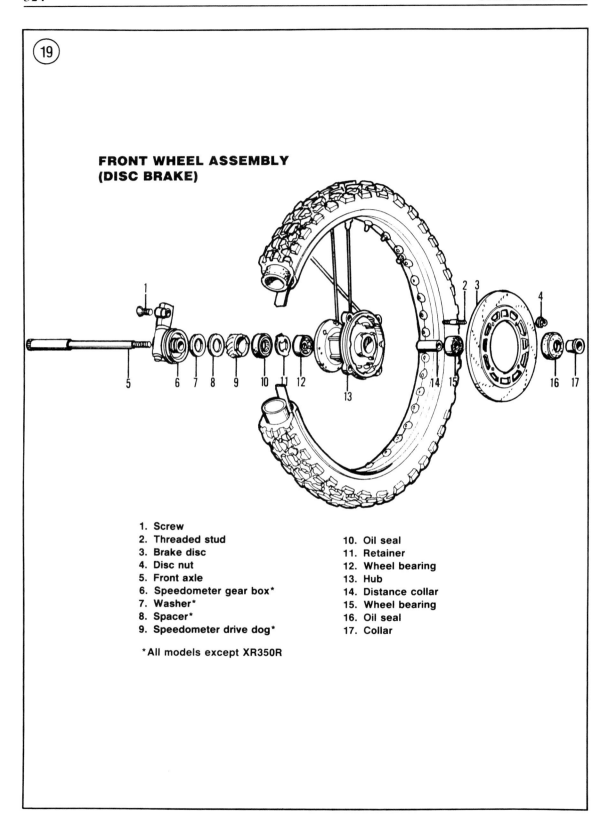

⑲

**FRONT WHEEL ASSEMBLY
(DISC BRAKE)**

1. Screw
2. Threaded stud
3. Brake disc
4. Disc nut
5. Front axle
6. Speedometer gear box*
7. Washer*
8. Spacer*
9. Speedometer drive dog*

10. Oil seal
11. Retainer
12. Wheel bearing
13. Hub
14. Distance collar
15. Wheel bearing
16. Oil seal
17. Collar

*All models except XR350R

4. Remove the dust seal (**Figure 20**) from the right-hand side.

5. On XR250R and disc brake models, remove the retainer.

6. On models equipped with a speedometer, remove the speedometer drive dog (A, **Figure 21**) and grease seal (B, **Figure 21**).

7. On disc brake models, perform the following:

    a. On models so equipped, remove the screws securing the plastic dust cover and remove the cover.

    b. Remove the nuts securing the brake disc and remove the disc.

    c. Remove the grease seal.

8. Before proceeding further, inspect the wheel bearings as described in this chapter. If they must be replaced, proceed as follows.

9A. A special Honda tool set-up can be used to remove the wheel bearings as follows:

    a. Install the 15 mm bearing remover (Honda part No. 07746-0050400) into the right-hand bearing.

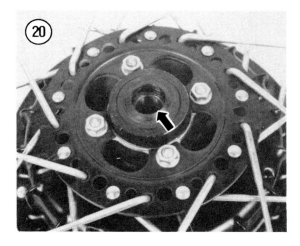

    b. Turn the wheel over (left-hand side up) on the workbench so the bearing remover is touching the workbench surface.

    c. From the left-hand side of the hub, install the bearing remover expander (Honda part No. 07746-0050100) into the bearing remover. Using a hammer, tap the expander into the bearing remover with a hammer.

    d. Stand the wheel up to a vertical position.

    e. Tap on the end of the expander and drive the right-hand bearing out of the hub. Remove the bearing and the distance collar.

    f. Repeat for the left-hand bearing.

9B. If special tools are not used, perform the following:

    a. To remove the right- and left-hand bearings and distance collar, insert a soft aluminum or brass drift into one side of the hub.

    b. Push the distance collar over to one side and place the drift on the inner race of the lower bearing.

    c. Tap the bearing out of the hub with a hammer, working around the perimeter of the inner race.

    d. Repeat for the other bearing.

10. Clean the inside and the outside of the hub with solvent. Dry with compressed air.

Assembly

1. On non-sealed bearings, pack the bearings with a good quality bearing grease. Work the grease in between the balls thoroughly; turn the bearing by hand a couple of times to make sure the grease is distributed evenly inside the bearing.

2. Blow any dirt or foreign matter out of the hub prior to installing the bearings.

> *CAUTION*
> *Install non-sealed bearings with the single sealed side facing outward. Tap the bearings squarely into place and tap on the outer race only. Do not tap on the inner race or the bearing might be damaged. Be sure that the bearings are completely seated.*

3A. A special Honda tool set-up can be used to install the wheel bearings as follows:

    a. Install the 32×35 mm attachment (Honda part No. 07746-010100) and the 15 mm pilot (Honda part No. 07746-0040300) into the right-hand bearing and drive in the right-hand bearing.

    b. Turn the wheel over (left-hand side up) on the workbench and install the distance collar.

    c. Use the same tool set-up and drive in the left-hand bearing.

3B. If special tools are not used, perform the following:

    a. Tap the right-hand bearing squarely into place and tap on the outer race only. Use a socket (**Figure 22**) that matches the outer race diameter. Do not tap on the inner race or the bearing might be damaged. Be sure that the bearing is completely seated.

    b. Turn the wheel over (left-hand side up) on the workbench and install the distance collar.

    c. Use the same tool set-up and drive in the left-hand bearing.

4. On disc brake models, perform the following:

    a. Install the grease seal.

    b. Install the brake disc and nuts. Tighten to the torque specifications listed in **Table 1**.

    c. On models so equipped, install the plastic dust seal and screws. Tighten the screws securely.

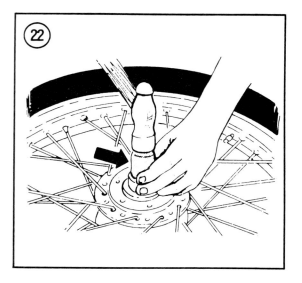

5. Install the grease seal (B, **Figure 21**) and the speedometer drive dog (A, **Figure 21**).

6. On models so equipped, on the right-hand side, align the tangs of the retainer with the slots in the hub and install the retainer. Push the retainer all the way down onto the surface of the bearing and the hub.

7. Apply grease to the dust seal and install the dust seal (**Figure 20**) next to the retainer.

8. On models equipped with a speedometer, align the tangs (**Figure 23**) of the speedometer drive dog with the notches in the front hub and install the speedometer gearbox.

> *NOTE*
> *Make sure the speedometer gear box seats completely. If the speedometer components do not mesh properly the wheel will be to wide for installation.*

9. Install the front wheel as described in this chapter.

WHEELS

Wheel Balance

An unbalanced wheel is unsafe. Depending on the degree of unbalance and the speed of the motorcycle, the rider may experience anything from a mild vibration to a violent shimmy which may even result in loss of control.

On spoke wheels, the weights are attached to the spokes on the light side of the wheel.

Before you attempt to balance the wheel, check to be sure that the wheel bearings are in good condition and properly lubricated and that the brakes do not drag. The wheel must rotate freely.

NOTE
When balancing the rear wheel, do so with the final drive sprocket assembly attached, as it rotates with the rear wheel and affects the balance. The front brake panel does not rotate with the front wheel so it should be removed from the front wheel.

1. Remove the wheel as described in this chapter or Chapter Ten.
2. Mount the wheel on a fixture such as the one shown in **Figure 24** so it can rotate freely.
3. Give the wheel a spin and let it coast to a stop. Mark the tire at the lowest point.

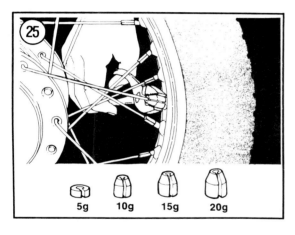

4. Spin the wheel several more times. If the wheel keeps coming to rest at the same point, it is out of balance.
5. Attach a weight to the upper (or light) side of the wheel at the spoke (**Figure 25**). Weights come in 4 sizes: 5, 10, 15 and 20 grams. They are crimped onto the spoke with ordinary gas pliers.
6. Experiment with different weights until the wheel, when spun, comes to a rest at a different position each time.

Spoke Adjustment

Spokes loosen with use and should be checked periodically. If all appear to be loose, tighten all spokes on one side of the hub, then tighten all spokes on the other side of the hub. One-half to one turn should be sufficient; do not overtighten.

After tightening the spokes, check rim runout to be sure you haven't pulled the rim out of shape.

One way to check rim runout is to mount a dial indicator onto the front fork so that it bears against one side of the rim.

If you don't have a dial indicator, improvise a device like the one shown in **Figure 26**. Adjust the position of the bolt until it just clears the rim. Rotate the wheel and note whether the clearance increases or decreases. Mark the tire with chalk or crayon at areas that produce significantly larger or smaller clearance. Clearance must not change by more than 2.0 mm (0.08 in.).

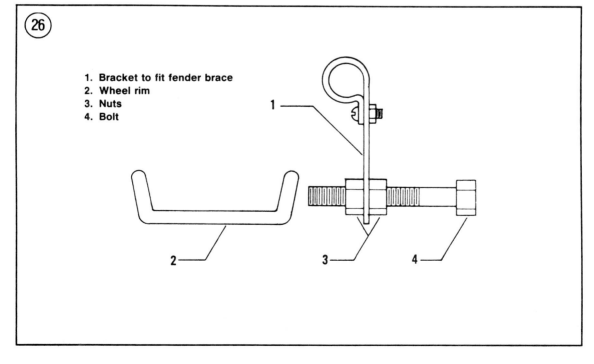

1. **Bracket to fit fender brace**
2. **Wheel rim**
3. **Nuts**
4. **Bolt**

To pull the rim out, tighten the spokes which terminate on the same side of the hub and loosen spokes which terminate on the opposite side of the hub (**Figure 27**). In most cases, only a slight amount of adjustment is necessary to true a rim. After adjustment is complete, rotate the wheel and make sure another area has not been pulled out of true. Continue adjustment and checking until runout does not exceed 2.0 mm (0.08 in.).

Wheel Alignment

Refer to **Figure 28** for this procedure.

1. Measure the tires at their widest point.
2. Subtract the small dimension from the larger dimension.
3. Make an alignment tool out of wood, approximately 7 feet long, with an offset equal to one-half of the dimension obtained in Step 2. Refer to (D).
4. If the wheels are not aligned as in (A) and (C), the rear wheel must be shifted to correct the alignment.
5A. On dual-shock models, perform the following:
   a. Loosen the rear axle nut.

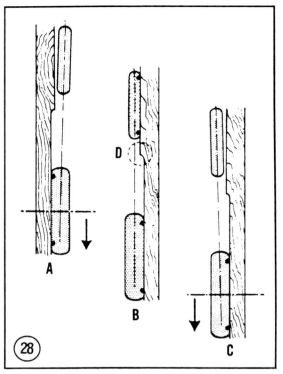

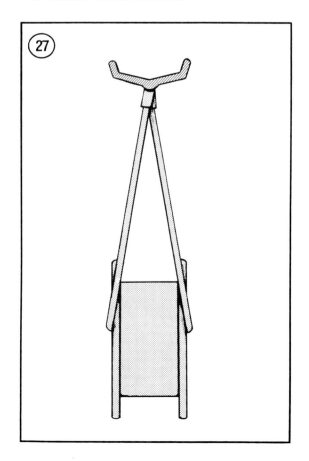

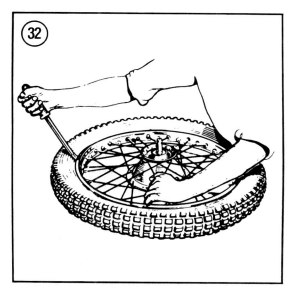

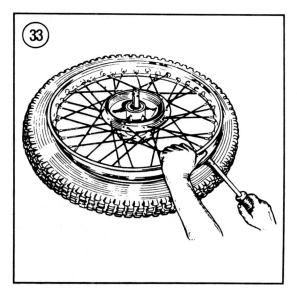

b. Loosen the drive chain adjuster locknut and turn the adjuster (**Figure 29**) until the wheels align.

5B. On Pro-Link models, perform the following:

a. Loosen the rear axle nut (A, **Figure 30**).

b. Turn both snail adjusters (B, **Figure 30**) in either direction until the wheels align.

6. Adjust the drive chain as described in Chapter Three.

TIRE CHANGING

Removal

1. Remove the valve core to deflate the tire. On models so equipped, loosen the rim locknuts (**Figure 31**) fully, but do not remove them.

2. Press the entire bead on both sides of the tire into the center of the rim.

3. Lubricate the beads with soapy water.

4. Insert the tire iron under the bead next to the valve (**Figure 32**). Force the bead on the opposite side of the tire into the center of the rim and pry the bead over the rim with the tire iron.

5. Insert a second tire iron next to the first to hold the bead over the rim. Then work around the tire with the first tire iron, prying the bead over the rim. Be careful not to pinch the inner tube with the tire irons.

6. Remove the valve from the hole in the rim and remove the inner tube from the tire.

NOTE
Step 7 is required only if it is necessary to completely remove the tire from the rim, as in tire replacement.

7. Stand the tire upright. Insert the tire iron between the second bead and the side of the rim that the first bead was pried over (**Figure 33**). Force the bead on the opposite side from the tire iron into the center of the rim. Pry the second bead off the rim, working around as with the first.

Installation

1. Carefully inspect the tire for any damage, especially inside.

2. A new tire may have balancing rubbers inside. These are not patches and should not be disturbed. A colored spot near the bead indicates a lighter point on the tire. This spot should be placed next to the valve stem or on models so equipped, midway between the 2 rim locks.

3. Check that the spoke ends do not protrude through the nipples into the center of the rim. If they do they will puncture the inner tube. File off any protruding spoke ends.

4. Make sure the rubber rim tape is in place with the rough side toward the rim.

5. Install the tube valve core into the tube valve. Place the tube into the tire and inflate it just enough to round it out. Too much air will make installing the tire difficult and too little will increase the chances of pinching the tube with tire irons.

6. Lubricate both beads of the tire with soapy water. Pull the tube partly out of the tire at the valve. Squeeze the beads together to hold the tube and insert the valve into the hole in the rim (**Figure 34**). The lower bead should go into the center of the rim with the upper bead outside it.

7. Place the lower bead of the tire into the center of the rim on each side of the valve stem. Work around the tire in both directions (**Figure 35**). Use a tire iron for the last few inches of bead (**Figure 36**).

8. Press the upper bead into the rim opposite the valve stem. Pry the bead into the rim on both sides of the initial point with a tire iron, working around the rim to the valve (**Figure 37**).

9. Wiggle the valve stem to be sure the tube is not trapped under the tire bead. Set the valve squarely in the rim hole before screwing on the valve stem nut.

10. Check the bead on both sides of the tire for even fit around the rim.

11. Bounce the wheel several times, rotating it each time. This will force the tire beads against the rim flanges. After the tire beads are in contact with the rim evenly, inflate the tire to seat the beads.

12. Inflate the tire to more than the recommended inflation pressure for the initial seating of the rim flanges. Once the beads are seated correctly, deflate the tire to the correct pressure described in Chapter Three.

13. Balance the wheel as described in this chapter.

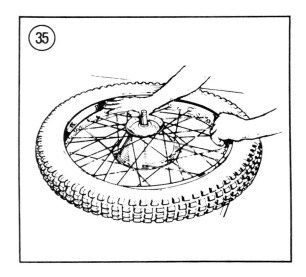

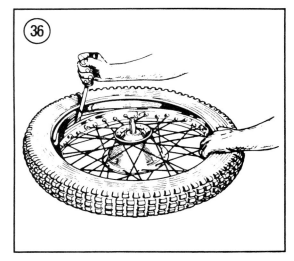

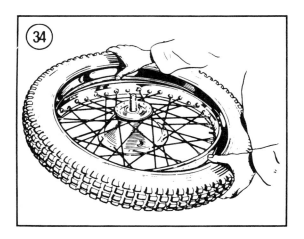

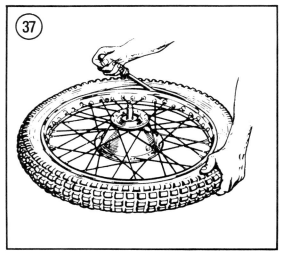

TIRE REPAIRS

Patching an inner tube on the road is very difficult. A can of pressurized tire sealant may inflate the tire and seal the hole, although this is only a temporary fix.

Another solution is to carry a spare inner tube that could be installed and inflated.

If you do patch the inner tube, do not run for any length of time as the patch may rub off resulting in another flat. Install a new inner tube as soon as possible.

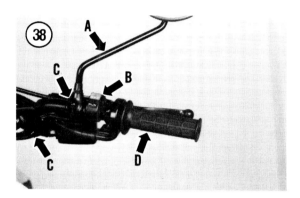

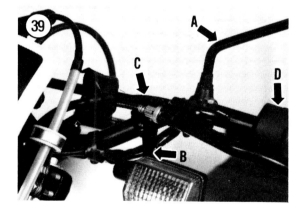

HANDLEBAR

Removal/Installation
(Drum Brake Models)

1. On XL series models, perform the following:

   a. Remove the right-hand rear view mirror (A, **Figure 38**).

   b. Remove the clamping screws on the turn signal bracket and remove the turn signal assembly from the handlebar.

2. Disconnect the brake light switch electrical connector.

3. Remove the screws securing the right-hand handlebar switch assembly (B, **Figure 38**) and remove the electrical wires from the clips (C, **Figure 38**) on the handlebar. Remove the switch assembly from the handlebar.

4. Remove the throttle assembly (D, **Figure 38**) and carefully lay the throttle assembly and cables over the fender or back over the frame. Be careful that the cables do not get crimped or damaged.

5. On XL series models, perform the following:

   a. Remove the left-hand rear view mirror (A, **Figure 39**).

   b. Remove the clamping screws on the turn signal bracket (B, **Figure 39**) and remove the turn signal assembly from the handlebar.

6. On models so equipped, perform the following:

   a. Disconnect the choke cable from the choke lever (C, **Figure 39**).

   b. Remove the bolt securing the clutch lever assembly.

7. Lay the clutch and choke (models so equipped) lever assemblies and cable(s) back over the frame or front fender. Be careful that the cables do not get crimped or damaged.

8. Remove the screws securing the left-hand handlebar switch assembly (D, **Figure 39**) and remove the electrical wires from the clips on the handlebar.

9. Remove the bolts (**Figure 40**) securing the handlebar upper holders in place. Remove the handlebar upper holders, then remove the handlebar.

10. To maintain a good grip on the handlebar and to prevent it from slipping down, clean the knurled section of the handlebar with a wire brush. It should be kept rough so it will be held securely by the holders. The holders should also be kept clean and free of any metal that may have been gouged loose by handlebar slippage.

11. Install by reversing these removal steps, noting the following.

12. Position the handlebar on the upper fork bridge so the punch mark on the handlebar is aligned with the top surface of the raised portion of the upper fork bridge (**Figure 41**).

13. Install the handlebar holders and install the bolts. Tighten the forward bolts first and then the rear bolts. Tighten all bolts to the torque specification listed in **Table 1**.

14. Apply a light coat of multipurpose grease to the throttle grip area on the handlebar prior to installing the throttle grip assembly.

> *NOTE*
> *When installing all assemblies, align the punch mark on the handlebar with the slit on the mounting bracket (**Figure 42**).*

> *WARNING*
> *After installation is complete make sure the brake lever does **not** come in contact with the throttle grip assembly when it is pulled on fully.*

15. Adjust the throttle operation as described in Chapter Three.

Removal/Installation
(Disc Brake Models)

1. Remove the headlight housing as described Chapter Eight.

2. Remove the fuel tank as described in Chapter Seven.

3. On XL series models, perform the following:
   a. Remove the right-hand rear view mirror.
   b. Remove the clamping screws on the turn signal bracket and remove the turn signal assembly from the handlebar.

4. Disconnect the brake light switch electrical connector.

5. Remove the screws securing the right-hand handlebar switch assembly and remove the electrical wires from the clips on the handlebar.

> *CAUTION*
> *Cover the frame with a heavy cloth or plastic tarp to protect it from accidental spilling of brake fluid. Wash any spilled brake fluid off any painted or plated surface immediately, as it will destroy the finish. Use soapy water and rinse thoroughly.*

6. Remove the bolts (**Figure 43**) securing the throttle assembly and carefully lay the throttle

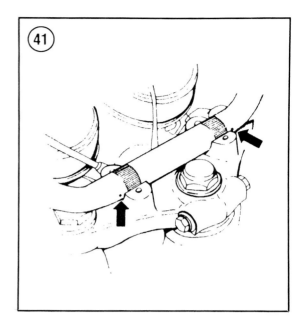

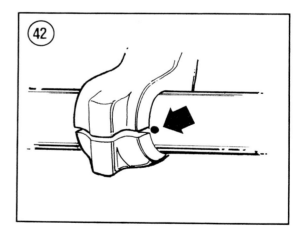

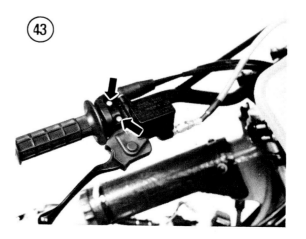

assembly and cables over the fender or back over the frame. Be careful that the cables do not get crimped or damaged.

7. Remove the bolts (**Figure 44**) securing the brake master cylinder and lay it over the frame. Keep the reservoir in the upright position to minimize loss of brake fluid and to keep air from entering into the brake system. It is not necessary to remove the hydraulic brake line.

8. On XL series models, perform the following:
    a. Remove the left-hand rear view mirror.
    b. Remove the clamping screws on the turn signal bracket and remove the turn signal assembly from the handlebar.

9. Remove the bolts securing the clutch lever assembly.

10. On models so equipped, disconnect the choke cable from the choke lever.

11. Lay the clutch and choke (models so equipped) lever assemblies and cable back over the frame or front fender. Be careful that the cables do not get crimped or damaged.

12. Remove the screws securing the left-hand handlebar switch assembly and remove the electrical wires from the clips on the handlebar.

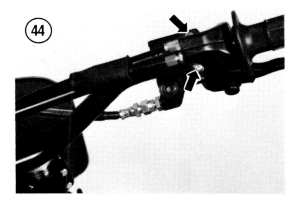

13. On 1985 XR350R models, disconnect the speedometer cable from the Digital Enduro Meter.

14. Remove the bolts (**Figure 45**) securing the handlebar upper holders in place.

15A. On 1985 XR350R models, remove the handlebar upper holders, the Digital Enduro Meter assembly and mounting brackets from upper fork bridge.

15B. On all other models, remove the handlebar upper holders.

16. Remove the handlebar.

17. Install by reversing these removal steps, noting the following.

18. To maintain a good grip on the handlebar and to prevent it from slipping down, clean the knurled section of the handlebar with a wire brush. It should be kept rough so it will be held securely by the holders. The holders should also be kept clean and free of any metal that may have been gouged loose by handlebar slippage.

19. Position the handlebar on the upper fork bridge so the punch mark on the handlebar is aligned with the top surface of the raised portion of the upper fork bridge (**Figure 41**).

20. Install the handlebar holders and install the bolts. Tighten the forward bolts first and then the rear bolts. Tighten all bolts to the torque specification listed in **Table 1**.

21. Apply a light coat of multipurpose grease to the throttle grip area on the handlebar prior to installing the throttle grip assembly.

NOTE
*When installing all assemblies, align the punch mark on the handlebar with the slit on the mounting bracket (**Figure 42**).*

22. Install the brake master cylinder onto the handlebar. Install the clamp with the UP arrow facing up and align the clamp mating surface with the punch mark on the handlebar. Tighten the upper bolt first and then the lower bolt.

WARNING
*After installation is completed, make sure the brake lever does not come in contact with the throttle grip assembly when it is pulled on fully. If it does the brake fluid may be low in the reservoir; refill as necessary. Refer to **Front Disc Brakes** in Chapter Eleven.*

23. Adjust the throttle operation as described in Chapter Three.

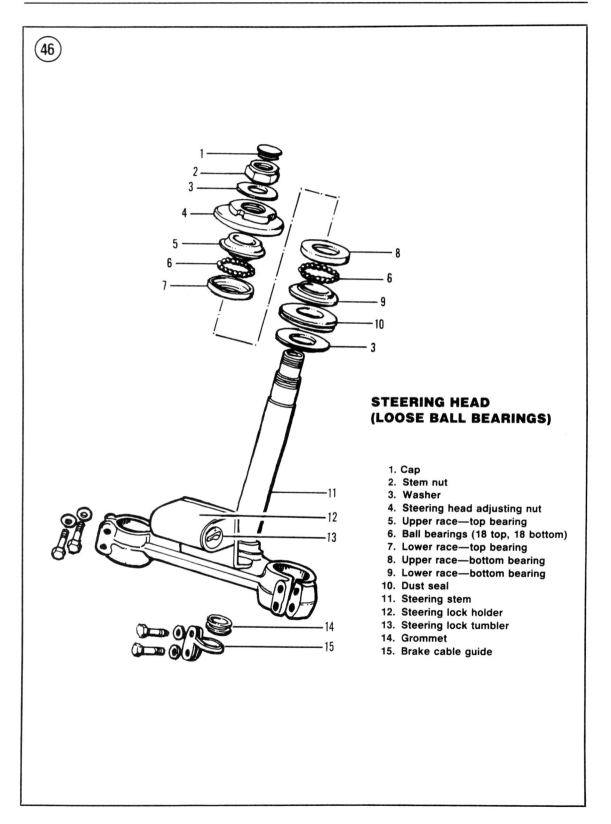

**STEERING HEAD
(LOOSE BALL BEARINGS)**

1. Cap
2. Stem nut
3. Washer
4. Steering head adjusting nut
5. Upper race—top bearing
6. Ball bearings (18 top, 18 bottom)
7. Lower race—top bearing
8. Upper race—bottom bearing
9. Lower race—bottom bearing
10. Dust seal
11. Steering stem
12. Steering lock holder
13. Steering lock tumbler
14. Grommet
15. Brake cable guide

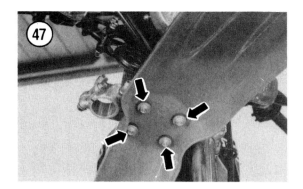

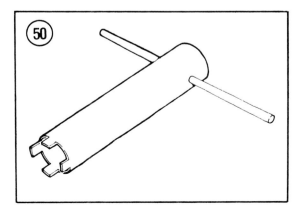

STEERING HEAD AND STEM (LOOSE BALL BEARINGS)

Disassembly

Refer to **Figure 46** for this procedure.

1. Remove the front wheel as described in this chapter.
2. Remove the handlebar as described in this chapter.
3. Remove the headlight and number plate assembly as described in Chapter Seven.
4. Remove the instrument cluster or speedometer as described in Chapter Seven.
5. Remove the horn as described in Chapter Seven.
6. Remove the ignition switch as described in Chapter Seven.
7. Remove the bolts (**Figure 47**) securing the front fender and remove the front fender.
8. Loosen the upper and lower fork bridge bolts (**Figure 48**) and slide out both fork tube assemblies.
9. Remove the steering stem nut and washer (**Figure 49**) and remove the upper fork bridge.
10. Loosen the steering stem adjust nut with the pin spanner provided in the factory tool kit, or use a large drift and hammer, or use the easily improvised tool shown in **Figure 50**.
11. Have an assistant hold a large pan under the steering stem to catch any loose balls that may fall out while you carefully lower the steering stem.
12. Lower the steering stem assembly down and out of the steering head.
13. Remove the upper race from the steering head.
14. Remove the ball bearings from the upper and lower race. There are 36 ball bearings total (18 in the upper race and 18 in the lower race).

Inspection

1. Clean the bearing races in the steering head and the bearings with solvent.
2. Check the welds around the steering head for cracks and fractures. If any are found, have them repaired by a competent frame shop or welding service.
3. Check the balls for pitting, scratches or discoloration indicating wear or corrosion. Replace them in sets if any are bad.
4. Check the races for pitting, galling and corrosion. If any of these conditions exist, replace the races as described in this chapter.
5. Check the steering stem for cracks and check its race for damage or wear. If this race or any race is damaged, the bearings should be replaced as a

complete bearing set. Take the old races and bearings to your dealer to ensure accurate replacement.

Steering Stem Assembly

Refer to **Figure 46** for this procedure.

1. Make sure the steering head and stem races are properly seated.

2. Apply a coat of cold grease to the upper bearing race cone and fit 18 ball bearings around it (**Figure 51**).

3. Apply a coat of cold grease to the lower bearing race cone on the steering stem and fit 18 ball bearings around it (**Figure 52**).

4. Install the steering stem into the head tube and hold it firmly in place.

5. Install the upper race of the top bearing.

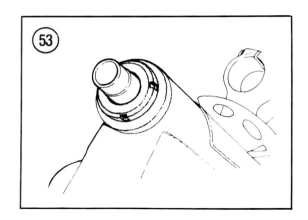

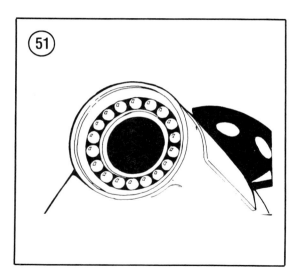

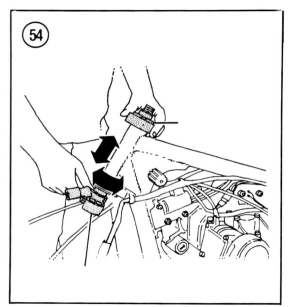

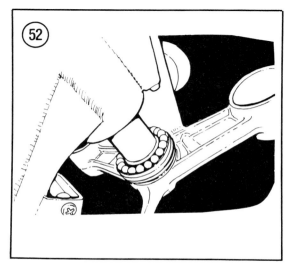

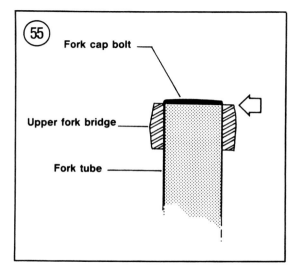

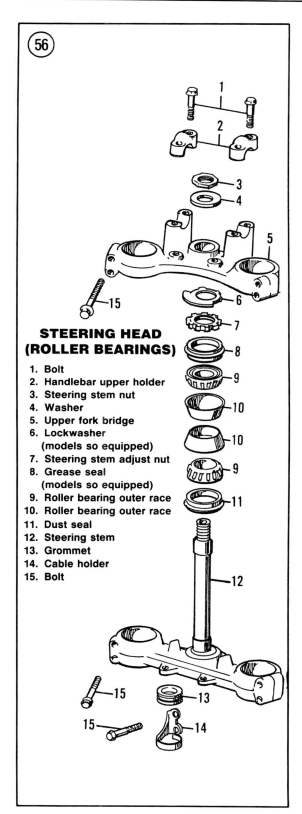

(56)

**STEERING HEAD
(ROLLER BEARINGS)**

1. Bolt
2. Handlebar upper holder
3. Steering stem nut
4. Washer
5. Upper fork bridge
6. Lockwasher
   (models so equipped)
7. Steering stem adjust nut
8. Grease seal
   (models so equipped)
9. Roller bearing outer race
10. Roller bearing outer race
11. Dust seal
12. Steering stem
13. Grommet
14. Cable holder
15. Bolt

6. Install the steering stem adjust nut (**Figure 53**) and tighten it until it is snug against the upper race, then back it off 1/8 turn.

NOTE
*The adjusting nut should be just tight enough to remove both horizontal and vertical play (**Figure 54**), yet loose enough so that the assembly will turn to both lock positions under its own weight after an assist.*

7. Install the upper fork bridge, washer and steering stem nut.

NOTE
Steps 8-10 must be performed in this order to assure proper upper and lower fork bridge to fork alignment.

8. Install the fork tubes so that the top of the fork tube aligns with the top surface of the upper fork bridge (**Figure 55**).
9. Tighten the *lower* fork bridge bolts to the torque specification listed in **Table 1**.
10. Tighten the steering stem nut to the torque specification listed in **Table 1**.
11. Tighten the *upper* fork bridge bolts to the torque specification listed in **Table 1**.
12. Install all items removed.
13. After a few hours of riding, the bearings have had a chance to seat; readjust the free play in the steering stem with the steering stem adjusting nut. Refer to Step 6.

Steering Stem Adjustment

If play develops in the steering system, it may only require adjustment. However, don't take a chance on it. Disassemble the stem and look for possible damage. Then reassemble and adjust as described in Step 6 of the *Steering Head Assembly* procedure.

**STEERING HEAD AND STEM
(ROLLER BEARINGS)**

Disassembly

Refer to **Figure 56** for this procedure.
1. Remove the front wheel as described in this chapter.

2. Remove the headlight and number plate assembly (A, **Figure 57**) as described in Chapter Seven.

3. Remove the speedometer (B, **Figure 57**) as described in Chapter Seven.

4. Remove the horn as described in Chapter Seven.

5. Remove the ignition switch as described in Chapter Seven.

6. Remove the bolts securing the front fender and remove it.

7. Remove the handlebar (A, **Figure 58**) as described in this chapter.

8. Remove the steering stem nut and washer (B, **Figure 58**).

9. Loosen the upper fork bridge bolts and remove the upper fork bridge (C, **Figure 57**).

10. On models so equipped, remove the lockwasher. Discard the lockwasher as a new one must be installed during assembly.

11. Remove the steering stem adjust nut. To loosen the adjust nut, use a large drift and hammer or use the easily improvised tool shown in **Figure 59**.

12. Lower the steering stem assembly down and out of the steering head (A, **Figure 60**). Don't worry about catching any loose steel balls as the steering stem is equipped with assembled roller bearings.

13. On models so equipped, remove the dust seal from the top of the headset.

14. Remove the upper bearing (B, **Figure 60**) from the top of the headset.

Inspection

1. Clean the bearing races in the steering head and the bearings with solvent.

2. Check the welds around the steering head for cracks and fractures. If any are found, have them repaired by a competent frame shop or welding service.

3. Check the rollers for pitting, scratches or discoloration indicating wear or corrosion. Replace them in sets if any are bad.

4. Check the races for pitting, galling and corrosion. If any of these conditions exist, replace the races as described in this chapter.

5. Check the steering stem for cracks, damage or wear. If damaged in any way, replace the steering stem.

Steering Stem Assembly

Refer to **Figure 56** for this procedure.

1. Make sure the steering head and stem races are properly seated.

2. Install the upper bearing into the steering head.

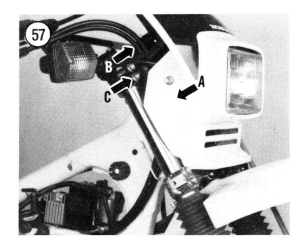

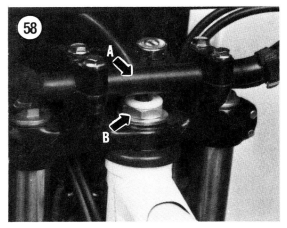

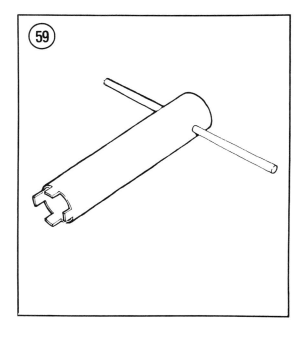

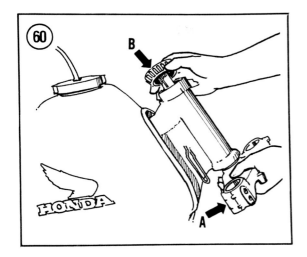

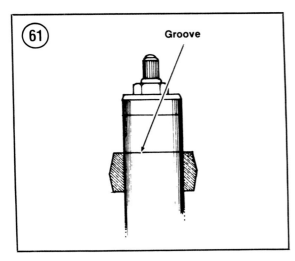

Groove

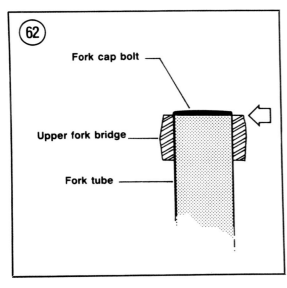

Fork cap bolt

Upper fork bridge

Fork tube

3. Install the steering stem into the head tube and hold it firmly in place.

4. Install the steering stem adjust nut and tighten it to about 1.0-2.0 N•m (0.7-1.5 ft.-lb.).

5. Turn the steering stem from lock-to-lock 4-5 times to seat the bearings.

6. Retighten the steering stem adjust nut to about 1.0-2.0 N•m (0.7-1.5 ft.-lb.).

7. Repeat Step 5 and Step 6 twice. If during these steps the adjust nut will not tighten, remove the nut and inspect both the nut and the steering stem threads for dirt and/or burrs. Clean both parts and repeat Steps 4-7.

8. On models so equipped, install a *new* lockwasher with the locking tab facing toward the rear of the bike.

9. Install the upper fork bridge, washer and steering stem nut only finger-tight at this time.

NOTE
Steps 10-13 must be performed in this order to assure proper upper and lower fork bridge to fork alignment.

10A. On 1981-1982 XR250R, XL350R and XR350R models, slide the fork tubes into position so the *lower* groove on the fork tube aligns with the top surface of the upper fork bridge (**Figure 61**).

10B. On all other models, slide the fork tubes into position so the top surface of the fork tube aligns with the top surface of the upper fork bridge (**Figure 62**).

11. Tighten the *lower* fork bridge bolts to the torque specification listed in **Table 1**.

12. Tighten the steering stem nut to the torque specification listed in **Table 1**.

13. Tighten the upper fork bridge bolts to the torque specification listed in **Table 1**.

14. On models so equipped, bend the lockwasher locking tab up against the back surface of the upper fork bridge.

15. Install all items removed.

Steering Stem Adjustment

If play develops in the steering system, it may only require adjustment. However, don't take a chance on it. Disassemble the stem and look for possible damage. Then reassemble and adjust as described in Steps 4-7 of the *Steering Head Assembly* procedure.

STEERING HEAD BEARING RACES

The headset and steering stem bearing races are pressed into place. Because they are easily bent, do not remove them unless they are worn and require replacement.

Headset Bearing Race
Removal/Installation

To remove the headset race, insert a hardwood stick or soft punch into the head tube (**Figure 63**) and carefully tap the race out from the inside. After it is started, tap around the race so that neither the race nor the head tube is damaged.   To install the headset race, tap it in slowly with a block of wood, a suitable size socket or piece of pipe (**Figure 64**). Make sure that the race is squarely seated in the headset race bore before tapping it into place. Tap the race in until it is flush with the steering head surface.

Steering Stem Bearing Race
and Grease Seal
Removal/Installation

1. To remove the steering stem race (bottom bearing lower race) try twisting and pulling it up by hand. If it will not come off, carefully pry it up with a screwdriver; work around in a circle, prying a little at a time.
2. On models with loose ball bearings, remove the bottom bearing lower race, dust seal and dust seal washer.

> *CAUTION*
> *On models with roller bearings, do not attempt to remove the lower bearing, inner race and dust seal from the steering stem. Removal of these components requires the use of a hydraulic press and special tools and should be entrusted to a Honda dealer or machine shop.*

3A. On models with loose ball bearings, install the dust seal washer and dust seal. Slide the lower race over the steering stem with the bearing surface facing up.
3B. On models with roller bearings, have the dealer or machine shop install the dust seal, and lower roller bearing and internal race.
4. Tap the lower race down with a piece of hardwood; work around in a circle so the race will not be bent. Make sure it is seated squarely and is all the way down.

FRONT FORK

The front suspension on all models uses spring controlled, hydraulically damped, telescopic fork.

Before suspecting major trouble, drain the front fork oil and refill with the proper type and quantity; refer to *Front Fork Oil Change* in Chapter Three. If you still have trouble, such as

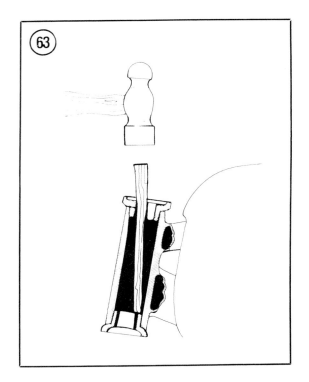

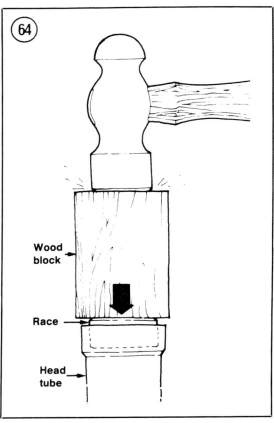

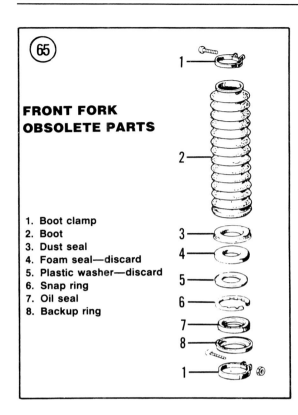

FRONT FORK OBSOLETE PARTS

1. Boot clamp
2. Boot
3. Dust seal
4. Foam seal—discard
5. Plastic washer—discard
6. Snap ring
7. Oil seal
8. Backup ring

poor damping, a tendency to bottom or top out or leakage around the rubber seals, follow the service procedures in this section.

To simplify fork service and to prevent the mixing of parts, the legs should be removed, serviced and installed individually.

Some of the fork assemblies used among the various models were originally equipped with a foam seal and a plastic washer.

These parts were located between the oil seal and the circlip (**Figure 65**). The manufacturer has determined that the foam seal may work its way down into the oil seal and give the appearance of a worn or leaking oil seal. Therefore on models so equipped, do *not* reinstall the foam seal and plastic washer under the dust seal during the assembly procedure. If you purchase a new seal kit that still contains these 2 parts in it, discard them; they are not to be used.

Figure 65 shows these 2 parts and indicates that they *should be discarded.*

Front Fork
Removal/Installation
(XL250S, XR250)

NOTE
The Allen bolt at the base of the slider has been secured with thread locking agent and is often very difficult to remove because the damper rod will turn inside the slider. It sometimes can be removed with an air impact driver. If you are unable to remove it, take the fork tubes to a dealer and have the bolts removed.

1. If the fork assembly is going to be disassembled, perform the following:
   a. Have an assistant hold the front brake on, compress the front forks and hold them in this position.
   b. Slightly loosen the Allen bolt at the base of the slider. If the bolt is loosened too much, fork oil may start to drain out of the slider. Release the front forks.
2. On XR models, remove the speedometer cable clamp in the left-hand fork slider (**Figure 66**).
3. Loosen the clamp screw (**Figure 67**) on the boot and slide the boot down.
4. Remove the front wheel as described in this chapter.
5. Remove the protective cap from the fork cap bolts.
6. Loosen, but do not remove, the fork cap bolts.
7. Loosen the upper and lower fork bridge bolts (A, **Figure 68**).

9

8. Remove the fork tubes (B, **Figure 68**). It may be necessary to slightly rotate the fork tube while pulling it down and out.

9. Install by reversing these removal steps, noting the following.

10. Insert the fork tube up through the lower and upper fork bridges.

11. Align the top of the fork tube with the top surface of the upper fork bridge (**Figure 62**).

12. Tighten the upper and lower fork bridge bolts to the torque specifications listed in **Table 1**.

Front Fork
Disassembly
(XL250S, XR250)

Refer to **Figure 69** for this procedure.

1. Clamp the slider in a vise with soft jaws.

2. If not loosened during the fork removal sequence, loosen the Allen bolt on the bottom of the slider.

> *NOTE*
> *This bolt has been secured with thread locking agent and is often very difficult to remove because the damper rod will turn inside the slider. It sometimes can be removed with an air impact driver. If you are unable to remove it, take the fork tubes to a dealer and have the bolts removed.*

3. Remove the 6 mm Allen bolt and gasket from the slider.

4. Hold the upper fork tube in a vise with soft jaws and loosen the fork cap bolt (if it was not loosened during the fork removal sequence).

> *WARNING*
> *Be careful when removing the fork top cap bolt as the spring(s) is under pressure. Protect your eyes accordingly.*

5. Remove the fork top cap bolt from the fork.

6A. On XL series models, remove the fork springs and flat washer.

6B. On XR series models, remove the fork spring.

7. Remove the fork from the vise, pour the fork oil out and discard it. Pump the fork several times by hand to expel most of the remaining oil.

8. Pull the fork tube out of the slider.

9. Remove the oil lock piece, the damper rod and rebound spring.

10. Remove the dust seal from the slider.

11A. On XL250S models, remove the set ring and oil seal from the slider.

11B. On XR250 models, remove the set ring (**Figure 70**), oil seal and backup ring from the slider.

> *NOTE*
> *It may be necessary to slightly heat the area on the slider around the oil seal prior to removal. Use a rag soaked in hot water; do not apply a flame directly to the fork slider.*

> *CAUTION*
> *Use a dull screwdriver blade to remove the oil seal (**Figure 71**). Do not damage the outer edge or inner surface of the slider.*

12. Inspect the components as described in this chapter.

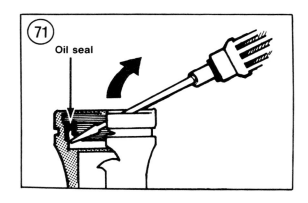

Oil seal

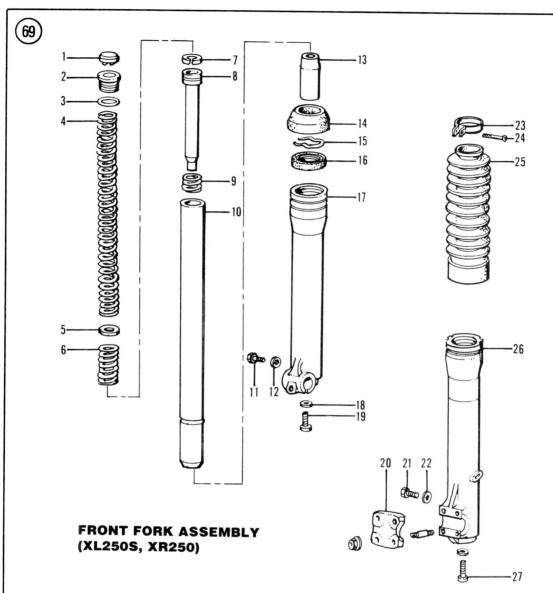

FRONT FORK ASSEMBLY (XL250S, XR250)

1. Protective cap
2. Fork cap bolt
3. O-ring seal
4. Fork spring "A"
5. Flat washer—XL series only
6. Fork spring "B"—XL series only
7. Piston ring
8. Damper rod
9. Rebound spring
10. Upper fork tube
11. Drain bolt
12. Drain bolt washer
13. Oil lock piece
14. Dust seal
15. Set ring
16. Oil seal
17. Fork slider—Model XL250S only
18. Gasket
19. Allen bolt
20. Axle shaft holder
21. Drain bolt
22. Drain bolt washer
23. Boot clamp—XR series only
24. Screw
25. Boot—XR series only
26. Slider—all models except XL250S
27. Allen bolt

Front Fork
Assembly (XL250S, XR250)

1. Coat all parts with fresh DEXRON automatic transmission fluid or fork oil prior to installation.
2. Install the rebound spring onto the damper rod and insert this assembly into the fork tube (**Figure 72**).
3A. On XL series models, temporarily install the fork springs. It is not necessary to install the flat washer at this time.
3B. On XR series models, temporarily install the fork spring.
4. Install the fork cap bolt to hold the damper rod in place.
5. Install the oil lock piece onto the damper rod (**Figure 73**).
6. Install the upper fork assembly into the slider (**Figure 74**).
7. Make sure the gasket (**Figure 75**) is on the Allen head screw.
8. Apply Loctite Lock N' Seal to the threads of the Allen bolt prior to installation. Install it in the fork slider and tighten (**Figure 76**) to the torque specification listed in **Table 1**.
9. To prevent damage to the inside of the new fork seal during installation, wrap the groove in the top of the fork tube with clear tape (something smooth and non-abrasive—do not use duct or masking tape).
10. On XR250 models, position the backup ring with the flange side facing up. Slide the backup ring down the fork tube and into the slider.
11. Install the new oil seal as follows:
   a. Coat the new seal with ATF (automatic transmission fluid).
   b. Position the seal with the marking facing upward and slide it down onto the fork tube.
   c. Drive the seal into the slider with Honda special tool Fork Seal Driver Body (part No. 07947-0010100) and Fork Seal Driver Attachment (part No. 07947-0010600); refer to **Figure 77**.
   d. Drive the oil seal in until the groove in the slider can be seen above the top surface of the oil seal.
   e. Remove the tape from the top of the fork tube.

NOTE
A piece of 2 in. galvanized pipe can also work as a tool. If both ends are threaded (a close nipple pipe fitting), wrap one end with duct tape to prevent the threads from damaging the interior of the slider.

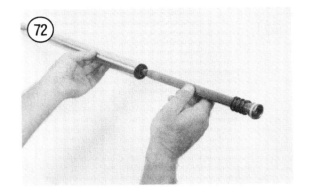

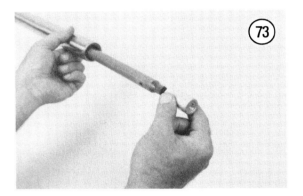

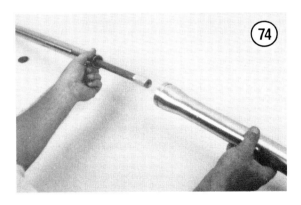

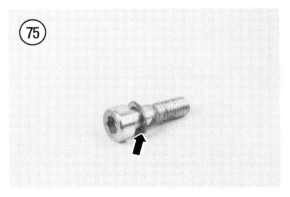

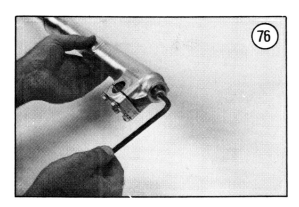

12. Install the set ring. Make sure the set ring is completely seated in the groove in the fork slider.
13. Install the dust seal into the slider (**Figure 78**).
14. Remove the fork cap bolt.
15A. On XL series models, remove the fork springs.
15B. On XR series models, remove the fork spring.
16. Fill the fork tube with the correct quantity of DEXRON automatic transmission fluid or fork oil. Refer to **Table 2**.
17A. On XL series models, perform the following:
    a. Install the short fork spring "B" (**Figure 79**) and the flat washer.
    b. Install the long fork spring "A" (**Figure 80**).

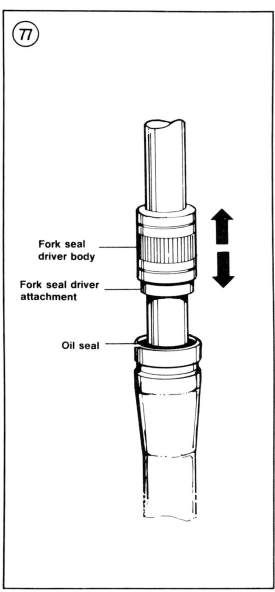

Fork seal driver body

Fork seal driver attachment

Oil seal

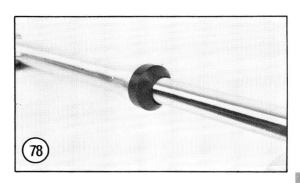

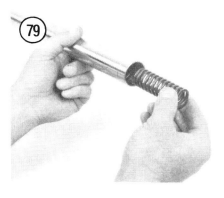

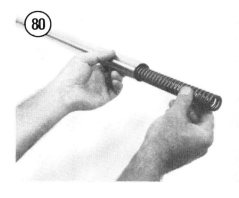

NOTE
Make sure the springs and flat washer
are installed as shown in ***Figure 81***.

17B. On XR series models, install the fork spring
(**Figure 80**).

18. Inspect the O-ring seal on the fork cap bolt;
replace if necessary.

19. Install the fork cap bolt (A, **Figure 82**). Make
sure the O-ring seal (B, **Figure 82**) is in place.

20. Push down on the spring(s) and start the bolt
slowly; don't cross-thread it.

21. Place the slider in a vise with soft jaws and
tighten the top fork cap bolt to the torque
specifications listed in **Table 1**.

23. Install the fork assemblies as described in this
chapter.

Front Fork
Removal/Installation
(1981-1982 XR250R)

1. Remove the air valve cap (**Figure 83**) and *bleed
off all air pressure* by depressing the valve stem.

WARNING
*Always bleed off all air pressure; failure
to do so may cause personal injury
when disassembling the fork assembly.*

WARNING
*Release the air pressure gradually. If
released too fast, fork oil will spurt out
with the air. Protect your eyes and
clothing accordingly.*

NOTE
*The Allen bolt at the base of the slider
has been secured with Loctite and is
often very difficult to remove because
the damper rod will turn inside the
slider. It sometimes can be removed
with an air impact driver. If you are
unable to remove it, take the fork tubes
to a dealer and have the bolts removed.*

2. If the fork assembly is going to be disassembled,
perform the following:
   a. Have an assistant hold the front brake on,
      compress the front forks and hold it in this
      position.
   b. Using a 6 mm Allen wrench, slightly loosen
      the Allen bolt at the base of the slider. If the
      bolt is loosened too much, fork oil may start to
      drain out of the slider.

3. Disconnect the brake and speedometer cables
from the left-hand fork slider (**Figure 84**).

4. Remove the front wheel as described in this
chapter.

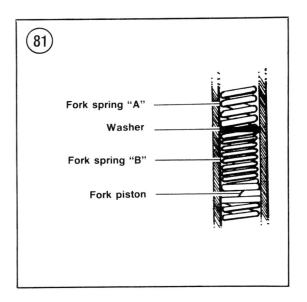

Fork spring "A"
Washer
Fork spring "B"
Fork piston

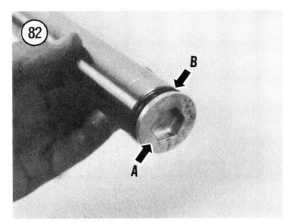

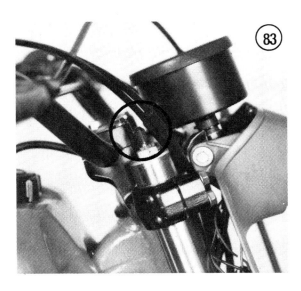

5. Remove the bolts securing the front fender (A, **Figure 85**) and remove the fender.

6. Loosen, but do not remove, the fork cap bolt/air valve assembly on each fork assembly.

7. Loosen the upper clamping band and slide the rubber boot (B, **Figure 85**) down and away from the lower fork bridge.

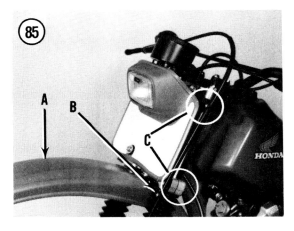

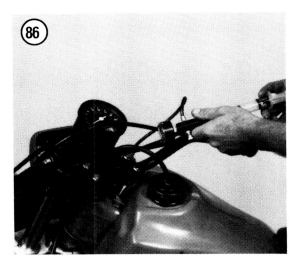

8. Loosen the upper and lower fork bridge bolts (C, **Figure 85**).

9. Remove the fork tube. It may be necessary to slightly rotate the fork tube while pulling it down and out.

10. Install by reversing these removal steps, noting the following.

11. Install the fork tube so the top of the fork tube aligns with the top surface of the upper fork bridge (**Figure 62**).

12. Tighten the upper and lower fork bridge bolts to the torque specifications listed in **Table 1**.

> *WARNING*
> *During Step 13, never use any type of compressed gas as an explosion may be lethal. Never heat the fork assembly with a torch or place it near an open flame or extreme heat, as this will also result in an explosion.*

> *CAUTION*
> *During the next step, never exceed an air pressure of 1.0 kg/cm² (14 psi) as damage may occur to internal components of the fork assembly.*

13. Inflate the front forks to the standard air pressure listed in **Table 3**. Do not use compressed air, use only a small hand-operated air pump (**Figure 86**).

14. Apply the front brake and pump the forks several times. Recheck the air pressure and readjust if necessary.

Front Fork
Disassembly
(1981-1982 XR250R)

Refer to **Figure 87** during the disassembly and assembly procedures.

1. Remove the rubber boot from the slider.

2. Clamp the slider in a vise with soft jaws.

3. If not loosened during the fork removal sequence, loosen the Allen bolt on the bottom of the slider.

> *NOTE*
> *This bolt has been secured with thread locking agent and is often very difficult to remove because the damper rod will turn inside the slider. It sometimes can be removed with an air impact driver. If you are unable to remove it, take the fork tubes to a dealer and have the bolts removed.*

4. Remove the Allen bolt and gasket from the slider.

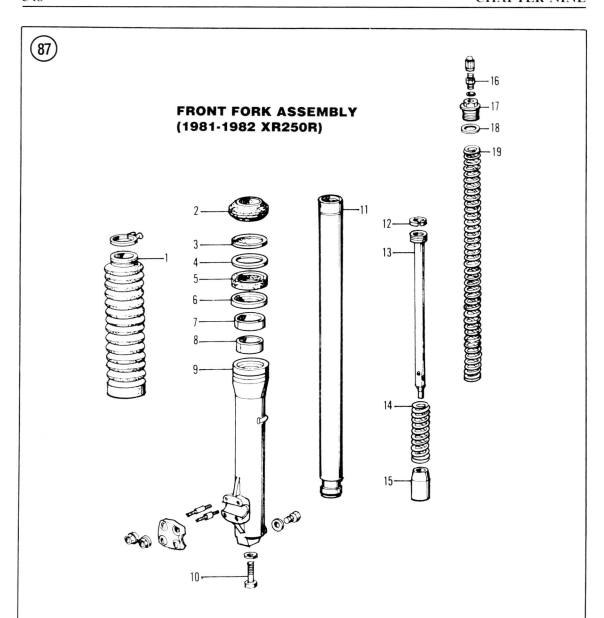

(87)

**FRONT FORK ASSEMBLY
(1981-1982 XR250R)**

1. Rubber boot
2. Dust seal
3. Circlip
4. Backup plate
5. Oil seal
6. Backup ring
7. Fork slider bushing

8. Fork tube bushing
9. Fork slider
10. Allen bolt and washer
11. Fork tube
12. Piston ring
13. Damper rod

14. Rebound spring
15. Oil lock piece
16. Air valve assembly
17. Top cap bolt
18. O-ring seal
19. Fork spring

5. Hold the upper fork tube in a vise with soft jaws and loosen the fork cap bolt/air valve assembly (if it was not loosened during the fork removal sequence).

WARNING
Be careful when removing the fork cap bolt/air valve assembly as the spring is under pressure. Protect your eyes accordingly.

6. Remove the fork cap bolt/air valve assembly from the fork.

7. Remove the collar, spring seat and the fork spring.
8. Remove the fork from the vise, pour the fork oil out and discard it. Pump the fork several times by hand to expel most of the remaining oil.
9. Remove the dust seal from the slider.
10. Remove the circlip (**Figure 88**) and the back up plate from the slider.

NOTE
On this type of fork, force is needed to remove the fork tube from the slider.

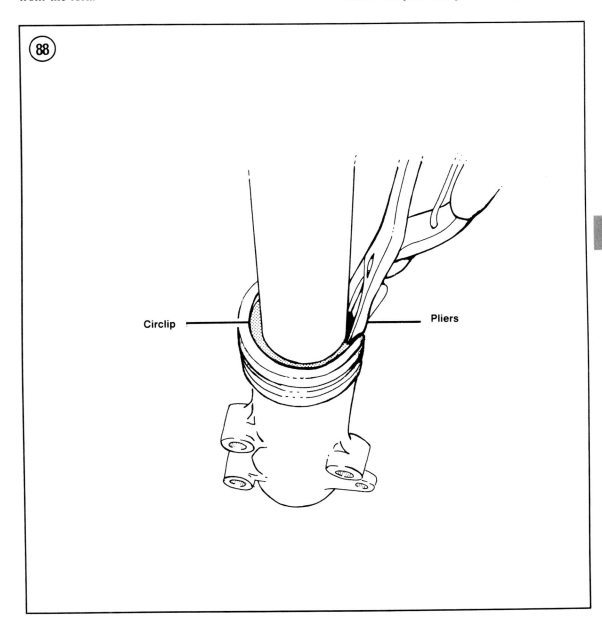
Circlip
Pliers

11. Install the fork slider in a vise with soft jaws.
12. There is an interference fit between the bushing in the fork slider and the bushing on the fork tube. In order to remove the fork tube from the slider, pull hard on the fork tube using quick in and out strokes (**Figure 89**). Doing this will withdraw the bushing, backup ring and oil seal from the slider.

> *NOTE*
> *It may be necessary to slightly heat the area on the slider around the oil seal prior to removal. Use a rag soaked in hot water; do not apply a flame directly to the fork slider.*

13. Withdraw the fork tube from the slider.

> *NOTE*
> *Do not remove the fork tube bushing unless it is going to be replaced. Inspect it as described in this chapter.*

14. Turn the fork tube upside down and slide off the oil seal, backup ring and slider bushing (**Figure 90**) from the fork tube.
15. Do not discard the slider bushing at this time. It will be used during the installation procedure.
16. Remove the oil lock piece, the damper rod and rebound spring.
17. Inspect the components as described in this chapter.

Front Fork
Assembly
(1981-1982 XR250R)

1. Coat all parts with fresh DEXRON automatic transmission fluid or fork oil prior to installation.
2. If removed, install a new fork tube bushing.
3. Install the rebound spring onto the damper rod and insert this assembly into the fork tube (**Figure 91**).
4. Temporarily install the fork spring, spring seat, collar and fork cap bolt/air valve assembly to hold the damper rod in place.
5. Install the oil lock piece onto the damper rod (**Figure 92**).
6. Install the upper fork assembly into the slider (**Figure 93**).
7. Make sure the gasket (**Figure 75**) is on the Allen bolt.
8. Apply Loctite Lock N' Seal to the threads of the Allen bolt prior to installation. Install it in the fork slider and tighten to the torque specification listed in **Table 1**.
9. Slide the fork slider bushing down the fork tube and rest it on the slider.

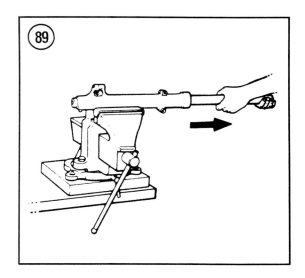

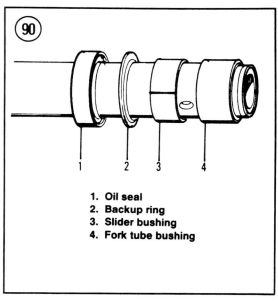

1. Oil seal
2. Backup ring
3. Slider bushing
4. Fork tube bushing

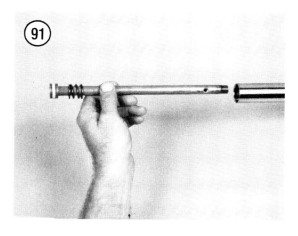

10. Slide the fork slider backup ring (flange side up) down the fork tube and rest it on top of the fork slider bushing.

11. Install the new slider bushing as follows:

   a. Place the old fork slider bushing on top of the backup ring.

   b. Drive the bushing into the fork slider with Honda special tool Fork Seal Driver Body (part No. 07947-0010100) and Fork Seal Driver (part No. 07947-3710101).

   c. Drive the bushing into place until it seats completely in the recess in the slider.

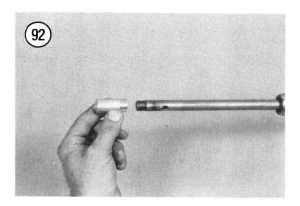

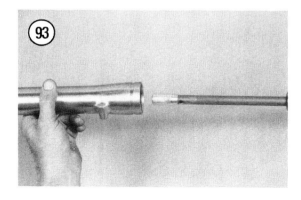

   d. Remove the installation tool and the old fork slider bushing.

NOTE
A piece of 2 in. galvanized pipe can also work as a tool. If both ends are threaded (a close nipple pipe fitting), wrap one end with duct tape to prevent the threads from damaging the interior of the slider.

12. Slide the oil seal backup ring (flange side up) down the fork tube and into the fork slider.

13. To prevent damage to the inside of the new fork seal during installation, wrap the groove in the top of the fork tube with clear tape (something smooth and non-abrasive—do not use duct or masking tape).

14. Install the new fork seal as follows:

   a. Coat the new seal with ATF (automatic transmission fluid).

   b. Position the seal with the marking facing upward and slide it down onto the fork tube.

   c. Drive the seal into the slider with Honda special tool Fork Seal Driver Body (part No. 07947-0010100) and Fork Seal Driver (part No. 07947-0010600); refer to **Figure 77**.

   d. Drive the oil seal in until the groove in the slider can be seen above the top surface of the oil seal.

   e. Remove the tape from the top of the fork tube.

NOTE
A piece of 2 in. galvanized pipe can also work as a tool. If both ends are threaded (a close nipple pipe fitting), wrap one end with duct tape to prevent the threads from damaging the interior of the slider.

15. Install the circlip with the sharp side facing up. Make sure the circlip is completely seated in the groove in the fork slider.

16. Install the dust seal onto the slider.

17. Remove the fork cap bolt/air valve assembly, collar, spring seat and the fork spring.

18. Fill the fork tube with the correct quantity of DEXRON automatic transmission fluid or fork oil. Refer to **Table 2**.

19. Install the fork spring into the fork tube.

20. Install the spring seat and the collar.

21. Inspect the O-ring seal (**Figure 94**) on the fork cap bolt/air valve assembly; replace if necessary.

22. Install the fork cap bolt/air valve assembly while pushing down on the spring. Start the bolt slowly; don't cross-thread it.

23. Place the slider in a vise with soft jaws and tighten the fork cap bolt/air valve assembly to the torque specifications listed in **Table 1**.

24. Slide the rubber boot down the fork tube and snap it into place in the groove in the fork slider. Tighten the clamping band screw securely.

25. Repeat this procedure for the other fork assembly.

26. Install the fork assemblies as described in this chapter.

Front Fork
Removal/Installation
(1982-1983 XL250R, XR350R)

WARNING
Always bleed off all air pressure in Step 1; failure to do so may cause personal injury when disassembling the fork assembly.

WARNING
Release the air pressure gradually in Step 1. If released too fast, fork oil will spurt out with the air. Protect your eyes and clothing accordingly.

1. Remove the air valve cap (**Figure 95**) and *bleed off all air pressure* by depressing the valve stem.

NOTE
The Allen bolt at the base of the slider has been secured with thread locking agent and is often very difficult to remove because the damper rod will turn inside the slider. It sometimes can be removed with an air impact driver. If you are unable to remove it, take the fork tubes to a dealer and have the bolts removed.

2. If the fork assembly is going to be disassembled, perform the following:
   a. Have an assistant hold the front brake on, compress the front forks and hold it in this position.
   b. Using a 6 mm Allen wrench, slightly loosen the Allen bolt at the base of the slider. If the bolt is loosened too much, fork oil may start to drain out of the slider.

3. On disc brake models, perform the following:
   a. Remove the bolts (**Figure 96**) securing the caliper assembly to the left-hand fork slider.
   b. Remove the bolts (**Figure 97**) securing the brake hose to the left-hand fork slider.
   c. Slide the caliper assembly off the brake disc.

   d. Tie the caliper assembly up to the frame with Bungee cord to take the strain off the brake hose.

4. Remove the front wheel as described in this chapter.

5. Loosen, but do not remove, the fork cap bolt/air valve assembly.

6. Loosen the upper and lower fork bridge bolts (**Figure 98**).

7. Loosen the clamping screws on the rubber boot bands. Slide the rubber boots down (**Figure 99**).

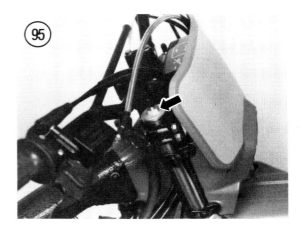

8. Remove the fork tube. It may be necessary to slightly rotate the fork tube while pulling it down and out.

9. Install by reversing these removal steps, noting the following.

10A. On XL series models, install the fork tubes so that the top of the fork tube aligns with the top surface of the upper fork bridge (**Figure 62**).

10B. On XR series models, install the fork tubes so that the *lower* groove of the fork tube aligns with the top surface of the upper fork bridge (**Figure 61**).

11. Tighten the upper and lower fork bridge bolts to the torque specifications listed in **Table 1**.

12. Install the rubber fork boots with the greater number of holes toward the rear of the bike.

> *WARNING*
> *During the next step, never use any type of compressed gas as an explosion may be lethal. Never heat the fork assembly with a torch or place it near an open flame or extreme heat, as this will also result in an explosion.*

> *CAUTION*
> *During the next step, never exceed an air pressure of 1.0 kg/cm² (14.2 psi) as damage may occur to internal components of the fork assembly.*

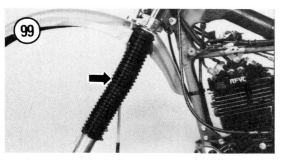

13. Inflate the forks to the standard air pressure listed in **Table 3**. Do not use compressed air, only use a small hand-operated air pump (**Figure 86**).

14. Apply the front brake and pump the forks several times. Recheck the air pressure and readjust if necessary.

Front Fork
Disassembly
(1982-1983 XL250R, XR350R)

Refer to **Figure 100** for XL350R and XR350R models or **Figure 101** for 1982-1983 XL250R models during the disassembly and assembly procedures.

1. Clamp the slider in a vise with soft jaws.

2. If not loosened during the fork removal sequence, loosen the Allen bolt on the bottom of the slider.

> *NOTE*
> *This bolt has been secured with thread locking agent and is often very difficult to remove because the damper rod will turn inside the slider. It sometimes can be removed with an air impact driver. If you are unable to remove it, take the fork tubes to a dealer and have the bolts removed.*

3. Remove the Allen bolt and gasket from the slider.

4. Hold the upper fork tube in a vise with soft jaws and loosen the fork cap bolt/air valve assembly (if it was not loosened during the fork removal sequence).

> *WARNING*
> *Be careful when removing the fork cap bolt/air valve assembly as the spring is under pressure. Protect your eyes accordingly.*

5. Remove the fork cap bolt/air valve assembly from the fork.

6. Remove the spacer, the spring seat and the fork spring.

7. Remove the fork from the vise, pour the fork oil out and discard it. Pump the fork several times by hand to expel most of the remaining oil.

8. Remove the dust seal from the slider.

9. Withdraw the fork tube from the slider.

10. Remove the oil lock piece, the damper rod and rebound spring.

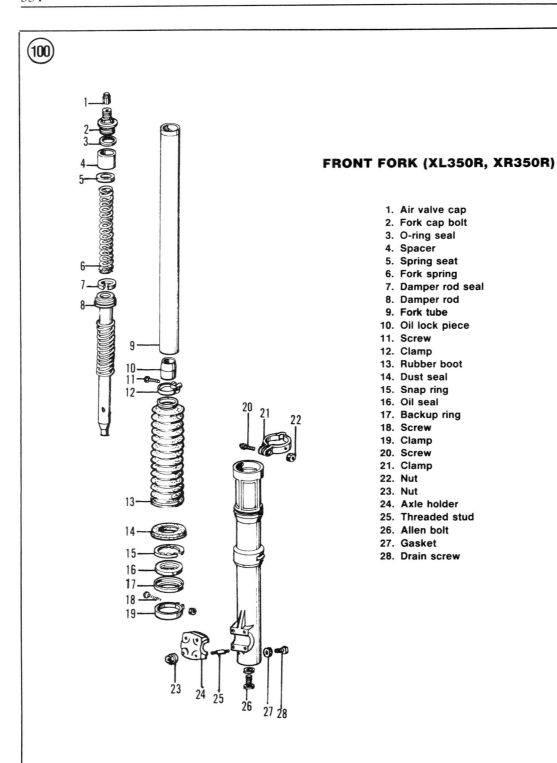

⑩

FRONT FORK (XL350R, XR350R)

1. Air valve cap
2. Fork cap bolt
3. O-ring seal
4. Spacer
5. Spring seat
6. Fork spring
7. Damper rod seal
8. Damper rod
9. Fork tube
10. Oil lock piece
11. Screw
12. Clamp
13. Rubber boot
14. Dust seal
15. Snap ring
16. Oil seal
17. Backup ring
18. Screw
19. Clamp
20. Screw
21. Clamp
22. Nut
23. Nut
24. Axle holder
25. Threaded stud
26. Allen bolt
27. Gasket
28. Drain screw

FRONT FORK (1982-1983 XL250R)

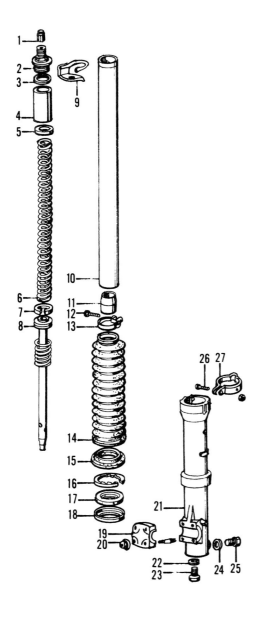

1. Air valve cap
2. Fork cap bolt
3. O-ring seal
4. Spacer
5. Spring seat
6. Fork spring
7. Damper rod seal
8. Damper rod
9. Clip
10. Fork tube
11. Oil lock piece
12. Screw
13. Clamp
14. Rubber boot
15. Dust seal
16. Snap ring
17. Oil seal
18. Backup ring
19. Axle holder
20. Nut
21. Slider
22. Gasket
23. Allen bolt
24. Gasket
25. Drain screw
26. Screw
27. Clamp

9

11. Remove the circlip (**Figure 102**), the oil seal and backup ring from the slider.

> *NOTE*
> *It may be necessary to slightly heat the area on the slider around the oil seal prior to removal. Use a rag soaked in hot water; do not apply a flame directly to the fork slider.*

> *CAUTION*
> *Use a dull screwdriver blade to remove the oil seal (**Figure 103**). Do not damage the outer edge or inner surface of the slider.*

12. Inspect the components as described in this chapter.

**Front Fork
Assembly
(1982-1983 XL250R, XR350R)**

1. Coat all parts with fresh DEXRON automatic transmission fluid or SAE 10W fork oil prior to installation.
2. Install the rebound spring onto the damper rod (**Figure 104**) and insert this assembly into the fork tube (**Figure 105**).
3. Temporarily install the fork spring, spring seat, spacer and fork cap bolt/air valve assembly to hold the damper rod in place.
4. Install the oil lock piece onto the damper rod (**Figure 106**).
5. Install the upper fork assembly into the slider (**Figure 107**).
6. Make sure the gasket (**Figure 108**) is on the Allen bolt.
7. Apply Loctite Lock N' Seal to the threads of the Allen bolt prior to installation. Install it in the fork slider and tighten to the torque specification listed in **Table 1**.
8. Slide the fork slider backup ring (flange side up) down the fork tube and rest it on top of the fork slider bushing.
9. To prevent damage to the inside of the new fork seal during installation, wrap the groove in the top of the fork tube with clear tape (something smooth and non-abrasive—do not use duct or masking tape).
10. Install the new oil seal as follows:
   a. Coat the new seal with ATF (automatic transmission fluid).
   b. Position the seal with the marking facing upward and slide it down onto the fork tube.
   c. Drive the seal into the slider with Honda special tool Fork Seal Driver Body (part No.

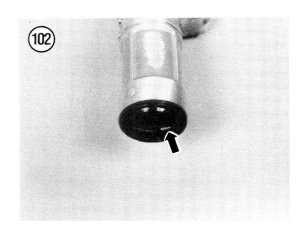

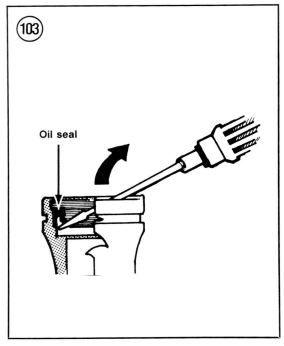

Oil seal

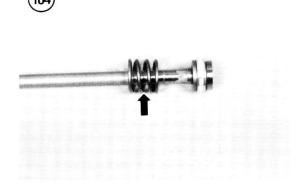

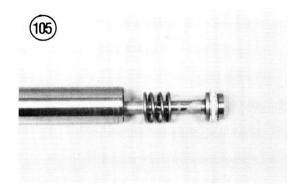

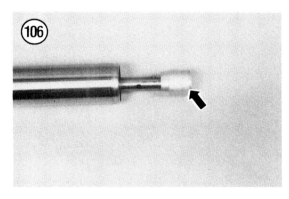

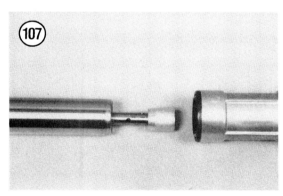

07947-KA50100) and Fork Seal Driver Attachment (part No. 07947-KF00100); refer to **Figure 109**.

d. Drive the oil seal in until the groove in the slider can be seen above the top surface of the oil seal.

e. Remove the tape from the top of the fork tube.

NOTE
A piece of 2 in. galvanized pipe can also work as a tool. If both ends are threaded (a close nipple pipe fitting), wrap one end with duct tape to prevent the threads from damaging the interior of the slider.

11. Install the circlip with the sharp side facing up. Make sure the circlip is completely seated in the groove in the fork slider.

12. Install the dust seal into the slider.

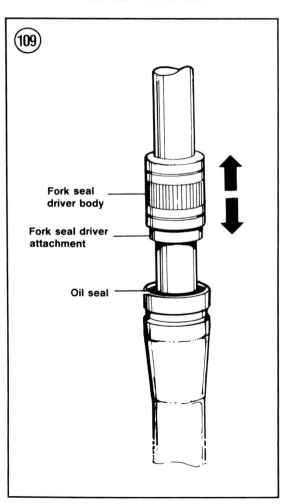

Fork seal driver body

Fork seal driver attachment

Oil seal

13. Refer to **Figure 110** and make sure that all components installed in Steps 8-12 are installed in their correct position.

14. Remove the fork cap bolt/air valve assembly, the spacer, the spring seat and the fork spring.

15. Fill the fork tube with the correct quantity of DEXRON automatic transmission fluid or fork oil. Refer to **Table 2**.

16. Install the fork spring with the tapered end (**Figure 111**) going in first.

17. Inspect the O-ring seal (**Figure 112**) on the fork cap bolt/air valve assembly; replace if necessary.

18. Install the spring seat, the spacer and the fork cap bolt/air valve assembly (**Figure 113**) while pushing down on the spring. Start the bolt slowly; don't cross-thread it.

19. Place the slider in a vise with soft jaws and tighten the top fork cap bolt to the torque specifications listed in **Table 1**.

20. Repeat for the other fork assembly.

21. Install the fork assemblies as described in this chapter.

Front Fork
Removal/Installation
(XR200R, 1984-on XL250R, 1984-on XR250R)

> *WARNING*
> *Always bleed off all air pressure in Step 1; failure to do so may cause personal injuiry when disassembling the fork assembly.*

> *WARNING*
> *Release the air pressure gradually in Step 1. If released too fast, fork oil will spurt out with the air. Protect your eyes and clothing accordingly.*

1. Remove the air valve cap (**Figure 114**) and *bleed off all air pressure* by depressing the valve stem (**Figure 115**).

> *NOTE*
> *The Allen bolt at the base of the slider has been secured with thread locking agent and is often very difficult to remove because the damper rod will turn inside the slider. It sometimes can be removed with an air impact driver. If you are unable to remove it, take the fork tubes to a dealer and have the screws removed.*

2. If the fork assembly is going to be disassembled, perform the following:

  a. Have an assistant hold the front brake on, compress the front forks and hold it in this position.

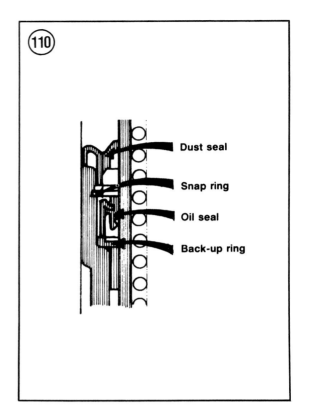

Dust seal

Snap ring

Oil seal

Back-up ring

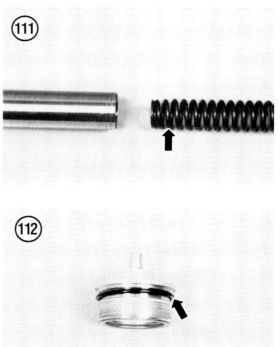

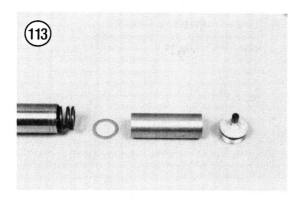

b. Using a 6 mm Allen wrench, slightly loosen the Allen bolt at the base of the slider. If the bolt is loosened too much, fork oil may start to drain out of the slider.

3. On disc brake models, perform the following:
   a. Remove the bolts (**Figure 96**) securing the caliper assembly to the left-hand fork slider.
   b. Remove the bolts (**Figure 97**) securing the brake hose to the left-hand fork slider.
   c. Slide the caliper assembly off of the brake disc.
   d. Tie the caliper assembly up to the frame to take the strain off the brake hose.

4. Remove the front wheel as described in this chapter.

5. Loosen, but do not remove, the fork cap bolt/air valve assembly.

6. Loosen the upper and lower fork bridge bolts (A, **Figure 116**).

7. Loosen the clamping screws on the rubber boot bands. Slide the rubber boots down (B, **Figure 116**).

8. Remove the fork tube. It may be necessary to slightly rotate the fork tube while pulling it down and out.

9. Install by reversing these removal steps, noting the following.

10A. On XL series models, install the fork tubes so that the top of the fork tube aligns with the top surface of the upper fork bridge (**Figure 62**).

10B. On XR series models, install the fork tubes so that the *lower* groove of the fork tube aligns with the top surface of the upper fork bridge (**Figure 61**).

11. Tighten the upper and lower fork bridge bolts to the torque specifications listed in **Table 1**.

12. Install the rubber fork boots with the greater number of holes toward the rear of the bike.

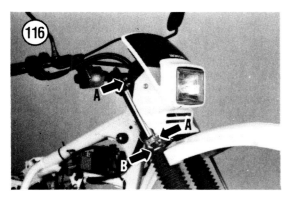

9

WARNING
During the next step, never use any type of compressed gas as an explosion may be lethal. Never heat the fork assembly with a torch or place it near an open flame or extreme heat, as this will also result in an explosion.

CAUTION
During the next step, never exceed an air pressure of 0.4 kg/cm² (6.0 psi) as damage may occur to internal components of the fork assembly.

13. Inflate the forks to the standard air pressure listed in **Table 3**. Do not use compressed air, only use a small hand-operated air pump (**Figure 117**).

14. Apply the front brake and pump the forks several times. Recheck the air pressure and readjust if necessary.

Front Fork Disassembly
(1984-1985 XR200R, 1984-1987 XL250R and 1984-on XR250R)

Refer to **Figure 118** for 1986-on XR250R models. Refer to **Figure 119** for the following models:

a. 1984-1985 XR200R
b. 1984-1987 XL250R
c. 1984-1985 XR250R

1. Clamp the slider in a vise with soft jaws.

2. If not loosened during the fork removal sequence, loosen the special Allen bolt on the bottom of the slider.

NOTE
This bolt has been secured with Loctite and is often very difficult to remove because the damper rod will turn inside the slider. It sometimes can be removed with an air impact driver. If you are unable to remove it, take the fork tubes to a dealer and have the special Allen bolts removed.

3. Remove the special Allen bolt and gasket from the slider.

4. Hold the upper fork tube in a vise with soft jaws and loosen the fork cap bolt/air valve assembly (if it was not loosened during the fork removal sequence).

WARNING
Be careful when removing the fork cap bolt/air valve assembly as the spring is under pressure. Protect your eyes accordingly.

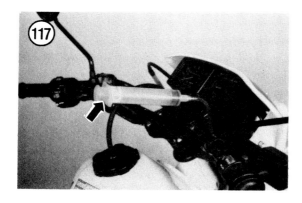

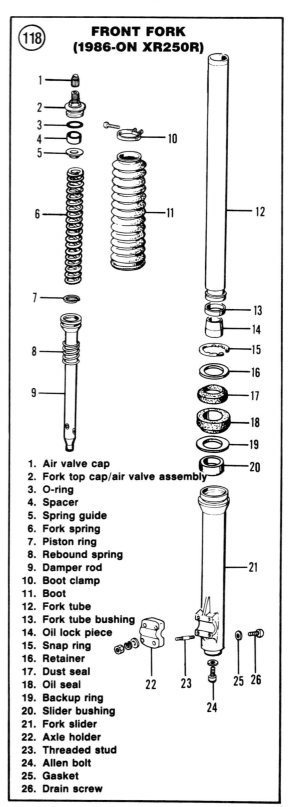

FRONT FORK (1986-ON XR250R)

1. Air valve cap
2. Fork top cap/air valve assembly
3. O-ring
4. Spacer
5. Spring guide
6. Fork spring
7. Piston ring
8. Rebound spring
9. Damper rod
10. Boot clamp
11. Boot
12. Fork tube
13. Fork tube bushing
14. Oil lock piece
15. Snap ring
16. Retainer
17. Dust seal
18. Oil seal
19. Backup ring
20. Slider bushing
21. Fork slider
22. Axle holder
23. Threaded stud
24. Allen bolt
25. Gasket
26. Drain screw

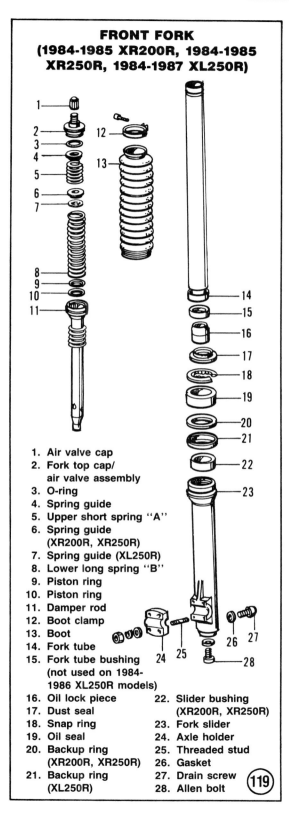

FRONT FORK
(1984-1985 XR200R, 1984-1985
XR250R, 1984-1987 XL250R)

1. Air valve cap
2. Fork top cap/
   air valve assembly
3. O-ring
4. Spring guide
5. Upper short spring "A"
6. Spring guide
   (XR200R, XR250R)
7. Spring guide (XL250R)
8. Lower long spring "B"
9. Piston ring
10. Piston ring
11. Damper rod
12. Boot clamp
13. Boot
14. Fork tube
15. Fork tube bushing
    (not used on 1984-
    1986 XL250R models)
16. Oil lock piece
17. Dust seal
18. Snap ring
19. Oil seal
20. Backup ring
    (XR200R, XR250R)
21. Backup ring
    (XL250R)
22. Slider bushing
    (XR200R, XR250R)
23. Fork slider
24. Axle holder
25. Threaded stud
26. Gasket
27. Drain screw
28. Allen bolt

(119)

5. Remove the fork cap bolt/air valve assembly from the fork.

6A. On 1986-on XR250R models, remove the spacer, spring guide and the fork spring.

6B. On all other models, remove the spring guide, the upper short fork spring "A," spring guide and lower long fork spring "B."

7. Remove the fork from the vise, pour the fork oil out and discard it. Pump the fork several times by hand to expel most of the remaining oil.

8A. On 1986-on XR250R models, remove the snap ring, retainer and dust seat from the slider.

8B. On all other models, remove the dust seal and snap ring (**Figure 88**) from the slider.

> *NOTE*
> *On all models except 1984-1986 XL250R models, force is needed to remove the fork tube from the slider. The 1984-1986 XL250R models are not equipped with a slider bushing or fork tube bushing.*

9. Install the fork slider in a vise with soft jaws.

10. On all models except 1984-1986 XL250R models, there is an interference fit between the bushing in the fork slider and the bushing on the fork tube. In order to remove the fork tube from the slider, pull hard on the fork tube using quick in and out strokes (**Figure 89**). Doing this will withdraw the slider bushing, backup ring and oil seal from the slider.

> *NOTE*
> *It may be necessary to slightly heat the area on the slider around the oil seal prior to removal. Use a rag soaked in hot water; do not apply a flame directly to the fork slider.*

11. Withdraw the fork tube from the slider.

> *NOTE*
> *On models so equipped, do not remove the fork tube bushing unless it is going to be replaced. Inspect it as described in this chapter.*

12. Turn the fork tube upside down and slide off the oil seal, backup ring and on models so equipped, the slider bushing (**Figure 90**) from the fork tube.

13. On models so equipped, do not discard the slider bushing at this time. It will be used during the installation procedure.

14. Remove the oil lock piece, the damper rod and rebound spring.

15. Inspect the components as described in this chapter.

9

**Front Fork Assembly
(1984-1985 XR200R, 1984-1987 XL250R and
1984-on XR250R)**

1. Coat all parts with fresh DEXRON automatic transmission fluid or SAE 10W fork oil prior to installation.
2. Install the rebound spring onto the damper rod (**Figure 120**) and insert this assembly into the fork tube (**Figure 121**).
3A. On 1986-on XR250R models, temporarily install the fork spring, spring guide, spacer and fork cap bolt/air valve assembly to hold the damper rod in place.
3B. On all other models, temporarily install the lower long fork spring ''B,'' spring guide, upper short spring ''A,'' spring guide and fork cap bolt/air valve assembly to hold the damper rod in place.
4. Install the oil lock piece onto the damper rod (**Figure 122**).
5. Install the upper fork assembly into the slider (**Figure 123**).
6. Make sure the gasket is on the special Allen bolt.
7. Apply Loctite Lock N' Seal to the threads of the special Allen bolt prior to installation. Install it in the fork slider and tighten to the torque specification listed in **Table 1**.
8A. On XL250R models, slide the fork slider backup ring (flange side up) down the fork tube and rest it on top of the fork slider.
8B. On all other models, slide the fork slider backup ring down the fork tube and rest it on top of the fork slider bushing.
9. On models so equipped, slide the fork slider bushing down the fork tube and rest it on the slider.
10. On models so equipped, install the new slider bushing as follows:
  a. Place the old fork slider bushing on top of the backup ring.
  b. Drive the bushing into the fork slider with Honda special tool Fork Seal Driver Body (part No. 07947-KA50100) and the following attachments.
  c. On XR200R models, use Fork Seal Attachment (part No. 07947-3710100).
  d. On XR250R models, use Fork Seal Attachment (part No. 07947-KA30200).
  e. Drive the bushing into place until it seats completely in the recess in the slider.
  f. Remove the installation tool and the old fork slider bushing.

NOTE
A piece of 2 in. galvanized pipe can also work as a tool. If both ends are threaded (a close nipple pipe fitting), wrap one

end with duct tape to prevent the threads from damaging the interior of the slider.

11. Slide the oil seal backup ring down the fork tube and into the fork slider.
12. To prevent damage to the inside of the new fork seal during installation, wrap the groove in the top of the fork tube with clear tape (something smooth and non-abrasive—do not use duct or masking tape).
13. Install the new fork seal as follows:
  a. Coat the new seal with ATF (automatic transmission fluid).

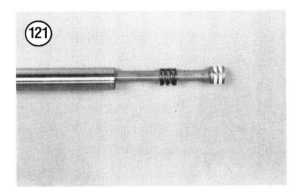

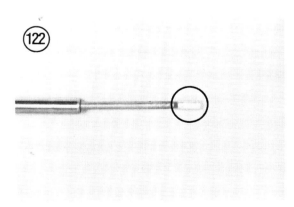

b. Position the seal with the marking facing upward and slide it down onto the fork tube.

c. Drive the seal into the fork slider with Honda special tool Fork Seal Driver Body (part No. 07947-KA50100) and the following attachments.

d. On XR200R models, use Fork Seal Attachment (part No. 07947-3710100).

e. On XR250R models, use Fork Seal Attachment (part No. 07947-KA30200).

f. On XL250R models, use Fork Seal Attachment (part No. 07947-KL40100).

g. Drive the oil seal in until the groove in the slider can be seen above the top surface of the oil seal.

h. Remove the tape from the top of the fork tube.

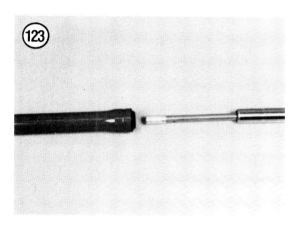

NOTE
A piece of 2 in. galvanized pipe can also work as a tool. If both ends are threaded (a close nipple pipe fitting), wrap one end with duct tape to prevent the threads from damaging the interior of the slider.

14. On 1986-on XR250R models, install the dust seal and retainer.

15. Install the snap ring with the sharp side facing up. Make sure the snap ring is completely seated in the groove in the fork slider.

16. On all models except 1986-on XR250R, install the dust seal onto the slider.

17A. On 1986-on XR250R models, remove the fork cap bolt/air valve assembly, spacer, spring guide and the fork spring.

17B. On all other models, remove the fork cap bolt/air valve assembly, spring guide, the upper short fork spring ''A,'' spring guide and lower long fork spring ''B.''

18. Fill the fork tube with the correct quantity of DEXRON automatic transmission fluid or fork oil. Refer to **Table 2**.

19A. On 1986-on XR250R models, install the fork spring, spring guide and spacer.

19B. On all other models, temporarily install the lower long fork spring ''B,'' spring guide, upper short spring ''A,'' and spring guide.

20. Inspect the O-ring seal (**Figure 94**) on the fork cap bolt/air valve assembly; replace if necessary.

21. Install the fork cap bolt/air valve assembly while pushing down on the springs. Start the bolt slowly, don't cross-thread it.

22. Place the slider in a vise with soft jaws and tighten the fork cap bolt/air valve assembly to the torque specifications listed in **Table 1**.

23. Slide the rubber boot down the fork tube and snap it into place in the groove in the fork slider. Position the boot with the breather holes to the rear of the bike. Tighten the clamping band screw securely.

24. Repeat this procedure for the other fork assembly.

25. Install the fork assemblies as described in this chapter.

Front Fork Inspection
(All Models)

1. Thoroughly clean all parts in solvent and dry them. Check the fork tube for signs of wear or scratches.

2. Check the damper rod for straightness. **Figure 124** shows one method. The rod should be replaced if the runout is 0.2 mm (0.008 in.) or greater.

3. Carefully check the damper rod and piston ring(s) for wear or damage. Refer to **Figure 125** or **Figure 126**.

4. Check the upper fork tube for straightness. If bent or severely scratched, it should be replaced.

5. Check the lower slider for dents or exterior damage that may cause the upper fork tube to hang up during riding. Replace if necessary.

6. Measure the uncompressed length of the fork spring (not rebound spring) as shown in **Figure 127**. If the spring has sagged to the service limit dimensions listed in **Table 4,** the spring must be replaced.

7. On models so equipped, inspect the slider and fork tube bushings. If either is scratched or scored, they must be replaced. If the Teflon coating is worn off so that the copper base material is showing on approximately 3/4 of the total surface, the bushing must be replaced. Also check for distortion on the check points of the backup ring; replace as necessary. Refer to **Figure 128**.

8. Any parts that are worn or damaged should be replaced. Simply cleaning and reinstalling unserviceable components will not improve performance of the front suspension.

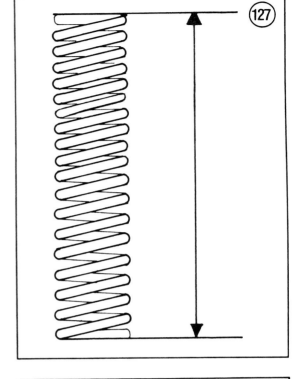

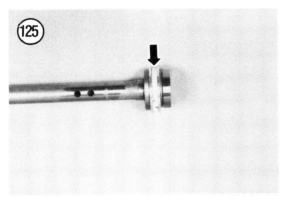

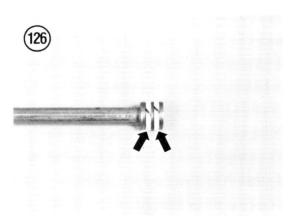

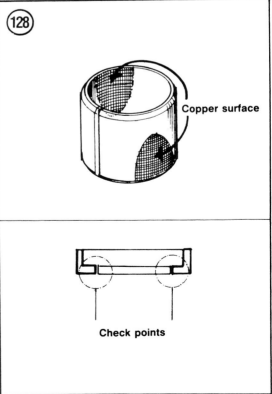

Copper surface

Check points

Table 1 FRONT SUSPENSION TORQUE SPECIFICATIONS

Item	N·m	ft.-lb.
Front axle	50-85	36-58
Front axle nut	50-85	36-58
Front axle holder nuts	10-14	7-10
Front axle pinch bolt (Model XL250)	23-28	17-20
Handlebar holder bolts	18-30	12-22
Upper fork bridge bolts		
XL250S, XR250	8-10	6-7
XR250R	18-25	13-18
XR350R	18-30	12-22
Lower fork bridge bolts		
XR350R	30-35	22-25
All other models	18-30	13-22
Steering stem nut		
XR350R	95-140	69-101
All other models	70-100	51-72
Front fork top cap bolt		
1986-on XR250R	25-35	18-25
All other models	15-30	11-22
Front fork Allen bolt		
1984-1985 XR200R	20-26	14-19
XL250S	8-12	6-9
XR250R		
1984-1985	32-42	24-30
1986-on	60-84	43-61
All other models	15-30	11-22
Brake disc mounting nuts	14-16	10-12

9

Table 2 FRONT FORK OIL CAPACITY*

Model	Standard capacity		Standard distance from top of fork	
	cc	fl. oz.	mm	in.
XR200R	397	13.4	–	–
Maximum	–	–	146	5.75
Minimum	–	–	186	7.32
XL250S	190	6.4	–	–
XL250R				
1982-1983	300	10.14	173	6.81
1984-on	293	9.91	195	7.68
XR250	202	6.8	–	–
XR250R				
1981	368	12.4	152	6
1982	395	13.4	156	6.125
1984-1985	397	13.4	–	–
Maximum	–	–	190	7.48
Minimum	–	–	150	5.91
1986-on	535	18.0	–	–
Maximum	–	–	165	6.5
Minimum	–	–	125	4.9
		(continued)		

Table 2 FRONT FORK OIL CAPACITY* (continued)

Model	Standard capacity		Standard distance from top of fork	
	cc	fl. oz.	mm	in.
XL350R	411	14.0	184	7.2
XR350R				
1983	553	18.7	132	5.2
1984-1985	563	19.0		
Maximum	-	-	152	5.98
Minimum	-	-	112	4.41

* Capacity for each fork leg.

Table 3 FRONT FORK AIR PRESSURE

Model	psi	kg/cm²
XL250R	0-2.8	0-0.2
All other models	0	0

Table 4 FRONT FORK SPRING FREE LENGTH

Model	Standard		Service Length	
	mm	in.	mm	in.
XR200R				
Spring A	NA	NA	87	3.42
Spring B	NA	NA	498	19.61
XL250S	501.9	19.76	483.5	19.04
XR250	562.4	22.1	551	21.7
XL250R				
1982-1983	579.9	22.83	568.3	22.37
1984-1986				
Spring A	102.2	4.02	100.1	3.9
Spring B	518.3	20.4	513.1	20.2
1987				
Spring A	102.2	4.02	100.1	3.9
Spring B	521.3	20.5	516.1	20.3
XR250R				
1981	562.4	22.1	551	21.7
1982	NA	NA	NA	NA
1984-1985				
Spring A	NA	NA	78.5	3.09
Spring B	NA	NA	504.5	19.86
1986-on	604.4	23.80	598.4	23.56
XL350R	571.4	22.50	565.7	22.27
XR350R				
1985	598.9	23.58	593.9	23.38
1986	559.9	22.04	554.3	21.82

NA = Information not available from Honda.

NOTE: If you own a 1990 or later model, first check the Supplement at the back of the book for any new service information.

CHAPTER TEN

REAR SUSPENSION

This chapter includes repair and replacement procedures for the rear wheel and rear suspension components. Tire changing and wheel balancing are covered in Chapter Nine.

Refer to **Table 1** for rear suspension torque specifications.

Tables 1-3 are located at the end of this chapter.

REAR WHEEL (DUAL-SHOCK)

Removal/Installation

1. Place wood block(s) under the skid plate to support the bike securely with the rear wheel off the ground.

2. Completely unscrew the rear brake adjusting nut (**Figure 1**) and pull the cable retainer and cable out of the brake arm.

3. Loosen the locknut and axle adjusting bolt (**Figure 2**) on each side.

4. Remove the cotter pin and loosen the rear axle nut (**Figure 3**).

5. Remove the screws (**Figure 4**) securing the drive sprocket cover and remove the cover.

6. Remove the bolts (**Figure 5**) securing the drive sprocket. Remove the sprocket retainer, the sprocket and the drive chain. Let the drive chain rest on the chain slider on the swing arm.

7. Remove the rear axle nut and withdraw the axle from the right-hand side.

8A. On 1978-1980 XL250S models, pull the wheel to the rear to disengage the brake panel from the swing arm.

8B. On 1981 XL250S models, perform the following:

a. Pivot the brake set plate down (**Figure 6**) and slide it off the brake torque link.

b. Remove the brake torque link from the brake panel (**Figure 7**).

c. Let the brake torque link pivot down and rest it on the floor.

9. Remove the drive chain from the wheel sprocket and remove the wheel.

10. Install by reversing these removal steps, noting the following.

11A. On 1978-1980 XL250S models, be sure to align the groove in the brake panel onto the boss on the swing arm.

11B. On 1981 XL250S models, be sure to install the brake set plate onto the brake panel and torque link (**Figure 6**).

12. If the drive chain master link was removed, install a new clip on the master link with the closed end facing in the direction of travel (**Figure 8**).

13. Install the rear axle in from the right-hand side.

14. Adjust the drive chain as described in Chapter Three.

15. Tighten the rear axle nut to the torque specification listed in **Table 1**.

16. Install a new cotter pin and bend the ends over completely.

17. After the wheel is installed, completely rotate it and apply the brake several times to make sure it rotates freely and that the brakes work properly.

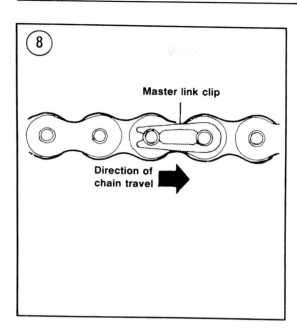

Master link clip

Direction of chain travel

18. Adjust the rear brake as described in Chapter Three.

REAR WHEEL (PRO-LINK)

Removal/Installation

1. Place wood block(s) under the skid plate to support the bike securely with the rear wheel off the ground.
2. Unscrew the brake adjust nut (**Figure 9**) and disconnect it from the brake arm.
3. Remove the rear axle nut (A, **Figure 10**).
4. On models so equipped, loosen the holder nut (**Figure 11**) on the snail adjuster.
5. Rotate the snail adjusters (B, **Figure 10**) toward the front so the wheel can be moved forward for maximum chain slack.
6. Move the wheel forward and position the notch in the snail adjusters onto the stopper pin on the swing arm.
7. Rotate the rear wheel and derail the drive chain from the driven sprocket.

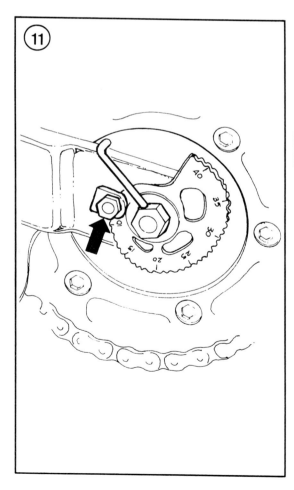

8. On the right-hand side, pull the stopper plate (**Figure 12**) off of the stopper pin on the swing arm.
9. Slide the wheel and axle assembly to the rear and remove it.
10. Install by reversing these removal steps, noting the following.
11. Make sure the groove in the brake panel is properly meshed with the tang on the swing arm. This is necessary for proper brake operation.
12. Adjust the drive chain as described in Chapter Three.
13. Tighten the rear axle nut to the torque specification listed in **Table 1**.
14. After the wheel is installed, completely rotate it and apply the brake several times to make sure it rotates freely and that the brake works properly.
15. Adjust the rear brake as described in Chapter Three.

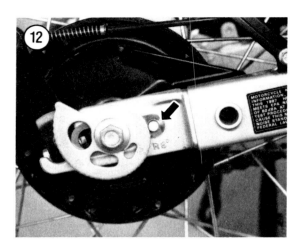

REAR WHEEL INSPECTION
(ALL MODELS)

Measure the axial and radial runout of the wheel with a dial indicator as shown in **Figure 13**. The maximum axial and radial runout is 2.0 mm (0.08 in.).

Tighten or replace any bent or loose spokes as described under *Spoke Adjustment* in Chapter Nine.

Check axle runout as described in this chapter.

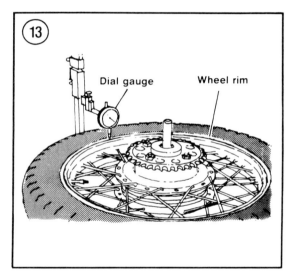

Dial gauge   Wheel rim

REAR HUB INSPECTION
(ALL MODELS)

Inspect each wheel bearing prior to removing it from the wheel hub.

> *CAUTION*
> *Do not remove the wheel bearings for inspection purposes as they will be damaged during the removal process. Remove wheel bearings only if they are to be replaced.*

1A. On XL250S, XL250R, XR250, 1981-1982 XR250R and XL350R models perform Steps 1-5 of *Disassembly* in this chapter.
1B. On 1984-on XR200R, 1984-on XR250R and XR350R, models, perform Steps 1-4 of *Disassembly* in this chapter.
2. Turn each bearing by hand. Make sure the bearings turn smoothly.

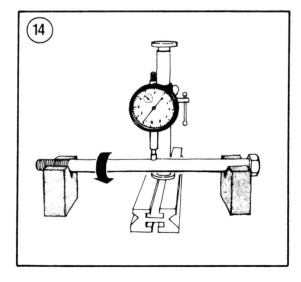

3. On non-sealed bearings, check the balls for evidence of wear, pitting or excessive heat (bluish tint). Replace the bearings if necessary; always replace as a complete set. When replacing the bearings, be sure to take your old bearings along to ensure a perfect match.

NOTE
Fully sealed bearings are available from many bearing specialty shops. Fully sealed bearings provide better protection from dirt and moisture that may get into the hub.

4. Check the axle for wear and straightness. Use V-blocks and a dial indicator as shown in **Figure 14**. If the runout is 0.2 mm (0.01 in.) or greater, the axle should be replaced.

REAR HUB (XL250S, XL250R, XR250, 1981-1982 XR250R, XL350R)

Disassembly

Refer to **Figure 15** for this procedure.
1. Remove the rear wheel as described in this chapter.
2. Pull the brake assembly straight up and out of the brake drum.

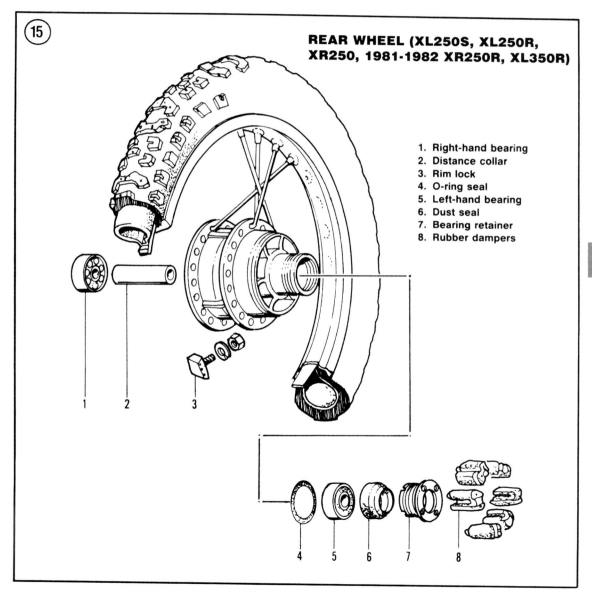

REAR WHEEL (XL250S, XL250R, XR250, 1981-1982 XR250R, XL350R)

1. Right-hand bearing
2. Distance collar
3. Rim lock
4. O-ring seal
5. Left-hand bearing
6. Dust seal
7. Bearing retainer
8. Rubber dampers

10

3. Remove the axle spacer (**Figure 16**).

4. To remove the bearing retainer (**Figure 17**), perform the following:

   a. Install the Honda special tool, Retainer Wrench Body (part No. 07710-0010401) in from the right-hand side (**Figure 18**).

   b. Install the Honda special tool, Retainer Wrench A (part No. 07710-0010200) on the left-hand side and onto the bearing retainer.

   c. Use a wrench (**Figure 19**) on the Retainer Wrench A and unscrew the bearing retainer.

   d. Remove the bearing retainer and the special tools from the rear hub.

5. Remove the dust seal.

6. Before proceeding further, inspect the wheel bearings as described in this chapter. If they must be replaced, proceed as follows.

7. To remove the right- and left-hand bearings (**Figure 20**) and distance collar, perform the following:

   a. Insert a soft aluminum or brass drift into one side of the hub.

   b. Push the distance collar over to one side and place the drift on the inner race of the lower bearing.

   c. Tap the bearing out of the hub with a hammer, working around the perimeter of the inner race.

   d. Repeat for the other bearing.

8. Clean the inside and the outside of the hub with solvent. Dry with compressed air.

Assembly

1. On non-sealed bearings, pack the bearings with a good quality wheel bearing grease. Work the grease in between the balls thoroughly; turn the bearing by hand a couple of times to make sure the grease is distributed evenly inside the bearing.

2. Blow any dirt or foreign matter out of the hub prior to installing the bearings.

> *CAUTION*
> *Install non-sealed bearings with the single sealed side facing outward.*

3. Pack the hub with wheel bearing grease.

> *CAUTION*
> *Install the standard bearings (they are sealed on one side only) with the sealed side facing out (**Figure 20**). Tap the bearings squarely into place and tap on the outer race only. Use a socket (**Figure 21**) that matches the outer race diameter. Do not tap on the inner race or the bearing might be damaged. Be sure that the bearings are completely seated.*

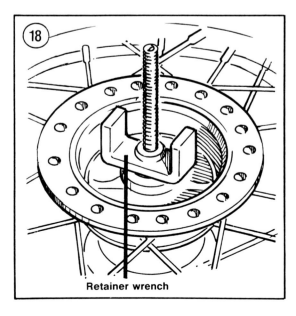

Retainer wrench

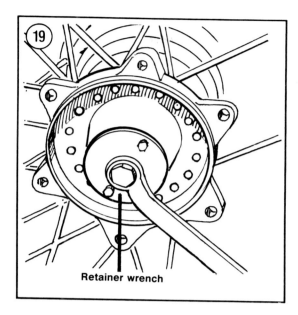

Retainer wrench

4. Install the right-hand bearing into the hub.

5. Press the distance collar into the hub from the left-hand side.

6. Install the left-hand bearing into the hub.

7. Inspect the bearing retainer threads for damage, replace if necessary.

8. Apply grease to the lips of the grease seal in the bearing retainer.

9. Screw the bearing retainer into the hub. Use the same tool set-up used in Step 4 of *Disassembly*.

10. After the bearing has been screwed into the hub, lock it in place by staking it with a center punch and hammer (**Figure 22**).

11. Install the rear brake assembly into the hub.

12. Install the rear wheel as described in this chapter.

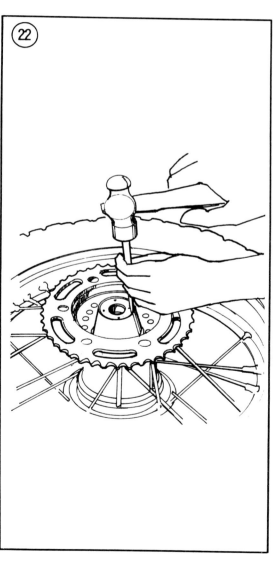

10

REAR HUB (1984-1985 XR200R, 1984-ON XR250R, XR350R)

Disassembly

Refer to **Figure 23** for this procedure.
1. Remove the rear wheel as described in this chapter.
2. Remove the bolts securing the driven sprocket and remove the sprocket.
3. Using 2 wide, flat-blade screwdrivers, carefully pry loose, then remove, the collar from the left-hand side.
4. To remove the bearing retainer, perform the following:
    a. Install the Honda special tool, Retainer Wrench Body (part No. 07910-3000000) in from the right-hand side (**Figure 18**).
    b. Install the Honda special tool, Retainer Wrench A (part No. 07710-0010100) on the left-hand side and onto the bearing retainer.
    c. Use a wrench (**Figure 19**) on the Retainer Wrench A and unscrew the bearing retainer.
    d. Remove the bearing retainer and the special tools from the rear hub.
5. Before proceeding further, inspect the wheel bearings as described in this chapter. If they must be replaced, proceed as follows.
6. To remove the right- and left-hand bearings and distance collar, perform the following:
    a. Insert a soft aluminum or brass drift into one side of the hub.
    b. Push the distance collar over to one side and place the drift on the inner race of the lower bearing.
    c. Tap the bearing out of the hub with a hammer, working around the perimeter of the inner race.
    d. Repeat for the other bearing.
7. Clean the inside and the outside of the hub with solvent. Dry with compressed air.

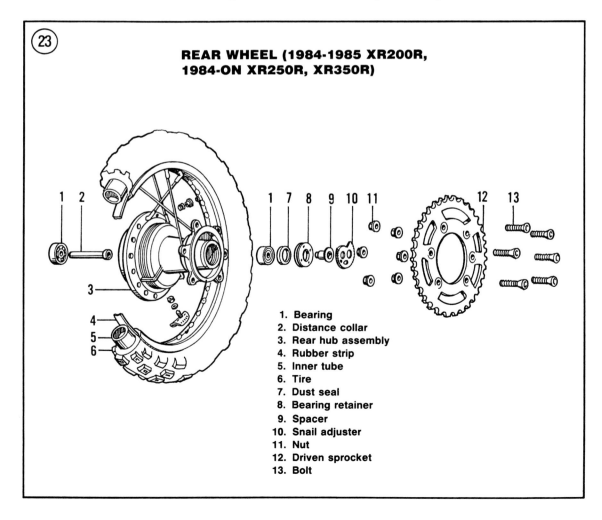

(23)

REAR WHEEL (1984-1985 XR200R, 1984-ON XR250R, XR350R)

1. Bearing
2. Distance collar
3. Rear hub assembly
4. Rubber strip
5. Inner tube
6. Tire
7. Dust seal
8. Bearing retainer
9. Spacer
10. Snail adjuster
11. Nut
12. Driven sprocket
13. Bolt

Assembly

1. On non-sealed bearings, pack the bearings with a good quality wheel bearing grease. Work the grease in between the balls thoroughly; turn the bearing by hand a couple of times to make sure the grease is distributed evenly inside the bearing.

2. Blow any dirt or foreign matter out of the hub prior to installing the bearings.

CAUTION
Install non-sealed bearings with the single sealed side facing outward.

3. Pack the hub with multipurpose grease.

CAUTION
*Install the standard bearings (they are sealed on one side only) with the sealed side facing out (**Figure 20**). Tap the bearings squarely into place and tap on the outer race only. Use a socket (**Figure 21**) that matches the outer race diameter. Do not tap on the inner race or the bearing might be damaged. Be sure that the bearings are completely seated.*

4. Install the right-hand bearing into the hub.

5A. On 1986-on XR250R models, position the distance collar with the "LH" mark facing toward the left-hand side. Press the distance collar into the hub from the left-hand side.

5B. On all other models, press the distance collar into the hub from the left-hand side. Either end can go in first as the collar is symmetrical.

6. Install the left-hand bearing into the hub.

7. Inspect the bearing retainer threads for damage. Replace the retainer if necessary.

8. Apply grease to the lips of the grease seal in the bearing retainer.

9. Screw the bearing retainer into the hub. Use the same tool set-up used in Step 4 of *Disassembly*.

10. After the bearing has been screwed into the hub, lock it in place by staking it with a center punch and hammer (**Figure 22**).

11. Install the driven sprocket and tighten the bolts to the torque specification listed in **Table 1**.

12. Install the rear wheel as described in this chapter.

FINAL DRIVEN SPROCKET
(XL250S, XL250R, XR250,
1981-1982 XR250R, XL350R)

Refer to **Figure 24** for this procedure. Models not listed in this procedure do not have a final driven sprocket assembly with rubber dampers. The sprocket is attached directly to the wheel hub.

10

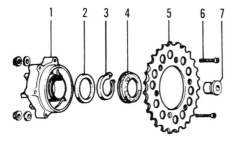

㉔

FINAL DRIVEN SPROCKET
ASSEMBLY (XL250S, XL250R,
XR250, 1981-1982 XR250R,
XL350R)

1. Drive flange
2. Thrust washer
3. Circlip
4. Dust cover
5. Sprocket
6. Bolt
7. Collar

Disassembly/Assembly

1. Remove the rear wheel as described in this chapter.
2. Remove the dust cover (A, **Figure 25**).
3. Remove the circlip and thrust washer.
4. Withdraw the final driven sprocket assembly straight up and out of the rear hub.

> *NOTE*
> *If the final driven sprocket assembly is difficult to remove, tap on the backside of the sprocket (from the opposite side of the wheel through the wheel spokes) with a wooden hammer handle hammer. Tap evenly around the perimeter of the sprocket until the assembly is free.*

5. If necessary, remove the Allen bolts (B, **Figure 25**) securing the driven sprocket to the driven flange.
6. Install by reversing these removal steps, noting the following.
7. The snap ring and dust cover must be installed as shown in **Figure 26**.
8. If the driven sprocket was removed from the flange, tighten the bolts to the torque specification listed in **Table 1**.

Inspection

1. Visually inspect the rubber dampers for signs of damage or deterioration. Replace as a complete set.
2. Inspect the driven flange assembly housing for cracks or damage. Replace if necessary.
3. Inspect the teeth (C, **Figure 25**) of the driven sprocket. If the teeth are visibly worn (**Figure 27**), remove the bolts and replace the sprocket.
4. If the sprocket requires replacement, also inspect the drive chain and the drive sprocket. They also may be worn and need replacing.

SWING ARM (DUAL-SHOCK)

In time, the bushings will wear and have to be replaced. The condition of the bushings can greatly affect handling performance and if worn parts are not replaced they can produce erratic and dangerous handling. Common symptoms are wheel hop, pulling to one side during acceleration and pulling to the other side during braking.

Removal/Installation

1. Remove both side covers.
2. Remove the rear wheel as described in this chapter.
3. Remove the lower mounting bolt securing each shock absorber.

> *NOTE*
> *It is not necessary to remove the shock absorber units, just pivot the units up and out of the way.*

4. Grasp the rear end of the swing arm and try to move it from side to side in a horizontal arc. There should be no noticeable side play. If play is evident, and the pivot bolt is tightened correctly, then the bushings or pivot collar are worn and require replacement.

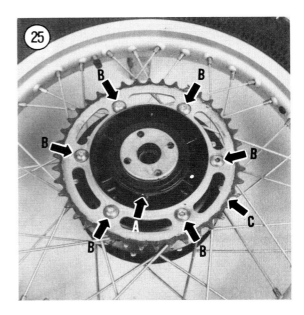

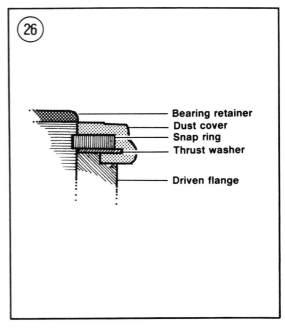

Bearing retainer
Dust cover
Snap ring
Thrust washer

Driven flange

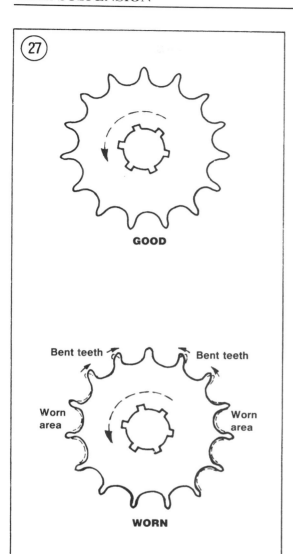

GOOD

Bent teeth   Bent teeth

Worn
area   Worn
                             area

WORN

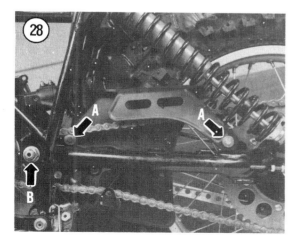

5. Remove the bolts (A, **Figure 28**) securing the drive chain cover and remove the cover.
6. On XL series models, remove the drive chain guide.
7. Remove the self-locking nut (B, **Figure 28**) and withdraw the pivot bolt from the right-hand side.
8. Pull back on the swing arm, free it from the frame and remove it from the frame.

NOTE
Don't lose the dust caps on each side of the pivot points; they may fall off during removal.

9. Install by reversing these removal steps, noting the following.
10. Position the swing arm into the mounting area of the frame. Align the holes in the swing arm with the holes in the frame.
11. Apply a light coat of grease to the pivot bolt prior to installation.
12. Tighten the pivot bolt to the torque specification listed in **Table 1**.
13. Move the swing arm up and down several times to make sure all components are properly seated.
14. Adjust the drive chain and rear brake as described in Chapter Three.

Disassembly/Inspection/Assembly

Refer to **Figure 29** for this procedure.
1. Remove the chain slider from the left-hand side.
2. Remove the dust seal from each side of the swing arm. Discard the dust seals.
3. Withdraw the pivot collar from the swing arm.
4. Secure the swing arm in a vise with soft jaws.
5. Using a suitable size drift or extension and socket tap the bushing out of one end of the swing arm (**Figure 30**).
6. Repeat Step 5 and remove the bushing from the other end.
7. Thoroughly clean out the inside of the swing arm with solvent and dry with compressed air.
8. Measure the outside diameter of the pivot collar at both ends. If the diameter is 21.35 mm (0.841 in.) or less at either end, the collar must be replaced.

NOTE
Always replace both bushings even though only one may be worn.

9. Measure the inside diameter of each bushing. If the diameter is 21.67 mm (0.853 in.) or greater on either bushing, replace both bushings as a pair.

DUAL-SHOCK SWING ARM ASSEMBLY

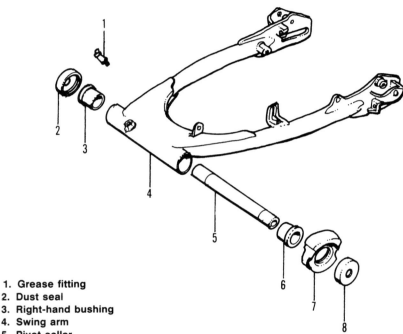

1. Grease fitting
2. Dust seal
3. Right-hand bushing
4. Swing arm
5. Pivot collar
6. Left-hand bushing
7. Chain slider
8. Dust seal

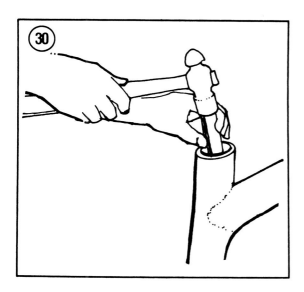

10. The maximum clearance between the bushings and the collar is 0.32 mm (0.013 in.). Replace one or all parts if this dimension is exceeded.

11. Apply a light coat of oil to the inside and outside surfaces of the new bushings prior to installation.

> *WARNING*
> *Never reinstall a bushing that has been removed. During the removal procedure it becomes slightly damaged and is no longer true to alignment. If reinstalled, it will damage the pivot collar and create an unsafe riding condition.*

12. Tap one bushing into place slowly and squarely into the swing arm with a block of wood (**Figure 31**). Make sure it completely seats and is not cocked in the bore of the swing arm.

13. Repeat Step 12 and install the other bushing.

14. Apply a light coat of molybdenum disulfide grease to the pivot collar and the inside surface of both bushings. Insert the pivot collar into the swing arm.

15. Install new dust seals. Apply a light coat of grease to their lips prior to installation.

16. Inspect the drive chain slider for wear; replace if necessary.

SWING ARM (PRO-LINK)

In time, the needle bearings or pivot collar will wear and will have to be replaced. The condition of the bearings can greatly affect handling performance and if worn parts are not replaced they can produce erratic and dangerous handling. Common symptoms are wheel hop, pulling to one side during acceleration and pulling to the other side during braking.

Removal
(1984-on XL250R, XL350R and XR350R)

1. Place wood block(s) under the skid plate to hold the bike securely with the rear wheel off the ground.

2. Remove the rear wheel as described in this chapter.

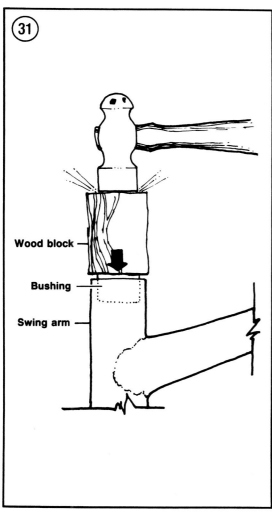

Wood block

Bushing

Swing arm

3. Disconnect the rear brake pedal return spring (A, **Figure 32**) from the swing arm.

4. Remove the upper pivot bolt and nut (B, **Figure 32**) securing the shock arm to the swing arm.

5. Remove the lower pivot bolt and nut (C, **Figure 32**) securing the shock arm to the shock link.

6. Grasp the rear end of the swing arm and try to move it from side to side in a horizontal arc. There should be no noticeable side play. If play is evident and the pivot bolt is tightened correctly, the bearings or pivot collar should be replaced.

7. Remove the self-locking nut (D, **Figure 32**) and withdraw the swing arm pivot bolt from the left-hand side.

8. Pull back on the swing arm, free it from the drive chain and remove the swing arm from the frame.

NOTE
Don't lose the dust seal cap on each side of the pivot points; they will usually fall off when the swing arm is removed.

9. Inspect the swing arm as described in this chapter.

Installation
(1984-on XL250R, XL350R and XR350R)

1. Make sure the dust seals are installed on the swing arm.

2. Position the drive chain over the left-hand side of the swing arm.

3. Position the swing arm into the frame mounting area. Align the holes in the swing arm with the holes in the frame. To help align the holes, insert a drift in from the right-hand side.

4. Apply a light coat of grease to the pivot bolt.

5. After the holes are aligned, insert the pivot bolt from the left-hand side and install the self-locking nut. Tighten the self-locking nut to the torque specifications listed in **Table 1**.

6. Move the swing arm up and down several times to make sure all components are properly seated.

7. Move the shock arm into position with the swing arm and install the shock arm pivot bolt (B, **Figure 32**) from the left-hand side. Install the nut and tighten to the torque specification listed in **Table 1**.

8. Make sure the dust seals are installed on the shock link.

9. Move the shock link up into position with the shock arm and install the shock arm pivot bolt (C, **Figure 32**) from the left-hand side. Install the nut and tighten to the torque specification listed in **Table 1**.

10. Attach the rear brake pedal return spring (A, **Figure 32**).

11. Install the rear wheel as described in this chapter.

12. Install the fuel tank, the seat and side covers.

13. Lubricate the swing arm pivot bolt and shock linkage as described in Chapter Three.

Removal (All Except 1984-on XL250R, XL350R and XR350R)

1. Place wood block(s) under the skid plate to support the bike securely with the rear wheel off the ground.

2. Remove both side covers and the seat.

3. Remove the fuel tank as described in Chapter Seven.

4. Remove the air filter case.

5. Remove the shock absorber (**Figure 33**) as described in this chapter.

6. Grasp the rear end of the swing arm and try to move it from side to side in a horizontal arc. There should be no noticeable side play. If play is evident and the pivot bolt is tightened correctly, the bearings or pivot collar should be replaced.

7. Remove the bolt and nut (**Figure 34**) securing the shock arm to the shock link.

8. Remove the rear wheel (A, **Figure 35**) as described in this chapter.

9. Remove the self-locking nut (B, **Figure 35**) and withdraw the pivot bolt from the left-hand side.

10. Pull back on the swing arm, free it from the drive chain and remove the swing arm from the frame.

11. Inspect the swing arm as described in this chapter.

NOTE
Don't lose the dust seals on each side of the pivot points; they will usually fall off when the swing arm is removed.

Installation (All Except 1984-on XL250R, XL350R and XR350R)

1. Position the drive chain over the left-hand side of the swing arm.

2. Position the swing arm into the mounting area of the frame. Align the holes in the swing arm with the holes in the frame. To help align the holes, insert a drift in from the right-hand side.

3. Apply a light coat of molybdenum disulfide grease to the pivot bolt and install the pivot bolt from the left-hand side.

4. Install the self-locking nut and tighten to the torque specification listed in **Table 1**.

5. Move the swing arm up and down several times to make sure all components are properly seated.

6. Locate the shock arm into position with the mounting holes in the shock link and install the bolt and nut. Tighten the bolt and nut to the torque specification listed in **Table 1**.

7. Install the rear wheel as described in this chapter.

8. Install the shock absorber as described in this chapter.

9. Install the air filter case as described in Chapter Seven.

10. Install the fuel tank, the seat and side covers.

11. Lubricate the swing arm pivot bolt and shock linkage as described in Chapter Three.

Disassembly/Inspection/Assembly

Refer to **Figure 36** for the following models:
  a. 1982-1983 XL250R
  b. 1982-1983 XR250R
Refer to **Figure 37** for the following models:
  a. 1984-1985 XR200R
  b. 1984-on XL250R
  c. 1984-on XR250R
  d. XL350R
  e. XR350R

1. Remove the swing arm as described in this chapter.

2. Remove the drive chain guard and mud guard from the swing arm.

3. Remove the drive chain slider from the left-hand side of the swing arm.

4. Remove the bolt and nut securing the shock arm to the swing arm.

5. Remove both dust seals if they have not already fallen off during the removal sequence.

6. Withdraw the pivot collar, clean in solvent and thoroughly dry.

NOTE
There are no factory specifications for the outside diameter of the pivot collar.

7. Inspect the pivot collar for abnormal wear, scratches or score marks. Replace if necessary.

NOTE
If the pivot collar is replaced, the needle bearing at each end must also be replaced at the same time.

10

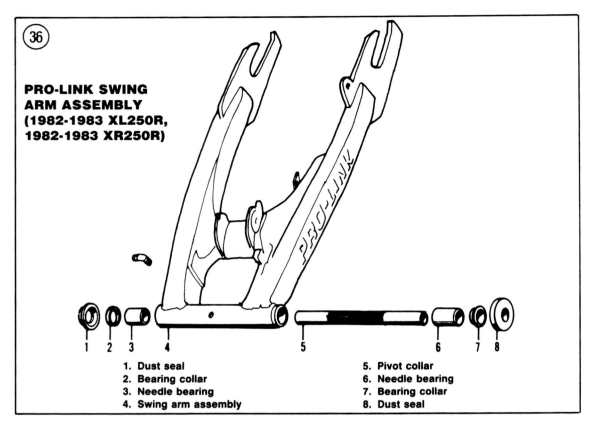

(36)

**PRO-LINK SWING
ARM ASSEMBLY
(1982-1983 XL250R,
1982-1983 XR250R)**

1. Dust seal
2. Bearing collar
3. Needle bearing
4. Swing arm assembly

5. Pivot collar
6. Needle bearing
7. Bearing collar
8. Dust seal

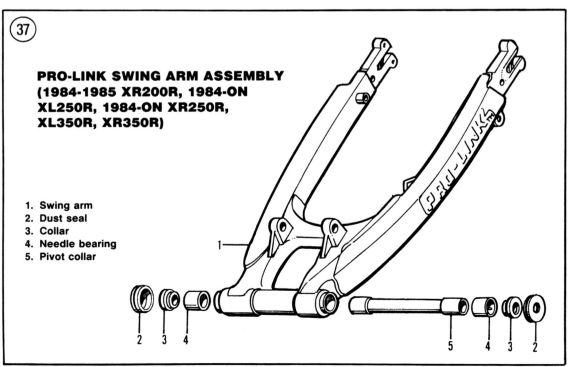

(37)

**PRO-LINK SWING ARM ASSEMBLY
(1984-1985 XR200R, 1984-ON
XL250R, 1984-ON XR250R,
XL350R, XR350R)**

1. Swing arm
2. Dust seal
3. Collar
4. Needle bearing
5. Pivot collar

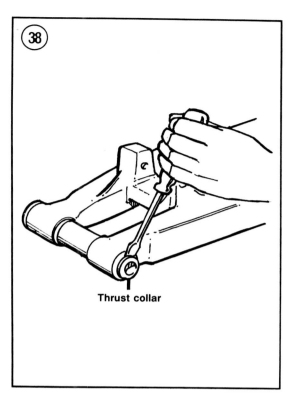

Thrust collar

8. Inspect the needle bearings as follows:
   a. Wipe off any excess grease from the needle bearing at each end of the swing arm.
   b. Turn each bearing with your fingers; make sure they rotate smoothly. The needle bearings wear very slowly and wear is very difficult to measure.
   c. Check the rollers for evidence of wear, pitting or color change (bluish tint) indicating heat from lack of lubrication.

NOTE
Always replace both needle bearings even though only one may be worn.

9. Prior to installing the pivot collar, coat the collar and both needle bearings with molybdenum disulfide grease.
10. Insert the pivot collar.
11. Coat the inside of both dust caps with molybdenum disulfide grease and install them onto the ends of the swing arm.
12. Install the drive chain slider, the drive chain guard and mud guard.
13. Install the swing arm as described in this chapter.

Needle Bearing Replacement
(1986-on XR250R, 1985 XR350R)

The swing arm is equipped with a needle bearing at each end. The bearing is pressed in place and has to be removed with force. The bearing will be distorted, so don't remove it unless absolutely necessary.

The bearings must be removed and installed with special tools that are available from a Honda dealer.

1. Remove the swing arm as described in this chapter.
2. Remove the dust seal from each side of the swing arm.
3. Secure the swing arm in a vise with soft jaws.
4. Using a wide, flat-blade screwdriver (**Figure 38**) carefully pry the thrust collar from each side of the swing arm.
5. Install the Honda special tool, Needle Bearing Remover (part No. 07931-MA70000) into one end of the swing arm.
6. Using 2 wrenches, turn the bolt heads on the remover and withdraw the needle bearing from the swing arm (**Figure 39**). Discard the needle bearing as it cannot be reused.
7. Turn the swing arm over in the vise and repeat Step 5 and Step 6 for the other side.

10

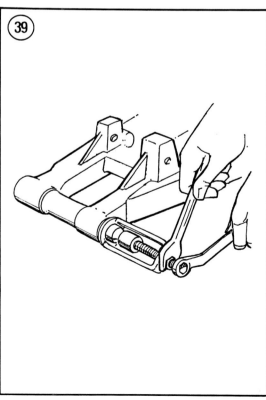

8. Thoroughly clean out the inside of the swing arm with solvent and dry with compressed air.

NOTE
Either the right- or left-hand bearing race can be installed first.

9. Apply a light coat of molybdenum disulfide grease to all parts prior to installation.

CAUTION
For correct alignment the new needle bearings should be pressed into place by a Honda dealer with the use of special tools and a hydraulic press. The following procedure is provided if you choose to perform this operation yourself. If done incorrectly, the needle bearing can be damaged during installation and may not be aligned correctly.

WARNING
Never reinstall a needle bearing that has been removed. During removal it becomes slightly damaged and is no longer true to alignment. If installed, it will damage the pivot collar and create an unsafe riding condition.

10. Position the new needle bearing with its marks facing up toward the outside.
11. Place the bearing collar onto the needle bearing and place them onto the swing arm.
12. Use the following Honda special tools:
   a. 20 mm Pilot: part No. 07746-0040500.
   b. 32×35 mm Attachment: part No. 07746-0010100.
   c. Driver: part No. 07749-0010000.
13. Place the Honda special tools onto the bearing collar and the needle bearing (**Figure 40**).
14. Using a hammer, slowly and carefully drive the needle bearing and collar into place squarely. Make sure it is properly seated.
15. Remove the special tools.
16. Repeat Steps 10-14 for the other needle bearing.
17. Install a new dust seal on each end of the swing arm.
18. Install the swing arm as described in this chapter.

Needle Bearing Replacement (All Except 1986-on XR250R, 1985 XR350R)

The swing arm is equipped with a needle bearing at each end. The bearing is pressed in place and has to be removed with force. The bearing will be distorted during removal, so don't remove it unless absolutely necessary.

The bearings must be removed with special tools that are available from a Honda dealer. The special tools are as follows:
   a. Bearing remover:
   XR250R—part No. 07936-3710000.
   All other models—part No. 07936-3710600.
   b. Handle: part No. 07936-3710200.
   c. Slide hammer weight: part No. 07936-3710200.

1. Remove the swing arm as described in this chapter.
2. Remove the dust seal and bearing assembly from each side of the swing arm.
3. Secure the swing arm in a vise with soft jaws.

NOTE
These special tools grab the inner surface of the bearing and then withdraw it from the swing arm with the use of a tool similar to a body shop slide hammer.

4. Either the right- or left-hand bearing race can be removed first.
5. Install the bearing remover through the hole in the bearing and expand the tool behind the bearing.

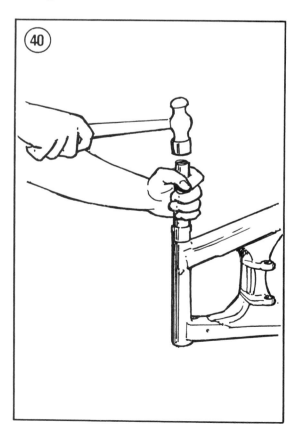

6. Attach the handle (slide hammer and handle) to the bearing remover.

7. Slide the weight on the hammer back and forth several times until the bearing and bearing collar are withdrawn from the swing arm (**Figure 41**).

8. Remove the bearing and bearing collar from the special tools.

9. Turn the swing arm over in the vise and repeat Steps 5-8 for the other bearing.

10. Thoroughly clean out the inside of the swing arm with solvent and dry with compressed air.

11. Apply a light coat of molybdenum disulfide grease to all parts prior to installation.

NOTE
Either the right- or left-hand bearing race can be installed first.

CAUTION
*For correct alignment the new needle bearings **should** be pressed into place by a Honda dealer with the use of special tools and a hydraulic press. The following procedure is provided if you choose to perform this operation yourself. If done incorrectly, the needle bearing can be damaged during installation and may not be aligned correctly.*

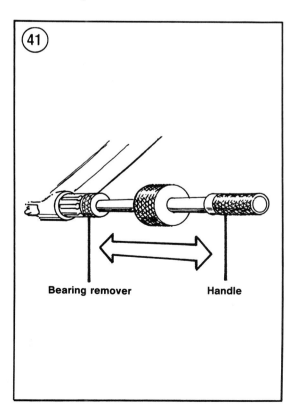

(41)

Bearing remover   **Handle**

CAUTION
Never reinstall a needle bearing that has been removed. During removal it becomes slightly damaged and is no longer true to alignment. If installed, it will damage the pivot collar and create an unsafe riding condition.

12. Position the new needle bearing with its marks facing up toward the outside.

13. Place the bearing collar onto the needle bearing and place them onto the swing arm.

14. Use the following Honda special tools:
   a. 20 mm Pilot: part No. 07746-0040500.
   b. 32×35 mm Attachment: part No. 07746-0010100.
   c. Driver: part No. 07749-0010000.

15. Place the Honda special tools onto the bearing collar and the needle bearing (**Figure 40**).

16. Using a hammer, slowly and carefully drive the needle bearing and collar into place squarely. Make sure it is properly seated.

17. Remove the special tools.

18. Repeat Steps 13-18 for the other needle bearing.

19. Install a new dust seal on each end of the swing arm.

20. Install the swing arm as described in this chapter.

DUAL SHOCK ABSORBERS

10

The rear shocks are spring controlled and gas charged. Spring preload can be adjusted on all models. The shock damper unit is sealed and cannot be serviced. Service is limited to removal and replacement of the damper unit and/or spring.

WARNING
Do not try to dismantle the gas filled shock damper unit or apply any form of heat to it. If the unit is heated in any way it will result in an extremely dangerous explosion.

Spring Preload Adjustment

XL250S models

1. Remove the right- and left-hand side covers.

WARNING
The cam ring must be set to the same setting on both sides or it will result in an unsafe riding condition.

2. Use the spanner wrench furnished in the factory tool kit. Rotate the cam ring (**Figure 42**) at the upper end of the shock to one of the 5 positions; *counterclockwise* to increase spring preload or *clockwise* to decrease spring preload.

XR250 models

1. Remove the right- and left-hand side covers.
2. Have an assistant pull down on the spring coils (A, **Figure 43**).
3. Make sure the adjust collar (B, **Figure 43**) slides down with the spring.

> *WARNING*
> *The set ring must be set to the same groove on both sides or it will result in an unsafe riding condition.*

4. Remove the set ring and reposition it into a different groove on the damper unit. *Down* to increase spring preload or *up* to decrease spring preload.

> *NOTE*
> *Make sure the set ring is correctly seated in the groove in the damper unit.*

5. After resetting, push down on the rear end of the bike several times to make sure the set rings have been properly seated.

Removal/Installation

Removal and installation of the rear shocks is easier if done separately. The remaining unit will support the rear of the bike and maintain the correct relationship between the top and bottom shock mounts.
1. Place wood block(s) under the skid plate to hold the bike securely with the rear wheel off the ground.
2. Remove both side covers and the seat.
3. Adjust both shocks to their softest setting.
4. Remove the upper and lower mounting bolts (**Figure 44**) securing the shock absorber to the frame. Remove the shock.
5. Install by reversing these removal steps, noting the following.
6. Tighten the upper and lower mounting bolts to the torque specifications listed in **Table 1**.
7. Repeat for the other side.

Disassembly/Inspection/Assembly

Refer to **Figure 45** for XL250S or **Figure 46** for XR250 models for this procedure.

> *WARNING*
> *Without the proper tool, this procedure can be dangerous. The spring can fly loose, causing injury. For a small bench fee, a dealer can do the job for you.*

REAR SHOCK—DUAL SHOCK (XL SERIES) ⓐ45

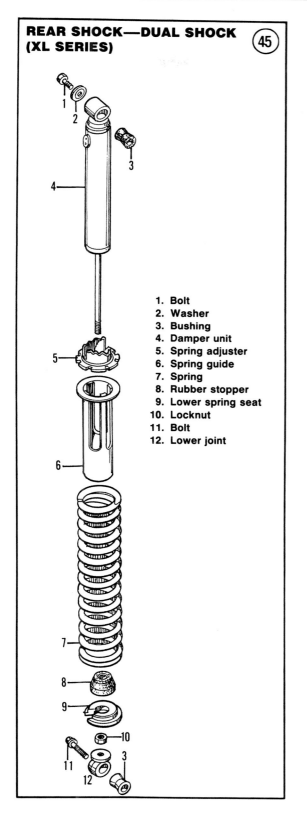

1. Bolt
2. Washer
3. Bushing
4. Damper unit
5. Spring adjuster
6. Spring guide
7. Spring
8. Rubber stopper
9. Lower spring seat
10. Locknut
11. Bolt
12. Lower joint

ⓐ46 REAR SHOCK—DUAL SHOCK (XR SERIES)

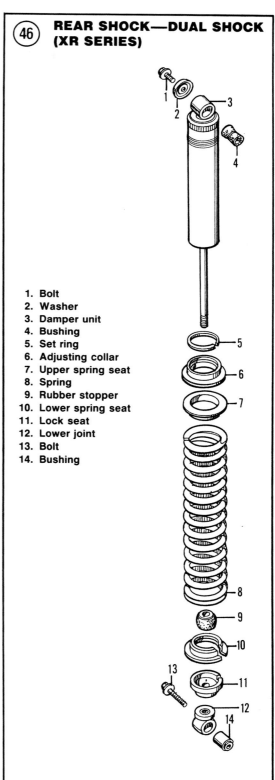

1. Bolt
2. Washer
3. Damper unit
4. Bushing
5. Set ring
6. Adjusting collar
7. Upper spring seat
8. Spring
9. Rubber stopper
10. Lower spring seat
11. Lock seat
12. Lower joint
13. Bolt
14. Bushing

10

1. Install the shock absorber in a compression tool as shown in **Figure 47**. This is a special tool and is available from a Honda dealer. It is the Shock Absorber Compressor Tool (part No. 07959-3290001).

> *CAUTION*
> *Be sure the compressor tool base is properly adjusted to fit the shock spring seat.*

2. Compress the shock spring just enough to gain access to the spring seat. Remove the spring seat.
3. Place the lower joint in a vise with soft jaws and loosen the locknut.
4. Completely unscrew the lower joint. This part may be difficult to break loose as thread locking agent was applied during assembly.
5. Release the spring tension and remove the shock from the compression tool.
6. Remove the spring adjuster, spring and spring guide from the damper unit.
7. Measure the spring free length (**Figure 48**). The spring must be replaced if it has sagged to the service limit listed in **Table 2** or less.
8. Check the damper unit for leakage and make sure the damper rod is straight.

> *NOTE*
> *The damper unit cannot be rebuilt; it must be replaced as a unit.*

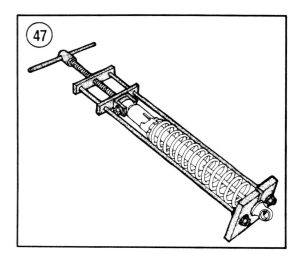

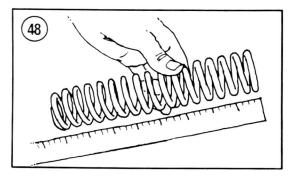

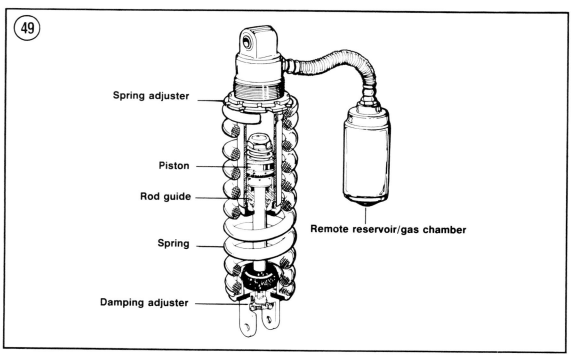

9. Inspect the rubber bushings in the upper and lower joints. Replace if necessary.

10. Inspect the rubber stopper. If it is worn or deteriorated, remove the locknut and slide off the rubber stopper. Replace with a new one.

11. Assembly is the reverse of these disassembly steps, noting the following.

12. Apply Loctite Lock 'N Seal to the threads of the damper rod prior to installing the locknut. Temporarily screw the locknut all the way down and tight against the end of the threads.

13. Apply Loctite Lock N' Seal to the threads of the damper rod prior to installing the lower joint. Screw the upper joint on all the way. Secure the lower joint in a vise with soft jaws and tighten the locknut along with the damper rod against the lower joint.

NOTE
After the locknut is tightened completely the locknut must be against the bottom surface of the upper joint and against the end of the threads on the damper rod.

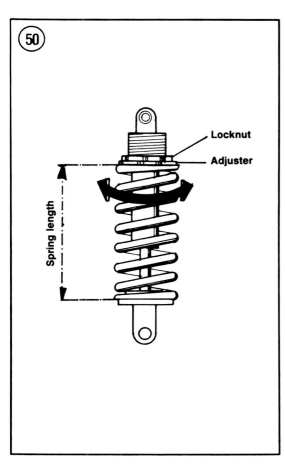

PRO-LINK SUSPENSION SYSTEM

The single shock absorber and linkage of the Pro-Link rear suspension system are attached to the swing arm just aft of the swing arm pivot point and to the lower rear portion of the frame and the shock absorber. All of these items are located forward of the rear wheel.

The shock link and shock arms working together with the matched spring rate and damping rates of the shock absorber combine to achieve a "progressive rising rate" rear suspension. This system provides the rider with the best of two worlds—greater rider comfort and better transfer of power to the ground.

As the rear suspension is moved upward by bumps, the shock absorber is compressed by the movement of the shock arm. As rear suspension travel increases, the portion of the shock link where the shock absorber is attached rises above the swing arm, thus increasing shock absorber travel (compression). This provides a progressive rise rate in which the shock eventually moves at a faster rate than the wheel. At about halfway through the wheel travel the shock begins to move at a faster rate than it did in the beginning.

SHOCK ABSORBER (PRO-LINK)

The single shock absorber (**Figure 49**) used in the Pro-Link suspension system has a remote oil/nitrogen reservoir on all models except the 1982-1983 XL250R and the XL350R.

The remote reservoir allows more rapid oil cooling and helps prevent the oil from frothing. The shock is adjustable for both shock rate and damping action.

Spring Preload Adjustment

There must be preload on the spring at all times. Never ride the bike without spring preload as possible loss of control will result.

The spring length (preload) must be maintained within the dimensions listed in **Table 3**.

1. Place wood block(s) under the skid plate to support the bike securely with the rear wheel off the ground.

2. Remove both side covers.

3. Remove the air filter air box.

CAUTION
After the air box is removed the carburetor throat(s) is exposed. Cover the opening with a clean shop cloth to keep out dirt and foreign matter.

4. Measure the existing spring length (**Figure 50**).

NOTE
Special Honda tools are required for the locknut and the adjuster. These are Pin Spanners, part No. 89201-KA4-810 and part No. 89202-KA4810.

5. To adjust, loosen the locknut and turn the adjuster (**Figure 51**) in the desired direction. Tightening the adjuster *increases* spring preload and loosening it *decreases* preload.
6. One complete turn (360°) of the adjuster moves the spring 1.5 mm (0.006 in.).

NOTE
*Remember, the spring length (preload) must be maintained within the dimensions listed in **Table 3**.*

7. After the desired spring length is achieved, tighten the locknut securely.
8. Install all items removed.

Rebound Adjustment

Rebound damping can be adjusted to 4 different settings. The adjuster knob is located at the base of the shock absorber (**Figure 52**) between the legs of the lower mounting bracket.

The rebound setting should be adjusted to personal preference to accommodate rider weight and riding conditions.

Make sure that the adjuster is located into one of the detents and not in between any 2 settings.

Removal

1. Place wood block(s) under the engine to support the bike securely with the rear wheel off of the ground.
2. Remove the seat and both side covers.
3. Remove the fuel tank as described in Chapter Seven.
4. Remove the muffler as described in Chapter Seven.
5. On XR350R models, disconnect the electrical connector to the rear brake light switch and move the wires out of the way.
6. On 1981-1983 XL250R, remove the bolts securing the drive chain mud guard and remove the mud guard.
7. On all models except 1981-1982 XL250R models, remove the air filter air box.

CAUTION
After the air box is removed the carburetor(s) throat is exposed. Cover the opening with a clean shop cloth to keep out dirt and foreign matter.

8. On 1984-on XL250R models, remove the battery as described in Chapter Three.

WARNING
On models so equipped, do not attempt to disconnect the reservoir from the shock absorber body. The compressed nitrogen within the system is pressurized to about 20 kg/cm² (285 psi).

9. On models so equipped, remove the bolts (A, **Figure 53**) and/or bands securing the remote reservoir to the frame. Don't lose the clamping bands.
10. Remove the upper mounting flange bolt (B, **Figure 53**) securing the shock to the frame. Some models have a nut on the bolt; on others the bolt is threaded into the other side of the mounting bracket.
11. Tilt the upper portion of the shock absorber toward the rear.

NOTE
The next step requires the aid of a helper. While raising the rear wheel, make sure the upper portion of the shock absorber clears any mounting

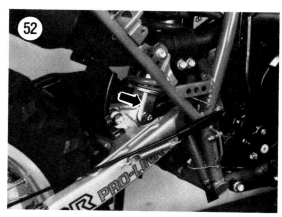

brackets on the frame. Do not damage the locknut and adjust nut threads on the upper portion of the shock.

12. Raise the rear wheel as far as possible and have the helper install wooden block(s) under the rear wheel (**Figure 54**).

13. Remove the shock absorber lower mounting bolt (and nut on models so equipped).

14. On models so equipped, note the location of the remote reservoir hose in relation to the shock absorber and the frame. The shock absorber must be reinstalled in the same direction so the remote reservoir will be on the correct side of the frame.

15. Carefully remove the shock absorber from the frame.

16. Keep the rear wheel in the raised position for the installation procedure.

Installation

WARNING
*All bolts and nuts used on the Pro-Link suspension must be replaced with parts of the same type. Do **not** use a replacement part of lesser quality or substitute design, as this may affect the performance of the system or result in failure of the part which will lead to loss*

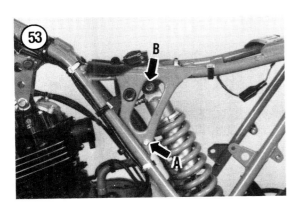

of control of the bike. Torque values listed must be used during installation to assure proper retention of these parts.

1. The rear wheel must be in the raised position as shown in **Figure 54**.

2. Apply a light coat of molybdenum disulfide paste grease to the upper mounting bracket on the frame.

3. Position the shock absorber assembly in the frame with the remote reservoir hose on the correct side as noted in Step 14 of *Removal.*

4. Apply a coat of molybdenum disulfide paste grease to the pivot points of the shock link.

5. Position the shock absorber onto the shock link and install the lower mounting bolt (and nut on models so equipped). Do not tighten the bolt at this time.

NOTE
The next step requires the aid of a helper. While lowering the rear wheel, make sure the upper portion of the shock absorber clears any mounting brackets on the frame. Do not damage the locknut and adjust nut threads on the upper portion of the shock. Also on models so equipped, make sure the remote reservoir does not get damaged.

6. Slowly lower the rear wheel and move the upper portion of the shock absorber into alignment with the upper mounting flange on the frame.

7. Install the shock absorber upper mounting bolt.

8. Tighten the upper and lower mounting bolts (and nuts on models equipped) to the torque specification listed in **Table 1**.

9. On models equipped with a remote reservoir, perform the following:

    a. Position the remote reservoir onto the frame.

    b. Attach to the frame with the mounting bands and/or bolts.

    c. Make sure the remote reservoir hose is correctly routed through the frame and is not kinked or touching any moving part of the bike.

10. Remove the wood block(s) from under the engine. Push down on the rear of the bike and make sure the rear suspension is operating properly. Make sure the remote reservoir hose is not rubbing on the shock absorber. Relocate if necessary.

11. On all models except 1981-1982 XL250R models, perform the following:

    a. Remove the shop cloth covering the carburetor(s) throat.

10

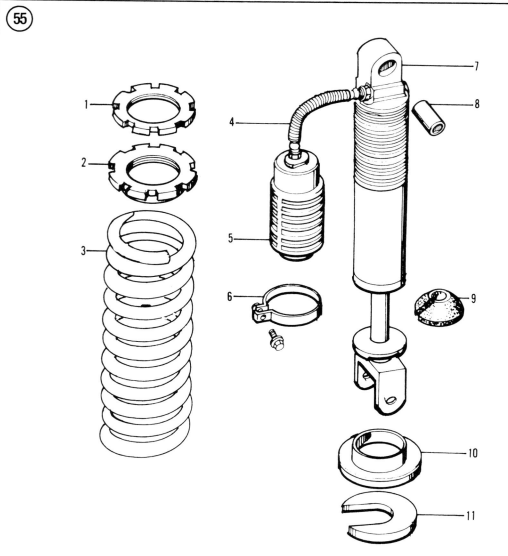

**REAR SHOCK ABSORBER—
PRO-LINK (1981-1982 XR250R)**

1. Adjuster locknut
2. Spring adjuster
3. Spring
4. Hose
5. Reservoir
6. Reservoir clamp band
7. Damper unit assembly
8. Bushing
9. Rubber stopper
10. Spring seat
11. Spring stopper

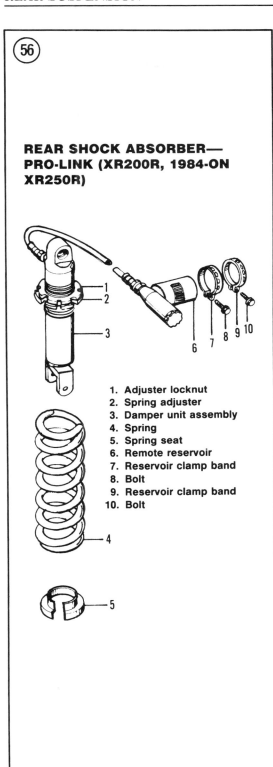

(56)

REAR SHOCK ABSORBER— PRO-LINK (XR200R, 1984-ON XR250R)

1. Adjuster locknut
2. Spring adjuster
3. Damper unit assembly
4. Spring
5. Spring seat
6. Remote reservoir
7. Reservoir clamp band
8. Bolt
9. Reservoir clamp band
10. Bolt

b. Install the air filter air box. Make sure all fittings are tight to avoid an air leak.

12. On 1984-on XL250R models, install the battery as described in Chapter Three.

13. On 1981-1983 XL250R, install the drive chain mud guard and bolts. Tighten the bolts securely.

14. On XR350R models, connect the electrical connector to the rear brake light switch.

15. Install the muffler as described in Chapter Seven.

16. Install the fuel tank as described in Chapter Seven.

17. Install the seat and both side covers.

Disassembly/Inspection/Assembly (XR200R, XR250R, 1983-1984 XR350R)

Refer to the following illustrations for this procedure:

a. **Figure 55**: 1981-1982 XR250R.
b. **Figure 56**: XR200R, 1984-on XR250R.
c. **Figure 57**: 1983-1984 XR350R.

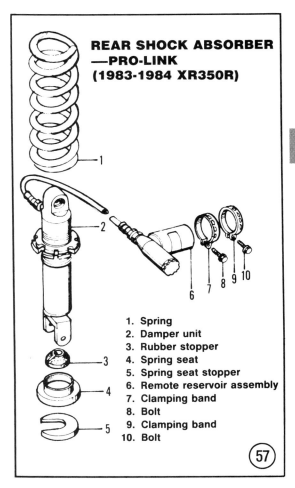

REAR SHOCK ABSORBER —PRO-LINK (1983-1984 XR350R)

1. Spring
2. Damper unit
3. Rubber stopper
4. Spring seat
5. Spring seat stopper
6. Remote reservoir assembly
7. Clamping band
8. Bolt
9. Clamping band
10. Bolt

(57)

10

Service by the home mechanic is limited to removal and installation of the spring. Under no circumstances should you attempt to disconnect the reservoir hose or disassemble the shock absorber unit or reservoir due to the high internal pressure of the nitrogen. If you are satisfied with the existing spring preload setting and want to maintain it, measure the spring length (**Figure 58**) prior to disassembly.

1. Hold the shock absorber upside down and secure the upper mounting portion (A, **Figure 59**) of the shock absorber in a vise with soft jaws. Be careful not to kink or damage the remote reservoir hose.

NOTE
Special tools are required to loosen the locknut and the adjuster. These are pin spanners, Honda part No. 89201-KA4-810 and 89202-K44-810.

2. Use special tools to loosen the locknut and spring adjuster (B, **Figure 59**). Unscrew them almost to the end of the threads. Do not completely unscrew either nut.

3. Remove the shock absorber from the vise.

4. From the lower portion of the shock absorber assembly, compress the spring.

5. On models so equipped, remove the spring seat.

6. Slide out the spring stopper.

7. Slide off the spring.

8. Inspect all components as described in this chapter.

9. Install the spring onto the damper unit.

10. Position the spring seat with the flange side toward the spring and install the spring seat.

11. On models so equipped, install the spring stopper.

12. Hold the shock absorber upside down and secure the upper mounting portion (A, **Figure 59**) of the shock absorber in a vise with soft jaws. Be careful not to kink or damage the remote reservoir hose.

13. Screw the adjuster and locknut on by hand until they contact the spring.

14. Use the special Honda tools used during disassembly and tighten the adjuster to the dimension taken prior to disassembly or to the standard spring length indicated in **Table 2**.

15. Hold onto the adjuster and tighten the locknut securely.

16. Remove the shock absorber from the vise.

Disassembly/Inspection/Assembly (XL250R, 1984-1985 XL350R)

Refer to the following illustrations for this procedure:
a. **Figure 60**: 1982-1983 XL250R.
b. **Figure 61**: 1984-on XL250R, 1984-1985 XL350R.

Service by the home mechanic is limited to removal and installation of the spring. Under no circumstances should you attempt to disconnect the reservoir hose or disassemble the shock absorber unit or reservoir due to the high internal pressure of the nitrogen. If you are satisfied with the existing spring preload setting and want to maintain it, measure the spring length (**Figure 58**) prior to disassembly.

1. Hold the shock absorber upside down and secure the upper mounting portion of the shock absorber in a vise with soft jaws. Be careful not to kink or damage the remote reservoir hose.

NOTE
Special tools are required to loosen the locknut and the adjuster. These are pin spanners, Honda part No. 89201-KA4-810 and 89202-KA4-810.

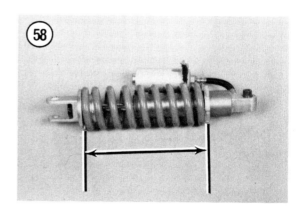

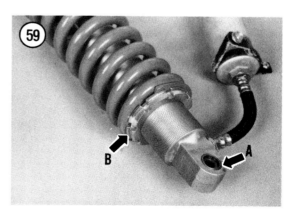

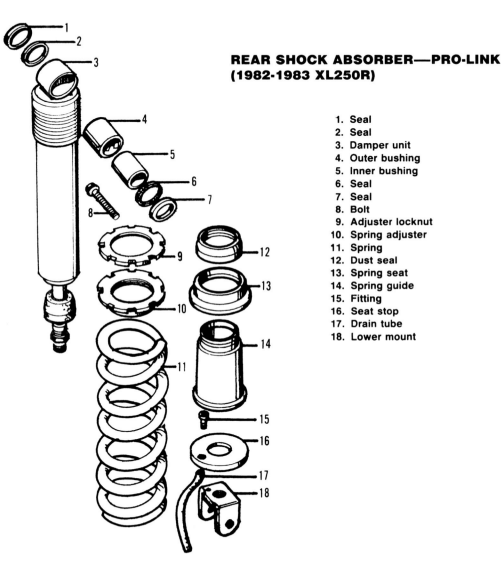

REAR SHOCK ABSORBER—PRO-LINK (1982-1983 XL250R)

1. Seal
2. Seal
3. Damper unit
4. Outer bushing
5. Inner bushing
6. Seal
7. Seal
8. Bolt
9. Adjuster locknut
10. Spring adjuster
11. Spring
12. Dust seal
13. Spring seat
14. Spring guide
15. Fitting
16. Seat stop
17. Drain tube
18. Lower mount

10

2. Use special tools to loosen the locknut and spring adjuster to almost the end of the threads. Do not completely unscrew either nut at this time.

3. Remove the shock absorber from the vise.

4. Completely unscrew the locknut and adjust nut from the damper unit.

5. Slide the spring off the damper unit.

6A. On 1984-on XL250R and 1984-1985 XL350R models, no further disassembly is required.

6B. On 1982-1983 XL250R models, perform the following:

   a. Secure the upper mounting portion of the shock absorber in a vise with soft jaws. Be careful not to kink or damage the remote reservoir hose.

   b. Loosen the locknut on the damper rod.

   c. Remove the shock absorber from the vise.

   d. Completely unscrew the lower mount from the damper rod.

   e. Slide off the seat stop, spring guide, spring seat and dust seal.

7. Inspect all components as described in this chapter.

NOTE
The damper unit cannot be rebuilt; it can be recharged with gas, the ATF fluid can be replaced or the entire unit can be replaced.

WARNING
The shock absorber damper unit and remote reservoir contain nitrogen gas compressed to between 142-284 psi (10-20 kg/cm²) (pressure varies, depending on year and model). Do not tamper with or attempt to open the damper unit or disconnect the reservoir hose from either unit. Do not place it near an open flame or other extreme heat. Do not dispose of the damper assembly yourself. Take it to a dealer where it can be deactivated and disposed of properly. Never attempt to remove the valve core from the base of the reservoir.

8. On 1982-1983 XL250R models, perform the following:

   a. Slide on the dust seal, spring seat (flange side toward the spring), spring guide and seat stop.

   b. Apply Loctite Lock N' Seal to the threads on the damper rod.

   c. Screw the lower mount. Align the locating pin on the seat stop with the notch on the lower mount.

   d. Secure the upper mounting portion of the shock absorber in a vise with soft jaws. Be careful not to kink or damage the remote reservoir hose.

   e. Tighten the locknut on the damper rod to the torque specification listed in **Table 1**.

9. Install the spring onto the damper unit.

10. Screw on the adjuster and locknut by hand until they contact the spring.

11. Hold the shock absorber upside down and secure the upper mounting portion of the shock absorber in a vise with soft jaws. Be careful not to kink or damage the remote reservoir hose.

12. Use the special Honda tools used during disassembly and tighten the adjuster to the dimension taken prior to disassembly or to the standard spring length indicated in **Table 3**.

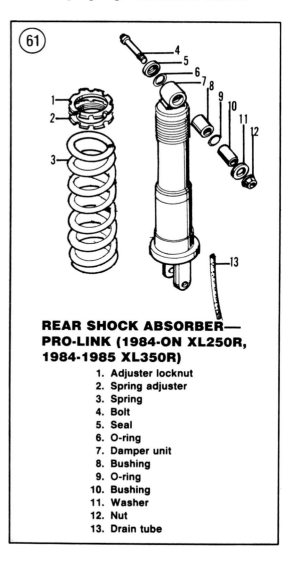

**REAR SHOCK ABSORBER—
PRO-LINK (1984-ON XL250R,
1984-1985 XL350R)**

   1. **Adjuster locknut**
   2. **Spring adjuster**
   3. **Spring**
   4. **Bolt**
   5. **Seal**
   6. **O-ring**
   7. **Damper unit**
   8. **Bushing**
   9. **O-ring**
   10. **Bushing**
   11. **Washer**
   12. **Nut**
   13. **Drain tube**

13. Hold onto the adjuster and tighten the locknut securely.

14. Remove the shock absorber from the vise.

Disassembly/Inspection/Assembly (1985 XR350R)

Refer to **Figure 62** for this procedure.

Service by the home mechanic is limited to removal and installation of the spring. Under no circumstances should you attempt to disconnect the reservoir hose or disassemble the shock absorber unit or reservoir due to the high internal pressure of the nitrogen. If you are satisfied with the existing spring pre-load setting and want to maintain it, measure the spring length (**Figure 58**) prior to disassembly.

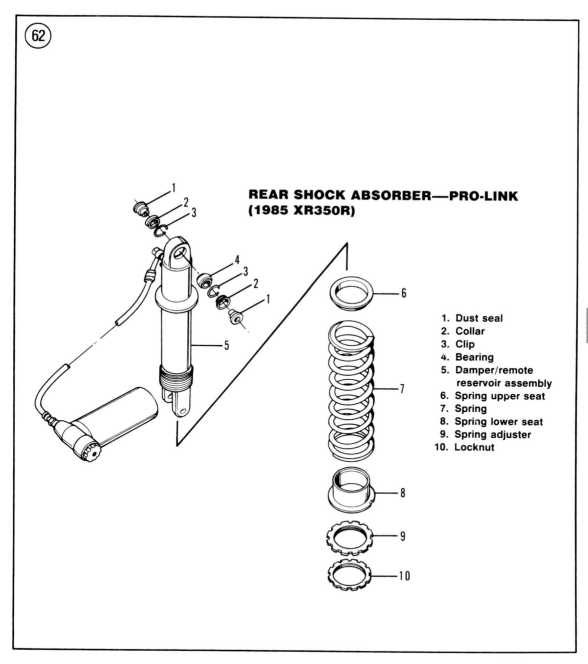

62

REAR SHOCK ABSORBER—PRO-LINK (1985 XR350R)

1. Dust seal
2. Collar
3. Clip
4. Bearing
5. Damper/remote reservoir assembly
6. Spring upper seat
7. Spring
8. Spring lower seat
9. Spring adjuster
10. Locknut

10

1. Hold the shock absorber upside down and secure the upper mounting portion of the shock absorber in a vise with soft jaws. Be careful not to kink or damage the remote reservoir hose.

NOTE
Special tools are required to loosen the locknut and the adjuster. These are pin spanners, Honda part No. 89201-KA4-810 and 89202-KA4-810.

2. Use special tools to loosen the locknut and spring adjuster (B, **Figure 59**) to almost the end of the threads. Do not completely unscrew either nut at this time.
3. Remove the shock absorber from the vise.
4. Completely unscrew the locknut and spring adjuster.
5. From the lower portion of the shock absorber, slide off the spring lower seat, the spring and the spring upper seat.
6. Inspect all components as described in this chapter.

NOTE
The damper unit cannot be rebuilt; it can be recharged with gas, the ATF fluid replaced or the entire unit can be replaced.

WARNING
The shock absorber damper unit and remote reservoir contain nitrogen gas compressed to between 142-284 psi (10-20 kg/cm²) (pressure varies, depending on year and model). Do not tamper with or attempt to open the damper unit or disconnect the reservoir hose from either unit. Do not place it near an open flame or other extreme heat. Do not dispose of the damper assembly yourself. Take it to a dealer where it can be deactivated and disposed of properly. Never attempt to remove the valve core from the base of the reservoir.

7. Onto the lower end of the damper unit, slide on the upper spring seat (flange side toward the spring), the spring and the spring lower seat (flange side toward the spring).
8. Hold the shock absorber upside down and secure the upper mounting portion of the shock absorber in a vise with soft jaws. Be careful not to kink or damage the remote reservoir hose.
9. Screw the adjuster and locknut on by hand until they contact the spring.

10. Use the special Honda tools used during disassembly and tighten the adjuster to the dimension taken prior to disassembly or to the standard spring length indicated in **Table 2**.
11. Hold onto the adjuster and tighten the locknut to the torque specification listed in **Table 1**.
12. Remove the shock absorber from the vise.

Inspection
(All Models)

1. Measure the free length of the spring (**Figure 63**). Replace the spring if it has sagged to the service limit listed in **Table 2** or less.
2. Check the remote reservoir hose for deterioration or damage. If damaged, have it replaced by a dealer.
3. Check the damper unit for dents, oil leakage or other damage. Make sure the damper rod is straight.

NOTE
The damper unit cannot be rebuilt; it can be recharged with gas, the ATF fluid can be replaced or the entire unit can be replaced.

WARNING
The shock absorber damper unit and remote reservoir contain nitrogen gas compressed to between 142-284 psi (10-17 kg/cm²). Pressure varies depending on year and model. Do not tamper with or attempt to open the damper unit or disconnect the reservoir hose from either unit. Do not place it near an open flame or other extreme heat. Do not dispose of the damper assembly yourself. Take it to a dealer where it can be deactivated and disposed of properly. Never attempt to remove the valve core from the base of the reservoir.

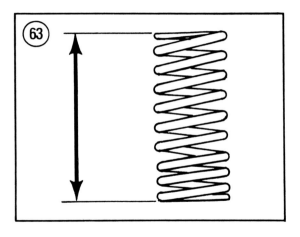

4. On 1985 XR350R models, the upper bearing must be removed and installed with a special tool and hydraulic press. This job should be entrusted to a Honda dealer or machine shop.

5. On models so equipped, on the upper mounting portion of the shock absorber, perform the following:

    a. Remove the dust seal on each side of the upper mounting bushing.

    b. Withdraw the bushings from the upper mounting flange.

    c. Inspect the bushings for wear or damage. Replace if necessary.

    d. Apply a coat of molybdenum disulfide grease to the upper mounting bushing and the inside and outside surfaces of the collar.

    e. Reinstall the bushings and the grease seals.

6. Check the remote reservoir hose for deterioration or damage. If damaged have the hose replaced by a dealer.

7. Check the damper unit for dents, oil leakage or other damage. Make sure the damper rod is straight.

PRO-LINK PIVOT ARM ASSEMBLY (1982-1983 XL250R, 1981-1982 XR250R)

Removal

Refer to **Figure 64** for this procedure.

1. Remove the shock absorber as described in this chapter.

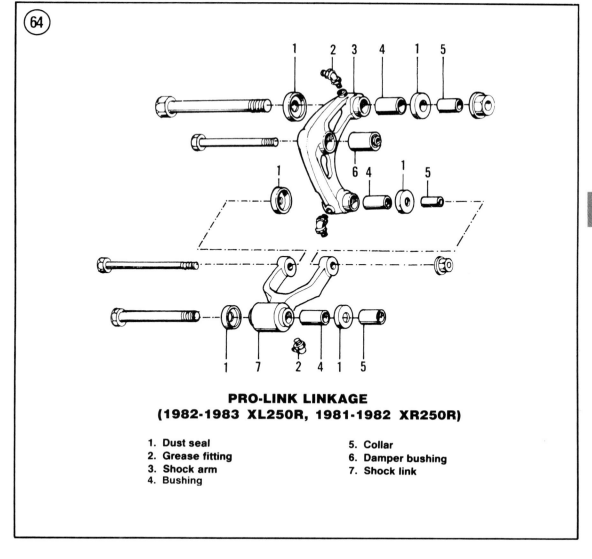

**PRO-LINK LINKAGE
(1982-1983 XL250R, 1981-1982 XR250R)**

1. Dust seal
2. Grease fitting
3. Shock arm
4. Bushing
5. Collar
6. Damper bushing
7. Shock link

10

2. Remove the shock arm pivot bolt (A, **Figure 65**).
3. From the lower portion of the frame, remove the bolt and nut securing the shock link to the frame (B, **Figure 65**).
4. Remove the bolt (**Figure 66**) securing the shock arm to the swing arm.
5. Remove the pivot arm assembly.
6. Inspect all components as described in this chapter.

Installation

1. Install the shock arm onto the swing arm and install the bolt from the right-hand side (**Figure 66**). Tighten the bolt to the torque specification listed in **Table 1**.
2. Install the shock link onto the frame and install the pivot bolt (B, **Figure 65**) in from the right-hand side. Install the nut and tighten the bolt to the torque specification listed in **Table 1**.
3. Make sure the dust seals are installed on the shock link.
4. Move the shock link up into position with the shock arm and install the shock arm pivot bolt (A, **Figure 65**) from the right-hand side.
5. Install the nut and tighten to the torque specification listed in **Table 1**.
6. Install the shock absorber as described in this chapter.

**PRO-LINK PIVOT ARM ASSEMBLY
(1984-1985 XR200R, 1984-ON XR250R)**

Removal

Refer to **Figure 67** for this procedure.
1. Place wood block(s) under the skid plate to hold the bike securely with the rear wheel off the ground.
2. Remove the rear wheel as described in this chapter.
3. Disconnect the rear brake pedal return spring (A, **Figure 68**) from the swing arm.
4. Remove the upper pivot bolt and nut (B, **Figure 68**) securing the shock arm to the swing arm.
5. Remove the lower pivot bolt and nut (C, **Figure 68**) securing the shock arm to the shock link.
6. Remove the self-locking nut (D, **Figure 68**) and withdraw the swing arm pivot bolt from the left-hand side.
7. Pull back on the swing arm, free it from the drive chain and remove the swing arm from the frame.

NOTE
Don't lose the dust seal cap on each side of the pivot points; they will usually fall off when the swing arm is removed.

8. Remove the bolt and nut securing the lower portion of the shock absorber to the shock arm. Remove the shock arm.
9. Remove the pivot bolt and nut (D, **Figure 68**) securing the shock link to the frame.
10. Remove the shock link from the frame.
11. Inspect all components as described in this chapter.

Installation

1. Install the shock link onto the frame and install the pivot bolt (D, **Figure 68**) in from the left-hand side. Install the nut and tighten to the torque specification listed in **Table 1**.
2. Install the shock arm onto the lower portion of the shock absorber and install the bolt from the right-hand side. Install the nut and tighten to the torque specification listed in **Table 1**.
3. Make sure the dust seals are installed on the swing arm.
4. Position the drive chain over the left-hand side of the swing arm.

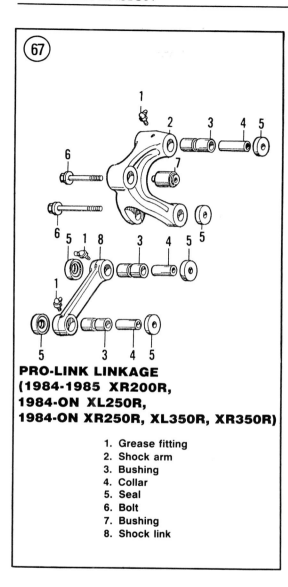

**PRO-LINK LINKAGE
(1984-1985 XR200R,
1984-ON XL250R,
1984-ON XR250R, XL350R, XR350R)**

1. Grease fitting
2. Shock arm
3. Bushing
4. Collar
5. Seal
6. Bolt
7. Bushing
8. Shock link

5. Position the swing arm into the frame mounting area. Align the holes in the swing arm with the holes in the frame. To help align the holes, insert a drift from the right-hand side.

6. Apply a light coat of grease to the pivot bolt.

7. After the holes are aligned, insert the pivot bolt from the left-hand side and install the self-locking nut. Tighten the self-locking nut to the torque specifications listed in **Table 1**.

8. Move the shock arm into position with the swing arm and install the shock arm pivot bolt (B, **Figure 68**) from the left-hand side. Install the nut and tighten to the torque specification listed in **Table 1**.

9. Make sure the dust seals are installed on the shock link.

10. Move the shock link up into position with the shock arm and install the shock arm pivot bolt (C, **Figure 68**) from the left-hand side. Install the nut and tighten to the torque specification listed in **Table 1**.

11. Move the swing arm up and down several times to make sure all components are properly seated.

12. Attach the rear brake pedal return spring (A, **Figure 68**).

13. Install the rear wheel as described in this chapter.

14. Lubricate the linkage as described in Chapter Three.

PRO-LINK PIVOT ARM ASSEMBLY (1984-ON XL250R, XL350R, XR350R)

Removal

Refer to **Figure 67** for this procedure.

1. Remove the shock absorber (A, **Figure 69**) as described in this chapter.

2. Remove the pivot bolt and nut (B, **Figure 69**) securing the shock link to the frame.

10

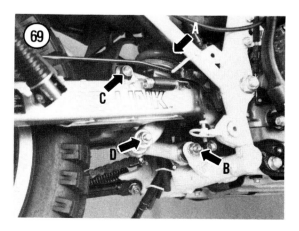

3. Remove the upper pivot bolt and nut (C, **Figure 69**) securing the shock arm to the swing arm.

4. Remove the lower pivot bolt and nut (D, **Figure 69**) securing the shock arm to the shock link.

5. Remove the pivot arm assembly.

6. Inspect all components as described in this chapter.

Installation

1. Install the shock link onto the frame and install the pivot bolt (B, **Figure 69**) in from the left-hand side. Install the nut and tighten to the torque specification listed in **Table 1**.

2. Install the shock arm onto the swing arm and install the bolt from the left-hand side (C, **Figure 69**). Install the nut and tighten to the torque specification listed in **Table 1**.

3. Make sure the dust seals are installed on the shock link.

4. Move the shock link up into position with the shock arm and install the shock arm pivot bolt (D, **Figure 69**) from the left-hand side. Install the nut and tighten to the torque specification listed in **Table 1**.

5. Install the shock absorber as described in this chapter.

6. Lubricate the linkage as described in Chapter Three.

Inspection (All Models)

Refer to **Figure 67** for this procedure.

1. Inspect the shock link and shock arm for cracks or damage; replace as necessary.

2. Remove the dust seals at all pivot points and push out the bushings.

3. Clean all parts in solvent and thoroughly dry with compressed air.

4. Inspect the bushings for scratches, abrasion or abnormal wear; replace as necessary.

5. Inspect the dust seals. Replace all of them as a set if any are worn or starting to deteriorate. If the dust seals are in poor condition they will allow dirt to enter into the pivot areas and cause the bushings to wear.

6. Coat all surfaces of the pivot receptacles, the bushings and the inside of the dust seals with molybdenum disulfide paste grease. Insert the bushings into the shock link and the shock arm and install the dust seals.

NOTE
Make sure the dust seal lips seat correctly. If not, they will allow dirt and moisture into the bushing areas and cause wear.

Table 1 REAR SUSPENSION TORQUE SPECIFICATIONS

Item	ft.-lb.	N•m
Rear axle nut (dual shock models)	70-110	51-80
Rear axle nut (Pro-Link models)		
1981 models	70-110	51-80
1982-1983 modles	80-110	58-80
Rear swng arm pivot bolt nut	70-100	51-72
Driven sprocket bolts	27-33	20-24
Shock absorbers mounting bolts		
and nuts (dual-shock models)		
Upper	8-14	6-10
Lower	30-50	22-36
Shock absorber mounting bolts		
and nuts (Pro-Link models)		
XR200R		
Upper and lower	40-50	29-36
XL250R		
Upper	40-50	29-36
Lower	38-43	28-31
XR250R		
1981-1982		
Upper	90-120	65-87
Lower	62-75	43-54
1984-1985		
Upper and lower	40-50	29-36
1986-on		
Upper	40-50	29-36
Lower	30-40	22-29
XL350R, XR350R		
Upper and lower	40-50	29-36
Pro-Link linkage		
XR200R, 1984-on XL250R,		
1984-1985 CR250R, XL350R, XR350R		
Shock arm to swing arm pivot bolt	90-120	65-87
Shock link to frame pivot bolt	40-50	29-36
Shock arm to shock link pivot bolt	40-50	29-36
Pro-Link linkage		
1981-1982 XL250R, 1981-1982 XR250R		
Shock arm to swing arm pivot bolt	90-120	65-87
Shock link to frame pivot bolt	60-75	43-54
Shock arm to shock link pibot bolt	60-75	43-54
Pro-link linkage		
1986-on XR250R		
Shock arm to swing arm pivot bolt	60-80	43-58
Shock arm to frame pivot bolt	40-50	29-36
Shock arm to shock link pivot bolt	40-50	29-36

10

Table 2 REAR SHOCK SPRING FREE LENGTH

Model	Service Limit	
	mm	in.
XR200R	267.5	10.53
XL250S	320.5	12.61
XR250	339	13.3
XL250R		
1982-1983	219	8.62
1984-on	274.5	10.81
XR250R		
1981-1982	244.0	9.56
1984-on	264.5	10.41
XL350R	280.2	11.03
XR350R		
1983-1984	264.8	10.43
1985	234.5	9.23

Table 3 REAR SHOCK SPRING PRE-LOAD STANDARD DIMENSION

Model	mm	in.
XR200R	199.5	7.85
XL250R	241	9.5
XR250R		
1981-1982	212.6	8.4
1984-1985	199.5	7.85
1986-on	203	8.0
XL350R	272.6	10.73
XR350R		
1983-1984	255.1	10.04
1985	237.5	9.35

NOTE: If you own a 1990 or later model, first check the Supplement at the back of the book for any new service information.

BRAKES

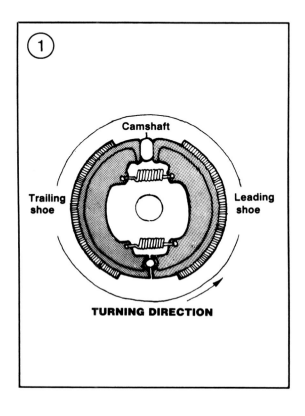

Camshaft

Trailing shoe

Leading shoe

TURNING DIRECTION

The brake system consists of either a drum brake or single disc on the front wheel and a drum brake on the rear.

Table 1 (drum brakes) and **Table 2** (disc brakes) list brake specifications. **Tables 1-3** are located at the end of this chapter.

DRUM BRAKES

The front brake on the 1981-1982 XR250R is a double leading shoe type. All other drum brake models are of the single leading shoe type.

Figure 1 illustrates the major parts of the brake assembly. Activating the brake lever or pedal pulls the lever which in turn rotates the camshaft. This forces the brake shoes out into contact with the brake drum.

Lever and pedal free play must be maintained on both brakes to minimize premature brake wear and maximize braking effectiveness. Refer to Chapter Three for complete adjustment procedures.

Each drum brake is equipped with a wear indicator (**Figure 2**). The indicators should be inspected frequently, especially if riding in competition. When the two arrows align it is time to replace the brake linings.

FRONT DRUM BRAKE

Disassembly

1. Remove the front wheel as described in Chapter Nine.
2. Pull the brake assembly straight up and out of the brake drum.

NOTE
*Prior to removing the brake shoes from the backing plate, measure them as described under **Inspection** in this chapter.*

3A. On double leading shoe models, remove the cotter pins and flat washers on both brake camshafts.
3B. On single leading shoe models, remove the cotter pin and flat washer from the brake backing plate (**Figure 3**).
4. Place a clean shop cloth on the brake linings to protect them from oil and grease during removal.
5. Remove the brake shoes from the backing plate. Pull up on the center of each shoe as shown in **Figure 4**.
6. Remove the return springs and separate the brake shoes.
7. Mark the position of the brake arm to the camshaft so it will be installed in the same position.
8. Loosen the clamp bolt on the brake lever.
9. Remove the brake arm, wear indicator, return spring and dust seal.
10. Withdraw the camshaft from the backing plate.

Inspection

1. Thoroughly clean and dry all parts except the brake linings.
2. Check the contact surface of the drum (**Figure 5**) for scoring. If there are grooves deep enough to snag your fingernail, the drum should be turned and new brake shoes fitted. This type of wear can be avoided to a great extent if the brakes are disassembled and thoroughly cleaned after riding in water, mud or deep sand.
3. Clean any oil or grease residue from the brake drum with a clean rag soaked in lacquer thinner. Do not use a solvent that will leave an oil residue.
4. Measure the inside diameter of the brake drum with vernier calipers (**Figure 6**). If the measurement is greater than the service limit listed in **Table 1**, the brake drum must be replaced.
5. If the drum can be turned and still stay within the maximum service limit diameter, the linings

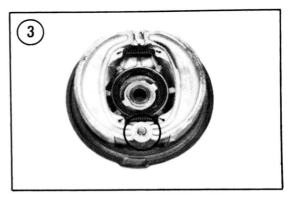

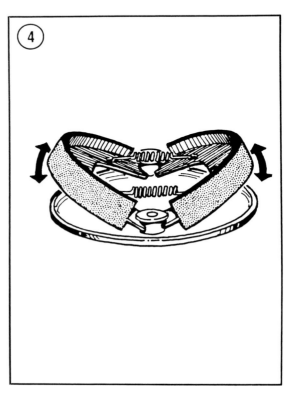

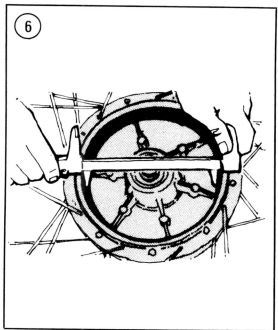

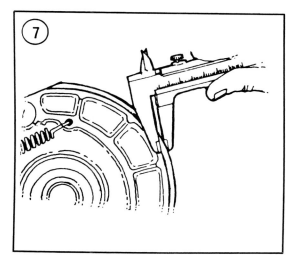

will have to be replaced and the new ones arced to conform to the new drum contour.

6. Inspect the linings for embedded foreign material. Dirt can be removed with a stiff wire brush. Check for any traces of oil or grease; if they are contaminated, they must be replaced.

7. Measure the brake linings with a vernier caliper (**Figure 7**). They should be replaced if the lining portion is worn to the service limit dimension or smaller. Refer to specifications listed in **Table 1**.

8. Inspect the cam lobe(s) and pivot pin area of the backing plate for wear or corrosion. Minor roughness can be removed with fine emery cloth.

9. Inspect the bearing surface for the camshaft(s) in the backing plate. If it is worn or damaged, the backing plate must be replaced. The camshaft(s) should also be replaced at the same time.

10. Inspect the brake shoe return springs for wear. If they are stretched, they will not fully retract the brake shoes. Replace as necessary.

Assembly

1. Grease the camshaft(s) with a light coat of molybdenum disulfide grease.

2. Install the camshaft(s) into the backing plate from the backside.

3. From the outside of the backing plate, install the return spring onto the camshaft.

4. Align the wear indicator to the camshaft as shown in **Figure 8**. Push it onto the camshaft and down all the way to the backing plate.

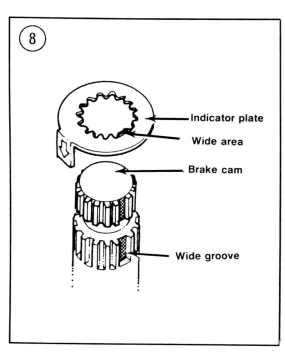

Indicator plate

Wide area

Brake cam

Wide groove

11

5. When installing the brake arm(s) onto the camshaft(s), be sure to align the marks on the two parts with the punch marks (**Figure 9**). Tighten the bolt and nut securely.

6. Grease the camshaft(s) and pivot post with a light coat of molybdenum disulfide grease; avoid getting any grease on the brake backing plate where the brake linings may come in contact with it.

NOTE
If new linings are being installed, file off the leading edge of each shoe a little so that the brake will not grab when applied (Figure 10).

7. Hold the brake shoes in a "V" formation with the return springs attached and snap them into place on the brake backing plate. Make sure they are firmly seated on it.

8A. On double leading shoe models, install the flat washers and the cotter pins. Bend the ends over completely.

8B. On single leading shoe models, install the flat washer and the cotter pin. Bend the ends over completely.

9. Install the brake panel assembly into the brake drum.

10. Install the front wheel as described in Chapter Nine.

11. Adjust the front brake as described in Chapter Three.

**Brake Arm, Brake Cam and Connecting
Rod Replacement
(1981-1982 XR250R)**

Refer to **Figure 11** for this procedure.

1. Remove the brake assembly and remove the brake shoes as described in this chapter.

2. Remove the bolts and nuts securing brake arm "A" and "B" to each brake camshaft.

3. Loosen both locknuts on the connecting rod.

4. Remove both brake arms and the connecting rod.

5. Unscrew the brake arms from the connecting rod.

6. Assemble by reversing these disassembly steps, noting the following.

7. Align the punch mark on the brake cams and the brake arms and tighten the bolts and nuts to the torque specification listed in **Table 3**.

NOTE
After the brake arms and connecting rod have been removed or replaced they have to be adjusted as follows.

8. Loosen both connecting rod locknuts.

9. Place a clean shop cloth on the brake shoes. With your hands, push both brake shoes together until they are tight against both brake camshafts with no free play.

10. Turn the connecting rod as indicated by direction "C" until there is free play between the connecting rod and the brake arm.

11. Now turn the connecting rod as indicated by direction "D" to just the point where the free play decreases (not any further).

12. Tighten the locknuts securely and recheck the free play. Readjust if necessary.

13. Remove the shop cloth and make sure that both brake cams are parallel to each other. If not, repeat this procedure until correct.

14. Move the brake lever and make sure that both brake arm "A" and "B" start to move at the same time.

FRONT DISC BRAKE

The front disc brake is actuated by hydraulic fluid and is controlled by a hand lever on the master cylinder. As the brake pads wear, the brake fluid level drops in the reservoir and automatically adjusts for wear.

When working on hydraulic brake systems, it is necessary that the work area and all tools be absolutely clean. Any tiny particles of foreign matter and grit in the caliper assembly or the master cylinder can damage the components. Also, sharp tools must not be used inside the caliper or on the piston. If there is any doubt about your ability to correctly and safely carry out major service on the brake components, take the job to a dealer or brake specialist.

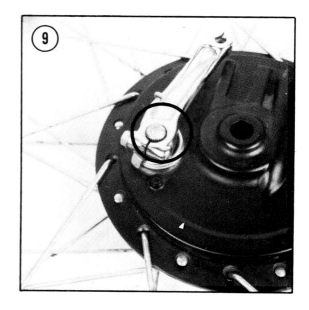

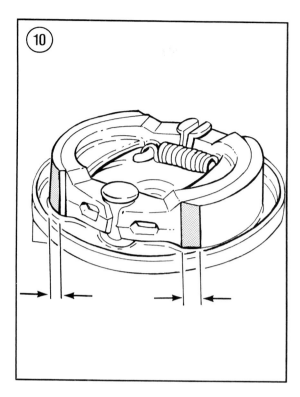

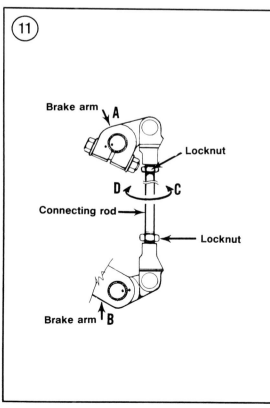

FRONT BRAKE PAD REPLACEMENT

There is no recommended mileage interval for changing the friction pads in the disc brake. Pad wear depends greatly on riding habits and conditions. The pads should be checked for wear every 6 months and replaced when the wear indicator reaches the edge of the brake disc. To maintain an even brake pressure on the disc, always replace both pads in the caliper at the same time.

CAUTION
Check the pads more frequently when the wear line approaches the disc. On some pads the wear line is very close to the metal backing plate. If pad wear happens to be uneven for some reason, the backing plate may come in contact with the disc and cause damage.

Refer to **Figure 12** for this procedure.
1. Unscrew the threaded plugs (**Figure 13**) covering the pad pins.
2. Loosen both pad pins (A, **Figure 14**) but do not remove them at this time.
3. Remove the bolts (B, **Figure 14**) securing the brake caliper assembly to the front fork.
4. Carefully slide the caliper assembly off the brake disc and remove the caliper assembly.
5. Remove both pad pins.
6. Remove both brake pads and the shim.
7. Clean the pad recess and the end of the pistons with a soft brush. Do not use solvent, a wire brush or any hard tool which would damage the cylinders or pistons.
8. Carefully remove any rust or corrosion from the disc.
9. Lightly coat the ends of the pistons and the backs of the new pads (*not* the friction material) with disc brake lubricant.

NOTE
When purchasing new pads, check with your dealer to make sure the friction compound of the new pad is compatible with the disc material. Remove any roughness from the backs of the new pads with a fine-cut file; blow them clean with compressed air.

10. When new pads are installed in the caliper, the master cylinder brake fluid level will rise as the caliper pistons are repositioned. Perform the following:
   a. Clean the top of the master cylinder of all dirt and foreign matter.
   b. Remove the screws securing the cover. Remove the cover, plate (models so equipped)

11

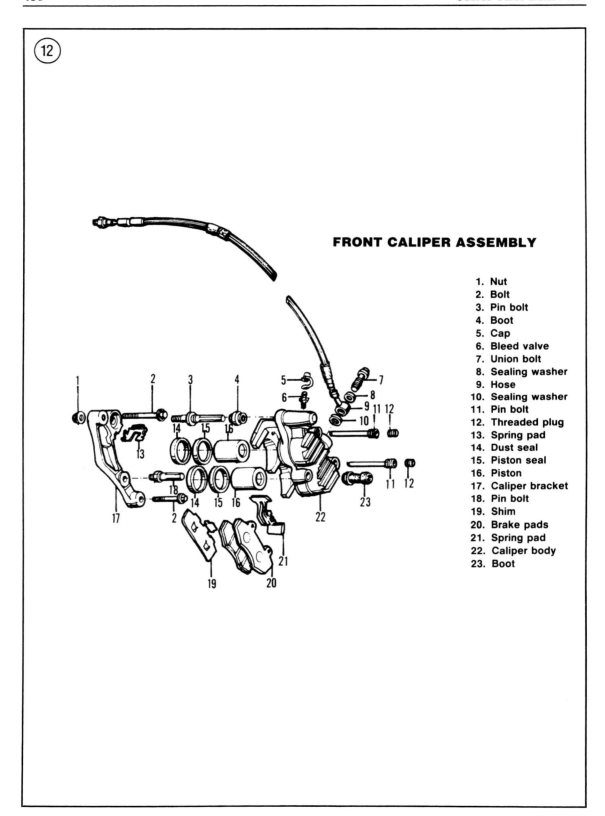

FRONT CALIPER ASSEMBLY

1. Nut
2. Bolt
3. Pin bolt
4. Boot
5. Cap
6. Bleed valve
7. Union bolt
8. Sealing washer
9. Hose
10. Sealing washer
11. Pin bolt
12. Threaded plug
13. Spring pad
14. Dust seal
15. Piston seal
16. Piston
17. Caliper bracket
18. Pin bolt
19. Shim
20. Brake pads
21. Spring pad
22. Caliper body
23. Boot

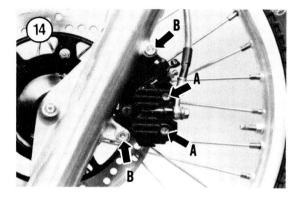

and the diaphragm from the master cylinder and slowly push the caliper pistons into the caliper. Constantly check the reservoir to make sure brake fluid does not overflow. Remove fluid, if necessary, prior to it overflowing.

   c. The pistons should move freely. If they don't, and there is evidence of them sticking in the cylinder, the caliper should be removed and serviced as described in this chapter.

11. Push the caliper pistons in all the way to allow room for the new pads.

12. Install the anti-rattle spring as shown in A, **Figure 15**.

13. Install the shim into the caliper (B, **Figure 15**).

14. Install the outboard pad (**Figure 16**).

15. Install the inboard pad (**Figure 17**).

16. Push both pads against the anti-rattle spring, then insert one of the pin bolts (**Figure 18**).

17. Install the other pad pin bolt (**Figure 19**).

18. Tighten the pad pin bolts only finger-tight at this time.

19. Carefully install the caliper assembly onto the disc, being careful not to damage the leading edge of the brake pads.

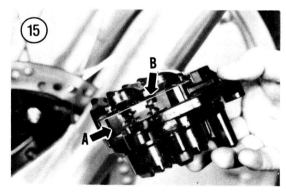

11

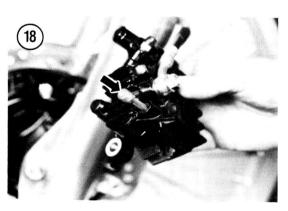

20. Install the bolts securing the brake caliper assembly to the front fork and tighten to the torque specification listed in **Table 3**.

21. Tighten the pad pin bolts to the torque specification listed in **Table 3**.

22. Install the threaded plugs and tighten securely.

23. Place wooden block(s) under the skid plate so that the front wheel is off the ground. Spin the front wheel and activate the brake lever as many times as it takes to refill the cylinder in the caliper and correctly locate the pads.

> *WARNING*
> *Use brake fluid clearly marked DOT 3 or DOT 4 from a sealed container. Other types may vaporize and cause brake failure. Always use the same brand name; do not intermix as many brands are not compatible. Do not intermix silicone based (DOT 5) brake fluid as it can cause brake component damage leading to brake system failure.*

24. Refill the master cylinder reservoir, if necessary, to maintain the correct fluid level as seen through the viewing port on the side. Install the diaphragm, plate (models so equipped) and cover. Tighten the screws securely.

> *WARNING*
> *Do not ride the motorcycle until you are sure the brakes are operating correctly with full hydraulic advantage. If necessary, bleed the brake as described in this chapter.*

25. Bed the pads in gradually for the first 10 days of riding by using only light pressure as much as possible. Immediate hard application will glaze the new friction pads and greatly reduce the effectiveness of the brake.

FRONT MASTER CYLINDER

Removal/Installation

1. On XL350R models, remove the rear-view mirror from the master cylinder.

> *CAUTION*
> *Cover the fuel tank, front fender and speedometer or instrument cluster with a heavy cloth or plastic tarp to protect them from accidental brake fluid spills. Wash brake fluid off any painted or plated surfaces or plastic parts immediately, as it will destroy the finish. Use soapy water and rinse completely.*

2. On XL350R models, pull back the rubber boot on the hand lever.

3A. On XL350R models, remove the bolt (**Figure 20**) and nut securing the hand lever and remove the hand lever.

3B. On all other models, remove the bolt and nut securing the hand lever and remove the knuckle protector and hand lever.

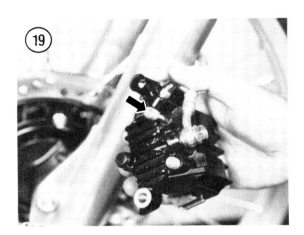

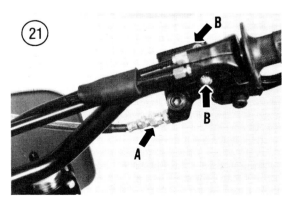

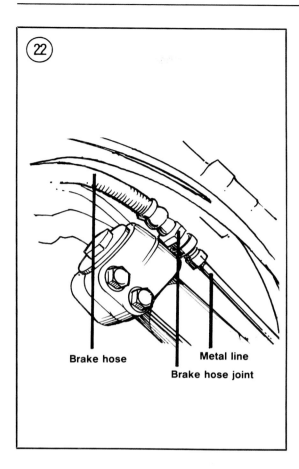

Brake hose **Metal line**
Brake hose joint

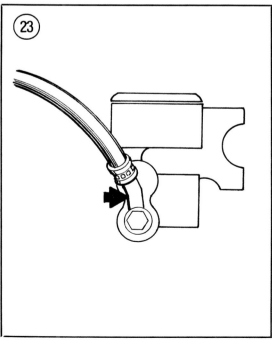

4A. On 1984-on XR200R, 1984-1985 XR250R and 1984 XR350R models, perform the following:

   a. Unscrew the fitting (A, **Figure 21**) securing the brake hose to the master cylinder.
   b. Remove the brake hose and tie it up, then cover the end to prevent the entry of foreign matter.

4B. On XL350R models, unscrew the fitting securing the brake hose to the metal brake line at the top of the upper fork bridge (**Figure 22**).

4C. On 1986-on XR250R and 1985 XR350R models, unscrew the union bolt and sealing washers securing the brake hose to the master cylinder. Remove the brake hose. Tie the brake hose up and cover the end to prevent the entry of foreign matter.

5. On XL350R models, disconnect the front brake light switch wires.

6. Remove the clamping bolts (B, **Figure 21**) and clamp securing the master cylinder to the handlebar and remove the master cylinder.

7. Install by reversing these removal steps, noting the following.

8. Install the clamp with the "UP" arrow facing up. Align the face of the clamp with the punch mark on the handlebar. Tighten the upper bolt first, then the lower to the torque specification listed in **Table 3**.

9A. On 1984-on XR200R, 1984-1985 XR250R and 1984 XR350R models, screw the brake hose fitting (A, **Figure 21**) onto the master cylinder. Tighten the fitting to the torque specifications listed in **Table 3**.

9B. On XL350R models, screw the brake hose onto the metal brake line at the top of the upper fork bridge (**Figure 22**). Tighten to the torque specification listed in **Table 3**.

9C. On 1986-on XR250R and 1985 XR350R models, perform the following:

   a. Place a sealing washer on each side of the brake hose fitting and install the union bolt.
   b. Position the brake hose as shown in **Figure 23** and tighten the union bolt to the torque specification listed in **Table 3**.

10. Bleed the brake as described in this chapter.

Disassembly

   Refer to the following illustrations for this procedure:

11

(24)

FRONT MASTER CYLINDER (1984-1985 XR200R, 1984-1985 XR250R, 1984 XR350R)

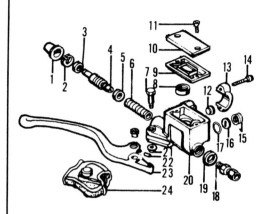

1. Rubber boot	13. Clamp
2. Circlip	14. Bolt
3. Secondary cup	15. Viewing port
4. Piston	16. Window
5. Primary cup	17. O-ring
6. Spring	18. Fitting
7. Bolt	19. Sealing washer
8. Separator	20. Body
9. Diaphagm	21. Nut
10. Cover	22. Pin
11. Screw	23. Hand lever
12. Plug	24. Rubber boot

(25)

FRONT MASTER CYLINDER (XL350R)

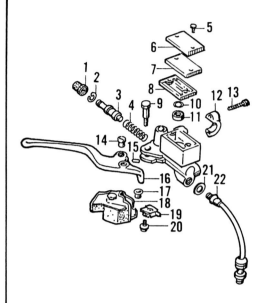

1. Rubber boot
2. Circlip
3. Piston
4. Spring
5. Screw
6. Cover
7. Diaphragm plate
8. Diaphragm
9. Bolt
10. O-ring
11. Separator
12. Clamp
13. Bolt
14. Screw
15. Pin
16. Hand lever
17. Nut
18. Rubber boot
19. Brake light switch
20. Screw
21. Sealing washer
22. Brake hose

(26)

FRONT MASTER CYLINDER
(1986-ON XR250R, 1985 XR350R)

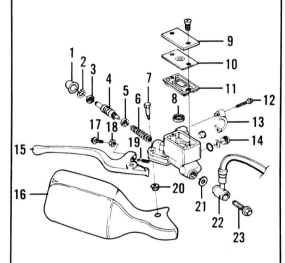

1. **Rubber boot**
2. **Circlip**
3. **Secondary cup**
4. **Piston**
5. **Primary cup**
6. **Spring**
7. **Bolt**
8. **Separator**
9. **Cover**
10. **Plate**
11. **Diaphragm**
12. **Screw**
13. **Clamp**
14. **Viewing port assembly**
15. **Hand lever**
16. **Knuckle protector**
17. **Adjuster screw**
18. **Locknut**
19. **Steel ball and spring**
20. **Nut**
21. **Sealing washer**
22. **Brake line**
23. **Union bolt**

a. **Figure 24**: 1984-1985 XR200R, 1984-1985 XR250R and 1984 XR350R.

b. **Figure 25**: XL350R.

c. **Figure 26**: 1986-on XR250R and 1985 XR350R.

1. Remove the master cylinder as described in this chapter.

2. On XL350R models, unscrew the brake hose and sealing washer from the master cylinder.

3. Remove the screws securing the cover and remove the cover, diaphragm plate (models so equipped) and diaphragm.

4. Pour out the brake fluid and discard it. *Never reuse brake fluid.*

5. Remove the rubber boot from the area where the hand lever actuates the internal piston.

6. Using circlip pliers, remove the internal circlip from the body (**Figure 27**).

(27)

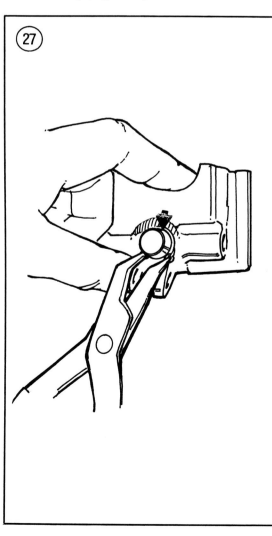

11

7. Remove the piston assembly and the spring (**Figure 28**).

8. On models so equipped, remove the brake light switch if necessary.

Inspection

1. Clean all parts in denatured alcohol or fresh brake fluid. Inspect the cylinder bore and piston contact surfaces for signs of wear and damage. If either part is less than perfect, replace it.

2. Check the end of the piston for wear caused by the hand lever. Replace if worn.

3. Replace the piston assembly if either the primary or secondary cup requires replacement.

4. Inspect the pivot hole in the hand lever. If worn or elongated it must be replaced.

5. Make sure the passages in the bottom of the brake fluid reservoir are clear. Check the reservoir cap and diaphragm for damage and deterioration and replace as necessary.

6. Inspect the threads in the bore for the brake line.

7. Check the hand lever pivot lugs on the master cylinder body for cracks.

8. Measure the cylinder bore (**Figure 29**). Replace the master cylinder if the bore exceeds the specifications given in **Table 2**.

9. Measure the outside diameter of the piston as shown in **Figure 30** with a micrometer. Replace the piston assembly if it is less than the specifications given in **Table 2**.

Assembly

1. Soak the new cups in fresh brake fluid for at least 15 minutes to make them pliable. Coat the inside of the cylinder with fresh brake fluid prior to the assembly of parts.

> *CAUTION*
> *When installing the piston assembly, do not allow the cups to turn inside out as they will be damaged and allow brake fluid leakage within the cylinder bore.*

2. Install the spring and piston assembly into the cylinder together. Install the spring with the tapered end facing toward the secondary cup on the piston.

3. Install the circlip and slide in the rubber boot.

4. Install the diaphragm, diaphragm plate (models so equipped) and cover. Do not tighten the cover screws at this time as fluid will have to be added later when the system is bled.

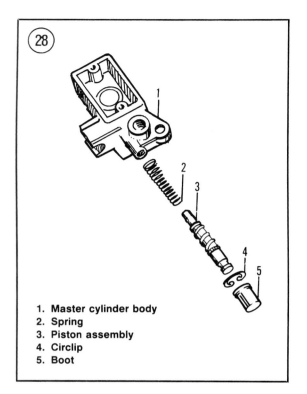

1. **Master cylinder body**
2. **Spring**
3. **Piston assembly**
4. **Circlip**
5. **Boot**

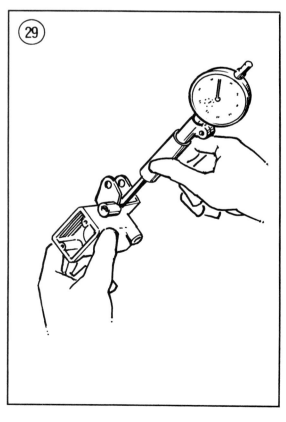

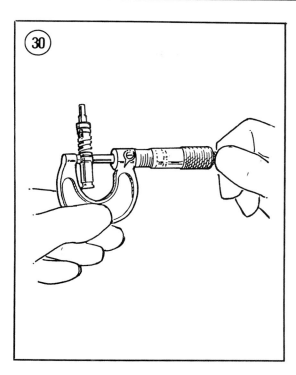

5. On XL350R models, perform the following:
   a. Install a sealing washer onto the brake hose and screw the brake hose onto the master cylinder body.
   b. Tighten the hose to the torque specification listed in **Table 3**.
6. If removed, install the brake light switch.
7. Install the master cylinder as described in this chapter.

FRONT CALIPER

Removal/Installation

Refer to **Figure 31** for this procedure.

It is not necessary to remove the front wheel in order to remove the caliper assembly.

> *CAUTION*
> *Do not spill any brake fluid on the front fork or front wheel. Wash off any spilled brake fluid immediately, as it will destroy the finish. Use soapy water and rinse completely.*

1. On XL350R models, remove the flexible brake line from the clamp on the left-hand fork slider. It

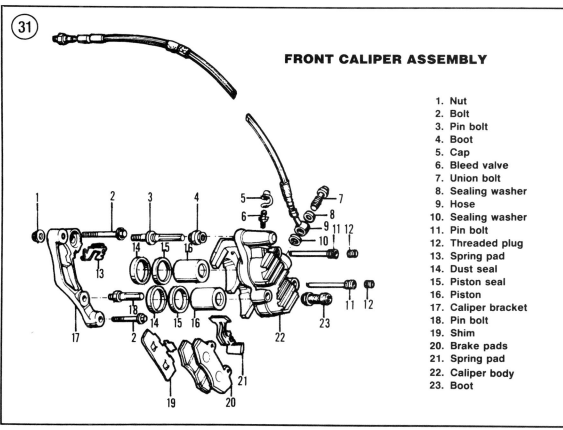

FRONT CALIPER ASSEMBLY

1. Nut
2. Bolt
3. Pin bolt
4. Boot
5. Cap
6. Bleed valve
7. Union bolt
8. Sealing washer
9. Hose
10. Sealing washer
11. Pin bolt
12. Threaded plug
13. Spring pad
14. Dust seal
15. Piston seal
16. Piston
17. Caliper bracket
18. Pin bolt
19. Shim
20. Brake pads
21. Spring pad
22. Caliper body
23. Boot

11

is not necessary to disconnect the metal brake line from the flexible brake line at this connection.

2. Clean the top of the master cylinder of all dirt and foreign matter.

3. Loose the screws securing the master cylinder cover. Pull up and loosen the cover, plate (models so equipped) and the diaphragm. This will allow air to enter the reservoir and allow the brake fluid to drain out more quickly in the next step.

4. Place a container under the brake line at the caliper. Remove the union bolt and sealing washers (A, **Figure 32**) securing the brake hose or metal brake line to the caliper assembly.

5. Remove the brake line and let the brake fluid drain out into the container. Dispose of this brake fluid—never reuse brake fluid. To prevent the entry of moisture and dirt, cap the end of the brake line and tie the loose end up to the forks.

6. Loosen the bolts (B, **Figure 32**) securing the brake caliper assembly to the front fork. Push in on the caliper while loosening the bolts to push the pistons back into the caliper bores.

7. Remove the bolts securing the brake caliper assembly to the front fork.

8. Remove the caliper assembly from the brake disc.

9. Install by reversing these removal steps, noting the following.

10. Carefully install the caliper assembly onto the disc, being careful not to damage the leading edges of the brake pads.

11. Install the bolts securing the brake caliper assembly to the front fork and tighten to the torque specifications listed in **Table 3**.

12. If the caliper bracket was removed from the caliper, lubricate the caliper pin bolts and pin bushing on the caliper bracket with silicone grease.

13. Install the brake hose or brake lines with a sealing washer on each side of the fitting, onto the caliper. Install the union bolt and tighten to the torque specifications listed in **Table 3**.

14. Remove the master cylinder top cover, plate (models so equipped) and diaphragm.

> *WARNING*
> *Use brake fluid clearly marked DOT 3 or DOT 4 from a sealed container. Other types may vaporize and cause brake failure. Always use the same brand name; do not intermix as many brands are not compatible. Do not intermix silicone-based (DOT 5) brake fluid as it can cause brake component damage leading to brake system failure.*

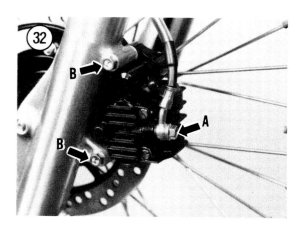

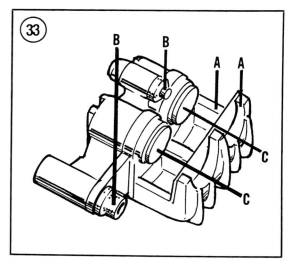

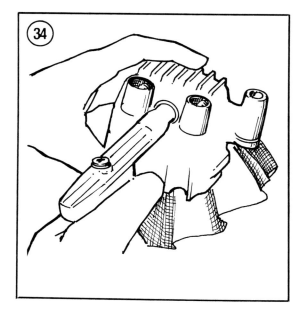

15. Place wooden block(s) under the skid plate to support the bike securely with the front wheel off the ground.

16. Spin the front wheel several times and activate the front brake lever as many times as it takes to refill the cylinders in the caliper and correctly locate the pads.

17. Refill the master cylinder reservoir. Install the diaphragm, plate (models so equipped) and cover. Do not tighten the screws at this time.

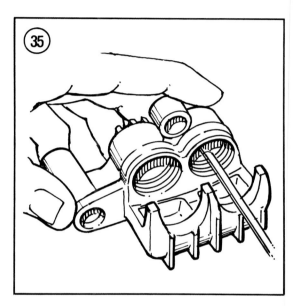

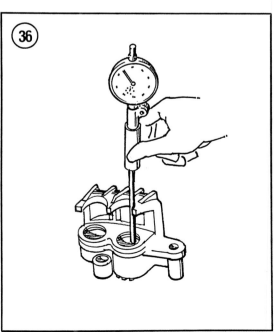

18. Bleed the brake as described in this chapter.

> *WARNING*
> *Do not ride the motorcycle until you are sure that the brakes are operating properly.*

Caliper Rebuilding

1. Remove the caliper and brake pads as described in this chapter.

2. If not already removed, remove the shim and pad spring (A, **Figure 33**).

3. Remove the caliper pivot boots (B, **Figure 33**).

4. Place a shop cloth or piece of soft wood in the area normally occupied by the brake pads.

5. Place the caliper assembly on the workbench with the pistons (C, **Figure 33**) facing down.

> *WARNING*
> *In the next step, the pistons may shoot out of the caliper body like bullets. Keep your fingers out of the way. Wear shop gloves and apply air pressure gradually. Do **not** use high pressure air or place the air hose nozzle directly against the hydraulic line fitting inlet in the caliper body. Hold the air nozzle away from the inlet, allowing some of the air to escape.*

6. Apply the air pressure in short spurts to the hydraulic line fitting inlet (**Figure 34**) and force both pistons out. Use a service station air hose if you don't have a compressor.

> *CAUTION*
> *In the following step, do not use a sharp tool to remove the dust and piston seals from the caliper cylinders. Do not damage the cylinder surface.*

7. Use a piece of plastic or wood and carefully push the dust and piston seals in toward the caliper cylinder and out of their grooves (**Figure 35**). Remove the dust and piston seals from both cylinders and discard all seals.

8. Inspect the caliper body for damage. Replace the caliper body if necessary.

9. Inspect the cylinders and the pistons for scratches, scoring or other damage. Light dirt and rust may be removed with fine emery paper. If rust is severe, replace the caliper body. Replace the caliper body if necessary.

10. If serviceable, clean the caliper body with rubbing alcohol and rinse with clean brake fluid.

11. Measure the inside diameter of both caliper cylinders (**Figure 36**) with an inside micrometer. If worn to the service limit dimension listed in **Table 2**, or greater, replace the caliper assembly.

11

12. Measure the outside diameter of the pistons (**Figure 37**) with a micrometer. If worn to the service limit dimension listed in **Table 2**, or less, replace the pistons.

> *NOTE*
> *Never reuse the old dust seals and piston seals. Very minor damage or age deterioration can make the seals useless.*

13. Coat the new dust seals and piston seals with fresh DOT 3 or DOT 4 brake fluid.
14. Carefully install the new dust seals and pistons seals in the grooves in each caliper cylinder. Make sure the seals are properly seated in their respective grooves.
15. Coat the pistons and caliper cylinders with fresh DOT 3 or DOT 4 brake fluid.
16. Position the pistons with the insulated ends or dished ends toward the brake pads and install the pistons into the caliper cylinders. Push the pistons in until they bottom out.
17. Inspect the caliper pin boots. Replace if damaged or starting to deteriorate.
18. Apply silicone grease to the caliper pivot boots and install the boots into the caliper body. Make sure the boots are properly seated in the caliper body grooves.
19. Install the brake pad shim and spring.
20. Install the brake pads and the caliper as described in this chapter.

FRONT BRAKE HOSE REPLACEMENT

There is no factory-recommended replacement interval but it is a good idea to replace all brake hoses every four years or when they show signs of cracking or damage.

The XL350R has a combination of 2 flexible brake hoses and 2 metal brake lines (**Figure 38**). On all other models there is only one flexible brake hose that runs from the master cylinder to the caliper assembly.

> *CAUTION*
> *Cover the front wheel, fender and fuel tank with a heavy cloth or plastic tarp to protect it from accidental spilling of brake fluid. Wash off any brake fluid from any painted or plated surface or plastic parts immediately, as it will destroy the finish. Use soapy water and rinse completely.*

1A. On XL350R models, remove the flexible brake line from the clamp on the left-hand fork slider. It is not necessary to disconnect the metal brake line from the flexible brake line at this time.

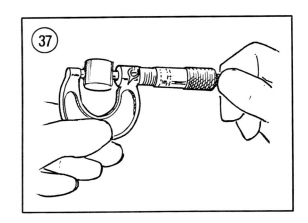

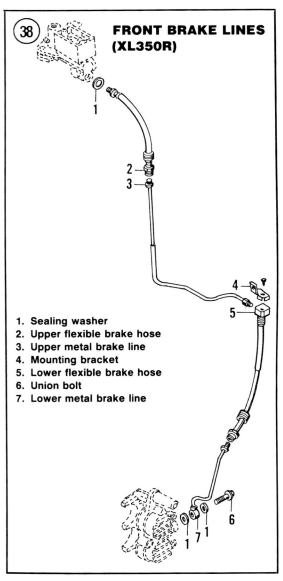

FRONT BRAKE LINES (XL350R)

1. **Sealing washer**
2. **Upper flexible brake hose**
3. **Upper metal brake line**
4. **Mounting bracket**
5. **Lower flexible brake hose**
6. **Union bolt**
7. **Lower metal brake line**

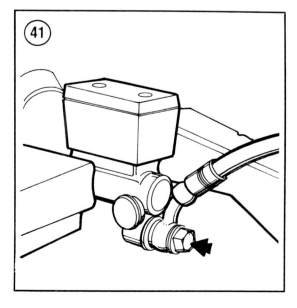

1B. On all other models, remove brake hose from the clip on the fender stay (**Figure 39**).

2. Clean the top of the master cylinder of all dirt and foreign matter.

3. Loosen the screws securing the master cylinder cover. Pull up and loosen the cover, plate (models so equipped) and the diaphragm. This will allow air to enter the reservoir and allow the brake fluid to drain out more quickly in the next step.

4. Place a container under the brake line at the caliper. Remove the union bolt and sealing washers (A, **Figure 32**) securing the brake hose or metal brake line to the caliper assembly.

5. Remove the brake hose or line and let the brake fluid drain out into the container. Dispose of this brake fluid—never reuse brake fluid. To prevent the entry of moisture and dirt, cap the end of the brake line and tie the loose end up to the forks.

> *WARNING*
> *Dispose of this brake fluid—never reuse brake fluid. Contaminated brake fluid can cause brake failure.*

6A. On 1984-on XR200R, 1984-1985 XR250R and 1984 XR350R models, perform the following:
  a. Unscrew the fitting (**Figure 40**) securing the brake hose to the master cylinder.
  b. Remove the brake hose and tie it up, then cover the end to prevent the entry of foreign matter.

6B. On XL350R models, unscrew the fitting securing the brake hose to the metal brake line at the top of the upper fork bridge (**Figure 38**).

6C. On 1986-on XR250R and 1985 XR350R models, unscrew the union bolt (**Figure 41**) and sealing washers securing the brake hose to the master cylinder. Remove the brake hose. Tie the brake hose up and cover the end to prevent the entry of foreign matter.

7. On XL350R models, to replace the upper brake hose, unscrew the hose from the master cylinder. Remove the brake hose and sealing washer.

8. On XL350R models, to replace the lower brake hose, perform the following:
  a. Unscrew the mounting bracket securing the upper portion of the lower hose at the lower fork bridge.
  b. Unscrew the lower hose from the metal brake line.
  c. Unscrew the lower hose from the lower metal brake line and remove the brake hose.

9. Install a new hose, sealing washers and union bolts in the reverse order of removal. Be sure to install new sealing washers in the correct positions.

11

10. Tighten the fittings and union bolts to the torque specifications listed in **Table 3**.

11. Refill the master cylinder reservoir, if necessary, to maintain the correct fluid level as seen through the viewing port on the side. Install the diaphragm, diaphragm plate (models so equipped) and cover. Tighten the screws securely.

> *WARNING*
> *Use brake fluid clearly marked DOT 3 or DOT 4 from a sealed container. Other types may vaporize and cause brake failure. Always use the same brand name; do not intermix as many brands are not compatible. Do not intermix silicone-based (DOT 5) brake fluid as it can cause brake component damage leading to brake system failure.*

> *WARNING*
> *Do not ride the motorcycle until you are sure that the brakes are operating properly.*

12. Bleed the brake as described in this chapter.

FRONT BRAKE DISC

Removal/Installation

1. Remove the front wheel as described in Chapter Nine.

> *NOTE*
> *Place a piece of wood or vinyl tube in the caliper in place of the disc. This way, if the brake lever is inadvertently squeezed the pistons will not be forced out of the cylinders. If this does happen, the caliper might have to be disassembled to reseat the pistons and the system will have to be bled. By using the wood or vinyl tube, bleeding the system is not necessary when installing the wheel.*

> *CAUTION*
> *Do not set the wheel down on the disc surface, as it may get scratched or warped. Set the wheel on 2 blocks of wood.*

2. Remove the nuts or bolts (**Figure 42**) securing the brake disc to the hub and remove the disc.

3. Install by reversing these removal steps, noting the following.

4. Tighten the disc mounting nuts or bolts to the torque specifications listed in **Table 3**.

Inspection

It is not necessary to remove the disc from the wheel to inspect it. Small marks on the disc are not important, but scratches deep enough to snag a fingernail reduce braking effectiveness and increase brake pad wear. If these grooves are found, the disc should be replaced.

1. Measure the thickness of the disc at several locations around the disc with a micrometer or vernier caliper (**Figure 43**). The disc must be replaced if the thickness in any area is less than that specified in **Table 2**.

2. Make sure the disc mounting nuts or bolts are tight prior to running this check. Check the disc runout with a dial indicator as shown in **Figure 44**.

3. Slowly rotate the wheel and watch the dial indicator. If the runout exceeds that listed in **Table 2** the disc must be replaced.

4. Clean the disc of any rust or corrosion and wipe clean with lacquer thinner. Never use a petroleum-based solvent that may leave a residue on the disc.

BLEEDING THE SYSTEM

This procedure is not necessary unless the brakes feel spongy, there has been a leak in the system, a component has been replaced or the brake fluid has been replaced.

Brake Bleeder Process

This procedure uses a brake bleeder that is available from motorcycle or automotive supply stores or from mail order outlets.

1. Remove the dust cap from the bleed valve on the caliper assembly. Refer to the following:
2. Connect the brake bleeder to the bleed valve on the caliper assembly.

CAUTION
Cover the front fender and front wheel with a heavy cloth or plastic tarp to protect it from the accidental spilling of brake fluid. Wash any brake fluid off of any plastic, painted or plated surface immediately, as it will destroy the finish. Use soapy water and rinse completely.

3. Clean the top of the master cylinder of all dirt and foreign matter.
4. Remove the screws securing the reservoir cover and remove the reservoir cover, plate (models so equipped) and diaphragm.
5. Fill the reservoir almost to the top lip; insert the diaphragm, plate (models so equipped) and the cover loosely. Leave the cover in place during this procedure to prevent the entry of dirt.

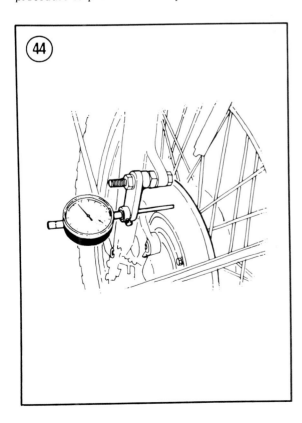

WARNING
Use brake fluid from a sealed container marked DOT 3 or DOT 4 only (specified for disc brakes). Other types may vaporize and cause brake failure. Do not intermix different brands or types as they may not be compatible. Do not intermix a silicone-based (DOT 5) brake fluid as it can cause brake component damage leading to brake system failure.

6. Open the bleed valve about one-half turn and pump the brake bleeder.

NOTE
If air is entering the brake bleeder hose from around the bleed valve, apply several layers of Teflon tape to the bleed valve. This should make a good seal between the bleed valve and the brake bleeder hose.

7. As the fluid enters the system and exits into the brake bleeder the level will drop in the reservoir. Maintain the level at about 3/8 inch from the top of the reservoir to prevent air from being drawn into the system.
8. Continue to pump the lever on the brake bleeder until the fluid emerging from the hose is completely free of bubbles. At this point, tighten the bleed valve.

NOTE
Do not allow the reservoir to empty during the bleeding operation or more air will enter the system. If this occurs, the entire procedure must be repeated.

9. When the brake fluid is free of bubbles, tighten the bleed valve, remove the brake bleeder tube and install the bleed valve dust cap.
10. If necessary, add fluid to correct the level in the reservoir. It should be to the upper level line.
11. Install the diaphragm, plate (models so equipped) and the reservoir cover. Tighten the screws securely.
12. Test the feel of the brake lever or pedal. It should be firm and should offer the same resistance each time it's operated. If it feels spongy, it is likely that there is still air in the system and it must be bled again. When all air has been bled from the system and the fluid level is correct in the reservoir, double-check for leaks and tighten all fittings and connections.

WARNING
Before riding the bike, make certain that the brake is operating correctly by operating the lever several times.

11

13. Test ride the bike slowly at first to make sure that the brakes are operating properly.

Without a Brake Bleeder

1. Remove the dust cap from the bleed valve on the caliper assembly.
2. Connect the bleed hose to the bleed valve on the caliper assembly (**Figure 45**).
3. Place the other end of the tube into a clean container. Fill the container with enough fresh brake fluid to keep the end submerged. The tube should be long enough so that a loop can be made higher than the bleed valve to prevent air from being drawn into the caliper during bleeding.

> *CAUTION*
> *Cover the front fender and front wheel with a heavy cloth or plastic tarp to protect it from the accidental spilling of brake fluid. Wash any brake fluid off of any plastic, painted or plated surface immediately, as it will destroy the finish. Use soapy water and rinse completely.*

4. Clean the top of the master cylinder of all dirt and foreign matter.
5. Remove the screws securing the reservoir cover and remove the reservoir cover, plate (models so equipped) and diaphragm.
6. Fill the reservoir almost to the cover lip; insert the diaphragm, plate (models so equipped) and the cover loosely. Leave the cover in place during this procedure to prevent the entry of dirt.

> *WARNING*
> *Use brake fluid from a sealed container marked DOT 3 or DOT 4 only (specified for disc brakes). Other types may vaporize and cause brake failure. Do not intermix different brands or types as they may not be compatible. Do not intermix a silicone-based (DOT 5) brake fluid as it can cause brake component damage leading to brake system failure.*

7. Slowly apply the brake lever several times as follows:
   a. Pull the lever in. Hold the lever in the applied position.
   b. Open the bleed valve about one-half turn. Allow the lever to travel to its limit.
   c. When this limit is reached, tighten the bleed screw.
8. As the fluid enters the system, the level will drop in the reservoir. Maintain the level at about 3/8 inch from the cover of the reservoir to prevent air from being drawn into the system.

9. Continue to pump the lever and fill the reservoir until the fluid emerging from the hose is completely free of bubbles.

> *NOTE*
> *Do not allow the reservoir to empty during the bleeding operation or more air will enter the system. If this occurs, the entire procedure must be repeated.*

10. Hold the lever in, tighten the bleed valve, remove the bleed tube and install the bleed valve dust cap.
11. If necessary, add fluid to correct the level in the reservoir. It should be to the upper level line.
12. Install the diaphragm, plate (models so equipped) and reservoir cover. Tighten the screws securely.

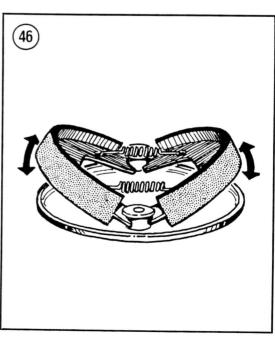

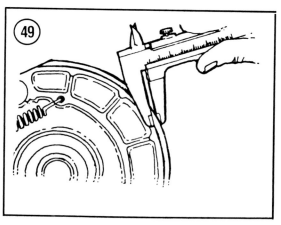

13. Test the feel of the brake lever. It should be firm and should offer the same resistance each time it's operated. If it feels spongy, it is likely that there is still air in the system and it must be bled again. When all air has been bled from the system and the fluid level is correct in the reservoir, double-check for leaks and tighten all fittings and connections.

WARNING
Before riding the bike, make certain that the brakes are operating correctly by operating the lever or pedal several times.

14. Test ride the bike slowly at first to make sure that the brakes are operating properly.

REAR DRUM BRAKE

Disassembly

1. Remove the rear wheel as described in Chapter Ten.
2. Pull the brake assembly straight up and out of the brake drum.
3. Prior to removing the brake shoes, inspect them as described under *Inspection* in this chapter.
4. Place a clean shop rag on the linings to protect them from oil and grease during removal.
5. Remove the brake shoes from the backing plate. Pull up on the center of each shoe as shown in **Figure 46**.
6. Remove the return springs and separate the brake shoes.
7. Remove the bolt and nut securing the brake arm and remove the brake arm, wear indicator and dust seal. Withdraw the camshaft from the backing plate.

Inspection

1. Thoroughly clean and dry all parts except the brake linings.
2. Check the contact surface of the drum (**Figure 47**) for scoring. If there are grooves deep enough to snag your fingernail the drum should be reground.
3. Measure the inside diameter of the brake drum with a vernier caliper (**Figure 48**). If the measurement is greater than the service limit listed in **Table 1**, the brake drum must be replaced.
4. If the drum can be turned and still stay within the maximum service limit diameter, the linings will have to be replaced and the new ones arced to conform to the new drum contour.
5. Measure the brake linings with a vernier caliper (**Figure 49**). They should be replaced if the lining portion is worn to the service limit dimension or less. Refer to specifications listed in **Table 1**.

11

6. Inspect the linings for embedded foreign material. Dirt can be removed with a stiff wire brush. Check for any traces of oil or grease; if they are contaminated they must be replaced.

7. Inspect the cam lobe and pivot pin area of the backing plate for wear or corrosion. Minor roughness can be removed with fine emery cloth.

8. Inspect the brake shoe return springs for wear. If they are stretched, they will not fully retract the brake shoes. Replace as necessary.

Assembly

1. Grease the camshaft with a light coat of molybdenum disulfide grease. Install the cam into the backing plate from the backside.

2. Install the dust seal from the outside of the backing plate.

3. Align the wear indicator to the camshaft as shown in **Figure 50** and push it down all the way to the backing plate.

4. When installing the brake arm onto the camshaft, be sure to align the punch marks on the two parts (**Figure 51**). Tighten the bolt and nut securely.

5. Grease the camshaft and pivot post with a light coat of molybdenum disulfide grease; avoid getting any grease on the brake backing plate where the brake linings may come in contact with it.

> *NOTE*
> *If new linings are being installed, file off the leading edge of each shoe a little so that the brake will not grab when applied.*

6. Hold the brake shoes in a "V" formation with the return springs attached and snap them into place on the brake backing plate. Make sure they are firmly seated on it.

7. Install the brake panel assembly into the brake drum.

8. Install the rear wheel as described in Chapter Nine.

9. Adjust the rear brake as described in Chapter Three.

BRAKE CABLE (DRUM BRAKE MODELS)

Front brake adjustment should be checked at the interval listed in Chapter Three as the cable stretches with use and increases brake lever free play. Free play is the distance that the brake lever travels between the released position and the point when the brake shoes come in contact with the brake drum.

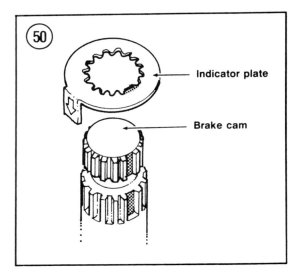

Indicator plate

Brake cam

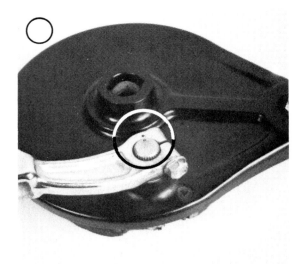

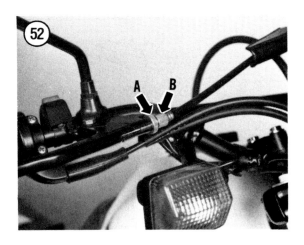

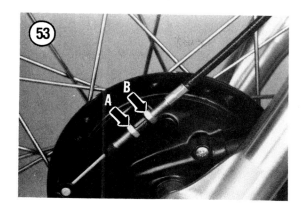

If the brake adjustment described in Chapter Three can no longer be achieved, the brake cable must be replaced.

Front Cable Replacement

1. At the brake lever, loosen the locknut (A, **Figure 52**) and turn the adjuster (B, **Figure 52**) all the way into the cable sheath.
2. At the brake panel assembly, loosen the locknut (A) and loosen the adjusting nut (B). Refer to **Figure 53** or **Figure 54**.
3. Disconnect the cable from the backing plate.
4. Pull the hand lever all the way back to the grip. Remove the cable nipple holder and remove the cable from the lever.

NOTE
Prior to removing the brake cable, make a drawing (or take a Polaroid picture) of the cable routing through the frame. It is very easy to forget how it was, once the cable has been removed. Replace the cable exactly as it was, avoiding any sharp turns.

5. On models so equipped, remove the screws on cable clip and remove the cable from the clip on the front fork (**Figure 55**).
6. Remove the brake cable from the loops on the front fork (**Figure 56**).
7. Install by reversing these removal steps, noting the following.
8. Adjust the front brake as described in Chapter Three.

Rear Cable Replacement (Models So Equipped)

1. At the brake panel assembly, unscrew the adjusting nut and the cable retainer (A, **Figure 57**).
2. At the brake pedal, remove the brakelight switch spring (A, **Figure 58**) from the cable end.

3. Remove the cable and retainer (B, **Figure 58**) from the brake pedal.

4. Pull the rear end of the cable out from the guide on the swing arm (B, **Figure 58**) and the frame guide (C, **Figure 58**).

NOTE
Prior to removing the brake cable, make a drawing (or take a Polaroid picture) of the cable routing through the frame. It is very easy to forget how it was, once the cable has been removed. Replace the cable exactly as it was, avoiding any sharp turns.

5. Install by reversing these removal steps, noting the following.

6. Adjust the rear brake as described in Chapter Three.

Table 1 DRUM BRAKE SPECIFICATIONS

Model	Standard		Service limit	
	mm	in.	mm	in.
Front brake drum ID				
XR200R	110.0	4.33	111.0	4.37
XL250S, XR250R	140.0	5.51	141.0	5.55
XR250,				
XL250R, XR350R	130.0	5.12	131.0	5.16
Rear brake drum ID				
XR200R	110.0	4.33	111.0	4.37
XL250S, XL250R	110.0	4.33	111.0	4.37
XR250, XR350R,				
XR250R	130.0	5.12	131.0	5.16
Brake shoe thickness	4.0	0.16	2.0	0.08

Table 2 DISC BRAKE SPECIFICATIONS

Model	Standard	Service limit
Master cylinder		
XL350R, 1983-1984 XR350R		
ID	12.7-12.743 mm (0.5000-0.5017 in.)	12.755 mm (0.5022 in.)
Piston OD	12.657-12.684 mm (0.4983-0.4994 in.)	12.640 mm (0.4976 in.)
1986-on XR250R, 1985 XR350R		
ID	11.0-11.042 mm (0.4330-0.4347 in.)	11.06 mm (0.435 in.)
Piston OD	10.957-10.984 mm (0.4314-0.4324 in.)	10.940 mm (0.431 in.)
Caliper		
XL350R, 1983-1984 XR350R		
ID	25.400-25.405 mm (1.000-1.0002 in.)	25.45 mm (1.002 in.)
Piston OD	25.318-25.368 mm (0.9968-0.9987 in.)	25.30 mm (0.9960 in.)
1986-on XR250R, 1985 XR350R		
ID	27.000-27.005 mm (1.0630-1.0632 in.)	26.99 mm (1.063 in.)
Piston OD	26.900-26.950 mm (1.0590-1.0610 in.)	27.00 mm (1.063 in.)
Brake disc		
Thickness		
1986-on XR250R	3.0 mm (0.12 in.)	2.5 mm (0.10 in.)
All other models	3.5 mm (0.14 in.)	3.0 mm (0.12 in.)
Runout	–	0.30 mm (0.012 in.)

Table 3 BRAKE TORQUE SPECIFICATIONS

Item	N•m	ft.-lb.
1981-1982 XR250R		
Brake cam and arm		
bolts and nuts	8-12	6-9
Caliper mounting bolts		
Upper and lower	20-30	15-22
Pin bolts	15-20	11-15
Caliper union bolt	30-40	22-29
Master cylinder		
Fitting	12-15	9-11
Union bolt	30-40	22-29
XL350R		
Brake hose-to-master cylinder	30-40	22-29
Brake disc mounting bolts or nuts	14-16	10-12

11

SUPPLEMENT

1990 AND LATER SERVICE INFORMATION

This chapter contains all procedures and specifications unique to the 1990-2000 XR250R models and the new XR250L model from 1991-1996. All other service procedures are identical to earlier models.

On all prior models and years, the XL series bikes were equipped with a battery and other related electrical components. The 1990 and later XR250L is a "XR Series" bike, *but* is equipped with many of the electrical components normally found previous only on the "XL Series" bikes. Where it is necessary in this supplement, reference is made for the correct service procedure to follow in the main body of this book for the 1990 and later XR250L models.

The chapter headings in this supplement correspond to those in the main body of this book. If a specific procedure is not included in this supplement, use the information given for the prior years in the main body of this book.

CHAPTER ONE

GENERAL INFORMATION

Table 1 lists the model, year and frame numbers for models covered in this supplement.

Table 1 MODEL, YEAR ENGINE AND FRAME NUMBERS

Model	Year	Engine beginning	Frame beginning
XR250R	1990	ME06E-5600001-on	ME060-LK600003-on
	1991	ME07E-5700001-on	ME060-MK700003-on
	1992	ME08E-5800001-5802103	ME060-NM800004-801509
	1993	ME09E-5900001-on	ME060-PM900001-on
	1994	ME06E-5000001-on	ME060-RM00001-on
XR250L			
49 STATE	1991	MD17E-2200007-2203139	MD220-MK000003-002363
California	1991	MD17E-2200017-2203321	MD221-MK00004-000649
49 STATE	1992	MD17E-2300007-2302230	MD220-NM100005-101850
California	1992	MD17E-2300042-2302476	MD21-NM100002-100572
49 STATE	1993	MD17E-2350005-2353313	MD220-PM200004-202684
California	1993	MD17E-2350100-2353530	MD221-PM200005-200793
49 STATE	1994	MD17E-2380001-2382087	MD220-RM300001-301835
California	1994	MD17E-2380001-2381567	MD221-RM300001-300230
49 STATE	1995	MD17E-2400001-on	MD220-SM400001-on
California	1995	MD17E-2400001-on	MD221-SM400001-on
49 STATE	1996	MD17E-2500001-on	MD220-TM500001-on
	1995	ME06E-5050001-on	ME060-SM100001-on
	1996	ME08E-200006-on	ME080-TM100004-on
	1997	ME08E-2100001-on	ME080-VM100001-on
	1998	NA	NA
	1999	NA	NA
	2000	NA	NA

CHAPTER TWO

TROUBLESHOOTING

12

EMERGENCY TROUBLESHOOTING

Choke Location (XR250R)

The emergency troubleshooting procedures are identical to prior years with the exception of choke operation. The choke is operated by a lever attached to the left-hand side of the carburetor, not by the choke lever and choke cable as on previous years.

The lever on the carburetor should be in the *raised* position (**Figure 1**) for a cold engine or *lowered* position (**Figure 2**) for a warm engine.

Main Fuse Location (XR250L)

The location of the main fuse is still next to the battery on the left-hand side of the bike. The main fuse is now in a fuse box along with 4 additional fuses as shown in **Figure 3**.

ENGINE STARTING

All engine starting procedures are identical to prior years, except the ignition system CDI pulse generator is now referred to as the ICM pulse generator. The ignition system operation is exactly the same, only the name of the component has been changed.

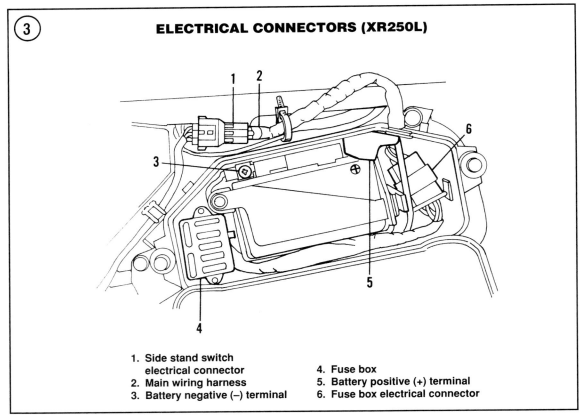

ELECTRICAL CONNECTORS (XR250L)

1. Side stand switch electrical connector
2. Main wiring harness
3. Battery negative (–) terminal
4. Fuse box
5. Battery positive (+) terminal
6. Fuse box electrical connector

CHAPTER THREE

LUBRICATION, MAINTENANCE AND TUNE-UP

ROUTINE CHECKS

Battery (XR250L)

The battery on these models is sealed and requires no routine service other than to keep the terminals free of corrosion and keep the terminal screws securing the harness leads to battery tight. The electrolyte level cannot be corrected on a sealed battery as the top is not removable.

Lights (XR250L)

Follow the procedure in Chapter Three in the main body of this book relating to the XL Series bikes.

BATTERY (XR250L)

NOTE
*Recycle your old battery. When you re-place the old battery, be sure to turn in the old battery at that time. The lead plates and plastic case can be recycled. Most motorcycle dealers will accept your old battery in trade when you purchase a new one, but if they will not, many automotive supply stores certainly will. **Never** place an old battery in your household trash since it is illegal, in most states, to place any acid or lead (heavy metal) contents in landfills. There is also the danger of the battery being crushed in the trash truck and spraying acid on the truck operator.*

Removal/Installation

Refer to **Figure 4** for this procedure.

1. Remove the left-hand side cover.

2. Unhook the rubber straps securing the battery case cover (1) and remove the cover.

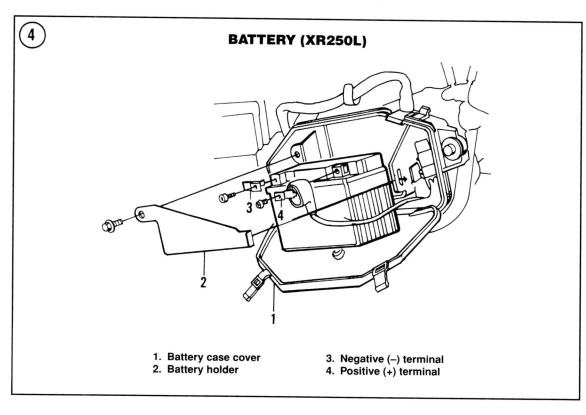

④ **BATTERY (XR250L)**

1. Battery case cover
2. Battery holder
3. Negative (–) terminal
4. Positive (+) terminal

12

3. Remove the bolt securing the battery holder. Hinge the holder out, disengage it from the battery case and remove the holder (2).

4. First disconnect the harness negative (–) lead (3) and then the positive (+) lead (4) from the battery terminals. Move the leads out of the way.

5. Carefully slide the battery out of the battery box.

6. Install by reversing these removal steps while noting the following:

    a. Clean the battery terminals, electrical cable connectors and surrounding battery case.

    b. Position the battery with the negative (–) terminal toward the *front* of the bike and install the battery.

    c. Coat the battery terminals with Vaseline or silicone spray to retard corrosion and decomposition of the terminals.

    d. Attach the positive (+) cable first then the negative (–) cable.

Inspection

For a preliminary test, connect a digital voltmeter across the battery negative and positive terminals and measure the battery voltage. A fully charged battery should read between 13.0 to 13.2 volts. If the voltage is 12.3 or less the battery is undercharged and should be recharged as described in this supplement.

Clean the battery terminals (**Figure 5**) and surrounding case and reinstall the battery as described in this section of the supplement. Coat the battery terminals with Vaseline or silicone spray to retard corrosion and decomposition of the terminals.

Charging

The battery is a sealed type and if recharging is necessary, a special type of battery charger must be used. The special type used has a built-in battery tester along with a timer. Take the battery to a Honda dealer to avoid damage to a good battery that only requires recharging. The following procedure is included if you choose to recharge the battery yourself.

CAUTION
Never *connect a battery charger to the battery with the battery cables still connected.* ***Always*** *disconnect the cables*

from the battery first. During the charging procedure the charger may damage the diodes within the voltage regulator/rectifier if the battery cables remain connected to the battery.

1. Remove the battery from the battery box as described in this section of the supplement.

2. Connect the positive (+) charger lead to the positive (+) battery terminal and the negative (–) charger lead to the negative (–) battery terminal.

CAUTION
*Do not exceed the recommended charging amperage rate or charging time on the battery charging label attached to the battery (**Figure 6**).*

3. Set the charger to 12 volts. If the output of the charger is variable, select the low setting. Use the suggested charging amperage and length of time shown on the charging label (**Figure 6**).

4. Turn the charger ON.

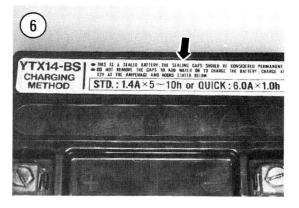

5. After the battery has charged for the specified amount of time, turn the charger off and disconnect the charger leads.

6. Connect a digital voltmeter across the battery negative and positive terminals and measure battery voltage. A fully charged battery will read 13.0-13.2 volts. If the voltage is 12.3 or less, the battery is still undercharged.

7. If the battery remains stable for 1 hour at the specified voltage, the battery is considered charged.

8. Clean the battery terminals (**Figure 5**) and surrounding case. Coat the battery terminals with Vaseline or silicone spray to retard corrosion and decomposition of the terminals.

9. Reinstall the battery as described in this section of the supplement.

New Battery Installation

Always replace the sealed battery with another sealed-type battery. The charging system is designed to have this type of battery in the charging system.

When replacing the battery, be sure to have it fully charged by the dealer before installing it in the bike. Failure to do will permanently damage the new battery.

PERIODIC LUBRICATION

Engine Oil Change

The engine oil change and filter replacement is the same as on previous models. For oil capacity for the XR250L models, refer to the XR250R (1985-on) specifications in **Table 5** located in Chapter Three in the main body of this book.

Front Fork Oil Change (XR250R)

The fork assembly on XR250R models is a cartridge-type and requires bleeding to properly remove any trapped air bubbles from within the upper fork chamber. Remove the fork assemblies as described in the Chapter Nine section of this supplement to change the fork oil.

Front Fork Oil Change (XR250L)

Refer to the *Front Fork Oil Change (With Air-assist)* procedure in Chapter Three in the main body of this book, then refer to the Chapter Nine section of this supplement for the recommended type of fork oil, correct fork oil capacity and oil level dimension as listed in **Table 3**.

PERIODIC MAINTENANCE

Drive Chain Adjustment (XR250R)

> *NOTE*
> *Honda does not provide service specifications for drive chain slack on XR250L models. Refer to **Drive Chain Adjustment (Pro-Link Models)** in Chapter Three in the main body of this book.*

Perform the drive chain adjustment procedure as described under *Drive Chain Adjustment (Pro-Link Models)* in Chapter Three in the main body of this book. The correct amount of drive chain slack is 35-45 mm (1 3/8-1 3/4 in.) on the top run of the drive chain as shown in **Figure 7**.

12

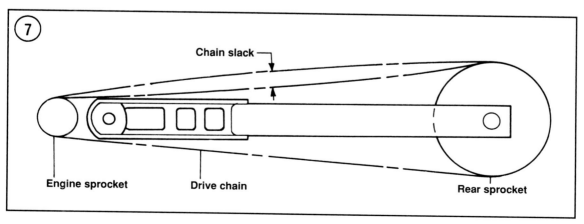

Figure 7 — Chain slack, Engine sprocket, Drive chain, Rear sprocket

Tighten the rear axle nut to 80-110 N•m (59-81 ft.-lb.).

Drive Chain Cleaning, Inspection and Lubrication

1. Shift the transmission into NEUTRAL.

2. Remove the master link retaining clip (**Figure 8**) and remove the master link. Roll the drive chain off the motorcycle. Handle the O-rings carefully when removing the master link.

> *CAUTION*
> *Clean the O-ring chain with a cleaner that has been recommended by the chain manufacturer. Most solvents and gasoline will cause the O-rings to swell, deteriorate and make the chain so stiff that it will not flex.*

3. Immerse the chain in a pan of kerosene and allow it to soak for about half an hour. Move it around and flex it during this period so that the dirt between the pins and rollers can work its way out.

4. Hang up the chain and allow it to dry.

5. Inspect the inner plate chain faces (**Figure 9**). They should be lightly polished on both sides. If they show considerable uneven wear on one side, the sprockets are not aligned properly. Severe wear re-

quires replacement of not only the drive chain but also the drive and driven sprockets.

> *WARNING*
> *Always check the master link spring clip after the bike has been rolled backwards such as when unloading from a truck or trailer. The master link retaining clip may get snagged on the chain guide or tensioner and become disengaged. Obviously, losing a chain while riding can cause a serious spill not to mention the chain damage which may occur.*

6. To measure drive chain wear, perform the following. Place a tape measure along the chain run and measure the distance between 107 pins in the chain.

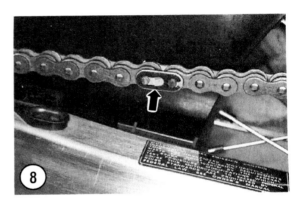

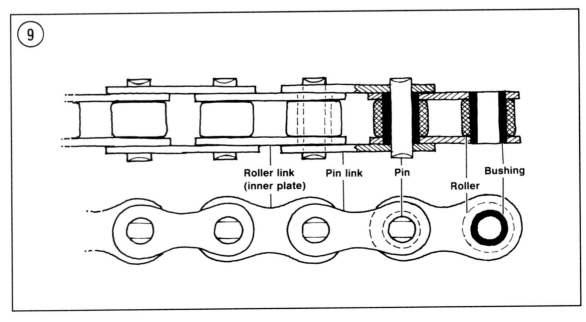

Roller link (inner plate)   Pin link   Pin   Roller   Bushing

If the link length is more than the limit of 1,716 mm (67.6 in.), install a new drive chain.

7. Install the chain on the motorcycle. Use a new master link retaining clip and install the clip so that the closed end of the clip is facing the direction of forward rotation of the chain as shown in **Figure 10**.

> *CAUTION*
> *Only a commercial lubricant that is formulated for O-ring chains should be used to lubricate the O-ring chain.*

8. Spray chain lube onto the sprocket side of the chain and rotate the chain for one complete rotation. Repeat for both sides of the drive chain. Then lube the outer sides of the rollers. Do not overlubricate as this will cause dirt to collect on the chain and sprockets.

9. Hold a clean rag on the chain, slowly rotate the rear wheel and wipe off excessive lubrication.

10. Wipe off excess lubrication from the rear hub, wheel and tire.

11. Drive chain replacement numbers are as follows:

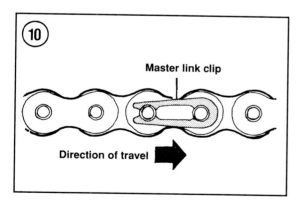

a. *XR250R:* Diado 520VC.3-108FJ, Takasago 520MO-108FJ.

b. *XR250L:*
  1991-on: Diado 520VC6-104LE.
  1991-1992: RK Excel RK520MO9-104LE.
  1993-on: RK Excel RK520M29-104LE.

Disc Brake Fluid Level

The hydraulic brake fluid in the reservoir should be kept at its maximum level (upper line) on the front and rear brake (**Figure 11**) master cylinders. If necessary, correct the level by adding fresh brake fluid.

> *WARNING*
> *Use brake fluid clearly marked DOT 4 and specified for disc brakes. Do not intermix different brands or types of brake fluid as they may not be compatible. Do not intermix silicone based (DOT 5) brake fluid as it can cause brake component damage leading to brake system failure.*

> *CAUTION*
> *Be careful when adding brake fluid. Do not spill it on plastic, painted or plated surfaces as it will destroy the finish. Wash off the area immediately with soapy water and thoroughly rinse it off with clean water.*

1. Clean any dirt from the area around the cover prior to removing the cover.

2. On the front master cylinder, perform the following:

  a. Turn the handlebar so the master cylinder reservoir is level.

  b. Remove the top cover screws and remove the top cover and diaphragm (Figure 12).

3. On the rear master cylinder, unscrew the top cover (**Figure 13**) and remove the plate and diaphragm.

4. Add fresh DOT4 brake fluid from a sealed container to bring the fluid to the correct level.

5. Reinstall the diaphragm and cover. On the front master cylinder, tighten the cover screws securely. On the rear master cylinder, tighten the top cover securely.

12

Front Disc Brake Lever Adjustment
(XR250R)

Brake pad wear is automatically adjusted as the pistons move outward in the caliper. However, the brake lever should be checked for adequate free play. Reduced free play can cause brake drag resulting in premature brake pad wear. The recommended amount of free play measured at the tip of the lever is 0.6-7.8 mm (1/4-5/8 in.) as shown in **Figure 14**.

To increase the amount of free play, loosen the locknut and turn the adjuster counterclockwise. To decrease the amount of free play, turn the adjuster clockwise. After the correct amount of free play has been achieved, tighten the locknut securely.

Rear Disc Brake Pedal Height Adjustment

Adjust the brake pedal to the desired height (personal preference)

1. Check that the brake pedal is in the at-rest position.

2. At the rear master cylinder; perform the following:

    a. Loosen the locknut (A, **Figure 15**).

    b. Turn the master cylinder pushrod (B, **Figure 15**) in either direction until the brake pedal is at the desired height.

    c. Tighten the locknut securely.

3. Apply the brake pedal several times and recheck the tightness of the locknut.

Air Filter Element
Removal/Installation

Remove and clean the air filter element at the interval indicated in **Table 2**. Replace the filter if it is damaged or deteriorating.

Air filter element cleaning is the same as on previous models except there is a cover over the air filter air box on all models.

1. Rotate the special bolt heads 1/2 turn and remove the side number plate (**Figure 16**) from the left-hand side. The special bolts are not loose and will stay with the side number plate.

2. Remove the air box cover (**Figure 17**).

3. Unhook the air filter element retaining strap (**Figure 18**).

4. Withdraw the element assembly from the air box.

5. Separate the element from the holder.

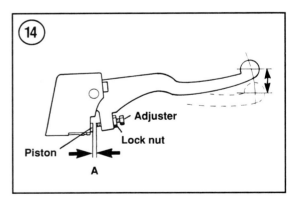

6. Wipe out the interior of the air box with a shop rag dampened with cleaning solvent. Remove any foreign matter that may have passed through a broken element.

7. Clean and re-oil the air filter element as described under *Air Filter Element Cleaning and Re-oiling*

(All Models) in Chapter Three in the main body of this book.

8. Install by reversing these removal steps. Make sure the element is correctly seated in the air box to prevent air leakage.

Evaporative Emission Control System (XR250L)

Refer to the Chapter Seven section of this supplement for correct hose layout of the evaporative emission control system.

TUNE-UP

The tune-up specifications are listed in **Table 4**.

Valve Clearance Adjustment

The valve clearance adjustment procedure is the same as on previous models with the exception of the clearance dimensions. The clearance dimensions are listed in **Table 4**.

Cylinder Compression

The cylinder compression test procedure is the same as on previous models with the exception of the pressure reading. The cylinder compression pressure is listed in **Table 4**.

Spark Plug Selection

Spark plug service procedures are the same as on previous models with the exception of the heat range and electrode gap. Refer to **Table 4** for specifications.

CDI Ignition Timing

The CDI ignition system is now referred to as the ICM (ignition control module) ignition system. The ignition system operation is exactly the same, only the name of the component has been changed. Checking the ignition timing is the same as on previous models.

12

Table 2 MAINTENANCE SCHEDULE

XR250R	
First week of operation or about 200 miles (350 km)	Change engine oil and filter Check and adjust valve clearance Inspect decompression system free play and adjust if necessary Check and adjust idle speed Clean and lubricate drive chain. Check free play and adjust if necessary Inspect drive chain slider for wear Inspect entire brake system Inspect clutch system and adjust clutch lever free play if necessary Check and tighten all frame component and engine mounting fasteners Check wheel spoke condition
Every 30 operating days or about 1,000 miles (1,600 km)	Inspect fuel lines for chaffed, cracked or swollen ends Clean fuel shutoff valve and strainer screen Check throttle operation and adjust free play if necessary Clean air filter element Inspect spark plug and regap if necessary Check and adjust valve clearance Change engine oil and filter Inspect decompression system free play; adjust if necessary Check and adjust idle speed Clean and lubricate drive chain. Check free play; and adjust if necessary Inspect drive chain slider for wear Check brake fluid level in both master cylinders; add fluid if necessary Inspect brake pad wear; replace if necessary Inspect headlight aim; readjust if necessary Inspect clutch system; adjust clutch lever free play if necessary Check side stand operation. Lubricate the pivot point Check all suspension components Check and tighten all frame component and engine mounting fasteners Check engine mounting bolts for tightness Clean spark arrester Check wheel spoke condition Check wheel runout Lubricate all control cables Lubricate front brake and clutch lever pivots Lubricate rear brake pedal pivot Inspect steering head bearings. Lubricate and adjust if necessary Check wheel bearings for smooth operation. Clean and repack bearings if necessary
Every 2 years	Replace brake fluid in both systems
XR250L	
Every 4,000 miles (6,400 km)	Inspect fuel lines for chaffed, cracked or swollen ends Clean fuel shutoff valve and strainer screen

(continued)

Table 2 MAINTENANCE SCHEDULE (continued)

Every 4,000 miles (6,400 km)
(continued)
	Check throttle operation, adjust free play
	  if necessary
	Clean air filter element
	Clean crankcase breather
	Inspect spark plug, regap if necessary
	Check and adjust valve clearance
	Change engine oil and filter
	Inspect decompression system free play,
	  adjust if necessary
	Check and adjust idle speed
	Clean and lubricate drive chain. Check free play,
	  and adjust if necessary
	Inspect drive chain slider for wear
	Check brake fluid level in both master cylinders,
	  add fluid if necessary
	Inspect brake pad wear, replace if necessary
	Inspect headlight aim, readjust if necessary
	Inspect clutch system, adjust clutch lever free play
	  if necessary
	Check side stand operation, lubricate the pivot point
	Check all suspension components
	Check and tighten all frame component and engine
	  mounting fasteners
	Check engine mounting bolts for tightness
	Check wheel spoke condition
	Check wheel runout
	Lubricate all control cables
	Lubricate front brake and clutch lever pivots
	Lubricate rear brake pedal pivot
	Inspect steering head bearings, lubricate and adjust
	  if necessary
	Check wheel bearings for smooth operation, clean
	  and repack bearings if necessary
	Lubricate swing arm bearings

Every 8,000 miles (12,800 km)	Inspect fuel lines for chaffed, cracked
	  or swollen ends
	Clean fuel shutoff valve and strainer screen
	Check throttle operation, adjust free play
	  if necessary
	Check choke operation
	Clean air filter element
	Replace spark plug
	Check and adjust valve clearance
	Change engine oil and filter
	Clean engine oil strainer screen
	Inspect decompression system free play,
	  adjust if necessary
	Check and adjust idle speed
	Clean and lubricate drive chain. Check free play,
	  and adjust if necessary
	Inspect drive chain slider for wear
	Check brake fluid level in both master cylinders,
	  add fluid if necessary
	Inspect brake pad wear, replace if necessary
	Check opertion of brake light switches
	Inspect headlight aim, readjust if necessary
	Inspect clutch system, adjust clutch lever free play
	  if necessary
	Check side stand operation, lubricate the pivot point

(continued)

12

Table 2 MAINTENANCE SCHEDULE (continued)

Every 8,000 miles (12,800 km)	Check all suspension components
	Check and tighten all frame component and engine
	  mounting fasteners
	Check engine mounting bolts for tightness
	Clean spark arrester
	Check wheel spoke condition
	Check wheel runout
	Lubricate all control cables
	Lubricate front brake and clutch lever pivots
	Lubricate rear brake pedal pivot
	Inspect steering head bearings, lubricate and adjust
	  if necessary
	Check wheel bearings for smooth operation, clean
	  and repack bearings if necessary

Every 12,000 miles (19,200 km)	Inspect the evaporative emission system Replace the brake fluid in both systems

Table 3 FORK OIL TYPE AND CAPACITY

		Distance from top of fork tube		
Fork oil type	**Quantity**	**Standard**	**Maximum**	**Minimum**
XR250R				
Pro-Honda	492 cc	128 mm	124 mm	150 mm
Susp. Fluid SS-7	(16.6 U.S. oz.)	(5.0 in.)	(4.9 in.)	(5.9 in.)
XR250L				
Pro-Honda	550 cc	139 mm	–	–
Susp. Fluid SS-8	(18.6 U.S. oz.)	(5.5 in.)	–	–

Table 4 TUNE-UP SPECIFICATIONS

Valve clearance	
Intake	0.03-0.07 mm (0.001-0.003 in.)
Exhaust	0.06-0.10 mm (0.002-0.004 in.)
Compression pressure	
XR250R	
1990-1991	184.9-213.3 psi (13.0-15.0 kg/cm^2)
1992-1995	170.7-184.9 psi (12.0-13.0 kg/cm^2)
XR250L	156-185 psi (11.0-13.0 kg/cm^2)
Spark plug type	
Standard heat range	
XR250R	ND X27GRP-U or NGK DPR9Z
XR250L	ND X24GRP-U or NGK DPR8Z
For cold climate	
XR250R	ND X24GRP-U or NGK DPR8Z
XR250L	ND X22GRP-U or NGK DPR7Z
For extended high speed riding	
XR250L	ND X27GRP-U or NGK DPR9Z
Spark plug gap	0.6-0.7 mm (0.024-0.028 in.)
Ignition timing @ "F" mark	
Initial	8° BTDC
Full advance	28 ± 2° BTDC @ 4,300 rpm
Idle speed	1,300 ± 100 rpm

CHAPTER FIVE

200 THRU 350 CC RFVC ENGINES

ENGINE REMOVAL/INSTALLATION

The engine removal and installation procedure is the same as on previous models with the exception of some bolt and nut torque specifications. Refer to **Table 5** for engine torque specifications unique to the 1990-on models.

On XR250L models, be sure to install the fuel tank rubber guard covers over the engine upper hanger plate bolts and nuts. These covers are necessary to prevent damage to the inner surface of the fuel tank adjacent to these bolt heads and nuts.

OIL COOLER SYSTEM
(XR250R)

Removal/Installation

The oil cooler removal and installation procedure is the same as on previous models with the exception of some torque specifications. Refer to **Table 5** for engine torque specifications unique to the 1990-on models.

BALANCER SYSTEM
(XR250L)

Disassembly/Inspection/Assembly

The balancer assembly is basically the same as used on previous models except there is only one balance weight on the assembly that is equipped with a split gear (**Figure 19**). Be sure to align the 2 mm pin holes in both gears prior to installing the circlip.

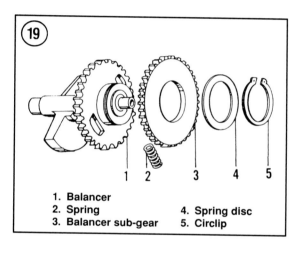

1. Balancer
2. Spring
3. Balancer sub-gear
4. Spring disc
5. Circlip

12

Table 5 ENGINE TORQUE SPECIFICATIONS

Item	N·m	ft.-lb.
Engine hanger bolts		
8 mm bolts	24-30	17-22
10 mm bolts	60-70	44-51
Oil cooler pipe bolts		
(XR250R)	32-40	23-29

CHAPTER SEVEN

FUEL AND EXHAUST

CARBURETOR SERVICE

Refer to **Table 6** for 1990-on carburetor specifications.

Single Carburetor
Removal/Installation
(XR250R)

Carburetor removal and installation are the same as on previous models except the 1990-on models are *not* equipped with a choke cable.

Carburetor Disassembly/Assembly
(XR250R)

The carburetor is 99% the same as on previous models with the slight exception of the appearance and location of some small parts. Refer to **Figure 20** when servicing the carburetor while following the procedure in Chapter Seven in the main body of this book.

New Pilot Screw Adjustment and
New Limiter Cap Installation
(XR250L)

The pilot jet is preset at the factory and adjustment is not necessary unless the carburetor had been overhauled or someone has misadjusted it.

The air filter must be cleaned before starting this procedure or the results will be inaccurate. Refer to Chapter Three in the main body of this book.

> *CAUTION*
> *Do not try to remove the limiter cap from the old pilot screw, as it is bonded in place. It will break off and damage the pilot screw and internal portions of the carburetor body if removal is attempted.*

1. For preliminary adjustment, carefully turn the new pilot screw in until it seats *lightly* and then turn it back out the number of initial opening turns listed in **Table 6**.

> *CAUTION*
> *The pilot screw can be damaged if the pilot screw is tightened too hard against the seat.*

2. Start the engine and let it reach normal operating temperature. Approximately 5-10 minutes of stop and go riding is usually sufficient. Shut off the engine.

3. Connect a portable tachometer following its manufacturer's instructions.

4. Restart the engine and turn the idle adjust screw in or out to obtain the idle speed listed in **Table 6**.

5. Turn the pilot screw 1/2 turn out from the initial setting obtained in Step 1.

6. If the engine speed increases by 50 rpm or more, turn the pilot screw out by continual 1/2 turn increments until engine speed does not increase.

7. Turn the idle adjust screw in or out to obtain the idle speed listed in **Table 6**.

8. Turn the pilot screw in until the engine speed drops by 50 rpm.

9. Turn the pilot screw 1/2 turn in from the position obtained in Step 8.

10. Turn the idle adjust screw in or out to obtain the idle speed listed in **Table 6**.

11. Shut off the engine and disconnect the portable tachometer.

12. Perform this step only if a new limiter cap is to be installed. Install the limiter cap as follows:

   a. Apply a thread locking compound to the new limiter cap.

   b. Position the limiter cap against the stop on the float bowl (**Figure 21**) so that the pilot screw can only turn *clockwise* toward a leaner mixture.

13. After this adjustment is complete, test ride the bike. Throttle response from idle should be rapid without any hesitation.

20

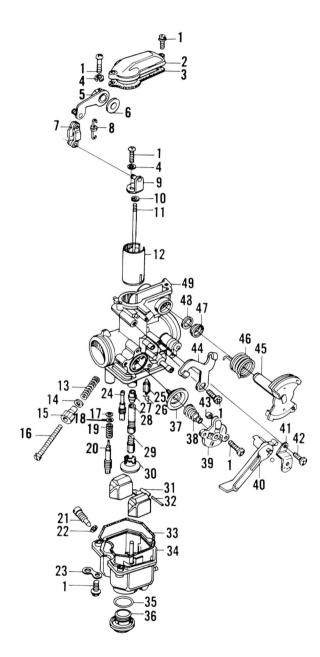

CARBURETOR (XR250R)

1. Screw
2. Top cover
3. Gasket
4. Lockwasher
5. Link arm
6. Plastic washer
7. Connector
8. Spring
9. Plate
10. Jet needle clip
11. Jet needle
12. Throttle valve
13. Spring
14. Washer
15. Throttle adjust knob
16. Screw
17. O-ring
18. Gasket
19. Spring
20. Pilot screw
21. Drain screw
22. Gasket
23. Hose guide
24. Slow jet
25. Float valve
26. Clip
27. Needle jet
28. Needle jet holder
29. Main jet
30. Plastic ferrule
31. Float
32. Float pin
33. Gasket
34. Float bowl
35. O-ring
36. Main jet cover
37. Air cutoff valve diaphragm
38. Spring
39. Cover
40. Choke lever
41. Bracket
42. Screw
43. O-ring
44. Bracket
45. Throttle pulley
46. Return spring
47. Seal
48. Washer
49. Carburetor body

12

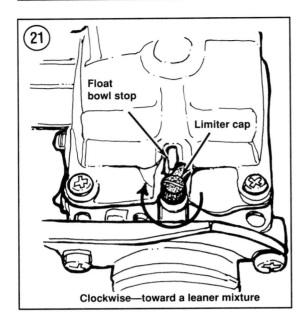

Float bowl stop

Limiter cap

Clockwise—toward a leaner mixture

FUEL TANK (METAL)

Removal/Installation (XR250L)

Fuel tank removal and installation is the same as on previous models, except there are 2 sets of bolts and washers securing the rear of the fuel tank to the frame.

EVAPORATIVE EMISSION CONTROL SYSTEM (CALIFORNIA MODELS)

The fuel evaporation emission control system is basically the same as on previous models except for the layout of some of the hoses. Refer to **Figure 22** for typical hose routing.

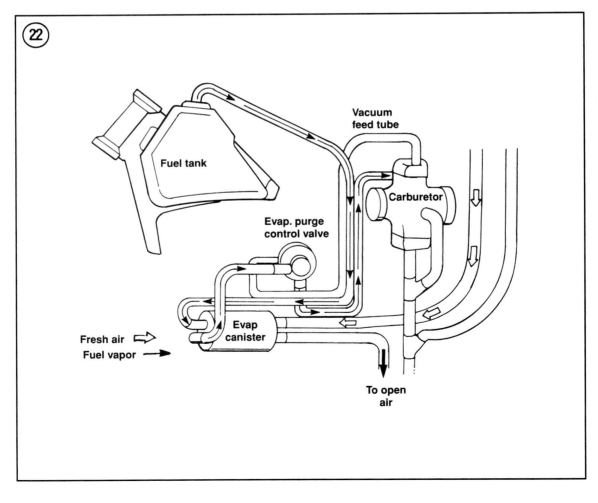

Vacuum feed tube

Fuel tank

Carburetor

Evap. purge control valve

Fresh air ⇨
Fuel vapor →

Evap canister

To open air

Table 6 CARBURETOR SPECIFICATIONS

Item	XR250R 1992-1995	1996-on
Model number		
49-state	PD05B	PDG1A
California	NA	PDG1C
Main jet number		
49-state	125	132
California	NA	122
High altitude main jet No.		
See *High-altitude and Temperature Adjustment* in main body of book.		
Slow jet	40	45
Initial pilot screw opening	2 1/4 turns out	1 3/4 turns out (1 3/8 CA)
Needle jet clip position from top	3rd groove	3rd groove
Float level	12.5 mm (0.49 in.)	12.5 mm (0.49 in.)
Item	XR250L 1991	1992 -1996
Model number		
49 state	PD79E	PD79G
California	PD70F	PD79H
Main jet number	122	122
High altitude main jet No.		
See *High-altitude and Temperature Adjustment* in main body of book.		
Slow jet	38	38
Initial pilot screw opening		
49 state	1 7/8 turns out	2 1/4 turns out
California	1 7/8 turns out	2 1/4 turns out
Needle jet clip position from top	3rd groove	3rd groove
Float level	14.0 mm (0.55 in.)	14.0 mm (0.55 in.)
Idle speed	1,300 ± 100 rpm	1,300 ± 100 rpm

CHAPTER EIGHT

ELECTRICAL SYSTEM

12

CHARGING SYSTEM
(XR250L)

The charging system on 1990 and later models operates same as previous models. The wire colors and component layout differ from previous years and the new layout is shown in **Figure 23**. All test procedure are identical to previous years and are described in Chapter Eight in the main body of this book.

Charging System Test

Honda does not provide charging system specifications for the XR250L models.

ALTERNATOR STATOR

Removal/installation

The alternator stator removal and installation procedure is the same as on previous models with the exception of the number of electrical connectors attached to the stator assembly.

On XR250R models, disconnect the 2 alternator stator electrical connectors. On XR250L models, disconnect the 3 electrical connectors and the screw and washer securing the ground connector to the engine.

Stator Coil Testing

Exciter coil (XR250R)

1. Remove the seat and side covers.
2. Locate the wiring harness, under the seat, coming from the alternator stator assembly.
3. Disconnect the black/red electrical connector.
4. Use an ohmmeter set at R × 1 and check for continuity between the black/red connector and ground. If there is continuity (low resistance) the coil is good. If there is no continuity (infinite resistance) the coil is defective and must be replaced.
5. Connect the electrical connector. Make sure the electrical connector is free of corrosion and is tight.
6. Install all items removed.

Lighting coil (XR250R)

1. Remove the seat and side covers.
2. Locate the wiring harness, under the seat, coming from the alternator stator assembly.
3. Disconnect the blue electrical connector.

4. Use an ohmmeter set at R × 1 and check for continuity between the blue connector and ground. If there is continuity (0.2-1.2 ohms) the coil is good. If there is no continuity (infinity) the coil is defective and must be replaced.
5. Connect the electrical connector. Make sure the electrical connector is free of corrosion and is tight.
6. Install all items removed.

Stator coil (XR250L)

1. Remove the seat and side covers.

2. Locate the wiring harness, under the seat, coming from the alternator stator assembly.

3. Disconnect the 3 yellow electrical connectors.

4. Use an ohmmeter set at R × 1 and check for continuity between each yellow connector on the coil side. Replace the stator coil assembly if any yellow connector shows no continuity (infinity) to any other connector. This would indicate an open in the coil windings.

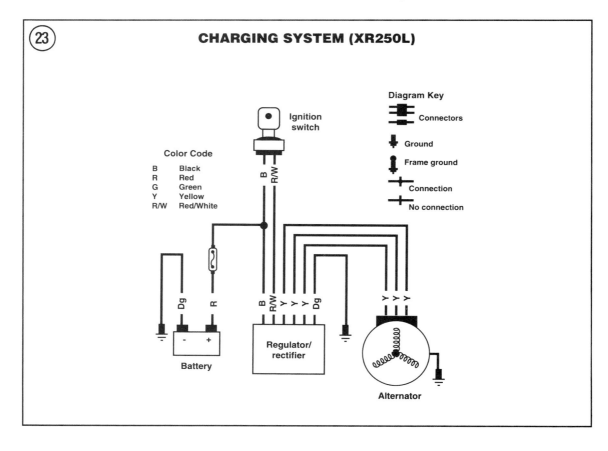

5. Use an ohmmeter set at R × 1 and check for continuity between each yellow connector and ground. Replace the stator coil assembly if any yellow connector shows continuity to ground. This would indicate a short within the coil windings.

NOTE
Prior to re placing the stator, check the electrical wiring from the stator coil assembly and the electrical connectors for open or short circuits.

6. Connect the electrical connectors. Make sure all electrical connectors are free of corrosion and are tight.

7. Install all items removed.

IGNITION SYSTEM

The ignition system on 1990 and later models operates same as previous models. The wire colors and component layout differ from previous years and the new layout for XR250R models is shown in **Figure 24** and the new layout for XR250L models in **Figure 25**.

The CDI unit is now referred to as the ICM (ignition control module). The ICM operates the same as the CDI unit.

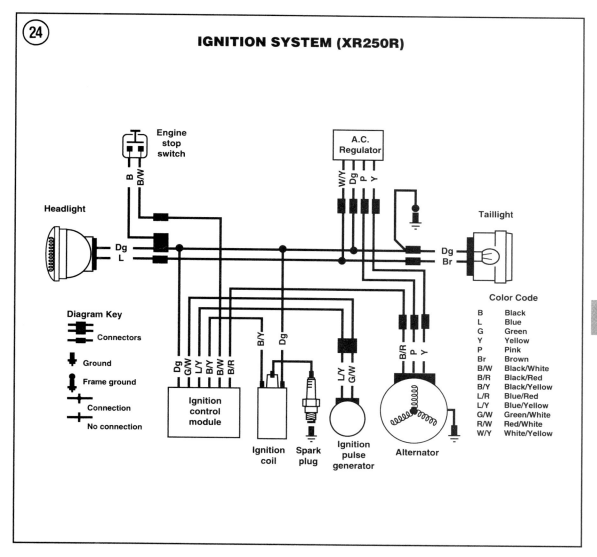

24

IGNITION SYSTEM (XR250R)

Engine stop switch

A.C. Regulator

Headlight

Taillight

Color Code

B	Black
L	Blue
G	Green
Y	Yellow
P	Pink
Br	Brown
B/W	Black/White
B/R	Black/Red
B/Y	Black/Yellow
L/R	Blue/Red
L/Y	Blue/Yellow
G/W	Green/White
R/W	Red/White
W/Y	White/Yellow

Diagram Key

Connectors

Ground

Frame ground

Connection

No connection

Ignition control module

Ignition coil

Spark plug

Ignition pulse generator

Alternator

12

SWITCHES

Side Stand Switch
(XR250L) Testing

1. Remove the left-hand side cover (**Figure 16**).

2. On the left-hand rear frame rail behind the battery case, disconnect the green 3-pin electrical connector (1, **Figure 26**) containing 3 wires (1 green/white, 1 yellow/black, 1 green).

3. Set the ohmmeter to the R × 1 scale and zero the test leads.

4. Use the ohmmeter and check for continuity between the switch side of the electrical terminals as follows:

   a. S*ide stand down:* there should be continuity (low resistance) between the yellow/black and green terminals of the electrical connector.

   b. *Side stand up:* there should be continuity (low resistance) between the green/white and green terminals of the electrical connector.

5. If the switch fails either of these tests, replace the switch.

6. Reconnect the 3-pin electrical connector and install the left-hand side cover.

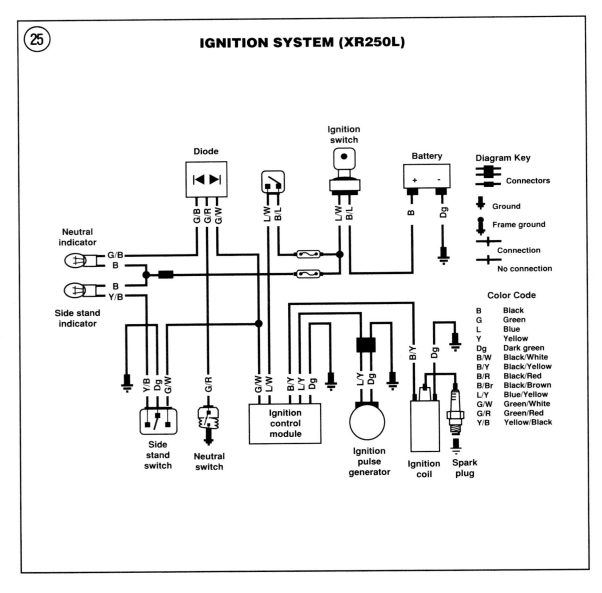

IGNITION SYSTEM (XR250L)

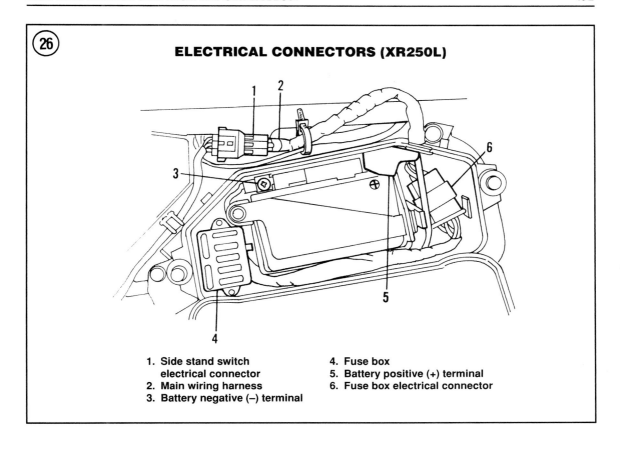

(26) **ELECTRICAL CONNECTORS (XR250L)**

1. Side stand switch electrical connector
2. Main wiring harness
3. Battery negative (–) terminal
4. Fuse box
5. Battery positive (+) terminal
6. Fuse box electrical connector

CHAPTER NINE

FRONT SUSPENSION AND STEERING

STEERING STEM AND HEAD (XR250L)

Disassemble the steering head periodically and pack the bearings with new grease. The XR250L is the only model covered in this manual to use assembled ball bearings in both the upper and lower bearing races. Use a good heavy water-resistant grease to lubricate the bearings.

Disassembly

Refer to **Figure 27** for this procedure.

1. Remove the fuel tank as described in Chapter Seven in the main body of this book.

2. Remove the headlight/number plate assembly (A, **Figure 28**) as described in Chapter Eight in the main body of this book.

3. Remove the speedometer (B, **Figure 28**) as described in Chapter Eight in the main body of this book.

4. Remove the bolts, collars and washers securing the front fender and remove the fender.

5. Remove the meter mounting bracket.

6. Remove the handlebar assembly (A, **Figure 29**) and the front forks as described in Chapter Nine in the main body of this book .

7. Remove the steering stem nut and washer (B, **Figure 29**) and remove the upper fork bridge (3, **Figure 27**).

12

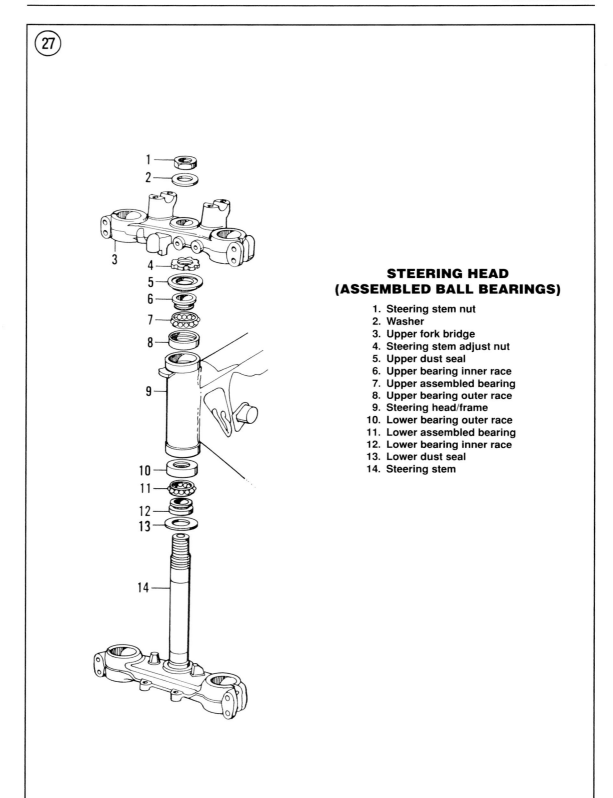

㉗

**STEERING HEAD
(ASSEMBLED BALL BEARINGS)**

1. Steering stem nut
2. Washer
3. Upper fork bridge
4. Steering stem adjust nut
5. Upper dust seal
6. Upper bearing inner race
7. Upper assembled bearing
8. Upper bearing outer race
9. Steering head/frame
10. Lower bearing outer race
11. Lower assembled bearing
12. Lower bearing inner race
13. Lower dust seal
14. Steering stem

8. Loosen the steering stem adjust nut using the Honda socket (part No. 07916-KA50100), an easily fabricated tool such as shown in **Figure 30** or a suitable spanner wrench (**Figure 31**).

NOTE
If you are careful, the steering stem locknut can also be loosened by tapped it loose with a screwdriver or punch and hammer.

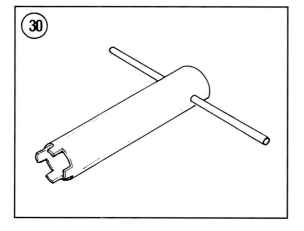

NOTE
Support the weight of the steering stem assembly after removing the stem adjust nut or the assembly will drop out of the motorcycle frame.

9. Hold onto the steering stem and remove the adjust nut (**Figure 31**).

10. Lift off the upper dust seal.

11. Gently lower the steering stem down and out of the steering head. Don't worry about catching any loose balls as the steering stem is equipped with assembled ball bearings. If the bearing cage is damaged, some loose balls may fall out.

12. Remove the upper bearing inner race and upper assembled ball bearing from the top of the steering head.

13. Carefully remove the lower assembled bearing from the lower bearing inner race on the steering stem.

Inspection

1. Clean the bearing balls and bearing inner race of both bearings with solvent.

2. Wipe the old grease from the outer races located in the steering stem, then clean the outer races with

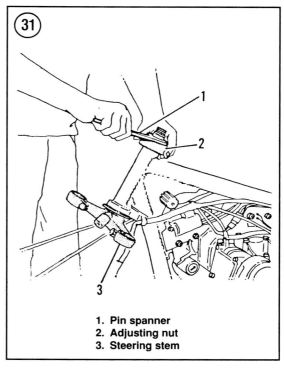

1. **Pin spanner**
2. **Adjusting nut**
3. **Steering stem**

12

a rag socket in solvent. Thoroughly dry with a lint-free cloth.

3. Check the welds around the steering head for cracks and fractures. If any damage is found, have the frame repaired by a competent frame shop or welding service.

4. Check the bearing balls in both sets of bearings for pitting, scratches or corrosion. If they are less than perfect, replace them as a set.

5. Check the steering stem outer races for pitting, galling and corrosion. If a race is worn or damaged, replace the races as described in Chapter Nine in the main body of this book.

6. Check the lower bearing inner race on the steering stem for damage or wear. Replace the bearing race if necessary as described in Chapter Nine in the main body of this book.

7. Check the lower steering stem assembly for cracks or damage. Replace the steering stem if not in perfect condition.

Assembly

Refer to **Figure 27** for this procedure.

1. Use a good quality heavy water-resistant grease and thoroughly pack the bearing balls in both bearing sets.

2. Apply a good coat of grease to the upper and lower bearing outer races in the steering head and to the lower bearing inner race on the steering stem.

3. Install the lower ball bearing onto the inner race on the steering stem.

4. Install the upper bearing into the upper bearing outer race in the steering head.

5. Have an assistant hold the upper bearing assembly in place and carefully slide the steering stem up into the frame. Take care not to dislodge the upper bearing assembly.

6. Install the upper bearing inner race into the upper bearing. Push it down until it is completed seated in the bearing assembly.

7. Apply a light coat of grease to the upper dust seal. Hold the steering stem in position and install the dust seal over the steering stem

8. Install the steering stem adjust nut. Use the same tool setup used during disassembly and tighten the steering stem adjust nut to the torque specification listed in **Table 7**. This fully seats the upper bearing balls and lower roller bearing into their races.

9. Move the steering stem back and forth from lock to lock 5 or 6 times to make sure the bearings are completely seated.

10. Loosen the steering stem adjust nut and retighten to the torque specification listed in **Table 7**. Once again, check that the steering moves freely from side to side.

11. Install the upper fork bridge, washer and nut. Tighten the nut only finger-tight at this time. Do not tighten the nut until the front forks are in place. This will ensure proper alignment between the steering stem and the upper fork bridge.

12. Install the front forks as described in Chapter Nine in the main body of this book. Tighten the upper and lower fork pinch bolts to the torque specification listed in **Table 7**.

13. Check the movement of the front forks and steering stem assembly. The steering stem must turn freely from side to side, without binding or free play when the fork legs are moved fore and aft.

14. Tighten the steering stem nut to the torque specification listed in **Table 7**. Recheck the movement of the front end and readjust if necessary.

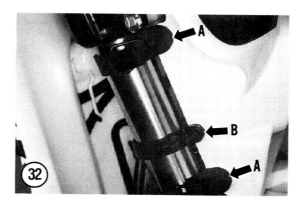

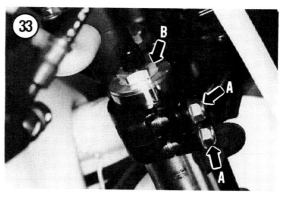

15. Install the handlebar (A, **Figure 29**) as described in Chapter Nine in the main body of this book.

16. Install the meter mounting bracket.

17. Install the front fender, collars, washers and bolts. Tighten the bolts securely.

18. Install the speedometer (B, **Figure 28**) as described in Chapter Eight in the main body of this book.

19. Install the headlight/number plate assembly (A, **Figure 28**) as described in Chapter Eight in the main body of this book.

20. Install the fuel tank as described in Chapter Seven in the main body of this book.

FRONT FORK
(XR250R)

Removal/Installation

NOTE
The bottom bolt at the base of the slider is secured with a thread locking compound and is often very difficult to loosen because the piston rod assembly

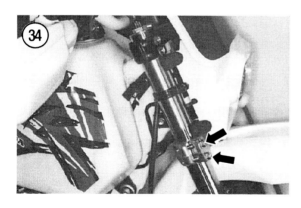

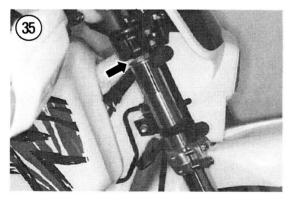

will turn inside the fork slider. It sometimes can be loosened with an air impact wrench. If you are unable to loosen the bottom bolt, take the fork assemblies to dealership and have the bolts loosened and removed.

1. Unhook the rubber straps (A, **Figure 32**), on each side, and move the front number plate out of the way or completely remove it.

2. If the fork is going to be disassembled, perform the following:

   a. Have an assistant sit on the bike, apply the front brake, compress the front forks and hold them in this position.

   b. Slightly loosen the bottom bolt at the base of the slider. If the bolt is loosened too much, fork oil may start to drain out of the slider. Loosen both bottom bolts.

   c. Release the pressure on the front forks.

   d. Loosen the upper pinch bolts (A, **Figue 33**) securing the fork tube to the upper fork bridge.

   e. Remove the air valve cap and bleed off any air pressure within the fork.

   f. Loosen the fork cap bolt (B, **Figure 33**) at this time.

3. Remove the front wheel as described in this chapter.

4. Loosen the screw securing the speedometer cable clamp (B, **Figure 32**) to the right-hand fork tube and the clamp on the front brake hose on the left-hand fork tube. It is not necessary to remove the clamps, just loosen them so the fork tube can slide out of them.

5. Remove the front brake caliper assembly from the left-hand fork slider as described in Chapter Eleven in the main body of this book.

6. Loosen the lower pinch bolts (**Figure 34**) securing each fork leg.

7. Carefully pull each fork leg down and out of the upper (**Figure 35**) and lower fork bridge clamps. It may be necessary to slightly rotate the fork tube while pulling it down and out (**Figure 36**).

8. Install by reversing these removal steps while noting the following:

   a. Install each fork tube so the fork cap is even with the top edge of the upper fork bridge (**Figure 37**).

   b. If the forks were disassembled, tighten the fork cap (B, **Figure 33**) after the fork tubes are installed and secured in the lower fork bridge.

12

Tighten the fork cap to the torque specification listed in **Table 7**.

c. Tighten the upper and lower fork bridge clamp bolts and the fork cap to the torque specification listed in **Table 7**.

d. Pull the rubber boot up so the top edge touches the lower surface of the steering stem (**Figure 38**). Position the boot clamp screw head toward the rear and tighten securely.

Fork Disassembly

Refer to **Figure 39** for this procedure.

1. Remove the front forks as described in this supplement.

2. Remove the fork boot clamps and remove the boot from the fork assembly.

3. If not loosened during the fork removal procedure, loosen the bottom bolt in the base of the slider.

4. Slowly unscrew the fork cap from the fork tube. The fork cap will not come completely free since it is still attached to the piston rod assembly within the fork assembly.

5. Turn the fork assembly upside down over a drain pan and drain out the fork oil.

6. Use a box wrench on the fork cap (A, **Figure 40**) and open-end wrench on the piston rod locknut (B, **Figure 40**).

7. Loosen, then completely unscrew the fork cap bolt from the piston rod.

8. Remove the washer, upper spring, washer, lower spring and on models so equipped, the lower washer and from the fork tube.

9. Over the drain pan, compress the fork tube into slider until it bottoms out.

10. Stroke the piston rod several times to pump out any remaining oil. Stand the fork tube upside down in the drain pan and allow the tube to drain for several minutes.

11. Remove the bottom bolt and gasket (**Figure 41**).

12. Withdraw the piston rod assembly (**Figure 42**) from the fork assembly.

13. Remove the wire stopper ring (**Figure 43**) from the slider groove.

14. Slide off the retainer and the dust seal.

15. Pad the jaws of a vise with wooden blocks or soft aluminum plates. Place the fork leg in the vise and clamp the vise securely on the axle mounting boss.

16. Use several quick slide-hammer motions (**Figure 44**) and remove the fork tube from the slider. The retainer, dust seal, oil seal/washer assembly, backup ring and the slider bushing are removed with the fork tube. Slide all of these part off of the slider.

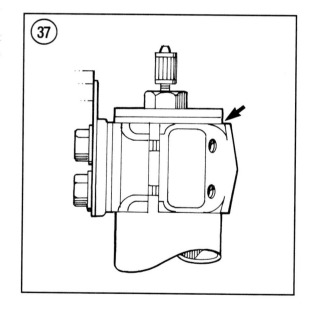

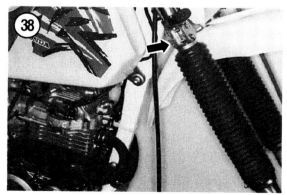

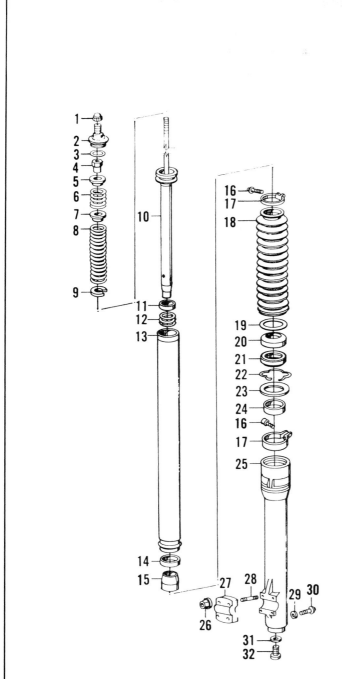

FRONT FORK ASSEMBLY (XR250R)

1. Valve cap
2. Fork cap
3. O-ring
4. Locknut
5. Washer
6. Upper spring
7. Washer
8. Lower spring
9. Washer (models so equipped)
10. Piston rod assembly
11. Piston ring
12. Rebound spring
13. Fork tube
14. Fork tube bushing
15. Oil lock piece
16. Screw
17. Clamp
18. Rubber boot
19. Retainer
20. Dust seal
21. Oil seal
22. Wire stopper ring
23. Backup ring
24. Slider bushing
25. Fork slider
26. Nut
27. Axle holder
28. Threaded stud
29. Washer
30. Drain bolt
31. Gasket
32. Allen bolt

12

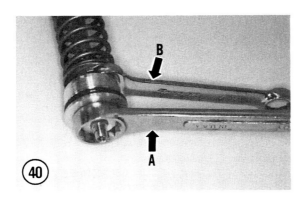

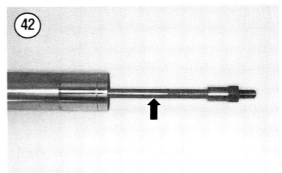

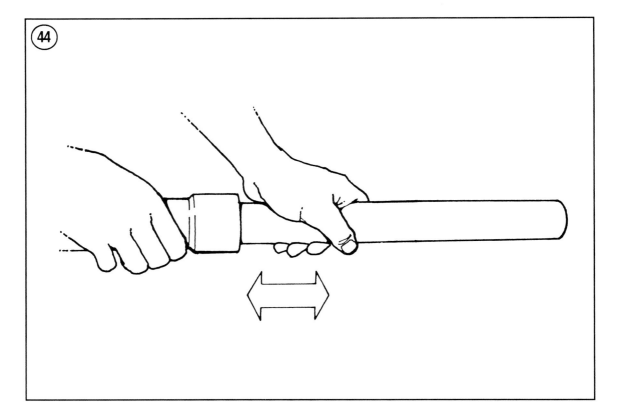

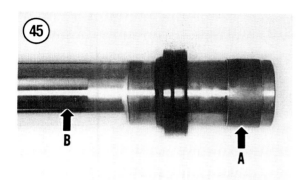

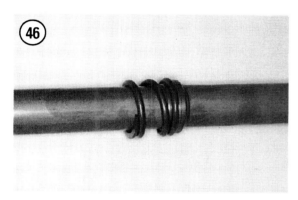

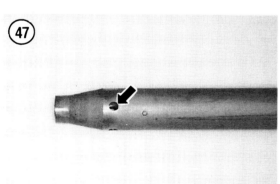

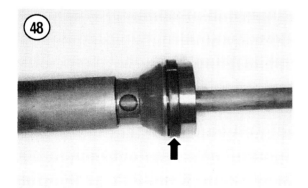

Discard the oil seal as it must be replaced every time it is removed.

NOTE
*Do not remove the fork tube bushing (A, **Figure 45**) unless it is going to be replaced. Inspect the bushing as described in this section.*

17. Remove the oil lock piece from the end of the fork tube.

18. Remove the piston rod assembly from the fork tube.

19. If necessary, unscrew and remove the locknut from the piston rod assembly.

Inspection

1. Thoroughly clean all parts in solvent and dry them completely.

2. Inspect the piston rod assembly (**Figure 46**) for damage or roughness. Check for galling, deep scores or excessive wear. Make sure the oil passages (**Figure 47**) are clear and free of sludge or dirty fork oil residue.

3. Inspect the piston ring (**Figure 48**) on the upper end of the piston rod for wear or damage. Replace if necessary.

4. Check the upper fork tube for straightness. Replace the tube if bent or severely scratched.

5. Carefully examine the area of the fork tube that passes through the fork seal in the slider (B, **Figure 45**). Any scratches or roughness on the fork tube in this area will damage the oil seal. If the fork tube is scratched or pitted, replace it.

6. Check the slider (**Figure 49**) for dents or exterior damage that may cause the fork tube to hang up during riding. Replace if necessary.

12

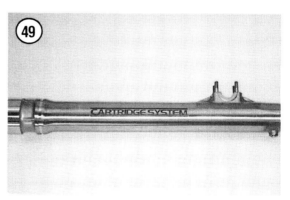

7. Check the axle holder threaded studs (**Figure 50**) on the right-hand fork tube for damage. If necessary, clean up with an appropriate size metric die or replace the threaded studs.

8. Inspect the slider and fork tube bushings. If either is scratched or scored, they must be replaced. If the Teflon coating is worn off so that the copper base material is showing on 3/4 of the total surface area, the bushing(s) must be replaced.

9. Separately measure the uncompressed free length of each upper and lower springs (**Figure 51**). If either spring is sagged to the to the service limit listed in **Table 8**, the spring(s) must be replaced.

10. Inspect each rubber boot for tears or abrasive damage. Clean out if necessary. A damaged boot will allow dirt and moisture to pack up next to the dust seal leading to early failure of the seal. Packed in dirt can scratch the surface of the fork tubes as well as damage the fork dust and oil seals. Install new fork boots if any damage exists.

11. Make sure the breather holes (**Figure 52**) in the base of the rubber boot are clear. Clean out if necessary.

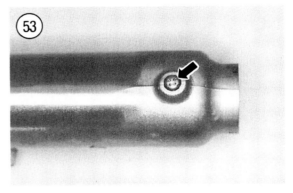

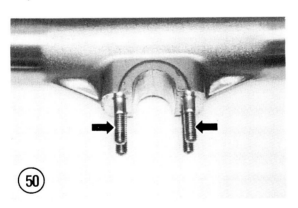

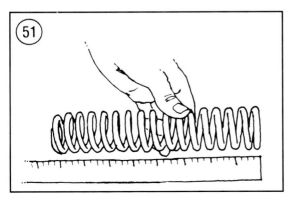

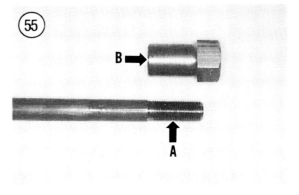

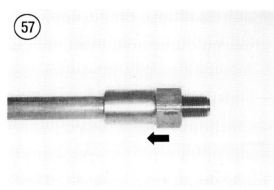

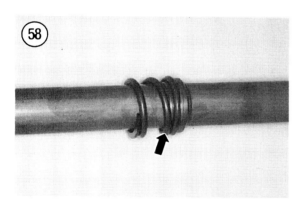

12. Inspect the dust seal for wear or damage. Replace if necessary.

13. Remove the drain bolt and washer (**Figure 53**) and inspect it. Replace if the threads are damaged or the washer is starting to deteriorate.

14. Inspect the air valve portion (**Figure 54**) of the fork cap for damage. Replace the fork cap if necessary.

15. Inspect the threads on top of the piston rod assembly (A, **Figure 55**) and the locknut (B, **Figure 55**) for damage. If necessary, clean up with the appropriate size metric tap and die.

16. Replace any parts that are worn or damaged. Simply cleaning and reinstalling unserviceable components will not improve performance of the front suspension.

Assembly

1. Make sure that all fork components are clean and dry. Wipe clean the oil seal bore in the fork slider (**Figure 56**) with a lint-free cloth.

2. If the nut was removed from the piston rod perform the following:

    a. The hex head portion of the nut must be positioned *up* toward the top so it will contact the bottom surface of the fork cap.

    b. Screw the locknut onto the piston rod. Screw it all the way *down* onto the end of the threads on the piston rod assembly (**Figure 57**). This is necessary to allow room for the correct installation of the fork cap.

3. If loose, install the rebound spring (**Figure 58**) onto the piston rod assembly.

4. Position the oil lock piece as shown in **Figure 59** and install the oil lock piece (**Figure 60**) into the end of the fork tube.

12

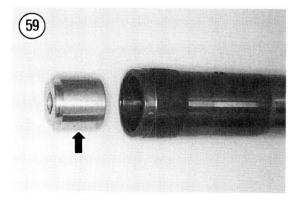

5. Install the fork tube into the slider (**Figure 61**) and push it down until it bottoms out (**Figure 62**).

6. Slide the fork slider bushing (**Figure 63**) down the fork tube and rest it on top of the fork slider.

NOTE
*The slider bushing can be installed using an oil seal driver (**Figure 64**) or a piece of tubing and suitable plate that fits over the fork tube. Oil seal drivers are available from Honda dealers and mail order tool suppliers.*

7. Drive the new slider bushing into the slider with the fork seal driver (**Figure 64**) or equivalent until it bottoms out. Remove the driver.

8. Slide the backup ring (A, **Figure 65**) down the fork tube.

CAUTION
To avoid damage to the oil and dust seals when installing them over the end of the fork tube, first place a plastic bag over the end of the fork tube. If using a recloseable type of bag, cut off the thick closing portion at the top of the bag. Then coat the exterior surface of the bag with fork oil.

9. Position the oil seal as shown in B, **Figure 65** and slide it and the washer (C, **Figure 65**) over the plastic bag and the fork tube.

10. Position the washer on the top of oil seal recess (**Figure 66**).

11. Use the same tool setup used in Step 7 and drive the oil seal into the slider until it bottoms out and the groove in the slider can be seen above the top surface of the oil seal. Remove the driver.

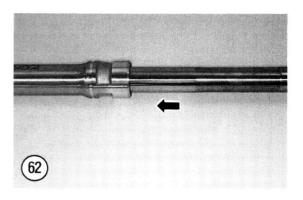

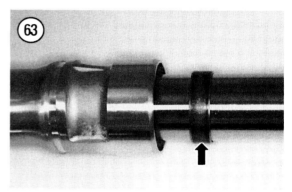

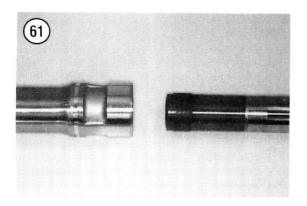

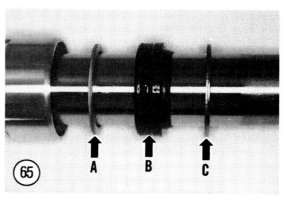

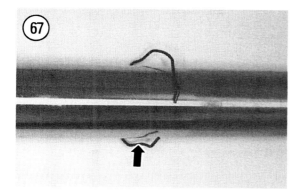

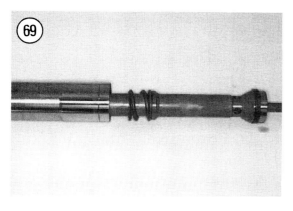

12. Secure the oil seal with the wire stopper ring (**Figure 67**). Make sure the stopper ring is locked into the groove in the fork tube (**Figure 68**).

13. Install the dust seal into the slider. Press it in until it is completely seated, then install the retainer.

14. Insert the piston rod assembly (**Figure 69**) into the fork tube. Push it down until it is completely seated.

NOTE
Steps 15-20 are used to hold the piston rod assembly in place while tightening the bottom bolt in Step 25.

15. Temporarily install the bottom bolt and washer to hold the piston rod assembly in place. Do not tighten the bolt at this time.

16. Compress the fork tube down into the slider to expose the upper end of the piston rod assembly. Make sure the locknut is still screwed all the way *down* onto the end of the threads on the piston rod assembly (A, **Figure 70**).

17. Install the lower spring (B, **Figure 70**) into the fork tube.

18. Install the lower washer (A, **Figure 71**), upper spring (B) and upper washer (C) onto the piston rod assembly.

19. Install the fork cap onto the piston rod and tighten hand-tight.

20. Push down on the fork spring and hand-tighten the fork cap onto the fork tube.

21. Remove the bottom bolt and gasket.

22. Clean the threads of the bottom bolt thoroughly with clean solvent or electrical contact cleaner to remove any remaining thread locking compound.

23. Make sure the gasket (**Figure 72**) is in place on the bottom bolt.

12

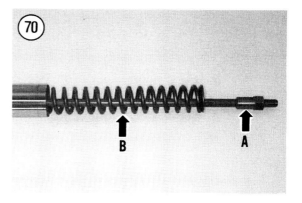

24. Apply ThreeBond No. TB1342 (blue), or equivalent, to the threads on the bottom bolt. Screw the bottom bolt (**Figure 73**) into the base of the slider.

25. Use an impact driver or an Allen wrench and tighten the bottom bolt to the torque specification listed in **Table 7**.

26. Unscrew the fork cap and remove the washers and both springs from the fork tube.

> *NOTE*
> *Honda recommends that the fork oil level be measured to ensure a more accurate filling which results in better handling of the bike.*

27. Hold the fork assembly vertical and compress the fork tube slightly.

28. Refer to **Table 8** and add one-half of the specified amount of fork oil to the fork tube.

29. Pour the remaining half of the fork oil into the top opening of the piston rod assembly until the fork oil flows out of the side breather holes.

30. Hold onto the fork slider and gently pump the fork tube and piston rod assembly up and down 8 to

10 times. This will distribute the fork oil and help bleed any air bubbles out of the upper and lower fork chambers.

31. Completely compress the fork tube into the slider. In a vertical mode, place the fork assembly aside for about 5 minutes to allow the any residual

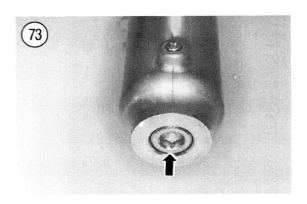

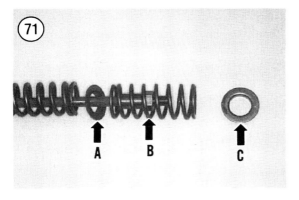

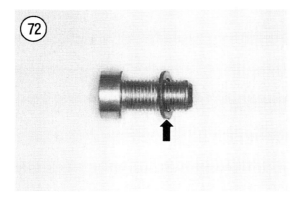

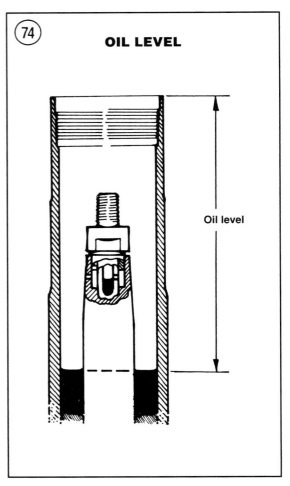

OIL LEVEL

Oil level

air bubbles to escape and allow the fork oil level to settle.

32. Use an accurate ruler or equivalent to achieve the correct oil level is as specified in **Table 8**. Measure the oil level (**Figure 74**) with the fork vertical, completely compressed and with the fork springs and washers removed.

NOTE
*An oil level measuring device can be fabricated as shown in **Figure 75**. Fill the fork tube with a few cc more than the required amount of oil. Position the*

lower edge of the hose clamp against the top edge of the fork tube and draw out the excess oil. Draw oil out until the level reaches the small diameter hole. A precise oil level can be achieved using this simple device.

33. Allow the oil to settle completely and recheck the oil level measurement. Adjust the oil level if necessary.

34. Remove the special tool. Keep the fork in the vertical position and pull the fork tube up until it stops.

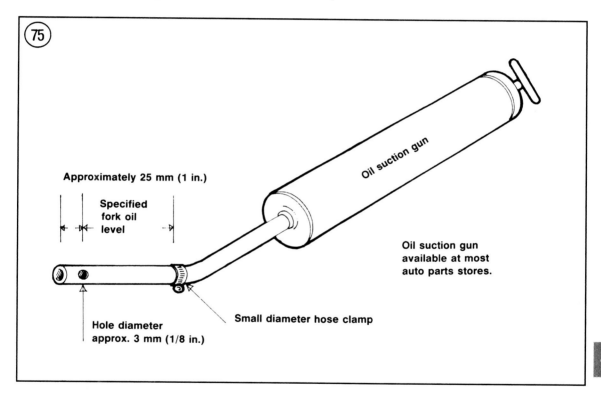

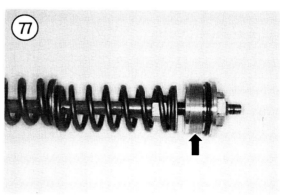

NOTE
The following photographs are shown with the fork on its side for clarity—keep the fork assembly vertical or some of the fork oil will drain out.

35. On models so equipped, install the washer.

36. Compress the fork tube down into the slider sufficiently to expose the upper end of the piston rod assembly. Make sure the locknut is still screwed all the way *down* onto the end of the threads on the piston rod assembly (A, **Figure 70**).

37. Install the lower spring (B, **Figure 70**) into the fork tube.

38. Install the lower washer (A, **Figure 71**), upper spring (B) and upper washer (C) onto the piston rod assembly.

39. Make sure the O-ring (**Figure 76**) on the fork cap is in good condition. Replace if necessary. Apply a light coat of fork oil to the O-ring.

40. Screw the fork cap (**Figure 77**) onto the piston rod assembly until it bottoms out.

41. Use a box wrench on the fork cap (A, **Figure 78**) and an open-end wrench on the piston rod locknut (B, **Figure 78**). Secure the fork cap and tighten the locknut up against the fork cap to the torque specification listed in **Table 7**. Remove the wrenches.

42. Pull up on the fork tube and have an assistant compress the fork spring. Carefully screw the fork cap onto the fork tube—don't cross-thread it. Tighten the fork cap only finger-tight at this time. The fork cap will be tightened after the forks have been installed on the bike.

43. Slide the fork boot onto the fork assembly and into position on the fork slider.

44. Position the breather holes toward the outside of the fork (when it is installed on the bike). Install the lower boot clamp and screw. Move the screw so the head is toward the rear.

45. Repeat for the other fork assembly.

46. Install the fork as described in this supplement. After installation, be sure to tighten the top cap and upper fork bridge bolts.

FORK SERVICE
(XR250L)

Removal/Installation

1. If the fork is going to be disassembled, perform the following:

    a. Have an assistant sit on the bike, apply the front brake, compress the front forks and hold them in this position.

    b. Slightly loosen the Allen bolt at the base of the slider. If the bolt is loosened too much, fork oil will drain from the slider. Loosen both bottom bolts.

    c. Release the pressure on the front forks.

    d. Loosen the upper pinch bolts securing the fork tube to the upper fork bridge (A, **Figure 79**).

    e. Remove the air valve cap and bleed off any air pressure within the fork (**Figure 80**).

    f. Loosen the fork cap bolt at this time.

2. Remove the front wheel as described in this chapter.

3. Remove the front number plate (B, **Figure 79**).

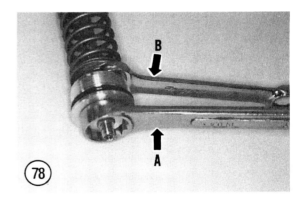

4. Remove the front brake caliper assembly from the left-hand fork slider as described in Chapter Eleven in the main body of this book.

5. Disconnect the speedometer cable from the fork clamp and move the cable out of the way.

6. Loosen the upper and lower pinch bolts securing each fork leg (A and C, **Figure 79**).

7. Carefully pull each fork leg down and out of the upper and lower fork bridge clamps. It may be necessary to slightly rotate the fork tube while pulling it down and out.

8. Install by reversing these removal steps while noting the following:

   a. Install each fork tube so that the fork cap bolt is even with the top edge of the upper fork bridge (**Figure 81**).

   b. If the forks were disassembled, tighten the fork cap after the fork tubes are installed and secure

in the lower fork bridge. Tighten the fork cap to the torque specification listed in **Table 7**.

   c. Tighten the upper and lower fork bridge clamp bolts and the fork cap to the torque specification listed in **Table 7**.

   d. Pull the rubber boot up so the top edge touches the lower surface of the steering stem (D, **Figure 79**). Position the boot clamp screw head toward the rear and tighten securely.

Disassembly

Refer to **Figure 82** for this procedure.

1. Remove the front forks as described in this chapter.

2. Remove the fork boot clamps and remove the boot from the fork assembly.

NOTE
When loosening the Allen retaining bolt in the bottom of the fork tube, leave the fork cap and fork springs installed until the Allen bolt is loosened and removed. The internal spring pressure against the damper rod assembly will hold it in place as the Allen bolt is being loosened and removed.

3. If the Allen bolt was not loosened prior to removing the forks from the bike, perform the following:

   a. Install the fork in a vise with soft jaws.

   b. Have an assistant compress the fork tube assembly as much as possible and hold it compressed against the rebound spring.

   c. Loosen then remove the Allen bolt at the base of the slider with the Allen wrench and an impact tool. Do not remove the Allen bolt at this time.

WARNING
Be careful when removing the fork cap as the spring is under pressure. Protect your eyes accordingly.

4. Slowly unscrew and remove the fork cap.

5. Remove the upper spring, the spring guide and the lower spring from the fork tube.

6. Turn the fork assembly upside down over a drain pan and completely drain the fork oil. Stroke the fork several times to pump out any remaining oil. Stand the fork tube upside down in the drain pan and allow the tube to drain for several minutes.

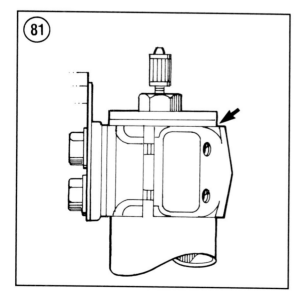

12

7. Remove the Allen bolt and gasket from the base of the slider.

NOTE
The oil lock piece is often stuck to the bottom of the slider and may not come out with the damper rod. Don't lose the oil lock piece.

8. Remove the oil lock piece from the end of the damper rod.

9. Turn the fork assembly upside down and slide out the damper rod assembly complete with the rebound spring.

10. Slide the dust seal off the fork tube.

11. Remove the stopper ring securing the oil seal.

NOTE
On this type of fork, force is needed to remove the fork tube from the slider.

12. Install the fork tube in a vise with soft jaws.

13. There is an interference fit between the bushing in the fork slider and bushing on the fork tube. To remove the fork tube from the slider, pull hard on the fork tube using quick in-and-out strokes (**Figure**

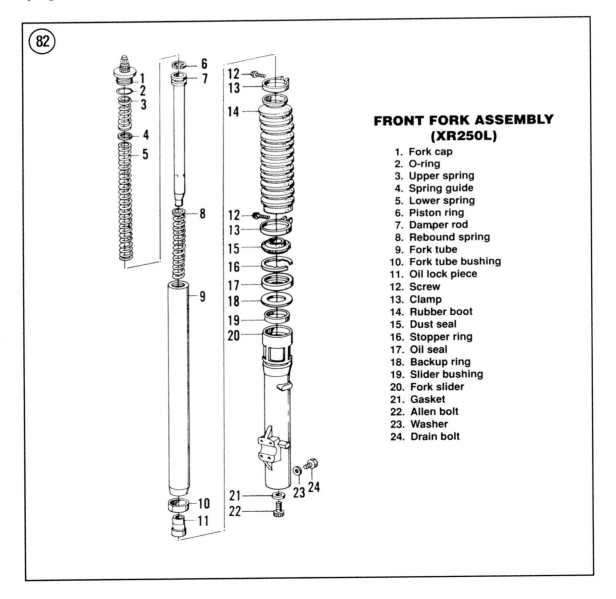

FRONT FORK ASSEMBLY (XR250L)
1. Fork cap
2. O-ring
3. Upper spring
4. Spring guide
5. Lower spring
6. Piston ring
7. Damper rod
8. Rebound spring
9. Fork tube
10. Fork tube bushing
11. Oil lock piece
12. Screw
13. Clamp
14. Rubber boot
15. Dust seal
16. Stopper ring
17. Oil seal
18. Backup ring
19. Slider bushing
20. Fork slider
21. Gasket
22. Allen bolt
23. Washer
24. Drain bolt

83). Doing so will withdraw the bushing, backup ring and oil seal from the slider.

14. Withdraw the fork tube from the slider.

NOTE
Do not remove the fork tube bushing unless it is going to be replaced. Inspect it as described in this section.

15. Remove the oil lock piece from the end of the damper rod.

16. Inspect all parts as described in this chapter.

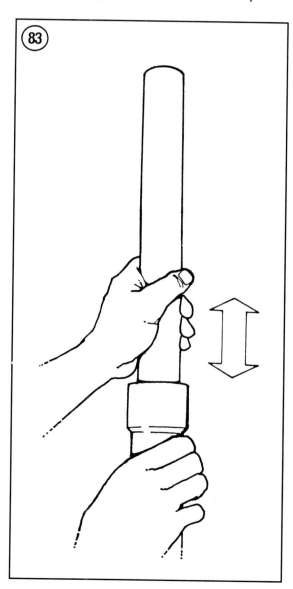

Inspection

1. Thoroughly clean all parts in solvent and dry them completely.

2. Inspect the damper rod assembly for damage or roughness. Check for galling, deep scores or excessive wear. Replace the parts as necessary. Make sure all the oil passages are clean and free of any sludge or oil residue.

3. Check the damper rod for straightness as shown in **Figure 84**. Replace if the damper rod if the runout exceeds 0.2 mm (0.008 in.).

4. Make sure the oil holes in the damper rod are clear. Clean out if necessary.

5. Inspect the piston ring (**Figure 85**) on the end of the damper rod for wear or damage. Replace if necessary.

6. Check the upper fork tube for straightness. Replace the tube if bent or severely scratched.

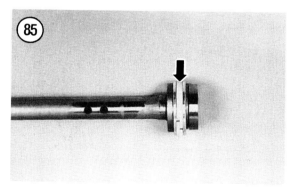

12

7. Check the slider for dents or exterior damage that may cause the fork tube to hang up during riding. Replace if necessary.

8. Measure the free length of the upper and lower fork springs, as shown in **Figure 86**. If the spring(s) is sagged to the to the service limit listed in **Table 8**, replace the spring(s).

9. Inspect the slider and fork tube bushings. If either is scratched or scored, they must be replaced. If the Teflon coating is worn off so that the copper base material is showing on 3/4 of the total surface area, the bushing(s) must be replaced.

10. Inspect the gasket (**Figure 87**) on the Allen bolt and replace if necessary.

11. Inspect each rubber boot for tears or abrasive damage. A damaged boot will allow dirt and moisture to pack up next to the dust seal leading to early failure of the seal. Packed in dirt can scratch the surface of the fork tubes as well as damage the fork dust and oil seals. Install new fork boots if any damage exists.

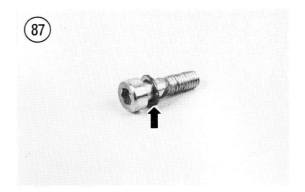

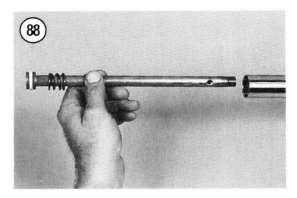

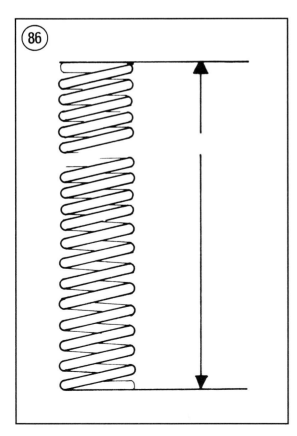

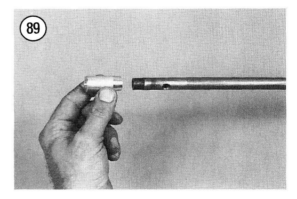

12. Make sure the breather holes in the base of the rubber boot are clear. Clean out if necessary.

13. Inspect the dust seal for wear or damage. Replace if necessary.

14. Replace any parts that are worn or damaged. Simply cleaning and reinstalling unserviceable components will not improve performance of the front suspension.

Assembly

Refer to **Figure 82** for this procedure.

1. Make sure that all fork components are clean and dry. Wipe clean the seal bore in the fork slider with a lint-free cloth.

2. Coat all parts with the recommended fork oil prior to installation. Refer to **Table 8**.

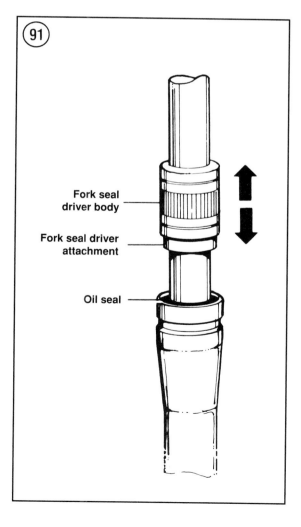

91

Fork seal driver body

Fork seal driver attachment

Oil seal

3. If removed, install a new bushing onto the fork tube.

4. Install the rebound spring on the damper rod and install the damper rod assembly into the fork tube (**Figure 88**).

5. Temporarily install the lower fork spring, spring guide, upper fork spring and fork cap to hold the damper rod in place. The tension of the fork springs will keep the damper rod in place through the end of the fork tube and ease the assembly process.

6. Slide the oil lock piece over the end of the damper rod assembly as shown in **Figure 89**).

7. Carefully install the fork tube and the damper rod assembly into the slider as shown in **Figure 90**.

8. Clean the threads of the Allen bolt thoroughly with clean solvent or spray contact cleaner. Make sure that the lockwasher is in place on the Allen bolt. Apply a couple of drops of a locking compound such as ThreeBond No. TB1360 (red) or Loctite No. 271 (red) to the bolt threads.

9. Install the Allen bolt and gasket and tighten to the specifications listed in **Table 7**.

10. Slide the fork slider bushing down the fork tube and rest it on top of the fork slider.

11. Position the backup ring with the chamfered side facing down, then slide it down the fork tube and rest it on top of the fork slider bushing.

NOTE
The slider bushing can be installed with an oil seal driver or a piece of tubing and suitable plate that fits over the fork tube. Oil seal drivers are available from Honda dealers and mail order tool suppliers.

12. Drive the new slider bushing into the slider with the fork seal driver, or equivalent, until it bottoms out.

13. Position the oil seal with the open groove facing upward and slide the oil seal down the fork tube.

14. Slide the fork seal driver and attachment down the fork tube (**Figure 91**) and drive the seal into the slider until it bottoms out and the groove in the slider can be seen above the top surface of the oil seal.

15. Secure the oil seal with the stopper ring. Make sure that the stopper ring is locked into the groove in the fork slider.

16. Install the dust seal (**Figure 92**) into the slider. Press it in until it is completely seated.

12

17. Remove fork cap, the upper fork spring, spring guide and the lower fork spring.

18. Refer to **Table 8** and add the specified amount of fork oil to the fork tube.

19. Position the lower fork spring with the closer wound coils going in first and install the lower fork spring.

NOTE
The upper spring is not directional, so, either end can be inserted first.

20. Install the spring guide and the upper fork spring.

21. Inspect the O-ring seal (**Figure 93**) on the fork cap; replace if necessary.

22. Install the fork cap and tighten only finger tight at this time. Tighten the top cap to the final torque specification after the fork has been installed.

23. Slide the fork boot onto the fork assembly and position it on the fork slider.

24. Position the breather holes toward the outside of the fork (when it is installed on the bike). Install the lower boot clamp and screw. Move the screw so the head is toward the rear.

25. Repeat for the other fork assembly.

26. Install the fork as described in this supplement.

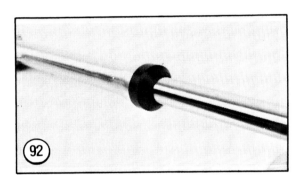

Table 7 FRONT SUSPENSION TORQUE SPECIFICATIONS

Item	N·m	ft.-lb.
Steering stem adjust nut		
Initial tightening	25	18
Final tightening	5	3.6
Steering stem nut	118	87
Upper fork bridge	24	17
Lower fork bridge	33	24
Bottom bolt		
XR250R	34-46	25-33
Fork locknut (XR250R)	15	11
Fork cap		
XR250R	25-35	18-25
XR250L	23	17

Table 8 FRONT SUSPENSION SPECIFICATIONS

Item	Standard	Service limit
Fork spring free length		
XR250R		
Upper spring	79 mm (3.1 in.)	78.2 mm (3.08 in.)
Lower spring	442 mm (17.4 in.)	438.6 mm (17.27 in.
XL250L		
Upper spring	88.1 mm (3.47 in.)	87.2 mm (3.43 in.)
Lower spring	544.6 mm (21.44 in.)	539.2 mm (21.23 in.
XR250R		
Fork oil type	Pro-Honda Suspension Fluid SS-7	
Fork oil capacity	492 ml (16.6 fl. oz.)	
Standard oil level	128 mm (5.0 in.)	
XR250L		
Fork oil type	Pro-Honda Suspension Fluid SS-8	
Fork oil capacity	550 ml (18.6 fl. oz.)	

CHAPTER TEN

REAR SUSPENSION

REAR WHEEL

Removal

1. Loosen the rear axle nut (A, **Figure 94**).

2. Support the bike securely with the rear wheel off the ground. If you don't have a bike stand, place wooden block(s) under the engine or frame.

3. Remove the rear axle nut (A, **Figure 94**) and on XR250L models, the washer.

4. Remove the snail adjusters (B, **Figure 94**) from the axle.

5. On XR250R models, remove the stopper plate (A, **Figure 95**) from the axle and from the locating pin (B, **Figure 95**) on the swing arm.

NOTE
The drive chain can be completely removed at this time, although it is not necessary in order to remove the rear wheel.

6. Hold onto the rear wheel and withdraw the rear axle from the rear wheel and swing arm.

NOTE
On models so equipped, note the location of the washer on the rear axle be-

12

tween the caliper mounting bracket and the swing arm. The washer must be in this location during wheel installation.

7. Push the wheel forward and derail the drive chain from the driven sprocket (**Figure 96**).

NOTE
The following photos are shown with the brake hose removed from the caliper for clarity. It is not necessary to disconnect it for this procedure.

8. On XR250R models, perform the following:
   a. Unhook the rear brake hose from the hose guides on the top surface of the swing arm.
   b. Slowly pull the rear wheel toward the rear to disengage the brake caliper mounting bracket from the boss on the swing arm (**Figure 97**).
   c. Carefully pull the rear wheel toward the rear, disengage the brake disc from the caliper assembly and the swing arm.
   d. Tie the rear brake caliper up to the fame with a piece of wire or string to avoid strain on the brake hose.

NOTE
The right- and left-hand axle spacers are not symmetrical. As soon as the front wheel is removed, remove the spacer from each side of the hub and mark them with a R or L. This will ensure that they are installed on the correct side of the hub during installation.

9. Don't lose the axle spacer on each side of the hub.
10. To avoid misplacing parts, reinstall the snail adjusters, spacers, washer and nut onto the rear axle.

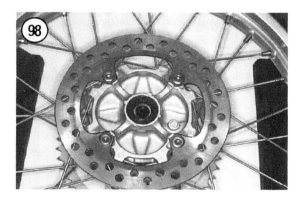

CAUTION
*Do not set the wheel down on the disc or sprocket surfaces as they may get scratched or warped. Set the sidewalls on 2 wooden blocks (**Figure 98**).*

NOTE
Insert a piece of vinyl tubing or wood in the caliper in place of the brake disc. Then, if the brake pedal is inadvertently applied, the caliper piston will not be forced out of its cylinder. If this does happen, the caliper must be disassembled to reseat the piston and the system will have to be bled.

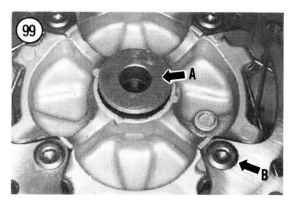

Inspection

1. If still in place, remove the right- (A, **Figure 99**) and left-hand (A, **Figure 100**) axle spacers.

2A. On XR250R models, inspect the right-hand oil seal (**Figure 101**) for excessive wear, hardness, cracks or other damage.

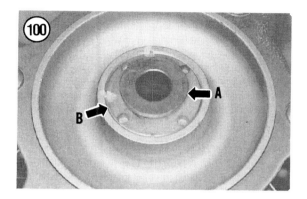

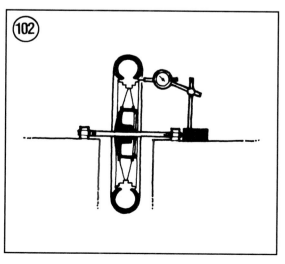

2B. On XR250L models, inspect the oil seal on each side for excessive wear, hardness, cracks or other damage.

3. Check the wheel bearings for excessive wear or damage. Turn the inner race with your finger. The bearing must turn smoothly without excessive play or other damage. Replace questionable bearings as described under *Rear Hub* in Chapter Ten in the main body of this book.

4. On XR250R models, inspect the left-hand bearing retainer (B, **Figure 100**) for wear, damage or looseness. If the retainer requires service, refer to *Rear Hub* in Chapter Ten in the main body of this book.

5. Clean the axle and spacers using solvent. Make sure all axle contact surfaces are clean and free of dirt and old grease prior to installation. If these surfaces are not cleaned, the axle may be difficult to remove later on.

6. Check the disc brake bolts (B, **Figure 99**) for tightness. Refer to **Table 9** and retighten if necessary.

7. Check the driven sprocket bolts and nuts for tightness. Refer to **Table 9** and retighten if necessary.

8. Measure the axial and radial runout of the wheel with a dial indicator as shown in **Figure 102**. The maximum axial and radial runout is 2.0 mm (0.08 in.). If the runout exceeds this specification, check the wheel bearing condition. If the wheel bearings are okay, tighten or replace bent or loose spokes. Refer to *Spoke Adjustment* in Chapter Nine in the main body of this book. Check axle runout as described under *Rear Hub Inspection* in Chapter Ten in the main body of this book.

12

Installation

1. Make sure all axle contact surfaces on the swing arm and axle spacers are free of dirt and small burrs.

2. Apply a light coat of grease to the axle, bearings, spacers and grease seals.

3. Remove the vinyl tubing or piece of wood from the brake caliper.

4. Make sure the right- and left-hand axle spacers are installed on the correct side of the rear hub.

5. Move the rear brake caliper into position on the swing arm.

6. Position the wheel into place and carefully insert the brake disc between the brake pads of the caliper assembly (**Figure 103**).

7. Carefully move the wheel forward and install the drive chain onto the driven sprocket.

8A. On XR250R models, install the snail adjuster onto the rear axle and insert the rear axle through the swing arm and rear wheel hub from the left-hand side.

8B. On XR250L models, install the snail adjuster onto the rear axle and insert the rear axle through the swing arm and rear wheel hub from the right-hand side.

9. On models so equipped, position the washer so it is located between the swing arm and the caliper mounting bracket.

10. On XR250R models, pull the rear wheel and rear axle back and slip the stopper plate over the rear axle (A, **Figure 95**) and onto the locating pin (B, **Figure 95**) on the swing arm. Make sure the stopper plate slot is correctly engaged with swing arm locating pin.

11. Install the snail adjuster, washer (XR250L models) and nut. Do not tighten the axle nut at this time.

12. Install the rear brake hose under the hose guides on the top surface of the swing arm.

13. Before tightening the axle nut, perform the drive chain adjustment procedure as described in this supplement and under *Drive Chain Adjustment (Pro-Link Models)* in Chapter Three in the main body of this book.

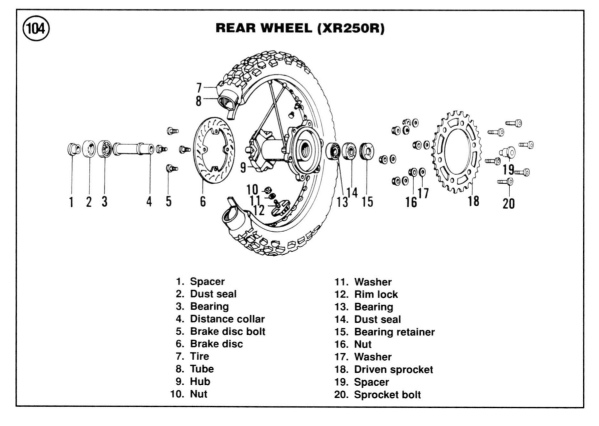

REAR WHEEL (XR250R)

1. Spacer
2. Dust seal
3. Bearing
4. Distance collar
5. Brake disc bolt
6. Brake disc
7. Tire
8. Tube
9. Hub
10. Nut
11. Washer
12. Rim lock
13. Bearing
14. Dust seal
15. Bearing retainer
16. Nut
17. Washer
18. Driven sprocket
19. Spacer
20. Sprocket bolt

14. After the wheel is completely installed, roll the bike back and forth and apply the brakes a couple of times to make sure the wheel rotates freely and the brake operates correctly.

REAR HUB

Refer to the following illustrations for this procedure:

    a. **Figure 104**: XR250R.
    b. **Figure 105**: XR250L.

Disassembly/Inspection/Assembly

Service procedures for the rear hub are the same as on prior models with the exception of the appearance of some of the components. Refer to the illustrations and to *Rear Hub* in Chapter Ten in the main section of this book.

SWING ARM AND SHOCK LINKAGE

Refer to the following illustrations for this procedure:

    a. **Figure 106**: XR250R swing arm.
    b. **Figure 107**: XR250L swing arm.
    c. **Figure 108**: Shock linkage.

All service procedures for the swing arm and shock linkage are the same as on prior models with the exception of the appearance of some of the components and the removal of the rear brake caliper and hydraulic hose. Refer to the illustrations and to *Swing Arm (Pro-Link)* in Chapter Ten in the main section of this book and to the Chapter Eleven section of this supplement for the removal of the brake caliper and brake hose.

SHOCK ABSORBER (PRO-LINK)

Spring Peload Adjustment

The adjustment procedure is the same as on previous models with the exception of the spring length. The spring length is as follows:

    a. XR250R: Standard length: 211 mm (8.3 in.).
        Maximum length: 218.5 mm (8.6 in.).
        Minimum length: 201.5 mm (7.9 in.).
    b. XR250L: Standard length: 206.5 mm (8.13 in.).

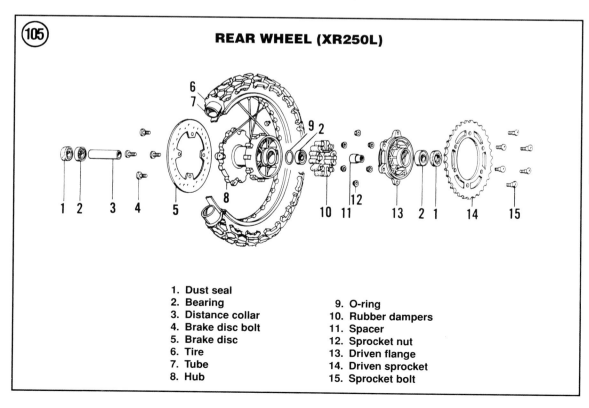

(105) REAR WHEEL (XR250L)

1. Dust seal
2. Bearing
3. Distance collar
4. Brake disc bolt
5. Brake disc
6. Tire
7. Tube
8. Hub
9. O-ring
10. Rubber dampers
11. Spacer
12. Sprocket nut
13. Driven flange
14. Driven sprocket
15. Sprocket bolt

12

106 ## PRO-LINK SWING ARM ASSEMBLY (XR250R)

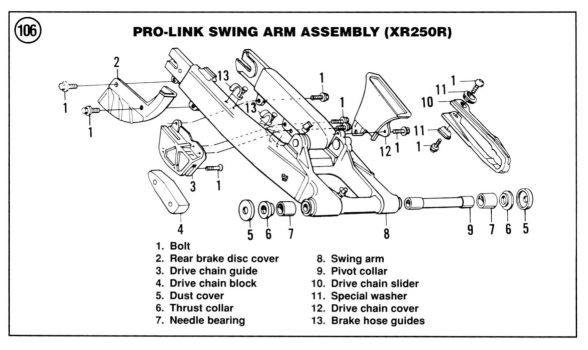

1. Bolt
2. Rear brake disc cover
3. Drive chain guide
4. Drive chain block
5. Dust cover
6. Thrust collar
7. Needle bearing
8. Swing arm
9. Pivot collar
10. Drive chain slider
11. Special washer
12. Drive chain cover
13. Brake hose guides

107 ## PRO-LINK SWING ARM ASSEMBLY (XR250L)

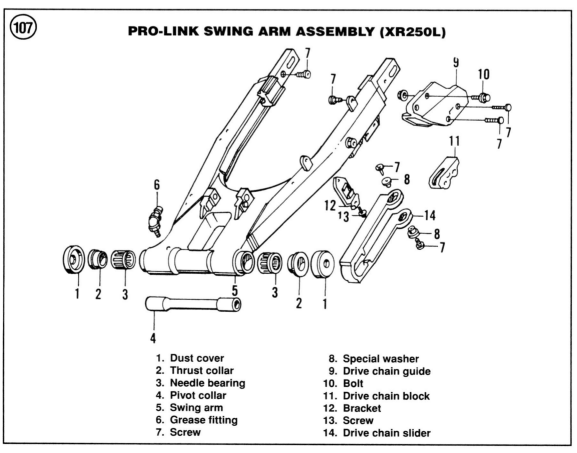

1. Dust cover
2. Thrust collar
3. Needle bearing
4. Pivot collar
5. Swing arm
6. Grease fitting
7. Screw
8. Special washer
9. Drive chain guide
10. Bolt
11. Drive chain block
12. Bracket
13. Screw
14. Drive chain slider

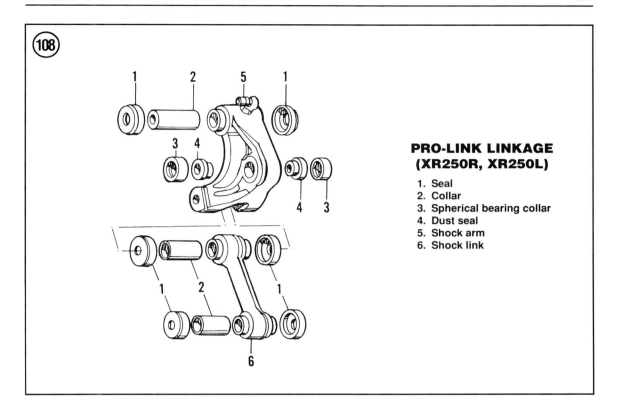

PRO-LINK LINKAGE (XR250R, XR250L)

1. Seal
2. Collar
3. Spherical bearing collar
4. Dust seal
5. Shock arm
6. Shock link

Table 9 REAR SUSPENSION TORQUE SPECIFICATIONS

Item	N·m	ft.-lb.
Rear axle nut	80-110	59-81
Rear disc bolts	40-45	29-33
Driven sprocket bolts and nuts		
XR250R	32-38	23-27
XR250L	37	26

12

CHAPTER ELEVEN

BRAKES

FRONT BRAKE PAD REPLACEMENT

There is no recommended mileage interval for changing the friction pads in the disc brakes. Pad wear depends greatly on riding habits and conditions. The pads should be checked for wear prior to each race or when the wear indicator reaches the edge of the brake disc.

To maintain an even brake pressure on the disc always replace both pads in the caliper at the same time. The caliper assembly does not have to be removed from the fork slider for brake pad replacement.

CAUTION
*Check the pads more frequently when the wear limit line approaches the disc. On some pads the wear line is very close to the metal backing plate (**Figure 109**). If pad wear happens to be uneven for some reason the backing plate may contact with the disc and cause damage.*

Refer to **Figure 110** for this procedure.

1. The pistons must be repositioned within the caliper to make room for the thicker replacement brake pads. When the pistons are repositioned, the master cylinder brake fluid level will rise and must be removed as follows:

a. Clean the top of the master cylinder of all dirt and foreign matter.

b. Remove the screws securing the cover and remove the cover and the diaphragm from the master cylinder.

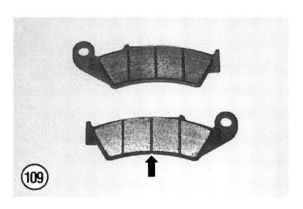

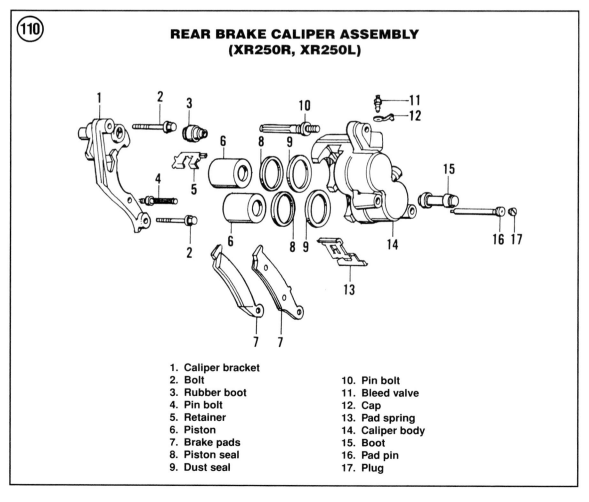

**REAR BRAKE CALIPER ASSEMBLY
(XR250R, XR250L)**

1. Caliper bracket
2. Bolt
3. Rubber boot
4. Pin bolt
5. Retainer
6. Piston
7. Brake pads
8. Piston seal
9. Dust seal
10. Pin bolt
11. Bleed valve
12. Cap
13. Pad spring
14. Caliper body
15. Boot
16. Pad pin
17. Plug

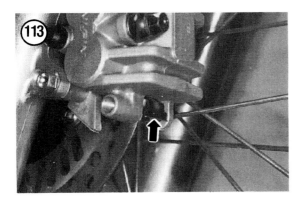

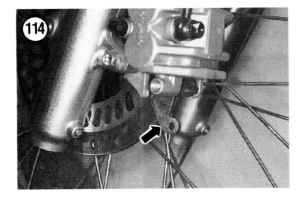

CAUTION
In the next step, do not push too hard on the caliper as the disc may become slightly distorted. The disc is relatively thin to dissipate heat and may be damaged from any excessive side pressure.

  c. Slowly, and carefully, push the caliper onto the disc to reposition the pistons back into the caliper body. Constantly check the reservoir to make sure brake fluid does not overflow. Siphon off fluid prior to it overflowing.

  d. The pistons should move freely back into the caliper. If they don't, and there is evidence of them sticking in the cylinders, the caliper should be removed and serviced as described in this section of the supplement.

2. Support the bike securely with the front wheel off the ground. If you don't have a bike stand, place wooden block(s) under the engine or frame.

3. Unscrew and remove the plug (**Figure 111**) from the pad pin.

4. Unscrew and remove the pad pin bolt (**Figure 112**).

5. Slide both brake pads out of the caliper assembly.

6. If necessary, carefully remove any rust or corrosion from the disc.

7. Lightly coat the backs of the new pads (*not* the friction material) with the disc brake lubricant.

NOTE
When purchasing new pads, check with your dealer to make sure the friction compound of the new pad is compatible with the disc material. Remove any roughness from the backs of the new pads with a fine-cut file; blow them clean with compressed air.

8. Make sure the pad spring (**Figure 113**) is still in place in the caliper body.

9. Install the outboard pad (**Figure 114**) into the caliper. Make sure it is correctly seated in the caliper.

10. Slightly press the outboard brake pad against the pad spring and partially install the pad pin (A, **Figure 115**) through the hole in the outboard pad (B, **Figure 115**).

11. Install the inboard pad into the caliper. Make sure it is correctly seated in the caliper.

12. Slightly press the inboard brake pad against the pad spring and push the pad pin through the hole in the inboard pad.

12

13. Screw the pad pin (**Figure 112**) into the caliper and tighten to the torque specification listed in **Table 10**.

14. Install and tighten the pad pin plug (**Figure 111**) securely.

15. With the front wheel still off the ground, spin the front wheel and activate the front brake lever as many times as it takes to refill the cylinders in each caliper and correctly locate the brake pads.

WARNING
Use brake fluid clearly marked DOT 4 from a sealed container. Always use the same brand name; do not intermix as many brands are not compatible. Do not intermix silicone based (DOT 5) brake fluid as it can cause brake component damage leading to brake system failure.

16. Refill the master cylinder reservoir, if necessary, to maintain the correct fluid level as seen through the viewing port on the side. Install the diaphragm and cover. Tighten the cover screws securely.

WARNING
*Do not ride the motorcycle until you are sure the brakes are operating correctly with full hydraulic advantage. If necessary, bleed the brake as described under **Bleeding the System** in Chapter Eleven in the main body of this book.*

17. Bed the pads in gradually at the first. If possible do some dirt riding prior to entering a race. Use only light pressure as much as possible. Immediate hard application will glaze the new friction pads and greatly reduce the effectiveness of the brake.

FRONT CALIPER

Removal/Installation

Refer to **Figure 110** for this procedure.

CAUTION
Do not spill any brake fluid on the front fork or front wheel. Wash off any spilled brake fluid immediately, as it will destroy the finish. Use soapy water to remove brake fluid then rinse completely.

1. If the caliper assembly is going to be disassembled for service, perform the following:

NOTE
By performing Step 1, compressed air may not be necessary for piston removal during caliper disassembly.

a. Remove the brake pads as described in this supplement.

b. Pull the backside of the caliper toward the brake disc. Do not come in contact with the disc.

CAUTION
Do not allow the pistons to travel out far enough to contact the brake disc. If this happens the pistons may scratch or gouge the disc during caliper removal.

c. Slowly apply the brake lever to push the pistons part way out of caliper assembly for ease of removal during caliper service.

2. Clean the top of the master cylinder of all dirt and foreign matter.

3. Loose the screws securing the front master cylinder cover. Pull up and loosen the cover and the diaphragm. This will allow air to enter the reservoir and allow the brake fluid to drain out more quickly in the next step.

4. Remove the union bolt and sealing washers (A, **Figure 116**) attaching the brake hose to the caliper assembly. Don't lose the sealing washer on each side of the hose fitting.

5. Place the end of the brake hose over an container and let the brake fluid drain out into the container. Dispose of this brake fluid properly—never reuse brake fluid.

6. Place the loose end of the brake hose in a reclosable plastic bag to prevent the entry of foreign matter and prevent brake fluid from dribbling out.

7. Remove the bolts (B, **Figure 116**) securing the brake caliper assembly to the front fork.

8. Remove the brake caliper assembly from the front fork and from the brake disc.

9. Install by reversing these removal steps while noting the following:

    a. Carefully install the caliper assembly onto the disc being careful not to damage the discs.

    b. Install the bolts securing the brake caliper assembly to the front fork and tighten to the torque specification listed in **Table 10**.

    c. Install a new sealing washer on each side of the brake hose fitting and install the union bolt. Screw the union bolt into the caliper and tighten to the torque specification listed in **Table 10**.

    d. Install the brake pads, as described in this supplement, and bleed the brake as described under *Bleeding the System* in Chapter Eleven in the main body of this book.

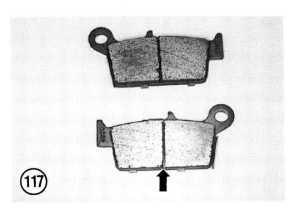

WARNING
Do not ride the motorcycle until you are sure that the brakes are operating properly.

Disassembly/Inspection/Assembly

Service procedures for the rear hub are the same as on prior models with the exception of the appearance of some of the components. Refer to **Figure 110** and to *Front Caliper Rebuilding* in Chapter Eleven in the main section of this book.

REAR BRAKE PAD REPLACEMENT

There is no recommended mileage interval for changing the friction pads in the disc brakes. Pad wear depends greatly on riding habits and conditions. The pads should be checked for wear prior to each race or when the wear indicator reaches the edge of the brake disc.

To maintain an even brake pressure on the disc always replace both pads in the caliper at the same time. The caliper assembly does not have to be removed from the fork slider for brake pad replacement.

CAUTION
*Check the pads more frequently when the wear limit line approaches the disc. On some pads the wear line is very close to the metal backing plate (**Figure 117**). If pad wear happens to be uneven for some reason the backing plate may come in contact with the disc and cause damage.*

Refer to **Figure 118** for this procedure.

1. The pistons must be repositioned within the caliper to make room for the thicker replacement brake pads. When the pistons are repositioned, the master cylinder brake fluid level will rise and must be removed as follows:

    a. Clean the cover of the master cylinder remote reservoir of all dirt and foreign matter.

    b. Unscrew the cover (**Figure 119**) and remove the diaphragm plate and diaphragm from the master cylinder remote reservoir.

CAUTION
In the next step, do not push too hard on the caliper as the disc may become

12

slightly distorted. The disc is relatively thin to dissipate heat and may be damaged from any excessive side pressure.

c. Slowly and carefully, push the caliper onto the disc to reposition the pistons back into the caliper body. Constantly check the reservoir to make sure brake fluid does not overflow. Siphon off fluid prior to it overflowing.

d. The pistons should move freely back into the caliper. If they don't, and there is evidence of

them sticking in the cylinders, the caliper should be removed and serviced as described in this section of the supplement.

2. Support the bike securely with the rear wheel off the ground. If you don't have a bike stand, place wooden block(s) under the engine or frame.

3. Unscrew and remove the plug (**Figure 120**) from the pad pin.

4. Unscrew and remove the pad pin bolt (**Figure 121**).

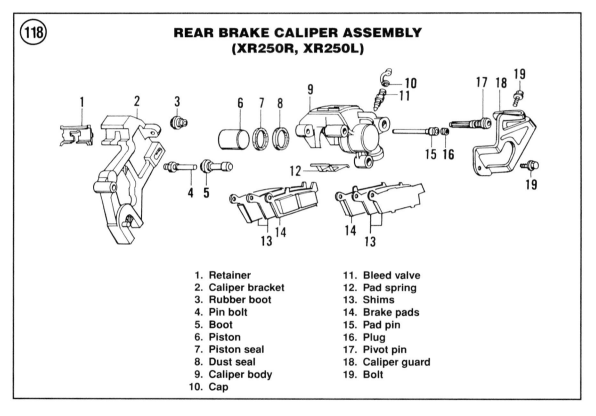

(118)

**REAR BRAKE CALIPER ASSEMBLY
(XR250R, XR250L)**

1. Retainer
2. Caliper bracket
3. Rubber boot
4. Pin bolt
5. Boot
6. Piston
7. Piston seal
8. Dust seal
9. Caliper body
10. Cap
11. Bleed valve
12. Pad spring
13. Shims
14. Brake pads
15. Pad pin
16. Plug
17. Pivot pin
18. Caliper guard
19. Bolt

(119)

(120)

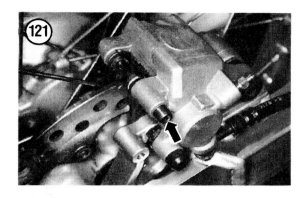

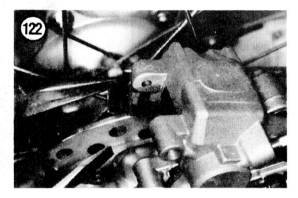

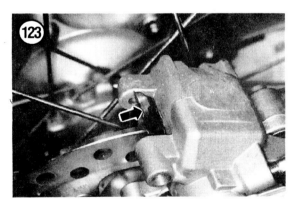

5. Slide both brake pads out of the caliper assembly.

6. If necessary, carefully remove any rust or corrosion from the disc.

7. Lightly coat the backs of the new pads (*not* the friction material) with disc brake lubricant.

NOTE
When purchasing new pads, check with your dealer to make sure the friction compound of the new pad is compatible with the disc material. Remove any roughness from the backs of the new pads with a fine-cut file; blow them clean with compressed air.

8. If removed, install the pad spring (**Figure 122**). Push it up and make sure it is correctly seated in the caliper (**Figure 123**).

9. Install the inboard pad (**Figure 124**) into the caliper. Make sure it is correctly seated in the caliper, then hold it in place

10. Install the outboard pad (**Figure 125**) into the caliper. Make sure it is correctly seated in the caliper.

11. Slightly press both brake pads against the pad spring and install the pad pin (**Figure 121**) through the hole in both pads. Screw the pad pin into the caliper and tighten to the torque specification listed in **Table 10**.

12. Tighten the pad pin plug securely (**Figure 120**).

13. With the front wheel still off the ground, spin the front wheel and activate the front brake lever as many times as it takes to refill the cylinders in each caliper and correctly locate the brake pads.

WARNING
Use brake fluid clearly marked DOT 4 from a sealed container. Other types may cause brake failure. Always use the same brand name; do not intermix as

12

many brands are not compatible. Do not intermix silicone based (DOT 5) brake fluid as it can cause brake component damage leading to brake system failure.

14. Refill the master cylinder reservoir, if necessary, to maintain the correct fluid level as seen through the transparent reservoir (**Figure 126**). Install the diaphragm, diaphragm plate and screw on the cover securely.

> *WARNING*
> *Do not ride the motorcycle until you are sure the brakes are operating correctly with full hydraulic advantage. If necessary, bleed the brake as described under **Bleeding the System** in Chapter Eleven in the main body of this book.*

15. Bed the pads in gradually at the first. If possible do some dirt riding prior to entering a race. Use only light pressure as much as possible. Immediate hard application will glaze the new friction pads and greatly reduce the effectiveness of the brake.

REAR CALIPER

Removal/Installation

> *CAUTION*
> *Do not spill any brake fluid on the rear wheel or swing arm. Wash off any spilled brake fluid immediately, as it will destroy the finish.*

> *NOTE*
> *By performing Step 1, compressed air may not be necessary for piston removal during caliper disassembly.*

1. If the caliper assembly is going to be disassembled for service, perform the following:
   a. Remove the brake pads as described in this chapter.
   b. Pull the backside of the caliper toward the brake disc. Do not come in contact with the disc.

> *CAUTION*
> *Do not allow the pistons to travel out far enough to contact the brake disc. If this happens the pistons may scratch or gouge the disc during caliper removal.*

c. Slowly apply the brake pedal to push the pistons part way out of caliper assembly for ease of removal during caliper service.

2. Clean the top of the master cylinder remote reservoir of all dirt and foreign matter.

3. Unscrew the cover (**Figure 119**) and remove the diaphragm plate and diaphragm from the master cylinder remote reservoir. This will allow air to enter the reservoir and allow the brake fluid to drain out more quickly in the next step.

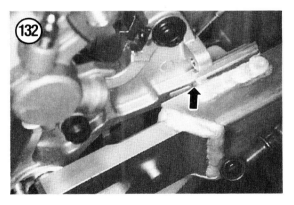

4. On XR250R models, remove the bolts securing the caliper guard (**Figure 127**) and remove the guard. Don't lose the spacer (A, **Figure 128**) on the rear bolt (B, **Figure 128**).

5. Remove the caliper mounting bolt (**Figure 129**) and pivot the caliper up and partially off the mounting bracket.

6. Remove the union bolt and sealing washer (**Figure 130**) attaching the brake hose to the caliper assembly. Don't lose the sealing washer on each side of the hose fitting.

7. Place the end of the brake hose over a container and let the brake fluid drain out. Dispose of this brake fluid properly—never reuse brake fluid.

8. Place the loose end of the brake hose in a reclosable plastic bag to prevent the entry of foreign matter and prevent brake fluid from dribbling out.

9A. On XR250R models, perform the following:

a. Remove the rear axle and derail the drive chain as described under *Rear Wheel Removal/Installation* in this supplement.

b. Pull the rear wheel toward the rear, then pivot the caliper assembly (**Figure 131**) up and away from the mounting bracket.

c. Hold onto the caliper assembly, pull the rear wheel farther toward the rear and remove the caliper assembly from the mounting bracket.

d. Remove the mounting bracket from the swing arm.

9B. On XR250L models,

a. Remove the rear wheel as described in this supplement.

b. Remove the caliper assembly.

10. Install by reversing these removal steps while noting the following:

a. On XR250R models, align the caliper mounting bracket slot with the locating tang on the swing arm (**Figure 132**).

b. Tighten the rear axle nut to the torque specification listed in **Table 9**.

c. Tighten the union bolt (**Figure 133**) to the torque specification listed in **Table 10**.

d. Bleed the brake as described under *Bleeding the System* in Chapter Eleven in the main body of this book.

WARNING
Do not ride the motorcycle until you are sure that the brakes are operating properly.

12

Disassembly

Refer to the **Figure 134** for this procedure.
1. Remove the caliper and brake pads as described in this chapter.
2. If still attached, remove the caliper assembly (A, **Figure 135**) from the caliper mounting bracket (B, **Figure 135**).
3. On XR250L models, remove the bolt securing the disc guard and remove the guard from the caliper bracket.

> *NOTE*
> *If the pistons were partially forced out of the caliper body during removal, Step 1, may not be necessary. If the pistons or caliper bores are corroded or very dirty, a small amount of compressed air may be necessary to completely remove the pistons from the body bores.*

4. Place a shop cloth or piece of soft wood over the end of the pistons.

5. Perform this step over and close down to a workbench top. Hold the caliper body with the piston facing away from you.

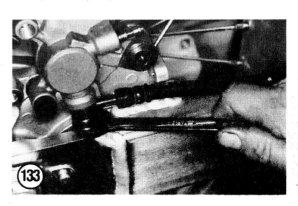

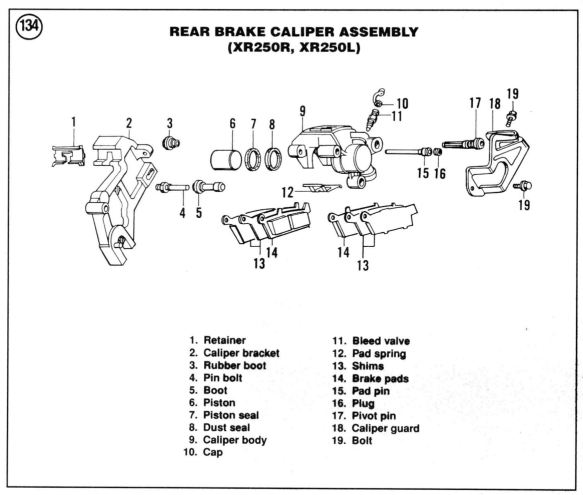

REAR BRAKE CALIPER ASSEMBLY
(XR250R, XR250L)

1. Retainer
2. Caliper bracket
3. Rubber boot
4. Pin bolt
5. Boot
6. Piston
7. Piston seal
8. Dust seal
9. Caliper body
10. Cap
11. Bleed valve
12. Pad spring
13. Shims
14. Brake pads
15. Pad pin
16. Plug
17. Pivot pin
18. Caliper guard
19. Bolt

WARNING
*In the next step, the piston may shoot out of the caliper body like a bullet. Keep your fingers out of the way. Wear shop gloves and apply air pressure gradually. Do **not** use high pressure air or place the air hose nozzle directly against the hydraulic line fitting inlet in the caliper body. Hold the air nozzle away from the inlet allowing some of the air to escape.*

6. Apply the air pressure in short spurts to the hydraulic fluid passageway and force out the piston. Use a service station air hose if you don't have an air compressor. Remove the piston from. the caliper cylinder.

CAUTION
In the following step, do not use a sharp tool to remove the dust and piston seals from the caliper cylinder. Do not damage the cylinder surface.

7. Use a piece of plastic or wood and carefully push the dust seal and the piston seal in toward the caliper

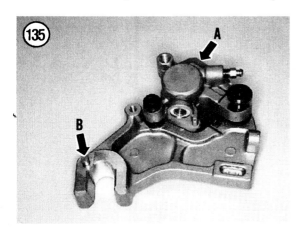

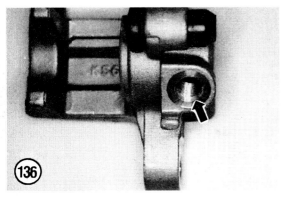

cylinder and out of their grooves. Remove the dust and piston seals from the cylinder and discard all seals.

8. Inspect the caliper assembly as described in this chapter.

Inspection

1. Inspect the pad pin bolt threaded hole in the caliper body. If worn or damaged, clean out with a thread tap or replace the caliper assembly.

2. Inspect the union bolt threaded hole (**Figure 136**) in the caliper body. If worn or damaged, clean out with a thread tap or replace the caliper assembly.

3. Remove the bleed screw and dust cap.

4. Inspect the bleed screw threaded hole in the caliper body. If worn or damaged, clean out with a thread tap or replace the caliper assembly.

5. Inspect the bleed screw. Make sure it is clean and open. Apply compressed air to the opening and make sure it is clear. Clean out if necessary with fresh brake fluid. Install the bleed screw and tighten securely.

6. Inspect the pad pin bolt and mounting bolt threads (**Figure 137**). If worn or damaged, clean with a thread die or replace the bolt(s).

7. Inspect the pad pin bolt threads (A, **Figure 138**), mounting bolt threads (B, **Figure 138**) and bleed screw threads (C, **Figure 138**) in the caliper body. If worn or damaged, clean with a thread tap or replace the body.

8. Remove the pad spring (**Figure 139**) from the caliper.

9. Inspect the caliper body (**Figure 140**) for damage. Replace the caliper body if necessary.

12

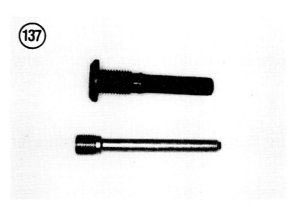

10. Inspect the seal grooves (A, **Figure 141**) in the caliper body for damage. If damaged or corroded, replace the caliper assembly.

11. Make sure the fluid opening (B, **Figure 141**) is open. Clean out if necessary.

12. Inspect the caliper bore (C, **Figure 141**) for cracks, deep scoring, or excessive wear. Measure the inside diameter of the cylinder bore (**Figure 142**) with a bore gauge (**Figure 143**). Replace the caliper assembly if the bore exceeds the service limit in **Table 11**.

13. Check the caliper piston (**Figure 144**) for scratches, scoring or rust. If rusty, replace the piston. Measure the piston outside diameter with a micrometer (**Figure 145**). Replace the piston if the piston outer diameter is less than the service limit in **Table 11**.

14. Inspect the union bolt and sealing washers (**Figure 146**). Make sure the fluid opening is clear in the union bolt.

15. Inspect the pad spring (**Figure 147**) for fatigue or damage and replace if necessary.

16. Inspect the rubber boot (**Figure 148**) for hardness or deterioration and replace if necessary.

17. The piston seal helps maintain correct brake pad to disc clearance. If the seal is worn or damaged, the brake pads will drag and cause excessive wear and increase brake fluid temperature. Replace the piston seal and the dust seal if the following conditions exist:

    a. Brake fluid leaks around the inner brake pad.

    b. Stuck piston seal.

    c. There is a large difference in the inner and outer brake pad thickness.

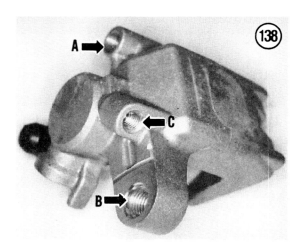

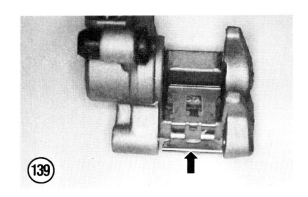

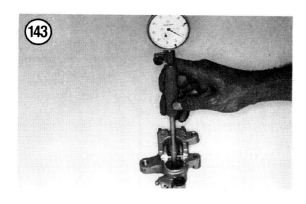

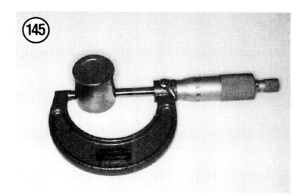

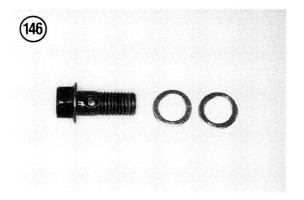

NOTE
Never reuse an old dust or piston seal. Very minor damage or deterioration can make the seals useless.

18. Measure the thickness of each brake pad with a vernier caliper or ruler and compare to the specification listed in **Table 11**. If the pad thickness is equal or less than the wear limit, replace the pads as a set.

19. Inspect the brake pads for uneven wear, damage or grease contamination. Make sure the shims (**Figure 149**) are secured on the backside of the brake pads.

NOTE
When the brake system is operating correctly, the inboard and outboard brake pads should show the same approximately amount of wear. If there is a large difference in pad wear, the caliper is not sliding properly along the support bracket shafts. This causes one pad to

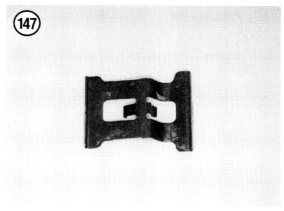

12

drag against the disc. Worn caliper piston seals will also cause uneven pad wear.

20. Inspect the caliper bracket (**Figure 150**) for cracks or damage and replace if necessary. Inspect the rubber boot (A, **Figure 151**) for hardness or deterioration and replace if necessary. Make sure the retainer (B, **Figure 151**) is in place.

21. If serviceable, clean the caliper body with rubbing alcohol and rinse with clean brake fluid.

Assembly

1. Coat the new dust seals and piston seals and piston bore with clean DOT 4 brake fluid.

2. Carefully install the new piston seal (**Figure 152**) into the lower groove. Make sure the seal is properly seated in its groove.

3. Carefully install the new dust seal (**Figure 153**) into the upper groove. Make sure the seal is properly seated in its groove.

4. Coat the piston with clean DOT 4 brake fluid.

5. Position the piston with the closed end facing out and install the piston into the caliper cylinder (**Figure 154**). Push the piston in until it bottoms out (**Figure 155**).

6. Install the pad spring (**Figure 139**) onto the caliper and lock it in place.

> *NOTE*
> *Prior to installing the caliper mounting bracket, apply silicone grease to the bracket pins and to the inside surfaces of the rubber boots on the caliper assembly. This makes installation much easier and ensures that the caliper will*

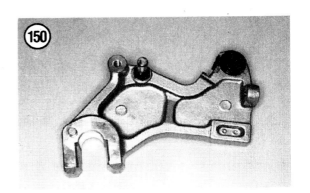

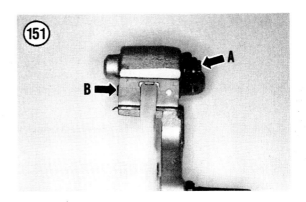

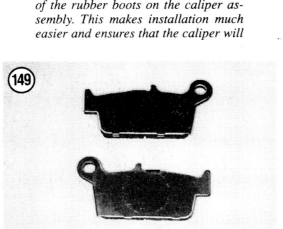

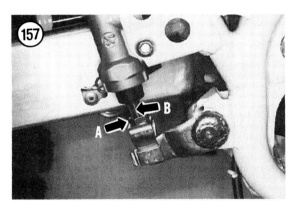

move easy after installation on the fork slider.

7. If removed, carefully install the caliper (A, **Figure 135**) onto the caliper mounting bracket (B, **Figure 135**). Push the caliper on until it bottoms out.

8. Install the caliper and brake pads as described in this chapter.

REAR MASTER CYLINDER

Removal/Installation

> *CAUTION*
> *Cover the swing arm and rear wheel with a heavy cloth or plastic tarp to protect them from accidental brake fluid spills. Wash brake fluid off any painted or plated surfaces or plastic parts immediately, as it will destroy the finish. Use soapy water and rinse completely.*

1. Place a shop cloth under the brake hose and the master cylinder union bolt to catch any remaining brake fluid that will leak out.

2. Unscrew the union bolt (A, **Figure 156**) securing the brake hose to the top of the master cylinder. Don't lose the sealing washer on each side of the hose fitting. Place the loose end in a reclosable plastic bag and close it to prevent the entry of moisture and foreign matter.

3. Loosen the locknut (A, **Figure 157**) on the master cylinder pushrod.

4. Remove the bolts (**Figure 158**) securing the master cylinder to the frame.

5. Carefully pull the master cylinder (A, **Figure 159**) toward the rear and away from the frame.

12

Release the hose clamp and disconnect the reservoir hose (B, **Figure 159**) from the master cylinder.

6. Unscrew the pushrod (B, **Figure 157**) from the fitting on the brake pedal assembly.

7. Remove the master cylinder from the frame. If the master cylinder is not going to be serviced, place it in a reclosable bag and close it.

8. To remove the reservoir and reservoir hose, remove the mounting bolt (A, **Figure 160**) then remove the reservoir and hose (B, **Figure 160**) assembly from the frame.

9. Wash off any brake fluid that may have been spilled during component removal.

10. Install by reversing these removal steps while noting the following:

  a. Be sure to locate the brake hose fitting up against the stopper post (B, **Figure 156**) on top of the master cylinder prior to tightening the union bolt.

  b. Place a sealing washer on each side of the brake hose fitting and install the union bolt and tighten the union bolt to the torque specification listed in **Table 10**.

  c. Bleed the rear brake as described under *Bleeding the System* in Chapter Eleven in the main body of this book.

Disassembly

Refer to **Figure 161** for this procedure.

1. Remove the rear master cylinder as described in this chapter.

2. Remove the circlip (A, **Figure 162**) securing the reservoir hose connector to the master cylinder body. Remove the connector (B, **Figure 162**) from the master cylinder.

3. Remove the O-ring seal (**Figure 163**) from the master cylinder body. Discard the O-ring as it must be replaced.

4. Slide the rubber boot (**Figure 164**) down and off the master cylinder push rod.

5. Using circlip pliers, remove the internal circlip (**Figure 165**) securing the pushrod assembly in the master cylinder body.

6. Withdraw the pushrod assembly from the master cylinder body.

7. Remove the piston assembly and the spring.

8. Pour out any residual brake fluid and discard it. *Never* re-use hydraulic fluid.

Inspection

1. Clean all parts in denatured alcohol or fresh hydraulic fluid. Inspect the body cylinder bore surface and piston contact surfaces (**Figure 166**) for wear and damage. If less than perfect, replace the master cylinder assembly. The body cannot be replaced separately.

2. Inspect the piston cups (A, **Figure 167**) for signs of wear and damage. If less than perfect, replace the piston assembly, the individual cups cannot be replaced.

3. Check the end of the piston (B, **Figure 167**) for wear caused by the push rod. If worn, replace the piston assembly.

4. Make sure the passage way (**Figure 168**) in the master cylinder body is clear.

5. Check the entire master cylinder body (**Figure 169**) for wear or damage. If damaged in any way, replace the master cylinder assembly.

6. Inspect the union bolt threads (**Figure 170**) in the master cylinder body bore. If worn or damaged, clean out with a thread tap or replace the master cylinder assembly.

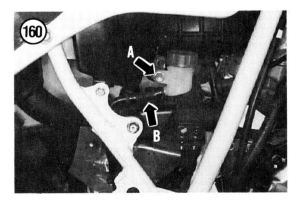

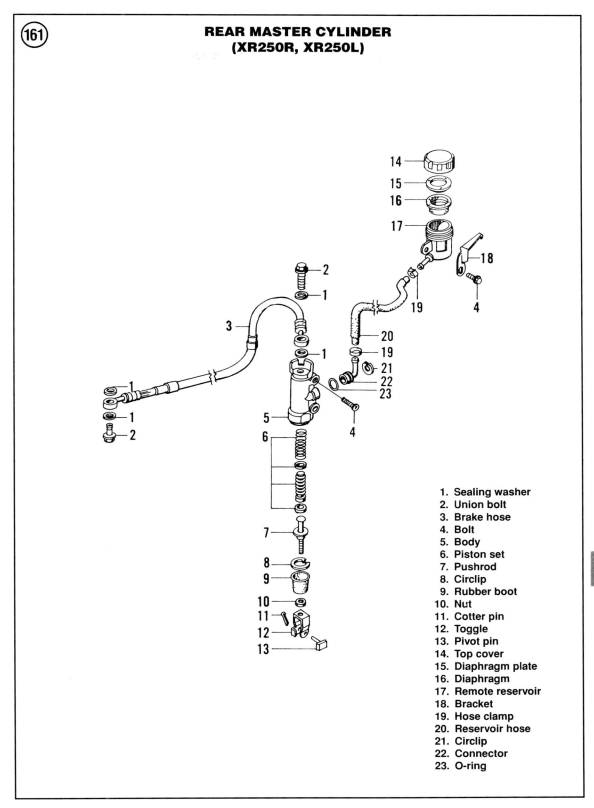

161

REAR MASTER CYLINDER
(XR250R, XR250L)

1. Sealing washer
2. Union bolt
3. Brake hose
4. Bolt
5. Body
6. Piston set
7. Pushrod
8. Circlip
9. Rubber boot
10. Nut
11. Cotter pin
12. Toggle
13. Pivot pin
14. Top cover
15. Diaphragm plate
16. Diaphragm
17. Remote reservoir
18. Bracket
19. Hose clamp
20. Reservoir hose
21. Circlip
22. Connector
23. O-ring

12

7. Measure the inside diameter of the cylinder bore with a small bore gauge (**Figure 171**), then measure the bore gauge with a micrometer. Replace the master cylinder if the bore exceeds the specification listed in **Table 11**.

8. Measure the outside diameter of the piston with a micrometer (**Figure 172**). Replace the piston/spring assembly if it less than the specification listed in **Table 11**.

9. Inspect the piston rod assembly (**Figure 173**) for wear or damage. Make sure the end (**Figure 174**) that contacts the push rod is not damaged.

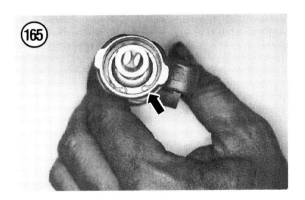

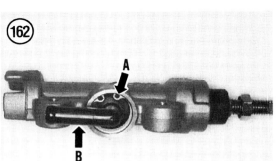

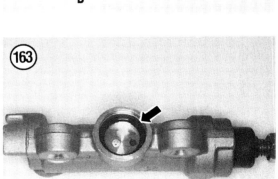

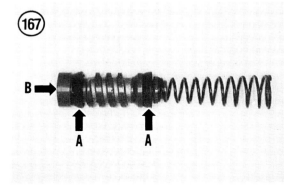

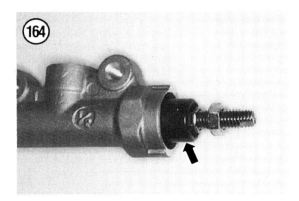

10. Inspect the rubber boot for tears, hardness or deterioration, replace if necessary.

11. Inspect the union bolt threads for damage. If damaged, clean out with a metric thread die or replace it (**Figure 175**). Make sure the brake fluid hole is clear. Clean out or replace if necessary.

12. Inspect the connector (**Figure 176**) for cracks or deterioration and replace if necessary.

13. Unscrew the reservoir top cap, diaphragm plate and diaphragm from the reservoir.

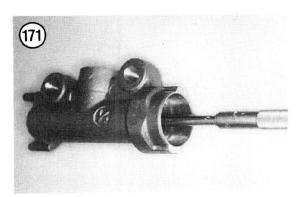

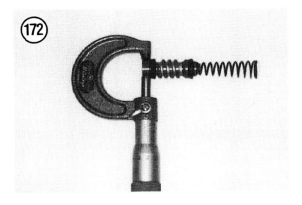

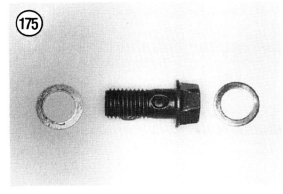

12

14. Check the reservoir top cap, diaphragm plate and diaphragm for damage and deterioration and replace as necessary.

15. Inspect the reservoir hose for wear or deterioration. Replace as necessary.

Assembly

1. Soak the new cups in fresh brake fluid for at least 15 minutes to make them pliable. Coat the inside of the cylinder bore with fresh hydraulic fluid prior to the assembly of parts.

CAUTION
When installing the piston assembly, do not allow the cups to turn inside out as they will be damaged and allow brake fluid leakage within the cylinder bore.

2. Position the spring with the larger diameter coils (A, **Figure 177**) going in first. Install the spring and piston assembly into the cylinder together (B, **Figure 177**). Push the piston assembly in (**Figure 178**) all way in until they bottom out (**Figure 179**).

3. Install the push rod assembly (C, **Figure 177**) up against the piston assembly (**Figure 180**) and push the piston cup assembly all the way in.

4. Hold the push rod assembly in and install the circlip and make sure the circlip is correctly seated in the groove (**Figure 165**).

5. Install the rubber boot over the pushrod and into the receptacle in the base of the master cylinder (**Figure 164**).

6. Refer to **Figure 181** and install a new O-ring seal (**Figure 182**) into the receptacle in the master cylinder body (**Figure 163**).

7. Install the reservoir hose connector (B, **Figure 162**) to the master cylinder body. Install the circlip (A, **Figure 162**). Make sure it is properly seated in the groove.

8. Attach the reservoir hose to the reservoir and install the clamp.

9. Install the diaphragm, diaphragm plate and cover. Do not tighten the cover at this time as hydraulic fluid will have to be added later when the system is bled.

10. Install the master cylinder as described in this chapter.

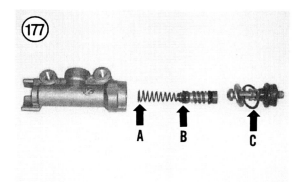

A   B   C

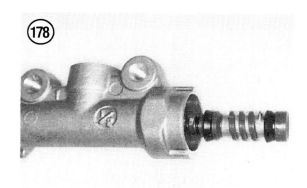

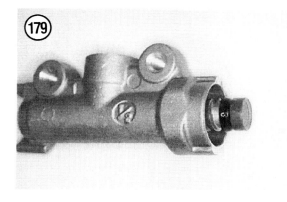

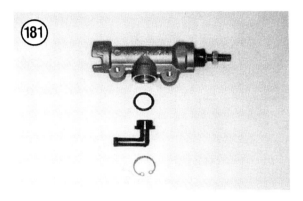

REAR BRAKE HOSE REPLACEMENT

There is no factory-recommended replacement interval but it is a good idea to replace all brake hoses every four years or if they show signs of cracking or damage.

NOTE
*The replacement procedure for the hose from the reservoir to the top of the rear master cylinder is covered under **Rear Master Cylinder** in this section of the supplement.*

CAUTION
Cover the surrounding area with a heavy cloth or plastic tarp to protect the components from accidental brake fluid spills. Wash brake fluid off any painted or plated surfaces or plastic parts immediately, as it will destroy the finish. Use soapy water and rinse completely.

1. Clean the top of the master cylinder remote reservoir of all dirt and foreign matter.

2. Loosen the master cylinder reservoir cover (**Figure 183**). Pull up and loosen the cover, plate and the diaphragm. This will allow air to enter the reservoir and allow the brake fluid to drain out more quickly in the next step.

3. On XR250R models, remove the bolts securing the caliper guard (**Figure 184**) and remove the guard. Don't lose the spacer (A, **Figure 185**) on the rear bolt (B, **Figure 185**).

4. Remove the caliper mounting bolt (**Figure 186**) and pivot the caliper up and partially off the mounting bracket.

5. Remove the union bolt and sealing washer (**Figure 187**) attaching the brake hose to the caliper

12

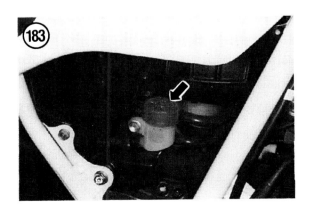

assembly. Don't lose the sealing washer on each side of the hose fitting.

6. Place the end of the brake hose over a container and let the brake fluid drain out. Apply the brake pedal several times to expel the brake fluid from the master cylinder and hose. Dispose of this brake fluid properly—never reuse brake fluid.

7. Remove the union bolt and sealing washer (A, **Figure 188**) attaching the brake hose to the top of the master cylinder assembly. Don't lose the sealing washer on each side of the hose fitting

8. Pull the brake hose out of the locating clamps on the swing arm. Remove the brake hose.

9. Wash off any spilled brake fluid that may have dribbled out of the hose during removal.

10. Install a new hose, sealing washers and union bolts in the reverse order of removal. Be sure to install new sealing washers and in their correct positions.

11. Be sure to locate the brake hose fitting up against the stopper post (B, **Figure 188**) on top of the master cylinder prior to tightening the union bolt.

12. Tighten the union bolts to the torque specifications listed in **Table 10**.

13. The brake hose must be routed correctly through the locating clamps on the swing arm. Make sure the hose is not touching the rear wheel.

14. Refill the master cylinder reservoir, if necessary, to maintain the correct fluid level as seen through the transparent side of the reservoir. Install the diaphragm, plate and cover. Do not tighten securely at this time.

> *WARNING*
> *Use brake fluid clearly marked DOT 4 from a sealed container. Other types may cause brake failure. Always use the same brand name; do not intermix as many brands are not compatible. Do not intermix silicone-based (DOT 5) brake fluid as it can cause brake component damage leading to brake system failure.*

> *WARNING*
> *Do not ride the motorcycle until you are sure that the brakes are operating properly.*

14. Bleed the brake as described under *Bleeding the System* in Chapter Eleven in the main body of this book.

REAR BRAKE DISC

Inspection

It is not necessary to remove the disc (**Figure 189**) from the wheel to inspect it. Small nicks and marks

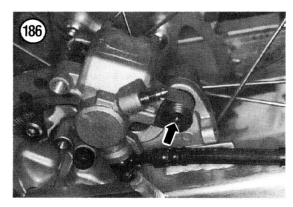

on the disc are not important, but radial scratches deep enough to snag a fingernail reduce braking effectiveness and increase brake pad wear. If these grooves are evident, and the brake pads are wearing rapidly, the disc should be replaced.

The Honda factory specifications for the standard and wear limits are listed in **Table 11**. Each disc is also marked with the minimum (MIN) thickness. If the specification marked on the disc differs from the that listed in **Table 11**, refer to the specified MIN thickness marks on the disc.

When servicing the brake discs, do not have the discs reconditioned (ground) to compensate for any warpage. The discs are thin and grinding will only reduce their thickness, causing them to warp quite rapidly. If the disc is warped, the brake pads may be dragging on the disc, causing the disc to overheat. Overheating can be caused when there is unequal pad pressure on both sides of the disc. Four main causes of unequal brake pad pressure are:

a. The floating caliper is binding on the caliper mounting bracket shafts, thus preventing the caliper from floating (side to side) on the disc.

b. The brake caliper piston seal is worn or damaged.

c. The small master cylinder relief port is plugged.

d. The primary cup on the master cylinder piston is worn or damaged.

NOTE
It is not necessary to remove the wheel to measure the disc thickness. The measurement can be performed with the wheel installed or removed from the bike.

1. Measure the thickness of the disc at several locations around the disc with a vernier caliper or a micrometer. The disc must be replaced if the thickness in any area is less than that specified in **Table 11** (or the marked MIN dimension on the disc).

2. Make sure the disc mounting bolts are tight prior to running this check. Check the disc runout with a dial indicator attached to the rear swing arm.

3. Slowly rotate the wheel and watch the dial indicator. If the runout exceeds that listed in **Table 11** the disc must be replaced.

4. Clean the disc of any rust or corrosion and wipe clean with lacquer thinner. Never use an oil-based solvent that may leave an oil residue on the disc.

Removal/Installation

1. Remove the rear wheel as described in this supplement.

NOTE
Place a piece of wood or vinyl tube in the caliper in place of the disc. Then, if the brake lever is inadvertently squeezed the pistons will not be forced out of the caliper cylinders. If this does happen, the caliper must be disassembled to reseat the pistons and the system will have to be bled.

CAUTION
Do not set the wheel down on the disc surface, as it may get scratched or warped. Set the wheel on 2 blocks of wood.

2. Remove the bolts securing the brake disc (**Figure 190**) to the hub and remove the disc.

3. Install by reversing these removal steps while noting the following:

CAUTION
*The disc bolts (**Figure 191**) are made from a harder material than similar bolts that are not used on the brake system. When replacing the bolts, always use the standard Suzuki brake disc bolts—never compromise and use a* cheaper bolt as they will **not** properly retain the disc to the hub.

a. Use a small amount of a locking compound such as ThreeBond No. TB1303 (green) or Loctite No. 242 (blue) on the brake disc bolts prior to installation.

b. Tighten the disc mounting bolts to the torque specification listed in **Table 10**.

Table 10 BRAKE TORQUE SPECIFICATIONS

Item	N•m	ft.-lb.
Pad pin bolts (front and rear)	15-20	11-14
Caliper mounting bolts		
XR250R	24-30	17-22
XR250L	25	18
Caliper union bolts	30-40	22-29
Brake disc bolts	43	31

Table 11 BRAKE SYSTEM SPECIFICATIONS

Item	Standard mm	Standard in.	Service limit mm	Service limit in.
XR250R				
Front caliper				
Cylinder bore diameter	27.00-27.05	1.063-1.064	27.06	1.065
Piston diameter	26.90-26.95	1.059-1.061	26.89	1.059
Brake pad thickness	4.4	0.17	3.4	0.13
Rear caliper				
Cylinder bore diameter	27.00-27.05	1.063-1.064	27.06	1.065
Piston diameter	26.93-26.96	1.060-1.062	26.89	1.059
Brake pad thickness	4.5	0.18	4.0	0.16
Rear master cylinder				
Cylinder bore diameter	12.70-12.74	0.500-0.502	12.76	0.502
Brake disc thickness				
Front	3.0	0.12	2.5	0.10
Rear	4.5	0.18	4.0	0.16
		(continued)		

Table 11 BRAKE SYSTEM SPECIFICATIONS (continued)

Item	Standard		Service limit	
	mm	in.	mm	in.
XR250L				
Front caliper				
Cylinder bore diameter	27.00-27.05	1.063-1.064	27.10	1.067
Piston diameter	26.90-26.95	1.059-1.061	26.84	1.057
Brake pad thickness	NA	NA	NA	NA
Rear caliper				
Cylinder bore diameter	27.00-27.05	1.063-1.064	27.06	1.065
Piston diameter	26.90-26.95	1.059-1.061	26.84	1.061
Brake pad thickness	NA	NA	NA	NA
Rear master cylinder				
Cylinder bore diameter	14.00-14.04	0.551-0.553	14.06	0.554
Piston diameter	13.95-13.98	0.549-0.551	13.95	0.549

12

INDEX

13

13

13

1979-1980 XR250

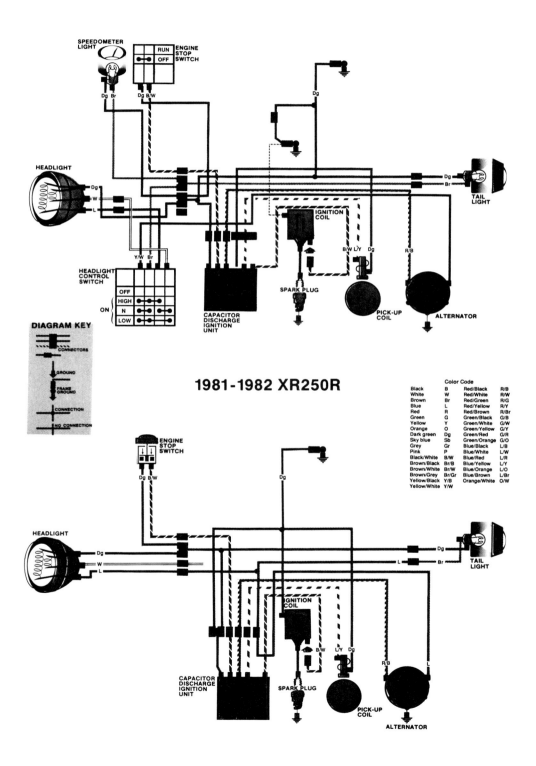

1981-1982 XR250R

Color Code			
Black	B	Red/Black	R/B
White	W	Red/White	R/W
Brown	Br	Red/Green	R/G
Blue	L	Red/Yellow	R/Y
Red	R	Red/Brown	R/Br
Green	G	Green/Black	G/B
Yellow	Y	Green/White	G/W
Orange	O	Green/Yellow	G/Y
Dark green	Dg	Green/Red	G/R
Sky blue	Sb	Green/Orange	G/O
Grey	Gr	Blue/Black	L/B
Pink	P	Blue/White	L/W
Black/White	B/W	Blue/Red	L/R
Brown/Black	Br/B	Blue/Yellow	L/Y
Brown/White	Br/W	Blue/Orange	L/O
Brown/Grey	Br/Gr	Blue/Brown	L/Br
Yellow/Black	Y/B	Orange/White	O/W
Yellow/White	Y/W		

1978-1981 XL250S

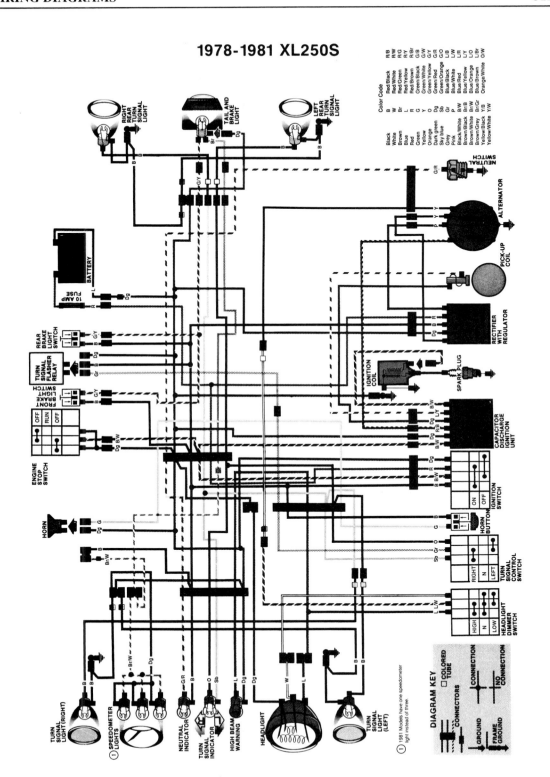

14

1982-1983 XL250R

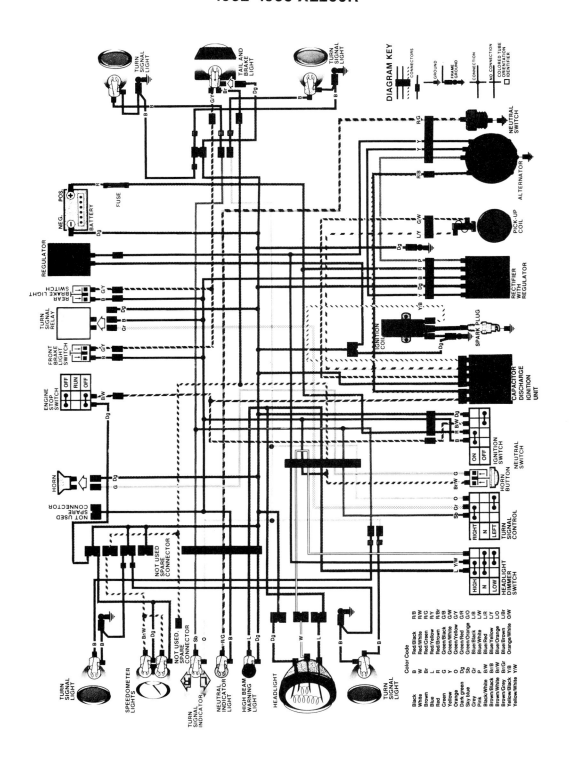

1983-1984 XR350R

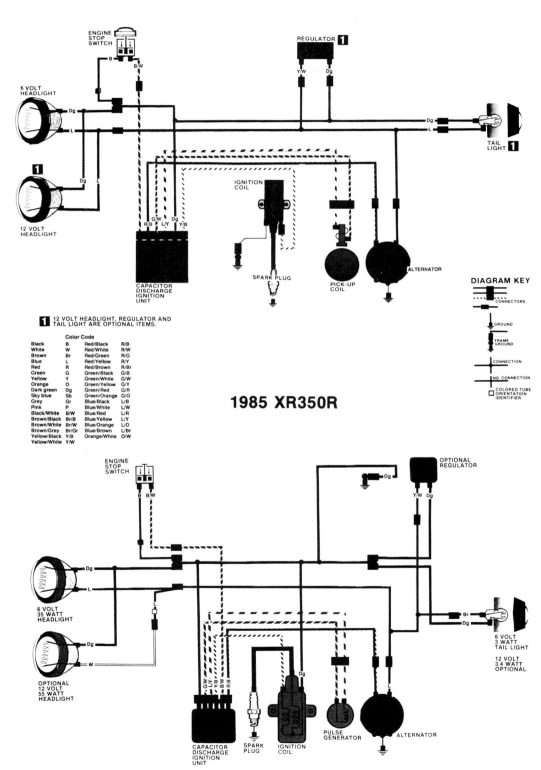

1985 XR350R

14

1984 XL250R

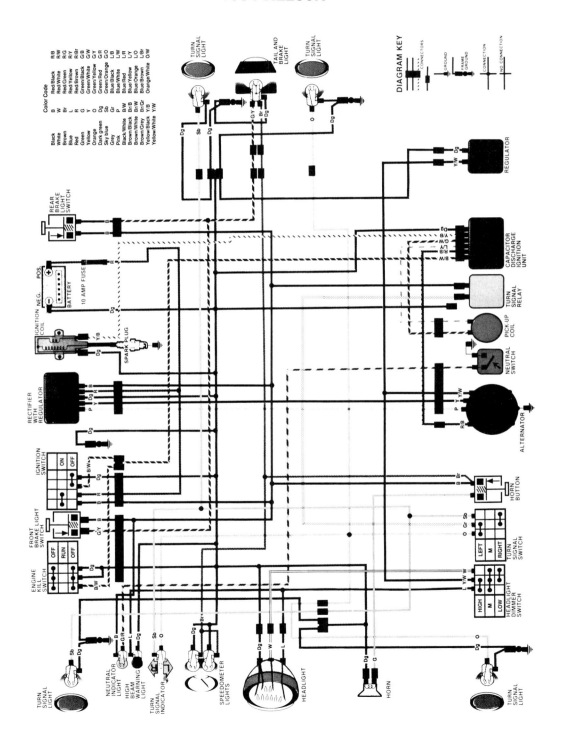

1984 XL350R

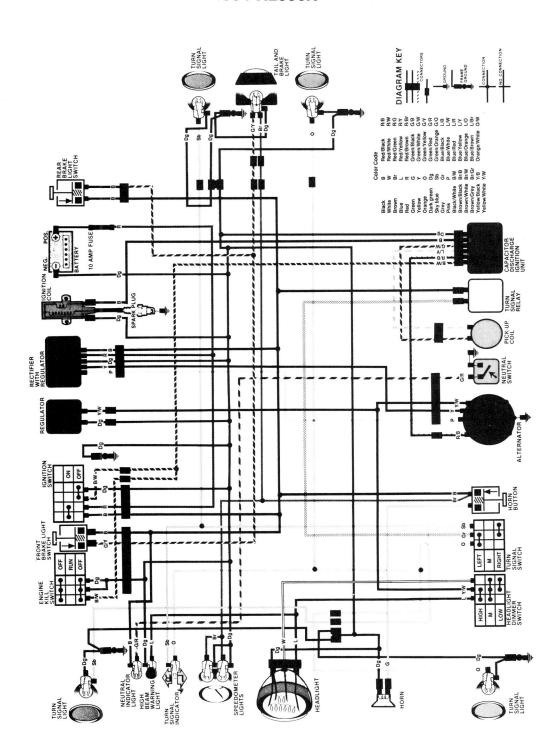

14

1984 XR200R/250R

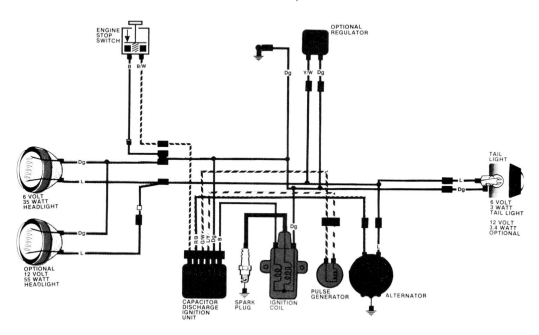

1985 XR200R/250R

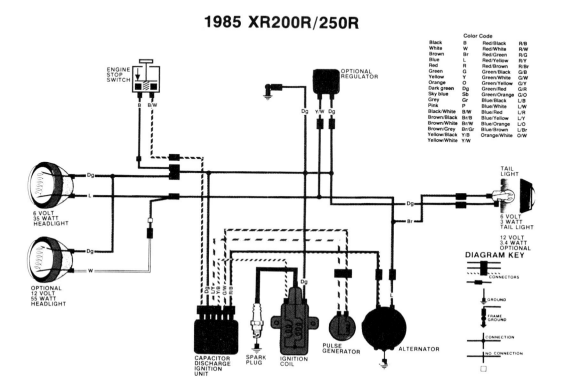

1985-1987 XL250R

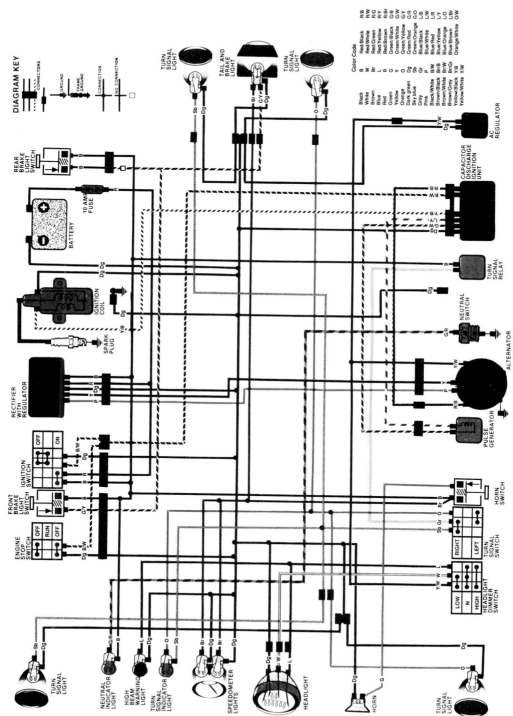

1985 XL350R

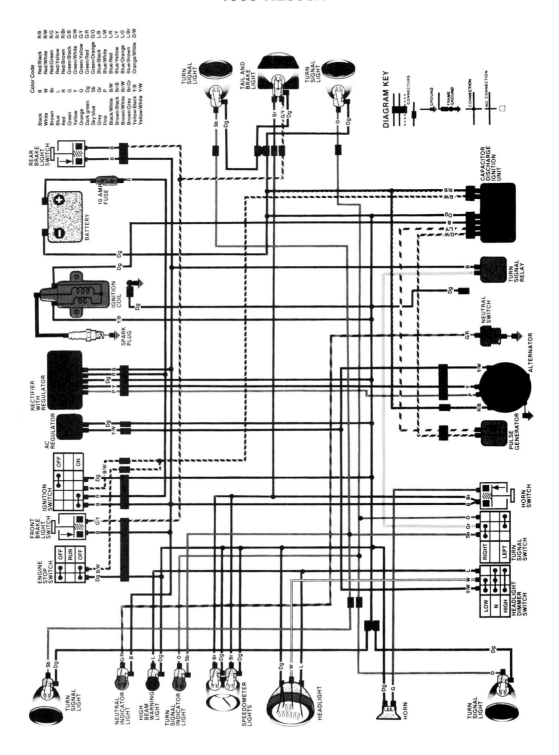

1986-1991 XR250R

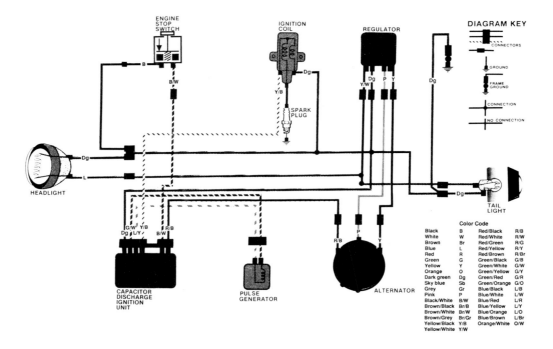

Color Code			
Black	B	Red/Black	R/B
White	W	Red/White	R/W
Brown	Br	Red/Green	R/G
Blue	L	Red/Yellow	R/Y
Red	R	Red/Brown	R/Br
Green	G	Green/Black	G/B
Yellow	Y	Green/White	G/W
Orange	O	Green/Yellow	G/Y
Dark green	Dg	Green/Red	G/R
Sky blue	Sb	Green/Orange	G/O
Grey	Gr	Blue/Black	L/B
Pink	P	Blue/White	L/W
Black/White	B/W	Blue/Red	L/R
Brown/Black	Br/B	Blue/Yellow	L/Y
Brown/White	Br/W	Blue/Orange	L/O
Brown/Grey	Br/Gr	Blue/Brown	L/Br
Yellow/Black	Y/B	Orange/White	O/W
Yellow/White	Y/W		

14

1991-1996 XR250L

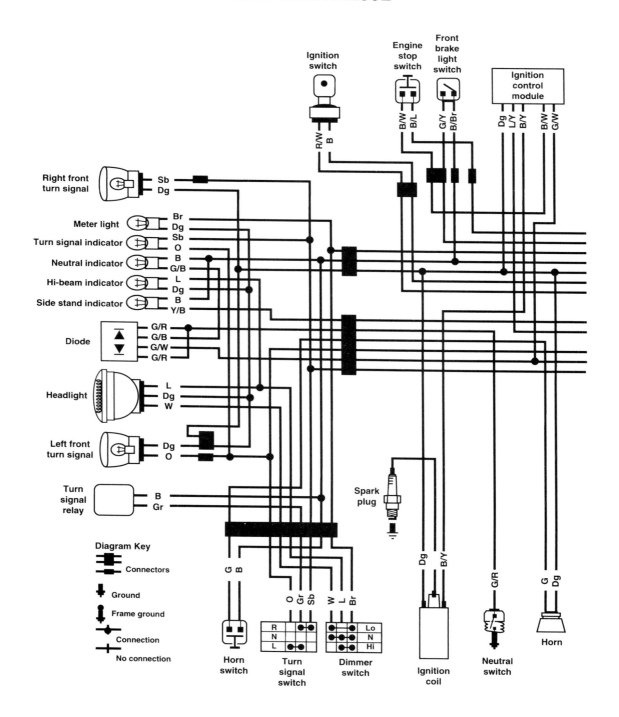

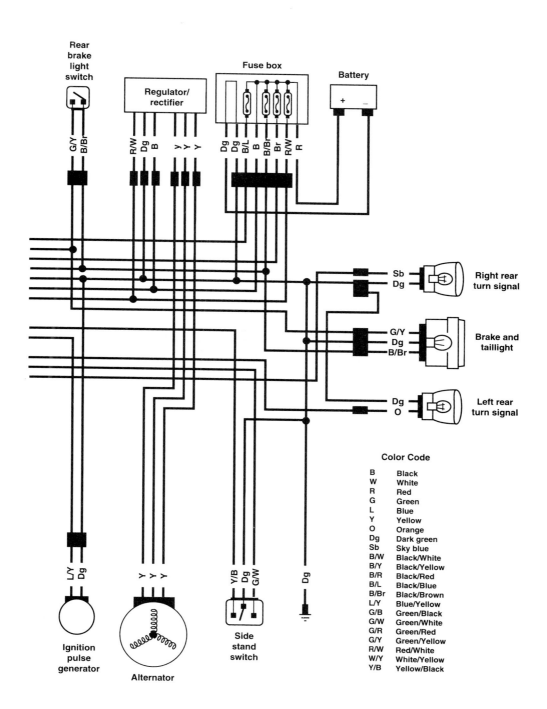

Color Code

B	Black
W	White
R	Red
G	Green
L	Blue
Y	Yellow
O	Orange
Dg	Dark green
Sb	Sky blue
B/W	Black/White
B/Y	Black/Yellow
B/R	Black/Red
B/L	Black/Blue
B/Br	Black/Brown
L/Y	Blue/Yellow
G/B	Green/Black
G/W	Green/White
G/R	Green/Red
G/Y	Green/Yellow
R/W	Red/White
W/Y	White/Yellow
Y/B	Yellow/Black

14

1992-2000 XR250R

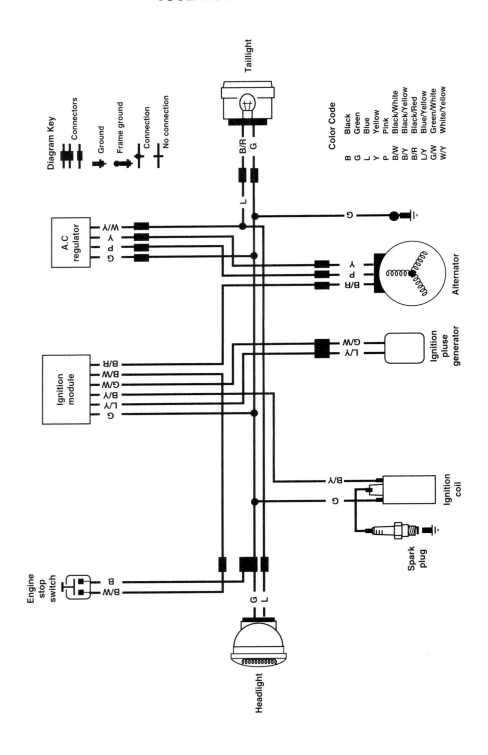